Library of
Davidson College

Pastoral Economics in the Kingdom of Naples

THE JOHNS HOPKINS UNIVERSITY STUDIES IN
HISTORICAL AND POLITICAL SCIENCE
106th Series (1988)

1. *Pastoral Economics in the Kingdom of Naples*
   by John A. Marino
2. *Death and Property in Siena, 1205–1800: Strategies for the Afterlife*
   by Samuel K. Cohn, Jr.
3. *Firstborn of Venice: Vicenza in the Early Renaissance State*
   by James S. Grubb

JOHN A. MARINO
Pastoral Economics in the Kingdom of Naples

THE JOHNS HOPKINS UNIVERSITY PRESS
BALTIMORE AND LONDON

© 1988 The Johns Hopkins University Press
All rights reserved
Printed in the United States of America

The Johns Hopkins University Press
701 West 40th Street   Baltimore, Maryland 21211
The Johns Hopkins Press Ltd., London

Library of Congress Cataloging-in-Publication Data
Marino, John A.
  Pastoral economics in the Kingdom of Naples.
  (The Johns Hopkins University studies in historical and political science ; 106th ser., 1(1988))
  Bibliography: p.
  Includes index.
  1. Wool trade and industry—Government policy—Italy—Naples (Kingdom)—History. I. Title. II. Series: Johns Hopkins University studies in historical and political science ; 106th ser., 1.
HD9905.I73N366   1988   338.1'763145'09457   87-9196
ISBN 0-8018-3437-6 (alk. paper)

The paper used in this publication meets the minimum requirements of American National Standard for Information Sciences—Permanence of Paper for Printed Library Materials, ANSI Z39.48–1984.

To the memory of my mother, Sadie Rose Lala Marino

CONTENTS

Illustrations and Tables   ix
Acknowledgments   xi
Introduction   1

PART 1   The Works and Days of the Dogana of Foggia   13
1 *Mediterranean Mestas and the Neapolitan Exemplar*   15
2 *The Georgics of the Tavoliere of Puglia*   40
3 *Explaining Economic Expansion and Contraction*   64

PART 2   La Ragion de' Locati   83
4 *The Graziers' Organization*   85
5 *The Conflict between Rich and Poor*   117

PART 3   La Ragion dello Stato   147
6 *Royal Patrimony, Royal Justice, Royal Office*   149
7 *The Competition between Wheat and Wool*   176

PART 4   La Ragion del Mercato   193
8 *The Fair of Foggia: Production and Prices*   195
9 *Sellers and Buyers at the Fair of Foggia*   212

PART 5   La Ragion Pastorale   243
10 *From Pastoral Models to Political Economy*   245

Conclusion   261

Appendixes   267
A *Weights and Measures*   267
B *Locazioni* and *Nazioni* in the Dogana   269
C *Doganal Social Structure*   270

D *Sheep and Income in the Dogana* 277
E *Production, Prices, and Product Value* 284
F *Enlightened Reformers on the Dogana of Foggia from the 1764 Famine to the 1806 Abolition of the Dogana* 298

Abbreviations 301
Notes 303
Manuscript Sources 363
Index 369

ILLUSTRATIONS AND TABLES

Illustrations

1 Foggia in the Sixteenth Century   3
2 A Physical Map of Capitanata   6
3 Sheepwalks and Holding Pastures of the Foggian Customhouse   43
4 Administrative Jurisdictions in the Foggian Customhouse   45
5 The Twenty-three General Locations   47
6 Sheepowners by Provincial Origin   93
7 Ownership by All *Locati* in the Seventeenth and Eighteenth Centuries   127
8 Ownership by *Padroni* Only in the Seventeenth and Eighteenth Centuries   127
9 Wealth of All *Locati* in the Seventeenth and Eighteenth Centuries   129
10 Wealth of *Padroni* Only in the Seventeenth and Eighteenth Centuries   129
11 Sheep in Foggia (1536–1805)   150
12 Sheep Income in Foggia (1536–1805)   151
13 The Location of San Andrea from Antonio de Michele's Maps (1686)   165
14 Detail from Antonio de Michele's Map of the Location of San Andrea   166
15 Total Wool Sold at Foggia (1623–1806)   199
16 *Voce* Prices of Staples (1731–1845)   209
17 *Voce* Prices of Staples, Base Year Comparisons (1731–1845)   210

Tables

1 Tavoliere Land Use in the Mid Eighteenth Century   51
2 Sheep Mortality in Harsh Winters   55
3 Comparative Sheep Numbers: Dogana of Foggia and Spanish Mesta   69

4   Comparative Income: Dogana of Foggia and Spanish Mesta   69
5   Comparative Wool Sales: Dogana of Foggia and Spanish Mesta   70
6   *Locati* in the Dogana (1591–1779)   89
7   Location Assignment of *Nazioni* by Fertility of Pasture   92
8   Wealth among Particular Deputies (1596–1754)   105
9   General Syndics' Budgets (1750–1774)   106
10 General Syndics' Budgets (1750–1774): Mean Annual Expenditures   108
11 Ownership and Wealth by Flock Size (1619–1779)   126
12 *Squarciafogli* Social Stratification: *Padroni* Only   131
13 *Squarciafogli* Social Stratification: All *Locati*   131
14 Ownership Status in the *Squarciafogli* (1591–1779)   133
15 Relationship between *Padroni* Heads of *Collettive* and Their *Padroncelli* (1591–1779)   134
16 Mean Flock Size by Ownership Status (1591–1779)   135
17 Large Holders and Social Orders in the Dogana (1591–1779)   136
18 Social Orders among All *Locati* (1591–1779)   137
19 The Foggian Customhouse Budget: Income   155
20 The Foggian Customhouse Budget: Expense   156
21 Wool Quantity and Sales at Foggia by Month   190
22 General Statistics from the Seventeenth-Century Foggian Fair   197
23 Wool Sellers' Origins: Quantity of Wool by Province (1670–1700)   216
24 Top Ten Wool Sellers' Towns of Origin (1670–1700)   216
25 Top Ten Wool Sellers (1670–1700)   219
26 Sellers and Sellers' Wealth by Social Order   220
27 Budgets of the Doria Sheep Industry at Melfi (1752–1763): Income   224
28 Budgets of the Doria Sheep Industry at Melfi (1752–1763): Expense   225
29 Top Five Wool Buyers (1625–1700)   228
30 Top Ten Wool Buyers' Towns of Origin (1625–1655)   229
31 Top Ten Wool Buyers' Towns of Origin (1670–1700)   230
32 Wool Buyers' Origins: Quantity of Wool by Province (1625–1700)   230
33 Top Four National Consumers of Foggian Wool (1625–1700)   232

ACKNOWLEDGMENTS

My work on the sheep customhouse (*dogana*) of Foggia has grown out of a Ph.D. dissertation (University of Chicago, 1977) on the sixteenth- and seventeenth-century pastoral economy of the Kingdom of Naples. With new research in the eighteenth century and in Spanish archives, my design and argument have assumed a wider focus than the regional world of the shepherds who wintered in Puglia. For the more insightful observations and suggestions along the way, I can name only a few of my many advisers and friends whose counsel and encouragement have seen me through this project.

Giuseppe Galasso, who first introduced me to the problem of the dogana of Foggia, has set the highest standards in his own research into provincial Neapolitan economy and society. Pasquale di Cicco, the director of the Archivio di Stato di Foggia, has been most generous in sharing his profound knowledge of doganal issues and sources and has always given me extraordinary freedom of action in the archives. Franco Venturi's special expertise on the *illuministi* has broadened my focus and sharpened my analysis of doganal reform through an understanding of Enlightenment economic philosophy. Above all, my advisers at the University of Chicago—William H. McNeill, Julius Kirshner, Eric Cochrane, Bernard Cohn, and Arcadius Kahan—have patiently taught me, each in his own way, what it means to be a historian. From the initial confrontation with the archives to the constant encouragement to strive for the big picture, Bill McNeill especially has been a model of a dissertation director. My colleagues at the University of California, San Diego—especially Stanley Chodorow, David Luft, Thomas Metzger, Allan Mitchell, Michael Parrish, Earl Pomeroy, David Ringrose, and Eric Van Young—have challenged me to make my rambling prose and penchant for detail intelligible to the general reader. A number of anonymous reviewers have also offered valuable suggestions.

Special thanks are due to Antonio Calabria, whose own research on related issues of Neapolitan state finances has often refined and always stimulated my own. His generous sharing of a personal inventory of the first fifty volumes of the *Sommaria Consultationum* in Naples opened up a major source of archival materials at an early stage of the research. Silvio Zotta introduced me to the Doria Pamphilj archives in Rome, and Alberto Grohmann shared microfilm that he collected from the *Dipendenze della Sommaria* in Naples. Elio Cerrito and Maria Nardella generously allowed me to read their *tesi di laurea*. Other colleagues have helped: Bruce Chapman, James T. Collins, Paul Gehl, Stephanie

Jed, David Quint, and Michael Sherman. Michael Himes, Eric Stout, Barbara Boyer, and Donna Andrews aided in computer preparation and analysis. Myrtali Anagnostopoulos prepared the maps and graphs. Stefan Fodor aided in preparation of the index. Henry Tom has been a demanding editor whose prodding has helped shape and tighten the manuscript. Giovanni Muto's contribution to the development of my archival sophistication and my growing knowledge of the history of the Kingdom of Naples is inestimable. Finally, Cynthia Truant has lived with my sheep almost as long as I. Her critical reading of the manuscript has forced me to rethink and clarify my arguments. Her support, enthusiasm, and sacrifices for this long-drawn-out enterprise have helped more than any other's to see it to its conclusion.

Research in Italy and Spain was made possible by grants from the Fulbright-Hayes program (Commissione per gli Scambi Culturali fra l'Italia e gli Stati Uniti), the Fondazione Luigi Einaudi, a National Endowment for the Humanities summer stipend, and the University of California, San Diego (Academic Senate, Department of History, and Regents' summer fellowship). The UCSD Subvention for Scholarly Publications provided a publication subsidy.

I wish to thank Douglas Wilson and Jane Daniel of the American Studies Center in Naples, Anna Maria Rao and Pietro Ciarlo, Giovanni Muto and Linda di Porzio, and Wym and Carla Phillips for their friendship, generosity, hospitality, and innumerable kindnesses. This book could not have been written without the patient concern of the archival and library staffs in Foggia, Naples, Rome, Vienna, Simancas, and Madrid. In particular, I am indebted to Viviano Iazzetti, Maria Nardella, and the personnel at the state archive and provincial library in Foggia.

Pastoral Economics in the Kingdom of Naples

INTRODUCTION

The wool trade in medieval and early modern Europe has long been of special interest to economic historians because woolen textiles were the dynamic core of preindustrial urban production and long-distance international trade. Furthermore, study of the wool trade traces economic exchange both to and from its urban focus of cloth production and market. Shepherds who tended sheep of their own or others, financiers who provided credit, middlemen who sold the raw wool, clothiers who oversaw textile production by some dozen specialized craftsmen, and merchants who sold the cloth at home and abroad formed a complex chain linking city and country, labor and capital, raw materials and finished goods, domestic and international policies, production, distribution, and consumption.

Dynamism in the wool trade is usually ascribed to changing demographic and economic conjunctures, international competition, and the free market—the Black Death of 1348, the seventeenth-century crisis, and "new draperies" over "old," English worsteds besting all. Such textbook formulas, however, gloss over the contradictory relationship between structure and change in the textile production cycle. The internal tensions holding together the various stages in the wool trade thus are usually ignored. Raw material supply (some one-third of manufacturing costs), for example, is rarely explored except as an instrument of state income and government protection, or intransigent sheep-owners versus urban "industrialists." How can a driving force of economic change like woolens begin its production cycle with a "backward" industry like pastoralism? Did the pastoral mode of production have no rationale of its own? Was the pastoral economy wholly subordinate to mercantile demand, extraction, and exploitation?

Southern Italy, after Castile continental Europe's largest supplier of raw wool and one of the twentieth century's hard-core examples of "underdevelopment," offers a model of pastoral production to help us escape from the dominant evolutionary models of economic development and redefine sheepherding in terms of its multiple relationships with agriculture, state, and market. Such specialized sheep farming produced wool and meat as cash crops in what was essentially a variant of capitalist agriculture developed to utilize the marginal zone. Pastoralism was part of a larger, interlocking system of state policy and agricultural production that teaches us much about the limits of economic growth. Despite intense conflict among the various groups within the system, sustained state intervention attempted to balance antagonists one against the other to prevent change. Development was neither inevitable nor desirable. And the royal sheep industry, in turn, became a cornerstone in holding the Old Regime monarchy of the Kingdom of Naples in place.

The royal sheep customhouse of Puglia (1447–1806), as this Italian equivalent to the better-known Castilian Mesta was called,[1] had its headquarters in Foggia. It was an administrative, fiscal, judicial, and commercial institution of the Kingdom of Naples whose power was grounded in land-based production. The dogana of Foggia maintained a vast network of sheepwalks between the mountains of the Abruzzi and the plains of Puglia. It rented winter pasture to sheepowners engaged in long-distance migration down from the mountains, as it regulated the land-use policy of indigenous landowners of the plains. Its tribunal moderated conflict between doganal participants in both civil and criminal cases. And finally, the customhouse served as economic consul between producers and merchants at the annual Foggian fair.

Foggia's urban topography remained relatively unchanged until the 1731 earthquake encouraged development outside the historic center.[2] One major street (Via Arpi) bisected the town horizontally, proceeding from the main gate on the east to one in the west (fig. 1). Intersecting Via Arpi, narrow alleyways ran about one block to the north and two or three to the south. Two other streets, which cut through the cramped space to southern gates, began at the town's two major squares—one in front of the cathedral and the other in front of the old doganal palace in use until the 1731 earthquake. The largest square (Piano delle fosse) lay outside the main gate and functioned as grain depository and marketplace. This extraurban center of the unwalled town emphasized the fact that Foggia's power did not reside in the town but in the countryside.

Foggia stood at the focal point of a vast plain with large farms engaged in cereal agriculture, some twenty-three official "locations" pasturing sheep, and only nine scattered villages of sparse population. During the summer heat, this hinterland was deserted and desiccated, its tenuous water resources perilously close to malarial swamps and evaporating salt pans. In the fall, an invasion of more than one million sheep and some five or six thousand shepherds came down from the mountains to fill up the empty expanse of the plain for winter shelter. Panpipes played until buyers and sellers drew all the animal products to Foggia for the spring fair. Shepherds then pulled up stakes for their summer retreat in mountain pastures, and desert summer returned to the plains.

The cyclical routine of this pastoral world was not that of a people without history, whose lulling rhythms only inspired idyllic dreams of idle poets. On the contrary, many of the great themes of early modern European history—the manifestation of social conflict, the emergence of the centralized state, the development of capitalism, and the expression of popular culture—are embodied in its history. The records of the dogana, especially those archives conserved in Foggia,[3] provide priceless and countless riches to view the complex interre-

FIGURE 1 Foggia in the Sixteenth Century

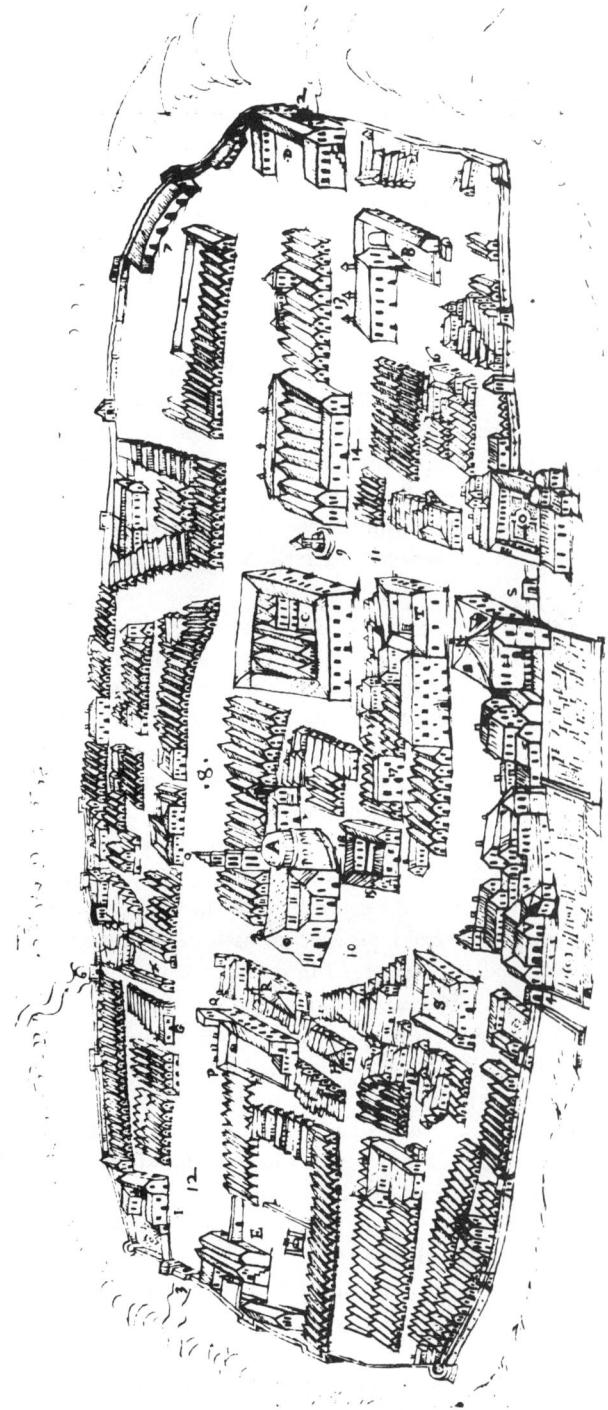

Source: Biblioteca Angelica, Rome, *Bancone stampe*, n.s. 56, c. 51, detail. Reprinted by permission.

lationship between socioeconomic reality and ideological rationalization in the early modern worlds of Mediterranean Europe.

Like the peasants of Le Roy Ladurie's Languedoc,[4] the shepherds who wintered in Puglia would seem to be unlikely candidates to reveal the structure and change of early modern European socioeconomic history. Both peasants and shepherds seem far removed from the dynamic centers of urban growth or the sophisticated courts of powerful elites. Both peasants and shepherds appear as unchanging fixtures in the rural landscape. Yet it is precisely their powerlessness and their slow-moving worlds that allow us to discern the patterns and turnings of the larger world more clearly.

The remoteness of peripheral regions like southern France and southern Italy as well as the monotony of their peasant and pastoral societies force us to reintegrate the varying timbres and tempos of society at large. As we begin to understand the labor that remained the basis for the production of early modern Europe's two most important commodities—the wheat that fed everyone's bodies and the wool that fueled their economy—we begin to see an interlocking system whose many parts simultaneously reinforced and undermined one another. How did such a system sustain itself? Why did the Old Regime endure so long?

Neither refeudalization by a resurgent nobility nor free market economics adequately explains the organization and stasis in much of preindustrial society. The pastoral society of the shepherds in Puglia, on the other hand, provides a convincing model for understanding the relationship between structure and change in that immobile premodern world. A structure of permanent conflict between competing interest groups prevented basic economic change because the centralizing power of the newly unified monarchies emerged to balance these conflicting antagonists. Thus, my five-part exploration of cultural geography, social structure, political action, market economy, and ideological rationale attempts to dissect and reassemble the shepherds' and early modern Europe's many worlds free from our anachronistic evolutionary bias.

Many worlds, indeed, converged in the dogana of Foggia. Two cultures and two peoples—the Abruzzesi mountain men and the Pugliesi plainsmen—met and worked in some 4,300 square kilometers of winter pasture in one of the largest plains in the Italian peninsula, the Tavoliere di Puglia (which had an area midway between those of Rhode Island and Delaware). Two livelihood systems—agriculture and pastoralism—competed with and complemented each other in the same ecological niche. Two modes of ownership—private enterprise and royal demesne—depended upon doganal income for rent and taxes respectively. Two production systems—the international market for wheat and wool and the local subsistence economy of provincial peasants and shepherds—laid claim to the same surplus. Two classes of holders—rich and poor, both large landholders and graziers versus small-time agriculturists and shepherds—demanded special favors and exemptions. Three levels of bureaucracy—officers resident in Foggia, the Regia Camera della Sommaria (the chief financial council) in Naples, and the royal court (resident Aragonese, 1443–1503; absentee Aragonese, 1503–17; absentee Spanish and Austrian Habsburgs, 1517–1734; and finally, the Neapolitan Bourbons, 1734–1806)—administered the dogana in light of their own policy and personal interests. The permutations become dizzying when one computes the variables: fiscal solvency, foreign exchange, international diplomacy, land management techniques, food production needs, rural pacification, bureaucratic abuse, entreprenurial risk, social stratification, class conflict, and livelihood competition. Factor in the three-hundred-fifty-year sweep of continuity and change, and the problems of the customhouse of Foggia transcend the provincial world of the Kingdom of Naples.

Capitanata, a province circumscribed by mountains and the mild Adriatic shore, was the winter domain of the sheep customhouse (fig. 2). Geographical descriptions of Capitanata provide a tangible example of these multiple, polyvalent oppositions underlying the structure of the Kingdom of Naples. Capitanata was the most fertile region of Puglia.[5] It exported grain and wool to Naples, to the rest of the Kingdom, and, from the thirteenth century, to many cities throughout the Italian peninsula.[6] Under Spanish administration this wealth in raw materials was further expanded and exploited. Despite its riches, however, Capitanata remained one of the harshest and most inhospitable provinces in the Kingdom. A report to the viceroy circa 1580 brought this point out clearly.

> It is a province very useful to the others of the Kingdom, but with regard to itself it is the most useless that there could be. It is thinly populated, has a bad climate, is deprived of trees and wood, and has extremely sparse water resources. Summer brings an [infernal] heat, innumerable flies, and a great quantity of snakes. Its men are unsuited for the army or for hard work. Its horses are weak by nature. On the other hand, the province produces wheat, barley, and other grains in such quantity that it can truthfully be called the granary not only of Naples and the Kingdom, but also of many cities of Italy.[7]

The peculiar inversion—fertile land inhospitable to man—points to the fundamental ambiguity circumscribing economy and society in the Tavoliere of Puglia. The tension between land use and natural landscape is the first of the contradictions that underlies and shapes social and economic conflict and weakens institutions throughout the Kingdom.[8]

The ambiguity of exchange, which assumes that one bargainer necessarily gets the better of another, is the source of a second underlying conflict in Neapolitan life.[9] Such inequality of exchange kept the customhouse in constant need of reform. Sheep taxes provided the Kingdom with its single most important source of revenue, while grain from Capitanata fed the Kingdom. Thus, since wheat and wool interests were in direct competition for the same land, land distribution was subject to legal exceptions and illegal abuses. Land management—grain yields, field rotation, sheep breeding, and wool produc-

FIGURE 2 A Physical Map of Capitanata

Source: G. B. Pacichelli, *Il Regno di Napoli in prospettiva*, 3 vols. (Naples: A spese del Parrino e del Mutio, 1703), 3:96a.

tion—was the concern of inimical interest groups. Power itself was contested by the state doganal officers, owners of the land, and the organization of shepherds. Conflict joined and separated livelihood groups and social classes.

How could the state harness these contending factions to work for everyone's mutual benefit? Law provided the means to create "good government" to resolve the tension underlying the Kingdom's institutions. Fostering harmony in the rural economy was a fiscal expedient, a food-provisioning necessity, and a means to control bandits. The state, therefore, was motivated to organize and protect the transhumant industry and to mediate the conflict between pastoralists and agriculturists, between large holders and small, in order to maintain itself and to prevent each party from destroying the other.

My study of the social and economic organization of the dogana of Foggia describes how the structures of rural life in the Kingdom modified the demands of nature and the market by means of political policy and cultural symbols. The rule of law was the organizing principle of doganal management. In order to defuse conflict, the state bureaucracy employed the tradition of law to define the economic exchange of the doganal system in terms of political patronage. Spanish centralization was based upon special privileges which kept antagonists separated from each other, yet tied to the state. For the participants in the dogana, on the other hand, the administration of that law and its circumvention defined utility and maximization in cultural terms. Profit for large holders was tied to the international wool market. Profit for the small provincial may not have been as important as honor, cleverness, and patronage, because playing the game was just as important to him as winning it.[10] Culture, therefore, institutionalized conflict as a cohesive norm.

The history of the royal sheep customhouse of Foggia was not the history of the transition from feudalism to capitalism in the Kingdom of Naples. By definition, from its foundations in the mid fifteenth century, the system of transhumance in southern Italy was a large-scale cash-cropping enterprise dependent upon private wealth (capitalist graziers, capitalist merchants, capitalist agriculturists) and public patronage (royal management, royal demesne, and royal justice). In controlling the movement of sheep from summer to winter pasture, the state placed itself in the center of a timeless tradition that amalgamated the realities of capitalist agriculture with the rationale of Arcadian pastoralism. Such institutional and ideological contradictions were typical of the complex logic and convoluted history of the Kingdom of Naples.[11]

The historiography of the dogana of Foggia has developed out of the rich legacy of the Neapolitan Enlightenment, whose concern for legal history and political economy focused attention on the long pastoral tradition and its need for enlightened reform. Two eighteenth-century lawyers intimately involved in doganal affairs wrote definitive histories that have continued to dominate scholarship. Stefano di Stefano labored more than thirty years in judicial cases at Foggia and wrote a two-volume, 1112-page treatise on the eve of his promotion to the doganal presidency.[12] Di Stefano drew upon his membership in the literary society of the Accademia degli Arcadi to write a kind of pastoral bible filled with literary allusions and legal precedents. Francesco Nicola De Dominicis produced a three-volume, 1409-page study based upon his access to the doganal archives and his personal eleven-year doganal experience.[13] De Dominicis emphasized the need for harmony between agricultural and pastoral livelihood systems in true Enlightenment fashion. In quality and quantity, their archival and juridical work cannot be replicated.

A third lawyer, Andrea Gaudiani, practiced in the dogana for some twenty-six years at the end of the seventeenth and beginning of the eighteenth centuries. Although his fifteen-year study of doganal history remained unpublished and unknown to contemporaries, its lucid style should make it the starting point for any serious student of the dogana.[14] Gaudiani's model is Tacitus, and Gaudiani's concern for good government reflects his master's practical, political orientation.

To this native legal tradition I have brought an *Annaliste* methodological orientation in an attempt to write a "total history" from *géographie humaine* to *mentalité*.[15] I have explored the newly reordered Foggian archives with special attention to quantitative social and economic analysis. Without the use of the computer, the kind of study that I have undertaken would be impossible. The sifting and sorting of taxpayers inscribed in the doganal tax rolls (*libri di squarciafoglio*) and buyers and sellers of wool recorded in the account books of the office of weights and measures (*libri di pesatori di lana*) provide the data to test hypotheses on social and economic change. Hard statistics on income, production, and prices, however, are only the beginning. My investigation leads to a whole series of issues outside the realm of mathematical manipulation and returns full circle to the chronology, laws, language, metaphor, and ideology of sage informants like Di Stefano, De Dominicis, and Gaudiani. If we take their rhetoric seriously and literally, we will rediscover that these innovators in classical economic theory did not believe in simplistic maximization but knew much more about the complex rationale of economic activity.

Before tackling the overriding questions of pastoral economics and early modern European history, we must first master the details of a lost world: the material foundation of that specialized form of pastoral nomadism called transhumance, the institutional organization of the customhouse, and its modification over time. Even as early as 1830, not yet twenty-five years after the demise of the doganal system and with almost one million sheep still grazing in Puglia, Luigi Granata believed that he had to clarify what were already "obscure and arcane" facts.[16] In part 1 I have done the same, hearkening back to an anonymous scribal prayer which introduced a doganal dictionary compiled for the Austrian Habsburgs as they were to assume the rule of the Kingdom in 1709. The invocation quoted St. Gregory the Great's reflections on Luke 12:35–40: "The exposition of these things is made so that the unknown may be made known and so that what is already known may not be too burdensome."[17] By reminding readers of the legal and institutional history of the dogana and of the minutiae of animal husbandry and land use, part 1 is meant to be a historical and geographical handbook which conveniently identifies documents and sources, summarizes the particulars of rural production, and explains the internal and external causes of continuity or change. As obscure as many of these facts of agricultural and pastoral production in the dogana of Foggia may appear, the analyses that follow will have little value unless understood in the specific context of tradition, law, land, man, animals, and economy in Puglia.[18]

Each of these contexts brings with it its own, often variant, chronology. The conjunctures of human and animal populations were not congruent; and they, in turn, diverged from political input into the system. Such contradictory time frames dramatize the ambiguity surrounding the rise and fall of the market. Market conjunctures can be readily defined and will be important guideposts throughout my analysis: 1447–1494, growth; 1494–1550, decline; 1550–1612, growth; 1612–1686, decline; and 1686–1806, growth. But the problem for the historian is not so much to pinpoint periods as to explain the mechanisms of change. Focusing upon a simplistic, monocausal variable does not do justice to the variegated evidence.

For both the individual graziers and the state administration, whose stories are really inseparable, the conflict between classes and the competition between livelihood groups provided an unabating dialectical pressure inimical to the dogana's existence. Part 2 describes the graziers' association and social stratification among sheepowners. The tension between rich and poor sheepowners demanded constant vigilance on the part of the state to ensure equitable distribution of pasture and to prevent the rich from squeezing out the poor. Part 3 explains the management strategy of the royal fisc to conserve and increase revenues, to administer justice, to staff the doganal bureaucracy, and to moderate the conflict between livelihood groups. Royal officers consciously intervened in the economic process, with mixed results, and often were interested only in their own aggrandizement. Part 4 describes the economic profile of the spring fair at Foggia and the competition between sellers and buyers. Large buyers, who had often originally financed the sellers and continually attempted to create monopolies to depress prices and ensure greater profits for themselves, were a constant source of sheepowner complaint and doganal lawmaking. Thus, these middle sections examine the structure and dynamic of the customhouse in its social, political, and economic organization.

The central government's support of a pastoral economy in the fertile plain of Puglia even in times of population growth, and its commitment to small and middling holders instead of the affluent class that should have been its natural ally, defied the conventional wisdom of rationalistic maximization in political economy. The problem of the dogana of Foggia, therefore, is to explain why state policy favored pastoralism over agriculture, and small holders over large. The solution to the paradox requires an understanding of how extraeconomic variables like kin, custom, religion or ideology, law, and politics operated on the conflicting needs and desires in the Kingdom between center and periphery, royal authority and private power, and the domestic and international markets. Such economic rationale did not engender a dialectic of change, but a synthesis of stability, as conflict fostered cohesion in the doganal provinces.

In order to defuse conflict, the central government manipulated the social structure of its provincial participants by dividing and conquering opponents. Economic cooperation and social equilibrium mediated the differences between farmer and shepherd or between rich and poor. The associational life of the grazier capitalists was encouraged to express itself in a kind of primitive parliament whose four deputies general worked together with the state bureaucrats in their economic and judicial functions. Thus, the sheep customhouse of Foggia developed a model for participatory democracy from below—even within the hierarchical world of an Old Regime monarchy.

Economic cycles and credit policies similarly demanded coordinated response from both pastoral investors and doganal managers. The state's attempts at good government, however, were often subverted by its own officers, whose collusion with mercantile interests created a third arena of conflict for the raw material producers. The final crisis came to the doganal system in the late eighteenth century when the state could no longer balance the overlapping and intertwining interests of the doganal partners in the face of the demands of the market for agricultural rather than pastoral products.

Part 5 explores the ideology of pastoral production and places the Foggian customs in the context of the early modern theory of political economy. The gradual transformation of feudalism to capitalism misidentifies the process of capital investment and cash cropping in the countryside, where sheepherding was the first link in the wool trade, late medieval Europe's most dynamic economic enterprise.[19] An economic system that could not grow beyond well-defined ecological limits likewise contradicts assumptions about ever-expanding, ever-developing enterprises. The multilayered interdependence of capitalist investment, rural labor, and state-leased land demanded a balanced rapport among sheepowners, landowners, workers, merchants, and government.

Here, deep in the rural soil of the early modern Kingdom of Naples, lie the roots of southern Italian underdevelopment, the "problema del Mezzogiorno." The doganal institution demonstrates the limits of diverse developmental models. Management expedients addressing the cyclical crises of capitalism attempted to manipulate the distribution of pasture and the taxation of sheep for the benefit of all parties. Thus, while good government fostered the growth of the central state, defused class conflict, and allowed for maximum exploitation of the land within contemporary technological limits, it elaborated a program of conservative defense of the status quo. How the ideology of *buon governo* and the literary image of the pastoral shaped the pastoral realities of the rural world into axioms of Neapolitan life is the meaning of pastoral economics.

INTRODUCTION

Pastoral economics was congruent with the ideology of hierarchical society. Like the biblical allusions to the shepherd king and the simpleton shepherd, like the harsh environment of pastoral livelihood and the ethereal peace of pastoral poetry, polar opposites were fused to create complex ideologies in support of an extremely powerful social and economic institution.[20] Like myths, both the institution and its ideology aimed at moderating conflict, resolving diametrically opposed forces, and explaining ambiguities.

It is my contention that models of political instability and economic backwardness only describe the surface phenomena in the Kingdom of Naples without understanding the hard realities and structural limits of production.[21] Seemingly rampant political upheaval and social chaos should not distract us from deciphering the deeper, structural antitheses embedded within the Kingdom's institutions and organization. Similarly, no inevitable industrial revolution should determine an evolutionary measuring rod for rural society and economy when, in fact, the cyclical repetition of early modern crises led to no such change on the continent. In the Neapolitan Kingdom, ever-present internal contradictions redefined theory and practice, appearance and reality, structure and antistructure into functional equivalents, and state policy manipulated these opposites into the means of maintaining the status quo, not revolutionary economic change.

Although the internal structure of the sheep customhouse may appear to be a disconnected and incongruous mosaic, the historical long term reveals a definite pattern. Reformers were constantly attempting to pluck the institution from the reality of abuses and return it to the ideals of its foundation, from the exploitation of large holders to an equality among all, from the tyranny of one of its participants to a symbiosis between agriculture and pastoralism. Pastoral economics was good government, and good government was a pastoral ideal.

PART I

The Works and Days of the Dogana of Foggia

An allusion to Hesiod's didactic poetry to begin an examination of material production in the pastoral economy of the Kingdom of Naples is not mere literary fancy. Labor, time, and imagination are what constituted the rural world of preindustrial society. Human agency as much as natural landscape created the pastoral preserve in the Tavoliere of Puglia. The timelessness of Mediterranean Europe's immutable pastoral structures can be understood only in terms of a specific set of historical circumstances common to both Spain and Italy in the mid thirteenth century, reinforced by the 1348 plague, and accelerated by the disruption of English raw wool exportation during the Hundred Years' War. Political decisions then established specific land-use patterns, pastoral divisions and distribution, tax rates and prices, even modifying the customary land rotation cycle during the 1548 general land survey in Puglia. Pastoral economics was not an illusory flight from the real world to the green cabinet, but an imposition of rational planning on the rural landscape.

1 Mediterranean Mestas and the Neapolitan Exemplar

Transhumance as an Economic and Political Decision

In the Mediterranean, the relationship between mountains, plateaus, and plains defined an ancient pattern of exchange.[1] Livelihood systems, political units, and religious movements converged and intermingled. Symbiosis, often antagonistic, characterized the dealings between men of these different regions. Geographic frontiers were continually broken by seasonal migrations, opportunities for work, and the pull of the city. As natural boundaries diminished in importance, social and cultural barriers were raised to distinguish the rude, traditional mountain folk from the more refined culture of the plain.

Topographical relief and seasonal variation appear to have governed the particulars of one of the Mediterranean's most spectacular migration patterns, transhumance. The harsh, cold winter at high mountain altitudes and the long, dry summer, which reduced the Tavoliere plain to semidesert, discouraged subsistence agriculture. Marginal land, however, could be transformed into a productive component of the rural economy if the animal products of cash-cropping pastoralists supplemented the unbalanced diets of cash-cropping agriculturists, and vice versa. Cheese and milk from the mountain folk exchanged for grains from the plainsmen made farmer and shepherd dependent upon each other for survival. Graziers, therefore, gathered their sheep together and descended upon the plains for dietary exchange, winter shelter, and spring markets. This kind of competitive exchange is characteristic of a limited agricultural economy which lives in symbiotic relationship with pastoralism.[2] The distinctive feature of this system of cooperation between shepherd and farmer was that both wool and grain production were destined for cash markets. With the appearance of merchants and money came government regulation and taxation.

The specific schedule of seasonal migration corresponded to the agricultural cycle. Pastoral movement from mountain summer to winter plains anticipated the first autumn rains in September or October. Simultaneously, however, wheat was being planted in those winter plains. Although animal manure was a welcome fertilizer for the fields, keeping grazing sheep out of sprouting wheat fields was no easy matter. With the drying up of spring grass by the end of April or May and the grain harvest due in late June or early July, the flocks were on the move once again. Sheep and grains were in competition for the same land at the same time. Some kind of cooperation or regulation was necessary to maintain the checks and balances that pastoral and agricultural economies imposed upon each other. Thus, no matter how the complementarity and conflict between farmer and shepherd were outwardly fashioned by mountains and plains, or affected by winter's severity and summer's drought, economics and politics rather than geography or meteorology primarily defined transhumance as a capital-intensive system of livestock farming.[3]

Man, not land, determined such a livelihood system. The specialist herder consciously chose to take numerous economic risks in order to exploit the natural environment. He maintained flocks far greater than his own land could pasture. He assumed that adequate pasture was available far afield and that he would be able to rent it. He expected to be able to reach it safely, without exorbitant tolls. He needed some kind of special tribunal or magistrates to settle disputes with agriculturists quickly. The cash-cropping pastoralist relied upon salaried shepherds working far from home. He depended on the external market and the international demand for wool. Thus, his economic fortunes were out of his own control as he gambled on profits that were contingent upon the ability of government to provide political stability, freedom from local tolls and bandits, expeditious justice, and free markets. Good government, not nature, ensured the success of such large-scale, capital investments.

Spain: The Castilian Mesta and the Aragonese Casa de Ganaderos

The Spanish system of transhumance, institutionalized in the Castilian Mesta (1273–1836), is the best known of the Mediterranean pastoral economies. The Spanish sheep-grazing industry is documented from Roman times and is believed to have existed among the indigenous people of Iberia long before the Roman era.[4] Although pastoralism continued through the Moorish period in a restricted range, it was only with the Reconquest that a definitive national transhumant structure established itself. With the expulsion of the Moors from the plains of Extremadura and La Mancha, northern graziers from the mountains in Galicia, Asturias, Leon, and Old Castile—especially the military orders, the Church, and privileged town councils with royal concessions for pastoralism beginning about 1156—extended their pastoral space at the expense of weaker entities and eventually initiated the great autumnal drives of sheep and cattle southward for milder winter grazing.[5] The monarchy consolidated these various local *mestas* ("reunions" or "councils" of graziers) into a national organization in order to facilitate tax collection. The earliest extant Mesta charter dates from 1273. Because it claims to replace older charters worn out by hard usage, the Mesta per se was probably founded a generation earlier, sometime between 1230 and 1263.[6]

At the time of the foundation of the Mesta, the Castilian economy was in a downward spiral of inflation and currency debasement because of only incipient industrial activity, the existence of a disproportionate market for luxury goods, and the needs of the public treasury. To counterbalance the outflow of capital, the monarchy organized and taxed the sale of wool to foreign merchants under the auspices of its royally sanctioned Mesta. The state monopoly was a way of creating a supraregional institution that could maintain order, administer justice, guarantee ease of movement, and protect grazing lands. Into the bargain, the herders were granted privileges and exemptions which were often at the expense of agricultural production.

The rapid rise of the Spanish Mesta in the thirteenth century, then, was due to a confluence of demographic, economic, and exogenous phenomena.[7] Late medieval population growth and increased commercial activity stimulated large wool-consuming markets, especially in Flanders and Italy. Increased demand for high-quality woolens strained the English suppliers, the chief European source of raw wool, at a time when England was engaged in political rivalries in France and Flanders. And in the fourteenth and fifteenth centuries, because of the effects of the Hundred Years' War and an increased domestic textile industry on English wool production and prices, cheaper wool was sought in alternate markets in Spain and North Africa.[8]

The characteristic sheep of Spain, the fine-wooled Merino, were not indigenous to the peninsula. They were probably introduced from North Africa by the mid fourteenth century.[9] Whether through the initiative of Spanish graziers themselves or at the suggestion of Genoese merchants, the sheep of the Banu-Marin (a Berber tribe of the southern Moroccan desert) were crossed with the native Spanish sheep. The Castilians refined this new breed into the world's best wool producers and established themselves as the dominant suppliers for the European market.

The Castilian Mesta remained a private monopoly subject to royal taxation in exchange for the personal patronage of the king. The dependence upon raw wool exports to maintain the balance of payments encouraged the monarchy to grant special privileges to pastoralists. The financial and political dominance of the nobility was grounded in their investment in the wool trade. Large sheepowners controlled the institutional structure of the Mesta, curtailed agricultural growth to retain their hold on the countryside, and attempted to block the growth of native textile industries in order to buttress their position against potential urban rivals. Despite some domestic production, Castile became a prisoner of her own success. Great wealth for the few inhibited expansion beyond the bounds of a one-product economy and a rigidified social structure.

In the short run, before the riches of the New World were realized, Castilian wool production was the cornerstone of the expansionist economic policy of the unified monarchy of Castile and Aragon. In each of his domains, Ferdinand the Catholic bolstered his power by strengthening existing institutions. In Castile he expanded Mesta privileges, increased pasture, and appointed a new chief officer dependent on the crown.[10] In Aragon he encouraged production (which had been on the rise since the mid fifteenth century) in the

Casa de Ganaderos (the "House of the Cattle Owners") of Saragossa, a native Aragonese *mesta* known since 1218, if not before.[11] In the Kingdom of Naples, after the disruptions of the French invasions (1494–1530), he reestablished the *dogana delle pecore* upon the model of his uncle, Alfonso the Magnanimous. Mesta-like institutions throughout the Spanish kingdoms brought ready cash to the royal treasury, guaranteed foreign exchange, and strengthened the centralizing tendencies of the new monarchy.

Italy: The Roman *dogana dei pascoli* and the Neapolitan *dogana delle pecore*

Although the governmental organization and sponsorship of transhumance in southern Italy followed a very different institutional history from that of its Spanish cousins, the political impetus and economic rationale of refoundation were strikingly similar. As in Spain, Italian transhumant sheep systems crossed diverse territorial jurisdictions and could only be maintained by a strong centralized state which was, for its part, further strengthened by the enormous and consistent revenues such institutions provided. Thus, a parallel pattern emerged in southern Italy: pre-Roman foundations, late antique and early medieval decadence, and refoundation in the late twelfth and early thirteenth centuries; but, because of dynastic rivalries, with relatively late definitive charters as compared to that of the Mesta in 1273.

The Papal States had its own sheep migration system, with the oldest extant privilege dating from Boniface IX in 1402.[12] The *dogana dei pascoli* ("customhouse of the pastures") of the Patrimonio di San Pietro in Tuscia provided Abruzzi flocks winter pastures extending from the gates of Rome to the borders with Tuscany and Umbria. Its origins stretch back to the ancients, with a modern foundation not much before 1289.[13] In the fourteenth century, the papal sheep industry provided meat and cheese for Rome and wool for Tuscan merchants, as well as a nascent native textile industry.[14] In 1452, after a half-century of continual warfare, brigandage, and depopulation in the Agro Romano, the reunified papacy in the person of Nicholas V promulgated a new constitution for its own dogana in response to the revived customhouse in Naples.[15]

The organizational structure of the Roman dogana was similar to the sheep customhouse in the Kingdom of Naples.[16] The Camera Apostolica appointed a doganiero annually to administer the system. Pastoralists were exempt from local gabelles, provided security and free rights of passage across private lands to arrive at guaranteed pasture, and promised special judicial privileges. Special statutes were established to distinguish between Roman citizens and Neapolitan foreigners. But income from the Roman dogana was only about 10 percent of that of its southern neighbor, as sheep numbered 106,530 head at mid fifteenth century, thus reflecting the smaller area available for winter grazing.[17]

In the Kingdom of Naples, the *dogana delle pecore* of Foggia also drew Abruzzi sheep down from the mountains for winter pastures,[18] but on the Adriatic side of the peninsula in Puglia, the "extremadura de este Regno."[19] Alfonso of Aragon, who had conquered the Kingdom in 1443, issued the founding charter for the sheep customhouse in 1447.[20] But transhumance in Puglia was neither a recent Aragonese nor, even earlier, a Roman invention. Continuity of the winter and summer migrations goes backward as well as forward from Roman times. Pliny called one of the two breeds of sheep *graeca*, and this name possibly recalled the early foundation of transhumance.[21] The Romans, having come late into Puglia, probably imposed their lordship over an already established Samnite system of animal migrations. From the time of the Greek colonies in the eighth century B.C., if not before, ancient Arpi (modern Foggia) had been an active agricultural and pastoral center.[22]

From early Roman times there is evidence of a transhumance industry in Puglia which was subject to the rule of commercial law.[23] *De re rustica*, the serious, scientific, agricultural treatise of M. Terentius Varro (116–27 B.C.), provides the earliest literary source on the Roman system of transhumance. "Hence flocks of sheep are driven all the way from Apulia into Samnium for summering and are reported to the tax collectors, for fear of offending against the censorial regulation forbidding the pasturage of unregistered flocks."[24] This description of sheep tolls emphasizes the major economic constraint to transhumance: state taxes. When taxes were paid, it was because herders feared (*paverint*) breaking the law. Whatever the motivation for obeying the law may have been, tax evasion must never have been far from the mind of the pastoralist.

With the breakdown of that law or that fear after the dissolution of the Roman Empire, the Lombard dukes of Benevento and the Byzantine emperors were in constant struggle for control of Puglia. Flocks contracted and transhumance declined as herders were content to stay closer to their homes in the hills of the Abruzzi and Molise rather than risk the uncertainties of the plain. Whenever any one party stabilized political power, sheep migrations increased. A cyclical pattern of large migrations, external disruption, decline in numbers, then reestablishment of enforceable sanctions and increased migrations characterized transhumance in Puglia throughout the early medieval period. The Norman conquest of southern Italy in the late eleventh century and the imperial policy of Frederick II in the early thirteenth decisively forged the links between raw material production in the southern countryside and urban markets in northern Italy.[25]

Two Norman laws, promulgated either by William I (1154–66) or by William II (1166–89), are the oldest extant post-Roman legislation defining the Puglia-Abruzzi axis.[26] In particular, the second law, *Cum per partes Apuliae*, focused on abuses in renting pasture. It fixed payment for sheepowners and forbade the withholding of pasture or the extortion of exorbitant rents. The law applied both to state officials in charge of the royal demesne and to private landowners. Transgressors were subject to the death penalty. Frederick II inserted both constitutions in his codex published at Melfi in 1231. He later modified the severity of punishment in two other constitutions, *Animalia in vineis* and *Ut delicti*, which substituted for the death penalty a fine of four times the amount extorted.[27]

By Frederick's 1231 constitution, the essential details of transhumance were reestablished. The state regulated sheep migrations and collected a tax (*fida*) for pasture. Administrators of the organization were provincial judges, procurators, and tax collectors (*giustizioni, maestri procuratori, baglivi*).[28] Private landholders could rent pasture for their own profit. And finally, two new forms of agricultural tenancy were introduced. "Royal land for planting" (*terre demaniali a coltura*) could be shared or rented to private parties, and "royal grazing land" (*terre demaniali salde*) could be divided up among private individuals for cultivation.[29] The first record of the institution's name, *dogana delle pecore*, is found in a budget entry of 1254, and the names of specific winter grazing areas, locations (*locazioni*), by 1270.[30] Like the Castilian Mesta, Aragonese Casa de Ganaderos, and Roman dogana, then, the Pugliese sheep transhumance institution grew from the exploitation of newly amalgamated territory in the twelfth century and had been officially chartered by the mid thirteenth century. But unlike Spain, the Kingdom of Naples, after the death of Frederick II in 1250, experienced dynastic rivalries, which again caused the number of sheep in transhumance to fluctuate with the power of the centralized bureaucracy to maintain political stability and a pro-pastoral policy.

Alfonso of Aragon's 1447 Charter

In the dynastic war between Angevins and Aragonese which followed the death of Giovanna II in 1435, feudal proprietors further encroached upon royal holdings in Puglia. Transhumance had fallen off drastically as the absence of state management allowed autonomous provincials to engage in open warfare: bandits preyed upon the shepherds during their migrations, and landowners gouged them upon arrival. In 1442/43, Alfonso of Aragon's first year in control of the Kingdom, his sheep toll institution collected only 18,168 ducats. Two Abruzzi natives, one from Sulmona and the other from Aquila, administered it, and it followed the 1423 charter of Alfonso's Angevin predecessor, Giovanna, in all particulars.[31] Alfonso's original foundation, therefore, was not based upon importing an Iberian institution, but rather upon reviving a native Neapolitan one.

In her 1423 charter, Giovanna appointed the chief officers from the two largest pastoral centers in the Abruzzi, Aquila and Sulmona.[32] The queen confirmed local power brokers already in existence, as in the early Catilian Mesta. She legitimized native leadership with appointments of men who were associated with the graziers or the wool merchants rather than the crown. The state had merely imposed itself upon a preexisting system to garner taxes.

Giovanna's 1423 register, similarly, established reciprocity between the monarch and her subject pastoralists in the form of legal ties. Giovanna ensured security to the owners of sheep, their servants, and shepherds from all kinds of molestation. A judicial system was even established to hear grievances. But most important, pasture land was assured to the graziers, and landholders were forbidden to take unjust advantages.

Landholders too had networks of exchange with the state. Special licenses were awarded that allowed them to graze their own animals on public pasture, send these animals outside the Kingdom, or rent their own pasture to third persons. Privilege and prerogative were still in the hands of the private property owners who continued to control the disposition and price of their pasture. In its provisions for the transhumant system, balance and exchange were the keystone of Angevin policy between the state and grazier, and between the state and landowner. The problem remained to maintain the balance between grazier and landowner.

In order to increase state revenues, Alfonso's charter of 1447 determined to strengthen this existing transhumant institution and expand its scope through an ideal good government. Like Giovanna, Alfonso bound the dogana to a double contract; one with the owners of land and pasture in Puglia, and the other with the owners of sheep in the Abruzzi, ensuring that both were evenly treated and well satisfied. But then he added an innovation. Private landowners lost control of their land and had to lease their pastures to the state, which then oversaw distribution and prices. For the pastoralists, Alfonso made it obligatory for his subjects to engage in the winter migration, and he lowered taxes across the board—even urging foreigners to cross over from papal territories by reducing their animal tax (*fida*) below that assessed on his own subjects.[33] In exchange for an animal head tax, the transhumant sheepowners would be assured free passage into and out of Puglia, protected from thieves and bandits, be given the pasture (*erbaggi*) necessary for wintering their herds at uniform prices, and provided with expeditious civil and criminal justice.[34] Further, Alfonso introduced the Merino sheep of Spain, called *gentili* in Puglia, in order to improve the local breed and cater to world demand for fine wool.[35] He also appointed a new doganiero, Francesco Montluber, a Catalan, with no ties in Puglia except to the king. In return, the state expected to receive its compensation in doganal taxes.

In the sheep customhouse, then, Alfonso's policies grew out of an amalgamation of two different traditions. He conserved the native Pugliese-Abruzzese system which had been inherited from the Angevins and refined in Giovanna's charter. At the same time, he amplified it with his own native Iberian transhumant tradition. Alfonso's solution to the political problems of land and office were what gave the *dogana delle pecore* the structural equilibrium to withstand four centuries of changing economic fortune.

For the land, Alfonso's policy of institutionalization and centralization halted the fragmentation of the countryside into the private domains of semi-independent barons. A strong state authority stood up against particularist interests. In response to the barons' petition in the parliament of 1443 to regain control of their own grazing land, Alfonso promised to maintain prices at a level at least equal to those under Ladislas at the beginning of the fifteenth century but made no mention of relinquishing the state's prerogative to dispense pasture.[36] Because this policy deprived the barons of extortionate profits, it made the dogana the first among the causes of Alfonso's unpopularity.[37] As a consequence of this policy, however, the number of sheep and the amount of revenue that could be collected increased proportionately to the removal of baronial tax barriers and their exorbitant local rates. Alfonso's policy of conciliar administration and bureaucratic centralization reaped economic rewards that established a model for a kind of political stability, uniform justice, and good government characteristic of southern Italy. A kind of "colonial" occupation reordered the traditional patron-client network by replacing the capricious power of independent barons with that of a state institution promising equal treatment under law.

The chief office (*doganiero*) of the sheep customhouse is a case in point. It was taken out of the hands of the wealthy sheepowning community and made directly dependent on the crown.[38] The new doganiero, Montluber, was, in fact, a surrogate for the king. The 1447 charter named him "Commissarius, Dohanerius, Procuratores, et Nuntius noster specialis." The legal formula identified four distinct offices as one. Montluber was to have the duties of a "custodian of credit," "officer of a tax institution," "purchasing agent," and "special royal envoy"; that is, the powers of his office extended beyond limited conventional appointments.[39] He was appointed for life, could make contracts, proclaim banns relating to doganal administration, regulate merchants, distribute pasture, set prices for cheese and wool, and exercise full and mixed judicial powers in both civil and criminal procedures (*cum plena Jurisdictione Civile et Criminali mero et mixto imperio ac gladii potestate*) like any baron.

The doganiero, however, was not autonomous, but responsible to the conciliar machinery of government. An official notary (*notarius credencerius*) oversaw his accounts for the ultimate arbiter of fiscal matters, the Sommaria in Naples. Its accountants (*rationales*), in turn, conducted audits.[40]

Alfonso's customhouse reforms, above all, aimed at a responsible fiscal policy to sustain his treasury. The results of Alfonso's policies were immediate. In 1444/45, income was 38,516.25 ducats, more than double that of two years before. Sheep numbered 424,642. But that was only the beginning. In 1448/49, sheep and income doubled again: 925,712 head and 92,972.52 ducats; in 1449/50, 1,019,821 sheep and 103,011.73 ducats; in 1450/51, 855,731 sheep and 87,798.16 ducats.[41]

The rural depopulation of the fifteenth century allowed for such spectacular expansion since sheep farming employed less manpower than agriculture. By mid century, at the low point of the demographic curve after the 1348 plague, there is no mystery in finding sheep transhumance systems institutionalized in southern and central Italy. Wheat prices could be artificially maintained with less land under the plow, more customs duties could be collected from the increasing sheep migrations, and hard currency could be accumulated from the sale of wool, meat, and cheese.

At the same time, the decline in English exports during the Wars of the Roses caused a vacuum in the international supply of raw wool. Political stabilization in the Papal States and the Kingdom of Naples made the Abruzzi ready to export wool from both the Roman and Foggian doganal outlets. New breeds and improved institutions provided both good quality and large quantities of raw wool. Abruzzese *matricina* (wool from ewes who have mothered lambs) thus captured the mid-fifteenth-century market, because the quality of Abruzzese wool was judged in Florence and Venice to be superior even to Catalan-Aragonese fibers. More than 70 percent of the raw wool sold by the Florentine import company of the Cambini to wool artisans between 1454 and 1480, for example, came from the Abruzzi.[42] Thus, rising wool prices and declining grain prices coincided to give the southern Italian transhumant industry a strong foothold in the international market.

By the end of the fifteenth century, the economic policies of the newly unified monarchy in Spain began to make their mark in the international wool market. Under the Catholic Kings, Mesta wool from Castile began to compete with the Abruzzese raw material in the 1480s and 1490s at just the moment when internal disorder and "barbarian" invasions once again disrupted the Italian peninsula. The Castilian wool pushed out Abruzzese wool and established itself as the dominant product in the Italian market until the middle of the seventeenth century.[43] Castilian success in Italy was political as well as economic, just as Alfonso's earlier success had been both political and economic.

The reforming spirit of Alfonso's policy was not limited to the sheep industry. It called for a complete reorganization of governmental machinery, finance, and defense, upon the model of most fifteenth-century European kings: transforming the administrative methods developed in the northern Italian cities for the purpose of running a whole kingdom.[44] Alfonso introduced conciliar government and tried to control, if not subjugate, baronial power and jurisdiction. The barons retained limited power on their own estates, but nowhere else. Catalans replaced Neapolitans in the councils, in the courts, and in command of fortresses.

The history of state sheep tolls in Puglia proves this model of Renaissance good government with a classical referent and a gradual refinement of state controls. From the earliest Roman times of state involvement in the transhumant economy, taxes were levied as a kind of payment—like a license issued in exchange for some government service, passage on roads, and rent of pasture. Throughout the medieval period, state revenues reflected fluctuation between state and baronial controls. The overwhelming thrust of Alfonso's foundation was continuity with the tradition. Emphasis on a bureaucratic customs agency was not a novel principle. Had the French invasions following 1494 been successful, would not a new foundation have been in order and the victorious French looked back to the model of Giovanna's 1423 constitution?[45] Ferdinand the Catholic's victory, however, confirmed southern Italian sheep transhumance in the pattern of his Aragonese forerunners. Change was defined by propaganda more than by fact. What Alfonso's foundation did was to ratify the state's role as protector and to alienate particularist and private patronage from interfering in transhumance. Alfonso's organizational genius envisioned the state as ideal arbiter between the participants in the pastoral economy. The doganal foundation was but one of the many attempts during his reign to integrate regional diversity into a unified administration.

Alfonso's policies defined the parameters of conflict but did not eliminate tension. The seeds of doganal struggle were embedded in the original foundation. The principle of institutionalized exchange had particularly narrow limits in a region with circumscribed physical boundaries and limited pastoral and agricultural resources. It was a false analogy to compare the Tavoliere of Puglia to the vast frontier of La Mancha or Extremadura. As the system on the Foggian plain prospered and herds grew, there was no possibility for unlimited growth. Maximum growth was an omnipresent reality defined by some 4,300 square kilometers of the Tavoliere itself. In such a closed system, the equality of economic exchange was undermined by the competition for limited resources. Different interest groups vied for their own advantage in the same niche—agriculturist against pastoralist, large holder of either kind against small holder. Livelihood competition and social conflict were explicit norms built into the dogana's foundation.

Competition meant unequal economic exchange through favoritism. This simple proposition kept alive distribution networks established by the older patronage system. Patron-client relationships had never really been wiped out, only modified and partially replaced. They operated simultaneously with the newer model of the centralized state, but in a different sphere, since Alfonso, (i.e., the state), never gave up his own claim to personal patronage. Royal concessions of free pasturage to barons, churches, monasteries, communes, and favorites of all kinds, vitiated the even-handed ideal of doganal administration.[46] Jealousies and resentment were the legacy of such favoritism. Official bureaucratic abuse fitted into this same framework. As time passed, the reality of competition and the longstanding patterns of patron-client relationships reestablished themselves despite the innovations of Alfonso's reform.

The Aragonese Legacy and Disruptions of War

In the year following Alfonso's death, the festering rivalry between Angevin and Aragonese erupted anew. From 1459 to 1464, civil war prevented his illegitimate son, Ferrante, from assuming effective control of the Kingdom. Duke John of Anjou (the son of René, Giovanna II's legal heir) occupied Puglia and appointed his own doganiero, Aloyse de Castellis of Aquila, to the *dogana delle pecore* in 1459. Only after Ferrante had defeated the rebels at Troia and expelled them from the Kingdom in 1464 could he begin to reorder the sheep customhouse.

Ferrante's policy was patterned on his father's: bureaucratic centralization, pastoral privileges, and pacification of the rebellious faction. In 1465 he replaced the Angevin doganiero with an Aragonese loyalist, Gasparo di Castiglione of Penne. He appropriated additional pasture lands from the confiscated territory of the defeated faction for the dogana's royal demesne. In 1468 he moved the seat of the dogana from Lucera to Foggia. The physical separation of the dogana (even if by only 19 km) from the provincial capital's law courts and hearth tax collection apparatus strengthened independent doganal administration. Doganal instructions in 1470 further enhanced the doganiero's power: he was allowed nine personal servants (five *cavallari*, three *famigli*, and one *ragazzo ad minus*) while the dogana's eighteen "cavalrymen" (*cavallari*) could be increased to twenty-two at his discretion.[47] The centralizing policies of the Aragonese were at work in creating an autonomous power in the dogana—a power which stood above and apart from provincial administration and baronial prerogatives.

Foggia, nevertheless, remained primarily an agricultural center in the fifteenth century.[48] The growing importance of the spring fair for animal products and the growing doganal bureaucracy soon altered the size and orientation of the city.[49] Two documents dated 31 October 1486 and 2 December 1506, which forbid the doganiero from moving his residence out of Foggia, however, suggest that there may still have been sentiment for running doganal affairs from Lucera; or, more likely, as a 1536 sheepowners' request makes clear, absentee officers attempted to live outside Puglia altogether.[50]

The effectiveness of administrative centralization in the dogana was tied to the ability of the pastoral lobby to supplant the native agricultural elite. The first list of royal concessions (*grazie*) of Ferrante, issued in 1470, addressed the issue directly by confirming the request of sheepowners for continued protection and privileges.[51] The eighteen chapters, which make up the requests presented by the three deputies of the graziers' organization, asked for a restitution of goods and privileges lost, maintenance of a subsidized price for salt bought and a guaranteed price for wool sold, control over the pretensions of rich and noble holders, and a tax consideration for sheep killed in harsh winters. The agricultural interests of Foggia were under attack by the monarchy's newly favored pastoral livelihood group, as a different relationship between city and countryside took shape under special Aragonese patronage.

Pastoral success did not depend upon victory over only one adversary. In addition to agriculturists, the graziers had to contend with state officials, foreign merchants, the weather, and especially one another. Items 9 and 14 of the list of royal concessions are suggestive of the kind of class conflict that was an ever-present reality in the doganal system.

9. Item, [the sheepowners] ask that your Majesty deign to command the doganiero to allocate all the sheep of the Signori [wealthy, noble holders] to one side of Puglia, that is, both those which are in place, and those which are in other pastures, awaiting the bread allowance, because the Trail Bosses and Company of the Signori have so much arrogance that they impede the other men wishing some better territory, taking up so much pasture that they usurp it with great damage to the other owners.

14. Item, [the sheepowners ask] that no one who buys summer pasture in the Abruzzi for grazing may buy from landowners at a low price and then resell it to sheepowners at a high price; but no one may buy pasture except for his own sheep or to resell it to associates at cost.

Rich holders tried to dominate their poorer competitors by occupying the best pasture in the winter, and by using their liquid capital to monopolize mountain meadows in the summer.

With the connivance of state officials, such frauds became commonplace. In 1474 the doganiero Gasparo di Castiglione was accused of mismanagement and favoritism in the distribution of lands. Castiglione had assigned pasture not to shepherds without prejudice, but to friendly graziers. They, in turn, used some of these pastures for draft animals or even plowed them up and planted grain. The scandal broke when a harsh winter found the sheep badly grazed on inferior land. More than 700,000 sheep died, more than 41 percent of the 1,700,000 reported.[52] Castiglione was prosecuted and dismissed. In 1478 Nicola Caracciolo, a Neapolitan noble, was appointed doganiero.

Patronage and collusion, however, were not limited to the doganiero and his favorites. Ferrante, like his royal predecessors and successors, considered the dogana to be his own private royal "industry" and dispensed privileges accordingly. In the same year as Caracciolo's appointment, Ferrante recommended to him a special exemption for one of the king's baronial clients. The duke of Calabria was to have his sheep assigned to the same pasture as the year before.[53]

The king concerned himself with administrative abuses in the dogana only when he was most directly affected, that is, when state revenues shrank. In 1479, Ferrante sent one of the ten presidents of the Sommaria, Niccolò de Statis, to collect unpaid accounts. The pastoral lobby presented additional requests to Ferrante in 1480.[54] Its twenty-one chapters repeated the petition for a separation of rich holders from poor and confirmation of past privileges and exemptions. These requests, however, had a new thrust. The majority of chapters addressed themselves to the excesses of agriculture and the usurpation of pasture. In 1483, Ferrante issued instructions granting the privileges requested by the pastoralists.[55] For the landowners, he decreed that all "extraordinary usual fodder" (*erbaggi straordinari soliti*), at the service of the dogana's pastoral needs from the time of the first doganiero Montluber, would remain under the future power of the dogana, at the same uniform price, in perpetuity.

The Great Conspiracy of the Barons (1485–86) intervened, and, after putting down the rebellion, Ferrante was once again forced to reorder the

Kingdom. In 1489, Colantonio Minadois was sent to visit the dogana in order to redistribute land usurped by nobles or squatters.[56] And again in 1492, Dottor Colantonio de Landes conducted a similar reintegration of pasture. Royal visitors, employed by the monarch in Naples and later Spain, frequently traveled to Foggia to ensure that his patrimony remained fiscally sound.

With Ferrante's death and the 1494 French invasions, the changing fortunes of the Italian Wars interrupted the smooth operation of the doganal system for almost forty years.[57] The dogana's wealth in 1496—1,700,000 sheep and more than 100,000 ducats in state income—proved to be too strong a temptation for the French who invaded Puglia proper in 1497 to collect doganal taxes. At the start of the new doganal year, Frederick, the last of the Neapolitan Aragonese, clarified royal favoritism further by restating the pastoralists' advantages in an eleven-item instruction.[58]

The importance of the Foggian customs in military strategy and diplomatic negotiations has been eloquently narrated by Guicciardini, Giovio, and Giannone.[59] The Treaty of Granada (11 November 1500) provides tangible evidence of the dogana's critical function as a "motive or at least a pretext" for war.[60] In the partitioning of the Kingdom, the dogana was specifically named and divided equally between Louis XII, who received the Neapolitan capital and the northern provinces, and Ferdinand the Catholic, who received the southern provinces. Hostilities over the collection of doganal taxes broke the uneasy peace in the spring of 1502 and opened the phase of fighting culminating in the Great Captain Gonsalvo di Cordova's 1 May 1503 Spanish victory near Cerignola in the middle of one of the doganal locations.

As a result of the wartime disturbances to the doganal system, private landowners (mostly resident in Naples) complained that they were not receiving their agreed-upon rents. The same request was stated in 1495 and repeated in 1496, 1503, and 1505. Ferdinand the Catholic granted this baronial and clerical request to regularize the payment of private pasture rents in 1505 and, again, in response to another parliamentary request, in 1507.[61] At the beginning of the transhumant season in August 1506, Ferdinand promulgated a twelve-item doganal constitution which reestablished the Foggian customs and initiated another period of reform and stability.[62] Provisions of this new charter forbade animal migrations to the Papal States, restored pastoral and mercantile privileges, reinstated the traditional tax structure, and redressed particular frauds and abuses. In 1508, in order to correct the numerous disorders and illegal land occupations caused by the wars, Annibale de Capua, another Neapolitan noble of the *seggio* or *piazza* of Nido (one of the five noble "seats" or quarters of the capital), was appointed doganiero, and Antonello Di Stefano, who was serving as fiscal procurator and one of the presidents of the Sommaria, was mandated to reintegrate usurped doganal territory. Di Stefano reclaimed former pasture land that had been turned over to cultivation and found that the doganal locations could winter 943,500 sheep without need of any extraordinary pasture.[63] New instructions were issued on the office of "ordinary cavalryman" (*cavallaro ordinario*) in order to stabilize their number at twenty-four (later increased to thirty), to stipulate their duties, to set down provisions to guard against abuses, and to make their appointment dependent upon the viceroy in Naples rather than the doganiero, who had been using them as a private army.[64]

In the midst of these reforms, baronial landlords tried to exploit the state's need for more revenues by attaching conditions before approving a proposed increase in the hearth tax. In the parliament of 1508, they reasserted their longstanding grievance on the terms of pasture distribution. One petition asked that the landowners regain their right to sell fodder to whomever they chose.[65] The viceroy, the conte di Ripacorsa, knowing full well that state control over transhumance depended upon the ability of the doganal bureaucracy alone to administer the renting of pasture, managed to avoid a confrontation. Mastering the barons in parliament, however, did not ensure their compliance. Ferdinand's measures to reinforce pastoral privileges and correct abuses did not reap the expected fiscal gains because of the state's inability to control the corruption of entrenched doganal officers and to enforce the reintegration of pasture on more powerful land usurpers.

Charles V's Refoundation

After Ferdinand's death in 1516, the future Charles V commissioned one of his Burgundian officers, Charles LeClerc, president of the Chambre des Comptes at Lille, to assess the Kingdom's fiscal resources.[66] At Foggia in 1518, LeClerc participated in the January sheep enumeration, intervened in a judicial case in March, and observed the April fair. He reported in 1521 that 100,000 ducats income were still collected in Foggia in the previous year.

Francis I's pretensions to Italy, however, once again put the Italian domains on the defensive. The French invaded the Kingdom's Adriatic provinces in 1528 under their captain general, Odet de Foiz, Monseigneur Lautrec, with more than 35,000 soldiers. Foggia's municipal archive burned during a battle for access to the city on 8 March. When Lautrec himself died of the plague later that year, the military threat disappeared, but his soldiers were not so easily dispersed. As late as 1531 marauding bands of renegade soldiers were still preying upon shepherds in the Abruzzi.[67]

In reordering the Kingdom after the wars, the new viceroy, Pedro de Toledo, began a thorough accounting in 1532, his first year in office.[68] In Capitanata, not only had population declined, but also sheep numbers and tax receipts were depressed. Therefore, in Toledo's second year in office, he appointed Juan de Figueroa, who was a regent of the Royal Chancellery (*Regia Cancellaria*), to investigate the effects of the war upon the pastoral industries. Figueroa proposed a complete cadastral survey (*reintegrazione*) of the Tavoliere in 1533, and three of his reforms were included in a twenty-eight-chapter petition that the graziers' organization presented independently to Charles V during his

Neapolitan visit from 25 November 1535 to 22 March 1536.[69] Charles confirmed their request, which called for a reestablishment of the ancient doganal privileges and maintenance of a just balance between planting and grazing.[70] The year 1535/36 thus marked a new beginning for the doganal system. An accurate head count recorded 1,048,396 sheep and a gross income of 90,827 ducats for the year.

With the death of the doganiero Miguel Jeronimo Sanchez in 1537, regent Gaspar de Basalis completed the term as acting doganiero, and regent Juan de Figueroa continued his monitoring of doganal affairs.[71] His report of 20 August outlined his original findings about doganal abuses. In surveying the first forty years of the sixteenth century, he found that the disruptions of the wars and official mismanagement had caused the usurpation of doganal lands by the baronial agricultural interest, illegal favoritism to large sheep holders (often baronial or clerical proprietors) in the distribution of pasture, and lateral migration to the Papal States by many Abruzzi shepherds—all to the disadvantage of both state finances and the wool trade.

According to Figueroa, the measuring rod for decline in the dogana was the fact that doganal sheep counts had dropped to 700,000 head, about one-third below the norm, and yet there was still insufficient fodder. The court had to buy some 6,000 ducats' worth of "extraordinary fodder" to sustain even these reduced herds. Here was a classic case of a downward economic spiral. Abruzzi herders were going to Roman pastures; the reduced number of sheep in transhumance encouraged private landholders to usurp more land; and the state was forced to expend a greater amount of its declining sheep revenues in order to pay those same landlords to provide fodder for the few sheep that did come down from the mountains. As the usurping landowners bribed state officials, less pasture was available for grazing, and more sheep stayed away.[72] The negative cycle intensified.

Figueroa's report concludes with the story of how the Abruzzi sheep breeders posted the 10,000 ducats needed to buy him the office of doganiero. His reforming stewardship stabilized sheep numbers between 1 and 1.1 million.

Upon Figueroa's transfer to Spain, Ferrante di Sangro, again a Neapolitan noble from the *seggio* of Nido, bought the office of doganiero in 1542 and, with the succession of his sons Gian Luigi and Fabrizio, kept it in the family until 1581. Only two other families had any success in passing on this venal office to kin, the d'Afflittos (1494–1506) and Bernaudas (1624–40); but neither family wielded the power or oversaw such major doganal changes as the di Sangros in their forty-year tenure. From the ten-year sheep average of 1,075,686 head (1538/39–1547/48) and the eight-year revenue average of 80,000 ducats (1540/41–1547/48), the dogana grew to reporting over 4.25 million sheep and 550,000 ducats in 1580/81, Fabrizio di Sangro's last year in office.[73]

What caused this phenomenal multiplication of doganal fortune? There is no simple answer.[74] Inflation, fiscal pressures, and changes in law, in grazing land, and in tax rates, all played their part. But most of this so-called growth was imaginary, a kind of accounting legerdemain. In actual fact, although net revenues doubled, sheep numbers could never have exceeded the ecological limit of 2.5 million head set by the Foggian plain.[75]

The most significant legal changes encouraging doganal growth (real and imaginary) came in the decade beginning in 1548 under the viceroy Pedro de Toledo. He commissioned a cadastral survey of the Foggian plain on 3 October 1548. The "general reintegration" continued from 1548 to 1553 under the direction of Alfonso Guerrero (a president of the Sommaria) and Francesco Revertera (regent of the Cancellaria). Pasture land in Puglia was measured and fixed, sheepwalks to and from the Abruzzi were cleared, extraordinary pastures in and out of Puglia were stabilized, and agricultural land was delimited. The final result: a new, definitive geographical framework demarcated the Tavoliere 58 percent pastoral, 42 percent agricultural.[76] At the same time, Pedro de Toledo issued a sixty-eight item list of instructions.[77] These laws precisely defined the seasonal timetable to guide state officials in overseeing the pastoral institution, provided for just and impartial pasture distribution, and even favored the poorer graziers over the rich. Moderating the tension between pastoralists and agriculturists as well as increasing state revenues were the primary motives of good government. Similarly, the price for "extraordinary unusual fodder" (*erbaggi straordinari insoliti*)—a continuing dispute between landlords and graziers—was fixed in 1551.[78] Further, the Foggian fair was unified, extended, and moved from March to April. Finally, a budget-saving measure in 1553 changed the method of sheep counting for all pasture assignments. A straightforward sheep census (*numerazione*) was replaced by a complex system of estimation called "free bidding" (*professazione voluntaria*).[79] Thus, land redistribution, legal reform, and fiscal expedience attempted to specify the limits of time and space in the dogana. Their unintended effects, however, only widened the disparities between privileged and plaintiff, between fact and fiction, between good government and anarchy.

The baronial landlords were the first to react. In the parliament of 1554, three *grazie* addressed the newly enacted reforms.[80] First, the barons argued that favoring pastoralism over agriculture was false economics for the royal treasury because it "would bring great [grain] scarcity to the Kingdom" as well as great damage to the king's friends, who would be "defrauded of their oldest source of income." Second, they intensified their demands to collect the rents due them by stipulating that they be paid before pastoralists left Puglia and before the court received its share. Finally, they again defended their right to rent pasture to whomever they chose, against the pretensions of the dogana.

The famine of 1555 proved them correct on the first count and forced a rethinking of the pastoral/agricultural land ratio.[81] One thousand *carra* of virgin agricultural land (*terre salde a coltura*), were reclaimed from pasture, and the land-use ratio came into relative parity, 52 percent pasture/48 percent cultivation. To make up for the revenue losses, the taxes on sheep (*fida*) increased in the spring of 1556 by 50 percent: from 8.8 to 13.2 ducats per 100 sheep and from 27.5 to 41.25 ducats per 100 larger animals.[82] The price revolution of the sixteenth century and the exigencies of the Spanish royal treasury provided constant external pressures stimulating so-called doganal growth. But that growth was often an illusory accounting fiction since any real growth was determined by the peculiar internal dynamic of the dogana— wheat versus wool, rich versus poor. If either party won out, the whole facade would come tumbling down.

Growth under Philip II

Roughly simultaneous with Philip II's second bankruptcy in 1575, the dogana of Foggia doubled its net contribution to the state treasury from 109,169 ducats in 1573/74 to 229,374 ducats in 1581/82.[83] This spectacular rise in doganal income was recorded because of Fabrizio di Sangro's manipulation of the new method of tax collection, free bidding (*professazione voluntaria*). Revenues squandered on unproductive military expenditures fought elsewhere in Europe by Spain fill the dogana's debit entries and underline the monarchy's suicidal logic. As one of the most important sources of viceregal revenue with 10 percent of net income, all collected in hard cash in one month, the dogana of Foggia remained a mainstay in the state's economic policy by bleeding itself dry.

In order to ensure continued doganal revenues, Philip II addressed numerous letters on the Foggian customs to the viceroys in Naples.[84] His active interest in doganal affairs helped ratify changes recommended by three meticulous investigations undertaken by visitors general or Sommaria presidents, and promulgated in six sets of instructions. Maintaining fiscal integrity and curbing official abuses were the primary mission of the visitors general.[85]

From 1559 to 1564, Gaspar de Quiroga y Vela examined the Spanish bureaucracy as it had operated in Naples from 1540.[86] During the visit, Gian Luigi di Sangro issued a twenty-four-item decree restating the calendar of doganal activities.[87] Quiroga's investigations reported that the dogana of Foggia was marred by abuses in the stewardship of Gian Luigi di Sangro and his father, Ferrante di Sangro. The visit notwithstanding, circumvention of doganal law continued, and in 1574, Fabrizio di Sangro, Gian Luigi's brother, issued an order which called for a return to the ancient laws.[88] His fifty-two items aimed at correcting current abuses which detracted from the state treasury and the privileges of pastoral livelihood. Because of the difficulty of enforcement upon large and powerful holders, the viceroy Antoine Perrenot, Cardinal Granvelle, reiterated the need for good government in the dogana later in the same year.[89] The twenty-three items of his decree of 19 June 1574 and the twenty-eight items of the pragmatic of 30 July 1574 once again stabilized doganal affairs with maximum clarity: such matters as pastoralists' rights, tax rates, pasture distribution, agricultural limitations, etc. were all set down again. Baronial discontent over doganal judicial prerogatives and prohibition of the right to rent their pasture as they wished led Granvelle to reissue his doganal laws on his last day in office, 1 July 1575.[90] Composed by the regent Revertera, Sommaria president Annibale Moles, and *avvocato fiscale* Marcello di Mauro, these new instructions, again divided into twenty-eight chapters, provided a commentary upon the earlier document.

Baronial protests only intensified between 1576 and 1579 as the feudal landowners of Capitanata and the Abruzzi filed a law suit in the Sommaria to curtail the doganal privileges of the grazier community. In 1577 and 1578 respectively, Francesco Alvarez de Ribera, a president of the Sommaria and Geronimo de Palazios, chairman (*luogotenente*) of the Sommaria, visited Foggia in order to oversee the distribution of pasture and report on the state of operations. Finally in 1579, Ribera issued a fifteen-point decree dismissing those baronial complaints which had aimed at undermining the royal customhouse; for example, doganal justice and doganal control of the distribution of pasture remained intact, but he sustained those grievances which addressed specific abuses of the existing laws like forbidding doganal officers from engaging in economic activity.[91] Amidst the state's attempts to moderate the wrangling between contentious doganal factions and its desire to improve its own fiscal profile, the state's officers played their own game with motives ranging from dedicated service to personal aggrandizement. Fabrizio di Sangro, for example, resigned the family office of doganiero in 1580 to become chief military disbursement officer (*scrivania di razione*) in Naples and thus to have a chance to move up the *cursus honorum*.[92]

In 1581 Lope de Guzmán began a three-year visit which again audited the entire viceregal administration in Naples. Six volumes of the twenty-five-volume report concerned the Foggian customs directly. Testimony from doganal participants, budgetary news, and miscellaneous reports documented doganal organization.[93] In order to prevent continued frauds, a royal letter of 1584 revoked the privileges of special locations for rich holders, assigned the "extraordinary unusual pastures" (*insoliti*) to places, not persons, and made free bidding secret.[94] The rich barons immediately protested against the frauds of the sheepowners in the parliament of 1586.[95] The visitor's final draft of charges was issued in 1588 and found the two doganieri Fabrizio di Sangro and Alfonso Caracciolo, two fiscal officers, and twenty-three *cavallari* guilty of corruption.[96] According to the seriousness of their offenses, the twenty-five minor defendants were expelled or suspended from office and assessed a mean fine of 77 ducats. The case against Caracciolo, who had died that year in office, was dismissed, but Fabrizio di Sangro was convicted of nine counts of fraud and was fined 10,000 ducats; that is, the price paid to buy the office or ten times his annual salary as doganiero.

Earlier in 1588, upon Caracciolo's death, Ferrante Fornaro, a Sommaria president, catalogued the excesses of doganal administration and examined the effects of the harsh winter of 1586.[97] Notorious abuses, like the renting of special pasture to the late doganiero's brother-in-law through a third party, resulted in a call for the abolition of venal offices in the dogana. Fiscal pressures forbade such a radical break with the common financial practices of early modern government. No new doganiero was appointed until 1592, however, and the office of doganiero was reformed. The Doganella d'Abruzzo (pasture for sheep migrating from the Marches and under separate administration) was removed from doganal supervision, and an independent administrator (*luogotenente*) was nominated by the Sommaria.[98] New instructions in twenty-two chapters were issued in April 1592; and, in a decree of 3 January 1593, Philip II ordered that a president of the Sommaria visit and inspect the dogana annually.[99] Philip demanded a strict accounting of revenues and from bureaucrats. In a royal letter of 5 September 1595, he was already laying the groundwork for a case against the new doganiero, the marchese di Padula.[100]

The Seventeenth-Century Crisis

Juan de Herrera visited the Kingdom in 1603 and uncovered fiscal irregularities from 1580.[101] In the Foggian customs, 500,000 ducats had been lost in that twenty-four-year-period—on the average, more than 20,000 ducats per year. Also in 1603, the marchese di Padula was indicted for extortion and suspended from office, and the doganiero's office was sold to Ferrante Monsorio. He, in turn, was indicted and suspended in 1605. Both were acquitted.

Built upon this reexamination and reform, doganal growth peaked in the decade after Philip II's death with 5.5 million sheep professed and 259,000 net ducats passed on to the court in 1604/05. Again, the ducats were real, but the sheep were not. Graziers professed highly overestimated numbers in order to ensure pasture. These inflated sheep numbers were an accounting fiction called *pecore in aerea,* in which the "sheep in the air" reflected the bidding war between pastoralists and agriculturists for land.[102] There were no winners: agriculturists were discriminated against, pastoralists were squeezed for taxes, and the state's short-term gains provided an income as illusory as the imaginary sheep.

From 1607 to 1612 Juan Beltrán de Guevara investigated the viceroyalty as visitor general.[103] In the dogana of Foggia he uncovered crimes and recommended punishments similar to those of his predecessor Guzmán. The new doganiero, Antonio Carafa, the marchese di Corato, was fined the office's purchase price and 2,000 ducats, for a total of 12,000 ducats. Three lieutenants of the doganella, seven fiscal officers of the dogana, three special commissioners, and twelve other doganal officers were assessed fines ranging from 6 to 3,000 ducats. In the middle of the Guevara visit, Giacomo Saluzzo, a Sommaria president, issued a scathing report on doganal abuses which included inequitable pasture distribution, agricultural kickbacks, circumvention of *fida,* archival mismanagement to cover up frauds, and uncollected back taxes.[104] Thus, the dogana declined slowly through maladministration until the catastrophic winter of 1611/12 when 69 percent of the sheep were killed.[105]

Fabrizio di Sangro, now duke of Vietri, was called back as doganiero in 1612; but, with depleted flocks, the graziers increasingly found it impossible to meet their tax obligations, further weakening the state treasury. In 1615, as part of a kingdomwide fiscal reorganization, the viceroy conte de Lemos sent the regent and Sommaria *luogotenente* Berardino Ramirez de Montalvo, marchese di San Giuliano, to initiate reforms in Foggia.[106] Lemos's reform substituted a "fixed tax arrangement" (*transazione*) for free bids (*professazione voluntaria*), and graziers paid an agreed-upon fixed sum of 182,000 ducats plus a 10,000-ducat levy (*donativo*). The *transazione* was renegotiated and increased at regular intervals for the next forty years.[107] With the decline in graziers' economic strength, the barons repeated their parliamentary complaints against the dogana in 1617 and 1621.[108]

At the same time the Spanish Habsburgs became embroiled in the Thirty Years' War, and their empire as a whole strained under a general economic depression. From 1628 to 1631, the visitor general to Naples Francisco Antonio de Alarçon attempted to reorder the chaotic finances of the Kingdom. Bankruptcy was declared in 1629, and payments of all debts were suspended.[109] In 1634, Alonso Guillen de la Carrera began a four-year visit to the Sommaria and the *dogana delle pecore*.[110] Juan Chacon Ponce de Leon, who journeyed to Naples in 1645 as visitor general with the charge to reform offices and to recover lost revenues, was still present in the city at the time of Masaniello's revolt.[111] In 1653 the king had decreed that debts should be paid at 10 percent of their value.[112] And the final blow was struck in 1656 when a new French invasion and an outbreak of the plague reduced the population in the Kingdom by 27 percent.

Meanwhile, the transhumant system of Foggia was in complete decline. Manfredonia, Foggia's nearby port, was sacked by the Turks in 1620. A devastating earthquake in Capitanata killed more than 20,000 people in 1627.[113] But the real institutional crisis was internal.[114] Graziers often refused or were unable to pay the fixed agreement tax. By 1639 wool production had fallen to about 40,000 to 60,000 *rubbi* (one *rubbi* = 8.91 kg), that is, between one-half to two-thirds of the 80,000-*rubbi* norm. Sheep numbered about 600,000 head. As a reform to improve doganal management, the office of doganiero was abolished in 1646, and presidents of the Sommaria were sent to attend to doganal administration.[115] But even the revolt of Masaniello had its repercussions in the countryside, and a Foggian notary, Sabato Pastore, led an abortive uprising in Foggia in the first months of 1648. For the majority of the graziers, the only remedy was a return to the old *modo di vivere*, free bidding (*professazione voluntaria*.)

In the 1660s the negative conjuncture reversed itself in Foggia. Neapolitan population decline after the 1656 plague shifted the rural economic balance from favoring agriculture to supporting sheep farming. The lower demand for grain reduced prices and discouraged production. Moreover, much less capital could be expended on the reduced work force needed to tend flocks. By 1671, for example, the prince of Melfi's flock increased from preplague levels of 1,000 head to over 8,500. This pastoral investment could reap a gross income far greater than that possible from wheat production in one of his territories like Forenza, while substantially reducing his overhead by employing about 10 percent of the comparable labor force.[116]

The state responded quickly. Free bidding was reinstated in 1661 in order to foster renewed pastoral investment.[117] In 1665 the new viceroy, Cardinal Pasquale d'Aragona, remitted the debts of poor holders and ordered them to reengage in transhumance.[118] Sheep professed in 1667 increased to 1,155,890 head. The investment system of the "public price" (*prezzo alle voce*) was introduced at the fair of 1667 and soon became standardized in the account books of the weighers of wool as investors reinfused credit into the countryside.[119] The viceroy Pietro Antonio d'Aragona published new instructions, the *Pramatica LXXIX de officio Procuratoris Caesaris*, restating the traditional rights and privileges, in 1668.[120] The Milanese Danese Casati acted as visitor general in the Kingdom from 1679 to 1682, with the commission to correct fiscal frauds and official negligence.[121] By the 1680s wool production in the dogana had broken out of its mid-seventeenth-century slump, and in 1686 the royal surveyor Antonio de Michele was commissioned to compile a topographic atlas of doganal territory.[122] During the last quarter of the seventeenth century, then, the economic profile of the dogana gradually improved.

The Eighteenth-Century Recovery

With this growing economic vitality, rich holders again sought to separate their pastures from those of poor holders. In 1685 the dogana initiated a policy of granting the excellent pastures of "fixed posts" (*poste fisse*) to particular favorites.[123] Similarly, the freedom of *professazione voluntaria* was attacked unsuccessfully in 1704, but it was gradually eroded by abuses later in the century. In 1705 a jurisdictional dispute erupted between the tribunal of the dogana and the Collateral Council (Council of State) in Naples over control of letters of exchange. Original doganal competence was confirmed in 1711 although not enforced until 1719.[124] Such administrative confusion in the first decade of the eighteenth century reflected the uncertainties of the Spanish succession. In 1708 the Neapolitan Andrea Natale addressed an unpublished manuscript, which included a detailed description of the *dogana delle pecore*, to the Austrian pretender, Charles III, who later became Holy Roman Emperor as Charles VI.[125] In 1709 the doganal governor, Andrea Guerrero y Torres, prepared a review of doganal abuses and their remedies, a brief chronological history of the Foggian customs, and a vocabulary of doganal terms. His new 20 percent surtax also demonstrated that doganal governors under the new Austrian viceroyalty were determined to increase state revenues.[126]

The 36 percent sheep mortality of 1726 again jeopardized the doganal system. Declining revenues led to a reform proposal by Tomaso Mancini. A commission of regents and Sommaria presidents met in Foggia in April 1729 to examine the situation.[127] Doganal documents from the 1670s were reviewed, and corrections for endemic abuses were discussed. The commission, however, could not agree upon an overall plan of reform. The War of the Polish Succession intervened as doganal revenues continued to decline and the work of the reform commission remained undone.

With the Kingdom's transfer from the Austrian Habsburgs to a new, independent Bourbon dynasty in 1734, the Foggian customs witnessed a rebirth of administrative efficiency and economic growth. Stefano di Stefano, the doganal commentator who had been serving as a legal counsel to the shepherds' organziation since 1698, was appointed governor general of the dogana in 1735 and set himself immediately to the task of reform.[128] In 1738, Charles III stabilized the election procedures and rights of the shepherds' organization with a decree of seven items.[129] In 1747 a thirty-four-chapter decree addressed the perennial questions of doganal abuse: corrupt officials, distribution of pasture, reintegration of usurped territories, competition between rich holders and poor.[130] In 1759, Charles abdicated to become king of Spain, but correspondence with his chief minister, Bernardo Tanucci, continued to betray a lively interest in the affairs of the Kingdom—even to the humdrum "wools of Foggia" and "the scarcity of pasture."[131] The royal surveyor Agatangelo della Croce dedicated his twenty-five years of labor (1735–60) on topographic and geometric maps of the twenty-three locations to the departing king.[132] In addition to patronizing Enlightenment culture, the Bourbons brought the Kingdom into a different international trade network. By 1779 one-half of Foggia's wool was exported in equal amounts to Venice and to France.[133] The resurgence of doganal production in the mid eighteenth century created a sense of tranquil cooperation in the countryside—a balanced harmony between pastoralism and agriculture which the doganal commentator De Dominicis described in 1781 as a pastoral interlude.

The Neapolitan school of political economy, as it examined the causes of the disastrous famine of 1764, provided the thunderbolts which burst the pastoral illusion of the Foggian customhouse.[134] Ferdinando Galiani, the brilliant Enlightenment economist who had become the enfant terrible of the Parisian salons, made the doganal dilemma famous.[135] Galiani mocked his native Naples as an extension of the African desert, a land as unenlightened as barbarous Tartary, because the dogana of Foggia favored pastoralism over agriculture. Galiani's one-paragraph salvo was not included in his first edition of *On Money* in 1751 but was appended to the second edition of 1780 as the pastoral policy of the dogana appeared in ever greater defiance of the logic of agricultural necessity after the 1764 famine. Population pressure, grain demand, and the evolutionary rules of civilization could not allow such backwardness. Other critics added their voices to the problem of agricultural reform necessitated by the doganal system's monopolization of the Puglian countryside: Cimaglia, Silla, and Patini in 1783; Targioni in 1786; Delfico and Filangieri in 1788; Palmieri in 1789; Longano and again Palmieri in 1790; Galanti in 1791; Camilli and Rosati in 1792; Di Merino and Marchesani in 1794; Vivenzio in 1796. As the *ancien régime* matured, the privileges and exemptions of the pastoral regimen received closer scrutiny.

In January 1806 the Bourbon king Ferdinand II fled the Neapolitan capital for Sicily. Soon after, the French entered the Kingdom and enacted the much-discussed programs of reforms. Joseph Bonaparte's personal visit to Foggia on 8 May was quickly followed by the first law of the new government, the law of 21 May 1806 on the reform of the Tavoliere di Puglia.[136] Its forty-four articles provided for the devolution of state-owned "virgin land used for planting" to its renter occupants, the annulment of the old location system of pasture leasing, the manumission of slaves on agricultural land, the perpetual leasing of Church-owned lands; in sum, the dissolution of Neapolitan "feudalism." The difficult process of transformation from state-owned and operated pastures to private plots was initiated. With the liquidation of royal demesne in Puglia, the doganal system of Alfonso of Aragon came to an end; that is, the state's management of pasture, not its use by graziers. In fact, a strong pastoral economy flourished in the Tavoliere past Italian Unification, and a circumscribed transhumance still continues today at about 5–10 percent of its early modern capacity.[137]

Pastoral Policy as Good Government

The interesting question about the sheep institutions of southern Italy (both Naples and Rome) and Spain (both Castile and Aragon) is not their similarity in foundation, organization, maintenance, and duration, but why they endured—in the case of Naples for over three hundred fifty years. Compared to the early Mesta charter in Spain, the definitive, doganal foundation diploma of 1 August 1447 by Alfonso came rather late. Even after the mid-fifteenth-century foundation by Alfonso, many later constitutions—the 1506 refoundation by Ferdinand the Catholic, the reordering of the Kingdom by Charles V and the new viceroy Pedro de Toledo in the 1530s, the Austrian Habsburg doganal reforms of 1709, and the stabilization of the Kingdom's institutions by Charles of Bourbon in 1734—were needed to reestablish the *dogana delle pecore* following foreign invasion, diplomatic negotiations, or dynastic readjustments. Similarly, the final doganal dissolution in 1806 and the anti-transhumance policy after Italian Unification in 1860 were both political decisions of new regimes. While engaging in sheep transhumance may have been good economics, maintaining the institution demanded good government.

Another way of answering the question of doganal longevity would be to define more precisely what a *mesta* was. A *mesta* was a council or reunion of graziers to ensure justice and good government.[138] It pitted the large pastoral holders against local nobility, agriculturists, and small holders. State patronage, above all, guaranteed their success.

Despite the jagged growth curve imposed upon the dogana of Foggia by war or economic conjectures, internal institutional modification and refinements established a definitive structure. The history of the sheep tolls administration in Puglia continued to reflect its own internal tensions between land and office, between privilege and faction. This internal balancing act provides a good barometer of administrative policies, population pressures, economic activity, and social rivalries in the Kingdom from the late medieval through the early modern period. The new state doganal institution at Foggia attempted to centralize power and allegiance in the hands of a strong monarch and his representatives in order to disrupt and supersede the diffused patron-client networks of the numerous local barons. With more than one such institution in the hands of the big winners, Alfonso of Aragon, Ferdinand the Catholic, and their Spanish Habsburg heirs, a different kind of external balancing act would have to be applied as the state monopoly in Castile, Aragon, and Naples competed for the same buyers in the international market. Internal institutional dynamic cannot be separated from the exigencies and articulation of Spanish policy throughout its empire. The fact that this ideal good government did not conform to reality is the story of the administrative structure of the dogana, the Kingdom, and the future Spanish Empire at large.[139]

Good government in the rural economy of the Kingdom of Naples, then, from the time of the mid-fifteenth-century foundation of the dogana of Foggia, had six distinguishing features related to increased taxes, centralized administration, control of the barons, and foreign policy. First, the double contract established bonds between state and landowners for their assured rental income, and between state and sheepowners in exchange for state revenue. Ensuring state control of pasture distribution was, above all, Alfonso's important innovation to reduce tension between landowners and sheepowners. Second, the state guaranteed equal and impartial justice for all in its courts and in its appointment of officers with monarchical, not provincial ties. Third, external concerns, like an antipapal policy which dictated the imposition of economic sanctions against Rome, and foreign wars, which affected international supply and demand, impinged upon domestic policy. Fourth, with the dogana's foundation at the low point after the plague, the state encouraged the smaller labor force to participate in a less labor-intensive enterprise. Contradictorily, however, it continued this policy thereafter, even in the face of a growing population's need for grain. Fifth, the state pacified the countryside and provided bread for the city. And sixth, remembering that Alfonso was a conquering usurper, as were his Spanish Habsburg heirs, we must never lose sight of the monarchy's desire to establish legitimacy with the tradition of law. Thus, for the new monarchies intent upon consolidating their power, good government meant vigorous political authority and aggressive economic intervention. Mediterranean sheep transhumance institutions were cornerstones in that policy of political stability by manipulating economic exchange and social solidarity.

2 The Georgics of the Tavoliere of Puglia

The Shepherds' Calendar

Before we can evaluate Capitanata's social and economic roots, we must try to assimilate the arcane details and understand the humdrum realities of a different conception of time and space. The material culture of the pastoral arts demands a familiarity with seasonal variation, geographical structures, and the technology of production—livestock and land management.

Transhumance, remember, cannot be understood by attempting to recreate some original landscape untouched by human agency, for man's law created an ideal time and an ideal space in the customhouse system.[1] Administrative time was reckoned from 30 August to 29 August, corresponding to the Kingdom's fiscal calendar, and roughly synchronized to the seasonal cycle of pastoral and agricultural life. The shepherds' calendar and the peasants' landscape formed a coherent, if not cohesive structure. One of the rules underlying the organization of the Kingdom of Naples is embodied in this complementary and contradictory tension between land use and natural landscape, between time and space.

In simplest terms, the doganal calendar was divided by the two feasts of St. Michael: a winter pasture season from 29 September to 8 May, and a summer pasture season from 8 May to 29 September. The beginning and end of the cycle corresponded to the busiest months for both pastoralists and agriculturists. Before the autumnal rains, sheep had to be brought down from the mountains and assigned winter grazing, while wheat fields had to be plowed and planted. Hard upon these tasks, almonds, grapes, and olives matured. In the spring, sheep were shorn, marketed, and returned to summer pasture, while garden and vineyard cultivation was readied and preparation for the wheat harvest made. The fever of activity slackened in the cold wet months and the hot dry months, but agricultural work still had a quotidian rhythm.

Even the less labor-intensive pastoral livelihood system demanded daily vigilance. While the small owners often accompanied their own sheep, the middling and large herders evolved an organizational hierarchy, refining methods of sheep breeding and management. The large companies established a definitive division of labor. The *massaro* was the head of operations, directly responsible to the owner. The *sottomassaro* or *casciero* was particularly responsible for sheep milk products. An assistant *casciero* concerned himself with personnel and provisioning. He was overseer of individual provisioning agents (*butteri*), who procured everything from wood to water. The shepherds (*pastori*) were themselves specialized: *agnellari* cared for lambs; *scortarellari*, pregnant ewes; *montonari* and *mulari*, rams, horses, and mules; and *quadrali* were menial workers from cooks to dog attendants.[2]

The Doria estates at Melfi demonstrated this division of labor among its approximately 87 shepherd employees. About 27 full-time shepherds (360 work days per year), about 31 additional shepherds at three-quarters time (at least 270 days), and another 29 shepherds for shorter periods were employed to tend 10,000 sheep and 1,000 goats in the eighteenth century. Mean salary expenditures of 1,463 ducats were paid for about 23,500 man-days of labor, that is, an annual salary of 22.7 ducats for a full-time shepherd.[3] Milking, cheese making, feeding the livestock, fuel gathering, and garden work were part of the daily routine, winter and summer, for both agriculturists who maintained draft animals and pastoralists who supplemented their diets with agricultural produce.

The physical layout of farms in the Tavoliere di Puglia reflected this cross-fertilization of wheat and wool. The livestock farms (*masseria di pecore*) were much more complex and took up much more area than the cereal farms (*masseria del campo*).[4] The livestock farms sprawled over two or three hectares and were composed of laborers' quarters, bedrooms, kitchen, well and watering place, dog kennels, animal stables, sheep pens, cheese processing building, threshing floor, and often a vegetable garden. The cereal farms, on the other hand, supported more people, but occupied less area and were more compact. They allocated space for both farming and some livestock pasture. Although cereal and sheep were the respective concerns of each kind of livelihood system, neither type of agricultural enterprise excluded the other. Through time and space, tasks mixed.

Since doganal management was predicated upon a time-space continuum, some familiarity with geography further clarifies the seasonal calendar. The river system of the Abruzzi defined convenient boundaries to moderate the flow of sheep down from the mountains. Doganal legislation attempted to prevent overgrazing during the autumnal migrations into Puglia. By 1549 sheep were not permitted to leave the Abruzzi before 15 September unless unseasonable rain, snow, or cold drove them down from the mountains, nor could they cross the Biferno River (the border between the Abruzzi and Capitanata) before 15 October, or the Fortore River (the northern border into the Tavoliere di Puglia) before 1 November.[5] Transhumance from summer to winter pasture followed this timetable:

8 May–29 September	Summer season
15 September–15 October	Migration to the Biferno River
15 October–1 November	Migration to the Fortore River
1 November–25 November	Holding pastures in Puglia

25 November–25 March   Winter season
25 March–8 May   Return to summer pasture[6]

Flocks thus descended the mountains gradually and did not consume winter pasture before its time.

The Pastoral Landscape

The principles of doganal foundation and administration were based upon the organization of the land: an abundant supply of pasture, its equitable distribution, and secure routes of access. Sheep moved along major sheepwalks (*tratturi*) and branch sheepwalks (*tratturelli* and *bracci*), browsing on side pastures (*riposi laterali*) along the way. In moderating their flow into Puglia, they awaited winter assignments in general holding pastures (*riposi generali*). Locations (*locazioni*) were the principal divisions of usual winter pasture (*fondi ordinari*) on the Tavoliere, either *generali* for the poor small owners or *particulari* for the rich large ones. Additional flocks were consigned "extraordinary pasture" (*erbaggi straordinari*), either "usual" or "unusual" (*soliti* or *insoliti*). Once on their location, graziers were further assigned posts (*poste*) for their flocks. Good government depended upon competent management of each of these land divisions.

From 1447, three major roads (*regi tratturi*) covered the 200 kilometers between the pastures of the Abruzzi and Puglia. These sheepwalks left Aquila, Celano-Sulmona, and Pescasseroli-Castel di Sangro trail heads respectively, arriving in the Tavoliere by different routes. Over time other sheepwalks were added. Among the major routes were trails between Castel di Sangro and Lucera, and in the south between Melfi and Castellaneta (fig. 3). A geography of production would assign approximately one-half of production to the Aquila trail head, one-third to Sulmona, and one-fifth to Castel di Sangro.

In order to accommodate the great numbers of sheep in transhumance, the doganal calendar budgeted six to eight weeks for the journey. Actual traveling time depended on distance—the longest journeys could cover over 700 kilometers. Travel time for any one flock averaged about twenty days.[7] Flocks larger than twenty head were required to engage in transhumance.[8]

The sheepwalks were extremely wide rights of way, measuring 60 *trapassi napoletani*, that is, about 111.11 meters. It was forbidden to encroach upon these trails by "maintaining vines, vegetable gardens, shrubs, grain crops, or enclosures."[9] Even when passing through private property, these routes were considered "regalia del Principe." They were free from any toll, subject to doganal justice, and removed from baronial jurisdiction.

Smaller routes led off of the major sheepwalks to holding pastures, locations, and posts. These minor sheepwalks measured 27 meters across. Such large rights of way guaranteed grazing grasses on the route between pastures.

From the very beginning barons and communes tried to impede sheep

FIGURE 3 Sheepwalks and Holding Pastures of the Foggian Customhouse

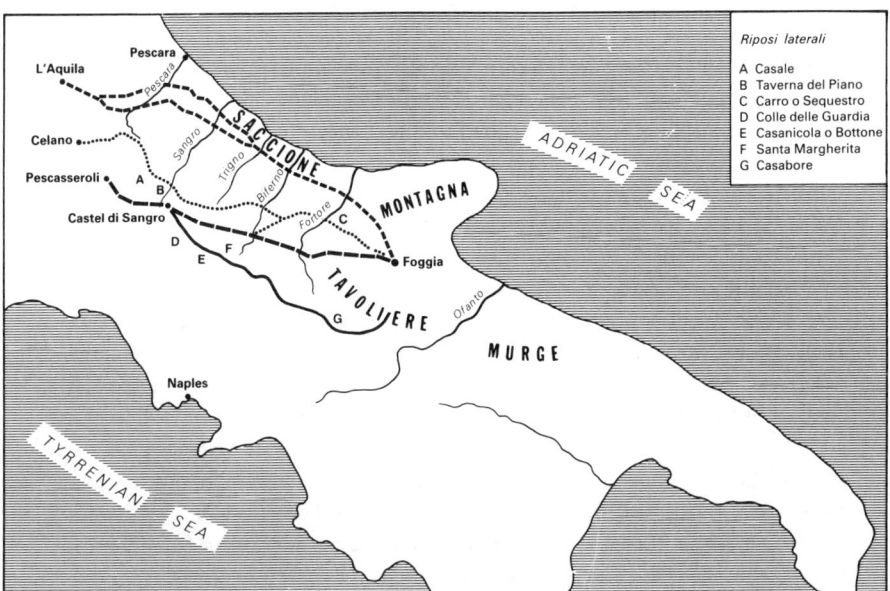

Source: Map adapted from Udo Sprengel, "La patorizia transumante," *Annali del Mezzogiorno* 15(1975):277, after "Carta dei Tratturi, Tratturelli, Bracci e Riposi" of the "Commissariato per la Reintegra dei R. R. Tratturi," Foggia.

migrations. Requests (*grazie*) addressed to Ferrante in 1480 invoked Alfonso's foundation in seeking protection for the sheepwalks.[10] Reordering of the sheepwalks, in fact, became a continual necessity. Important reforms were carried out in 1533 (Figueroa), 1574 (Fabrizio di Sangro), 1601 (Mastrillo), 1645 (Capece Galeota), 1648 (Capecelatro), 1712 (Crivelli), 1810 (d'Ecclesia), 1826 (Iannantuono), and 1875 (Avellino). The seriousness of the crime and, possibly, the frequency of abuse can be judged by the severity of punishment. In 1574 fines of 1,000 ducats were to be levied against sheepwalk encroachment. In 1575 the death penalty was added to the fine.[11]

Along the sheepwalks, nine side pastures were established to sustain the migrating herds. Transhumant sheep could rest in these "particular holding pastures" up to twenty-four hours before resuming their journey. But the graziers' immediate goal was to reach the three large "general holding pastures" which formed an arc around the Tavoliere: the Saccione, extending between the Fortore, Trigno, and Sangro rivers north of Capitanata along the Abruzzi coast; the Montagna dell'Angelo, covering the Gargano from Apricena to Vieste; and the Murge, formed from lands of Andria, Corato, Ruvo, and Bitonto south of

Capitanata in Terra di Bari.[12] Sheep pastured in these holding pastures until 25 November, the official opening of the Tavoliere winter season.

From the general holding pastures, flocks were obligated to proceed to their assigned locations in the company of representatives of the customhouse (*cavallari*) and of the posts (*postaioli*). In order to ensure compliance with their pasture assignments, the graziers had to direct their sheep by way of one of the six passes: Guglionisi, Ponterotto, La Motta, Biccari e San Vito, Ascoli e Candela, Melfi e Spinazzola. Upon closure of the winter season, departing transhumants once again passed through them and presented papers (*passate*) to verify that they had paid their sheep tax.

At the end of the road of march, five administrative jurisdictions called *ripartimenti* provided pasture (fig. 4).[13] Three fiscal units—Trigno, from the Trigno to the Sangro rivers; Saccione, from the Fortore to the Trigno rivers; and Montagna, the Gargano peninsula—grazed mostly heartier livestock like cattle and horses which remained closer to their native territory.[14] The fourth and major *ripartimento* for sheep was Puglia, named after its primary preserve in the Tavoliere, but also including other pasture in the provinces of Capitanata, Principato, Basilicata, Bari, Otranto, and Terra di Lavoro. A fifth *ripartimento*, the Doganella d'Abruzzo, was organized for the herds coming from the Papal States, the Marches, and the Abruzzi which did not go down into Puglia.[15]

Puglia, to reiterate, was the largest and most important administrative unit in the doganal system. It was open as winter grazing land (*erbaggi vernotici*) from 29 September to 8 May, that is, from one feast of St. Michael to the other. During the summer months between the feasts of St. Michael, 8 May to 29 September, the same land, now called summer grazing land (*erbaggi statonici*), reverted to its private owners, who could use it as they saw fit—usually to graze draft animals.

The saint's days were not merely a way of reckoning time but were above all a reminder of man's communion with God and nature. Religious enthusiasm reinforced the doganal calendar for both pastoralist and agriculturist. The powerful warrior-archangel Michael was a special patron in the region because he had appeared (8 May) in the Gargano in the fifth century. In his honor, medieval pilgrimages to the shrine at Monte Sant'Angelo fostered another kind of annual migration.[16] Among these pilgrims were the Normans, whose angelic visions in 1016/17 led to their conquest of southern Italy. One wonders if the riches of the Tavoliere were included in their visions. In the farmland of the Tavoliere, a second sanctuary, that of the Virgin in the Sacred Wood of Incoronata, became a pilgrimage shrine from 1066. The feast of this black madonna is celebrated in the last week of April, at the end of the winter grazing season, with a vesting of the Madonna and a cavalcade of angels.[17] Apparitions, pilgrimages, and black madonnas in agricultural and pastoral settings of the ancient and modern world, as well as the old world and the new, raise many striking parallels, since the solitary shepherd has so often been the focus of supernatural attention as an intermediary between nature and culture.[18]

FIGURE 4 Administrative Jurisdictions in the Foggian Customhouse

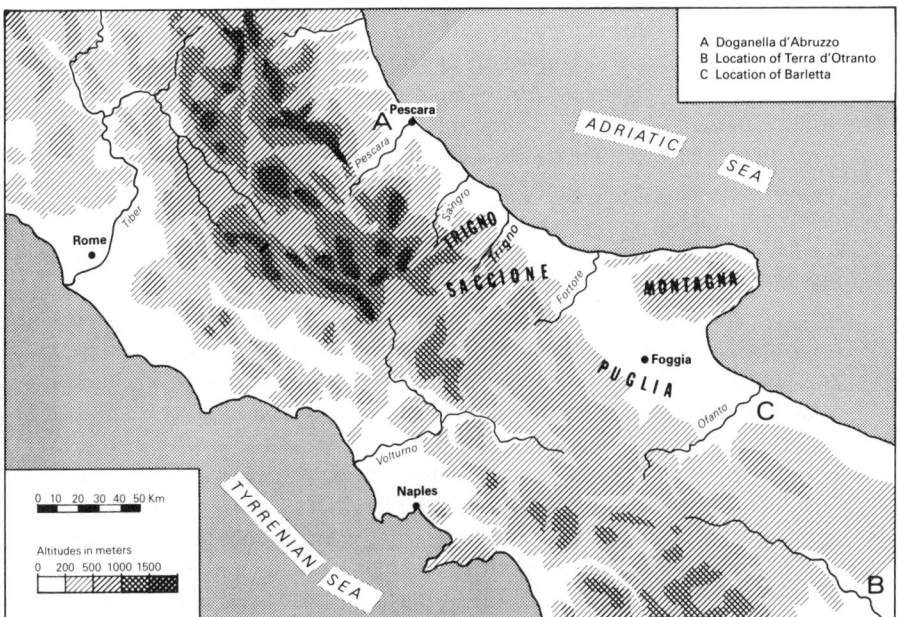

Source: See fig. 3, Sprengel, p. 273.

Back on earth, doganal grazing areas were divided, in turn, into two jurisdictional categories: ordinary and extraordinary pastures (*fondi ordinari* and *erbaggi straordinari*). The ordinary pastures were made up of the royal demesne proper and certain private holdings. When royal lands were filled up, private lands ensured additional pasture. The first doganiero, Montluber, negotiated with private proprietors to obtain the authority to allocate all pasture. He acquired for the state the proprietary rights to administer these lands in perpetuity, to distribute them among the graziers, and to collect taxes for the vicergal treasury as well as rent for the landlords.

The ordinary pastures were divided into locations of two kinds: general (*generale*), also called "original," "ordinary," or "of the poor"; and particular (*particolari*), also called "added," "extraordinary," or "of the rich." These locations, assigned to rich and poor, separated the small and middling sheepowners from the wealthy owners and feudal proprietors. Such doganal divisions provided for an important element of internal organization, as well as a means to reduce conflict among the graziers. Fornaro's reforms of 1588 abolished such special privileges, but they were reinstated in 1685.

Doganal tax lists (*squarciafogli*) almost always ordered the general locations geographically from north to south, as in the 1548 cadastral survey, except for Guardiola (the only site on the eastern slope of the Apennines) which was invariably placed last (fig. 5). There were twenty-three general locations and twenty extraordinary locations. The doganal system was not frozen in time; the number of locations changed, as did their size. In 1581, for example, the *credenziero* Gian Domenico Chirico listed twenty-four ordinary locations (including Barletta and Terra d'Otranto, excluding Camarda) and twenty-five particular locations.[19] Therefore, while the following structure is normative, the particulars are not definitive.

Each location was precisely measured for a fixed pasture/agriculture ratio, but measurements were constantly adjusted according to policy or legal action. The initial survey of the 1548 reintegration, for example, revealed 15,641 *carra*, which were divided 45 percent pasture and 55 percent agriculture.[20] After the deliberation in the Neapolitan councils of the Collaterale and Sommaria, the state determined that the cadastral survey should redistribute the dogana according to a 15,645-*carra* plan with 59 percent pasture and 41 percent agriculture.[21] The actual *reintegra* transferred 2,060 *carra* to pasture for a 58 percent pasture/42 percent agriculture ratio.[22] Since 20 percent of agricultural land was declared *mezzane* (grazing for draft animals), about 8 percent of the total land was given over to grazing oxen. Similarly, the two-field rotation system of Puglia provided that one-half of the cultivated land be fallow and open to doganal pasture, giving another 17 percent of the total to grazing. The effective pasture/arable ratio, then, was 83 percent pasture to 17 percent arable. The famines of 1555, however, forced the state to return 1,000 *carra* of pasture to agricultural use as virgin land used for planting (*terre salde*), reducing the disparity between pasture and agriculture to 52 percent versus 48 percent.[23] Although doganal measurement changed over the long term, as the 1760 cadastral survey of Della Croce, which measured 18,600 total *carra*, attests, pasture and agriculture ratios remained at their 52 percent/48 percent level.[24] By 1800 the 16,346 *carra* of the Tavoliere had a pasture/agriculture ratio of 54 percent : 46 percent.[25] State policy established and maintained this equilibrium in rough parity according to its principles of good government.

Their geographic setting fashioned the varying size and value of each location. Some were pastoral enclaves like Andria (100 percent) and Cave (95.9 percent), others were split between pasture and agriculture like Casalnuovo (50.3 percent : 49.7 percent) and San Giuliano (50.5 percent : 49.5 percent), while some, like Canosa (53.1 percent) and Trinità (51.6 percent), had more land under the plow. I have selected the following eight representative ordinary locations for much of my statistical analysis. The best grazing locations were Orta and Ordona, heavily plowed agricultural centers.[26] Also excellent grazing locations were Lesina and Arignano on the northern border of the Tavoliere, protected from harsh winters by the Gargano on their eastern flank.[27] Average locations were Salpi and Trinità, typical flat sites that bordered the salt pans of the sea of Barletta and were subject to sharp Adriatic winds. Among the worst locations were Cave and Canosa on the borderlands of the Tavoliere, marginal

FIGURE 5   The Twenty-three General Locations

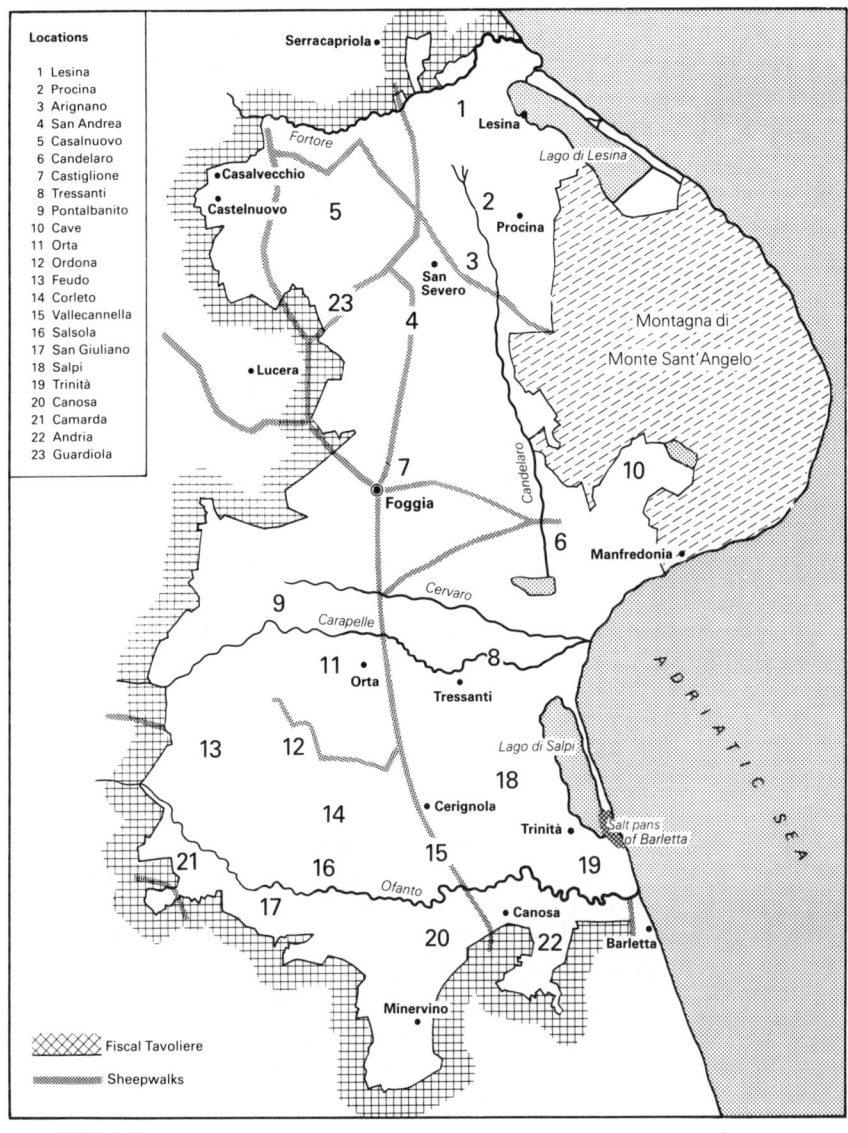

Locations

1 Lesina
2 Procina
3 Arignano
4 San Andrea
5 Casalnuovo
6 Candelaro
7 Castiglione
8 Tressanti
9 Pontalbanito
10 Cave
11 Orta
12 Ordona
13 Feudo
14 Corleto
15 Vallecannella
16 Salsola
17 San Giuliano
18 Salpi
19 Trinità
20 Canosa
21 Camarda
22 Andria
23 Guardiola

Sources: No general map of the locations in the Tavoliere existed before Agatangelo Della Croce's 2 × 1.95 m. eighteenth-century map, which was destroyed in World War II (but is partially reproduced in Andrea Gaudiani, *Notizie per il buon governo,* ed. Pasquale Di Cicco [Foggia: Editrice Apulia, 1981], p. 147). My map approximates the distribution of the individual locations on a base map adapted from Della Croce's 1765 map of entities not subject to the dogana, BNN, MS. Bᵃ 5ᴰ (15.

lands verging on the Gargano to the north and on the Murge to the south respectively.

Each location was rated for a fixed number of sheep. The maximum number that a pasture could sustain, the "possible" (*possedibile*), was determined by the quality and quantity of its pasture, both for ordinary and extraordinary locations. The possible of each location was calculated on the basis of 1,000 sheep for each 10–14 *carra* of land, depending upon its quality. According to this calculation, one *carro* could graze 100, 91, 83, or 77 sheep.[28] In the 1548 cadastral survey, the possible was established at 5 percent above the actual rating of each location.

Animals other than sheep could be grazed on the locations. Pasture was assigned to large animals such as cattle, horses, and mules and to small animals such as sheep, pigs, goats, and kids in fixed proportions. The 10–14 *carra* per 1,000 sheep ratio was doubled, 20–28 *carra*, for large animals. The possible was calculated on grazing demands in comparison to sheep: 3 lambs = 1 sheep; 1 pig = 2 sheep; 1 ass = 5 sheep; 1 horse or ox = 10 sheep.[29]

The 1548 cadastral survey provided for 735,009 sheep on the twenty-three general locations:

11 locations at 10 *carra* per 1,000 sheep grazed 404,163 (55 percent)
6 locations at 11 *carra* per 1,000 sheep grazed 152,983 (21 percent)
2 locations at 12 *carra* per 1,000 sheep grazed 73,197 (10 percent)
4 locations at 13 *carra* per 1,000 sheep grazed 104,666 (14 percent)

The best land grazed about 55 percent of the sheep, and the top two land qualities nourished more than 75 percent of the herds. But what about the remaining 25 percent? Gaudiani described the location of Guardiola, for example, as "the worst, the torment of the *locati* and of those who govern."[30] Obviously, quality grazing land was a privilege to be fought over. Nevertheless, by the quality rating system, the state attempted to compensate for the inequality between good and poor pasture by assigning fewer sheep per *carro*, or giving more land per sheep, to pasture in poorer locations. Increased quantity was to substitute for high quality. But since wool, meat, and cheese quality depended partially upon diet—what, not how much, an animal was fed—such compensation was necessarily inequitable.

To moderate this conflict all the more, the particular locations were created to protect the small holders from the large. The particular locations were also located in the plain of Puglia and were associated with a specific general location. After the 1548 cadastral survey, the 2,977 *carra* of the particular locations grazed 176,255 sheep:

9 locations at 10 *carra* per 1,000 sheep grazed 102,008 (58 percent)
8 locations at 11 *carra* per 1,000 sheep grazed 70,554 (40 percent)
0 locations at 12 *carra* per 1,000 sheep
1 location at 13 *carra* per 10,000 sheep grazed 3,693 (2 percent)

Note that the particular locations were more fertile areas: 98 percent of the land was rated 10 or 11 *carra* per 1,000 sheep, and 98 percent of *particolari* sheep grazed there. The proportion of pastoral use (56.9 percent) to agricultural use (43.1 percent) was also slightly higher than in the general locations. Further, the possible of the particular locations dramatized their richness. While the 10 *carra* per 1,000 head pasture had a normal possible of 4.76 percent above its rating (like the possible for the general locations), the 11 *carra* per 1,000 head particular locations were 15.24 percent above their rating. What did such an unlikely rating mean? If these 673 *carra* 9 *versure* are computed at the 10 rating rather than the 11, the 70,554 possible would also be 4.76 percent above that rating. In other words, despite their 10 or 11 designation, both categories of particular locations were rated at 10 *carra* per 1,000 head to compute the possible. The reintegration, thus, allowed about 20 percent of ordinary doganal sheep to be grazed in these special, rich-holder preserves and assigned 98 percent of the rich relatively equal pasture. Total *carra* of the ordinary pasture, in sum, measured 15,592 and accommodated 911,264 sheep.

After all the ordinary pasture had been dispensed, remaining sheep were assigned to the extraordinary pastures, called either usual (*soliti*) or unusual (*insoliti*). The extraordinary pastures were private lands that had been expropriated by the state for grazing assignment as the customhouse system expanded in the fifteenth century. The usual extraordinary pasture (also called *ristoro*) was land added to the dogana at the time of Montluber in order to accommodate the ever-increasing numbers of migrant sheep.

The extraordinary usual were often high mountain pastures for castrated and large animals which were more resistent to cold and inclement weather. The topography was rugged and the pastoral landscape more uniform than the complex land-use patterns of ordinary pastures. Twenty-one divisions made up the usual extraordinary pasture of Monteserico, 697 *carra,* feeding 140,424 sheep.[31] Eighteen other enclosures (*difense*) of the usual extraordinary pastures comprised 618 *carra* and grazed 91,730 sheep. Finally, another 27 royal plots (*demanii*) were not precisely measured but could graze some 179,260 sheep. Usual extraordinary pastures had a total possible of 411,414 sheep.

When the ordinary and the usual extraordinary pastures were insufficient, the dogana had the right to dispense unusual extraordinary pasture—private land first subjugated by Ferrante after he regained the Kingdom in 1465. Much of it was in Basilicata, at a greater distance from the more fertile centers of winter pasture. Any elasticity in the growth of herds, either actual or fictitious, was recorded in the unlimited possible of the unusual pastures. They were the pastures most constantly involved in fraud, the object of baronial complaints, and those used to record windfall profits for the state when it collected taxes on the *pecore in aerea*.[32]

A number of miscellaneous locations were included in Puglia's fiscal definition. The location or *mosciali* of Barletta was made up of five posts between Barletta and Andria.[33] Its 30 *carra* serviced 12,000 sheep of inferior wool, *moscia*. The location of Terra d'Otranto was an original usual extraordinary pasture whose designation was changed in the sixteenth century.[34] Terra d'Otranto per Cerreto had three posts and 9,700 sheep. Terra d'Otranto per Castellaneta measured 140 *carra* for 7,200 sheep. The *transazione* ("agreement") of Basilicata taxed sheep grazed in that province, a matter of dispute at the beginning of the eighteenth century.[35]

By the mid sixteenth century each location was occupied by a particular *nazione* (town of grazier origin). *Locati* (sheepowners who were placed on, leased, or assigned pasture in exchange for paying the dogana *fida*) were forbidden to pass from one location to another. This meant that there should have been, theoretically and legally, no competition for pasturage among the *locati* of different regions. Since the quality of the location varied considerably even though it was rated proportionately, a fixed hierarchy of privilege was established.

The smallest subdivisions of the locations were assigned to individual *locati* in measured posts where the shepherds' huts (*capanne*) stood in the center of pens fenced in by a variety of the fennel plant (*ferule*).[36] More than one *locato* could share a post. The exact number of posts in the Tavoliere would be difficult to fix. They were constantly changing and being measured and reassigned. In 1731, for example, Di Stefano listed 352 posts, while the surveyor (*compassatoro*) Della Croce counted over 500 some thirty years later. In the sixteenth century the most important question about posts centered on the privilege of fixed posts.

Fixed posts were assigned every year to the same great proprietor, noble, or religious community:

> Paglia (Tressanti) to the Santissima Annunziata of Sulmona for 3,500 sheep
> Parite (Candelaro) to Santo Spirito of Sulmona for 2,200 sheep
> Santa Agata (*extra locationes*) to the abbey of Tremiti for 3,000 sheep
> Serrone and Contessa (Pontalbanito) to the duke of Bovino for 4,000 sheep
> Schifara (Casalnuovo) to the Della Posta family of Foggia for 2,236 sheep
> Bombacili (Guardiola) to the duke of Montecalvo for 12,675 sheep
> Canestriello grande (Vallecannella) to the prince of Melfi for 3,437 sheep[37]

Both the Sommaria and the small owners fought this kind of privilege as an abuse undermining the principle of equal exchange in the dogana.

To summarize; the fiscal designation, Tavoliere of Puglia, did not correspond to the physical plain.[38] As sheep spilled over into the provinces to the south, the fiscal Tavoliere included even more area than the 4,300-square-kilometer plain lying between the Apennines on one side and the Gargano peninsula and Gulf of Manfredonia on the other. In addition, the fiscal Tavoliere

TABLE 1 Tavoliere Land Use in the Mid Eighteenth Century (In *Carra*)

Land Use	Area	Percentage	Area	Percentage
Pasture for sheep			8,524.75	(45.8)
Agriculture			7,536.70	(40.4)
Terre salde in the Church's tenth (*decima*)	1,145.05	(6.2)		
Terre salde beyond the Church's tenth (*decima*)	454.70	(2.4)		
Draft animal pasture for *terre salde*	320	(1.7)		
Regular agricultural plots (*portate*)	4,566.05	(24.5)		
Draft animal pasture for regular plots	1,050.60	(5.6)		
Private lands			2,311.90	(12.4)
Private lands in locations	926.50	(5.0)		
Private lands outside locations	1,385.40	(7.4)		
Miscellaneous			226.15	(1.3)
Total			18,599.50	(99.9)

Source: ASFg, *Dogana,* serie I, fas. 21 III, 91r, Agatangelo Della Croce's 1735–60 survey.

was not a contiguous unit. It was spread out over the plain in discrete units separated one from another by feudal, religious, or communal lands. The 1760 cadastral survey, for example, measured some 12 percent of the land in private hands (table 1).[39] Even the locations themselves were not endless fields of uninterrupted pasture. The land of the locations was divided into three categories: *saldo vergine,* assigned exclusively for animal pasturage; *portate,* given to cultivation; and *mezzane,* restricted for oxen used in agriculture.

Animal Husbandry

The *saldo vergine* ("virgin range-land"), the largest area of the Tavoliere, was given over to sheep grazing, and apportioned as we have seen:

    911,264 sheep—ordinary pastures:
        general locations   (735,009 sheep)
        particular locations   (176,255 sheep)
    411,414 sheep—usual extraordinary pastures:
        Monteserico   (140,424 sheep)
        18 enclosures   (91,730 sheep)
        27 demesnial lands   (179,260 sheep)
    indefinite—unusual extraordinary pastures

Total possible for the fiscal Tavoliere di Puglia was 1,322,678 sheep. But more sheep could be grazed in the marginal, expandable unusual extraordinary pastures; geographical evaluation of doganal pasture reveals that total sheep could expand to an upper limit of almost twice the 1.3 million estimate, to a little more than 2.5 million sheep.[40]

The most plentiful breed grazing on this pasture, the so-called *pecora gentile,* descended from the crossing of the native Puglian stock with Alfonso of Aragon's imported Merinos. They were raised for their fine wool, sometimes called *Lucoli* (after the Abruzzo Ultra town near Aquila) or *Scanno* (after the Abruzzo Citra town near Sulmona). A second breed, *moscie* or *carfagne,* was of heartier stock, but coarser wool. In addition to wool, both breeds were economically valuable for meat, milk (cheese), and skins. Some details of animal husbandry—wool qualities, sheep categories, and breeding technique—will help clarify the material foundations of the shepherds' life.

Sheep were shorn in April or May because new wool starts to grow at that time. The best wool was called *maggiorina* and accounted for about 80 percent of the spring yield. *Agnellina* or *ainina* came from lambs, *negra* or *nera* from black sheep; and each accounted for about 10 percent of total spring wool production. Average yield was 2–3 *libbre* (1 *libbra* = about 0.33 kg) per mature sheep in spring, 1 *libbra* less for lambs, 1 *libbra* more for castrated rams. A second shearing, the *agostina,* was done in July or August in the mountains and yielded only from one-third to one-half that of the May white wool. Total spring yield, measured in Neapolitan *rubbi* (8.91 kg), can be conveniently calculated at 8 percent of the total number of sheep; thus, 1 million sheep produced 80,000 *rubbi* of May wool. August wool would account for about another 35,000 *rubbi*. The white wool clip was valued at about one-third of the sheep's value on the hoof, comparable to the wool/sheep ratio in Tudor and Stuart England.[41]

Wool quality was differentiated by six objective criteria: color, length, thickness, texture, strength, and flexibility. Categories like thickness could be further subdivided: superfine, fine, medium, thick, and superthick. Different kinds of wool came from different parts of the sheep's body. Ensuring good yields and high-quality wool required constant attention to detail. Acquiring sufficient lush pasture for nutrition, overseeing selective breeding for height and color, and maintaining optimum age/sex ratios in the herds, for example, were necessary to prevent degeneration of one's holdings.[42]

The white wool of the *pecore gentili* was marketed in three grades according to quality.[43] Wool of the first "condition" commanded the best price and came from around the *nazione* of Lucoli in Abruzzo Ultra because its good mountain pasture produced very fine wool of perfect quality. Wool of the second condition came from Abruzzo Citra, around the area of the Lago di Fucino. Because it was not as fine, it was valued at 1.5 *carlini* per *rubbio* less than wool of the first condition and equal to wool from castrated rams (*castratina* from *castrati*). Wool of the third condition was valued at another 1.5 *carlini* per *rubbio* less than that of the second quality.

Ainina and *negra* were equal in value. From 1729 to 1781, lambswool and black wool were worth 1.5 *carlini* per *rubbio* less than white wool of the third condition; from 1782 to 1793, 3 *carlini* per *rubbio* less, and from 1795 to 1807, the same as third-condition white. For the greater part of the eighteenth century, then, wool prices differed according to quality in this proportion, with first-condition white wool at base 0.00:

First condition	0.00
Second condition	−0.15
Third condition	−0.30
Castratina	−0.15
Negra	−0.45
Agnellina	−0.45

Heartier breeds of sheep produced poorer-quality wool. *Carfagna* and *canina* (coarse and of mixed colors), *moscia* (long and thick, used for mattresses), *carapellesi* (white roots but black extremities), *ghezze*, and *pezzate* were all recorded qualities.[44]

Sheep and wool were also designated by age. *Ciavarrina* wool came from lambs of one year. *Recchiarelle* sheep were fertile but not yet pregnant ewes. *Matricina* wool came from pregnant ewes. *Fellate* (ewes after first pregnancy), *sterpate* (ewes that did not give milk), *lunari* or *sorde* (sterile sheep), *serroni* (those past reproductive age), and *vecchie* (those destined for the butcher) were all categories which emphasized the economic value of a particular animal.

Such categories reflected the diligence of graziers in maintaining flocks with graduated age pyramids. Biological life span of the species was about 13 years; but in practice, maximum age rarely exceeded 7 years.[45] Sheep remained fertile from about 18 months to 8 years but reached their prime breeding age at 3 years. Although biologically one vigorous male breeding sheep (*montone*) could impregnate 50–60 females (*pecore*), 5 rams were kept for every 100 ewes in order to produce more robust lambs. In theory, then, rams could fertilize 15 to 20 ewes per year, who, in turn, could bear one or two lambs. In practice, however, the lambing rate was closer to 0.5 lambs per ewe per annum.[46] Given such biological constraints, graziers attempted to maximize wool, meat, and cheese production by ensuring that flocks aged uniformly and that replacement lambs born from robust sheep under 4 years of age were annually added to their stock.[47] One million sheep thus birthed a maximum of 450,000 lambs, one-third of which (15 percent of 1 million) were reserved for stock rotation. Fixed capital—the flock itself—was constantly rejuvenated.

The gestation period was about five months, with a range of 136–160 days. Sheep breeding was, therefore, limited to four seasons, immediately before or immediately after the transhumant journey up or down the mountains. The best breeding months were June and July, when the sheep returned to summer pasture. *Vernarecci* lambs were born five months later at the beginning of winter in November or December. Most of these lambs were destined for market, especially males castrated 8 to 10 days after birth to improve the quality of their meat. Some of these winter lambs, however, were preserved to replenish the stock because they had the winter months to strengthen themselves for the following long transhumant trip. Sheep which were bred in September before leaving summer pasture gave birth to lambs in late February. Because of the scarcity of winter fodder, these lambs were almost all slaughtered for meat. Similarly destined for the butcher were those born to sheep arriving in winter pasture and bred in November. These lambs were born in late March and April in time for the spring fair. Both these groups of lambs born during the Tavoliere winter season were called *cordeschi*. Sheep bred in late March or early April, at the end of the winter season, produced *primaticci* lambs, which were born in August or September in Abruzzi summer pastures. They were marketed at the great animal fairs of the Abruzzi: Lanciano (the last 15 days of August), Aquila (20 days at the beginning of September), and Tagliacozzo (12 days in mid September). In the eighteenth century, *primaticci* lambs brought prices which were double those of the *vernarecci*.[48]

All of these newborn lambs demanded a constant milk supply from their mothers. And that same milk supply could be turned into profit as cheese. Each nursing ewe could produce enough milk for four *rotola* of cheese. With 450,000 lambs born to 1 million sheep, lactating ewes could produce enough milk for 82,000 *pesa* (wheels of 19.6 kg) of cheese.

Maintaining the relative weight of gross income—wool 50 percent, meat 30 percent, cheese 20 percent (according to Coda's 1666 estimate) or wool 50 percent, meat 40 percent, cheese 10 percent (according to the eighteenth-century Doria account books)—required constant vigilance. The rational management of flock size by means of selective breeding, rotation of stock age by selling off old and infirm animals and replacing them with younger ones, maintaining a supply of fertile and lactating females for lamb and cheese production, and selling off surplus lambs as meat are all strategies confirmed in the account books of the Doria holdings at Melfi.[49] In a normal year, three important breeding variables remained relatively uniform: (1) sheep deaths caused by such factors as old age, weather, or migration were about 15 percent (10 percent in winter, 5 percent in summer); (2) newborn lambs numbered about 42 percent of September herd size; and (3) 35 percent of these lambs were retained to replenish the stock. To summarize, a population of 100 sheep (5 males, and 95 females) would lose 15 animals by natural causes over the year. But 42 births meant that about 44 percent of the 95 females in the population bore young; and of these, about 67 percent would be sold for meat and 33 percent would be added to the flock. Thus, the 15 percent loss would be replaced by a 15 percent stock increase in order to keep the flock stable at 100 animals.

The caprice of nature, however, could easily disrupt the ideal practice of animal husbandry. Drought could desiccate the pastures, and fewer sheep could graze on doganal land. In 1611, for example, a seven-month drought left poor grazing grass, which only weakened the flocks before the disastrous winter to come.[50] Much worse, such harsh winters periodically hit the plain of Puglia. Frost or snow was recorded in 24 winters during the 350-year doganal history, on an average of every 15 years. The cold itself rarely killed off the sheep, but snow on the ground prevented easy grazing on pasture and caused starvation or malnutrition.[51] In ten cases, weather-related sheep deaths were significant (table 2).

TABLE 2 Sheep Mortality in Harsh Winters

Year	Deaths	Percentage of Total
1474	700,000	41
1561	290,000	16.67–25
1570	490,000	42
1586	530,000	26
1612	1,300,000	69
1622	ca. 600,000	67
1716	300,000	24
1726	500,000	36
1755	318,000	22
1788	273,000	25

Sources: Stefano Di Stefano, *La ragion pastorale over comento su la Prammatica LXXIX de offitio Procuratoris Caesaris,* 2 vols. (Naples: Domenico Roselli, 1731), 1:219–28. For 1561, ASFg, *Dogana,* serie I, fas. 36; for 1622, ASFi, *Mediceo,* fas. 4101, letter of sig. Vincenzo Vettori of Naples (5 May 1622); for 1755, ASFg, *Dogana,* serie I, fas. 42, ff. 184–87; for 1788, Viviana Bonazzoli, "La economia agraria nella società della Puglia cerealicolo-pastorale nel XVIII secolo," *Annali dell'Istituto Italiano per gli Studi Storici* 4 (1973–75): 112–15.

Note: Minor sheep deaths were reported for 1531, 1668, 1687, 1693, 1731, 1739, 1745, 1750, 1760, 1766, 1776, 1779, 1782, and 1802.

Again the Doria holdings offer exemplary evidence for generalizing upon the significance of unusually unfavorable weather in the Tavoliere. In the severe winter of 1726, the Doria flock was reduced by 43 percent (12,140 minus 5,206 head). That loss could not be compensated for by births: the flock was increased by a mere 7 percent in lambs (852 head) because only 17 percent of the newborns survived the winter to be added to stock. In the following year the Doria overseers began to build up herd size from its low of 7,786 head. The percentage of newborn lambs to sheep was increased from 15 percent in the preceding two years to 57 percent (4,417 lambs/7,786 sheep). From these newborns, 47 percent (2,060 lambs) were kept for stock breeding at an atypical sex ratio of 11 percent male/89 percent female (202 male/1,859 female lambs). The result was an increase of herd size by 1,012 animals by the beginning of 1727/28. Another 851 head were added in that year by the same extraordinary means: 50 percent newborn lambs to sheep ratio, and 50 percent of them retained for breeding with an 8 percent male/92 percent female ratio.

What was happening? The Doria shepherds were increasing the proportion of females bearing lambs to the entire female population, increasing the proportion of males in the flocks, in absolute numbers adding more female lambs as replacement stock, and selling off fewer lambs as meat in both absolute and percentage figures. In other words, in their attempts to return herd size to optimum numbers, a set of economic decisions was being made within the constraints imposed by the demography of the sheep. The Doria sheep industry was reducing its profit margin from meat revenues and transferring that capital, in the form of animals on the hoof, to its current stock. The problem was straightforward: how many more lambs could be retained as breeding stock (both male and female), instead of being sold off as meat profit, and still allow for balanced accounts? The Doria solution was an increase of replacement lambs by 12 percent per year. After flock devastation, sheep owners were faced with the same kind of problem as modern industrialists whose fixed capital, like factories and machinery, were destroyed by fire—only without insurance.[52] The dogana reimbursed taxes paid for dead sheep but could not replace lost capital. For the Doria, the result was a slow flock build-up that would have taken six years to return herd size to the 1725 starting point had not a bitter winter and earthquake in 1730/31 killed 26 percent of the sheep.

Other sheepography conclusions can be drawn from the Doria evidence. Deaths were unevenly distributed through the sheep population. First, lambs were the most vulnerable. In 1755, for example, although only 22.3 percent of the total doganal sheep were killed (317,788), more than 54.1 percent of the newborn lambs died (218,051).[53] Similarly, different locations were more severely affected than others. On 12 January 1779 an agent at Minervino in the location of Canosa, south of the Tavoliere itself, reported that six *palmi* of snow had fallen.[54] On the other hand, in 1560, Lesina, in the north, reported 6,192 sheep deaths and Camarda, in the south, none.[55] Finally, although sheep deaths in years when bad weather struck were immediately limited to direct exposure losses plus indirect losses from respiratory infection, malnutrition, and so forth, the surviving sheep were not necessarily the fittest, but generally older and less fertile. Residual effects like sterility and shortened life spans probably continued to reduce wool and lamb yields for some time. Increasing the newborn lamb/sheep ratio compensated for such losses in fertility but could also affect the longevity of the pregnant ewes as well as the robustness of their offspring. Thus, some graziers suffered far worse than others. It was likely that some individual small holders could be completely wiped out while others were almost unaffected. With older, less fertile herds, often greatly diminished, individual small proprietors, who were unable to draw upon liquid capital resources or to reduce their profit margin by restocking rather than selling off newborn lambs to compensate for the vicissitudes of climate, were the ones most likely to go under.

Disease could play a similar role. In 1736, for example, an animal epidemic swept through the Kingdom and curtailed transhumance.[56] By 1740 ambassadorial dispatches to Spain report that the disease had subsided.[57] But during the four-year interval, there was no cure except quarantine of animals and trust in God's favor. By 1738 the epidemic had jumped across political borders into the Papal States and was threatening the sheep in the grazing land of the garrisons in Tuscany. The Spanish ambassador in Florence reported on what must have been an emergency response.[58] Beginning on 21 November, public prayers were offered in the cathedral of Florence for three days. At the same time, some forty soldiers from the new battalion at Livorno arrived to strengthen the local militia and formed a cordon sanitaire at the frontier with the Papal States to prevent infected sheep from crossing the border.

Such "sheepography" teaches us three important lessons about economic decision making in the dogana. First, herds were slow to return to their original size after harsh winters. By applying the Doria standards of breeding experimentation—that is, by increasing replacement lambs 12 percent more than the norm—a mathematical model (not unlike compound interest) would predict that sheep deaths of 25 percent would require three years for regeneration; deaths of 33 percent, four years; deaths of 50 percent, six years; and deaths of 67 percent, ten years. Doganal income would decline accordingly, and the state would be in the same economic bind as the graziers. It was no coincidence that the 1611/12 sheep deaths led to a new system of fixed taxation three years later.[59] Second, meteorological statistics do not reflect the capriciousness of the weather. Regeneration predictions are based on the climatic assumption that the years following a bad winter would be mild. But new storms could wipe out pain-staking gains made in stock replacement. Weather comes in cycles, not discrete fifteen-year averages. Snow was recorded in the Tavoliere five times in the twenty-two year period between 1760 and 1782, but not again for another twenty years until 1802.[60] In 1788, however, exceptional cold rather than snow devastated the coast, but not the interior; 273,000 sheep (25 percent of total flocks) and 400,000 lambs were left dead.[61] Because cold and snow could strike unevenly in time and place, some holders were affected more than others. And finally, small holders were most penalized by climatic variation. They were less likely to be able to reduce meat sales and lower profit margins to rebuild herds. Economies of scale worked against small and middling holders. Sheepography argues for a kind of survival of the biggest—the rich getting richer and the poor getting poorer.

Agricultural Management

As with the pastoral industry, a wealth of literature and tradition exists on agricultural management in Capitanata. Tavoliere farming land (*portate*) was divided into "old farms" (*masserie vecchie* or *antiche*) and "new farms" (*masserie nuove* also called *fiscali, di Corte,* or *terre salde di Regia Corte a coltura*). Because of the growing population and overworking of the old farmland by the mid sixteenth century, about 1,500 *carri* of pasture land (new farmland) was added to cultivation. Both designations were subject to the custom of Puglia, a variant of the two-field rotation system.

According to testimony taken in preparation for the 1548 cadastral survey, arable land was managed in a six-year cycle with three years planted in grain and three years fallow.[62] Five witnesses were called. The first, fifty-five-year-old Sebastiano di Bellovedere from Foggia, offered this model: on 20 *carra* of land, 10 *carra* are planted, 3 *carra* 6 *versure* are placed in fallow (*maiese*) on 17 January, and the rest in "fallow open to grazing" (*restoppie*). The next three witnesses (Cornelio Caracciolo and Angelo de Atello, both sixty years old and from Foggia; and Petro Castello, a Florentine factor for the Abbey of San Leonardo delle Matine of Siponto) agreed on a similar model: on 30 *carra* of land, 15 *carra* are planted, 5 *carra* are in *maise,* and 10 in *restoppie*. A fifth testimony was taken from Federico de Minadois of Manfredonia, who could well have been the former pro-French doganiero of 1501 or an heir with the same name.[63] His 50-*carra* model provides for a seven-year turnaround, as in the previous testimony, but his mathematics are unclear: a 17-*carra* division is further divided, 5 *carra* into *maiese* and the rest *restoppia* of the first and second year of sowing.

The six-year cycle, thus, was a variant of the two-course system. Two years of wheat and one year of barley were followed by three years of repose. In the first two years of repose, the *locati* were free to graze their sheep; and, consequently, the fields were fertilized before being left completely vacant for one-half year of *maiese*. From 17 January these fallow plots in *maiese* were prepared for planting in the following autumn, between mid October and the end of November, to be harvested in July.[64] The six-year rotation modification of the two-course system, therefore, allowed Puglia to enjoy yields equal to land management systems employing the more productive three-course system.

As a result of the general reintegration, this six-year cycle was replaced by a more careful policy of fertility restoration.[65] The two-field rotation system remained customary, but soil exhaustion demanded a four-year cycle. The real foundation of long-term rapport between pasture and agriculture in the dogana thus dates from the 1548 reintegration.

An oft reduplicated geometrical diagram dating from Gaudiani's early eighteenth-century manuscript illustrates the reformed land-use pattern on agricultural plots in the dogana's jurisdiction.[66]

THE GEORGICS OF THE TAVOLIERE OF PUGLIA

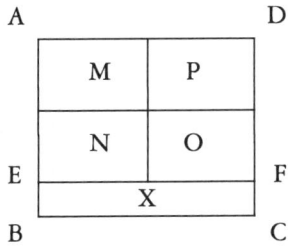

If the rectangle ABCD has an area of 60 *carra*, one-fifth of it would be assigned as *mezzana* for pasturing plow animals. These 12 *carra* are represented by area x. The remaining 48 *carra* are divided equally into four fields with area M, N, O, and P respectively. Wheat is planted in M after it has lain fallow for two years. Plot N is in the second year of cultivation. After two years of planting, field O is in *restoppia*, open to grazing. Plot P is in its second year of repose, called *nocchiarica*. After 15 January it will be left fallow and prepared for planting in the following autumn. In the second year, fields M and P would be in cultivation, while N would be in *restoppia* and O in *nocchiarica*. The cycle continues in this pattern, with two of the plots in seed and two in fallow. To summarize, plots were planted for two consecutive years—the first year in wheat; the second in either wheat, barley, oats, or fava beans according to either soil quality or demand. In the third year this field remained untilled in *restoppia* and the land was open to animal grazing. In the fourth year the plot was untilled and left in *nocchiarica*. It was open for sheep grazing until 17 January, when it was officially given back to the agriculturists. From 17 January, the *nocchiarica* lay fallow and was prepared for planting in the following autumn, when it returned to the beginning of the four-year cycle.

The two systems agree on the 1:5 proportion of *mezzane* (grazing land for oxen used in agriculture) to arable.[67] According to the first question answered in the sixteenth-century testimony, 1 *carro* of *mezzane* provided enough fodder for 16 oxen (with a range of 12 to 20 depending upon the quality of the pasture). In response to a second question, the five witnesses agreed that a total of 8 oxen were needed per *carro* of grain. Six oxen were needed to plow 1 *carro*, and 2 more were required for hauling grain to market or to the shipping docks. This means that 1 *carro* of *mezzane* grazed the oxen needed to plow 2 *carra* of cultivated land. For agricultural animals, then, the sixteenth-century testimony confirms the customary land management pattern in Puglia. The *mezzane*/cultivated/repose ratio (1:2:2) remained constant. The *mezzane* was immutably assigned to draft animal grazing.

One striking difference emerges, however, between the pre- and post-*reintegra* rotation systems with regard to planting and repose of the arable land. Instead of the earlier field division in the six-year cycle:

| wheat | 33.33 percent | sheep grazing | 33.33 percent |
| barley | 16.67 percent | complete repose | 16.67 percent |

the doganal reform distributed land use in the four-year cycle according to new proportions:

| wheat | 25 percent | sheep grazing | 25 percent |
| barley | 25 percent | complete repose | 25 percent |

Sheep grazing lost to land in complete repose, while the wheat and barley ratio underwent a similar shift. Increased soil exhaustion from overplanting forced the custom of Puglia to conform to the four-year variant of the two-field system because it put more land in barley and in complete repose.

Federico de Minadois, the distinguished witness of 1549 whose repetition of the words *hoggi* ("today") and *però* ("however"), in a parenthetical, derogatory manner suggest an older man who had seen better times, argued forcefully that the planters were constrained against their will by the division into posts to provide sheep pasture.[68] If left on their own to plant honestly and without interference from the dogana, they would willingly adopt a three-field rotation system. State intrusion, however, made it impossible to govern one's fields to one's best advantage. Consequently, agriculturists compounded the uncertainty of good harvests by planting in exhausted plots. Let us look at the implications of the Minadois observation.

In his study of Western European agricultural history, Slicher Van Bath identifies the size of the farm, especially the arable/pasture ratio, as the most important internal factor (within certain limits) determining the farm's productivity.[69] Puglia's particular land management system ensured that a large number of draft animals could be kept on the *mezzane* because there was a substantial supply of manure from migratory sheep. Grazed on the arable in years of repose, one sheep could fertilize an area about ten square feet.[70] Thus, the internal organization of the farm maintained a harmonious balance between livestock and tillage demands. Agricultural production could be geared to cash cropping because of the optimal proportions established between farm size, haulage, power, manure, household size, and field allocation.

Slicher Van Bath continues by explaining the critical corollary derived from the arable/pasture ratio, namely, yield in relation to seed sown. The average seed/yield ratio through the eighteenth century in Western Europe was 1:3 or 1:4.[71] This relatively low proportion of seed to yield meant that one-third or one-fourth of the whole arable land had to be used to raise the seed for the following year. If we recall that the three-field or two-field rotation kept one-third or one-half of the arable land fallow and sowed one-third or one-fourth of it in spring crops like barley and oats, the implications of seed/yield ratio become clearer. In the case of the three-field system, about one-third of the arable was left for bread grain; in the two-field rotation, one-fourth of the arable. Grain available for human consumption, therefore, was limited to an even smaller area of the total arable land. When the seed/yield ratio was 1:3, 22.2 percent of the arable land produced grain for human consumption in the three-course rotation; and only 16.7 percent in the two-course rotation. With a

1:4 seed/yield ratio, 25 percent of the arable was planted for human consumption in the three-course; and in the two-course, only 18.75 percent of the arable. Slicher Van Bath concludes: "A rise in yield from 3 to 4 has the result of increasing the crop grown on the original area by one-third, and, furthermore, barely one-quarter of the farmland, instead of one-third as before, has to be reserved for seed, so that the area which can be sown with cereals for consumption is increased by one-twelfth. The rise in yield has a cumulative effect in that the larger proportion of land that can now be used for food crops is added to it."[72] In other words, the relationship between seed/yield ratio and area of cultivation is exponential. As seed/yield ratio increases, less land is needed for seed; more land can be planted for human consumption. The cumulative effect of getting yield from land formerly left in seed follows a hyperbolic curve. As seed/yield ratio rises, the cumulative effect diminishes because less and less land is actually freed for yield. Some land must always remain in seed. The rise from 3 to 4 in the seed/yield ratio is more advantageous than one from 9 to 12 or 12 to 16. This exponential relationship explains the limits upon expansion of cultivation to marginally fertile land.

In Puglia seed/yield ratios were normally within the range of the Western European rule for the principal cereals. Onorati gives an eighteenth-century figure for the best of years as approaching 1:7.[73] Even if, in the sixteenth century, wheat yields in the Tavoliere's plots of virgin land used for planting reached record ratios, 1:20 and 1:30,[74] such rates would not in themselves have been very significant because of the declining limits of the exponential curve. In the four-year cycle standardized by the 1548 cadastral survey, the 21.4 percent of the arable land which produced cereals for human consumption with a 1:7 seed/yield ratio would have increased only to 23.75 percent with 1:20 yields, and to 24.2 percent with 1:30 yields.

What made the seed/yield margin in Puglia exceptional vis-à-vis other grain-producing regions using the two-course system was that sheep fertilizer helped rejuvenate the soil of wheat fields in fallow. By dividing the fallow into *restoppia* and *nocchiarica,* pastoralism was intimately tied to soil replenishment. Capitanata's characteristic land management system, linked as it was to sheep transhumance, was the reason why its Tavoliere plain was the granary of the Kingdom.

No wonder that there was competition for land ownership. Depending on the market, pasture land could be rented for cultivation, or vice versa. Agricultural or pastoral investment in Puglia guaranteed high profits. The price paid for mismanagement of the land, however, was also high. Agricultural or pastoral abuses from soil exhaustion or overgrazing were, nevertheless, not as costly as upsetting the balance between agricultural and pastoral livelihood systems.

External factors such as climate, environment, and economic conditions were also variables in determining grain production in Puglia.[75] The quality of its wheat was particularly dependent upon the Tavoliere's weather. Modern rainfall statistics reveal that the Tavoliere averages less than 500 millimeters of precipitation annually.[76] The hilly flanks surrounding the plain of Foggia receive only 500–600 millimeters annually. Rain falls only 60–70 days in Foggia and 70–80 days on the surrounding plain. Most of the rainfall is measured in autumn and winter, whereas summers are extremely dry: autumn receives 39.2 percent of the annual precipitation; winter, 31.6 percent; spring, 20.8 percent; and summer, 8.4 percent. The growing season reflected this rainfall pattern and crops were selected to conform to it.

In short, that environment is not particularly well suited for wheat production.[77] The Tavoliere has short, warm winters; long, hot summers; a paucity of rain; and above all, dry rivers by early summer—all of which are inimical to wheat cultivation. Nutritive elements and the low water table in the Tavoliere are also insufficient for cereal demands. But it is precipitation and temperature which are most crucial to grain cultivation. Short, wet winters are mild. But the optimum conditions for wheat are dryness, not mildness. An old proverb has it: "Dry January, rich farmer."[78] The violence of the January storms and the absence of a protective snow cover often prevent germination and retard growth if it has begun. The influence of the sea allows the temperature to rise too quickly in early spring, hurrying the biological cycle of wheat. Or the absence of rain coupled with heat late in the spring dries up the soil when the ripening wheat needs water most. Interruption of the maturation process dries out the stalk and can reduce yields by 50 percent. Grain cultivation in the Mediterranean basin is always a precarious proposition.

The primary grain was "strong" or "hard" wheat (*grani forti* or *duri*), popularly called *Saragolle*.[79] There was a secondary "sweet" or "white" wheat (*grani dolci* or *bianchi*), called *Majoriche*, or *Caroselle*. The sweet wheat was best suited for weaker soils and those that were not rotated. Its straw did not have to be broken up for fodder and was fed directly to horses. The hard grain was particularly adapted to the climatic conditions in the Tavoliere and produced its big yields with the aid of animal fertilizer. It quickly wore out the soil and was, therefore, grown in the rotated fields. Its straw had to be broken up before it could be used as animal fodder. This hard quality, however, also made it ideally suited for the long voyages necessary for exportation.

Storage was the key to the success of the hard wheats. Stockpiles of grain could be built up from the surplus and provide safeguards against famine. In the Tavoliere, underground pits or silos (*fosse* or *fovea*) were present from the time of prehistoric settlements.[80] These storage vaults are often credited with giving Foggia its name, although a good argument can also be made for derivation from the nearby bogs and standing water (*foya* or *fogiae*).[81] Municipal silos were concentrated at Piano della Croce, just outside the main population area, at the beginning of the Porta Grande, which opened onto the Foggia-Manfredonia road. They could preserve hard wheat for five years without its becoming damp or rotting in the summer heat.[82] Two companies of *sfossatori* maintained them, one called S. Rocco, the other S. Stefano.[83] Mean quantity put in storage annually by the two companies at Foggia for thirty-nine of the years between 1730 and 1774 was 2,311 *carra;* for the twenty-one years with accumulated grain, mean storage was 3,391 *carra*.[84]

Cash cropping of both wheat and wool, thus, was a mutually dependent economic strategy to exploit the Tavoliere of Puglia. The word *tavoliere* means "checkerboard."[85] Islands of cultivation dotted the pastoral sea of the Foggian plain, a vast but far from limitless open expanse. Similarly, this flat tableland under royal control was checkered with noble fiefs and ecclesiastical holdings. These patches of agricultural production and private enterprise were essential to the mixed livelihood system fostered in the royal demesne. In the cash cropping for wool and wheat, public pasture and private arable cooperated and competed for a circumscribed area. Past and present were fused within the ever-present establishment of special legal exemptions and extralegal frauds. Without an understanding of these individual foundations and their conflicting interest, privilege and power in the dogana makes little sense. The state machinery in Foggia attempted neither to reinforce nor to subvert agricultural or private interests. On the contrary, by administering all concerns through the bureaucracy, the state hoped to moderate conflict for the mutual benefit of all parties—graziers and agriculturists—whether they be commoner, aristocrat, cleric, or king.

3 Explaining Economic Expansion and Contraction

Although the customhouse of Foggia maintained a relatively uniform structure in the face of three hundred fifty years of conflict and change, exceptions, in the form of exemptions and contraventions, nevertheless, often seemed more the rule than the laws themselves. By 1770, for example, a sympathetic doganal jurist deliberately attempted, despite his advanced age, "to leave an instruction in ordinary [language] on this extraordinary material, so confused in practice."[1] My brief chronological review of law, privilege, abuse, official visitation, and reform in chapter 1 and the survey of geographical and technological constraints in chapter 2 may only have multiplied the confusion. But both the chaotic surface structure and the unstable deep structure of the customhouse (and the Kingdom for that matter) can be better understood by pinpointing the internal and external causes of change and by dividing the dogana's long-term history into periods defined by these problems.

The dogana's expanding and contracting economic cycles corresponded to the dominant European conjuncture during the early modern period. After all, the Foggian customhouse was an important but secondary raw material market subject to various overlapping and interconnected forces that acted cumulatively to set the moments of crisis and change. Thus, demography, the vagaries of the weather, political upheaval, and merchant demand operated beyond doganal power.

The success and failure of the doganal economy, however, was not simply a free market solution to economic challenge. Built into the dogana's structure was an uneasy balance between rich and poor, as well as between wheat and wool interests, that affected production and prices. Legal privileges and political will often operated in the face of external trends to retard or sometimes to stimulate economic activity and to hold the dogana to its course. The state's manipulation of the dogana's internal antagonisms kept it responsive to changing market conditions.

The interplay of exogenous and endogenous economic variables gave the dogana that vibrancy or resilience which determined its multifaceted history. External factors set the parameters for growth and decline in the dogana, but the institution's internal logic governed investment strategy and land exploitation. Analyzing the economic profile of the dogana of Foggia and understanding the variant pressures and conjunctures operative in the rural economy provide insight into the apparent instability of the Kingdom and the native Neapolitan response to the development of capitalist agriculture.

Periodization by External Variables

Demography forms the first external mechanism which governed doganal growth and decline.[2] The first demographic intervention, as we have already seen in the discussion of Alfonso of Aragon's doganal foundation in 1447, corresponded to the time when population had dropped to its lowest point as a result of the 1348 plague. In all, five important demographic "moments" can be pinpointed:

1. 1447 Alfonso's foundation
2. 1533–36 Charles V's refoundation
3. 1560 renting of former pasture land for agriculture
4. 1656 plague
5. 1759–66 famine

The second demographic shift was the reordering of the Kingdom by Charles V after the war of Lautrec in 1528. War, plague, and famine had "finished Puglia and part of the Abruzzo." Lucera's 1,520 hearths had been reduced to 120 and San Severo's 1,720 were down to 70. "There was a scarcity of everything: liberty, honor, justice, and provisions. . . . All fiscal mechanisms and payments were lost and reduced to nothing."[3] Thus, when hearth counts were taken by the new viceroy, Pedro de Toledo, in his first year in office, 1532, Capitanata was the only province in the Kingdom to have suffered population decline. Hearths fell 9.5 percent overall since the last hearth count in 1505, while those in the Kingdom at large increased 24 percent.[4] As a logical consequence to depopulation and revenue needs, Charles ordered a new cadastral survey for the dogana in 1533.

The third moment began to be perceived by the mid 1550s. According to the hearth counts, which did not include the city of Naples itself, population in the countryside grew 33 percent from 1532 to 1545; 14 percent from 1545 to 1561; and 12 percent from 1561 to 1591. The total provincial growth from 1505 to 1595 was a net doubling, a 112 percent increase. In an exchange of letters in 1560 on the crisis of population growth in the capital, Philip II and the viceroy, the duke of Alcala, agreed to meet the city's provisioning needs by turning over to agriculture some of the pastures on which shepherds had been wintering their sheep in the Tavoliere.[5]

The fourth demographic shift followed the plague of 1656. Rural population in the Kingdom fell 27 percent between the hearth counts of 1648 and 1669. Because of the decimated agricultural labor force, the great grain barons such as the prince of Melfi (the heir of Andrea Doria and still resident in Genoa through the eighteenth century) shifted their investment strategy to the less labor-intensive demands of sheep farming.[6]

The fifth moment corresponded to the recurrent famines of the mid eighteenth century. Strong demographic growth in the Kingdom continued from the late seventeenth century, then especially after 1730, and ended with the dramatic famine of 1759–66—200,000 people, about 5 percent of the population, died in 1764 alone. After this food provisioning crisis, new population pressure strained the Kingdom: 5.4 percent growth in 1765–67 and 12.4 percent in 1767–80.[7] In this context, Galiani's mocking indictment of doganal barbarism in 1780 was grounded in a profound commitment to eradicate the Kingdom's contradictions; in this case, state support of a pastoral economy in a fertile plain.

Climatic fluctuation and its effect upon animal population offer a second external variable to determine doganal periodization.[8] Winter temperature in Puglia rarely reached freezing. But when it did, and heavy snows fell, there were disastrous results for the sheep industry. As we have already seen, harsh winters devastated the flocks at least ten times (damaging them some twenty-four times in all) during the dogana's three-hundred-fifty-year history. The most serious natural disaster was in 1611/12, when 69 percent of the sheep were destroyed. On the basis of sheep reproductive cycles, life span, a 5 percent male/95 percent female flock ratio, and high mortality rates for newborn lambs, it is possible to predict the time necessary to replace flocks after such catastrophes.[9] Sheepography statistics are not just tongue-in-cheek economic theory but emphasize that in the great 69 percent mortality of 1611/12, flocks needed at least ten years to return to their original size. It should be no surprise that this rupture in raw wool production was directly connected to successive failures in commerce and industry that marked the origins of the seventeenth-century crisis.[10] The critical decade 1611/12–1621/22 divides doganal history into two periods of growth from meager to maximum flock size: 1447–1612, 250,000 to 2 million; and 1612–1806, 500,000 to 2 million.

Politics—the disruptions of war, dynastic rivalry, and baronial revolt which prevented graziers from making their trek from summer pasture in the mountains of the Abruzzi to winter grazing in the plain of Puglia—are the third external mechanism of doganal growth and decline. The 1447 foundation diploma of Alfonso of Aragon followed his pacification and conquest of the Kingdom in 1443. Ferdinand the Catholic reordered the dogana in 1506 after the French invasions of Charles VIII and Louis XII had been turned back. Charles V reestablished the doganal system in 1536 after the expulsion of the last French expeditionary force under Lautrec in 1528. The Austrian Habsburgs refounded it in 1709 after receiving Naples in the struggle over the Spanish succession. Finally, Joseph Bonaparte's land reform of 1806 abolished the doganal system and established a new jurisdiction called the Tavoliere di Puglia in the wake of the victorious Napoleonic armies. Four neat periods defined by legal charters emerge:

1. 1447–1506 Alfonso's foundation
2. 1506–1535 Aragonese control
3. 1536–1709 Spanish Habsburg viceregal administration
4. 1709–1806 Austrian Habsburg and native Bourbon florescence

Commercial demand is the fourth external factor affecting the doganal conjuncture and can be divided into five periods. In the first, from the foundation of the dogana by Alfonso in the mid fifteenth century through the French invasions, Abruzzese wool enjoyed premium prices in Florence and Venice. With the Hundred Years' War curtailing English wool supply and before Castilian wool replaced it, Abruzzese wool dominated the market. In period 2, however, the French Wars in Italy and the economic policies of the Catholic Kings to export Spanish wool eliminated Abruzzese production from the market until Pedro de Toledo began to revitalize the dogana after 1533.

By period 3, the middle of the sixteenth century, northern Italian merchants enjoyed a respite from war and began an economic recovery. Wool from the dogana of Foggia (about 80,000 *rubbi* annual production) was prized by the wool industry of Venice, Bergamo, and Como as well as native Neapolitan manufacturers. Research in the northern Italian textile manufacturing centers confirms this conjecture. Florentine production doubled from 1553 to 1560, registered 33,212 cloths in 1572, but fell in the 1580s.[11] Venetian wool production rose phenomenally (9.6 percent per annum) from 1521 to 1569 and continued to grow to its peak of 28,729 pieces in 1602.[12] After the 1559 Peace of Cateau-Cambresis, competition picked up from other northern cities, especially in the duchy of Milan. In 1580, Como's industry was booming; Bergamo produced 26,500 cloths in 1596. The simultaneous peaking of wool manufacture in the North and sheep grazing in the South was not mere coincidence.

Period 3 saw the Indian summer of the Italian economy peak as Spanish finances worsened. Fabrizio di Sangro stimulated maximum doganal growth to meet demand and manipulated the tax method of "sheep in the air" (*pecore in aerea*) to double doganal revenue. In period 4, production for the home market remained a constant of 40,000–60,000 *rubbi* through the crisis following the 1611/12 sheep mortality disaster, but foreign commerce virtually stopped.[13]

Finally after 1686, demand reasserted itself in period 5. Two-thirds of production remained in the Kingdom, and one-third was exported to northern Italian manufacturers. Eventually in the late eighteenth century, the home manufacturers consumed one-half of production; northern Italy and France divided the remaining half.

The five periods of commercial demand are:

1. 1447–94 establishment at 80 percent of mean wool sales and growth to 175 percent
2. 1494–1550 disruption and decline because of war
3. 1550–1612 a spectacular doubling to 200 percent

    4. 1612–86   depression and drift of 50–75 percent
    5. 1686–1806   slow recovery to 100 percent, then 125 percent

The international market was the single most important variable determining raw wool production. Rough comparison with the Spanish Mesta confirms this same conjuncture.

Comparing Production and Revenues in the Spanish Mesta

The description of the Spanish wool industry in a 1795 *informe* of Don Gaspar Melchor de Jovellanos, as developed by Felipe Ruiz Martín, also divides Mesta wool production into five periods:

    1. 1450–1526   norm, 100 percent
    2. 1526–78   doubling to 200 percent
    3. 1578–1602   decline to norm, 100 percent
    4. 1602–86   depression to 50–75 percent
    5. 1686–1795   recovery to 100–200 percent[14]

The Italian Wars caused the difference between Castile and Puglia in periods 1, 2, and 3. With the Foggian supply disrupted from the end of the fifteenth century, Castilian wool had a clear field to expand in Italian markets. The reorganization of the pastoral industries in Naples by the mid sixteenth century, however, allowed Foggian wool to challenge the Castilian monopoly. But internal factors played their part as well. Droughts around 1560 desiccated Mesta pastures for transhumant sheep and caused limited resources to be reassigned to pressing agricultural needs. Simultaneously, market demand also affected raw material supply. The Castilian economy began to diversify, and wool was finished in home industries especially after the late 1550s. Spanish exports shifted from northwest Europe to northern Italy after 1560 with the resurgence of Italian industry and the disruptive hostilities of the Dutch Revolt beginning in 1568. Thus, with the refueling of the northern Italian market, the increase in production of lower quality woolens, and the development of more domestic industry in Spain, the native southern Italian suppliers (under the political direction of the Spanish monarchy) increased their production in period 3 to take up the Spanish export slack.

A comparison of three measures of pastoral vitality—sheep counts, tax revenues, and wool—gives an indication of the strength of the Foggian customs in the international market (tables 3, 4, and 5). The dogana administered an institution about one-third the size of the Spanish Mesta in terms of sheep numbers and wool sales. Revenues were another matter, however. Despite the dogana's smaller size, its income was consistently greater than Mesta income since it was collected at a much higher rate or included pasture rent as well as road tolls—possibly as a kind of Castilian protectionist policy.

The Castilian crown compensated for lower taxes from Mesta tolls (*servicio*

TABLE 3 Comparative Sheep Numbers: Dogana of Foggia and Spanish Mesta

Period	Years	Dogana Sheep	Years	Mesta Sheep
1	1447–94	Growth to 1.7 million	1511–40	Growth, 3.5–4.5 million (2.5 million in transhumance; 1.5 million nontranshumance)
2	1494–1550	600,000 during French Wars; mean = 1 million	1540–63	Stable, 2.5–3 million in transhumance; ? nontranshumance
3	1550–1611	1–2.4 million; mean = 1 million	1563–1621	Crisis and decline
4	1612–90s	500,000–750,000	1621–84	Depression, 1.5–2 million total
5	1690s–1806	1–2 million; mean = 1.3 million	1684–1709	Growth, 1705–80: 2.4–3.5 million

Sources: Chap. 6; Jean Paul Le Flem, "Las cuentas de la Mesta (1510–1709)," Moneda y Crédito, 121 (1972):27–38.

TABLE 4 Comparative Income: Dogana of Foggia and Spanish Mesta

Period	Years	Dogana Income	Years	Mesta Income
1	1447–94	100,000 Neapolitan ducats (83,300 Castilian ducats)		
2	1494–1550	100,000 Neapolitan ducats (83,300 Castilian ducats)	1510–62	2 to 4 million *maravidís* (5,333–10,666 Castilian ducats)
3	1550–1611	450,000 Neapolitan ducats, gross (374,850 Castilian ducats) 150,000 Neapolitan ducats, net (124,950 Castilian ducats)	1563–1664	20–50 million *maravidís* (133,333 Castilian ducats)
4	1612–90s	200,000 Neapolitan ducats (139,000 Castilian ducats)		
5	1690s–1806	250,000 Neapolitan ducats (173,750 Castilian ducats)	1686–1709	10 million *maravidís* (26,666 Castilian ducats)

Sources: Chap. 6; Jean Paul Le Flem, "Las cuentas de la Mesta (1510–1709)," Moneda y Crédito, 121 (1972):38–44.
Note: 1 Neapolitan ducat = 0.833 Castilian ducat before 1611 and 0.695 Castilian ducat after 1611; 375 *maravidís* = 1 Castilian ducat.

TABLE 5 Comparative Wool Sales: Dogana of Foggia and Spanish Mesta

Period	Years	Dogana Wool Sold	Years	Mesta Wool Exports
1	1447–94	Lacunae, probably <60,000 *rubbi* (<530,000 kg)	1500–1520s	150,000 *arrobas* (1.7 million kg)
2	1494–1550	40,000–80,000 *rubbi* (350,000–710,000 kg)	1520s–82	Increase to 250,000 *arrobas* (2.8 million kg), with 575,000 *arrobas* max. (6.5 million kg) and 325,000 *arrobas* at close (3.7 million kg)
3	1550–1611	80,000 *rubbi*, probably doubling to 160,000 *rubbi* (710,000–1.4 million kg)	1582–1606	Stable, 175,000–250,000 *arrobas* (2.0–2.3 million kg)
4	1612–90s	40,000–60,000 *rubbi* (360,000–530,000 kg)	1606–80s	Decrease from 250,000 to 100,000 *arrobas* (from 2.8 to 1.1 million kg)
5	1690s–1806	80,000–100,000 *rubbi* (712,800–891,000 kg)	1692–1730	Doubling from 136,000 to 225,000 *arrobas* (from 1.5 to 2.6 million kg)
			1730–80	Doubling again from 225,000 to 400,000 *arrobas* (from 2.6 to 4.5 million kg)

Sources: Chap. 8; Carla Rahn Phillips, "The Spanish Wool Trade, 1500–1780," *Journal of Economic History* 42, no. 4 (1982):777–89.
Note: 1 *rubbio* = 8.91 kg; 1 *arroba* = 11.36 kg.

y montazgo) by collecting export taxes on wool (*nuevo* and *antiguo derechos*).[15] These added taxes were gathered at numerous exit ports at variable rates. By contrast, the dogana of Foggia's attraction for the Neapolitan state treasury was its high guaranteed revenues. The sheep customs comprised the Kingdom's single most important tax source, contributing about 10 percent of net patrimonial income, all collected in cash within one month at the same place.[16]

But state income was only part of the economic picture. The focal point of the doganal season was the spring fair of late April and early May. For no less a monetary expert and later doganal opponent than Ferdinando Galiani, the Foggian fair was the heart of the Kingdom of Naples because of its ability to attract foreign specie.[17] Total monetary value in the fair was a function of the pastoral products—wool, meat, cheese, and skins, which brought in approximately one-half, one-fourth, one-fifth, and one-twelfth of the fair's income respectively. We can estimate gross product at the fair during the second half of the eighteenth century at 600,000 ducats.[18] Although it is difficult to judge the relative weight of this enormous sum, if we assume that one-third of these pastoral products were exported according to the Kingdom's customary law, it would not be an exaggeration to estimate that doganal exports accounted for 10 percent of all exports kingdomwide.[19]

Variable Internal Structures

Internal economic structures of tax collection, rural credit, and location assignment were sensitive to external economic variables. As the changing external variables sharpened the conflict between rich and poor, between agriculturists and pastoralists, between the state and its subjects, between merchants and raw material producers, the internal structures shifted gears to mediate tension. Through the dogana's internal mechanisms, then, state policy manipulated the antagonisms of the vying participants in the rural economy and, in turn, helped to determine pastoral production and price curves.

The first of these internal structures, the method of tax collection, reflected doganal growth and decline.[20] From 1447 to 1553, sheep were actually counted for tax purposes. The expenses and frauds associated with the count could be saved with the new taxation policy which tied sheep estimation to the amount of pasture received. In 1553 a system of free bidding (*professazione voluntaria*) was exploited by the state to increase revenue. *Professazione* worked like a kind of market value escalator, easily manipulated by the state to create parity between what pastoralists and agriculturists paid for the land they used.[21] The estimated sheep numbers were a kind of index of the competition for land between livelihood groups and social classes. In 1615, as part of the fiscal reforms of the viceroy conte de Lemos, a new system, "forced bidding" (*professazione forzosa*), was introduced. The 1611/12 sheep mortality had so reduced herd size that a fixed tax agreement (*transazione*) was needed to make up for the loss in state income. Only after 1661, to the great relief of the graziers, was the method of free bidding reestablished. The graziers of the dogana referred to each system of taxation as their *modo di vivere*. Dividing up doganal history according to its "way of living" emphasizes the interrelationship between the pastoral lobby and the state. Fiscal viability for the state and economic growth for the shepherd depended upon how they made their living and how heavy the tax bite was. Thus, the internal structure of the dogana's *modo di vivere* defined four periods:

1. 1447–1552   sheep numeration
2. 1553–1614   free bidding
3. 1615–60   fixed taxes
4. 1661–1806   free bidding reinstated

Taxes in the pastoral industry, we must remember, came from pasture rental and thus depended upon the value of land. The competition between grazing and agriculture and the comparison between wheat and wool markets dominated all fiscal and monetary policy in Puglia. The sixteenth-century change in the *modo di vivere* from sheep numeration to free bidding meant that the price of fodder for sheep (*fida* for *erbaggi ordini*) was directly tied to the price of *terre salde* rent. Thus, the system of free bidding, which was a mechanism of sheep estimation, a kind of competitive bidding to obtain adequate pasture, reflected agricultural as well as pastoral demand.[22] Initially, rising cereal prices placed agricultural land at a premium. Even at the new, increased rate of 13.2 ducats per *carro* for grazing 100 sheep, the 1,000 *carra* of *terre salde* rented in 1562 at 30 or 40 ducats per *carro* netted a 15,723-ducat profit over the *fida* rate, 32,500 ducats versus 16,777 ducats. Similar calculations included in a 1567 *consulta* give a nearly equivalent profit, 13,301 ducats, but on only 500 *carra* of *terre salde*, 21,227 ducats versus 7,927 ducats.[23] This doubling of profit in the five years between 1562 and 1567 was caused by the introduction of state-sponsored auctions *alla candela*. Before the candle burned out, prospective agriculturists bid against one another. If more than one bidder remained, another candle would be lighted to a maximum of three.[24] The market set the price of land. The 500.33 *carra* of 1567 were rented at rates ranging from 40 to 51.5 ducats per *carro*. The mean price was 42.4 ducats per *carro*, more than one-third higher than the 1562 mean of 30.7 ducats.

The price of *terre salde* plots mirrored the supply of and demand for grain. In the autumn of 1591 acute famine and fiscal pressures caused normal channels to be by-passed.[25] Because of the late date for renting agricultural land, the usual candle auction was suspended in order to rent to those able to break ground immediately and plant for next year's harvest. Fixed prices were set at 60 ducats per *carro* per year for four years. But by the 1590s land had become so attractive that these 1,011.5 *carra* were rented at 85,400 ducats per year. Although the mode and median price was 80 ducats per *carro*, diverse plots were rented for as much as 121 ducats per *carro*, which raised the mean rent to 84.45 ducats per *carro*. The 1591 *consulta* noted that this rental income amounted to 65,381.8 ducats more than the *fida* rate, that is, four times the profit margin of 1562. As famine and population pressure created an insatiable demand for grain, prices rose, and sharp competition for investment and profit in the wheat market increased. At the same time, the state encouraged higher prices because its own financial profile was deteriorating rapidly after the defeat of the Armada.[26]

Given the fiscal and provisioning pressures of the Kingdom, it may seem surprising that all the land of the dogana of Foggia was not rented as *terre salde*. At the rate of 40, 50, or even 60 ducats per *carro*, the state would be making three, four, or five times the amount that the 13.2 ducats per *carro* sheep *fida* paid. At a price of 9 to 18 *carlini* per *tomolo*, agriculturists were also coming out ahead. Geography and economics, however, circumscribed profit taking. First, the Tavoliere was not an ever-expanding frontier with unlimited arable. The symbiotic relationship between sheep and soil, especially in terms of fertilizer during fallow periods, was what had made the newly rented animal pasture (*saldo vergine*) more attractive than exhausted, regular cultivated land (*portate*). Further, marginal land best suited for grazing could not be turned over to agricultural needs. Second, the growth in grain supply eventually had predictable effects upon prices. By 1608 agricultural prices in general, but especially that of wheat, began to fall.[27] *Terre salde* rent remained at 80 ducats per *carro* from 1608 to 1612; dropped to 60 ducats per *carro* in 1613; and fell to 50 ducats per *carro* from 1637 to 1661.[28] Agricultural success on the *terre salde* helped to lower grain prices, which in turn meant less demand for agricultural land. The agricultural depression in seventeenth-century Puglia was partly a result of past success.[29]

A similar kind of market mechanism operated, as we have seen, in the setting of sheep pasture taxes vis-à-vis agricultural plots. From 1553/54 sheepowners were required to estimate their herds in an attempt to ensure that small holders could obtain optimum quantity and quality of pasture. The more sheep one declared, the better one's chance to receive good pasture and, possibly, even secure better credit terms. The overestimation of tax, therefore, was extremely rational. Sheepowners were bidding competitively for a limited amount of land; and sheep numbers, as an index of pasture price, rose accordingly. The idiosyncratic notation of the free bidding "tax" reflected the market price of land in the Tavoliere.

Government intrusion into the price-setting mechanism of the market artificially fixed the price of pasture at the same high level as agrarian land. The state reimbursed graziers who professed imaginary sheep (*pecore in aerea*) for that portion of the *fida* which would have been paid to the owners of pasture (105 out of 132 ducats per 1,000 sheep, and 102 ducats after 1584). The tax portion (27 ducats per 1,000 *pecore in aerea* before and 30 ducats after 1584) was added to the royal treasury. Gross income quadrupled, while net income grew by 68 percent.

To understand the eccentricities of the free bidding system, two points must be kept in mind. Why did prices rise so high? Grain demand made agricultural land more valuable, and it in turn forced pasture prices up to that level. Why did the state rebate 75 percent of the pasture purchase price? The state maintained a special relationship with the graziers, offering them security in transit, adequate pasture, and special juridical protection in exchange for guaranteed revenues, foreign exchange at the Foggian fair, and control of violence in the countryside. The taxes paid on imaginary sheep expressed simple rate increases in an inverted notation which kept rates constant but forced bidders to increase their assessment of their holdings beyond what they really held. Neither state nor sheepowner was pulling the wool over the other's eyes. The system of free bidding had an eminent economic logic. It worked like an anti-inflationary indexing plan to ensure revenue for the state without gouging the grazier taxpayer. Thus, overestimated taxes bought pasture, justice, and profit for the grazier and brought income, markets, and internal peace to the government.

A second internal fiscal mechanism, which affected prices and production as much as the *modo di vivere,* was the practice of setting official prices. The common Neapolitan credit instrument, the *contratto alla voce,* applied to wool, cheese, meat, grain—all agricultural commodities.[30] The "public" contract or "public" price was introduced in Foggia in 1667, and in the 1680s the account books of the wool weighers stopped including the real price for each wool sale and substituted the phrase "at the price of the Royal Court."[31] The *voce* pricing mechanism was, in effect, a guarantee of profit for merchants who were thus willing to advance capital in a kind of futures market. With this infusion of credit to sheep graziers, the dogana came out of its long seventeenth-century slump. Two periods can be defined, pre- and post-1680.

If the state customhouse initiated *voce* pricing of wool in 1667 and established it in the weighers' account books after 1680, the tradition of *voce* credit went back a long time. The earliest *voce* wool contract found by Maria Nardella in the Lucera notarial archives dates from 1635.[32] Earliest evidence in the laws of Foggia goes back to Charles V's refoundation in 1536, when *voce* prices were regulated by the customhouse for the poorest sheepowners.[33] Their total sale, however, was a small 10,000 ducats, less than 5 percent of product value. Despite the small amounts of charity wool in question, large sellers still attempted to defraud small ones by receiving these tax advantages illegally, by buying old season's wool at discount and passing it off as new charity wool, or by paying to enter the charity rolls in order to save 100 ducats in taxes.[34]

The important variables are worth reiterating: how the price was set, who forwarded the cash, and how it was repaid. Two accounts from the 1580s clarify the last two points.[35] Raniero Capece, a grain merchant, made 41 *voce* contracts between 1581 and 1584. He lent a total of 2,524.7 ducats at a mean transaction rate of 90 ducats. His was not a big-time operation; the minimum loan was 15 ducats, the maximum, 240 ducats. Baldassare Caracciolo, another grain merchant, contracted 56 *voce* agreements in this same period. He ran a bigger clearing house in both quantity and quality. He lent 6,765 ducats at a mean of 121 ducats per transaction, with a maximum loan of 1200 ducats. Only one of his contracts was for noncereal produce: 74 ducats for vines. The loan entries were standardized: "On date x (usually winter or spring), borrower Q received N ducats from lender (Capace or Caracciolo) to be paid back in an equivalent amount of grain at the *voce* price of S. Giovanni Rotondo at the time of the July harvest." In other words, cash loans made during the year were repaid in kind at harvest time when abundant supply had lowered price to its annual minimum. Sellers hoped for high *voce* prices to repay their debts with less product; buyers preferred lower *voce* prices to gain more in-kind repayment. Creditor-buyer advantage came from this seasonal price differential and from control of the harvest. Indebtedness, thus, depended on how the public price was set.

On 19 June 1582 a commission under Ferrante Fornaro had ordered that *voce* prices at San Giovanni Rotondo were to be set "without fraud or deceit by expert men of authority, integrity, and intelligence."[36] Price-setting decisions were to be made "without any respect except what comes from the right rationale, by men holding Our Lord God before their eyes, considering the public good and not the particular interest, and chosen so as not to be interested persons, but men without interest, of good life, reputation, and condition."

The Capece and Caracciolo accounts were, therefore, not randomly preserved. The former was a brother-in-law and the latter a brother of the Foggian dogàniero, Alfonso Caracciolo. Credit networks and even collusion between financiers, merchants, and customhouse officers were common in the rural economy. Another document in the Spanish visitor's report of 1582 emphasized how nepotism greased the wheels of bureaucracy and commerce.[37] The results of marriage alliances Neapolitan style were personal profits through fraud. Was it purely coincidental that the commissioner of the royal mint had a niece who was married to the son of the head of the stamping division; that the head of the stamping division was the godson of the head of the bank, who in turn was brother-in-law of the foundry smelter, who was godson of the chief accountant? Obviously, the bureaucrats practiced endogamy within their social class, which kept blood, money, and favors in the family. But such familial connections did not inspire the objectivity demanded by the law for men above suspicion who possessed no insider information.[38]

Who were these disinterested good men in Foggia? Representatives from the three interested parties—state officers, buyers, and sellers—met to establish the public wool price.[39] What criteria did they use? They employed objective market mechanisms—wool unsold from the previous year, supply of wool in the current year, quality, price of wool already sold, demand, and restrictions on commerce.[40] Was there a mechanism or formula to compute each year's *voce?* A series of nineteenth-century documents spells out the procedures for computing public prices of wool, cheese, and grain. Nothing was left to chance.

In 1806, in the midst of the Napoleonic Wars and French conquest of the Kingdom, a memorial on the public price of wool and cheese was prepared for the sheepowners because merchants had delayed in setting prices, "exaggerating the damages and obstacles from the maritime trade of wool, then minimizing those for cheese."[41] This extraordinary document begins with the theory of prices. Just prices are formed from the "intrinsic" and "eventual" price of things, what Marx would call their labor value and their exchange value.[42] On the other hand, sellers must establish a commodity's price "on the relationship between expenses, labor, and capital investment." One does not sell at ten what costs thirty to produce. But, at the same time, "natural justice" demands that neither seller, merchant, nor consumer is damaged. "It would be a very stupid economist" who would gouge buyers for short-term profits, because in a few short years they would turn the tables on him. The scholastic theory of just prices, thus, modifies the classical economics inherited by our pastoral sellers in Foggia. They believed in the "opinions of the moralists and the doctors" which made it illegal to sell goods before harvest because of the injustice and inequity between "eventual" and "intrinsic" prices.

We might remember that the public price was usually set between 15 and 20 May, but not later than 25 May.[43] It was a form of disguised and often exorbitant interest which could reach as high as 20 percent and even 40 percent.[44] Since the merchants and financiers called the shots, the actual market price of wool was usually 4 to 7 *carlini* less than the *voce*. Merchants made an extra 6 to 7 *carlini* profit at the expense of poor sellers, whereas rich sellers might have to pay only 3 to 4 *carlini* of these charges.[45] Beyond the effects of the *voce* system on rural credit and indebtedness, its price quotations often served as models for agrarian contracts not paid with *voce* agreements, such as those of big sellers like the Doria. Thus, rich sellers might be able to set their contracted price at first-condition *voce*, poor sellers at second-condition *voce*, regardless of the quality of their wool.[46] The precarious viability of the small producer depended on his access to credit, and the *voce* system only perpetuated his exploitation.

To return to the sheepowners of Foggia in 1806, they argued that the *voce* prices for wool and cheese had been formulated without consideration of each product's intrinsic cost, that is, the producers' costs.[47] Instead, wool had been erroneously undervalued by the Foggian customhouse only according to the wool's eventual or exchange value. The sheepowners then examined a series of factors which influenced price: wool supply, the difference between last year's and this year's prices, risk and demand because of the war, money and exchange rates, and maritime trade. Their conclusion charged that the merchants were using "equivocations and double-talk" to exaggerate the effect of the delay in wool sales on prices. By no means should wool prices be reduced 10 percent. The merchants were, after all, buying wool at prices disadvantageous to the sellers for the purpose of reselling it at even higher prices in foreign markets. Actual market prices did not warrant such exorbitant *voce* increases. Surprisingly, the sheepowners' arguments must have convinced the customhouse, since the final public wool price for 1806 was only 82.8 *carlini* per *rubbio,* up 0.3 *carlini* from the previous year.

The complicated method for calculating *voce* prices may help explain the variables considered in the formulation of the "public" price. An 1827 reform project of the intendant of Capitanata, Nicola Santangelo, gives the formulas which had been followed "for many centuries" in order to compute the wool, cheese, and cereal *voce* prices.[48]

Wool: [(low price of new year − low price of old year) + (high price of new year − high price of old year)] / 2 = new difference.
   Old year *voce* + new difference = *voce* for new year.
Cheese: (median price at various towns − transportation costs − costs for

dividing cheese into smaller pieces − gabelles) / number of towns ×
140 *cantaio* of cheese + (price of *ricotte* at Foggia on Easter × 25
cantaio) − expenses / 1,000 *pesa* = *voce* per *pesa*.
Bread: [(sum of median price in months of October through May / 8
months × 36 *tomoli*) + 7.20 (i.e., cost of making bread, 20 *grana* per
tomolo)] / 147 *pesa* (15 *rotoli* each, quantity derived from 1 *carro* of
wheat) = *voce* per *pesa*.

No wonder Ludovico Bianchini, a nineteenth-century financial minister and economic historian, called this "uno strano calcolo."[49] Bianchini emphasized that "the defects, inconveniences, and disorders of this system" were "the cause of the most grave damage to our economy" inasmuch as two prices existed at the same time, the free one and the forced one.[50] Galiani, the master of monetary theory, argued that the *voce* price was a "fixed price, but not a forced one," that it was not a "true price," but 8–10 percent lower.[51] Gaudiani's 1715 judgement, on the other hand, was the same as Bianchini's 1859 condemnation; namely, the *voce* was a forced price. The *voce* price only "increased the rancor of poor sheepowners . . . because it denied them the liberty to make contracts, which is in the natural law, something no human authority can change because it is absolute."[52] The distinctions between intrinsic (labor value) and eventual (exchange value), between free and forced, between natural and legal prices point to the crux of the problem between sellers and buyers.

The 1827 reform focused on this issue—how prices were set—as what was "capricious" and "presumptuous" about the *voce* system. Simply, when the *voce* price was computed, random price quotations (*prezzi rotti*) had to be garnered to test the market value of high and low prices. They depended upon knowledge of that year's wool harvest. But who had such accurate knowledge of supply? Who had knowledge of buyers' demand? No secure means of gathering the relevant data existed.

According to the 1827 projected reform, as in Gaudiani's 1715 analysis, the result was an artificially elevated *voce* price, some 4 to 12 *carlini* per *rubbio* higher than current market price (*prezzo corrente*). The remedy was twofold. First, effective measures had to be taken to eliminate the "conjectures" used in setting prices. Santangelo's proposal, then, aimed at naming the personnel who would set the *voce* price. He established criteria for evaluating price quotations, such as the person who contracted the sale and the effect of quality and quantity on price. Second, other kinds of contracts (*sotto-voce* or *a provvisione*) had to be prohibited so that the public price would be nothing other than the market price. "For only market prices could give [a commodity's] real value." The intendant, G. Lotti, offered a minor correction to the proposal for the wool *voce* in 1834.[53] And the same method was still in force for wool, cheese, and bread *voce* as late as 1852.[54]

Finally, the third variable internal mechanism, the policy of the state transhumance institution toward large holders, is instructive for our understanding of how doganal law attempted to maintain the status quo in light of the changing economic conjuncture. The competition between the rich (*ricchi*) and the poor (*poveri*) for access to the best, but limited, grazing land was subject to doganal control. The state varied its policy:

1. 1447–70   No distinction between rich and poor
2. 1470–1586 Rich and poor separated
3. 1586–1685 No distinction between rich and poor
4. 1685–1806 Rich given fixed posts

The oscillations of the economic curve provided the rationale for these reversals in policy which established or abolished the division of the locations into general and particular ones.

First, in period 1 no distinctions were made between rich and poor. Despite Alfonso of Aragon's egalitarian ideology in his foundation charter of 1447, some large holders were given special privileges from the beginning. Of course, no Neapolitans could rival the incredible wealth of the largest holders in Spain. Don Gutierre de Sotomayer, Master of Alcántara, for example, left as part of his personal estate (apart from that of his order) 195,000 sheep upon his death in 1453.[55] The southern Italian cousins, nevertheless, competed in the manipulation of raw power and personal prerogatives.

Item 11 of Ferrante's first concessions of 1470 described how the rich lorded it over the poor in the most blatant, yet petty of terms.[56] The excesses of the rich at the time of pasture assignment made the king so critical of the pretensions of rich holders that he forbade them to appear in the doganal palace costumed in the honors and dignities of their station. Such "arrogance and presumption" was prejudicial to the average *poveri homini* because it undermined the dogana's Arcadian egalitarianism, and because it could either intimidate or tempt the doganiero to favor them.

Still, illegal favoritism given to large holders, especially their exploitation of grazing assignments in both winter and summer, led to the second period of state policy on doganal management.[57] In period 2 rich and poor were separated for more than one hundred years. For the purpose of doganal harmony, the establishment of particular locations under Aragonese rule defused class conflict. Titled and wealthy holders were automatically assigned the best grazing land and separated from the mass of sheepowners in the general locations. This formula of pasture allocation was acceptable both to the rich, who enjoyed the privileges, and to the poor, who were freed from encroachments on their own rights.

In the reforms following the cadastral survey of 1548, however, the method of tax payment (*modo di vivere*) was changed from exact sheep numeration to a kind of estimated bid (*professazione voluntaria*). As I have already noted, the free bid was linked to pasture allocation in order to prevent tax underestimation of *locati*'s herds. In other words, underbidding sheep numbers would result in less fodder; and consequently, the prudent sheepowner would be well advised to overbid and pay slightly more tax rather than run the risk of not having enough grazing land for his herds. Simultaneously, prices on agricultural land (often adjacent to and undiscriminated from the *terre vergine* used for pasture) were rising three- and fourfold. Since the total area of doganal winter pasture was strictly circumscribed by the physical features of the Tavoliere di Puglia, land was at a premium, and the rich, who had a monopoly on the best parcels already, began to intrude into the good pastures of the general locations. Thus, for the rich, favoritism was not enough. Their greed drove them to disrupt the precarious balance between livelihood groups and social classes.

Upon assuming the office of *credenziero* in 1581, Gian Domenico Chirico provided a detailed description of affairs in the *dogana delle pecore* at the height of this large holder power in period 3 of economic production (1550–1612). His discourse identified four problems faced by the poor in the general locations: (1) *locati* changed location assignments, illegally usurping the places of the poor; (2) rich owners registered false sheep and resold assigned pasture at three and four times the official rate; (3) abuses disadvantaged the poor in the renting of usual extraordinary pasture, which pastured an additional 281,380 sheep; and (4) measurement of land favored barons, rich individuals, and agriculturists.[58] In describing the second problem, Chirico used a tortured metaphor of bread and blood which emphasized the level of doganal conflict. "Some titled, baronial, and other possessors of particular location status who were the richest and most powerful owners in the dogana" were taking the bread from the mouths of the poor and then reselling it to them for its weight in blood.

The visitor general Lope de Guzmán received an anonymous *locato* complaint in 1583 with a similar eating-blood image. Here eighteen items listed how the *poveri locati* and the dogana itself were being ruined by the rich. The rich and powerful *locati* received special consideration from doganal officials, who dispensed the best pasture to them and left the *poveri locati* with the worst pasture. The poor, then, in order not to lose their animals, were forced to repurchase good pasture at excessive prices (item 1). Corrupt doganal officials were "eating up all the poor" by charging rates four and five times the established prices and even introducing new payments (item 2), while the rich were reselling pasture "at the price of blood" (item 18).[59]

Thus, in order to prevent continued frauds, Philip II sent a royal letter on 4 November 1584 which eliminated the privilege of particular locations for rich holders, gave extraordinary unusual pasture to places, not persons, and ordered free bidding to be secret.[60] Three ministers from the Collateral and Sommaria councils (Francescantonio David, Francescantonio Lanario, and Ferrante Fornaro) were sent to Foggia to investigate further Philip II's directive, and at the beginning of the next doganal year, 24 September 1585, they instructed the doganiero to implement the changes.[61] The general and particular locations were to be united in order to prevent the kind of extortion practiced by the rich, who could purchase pasture at a low price and resell it at inflated profits. According to the new rule, all parties would be equal and engage in the same bidding competition for pasture, as the system of free bidding intended. Any windfall profits, then, would devolve to the royal fisc, which kept the taxable portion of the payment and offered rebates disguised as unusual extraordinary pasture expenditures to the sheepowners. The reforms were finally put in place in 1586, but a harsh winter negated any immediate revenue gains until the 1590s.

At the same time, proposals to resolve conflicts between pastoralists and agriculturists were also instituted. Prices for *locati* provisions, especially bread, were to be controlled by a five-man commission consisting of two elected representatives each of the sheepowners' guild and the commune of Foggia, and the doganiero.[62] With conflicts addressed among pastoralists, between farmers and graziers, and between state officials and the king's subjects, a new period of state policy had begun. Finally, after the death of the doganiero Alfonso Caracciolo in 1588, Ferrante Fornaro led an inquiry into official frauds and favoritism.[63] He concluded, completely contrary to sixteenth-century practice, that venal offices should be abolished.

This third period of pasture policy, which made no distinction between rich and poor, endured for one hundred years, from 1586 to 1685. With the disastrous fall in sheep numbers in 1612 and the consequent change of the *modo di vivere* to a fixed agreement tax in 1615, however, the doganal harmony hoped for from the union of the rich and poor in the same location did not materialize. The difficulties of rebuilding flock sizes, in meeting the new tax schedules, and in breaking out of the long depression of the seventeenth century once again ignited class conflict. During the practice of fixed agreement from 1615 to 1660, both the rhetoric of *locati* complaints and the logic of Sommaria policies expressed the tension between rich and poor holders. In May 1620, for example, a new fixed agreement contract was worked out between state and shepherds, but in its three years the abuses between rich and poor resurfaced. The "poor and simple shepherds" were "disgusted" by the "cupidity" of the minor officials who exhibited "scandalous partiality in favor of the very rich and powerful either in pasture distribution or sheep enumeration."[64]

Finally, period 4 began when the state provided a decisive boost to recovery in 1685. The locations were again separated, and fixed posts were assigned every year to the same large holder, noble, or religious institution.[65] Period 5 of economic activity (1686–1806), then, repeated the abuses of the 1580s before the union of the locations. These abuses, for their part, spawned the Enlightenment condemnation of the irrationality of the doganal system as if the involution of the eighteenth century had been the norm throughout doganal history.

Balancing the interests of rich and poor at the time of pasture distribution was the primary means of sustaining doganal growth. Among the seven summary conclusions of the 1729 *giunta* recommendations, item 5 argued that "the fundamental basis of all the good effects of this most important work consists in instructing ministers who assist at the November assignment of pastures and the rent of the locations of Lesina and Castiglione to proceed in a manner in which the weight is equal and does not fall on the poor."66 Soon after, as governor of the dogana, Stefano di Stefano signed an order during the 1735 assignment of pastures which stated official doganal policy as "maintaining among *locati* good, correct, and equal distribution of pasture."67 Similarly, De Dominicis concluded his 1781 tome with the hope that once his "clementissimo MONARCA" understood the particulars of doganal care, he would abolish abuses and improve pastoral affairs. Most notably De Dominicis deplored the unjust "liberty" given to a few *locati* of Castiglione over their fellows contrary "to that impartial equality in which the wise economic laws of the dogana have always and constantly been inculcated as the unique foundation of pastoral felicity."68

The doganal tax collection systems, price fixing methods, and pasture distribution policy were far from free market solutions to production. Although determined by the variable of pasture supply and the competitive demand for grain and wool, they were always subject to strict moderation by the central government's administrative goals. In practice, however, the ideal of good government in the country and the city, which was meant to maintain the uneasy structural balance between contending interest groups, was altered from governor to governor as favoritism, power, and capital exerted their influence.

The drift toward particularism and privilege in the dogana was the legacy of the Kingdom's baronial factionalism, dynastic instability, and economic exploitation. Constant doganal decay and decline demanded continual vigilance from a strong central authority intent on preserving law and order in accordance with the principles of the institution's foundation. Only the rule of law could maintain the doganal balancing act in the face of the secular trend, foreign capital, and native intransigence.

The rule of law, nevertheless, was an ideal. No "historical exposition" of the laws nor "examination of their various changes" could explain daily practice, which spawned, "in the confusion and ignorance of these fundamental laws, abuses and contrary economic maxims prejudicial to pastoralism, agriculture, and royal finances."69 As practice challenged theory in the Kingdom, laws multiplied. Even the lawyers themselves recognized the futility. Gaudiani quoted Tacitus' review of the history of Roman law to the effect that the most corrupt societies had the most laws. "And now bills began to pass, not only of national but of purely individual application, and when the state was most corrupt, laws were most abundant."70 Theory and practice, as in all institutions, were never congruent, and the history of the dogana does not reside in its shifting laws or their circumvention, but in the interaction and conflict between the parties making, breaking, and keeping the law. Let us turn from the ideal to the real.

PART 2

La Ragion de' Locati

The economic and societal pressures outlined in part 1—geography, climate, demography, laws, government, loans, prices, markets—were all risks and challenges that each individual sheepowner had to face. The popular wisdom of pastoral society applied these practical concerns of sheepherding and wool production to the problematic relationship between self and society. In the process of anthropomorphizing sheep and wolves and of moralizing upon labor, wealth, power, and success, pastoral society coined proverbs which expressed a common attitude toward the role of the individual in shaping his fortune. The poor and the weak were like sheep—docile, abused, and exploited. Poverty was the result of ineffectual labor, success the reward for ability and knowledge. Men of power, who looked after their own self-interest and were not, like sheep, dependent on others for the clipping and weighing of their wool, acted aggressively to take charge. Thus, the weak and the strong could be differentiated on a continuum from negative to positive according to their personal ability, their honor, and their charisma. In this individualistic, interpersonal world view of an exclusively male, salaried or self-employed, nonsubsistence population without a fixed abode, what the individual did mattered.

Such a strident, agonistic self-image is the common property of all pastoral societies. Yet in the reality of the dogana of Foggia, this mentality was illusory because the individual units engaged in transhumance, namely, the large and small sheepowners who practiced pastoral capitalism, had to work and live together if all were to survive. How such self-professed individuals organized themselves and how they resolved tensions constituted the true rationale of the sheepowners located in the winter pastures of Puglia. Social organization and social stratification, both responsive to the economic constraints of pastoral livelihood, circumscribed pastoral freedom.

4 The Graziers' Organization

Generalità de' Locati as a Commune

A grievance which brought "all of the dogana and its *generalità* into Napoli" in 1563 dramatizes the cleavage between pastoral and agricultural interests. "Last year, 1563, the taxpayers who were assigned pasture in the royal dogana, that is, the shepherds and owners of sheep, were almost all in Naples at the service of the doganiero in order to right the wrongs of said dogana; and in particular, because they did not want the agriculturists to possess [the newly created] *terre salde* (former pasture used for planting.)"[1] The horde of pastoral migrants who had descended upon the city of Naples were not the benign Abruzzesi shepherds who would charm twentieth-century Roman holiday shoppers with their delightful pipes. The sixteenth-century *locati* had not gathered to remind the weary city dwellers of the simplicity of station which, the gospels proclaim, allowed God to favor the shepherds at the birth of his Son. No, no Arcadian Christmas pageant was this marshaling of forces marching upon the Neapolitan capital. Little imagination is needed to reconstruct the impact that over seven hundred graziers and even a small contingent from their gun-toting, unkempt, seven-thousand-strong shepherd army had upon the citified bureaucrats running things in Naples.[2]

What kind of organization could mobilize the pastoralists of the Abruzzi to trek to Naples? Had the shepherds who came "in the name of the doganiero" responded to his orders or to their own interests in maintaining pasture? Who were the participants in such an extraordinary demonstration? What links did they have to one another? What hope of success could such a disgruntled mass envision? Are we to believe, as the traditional historiography tells us, that the dogana of Foggia was organized by the state from the top down and, unlike its Spanish Mesta cousin, had no indigenous forms of voluntary association?

These protesting shepherds represented the *generalità de' locati,* or the *università de' padroni di animali,* that is, "an assembly of graziers and a union of animal owners, who were registered in the books of the Royal Dogana." Like all "political bodies" which have their divisions into "branches, parliaments, provinces, chambers, and members," the *generalità* ("meeting") elected deputies and acted in concert like a primitive democracy.[3]

This analogy to the Neapolitan *università* ("commune") which Stefano di Stefano, the great eighteenth-century doganal commentator, used to explain the rationale of the *generalità* was not idiosyncratic metaphor. A decree of Charles III codifying the election of the deputies of the *generalità* specifically draws the same comparison to the communes in legal terms.[4] Chapter 2 of the king's decree declares that the deputies must submit their budget upon the completion of office "under penalty prescribed in the Royal Pragmaticas for the respective commune," and chapter 7 confirms that, in the initiation of lawsuits, the *generalità* "ought to observe and execute that which is prescribed for syndics, elected representatives, and communes of the Kingdom in Pragmatica 3 *de Procuratoribus* (26 January 1599)."[5]

The *generalità*, however, differed in order of magnitude from other communes, each of which required only ten members. The *generalità* was, in fact, "the most numerous and extensive commune in the Kingdom since it was composed of both rich and an infinite number of poor who worked all year long for the utility of the Royal Fisc."[6] Its citizens (both rich and poor) were the *locati*, those graziers who migrated along the public sheepwalks, who wintered on the locations of the Tavoliere of Puglia, and who paid tax for that pasture to the royal court.[7] Membership, like that in the Spanish Mesta, was not determined by the number of animals owned, but by the mere payment of the animal tax (*fida*).[8]

Where did the *generalità* come from? The name *generalità* was undoubtedly of Catalan origin and imported into the dogana as part of Alfonso's formative legacy.[9] Di Stefano was aware of the Catalan influence and cited a learned Neapolitan lawyer, Domenico Aguirre, a member of the Sacro Regio Consiglio, whose work *Discursus super officiis venalibus Generalitatus Cathaloniae* explained the Catalan-Neapolitan connections in the nature of the deputies' duties.[10]

Di Stefano, as always, did not remain content with only one historical precedent but even claimed that the doganal deputies were like the *Nomophylakes* of ancient Athens "who. crowned with white fasces, assisted the prefects in Council."[11] What is important to remember about the Catalan precursor, a fact which the Athenian example may underscore, is that it was a parallel, not a borrowed institution. Like the Castilian *mesta*, the Catalan *Generalitat*, was, above all, a delegation, a meeting, or an assembly of "elected" representatives. With its competence in law and finances, then, it may have given definitive constitutional shape to an already existent and functioning, native institution, the assembly of Abruzzesi graziers.

The true lineage of the *dogana delle pecore*, however, must begin with the voluntary association of sheepowners on the march and far from home in winter pasture. The earliest doganal documents make it clear that the foundation of the dogana was not the state's invention, nor the transplanting of a foreign institution, but the state's response to an already operative economic system. Both the foundation charters of Giovanna II in 1423 and Alfonso in 1447 addressed real, not fictitious graziers.[12] Giovanna granted her concessions to sheepowners (*padroni*), trail bosses (*gregarii*), shepherds (*pastores*), and others engaged in transhumance. Alfonso, in turn, appealed to a formulaic host of both natives and foreigners of every "state, grade, condition, and dignity" including nobles, communes, merchants, drovers, shepherds, and factors. The decrees spoke not to imaginary, hoped-for sheepowners, but to an already existent corps of graziers engaged in an already active market.

In 1423, Nuncio de Fonte of Aquila and Giovanni Onufri Amico of Sulmona, whom Giovanna commissioned chief officers—not doganieri, but Mesta-like "judges of awards"—were probably the leaders of the graziers' organization. Note that Aquila and Sulmona were the leading cities of the two provinces (Abruzzo Ultra and Citra) which continued to elect syndics of the *generalità* up to 1806. Similarly, in 1425 another letter of Giovanna named two new chief officers or judges with doganal ties, one from Florence (Agostino di Paolo Tinacio, a resident citizen of Aquila) and one from Castro di Valle in Sulmona's province of Abruzzo Citra (Antonuccio di Nicola del Buccio).[13]

Why were new officials commissioned after such a short interval? Were they possibly newly elected grazier representatives? The sheepowners probably already ruled themselves through a strong, indigenous graziers' association. The crown only sanctioned their independent organization. Why else would Alfonso in 1442/43 have continued the tradition of appointing Abruzzesi of the two provinces by confirming Restanuccio Capograsso of Sulmona and Bartolomeo della Torre of Aquila? The appointment of the Catalan Francesco Montluber in 1447 can thus be understood as an Aragonese innovation to assert royal authority and put the sheepowners' association under royal control, not as originally constituting transhumance *de novo*.

The first mention of the sheepowners' association per se is recorded in the *Prime Grazie del Re Ferdinando I* of 1470. Three elected syndics, Domenico del Fonte (of the same Aquila family as the 1423 appointee), Georgio de Marino of Aquila, and Notar Corrado de Notorio of Castel del Monte, humbly beseeched the king for eighteen favors in the name of all the "sheepowners, trail bosses, and shepherds of the *dogana delle pecore* of Puglia."[14] Again, pastoralists from both Abruzzo Ultra and Citra represented the sheep industry of Foggia.

Locati Rights

The 1470 *grazie* along with the *grazie* of the 1480, 1536, and 1615 petitions add up to 88 specific items which chronicle the *generalità*'s purpose. It concerned itself with five charges: traditional privileges, governmental responsibilities, doganal officers' obligations, economic advantages, and conflict between participants. First, the *generalità* constantly reiterated its traditional privileges in terms of land and justice: access to pasture and water, freedom from illegal tolls and gabelles, expeditious and impartial justice, and the right to bear arms. Second, governmental responsibilities were usually particular requests aimed at immediate grievances: to repair bridges, not to tax horses used by shepherds in their work, to provide protection from bandits, to ban pigs from the sheepwalks and Tavoliere, to measure the sheepwalks and pasture in order to prevent enclosure by barons, communes, or large holders. Third, doganal officers, for their part, were often importuned to remain incorruptible, requested to be experienced, supported for wage increases, and charged not to demand extra recompense beyond their salary from the *locati*. Fourth, economic advantages for pastoralists were aimed at limiting agriculturists and at gaining privileges in the market. They included price supports for pastoral products, restraint of trade, exclusion of nondoganal pastoral products, tax rebates, maintenance of plowing rules, curbs on planting of *terre salde*. These first four rubrics, then, covered the privileges, exemptions, and expectations of the juridical and economic relationship between state and shepherd.

Later in the eighteenth century, Gaudiani (1715) and Grana (1770) summarized these rights and duties in a shepherds' "bill of rights," condensed into eight and ten articles respectively. Gaudiani's eight articles were:

1. Right to free passage and pasture for 24 hours on sheepwalks
2. In disputes, no payments for indemnities, but only for reparations
3. Exemption from all kinds of gabelles, taxes, and tolls, especially those on bread
4. Right to exclusive justice in doganal courts
5. Exemption from all tolls on passes, bridges, etc.
6. Right to summer as well as winter pasture
7. Right to wood, straw, water, and grass in passage and pasture
8. Right to bear arms[15]

Simply, the *generalità* safeguarded the reciprocal relationship between pastoralists and the crown.

The fifth category of request, the emphasis upon internecine rivalry, has already been noted as an extraordinary characteristic of the graziers' concerns about inequity in the system.[16] Obviously, it would not have been so often repeated if inequality were not rampant in the dogana. The egalitarian aspect of the *generalità*'s ideology led it to condemn the prerogatives practiced by rich holders. The *poveri homini* expressed this operative rationale in all the requests, especially in the class-conscious, economic ones. The tax reimbursement of item 12 of 1470, and the price supports for wool of item 27 of 1536 were exemplary. The references to poor men and *padroncelli* were not rhetorical embellishment meant to move the king to tears of pity. These *locati* were the guts of the dogana and, as such, confirmed what Alfonso's founding charter had sought to legitimate. The equality under the law of every "state, grade, condition, and dignity" was the cornerstone of the graziers' associational life, of their economic strength. and of their judicial privileges.

Generalità Membership

The tax lists of the dogana, which were compiled in November as part of the sheep estimates submitted for the assignment of pastures, provide an approximate count of the *locati*. Two kinds of lists were maintained, the original record (*squarciafogli*) of all taxpayers, and a simplified list (*squarciafoglietti*) of owners only. without dependents.[17] From a random eleven-year sample, the mean number of *locati* from the global lists was 2,306 and from the condensed lists of owners only, 1,223 (table 6). Averages are deceiving. however, since doganal investors fluctuated according to the economic conjuncture, with about 3,000 *locati* from the late sixteenth to mid seventeenth century and about 2,000 in the eighteenth century.

Three categories can be differentiated among those making the tax declarations: (1) individual *padroni,* sheepowners professing alone (mean of 811 or 35.2 percent); (2) *padroni* heads of *collettiva,* sheepowners with dependents or associates listed in separate entries below their names (mean of 412 or 17.9 percent); and (3) *padroncelli,* the dependent owners (mean of 1,083 or 47.0 percent). Again averages distort membership rolls over time. While the *padroni* with dependents form a relatively stable percentage of membership, the *padroni* professing alone and the *padroncelli* are in inverse proportion to one another. As the *padroncelli* declined at the end of the seventeenth-century crisis (1659 and 1679 lists) the independent *padroni* increased. In the eighteenth century, this cycle repeated itself: high *padroncelli* numbers in 1699, 1719, and 1739 fell to low ones in 1759 and 1779 as low independent *padroni* numbers increased. Thus, by the end of the period, the percentage of *locati* in categories 1 and 3 were reversed.

In each of these entries, sheepowners could be individuals, blood rela-

TABLE 6   *Locati* in the Dogana (1591–1779)

Year	1 Padroni Alone	2 Padroni with Dependents	3 Padroncelli Dependents	Squarciafoglietti Owners 1 + 2	Squarciafogli Owners 1 + 2 + 3
1591	610 (21%)	515 (18%)	1,760 (61%)	1,125 (39%)	2,885
1604	959 (35)	536 (19)	1,284 (46)	1,495 (54)	2,779
1619	487 (15)	646 (20)	2,085 (65)	1,133 (35)	3,218
1639	712 (30)	453 (19)	1,203 (51)	1,165 (49)	2,368
1659	1,696 (61)	387 (14)	707 (25)	2,083 (75)	2,790
1679	483 (41)	274 (23)	433 (36)	757 (64)	1,190
1699	627 (32)	430 (22)	893 (46)	1,057 (54)	1,950
1719	505 (21)	483 (20)	1,382 (58)	988 (42)	2,370
1739	574 (28)	380 (19)	1,097 (53)	954 (47)	2,051
1759	932 (57)	204 (12)	508 (31)	1,136 (69)	1,644
1779	1,333 (63)	226 (11)	564 (27)	1,559 (73)	2,123
Mean	811 (35)	412 (18)	1,083 (47)	1,223 (53)	2,306

Sources: ASFg, *Dogana,* serie V, *Squarciafogli,* regg. 747 (1591); 767 (1604); 795 (1619); 850 (1639); 876 (1659); 899 (1679); 933 (1699); 967 (1719); 1004 (1739); 1044 (1759); 1084 (1779).

tives, or unrelated partners. Gérard Delille's examination of the relationship between economic structures and demographic profiles in the Kingdom has demonstrated a significant correlation in terms of the type of agricultural system, plot or herd size, work hours, productivity, social structure, birth and death rates, and standard of living.[18] What Delille's demography tells us about pastoralists is that a nuclear family's subsistence needs required a flock of at least 80 sheep or goats. But, at the same time, such a family could not find within itself either the manpower or the money to provide a shepherd to work such a herd. Three possible solutions could resolve the problem of the pastoral work force: the grouping together of an extended family, which could provide four to six mature men, enough to work a herd of 500 to 600 animals; the grouping together of four or five unrelated nuclear families, which would provide the same benefits; or a kind of capitalist pastoralism in which large herds of more than 2,000 head, owned by a large sheep rancher, hired salaried employees.

The actual number of *locati*, therefore, would be greater than the computed number of "companies" or "families" registered in the tax lists. In 1679, for example, the complete tax rolls (*squarciafogli*) list 1,190 *locati*, but a *generalità* petition to the Sommaria claims more than 5,000 *locati*.[19] Thus, for 1783, when Silla counted some 2,315 *locati* families and claimed that 6,000 other families served as shepherds, we can estimate about 37,500 individuals, 0.8 percent of the total Kingdom's population (about 4 percent of the population of the four provinces Abruzzo Citra, Abruzzo Ultra, Capitanata, and Molise) owned or shepherded sheep in the dogana of Foggia.[20]

Abruzzesi Dominance

Membership in the *generalità de' locati* originally came from the two provinces of the Abruzzi, and then extended to Capitanata, Contado di Molise, and other places in the Kingdom. Each of the twenty-three locations was assigned to a particular *nazione* or town of origin in the Abruzzi. The one-to-one identification of locale and location is not perfect; but, within limits, each location was dominated by men from a particular town or towns.

In his 1670 compendium of Sommaria edicts, Annibale Moles identified the *nazioni* of the locations as still overwhelmingly Abruzzese: nine locations were inhabited by men from Abruzzo Citra, nine from Abruzzo Ultra, three from Molise, one from Principato Ultra, and one not given.[21] My global survey of the twenty-three locations listed in the *squarciafoglio* tax rolls for eleven selected years from 1591 to 1779 reveals little variation from Moles. The unassigned location of Camarda can be identified with large holders from Nusco in Principato Ultra and the prince of Melfi in Basilicata. Moles assigns Casalnuovo and Andria to Carapelle rather than Santo Stefano and San Demetro, but all are near Aquila in Abruzzo Ultra (appendix B).

Few of the locations were completely occupied by one *nazione* as was San

Giuliano by the men of Castel del Monte, who specialized in the production of black wool.[22] In his 1783 count, Silla numbered some three hundred fifty different towns registered in the accounts. Obviously, more than one town was usually present in each of the twenty-three locations. Even in Castiglione, the location surrounding Foggia, which was dominated by the men of Lucoli, who gave their town's name to the best white wool of the dogana, one could find the sheep of men from other *nazioni* as far away from Lucoli as Ortona de' Marsi in 1699 and Castel del Sangro in 1739, both on different sheepwalks. In other locations men from neighboring towns shared grazing rights with the chief designate; for example, Barrea and Rivisondoli were associated with Rocca del Raso in Candelaro; Pettorano with Rocca Valle Scura in Pontalbanito; and Vasto Girardo and Pesco Lanciano with Amatrice in Vallecannella. The locations were not exclusive preserves of a single *nazione*.

Similarly, the nation/location relationship varied over the course of doganal history just as we have seen the size of each location vary over time. In 1676 the doganal governor Nicolo Gascon proposed that unused extraordinary pasture in Guardiola, Castiglione, Arignano, Lesina, Casalnuova, Orta, and Cornito be rented by auction because "there were insufficient Locati Nazionali."[23] Lesina and San Andrea soon thereafter dropped out of the tax rolls. Lesina and later Castiglione were auctioned off to the highest bidders. San Andrea was assigned to the prince of San Severo for his 12,000 sheep during the eighteenth century.

The continuities in *nazioni* assignment are, however, more instructive. The Abruzzesi received the best pasture and wintered the most sheep. If we recall the evaluation of each location by rate of fertility—eleven locations rated at 10 *carra* per 1,000 sheep, six at 11 *carra,* two at 12 *carra,* and four at 13 *carra* per 1,000 sheep—it is clear that the *nazioni* of the Abruzzi received the most desirable winter land, monopolizing the locations rated at 10 *carra* per 1,000 sheep (table 7).

Similarly, in terms of sheep wealth, the dogana's winter pasture was dominated by Abruzzesi, who owned 67–75 percent of the sheep. The breakdown of sheep wealth by province of origin is uniform over time and corroborated in diverse measures: Abruzzo Citra, 40 percent; Abruzzo Ultra, 30 percent; Molise, 10 percent; Capitanata, 10 percent; Principato Ultra, 5 percent; and miscellaneous, 5 percent.[24] The dominance of Abruzzesi sheepowners confirms that the doganal system was what geographers call inverse transhumance; that is, pastoral migrations from the mountains to the plains and back were the norm. (fig. 6).

Abruzzesi control of the *generalità* was jealously guarded in accordance with the structure of privilege and wealth. The first two of the four elected *generalità* deputies were to be men from Abruzzo Citra with the assent of the men from Molise, while the other two deputies represented Abruzzo Ultra. In a 1749 letter to the king which was signed by 63 *locati* who opposed the election of a non-Abruzzesi deputy, the *generalità* expressed its will in terms of a

TABLE 7 Location Assignment of *Nazioni* by Fertility of Pasture

Province of Origin	10 Carra per 1,000 Sheep	11 Carra per 1,000 Sheep	12 Carra per 1,000 Sheep	13 Carra per 1,000 Sheep
Abruzzo Citra (9)	5	2	0	2
Abruzzo Ultra (9)	6	2	1	0
Contado di Molise (3)	0	0	1	2
Principato Ultra (2)	0	2	0	0
Total locations (23)	11	6	2	4

Source: See appendix B.

continuous tradition "from the most ancient times . . . from time immemorial . . . for so many centuries."[25] No *locato* from a *nazione* outside the Abruzzi had ever been elected. Even if an old, established Abruzzese family should move, like the Marchesano, who had become residents in Foggia only fifty years earlier, they would not be eligible for election despite past deputies in the family in 1655 and 1679. The specific proposal to allow the *locati* of Puglia to nominate one of the deputies was derided as a "grave and scandalous abuse" which reflected the Pugliesi's "pretensions" and "caprice" and was part of a "vendetta" against the poor *locati* of the Abruzzi who would be forced to pay "extravagant prices" for pasture controlled by these same Pugliesi. The rationale of the Abruzzesi graziers clarified their continued reference to themselves as *poveri locati*. The upstart sheepowners from Puglia had increased their herds to make money. The profit motive, on the other hand, did not determine Abruzzesi investment in pastoralism. For good or ill, they had no choice. Necessity demanded that they engage in transhumance because "in their country they had neither vines, fields, nor other means to sustain their homes, families, and other burdens." In sum, the "beautiful union, and harmony" of the *generalità* was in jeopardy because Pugliesi opportunists were investing in sheep as a chosen strategy of economic gain while the *poveri* Abruzzesi were constrained by land and climate to tend their flocks as a means of livelihood.

The self-identification of the Abruzzesi sheepowners as simple, poor shepherds, however, was misleading. The ideology of the *generalità* defined itself as an aggregate of "hundreds and thousands, an infinite number of poor persons and religious foundations which came without contradiction to enjoy all the privilgese granted to minors, wards, widows, the Church, and all other privileged persons." Giving privileges to the "underprivileged" helped the monarchy's antibaronial policy of centralization, but the *locati* were not exclusively "every kind of humble and low-born person." Even though the dogana "was marked by humble facts and base practice," many *locati* were themselves barons. "Even princes, dukes, marquises, counts, barons, prelates, religious foundations, and other ecclesiastics, both regular and secular clergy, did not think themselves unworthy to fraternize [in the dogana]." And, at the same

FIGURE 6 Sheepowners by Provincial Origin

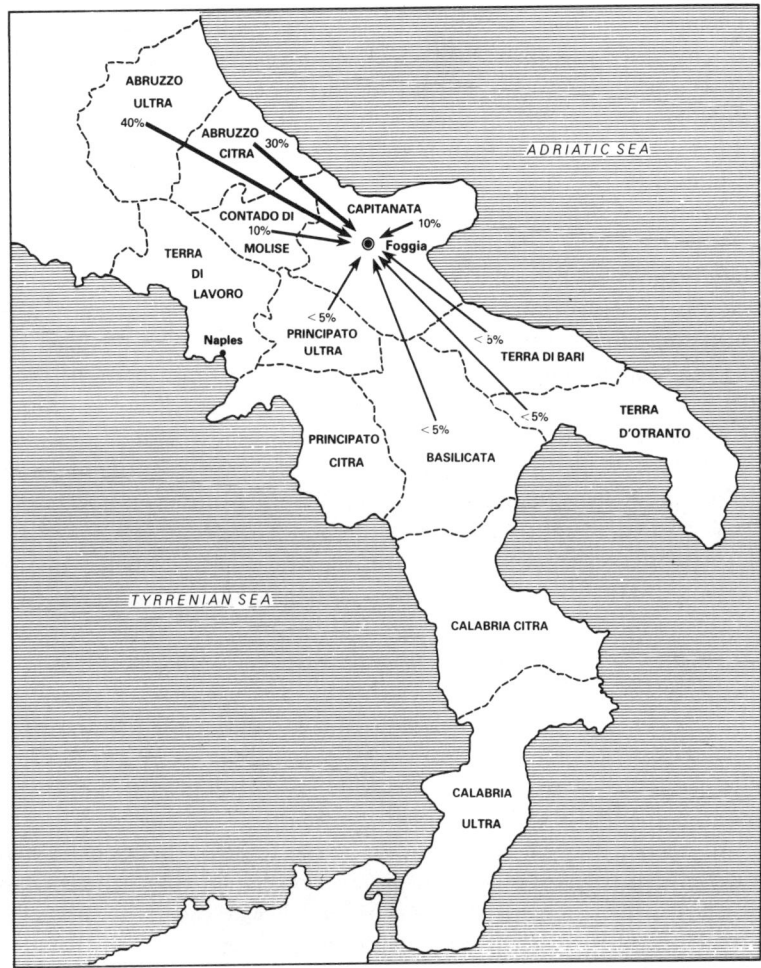

Sources: Map adapted from Giovanni Antonio Magini, *Italia* (Bologna, 1620). ASFg, *Dogana,* serie V, regg. 1999–2551 (a. 1623–1801), "Libri dei pesatori di lana," for production statistics.

time, many non-nobles were far from poor, subsistence sheep farmers. Di Stefano maintained that "the *generalità* was only concerned with profit."[26]

Age Pyramids and Economic Vitality

A demographic profile of the *locati*, drawn from homogenous data taken at a particular moment in the sixteenth century, clarifies the meaning of pastoral profit. During three years of interviews (1582–84) collected in four books of general testimony by the agents of the visitor general Guzmán, 426 individuals gave depositions which included their age, years of doganal service, and occupation.[27] Of the 394 witnesses whose occupation can be identified, 260 (66 percent) were sheepowners (208) or their shepherds (52). Vital statistics given by 248 of these identifiable pastoralists give a portrait of the *locati*'s age structure and suggest the importance of the profit motive for their participation in transhumance.

The ranges of age and experience are striking. Gian Battista di Nardis of Aquila, who was 25, claimed to have participated in the dogana from his earliest memories. One of the oldest *locati*, Marino de Pace of Lucoli, aged 70, attested to 60 years of doganal service, and he continued the doganal tradition by initiating his son, Pace de Marino Pace—another witness, now aged 19—when the boy was only 9. The youngest *locato* testifying before the visitors general was the 16-year-old baron delle Pizonne, Francesco Antonio Marchesano of Rocca di Cinquemiglia, who was later elected as a deputy in 1615. Paduano de Lettiero of Agnone, a 60-year-old shepherd working for the marchese di Montenegro, remembered that his transhumant marches began at age 7 (the youngest age cited by the employees). The oldest *locato*, the 75-year-old Virgilio de ColaAngelo of Pacentro, who was now a rich holder of 6,000 sheep, recalled that he had been active in the dogana since 1524, some 59 years ago.

Despite the range of ages, the *locati* in 1582–84 were a relatively uniform, aging population. The median age of the grazier witnesses was 40 years, with 20 years of doganal service behind them. Middle-aged owners were much more numerous than might be expected: 112 (56 percent) aged 30–49. If we add the 69 individuals (34 percent) over 50 years old to the middle-aged, it can be seen that 90 percent of these graziers were over 30.

Curiously, however, most of the graziers had entered the dogana as young men, 72 (62 percent) of the 117 identifiable grazier witnesses at 15–29 years old. The biggest bulge was at 15–25 years old, with 60 (51 percent) of the cases. Seventy-seven percent of the graziers had doganal experience before the age of 30. How can we account for the discrepancy between the age of the population present in 1582–84 (90 percent over 30) and the fact that 77 percent of them had joined the dogana before the age of 30?

Were shepherds living longer in the second half of the sixteenth century? Or was the slowing down of the sixteenth-century demographic surge after 1560 being reflected in the stability of the adult population? Was enrollment closed to the younger generation whereas it had not been earlier? Was it more difficult for young men to get their hands on money to invest in pastoralism by the 1580s? Or possibly, were the witnesses who were interrogated in our survey not randomly selected, but chosen for their knowledge of doganal affairs? The sample of 202 sheepowner witnesses was, after all, only about 7 percent of total *locati,* if the 1591 complete tax roll totals can be read backward to apply to 1582–84.

The length of doganal service given in 121 cases helps clarify the age pyramid and membership closure. First, charting the years of service by 5-year intervals demonstrates that there is little variation in the numbers of members in each 5-year category. The witness sample does indeed appear to have been random. Second, specifying age of entrance reveals that only 27 graziers (22 percent) became involved in doganal affairs less than 10 years before 1582–84, and only 42 (35 percent) less than 15 years before. The majority of graziers, 63 (52 percent) had enrolled in the dogana sometime between 15 and 35 years earlier. That 20-year period begins with the 1548/49 cadastral survey, ends about 1570, and corresponds to a favorable economic conjuncture for wool vis-à-vis wheat. The 1582–84 profile, therefore, seems to be a function of the strength and fall of the international market for wool and its patronage in the Kingdom of Naples. Other explanations may be partially correct but are questionable because of the rather uniform rate of membership in each 5-year interval. Although the 1582–84 population may have been atypical of doganal age structure over the long term, pinpointing the 1548/49–1570 conjuncture emphasizes the positive relationship between state policy and the market upon doganal investors.

One final measure of economic activity which can be inferred from the visitor general's investigation confirms this economic explanation. Comparing the signatures of graziers (ability to sign their name versus only making their mark) reveals that, among the sheepowners, 137 (66 percent) were literate and 72 (34 percent) were not. Not surprisingly, among the shepherds, the percentages are almost reversed, 27 (42 percent) literate and 30 (58 percent) illiterate. The high rate of literacy among the predominantly Abruzzesi population of pastoral investors suggests that these were not the stereotypical uneducated provincials of popular caricature. Business success required a facility with numbers, words, laws, and contracts. Even their employees were not the dumb shepherds often depicted in the Christmas crèche (*presepe*), but their relatively high percentage of literacy may have reflected the need to act in their employer's stead during the demanding economic calculations with other shepherds and the state's officers.[28]

Generalità as a Republic

Because of the complexity of their economic relations with the state, with merchants, and among themselves, these sheepowners joined together in collective organization in order to derive strength from their union. Twice a year the *locati* of the twenty-three locations would meet in general council when they gathered in Foggia for the fall assignment of pastures and for the spring fair. Initially, as in the general parliaments of the sixteenth century, as many *locati* as possible participated: 170 in November, 1578; 136 in November 1582; and 100 in November 1583.

The sixteenth-century parliaments usually addressed one or two specific issues. In 1578 two problems—unusual extraordinary pasture and the office of doganiero—were examined. In 1582/83, three meetings were recorded because sheep mortality in that harsh winter brought extra judicial business in the spring. The fall parliament expressed *locati* opposition to the taxation of imaginary sheep according to the system of *pecore in aerea*. The consequences of the sheep mortality dominated the two spring meetings, but discussion was also given to *generalità* elections, the doganal hospital in Foggia, and a monastic request for charity. Again, in the fall of 1583, the question of sheep mortality was still at issue as well as the *generalità*'s continual concerns over taxation, pasture rights, and their traditional privileges.[29]

Critical to the effectiveness of the pastoral voice was community action. When the individual members of the sheepowners' association came together in general parliament to express their position, as they did on 4 May 1615 in response to the fiscal reforms of the conte de Lemos, other issues came to the fore. In exchange for their acceptance of the new forced tax system, graziers demanded redress of two long-standing grievances: the abuse of officers and mercantile exploitation. Class conflict among themselves (the "simple shepherds") could be forgotten when they confronted their common enemies: the "insolent" doganal officers and the "cunning" merchants. Despite the unanimity of their resolve, the sheepowners found that their political fusion could nevertheless be encumbering.

The sheepowners recognized that the "annoyance and difficulty of congregating said commune, [given] every bit of minutia which [would] occur in this most grave negotiation," necessitated an expedient to prevent the multitude from falling into confusion without resolving anything. Each location, therefore, was charged to elect special deputies in addition to their ordinary syndics. The formula of an individualistic society reluctantly delegating authority is striking. The *locati* agreed that majority rule would "remain firm, valid, and, if necessary, inviolably executed, although everyone maintains his own opinion in this and every other case."[30]

In addition to the right to disagree, the *locati* recognized the right to fair and equal representation. Locations elected one, two, or three syndics, depending on their size. In 1615, for example, thirty-seven special deputies who were "the most experienced, expert, wealthy men" were selected from the twenty-three locations: one location (Candelaro) with three representatives, twelve with two, and ten with one.

Elected particular syndics who represented each location at moments of grave necessity became the parliamentary model. In the formula of the 1615 general parliament, each location was to choose one or two of its "most experienced, expert, and rich" *locati* "to represent all of their needs and troubles." In turn, location representatives (*sindaci particolari*) elected four general syndics (*sindaci generali*) from the *generalità* at large who formed their own ongoing "private parliament."³¹ The four general syndics thus formed a working cabinet to represent the interests of *locati* before customhouse officials and to arbitrate disputes between *locati*. In the words of Di Stefano, the *generalità* was a legal fiction. "Every community is a fictitious body and a figurative person without senses, will, or other powers," like all corporations, which can only exercise power in the person of designated representatives.³²

In a 1738 reform a quorum consisted of two of the four general syndics and a majority of the particular syndics, that is, at least one from each location.³³ Fewer participants or not, the eighteenth-century parliaments still sounded their consistent theme on the "present miserable state" of the *locati*. In 1727 and 1734 the *generalità* grievances continued to focus on official doganal policy reminiscent of issues over two hundred years old.³⁴ The *locati* expected greater leniency and sympathy on the part of the state tax collectors in light of the extraordinary 600,000 sheep mortality in 1725/26. The sheepowners unwillingly suffered the injustice of forced professions, despite doganal prohibitions. And finally, a traditional complaint in a new guise, the *locati* opposed high taxes, especially the newly initiated 20 percent surtax of 1709.

Di Stefano's equations of *generalità* as parliament or commune were only two of a series of comparisons that he employed to describe the role of the graziers' organization in doganal life. Three other similes, likewise, bear the weight of literal interpretation. The *generalità* was like a great city divided into various *piazze* or quarters, like a religion divided into various monasteries, and especially like the Arcadian Academy of Rome (the literary guild founded in 1690), which was divided into colonies. All five of these exemplary institutions shared a common identity. Each was a kind of universal republic.³⁵

For Di Stefano, two aspects of republicanism were of paramount importance: egalitarianism, and individuality within indivisibility. First, the law made no distinction between rank or status. Rich and poor, noble and commoner, clergy and laity enjoyed the same privileges. Second, each division of the whole was free to pursue its own rule, order, and uniqueness without losing sight of its links to the community at large. Individual interests separated each subdivision, yet their common needs drew them together. Each of these republics was bound tightly together, but it had the flexibility to accomodate diversity and the elasticity to spring back into shape when need be. The power inherent in such a relationship depended upon the balance of competing forces so that unchecked tensions did not snap the institution's resilience and, consequently, destroy each individual member.

The *generalità de' locati*, like a parliament, a commune, a great city, a religion, and above all the "ingenious" Accademia degli Arcadi, was "an ideal and fictitious body" that mirrored all republican and idealistic institutions.³⁶ The boundless energy of primitive democracy resulted from its open membership policy, egalitarian values, and individual freedom. These same forces, however, circumscribed the institution's power. The contradictory interests of its members necessitated watchful governance. As the state bureaucracy in Foggia, Naples, and Madrid exerted more and more control over doganal management, the essential features of the liberty of the pastoral world became obscured.

Generalità Elections and Representatives

The state bureaucracy attempted to tame the graziers' republic by coopting the *generalità* representatives. The fission-fusion model of pastoral society works not only to unite its members in emergency, but also to divide and conquer them in both good times and bad. My reading of doganal history underlines the state's efforts to manipulate interest groups and play them off against one another for the state's own advantage. Thus, some representatives, by virtue of their birth, wealth, character, and/or experience, often found themselves more sympathetic and responsive to government rather than grazier interests. It is important to emphasize this bipolar pull upon *generalità* representatives if we are to understand how their parliament functioned.

Procedures and criteria of *generalità* elections were, therefore, critical in determining the degree of cooperation and conflict between the state and the shepherds. In early May banns announced to all *locati* of every grade and condition the coming election to be held a few days later, but not later than 16 May.[37] *Locati* were required to present themselves in person before the doganal governor in the doganal palace at a given hour, usually early afternoon.[38] Fines were levied against absentees—1,000 ducats in 1596, 20 ducats in 1738, and 500 ducats in 1743.[39] The *locati*'s charge was to elect four new deputies for three-year terms. Each outgoing general syndic nominated a successor who was, in turn, voted upon independently in a secret ballot. (The elections of 1596 and 1682, however, record a different method, election by plurality.) Afterward, those elected were confirmed by the doganal governor.

The linkage between outgoing and incoming syndics on a one-to-one basis reflected the specific local character of the office.[40] These were not four deputies chosen at large from the sheepowners' community, but Abruzzesi who represented local interests. The first two were from Abruzzo Citra between the Trigno and Pescara rivers, the second two from Abruzzo Ultra between the Pescara and Tronto rivers.[41] This regional identification was further maintained in the electoral procedures following a deputy's death in office. He would be replaced at the next general parliament, and the new candidate would be nominated by his fellow syndic from Abruzzo Citra or Ultra.[42]

Not all nominees were automatically approved by the *locati*. In 1655, for example, three ballots were needed to select a syndic in two different cases.[43] Similarly, in the regular election of 1731 and in a special replacement election in 1732, one candidate, Ferdinando d'Alena, was rejected three times.[44] While all those elected in 1731 had more than 90 percent majorities, three of the eight elected in 1746 had less than 67 percent majorities, that is, more than 80 out of 250 voters opposed their election.[45]

Given this method of nomination, it was necessary to prevent the old syndics from perpetuating familial or personal power since there was no guarantee that the *locati* would reject all unacceptable candidates. Restrictions were legislated to prevent nomination of a new syndic within three degrees of consanguinity; and to prevent a syndic from succeeding himself.[46] Normally, individuals could not return to office for six years. Such impediments, however, were meant to be circumvented. In cases of "public utility," and then only with unanimous assent, not by majority vote, exceptions could be made and deputies reelected, as was Giuseppe de Mayo in 1699.[47]

Despite the legal safeguards, abuses among the general syndics were notorious, as the 1729 *giunta* reported. "Deputies work for their private interests, for the dogana itself or for powerful reasons . . . They have forgotten their proper function and obligation . . . changing their voices . . . bringing more miseries and embarrassing everyone they should be helping . . . They foment quarrels among the *poveri locati* . . . oppress and extort the poor . . . betray their confidences . . . and render insufferable that burden which should be mild."[48] The three-man *giunta* of Regent Ventura and Presidents Ram and Vespoli specifically identified the 1728 syndics in this corrupt tradition. Gian Lorenzo Centi was an agriculturist (*massaro di campo*), not a sheepowner at all; Gian Andrea Mosca was a dependent of the Church (citizen of the Papal States?) ineligible for election; Lorenzo Angelone was a former deputy with questionable financial dealings during his administration and outstanding debts; and Gian Francesco Ciancarella had never even engaged in transhumance.[49] The *giunta*, therefore, determined to remove them from office and to hold a new election in the spring of 1729 so that the new general syndics "would not be whom the previous deputies wanted, but whom the *locati* desired." The *locati* were free to "nominate whom they wanted without fear" and spent eight hours at the task of electing Isidoro de Marco and Biase Colabianco, who had been responsible for the 1719 *donativo;* Nicola d'Andrea, a "galantuomo"; and Filippo Baccaro, an "honest and well-known person who was a cousin of the viceregent of Rome."[50]

Not everyone agreed with this decision to hold new elections. In a special debate before the *giunta*, four senior bureaucrats with doganal experience (Regent Paterno, Avvocato Fiscale de Ferrante, Regent Castelli, and President Aguirre) sided with the *locati* who had supported the old syndics of 1728.[51] The old syndics, at least, had been elected legally, for the specified three-year term, and were able, experienced men from the Abruzzi. The election procedures for the new syndics, on the other hand, were patently illegal.[52] The old syndics were forbidden attendance and were actually given twenty-four hours to get out of town by twenty miles. So few *locati* arrived at the appointed hour that a second call, which threatened a 500-ducat fine for absence, was issued. Most *locati* still defied the *giunta* and declared its actions null and void. Finally, the new syndics were hardly exemplary choices. Isidoro di Marco owned no sheep, had been in prison for debts, and still owed money to the prince of San Severo. Biase Colabianco owned very few sheep as a dependent and debtor of the large enterprise of the Congregazione del Sanctissima d'Ovindoli. Nicola d'Andrea, the son of the baron of Sassano, was a notorious debtor with over 20,000 ducats in arrears to the royal fisc. Worse, none of these three knew anything about doganal law, and their election was contrary to the 1716 Collateral Council decree which stipulated that syndics should be in good standing among the *locati*, own large flocks, and have doganal experience. Finally, Filippo Baccaro. although he met some of these criteria, may have been the most ill-advised selection. He had never grazed his flocks in the dogana at all but, against all doganal law, had always driven them to winter pasture in the Papal States.

What were the *locati* and the *giunta* fighting about? The argument was not over the competence or abuses of the syndics since neither old nor new syndics seem to have been without faults. The important question was one of politics: who nominated the syndics and to whom they were loyal. In real terms, the test of will between the *giunta* and the *generalità* was one over taxes and royal income. The old syndics represented more traditional opposition by *locati* to higher taxes; the new syndics were more favorable to the doganal administration.[53]

Electoral manipulations and incompetent syndics were not an isolated phenomenon in the rivalry between state and shepherds. Elected syndics could be the pawns of large holders and/or consumed by self-interest. After the 1756 election, the *locati* expressed their outrage that all four syndics were unacceptable. Donatanonio Ciotti was the cousin of a deputy and, therefore, disqualified by law. Gioacchino del Monaco was illiterate. Baron Fabritio Petricone was too young and weak. Pasquale Incarnato was of base origins. Instead of choosing *locati* who were "honest, rich, and able to carry out their office without prejudice," the general parliament had been dominated by the "particular interests" of "vile and mercenary men." A list of sixteen former syndics, seven of whom were titled nobility, exemplified what was meant by "the most incorruptible, rich, and ablest men."[54]

These exceptions to doganal law prove the rule that the general syndics had real power. A review of the names of identifiable general syndics reveals the dominance of a finite number of families, alliances between them, the personal power or powerful connections of a few extraordinary individuals, and the overwhelmingly noble status or judicial expertise of all those elected. The power and rewards of office are what attracted men, good and bad, strong and weak, patron and client.

Out of 109 identifiable general syndics for the two-hundred-year period from 1563 to 1759, 9 families with 3 or more representatives accounted for more than one-third of the deputies. The Moscas, whom Di Stefano identified as Roman nobles, and to whom, as men from Lucoli, Moles assigned the particular location of Fontanelle, placed 6 members of their family in office in the eighty-six years from 1652 to 1738, while the Marchesanos placed 4 members from 1583 to 1679. Others like the Aniellis (1646, 1652, 1655, 1676), the Cerices (1643, 1652, 1655), the Marinanzis (1682, 1699, 1738), the Angelones (1719, 1728, 1746), the Colabiancos and the d'Andreas (both 1729, 1731, 1741) had their representation concentrated into a relatively limited time span. This specificity of syndic office holding may have reflected the peaking of their family fortunes or an exceptionally active participant like Nicola d'Andrea, who alone was elected 3 times. Six other individuals appear in the syndic list at least twice, while Di Stefano named a number of fathers and sons, for example, Giacomo Antonio del Baccaro (1696) and his father Filippo (no date).[55]

The general syndics of the mid seventeenth century give some indication of the intertwining familial alliances which lay behind the nomination of new syndics by their predecessors. When Cristofaro Mosca, representative of Abruzzo Ultra, died in office, his colleague Girolamo d'Anielli from Santo Stefano nominated Francesco Antonio Cerice, baron of Rosciano, to complete the 1652–55 term. In the 1655 election, Cerice attempted to reinstate the Mosca family, but both his first nominee, Tomasso Mosca, and his second, Pompaneo Mosca, were defeated.[56] He then nominated one of the Aniellis who had supported him, Gian Caterina d'Anielli. Because of the impediment against succession, Gian Caterina had not held office for six years from his term as a syndic in 1646–49. Cerice's nomination of Gian Caterina paid back his own appointment by Girolamo d'Anielli by circumventing the nepotism impediment which would have prevented Girolamo from nominating Gian Caterina.

Above all, the general syndics were nobles and lawyers. My partial list counts twenty-two titled cases, and Di Stefano enumerates some fifteen families. Further, Di Stefano makes much of the contribution of syndics of the robe like himself. Domenico de Rubbeis had been elected syndic from the office of legal counsel of the *generalità* (*avvocato della generalità*) in 1668, and Francesco Giuseppe de Angelis (syndic in 1685) had published numerous legal tracts.[57] Similarly, other persons, like Marc Antonio Coda, Giovanni Domenico Vitorando, Giulio Cesare Calvanese, and Pasquale Longo, were desirable candidates for syndic because of their legal training, even though they themselves were not *locati*.[58]

Di Stefano cites the banns of election for 21 May 1646 to demonstrate the *generalità*'s conscious desire to select general syndics who were "nobles, lawyers, or other rich, cultured, and substantial gentlemen."[59] The general syndics were to be "strong, upright, and honest" because of the importance of their duties "to judge lawsuits, to render opinions, to set taxes, to give orders, to deal with the ministers and persons of authority, to administer sums of money, and to negotiate important matters."[60] Di Stefano concludes that they were not only to be "rich and honest, but to have substantial holdings in the dogana."

Such representatives would be less corruptible, command greater respect, and in working for their private advantage would be furthering the common good.

Of course, not all syndics lived up to the ideal. In 1678 a complaint signed by 114 *locati* bemoaned the "ruin" caused by the neglect of their interests by the four syndics.[61] The elected deputies had misappropriated their stipends for their own use without providing any services to the *locati*, even those of their own locations. Not all private interests benefited the community. The *locati*, therefore, proposed a series of reforms to check the general deputies' powers and to ensure greater accountability. Their petition attempted to strengthen the input of each location in the persons of their particular syndics, who were to assist the general syndics and have the right to veto new appropriations.

Similar reforms were recorded in 1722 and 1738. The 1722 election report on the four general syndics included nine items for which the newly elected syndics would be held responsible. The first five provisions emphasized that the general syndics were dependent upon the general parliament for advice and consent. No debts or expenditures could be incurred, no embassies could be sent to Naples, no new taxes could be levied "without the express consent and knowledge of the particiular syndics of the locations."[62] Again, in the king's confirmation of election reform in 1738, item 4 made it clear that the general syndics were not autonomous autocrats.[63] They were representatives of the *generalità* who were charged to consult the particular syndics and to execute their decisions legally and above board. The growing importance of the particular syndics in the eighteenth century cannot be doubted.

Particular Syndics and the Rise of Middling Holders

The earliest list of the particular syndics comes from the election of the four general syndics of 1596.[64] Each of the 21 *locati*, who represented 19 locations, was given 4 votes. The general syndics were elected in order by number of votes: Cesare Pignatello received 21 votes (100 percent); Fabrizio de Nolfi, 16 (76 percent); Antonio Bruno, 14 (67 percent); and Sinaballo Bucciarella, 10 (48 percent). The next candidates registered 8 and 7 votes respectively, with one other loser gathering 4, and four losers scoring 1 each. While this system of voting ensured that a popular candidate like Pignatello might be named on all 21 ballots (first on 18), it also allowed someone like Bucciarella, who gained less than half-hearted support (fourth on 7 ballots), to be elected.[65]

The candidates were largely drawn from the electors. Only three of the eleven nominees were not particular syndics: two of the winners, Pignatello and Bruno; and the number-five vote getter, the ex-doganiero Fabrizio di Sangro, who still retained some of his investments in the dogana (at least 2,163 sheep *extra-locazione*) and obviously maintained the high regard of at least 38 percent of the grazier community. The two elected syndics who were not voters must also have been well known as among the largest holders in the whole dogana. Pignatello professed 18,000 sheep and was the leading investor in Orta; in addition, he professed 3,646 sheep *extra-locazione* and 500 more in Canosa. He came from Naples and, as a member of a wealthy, noble family, undoubtedly had close ties to the viceregal administration. Bruno came from Gildone in Capitanata and professed 10,000 sheep. Along with two other *locati* professing the same number, he shared first place in his location of Canosa.

The relative wealth invested in the dogana is a relevant measure for both electors and nominees. Of the 19 identifiable particular deputies, 12 were named in the complete tax rolls of 1595/96.[66] Eleven of the 12 were among the 10 largest *locati* registered in their location: 3 were first; 4, second; 2, third; 1, sixth; and 1, ninth. Even the twelfth elector enrolled in the complete tax rolls, however, professed 2,600 sheep, so that his twenty-sixth ranking out of 49 *locati* in Ordona still made him one of the rich holders in the dogana at large. Among the nominees, Bucciarella and Francesco Antonio Marchesano were the largest holders with 29,000 sheep in Salpi and 20,000 sheep in Tressanti respectively.

The one other extant record of a *generalità* election (1682) that followed the same procedure as the 1596 election can be examined with the same kind of precision.[67] All twenty-three locations were represented by 22 particular syndics (Camarda and Salsola had the same representative). Their 88 votes elected 4 general syndics by plurality. None of the elected syndics was drawn from the electors, although there was greater consensus: Giuseppe Francischelli, 20 votes; Giuseppe Mancini, 17; Antonio Castruccio, 18; and Giuliano Marinanzi, 20. Only 13 other votes (4 of them by the delegate from Casalnuovo) were cast for some 7 candidates; 1 lone vote for a particular syndic.

In the 1682 election, 11 of the 22 electors can be identified in the complete tax rolls of 1681/82.[68] They are on the whole much smaller holders than their 1596 colleagues: only 1 professed more than 2,000 sheep (2,500); 5, between 1,000 and 2,000; 3, between 200 and 1,000; and 2, less than 200. Among the 2 identifiable winners, Castruccio and Marinanzi had 900 sheep in Feudo and 1,700 sheep in Tressanti respectively. Doganal wealth was not a criterion for election for either particular or general syndics, but it helped.

In 1722 the procedures for election conformed to my earlier model, with outgoing syndics nominating their successors. Particular syndics still met at the time of the May fair to elect general syndics, but larger locations sent more delegates. Theoretically, locations with more than 40,000 sheep (twelve in all) could elect 2 deputies, while locations with fewer than 40,000 sheep (eight remained) were still entitled to 1 each; that is, 32 electors from 20 locations.[69] In practice, affidavits dated 13–14 May 1722 named 35 electors from twenty-two locations (thirteen with 2, and nine with 1 elector).[70]

These 35 particular deputies elected 4 general syndics, only 1 of whom was drawn from their number. Almost two-thirds of the electors (23 out of 35) are identifiable in the *squarciafoglio*.[71] Only 1 was a small holder, professing 125 sheep in Guardiola. Middling holders professing sheep between 200 and 2,000 head numbered 12; the elected syndic Giuseppe Antonio Vespa fell into this category with 1,410 sheep in Andria. Finally, 10 particular syndics were large holders of 2,000 head or more. One of the unidentifiable, non-*locati* electors, Antonio Manpietro from Casalnuovo, was a trail boss for 32 *locati*.

An examination of deputies' wealth in mid-eighteenth-century grazier parliaments changes this earlier portrait of dominance by the rich. Deputies from nine meetings between 1738 and 1754 included an average of forty-nine voters, who represented twenty locations which sent 1 to 4 particular deputies.[72] Comparison of the 1751 electors with their sheep estimate registered in the complete tax rolls suggests that the middling holders became the favored representatives.[73] Thirty-four out of 51 deputies (67 percent) are identifiable. More than 79 percent (27 out of 34) were middling holders, with only five large and two small owners. Even if all the 17 unidentifiable particular syndics were big-time investors not professing sheep, the middling holders would still hold 53 percent of the vote. And this same predominance of middling holders remained true in the 1754 election. Thus, the economic status of particular syndics had changed since the late sixteenth century (table 8). Middling holders had made a strong comeback. Particular syndics were not the rich, noble, or legal class who filled the ranks of the general syndics.

The nine issues examined by the 1754 general parliament, with its forty-one voting members, confirmed this pattern of increasing particular syndic impact upon *generalità* decision making.[74] The first four items concerned special expenditures: on the general syndics' budget, 78 percent in favor; on payment of *generalità* lawyers and procurators in Naples, 100 percent in favor; on three specific proposals regarding extraction of animals from the Kingdom, contraband, and the duke of Calabritto, 80 percent in favor; and on increasing the salary to legal counsel Orazio Cimaglia, 60 percent in favor. Three items reiterated the pastoralists' traditional privileges vis-à-vis agriculturists and the state: a proposal to allow Prince Paolo Imperiale to exchange 500 *carra* of land in repose was defeated unanimously; and resolutions banning plow and draft animals from doganal pastures after 29 September and affirming *locati* immunity from a cadastral survey passed unanimously. Two other proposals, on election procedures for lawyers and procurators, and on a request for charity from a convent in Sulmona, passed unanimously. The responsibilities and rights of the *generalità* were thus exercised and protected in general parliament.

At about the same time—in 1741, 1749, 1756, and 1769—the general syndics began to increase their terms in office from three years to six years. What the general parliaments took away on the one hand, then, was compensated for in longer tenure. But above all, particular syndics were virtually excluded from election to the higher rank of general syndic as the general syndics emerged as an intermediate bureaucratic layer between state and graziers.

TABLE 8 Wealth among Particular Deputies (1596–1754)

Year	Particular Deputies	Deputies Identified in Squarciafogli	Small Holders <200	Middling Holders 201–2,000	Large Holders >2,000
1596	21	12 (57%)	—	—	12 (57%)
1615	37	21 (57)	1 (3%)	18 (49%)	2 (5)
1682	22	11 (50)	2 (9)	8 (36)	1 (5)
1722	32	23 (72)	1 (3)	12 (38)	10 (31)
1738	48	22 (46)	6 (13)	12 (25)	4 (8)
1741	47	14 (30)	2 (4)	10 (21)	2 (4)
1743	50	22 (44)	8 (16)	11 (22)	3 (6)
1746	52	26 (50)	5 (10)	17 (33)	4 (8)
1747	53	24 (45)	2 (4)	20 (38)	2 (4)
1748	49	19 (39)	2 (4)	14 (29)	3 (6)
1749	43	19 (44)	2 (5)	15 (35)	2 (5)
1751	51	34 (67)	2 (4)	27 (53)	5 (10)
1754	42	28 (67)	4 (10)	21 (50)	3 (7)
Mean			(7)	(36)	(6)

Sources: ASFg, Dogana, serie I, fas. 108, n. 1740, 7r–9v (1596); fas. 2, 181r–198v (1615); fas. 108, n. 1750, 1 bis–28v (1682); n. 1745, 4r–v (1722); fas. 109, n. 1753, 12r–13r (1738); 83r–v (1741); 104v–105r (1743); n. 1758, 22r–23r (1746); n. 1753, 142v–143v (1747); 150r–v (1748); n. 1760, 3r–v (1749); n. 1753, 176r–v (1751); 189r–v (1754).

General Syndics' Duties and Budgets

The sharing of decision making by the general syndics with their *locati* constituency did not, however, diminish the syndics' duties. They were still responsible for two major judicial charges: to represent *locati* interests before the Collateral Council and the Sommaria in defense of traditional privileges and in prosecution of *generalità* cases; and to arbitrate disputes between *locati*.[75] The syndics' budgets summarize their day-to-day activities and give some idea of the range of their responsibilities. The general syndics' actions are our best source in defining the meaning of the graziers' organization.

Two kinds of general syndic budgets are preserved: ordinary expenses based on their salary and duties, and grain procurement expenses relating to the care and feeding of the pastoralists wintering in Foggia.[76] From the 1738 reform, the triennial, ordinary budgets of the general syndics were required for inspection by the general parliament. Extant budgets for the twenty-five-year period between 1750 and 1774 provide statistics on income for only fifteen of the years (table 9). Income fluctuated from a low of 600 ducats in 1760 to more than three times that, 1,915 ducats in 1761. The mean of 1,266 ducats, however, fits neatly with the income sources available.

The *locati* taxed themselves in public parliament at the rate of 4 *carlini* per

TABLE 9 General Syndics' Budgets (1750–1774) (In Ducats)

Year	Income	Expenses	Difference
1749/50		1,351.23	
1750/51		1,863.89	
1751/52		832.01	
1752/53		982.63	
1753/54		878.95	
1754/55		1,117.70	
1755/56		702.63[a]	
1756/57	914.76	1,209.47	−294.71
1757/58	886.77	1,162.99	−276.22
1758/59	815.00	1,780.79	−965.79
1759/60	600.00	1,412.17	−812.17
1760/61	1,914.84	1,625.00	289.84
1761/62	1,817.00	705.70	1,111.30
1765/66	1,647.63	1,863.29	−215.66
1766/67	1,121.93	1,503.38	−381.45
1767/68	1,802.83	1,722.62	80.21
1768/69	1,483.40	1,782.86	−299.46
1769/70	1,172.40	1,231.13	−58.73
1770/71	1,640.00	1,182.99	457.01
1771/72	1,282.80	1,292.55	−9.75
1772/73	1,082.60	1,113.30	−30.70
1773/74	803.00	995.70	−192.70
Mean	1,265.67	1,286.95	−106.60

Sources: ASFg, Dogana, serie I, fas. 110–111, n. 1766 (1750–56), n. 1770 (1757–62), n. 1773 (1766–68), n. 1775 (1769–74).

[a]Adjusted expenses do not include 1,652.82 ducat loan.

1,000 sheep for a total of 560 ducats to cover the general syndics' expenses. The general syndics received an annual stipend from the *locati* which was paid out before any other expenditures were debited. In 1564 each syndic received 110 ducats beyond expenses, in salary.[77] By 1596 the syndics were each paid 100 ducats in salary.[78] In addition to the *locati* stipend, by 1649 the royal fisc paid out 700 ducats each May as a kind of bribe to ensure the syndics' good offices for the state.[79]

By 1679 *locati* payments had increased. The four deputies were paid 170 ducats each.[80] Since about one-third fewer sheep were reported in transhumance in 1679 than in 1564 (only 456,347 in the complete tax rolls), the *locati* would have to have paid higher taxes to support their syndics unless alternative revenue sources could be exploited. One such source came from renting the monopoly, which the city of Foggia held on the sale of wine to *locati* and their dependents. The *franchi,* as it was called, contributed 600 ducats to the four deputies in 1679. By the 1730s, Di Stefano records that it provided 1,300 ducats.[81] The syndic budgets of 1749–56 confirm that income from taxes on the *locati*'s sheep holdings and from wine monopoly rents brought in the largest part of *generalità* revenues. Each provided about 45 percent of *generalità* credits. The remaining 10 percent came from *scomissioni* (fines for early or illegal grazing) and the salt tax.[82]

One other revenue source of immense importance to the *generalità* was the assignment after 1714 of the 8,000-ducat annual income from the locations of Lesina and Castiglione.[83] In the budgets of 1739–41, for example, that income accounted for almost 96 percent of *generalità* resources, some 25,100 ductas (more than 9,000 ducats for two years and only 6,000, the third).[84]

Extraordinary expenditures like the 8,000-ducat levy (*donativo*) collected in 1741 for the queen could only be approved in general parliament with special financing. Thus, in addition to revenues from the renting of Lesina and Castiglione, twenty-two locations were assessed a special 6.275 ducats per 1,000 possible sheep for a total of 6,860.5 ducats.[85] In 1702 an extraordinary tax of one *carlino* per *rubbio* of wool, a tax destined for the Collateral Council in Naples, was opposed by many *locati*. Only 1,500 ducats (less than 20 percent of the sum possible) was collected since the *locati* were not obligated to comply.[86] In 1719, however, the *locati* concurred and the general syndic Isidoro de Marco paid a *donativo* of 10,000 ducats for the urgent needs of war in Sicily.[87]

Normal expenditures, on the other hand, were recorded in twenty-two of the twenty-five years in the 1750–74 budgets. With expenditures as a mean total of 1,287 ducats, it appears that debits outran credits by only 20 ducats per year. Even the mean difference for the fifteen years with complete accounts produces only a 100-ducat annual deficit. The expenditure mean, however, is skewed downward by the seven earliest accounts without record of income. An analysis of the fifteen dates with both income and expenditures, moreover, suggests that comparing mean totals does not reveal the real crisis in *generalità* finances. The averages are distorted by the unusually low expenditure and, consequently, high balance for 1762. The median deficit was −276 ducats; and, if only the eleven deficit years are counted, their mean drops to −322 ducats. With deficits of 20 percent, the *locati* had good reason to oversee general syndic expenses.

In the sixteenth-century budgets, entries were listed chronologically. By the 1739–41 budget, expenses were divided into twelve rubrics. Expenditures were grouped into seven entries in the budgets for 1750–56, and five entries for those thereafter (table 10). This process of simplification, no doubt, aided *generalità* analysis, but also helps us see the *generalità*'s function more clearly.

The categories are not necessarily exclusive, however. Payment to musicians playing for liturgical ceremonies was listed under services from 1750 to 56, but under novenas from 1739 to 41. Some postal charges, gifts, and salaries were paid under miscellaneous in all of the 1750–56 budgets even though they had separate headings. In 1770 no entry was given for tribunal costs, but the

TABLE 10   General Syndics' Budgets (1750–1774): Mean Annual Expenditures (In Ducats)

Entry	1750–56	1757–62	1766–68	1769–74
Tribunal	129 (12%)	315 (24%)	940 (55%)	287 (23%)
Gifts	199 (18)	249 (19)	65 (4)	86 (7)
Novenas and charity	196 (18)	88 (7)	252 (15)	217 (17)
Services	150 (14)	— —	— —	— —
Carriages and mail	33 (3)	— —	— —	— —
Salaries	289 (26)	477 (36)	371 (22)	450 (36)
Miscellaneous	108 (10)	187 (14)	68 (4)	227 (18)
Total	1,104 (101)	1,316 (100)	1,696 (100)	1,267 (101)

Source: See table 9.

miscellaneous debits were uncharacteristically tripled. Similarly, not all debits for a given year were paid on time. No salaries were included in the 1750 budget, but in 1751, three years' salaries were paid.

My comparison of budget expenses is, therefore, not based upon the twenty-two years' cumulative averages but is divided into four periods which conform to the four general syndic administrations reporting. Their four budget accounts are preserved in homogeneous sources and reflect the particular problems and priorities of each group of syndics. Thus, if religious ceremonies were peculiarly expensive, as in 1750 to propitiate God for the harsh winter (539 ducats versus a mean of 139, with a maximum variation of only 8 ducats, in the other six years of the accounts); or if legal fees were unusually high, as in 1759 (628 ducats doubled the mean, and was five times greater than the 1762 low), each administration had to balance and compensate. The 1766–68 budgets demonstrate this principle neatly. As litigation doubled and tripled to a mean 940 ducats, gifts and miscellaneous expenses declined both absolutely and as a percentage of the whole. Given the possibility of such elasticity in some entries, the 1766–68 expenditures, nevertheless, still far exceeded all other debit accounts.

This first category, tribunal expenses, is the most important budget entry. Tribunal expenses were paid for depositions, information, copies of decrees and dispatches, the services of scribes on the salt, cheese, and wool account books, assistance in the numeration of horses and cattle at the time of the fair, extra archival assistance, and a number of minor officials' supplementary salaries. The specific entries underline the twofold judicial charge of the syndics: defense of *generalità* rights and arbitration of *locati* disputes.[88] The syndics intervened in matters large and small—for example, in 1750 when the rights of wool buyers were threatened by the Dogana of Salerno, in 1754 when meat merchants were guaranteed free passage for purchased lambs, and again in 1754 when the baron of San Ippolito, Paolo Nicola del Angelis, and Nicola Patini were arrested for contraband.

Legal fees coupled with the rubric for salaries, which were mostly paid to lawyers, amounted to more than one-half of *generalità* expenditures. The *generalità*'s critical function of legal representation could not have been more pointedly stated. Just as the state and its court promised to ensure equal and expeditious justice, so too the *locati* were deeply involved in the same process.

In the sixteenth century, the number of advocates for *locati* causes so overwhelmed the doganal burearacy that in Cardinal Granvelle's twenty-eight-item decree of July 1574 he limited *locati* representation to two lawyers and four syndics. This order, item 23, was countermanded within the year, however, in Granvelle's 1 July 1575 commentary on the twenty-eight items.[89] The cause of revocation may not have been the limitation on *locati* representation as much as the appointment of those officials by the doganiero rather than by the sheepowners themselves.

Regular *generalità* lawyers, nevertheless, were eventually appointed by the syndics with the consent of the doganiero and were paid by the *locati* at large. In 1596 the *generalità* lawyer, Giovanni Battista d'Afflitto, received 65 ducats per year, as did the *generalità* lawyer resident in Naples in 1679. In the budgets of 1751, 1752, and 1753, three lawyers (Sassinotto, Pauletta, and Ciancerella) received an annual salary of 60 ducats each, and one (Cimaglia), 20 ducats.

In addition to these salaried employees, extraordinary legal aid was brought in for specific cases. In the 1754 parliamentary debate over legal counsel Orazio Cimaglia's extra services, as we have seen, a narrow vote awarded Cimaglia another 150 ducats above his normal 20-ducats honorarium.[90] Other special appropriations of this sort were common under the headings of both salaries and miscellaneous. Two extra lawyers (Celentano and Manna), for example, received a total of 150 ducats in 1751.

Other salary and salarylike expenditures were paid on a regular basis. A *generalità* procurator received 10 ducats per year, and a notary or registrar received 50. Officials who weighed and measured bread, cheese, and wool were paid a small stipend for their participation in the annual setting of the *voce* price. The doganal archivist received 10 ducats annually for his scribal services. Laborers were paid 2 ducats each time they set up stalls for the annual May fair or carried benches and seats for the meetings of the general parliament. Even the sextant of the Church of Santa Maria Addolorata, where parliament met in the 1750s, received a small stipend for his "overtime" assistance up to 8:00 P.M. in 1750 and to 10:00 P.M. in 1755. The *generalità* had to pay for these late hours again in the debit for candles, as in the 3.1 ducats expended in the 1756 syndic election.

In addition to their salaries, *generalità* syndics and lawyers received per diem expenses for work outside Foggia. In 1567, 27 days in Naples were paid at 22 *carlini* per day, and in 1568, two stays of 93 days and 18 days were paid at the rate of 20 *carlini* per day. During two trips in 1597, the per diem was limited to a horse, lodging, and servant at 8 *carlini* per day for 43 days, and again for 30 days. In the 1739–41 budget, syndic Alessandro Sardi was paid an expense allowance of 80 ducats for five months' residence in Naples, that is, about 5 *carlini* per day, whereas his colleague, Oduardo Grillo, received the same 80-ducat assistance for a stay of a little more than two months, some 13 ducats per day. Finally, in 1751 and 1755, Bernardo Mosca received a 20 *carlini* per diem for 35 and 42 days in Naples. Over the course of two centuries, 20 *carlini* or 2 ducats would seem to be about the agreed-upon per diem for Naples.

The actual journey from Foggia was also reimbursed. In June 1597 the syndic Fabrizio Nolfi received 2.7 ducats for his horse and servant for 6 days on the road to Naples. For the same trip at the beginning of March, however, Nolfi received the same travel allowance for a 12-day journey. The 12-day itinerary was closer to the normal 10-day traveling time between the Neapolitan capital and its Foggian bureaucracy.[91]

All debit entries, in fact, can be construed as legal or quasi-legal services. The gifts, for example, were not given without purpose. In the later budgets, this entry was called "Recognizioni e Complimenti" (1757–62) and "Inserta del St. Natale" (1766–74). They were given, in other words, at Christmastime to officials and their families in recognition of their friendship and in gratitude for their favors to the *locati*. Minor functionaries like the *portiere*, bailiffs, and messengers were not forgotten, but most important were the ministers, secretaries, lawyers, and accountants of the dogana. Last but not least, the largest gift, 100 ducats, was given to the doganal president. In 1750, to make their point, the syndics gave the president two 100-ducat gifts because the previous deputies had been negligent. This kind of gift giving expressed the social bonds that tie patron and client, employer and employee. Such Christmas presents bespeak a practical social and economic relationship above and beyond any religious, holiday sentiment.

In the same way that they kept channels open to state authorities, the syndics also were responsible for maintaining a good relationship with divine authority. About 200 ducats per year were spent on masses and charity to beseech God for mild weather and for eternal salvation. In normal years like 1750, most of the religious contributions (71 percent) went for novenas: "at the beginning of November for the intentions of the *locati*" (101 ducats), "between the end of November and the beginning of December for the same reason" (141 ducats), that is, to bless the coming doganal season; and "at the beginning of January for the very great danger in which the *poveri locati* found themselves" (139 ducats). In 1751 and 1752 harsh winters worried the *locati*, and masses were celebrated "to implore divine assistance in the bad weather which came between January and February" and "for the weather which threatened to cause damage." The exceptionally low expenditure of 80 ducats in 1757–62 reflected the good winter weather during those years which allowed for some cost saving. Novenas to the Blessed Virgin and for the souls in Purgatory were also on the agenda, as in the 1739–41 budgets, when 225 ducats or 17 percent of novena payments were dedicated to them. The favorite church in Foggia was the Santissima Iconavetera, the patroness of the shepherds, although all churches in and around Foggia were remembered.

Charity was given at Christmas, Carnival, and Easter to the mendicant friars, to the sick, and to the imprisoned. Processions and festivals were underwritten. Individuals, such as the widow of Tomasso Manzino, who received 50 ducats in 1739–41, or the unnamed, newly penitent *povero* who received 2 ducats in 1750, partook of the *generalità's* alms.

One of the most important functions of the *generalità* as a confraternal organization was mutual aid. The 26 April 1583 parliament, for example, discussed one such enterprise, finances and overseers for the foundation of a doganal hospital.[92] In the second half of the sixteenth century, new hospital foundations proliferated in Naples because they were no longer under episcopal jurisdiction.[93] Presumably, a provincial hospital like that at Foggia would similarly find that its *locati* founders would be rectors free from ecclesiastical control.

The 1583 parliament debate began with an expression of the long-standing doganal need to help the sick and the poor who died without assistance. The hospital foundation was to be a joint venture between state and sheepowners—parliament and doganiero retaining the right of advice and consent. Funding came from an initial state grant of 3,000 ducats set aside by the 1539–42 doganiero, Juan de Figueroa. At 4.67 percent annual interest, the capital yielded 140 ducats per year, of which 1,200 ducats still remained.[94] With additional ducats lent by Francesco Antonio Pietro Paulo which the *locati* planned to repay with a 240-ducat annual tax, the 1,670 ducats were deemed sufficient to proceed. Three deputies—Marco Marchesano of Rocca di Cinquemiglia, Fabritio de Alfiero of Aquila, and Victorio Machio of Lucoli—were appointed to govern the hospital and to keep annual accounts. This fledgling charity received an added boost in 1588 when Guzmán's visit ruled that 2,000 ducats of the 10,000-ducat fine levied against the ex-doganiero, Fabrizio di Sangro, for abuse of office should be applied to the "construction, benefit, and utility of the Hospital of the Sheep Customhouse."[95] Thus, ongoing works of mercy were part of the *generalità's* pious duties and associational responsibilities.

Finally, the second kind of syndic budget, that of grain procurement, demonstrates even more dramatically the corporate consciousness of the *locati* as the *generalità* provided for their daily bread. In the 1596/97 budget, 36,989.65 ducats were expended out of 35,293.97 ducats in income.[96] These figures are nearly twenty-seven times the normal syndic budgets because 34,223.7 ducats purchased cereals for *locati* consumption at extremely high prices. To deal with those large sums an additional 1,624.2 ducats were spent on exchanging money at rates which varied from 1.1 percent, 1.67 percent, to 2.14 percent.[97]

The extraordinary grain budget of 1597 purchased 309 *carra*, 33.5 *tomoli* (11,157.5 *tomoli*) of wheat at a mean price of 2.6 ducats per *tomolo*, and 209 *carra*, 28 *tomoli* (10,060 *tomoli*) of barley at a mean price of 0.54 ducats per *tomolo*. From these figures we can estimate that shepherds consumed about 2.85 *tomoli* of grain per head, roughly equivalent to the consumption of agriculturists.[98] The prices paid for that grain by the *generalità* in 1597 reflected the deepening agricultural crisis at the turn of the century.[99] Even in the midst of agricultural crisis in Puglia, the *generalità* had power in numbers, wealth, and influence to protect its members and prosper by ensuring a supply of grain at reasonable prices.

The *locati*, of course, eventually paid for their success. On 26 November 1606, at the beginning of the new doganal season, the famine had become so extreme that the four syndics presented themselves before the doganiero to seek some kind of solution to prevent the *locati* "from abandoning their sheep."[100] The agreement to pay taxes at four, five, or more times the number of real sheep in each location in exchange for 20,000 *tomoli* of grain was signed by Francesco Filesio, the general council of the deputies, and 101 other *locati*.[101] The state and shepherds reinforced their partnership in adversity, but the price each paid was indeed high. The state risked riots in the cities and had to rely on imports of foreign grain.[102] The graziers, for their part, risked high taxes and even higher grain prices in the hope of reaping a profit from the sale of their wool in the international market. By 1607, at the height of the crisis, wheat was so scarce that the *generalità* had to pay skyrocketing prices of between 115 and 158 ducats per *carro* for some 32 *carra*.[103] By the spring of 1609 they were still paying 130 ducats per *carro* for only 40 *carro* and 120 ducats per *carro* for 5.5 other *carra*.[104]

As a summary of the legal counsel and mutual aid provided by the *generalità*, Di Stefano specified six administrative and economic functions which kept the general syndics busy.[105] First, they appointed the *generalità* lawyers and procurators in Foggia and Naples. Second, from the mid seventeenth century, they appointed the commissioners who guarded passes during the transhumant journey back to the Abruzzi in May and June. Third, they countersigned the state requisitions for the distribution of salt (some 15,000–18,000 *tomoli* to the *locati* for their sheep), for the *utilità del pane* (the 4,000-ducat doganal income derived from *locati* payment for the shepherds' bread), and for the *deduzione di erbaggi* (the pasture in the locations not used for transhumant sheep). Fourth, the general syndics made monthly checks of weights and measures used for shepherd provisions of bread, meat, and wine. Fifth, they represented the sheepowners at the annual meeting of merchants, buyers, and state bureaucrats which set the *voce* prices for wool and cheese. Finally, as rectors of the *generalità*, the syndics had to work for its collective interests in the maintenance of law and privileges, in guarding against *scomessi* (grazing in another's assigned area or before assignment in the locations), in establishing just prices, and in providing the food staples and material goods which the shepherds needed to graze their flocks. Aiding in the reconciliation of possible doganal conflicts—grazier against state, grazier against farmer, grazier against merchant, and grazier against grazier—was a full-time job.

The *Generalità*'s Power and Significance

This tetrad of relationship reminds us that the *generalità* was not the customhouse per se but comprised only one part (albeit the most important one) of Di Stefano's republic.[106] The *locati* of the *generalità*, who "owned animals and rented royal land for pasture," were partners with the agriculturists (*masserie di campo*), who "rented *terre salde* for cultivation." The royal custom house's laws united and protected both pastoralists and agriculturists, as well as their "wives, children, employees, servants, all of their families, horseman guards, surveyors, weighers, shearers, furriers, bakers, shoemakers, ropemakers, messengers, accountants, and other officials, workers, and assistants to these officers."

Grouped among the trades in such a list, the *generalità de' locati* appears to take its rightful place as an *arte* or guild in the corporate structure of Old Regime society. Di Stefano further demonstrated how the *generalità* elected representatives just as other corporations did.[107] The comparisons could continue, as we have seen: the *generalità* limited itself to an exclusive membership (the Abruzzesi), it boasted special rights and privileges, it protected its members as a legal defense fund and a mutual aid society, and, above all, it mediated the ambiguity between equality and anarchy common to all businessmen who share the same market, yet are in competition with one another.[108]

Gaudiani, however, cautions us to beware of the facile identification of the *locati* with other guilds. The renters of the pasture "must be thought about with another kind of intelligence" because they contributed to the wealth of the royal patrimony, whereas no other *arte* could make such a claim.[109] Thus, if we follow Gaudiani's reasoning and seek a special kind of rationale for the *generalità* beyond Di Stefano's legal-pastoral-poetic aesthetics, the reality of the *generalità* far exceeds the similes of commune, parliament, and guild. From what we know so far, we can, in fact, draw out these connotations from the traditionally narrow, fiscal denotation of the *generalità* and even break through the temporally bound arguments which have depicted the dogana (and the Mesta in Spain, for that matter) as regressive institutions typical of the intransigence of privilege in late medieval and early modern European society.

Pastoralism is a livelihood strategy that long preceded the burgeoning world of capitalism and cities that grew up in Europe after the eleventh century. The generative principle for all pastoral societies is resource exploitation in marginal agricultural zones. The problem of resource management in that circumscribed environment, however, is compounded because of the nomadic character and warlike posture of the invading pastoral populations. The *generalità de' locati* provided an egalitarian forum to express the unbridled individualism and inequality which came from pastoral wandering and pastoral wealth, while it resolved the conflicts that arose from the competition over pastoral resources and pastoral exchange. The sheepowners' organization, then, was an indigenous invention to establish and enforce a set of norms to allow for continued economic cooperation among the pastoral population. From the southern European transhumant cousins—Mesta and dogana—the centralizing medieval state incorporated these already existent sheepowners' institutions as partners in the royal plan to pacify and profit from the marginal zone.

Herein lie the meanings derived from Gaudiani's observation on the royal patrimony. First, the *generalità de' locati* was much more important than any other royally patronized corporation because of its primacy as an association which antedated effective state control of the land. Second, the transhumant economy was one of profit, not subsistence; thus, it not only gave to the royal fisc a ready income but also generated capital in domestic and international trade. Third, its social structure was extremely fluid since it reflected the rise and fall of the market. Whether it be demographic profiles, social stratification, or the eclipse of general syndics by particular syndics, the economic conjuncture set the pattern of social organization.

One measure of the *generalità*'s significance was its influence on the duties and personnel of the royal dogana offices. Not only did the *locati* steadfastly elect their own *generalità* officers, but they often could affect the appointment of doganal officers by the viceroy. In August 1537 the viceroy, Pedro de Toledo, had already sold the office of doganiero, which had been vacated by the death of Miguel Sanchez, to Francesco Carroz for 10,000 ducats when the doganal syndics approached him at Otranto with their own candidate. They supported a Castilian bureaucrat of experience and impartiality, Regent Juan de Figueroa, who had twice before been mandated by Toledo to adjust doganal affairs. After Toledo unsuccessfully attempted to persuade Carroz to renounce his recent appointment, the doganal deputation, with the intervention of the duke of Termoli (Vincenzo de Capua) and other baronial *locati* at their side, "insisted" on the Figueroa appointment. Toledo met with Carroz a second time and, "out of respect for me," Toledo wrote to the king, Carroz withdrew. He was reimbursed the purchase price, and the Abruzzesi sheepowners put up the money to buy the office for Figueroa.[110]

Similarly, the *generalità* could affect doganal policy on the continuity of officers' duties. In 1627, following the death of the *auditore*, Maurizio Moles, in the previous year, the deputies of the *generalità* sent a memorial to the Sommaria in order to establish rules for temporary replacements in cases of "sickness, absenteeism, death, or other impediment to the *auditore*."[111] Because of the importance of the *auditore* in the administration of the jurisdiction of the doganal tribunal, the *locati* requested that the duties of this office be assigned to the oldest of the *credenzieri* until a successor was appointed. Their request was tied retroactively to the most recent three-year contract on fixed taxes (November 1626) and confirmed like a *grazia* by the Sommaria.

Further, the *generalità* could lodge protests against and win impeachment for abuses of office. In 1699 it initiated procedures against the two *credenzieri* Giustiniano Freda and Giuseppe Giordano. Twenty-one charges were filed against them. The Sommaria appointed Gaetano Longo in Freda's place, and the *generalità* bought back the other position in perpetuity.[112]

The real test of the *generalità*'s power was thus its longevity and its lobby. No decade illustrates that power better than the 1640s. In the lingering economic doldrums which preceded the Masaniello revolt, the *generalità* celebrated its greatest victory.

Even though the Parlamento Generale of the Kingdom often voted forced levies (*donativi*) to the king, the king suspended it in 1642.[113] The representatives of the Kingdom of Naples were never recalled and even the facade of a domesticated parliament never resumed. Soon thereafter, however, the parliament of the *locati* of the dogana, far from being permanently dissolved, negotiated two important concessions from the state.[114] First, a new three-year contract replaced the fixed agreement method of tax collection, which dated from 1615, with the reestablishment of "spontaneous bidding" (*professazione spontanea*). But even more noteworthy, the *generalità* purchased the office of doganiero for the same 37,000-ducat price as its previous occupant, Giacomo Moneglia, had paid. Not the parliament, but an office, which from the foundation of the royal customhouse had symbolized the assertion of monarchical power, had been abolished. A noble of the robe from the Collateral Council or Sommaria continued to act as an impartial biennial governor, instead of the independent, life-term doganiero.[115] Further, in 1649 the *generalità* flexed its muscles to the point of requesting (unsuccessfully) that its own syndics be given nine- or ten-year terms instead of their three-year tenure.[116] The state, not the *generalità*, was in retreat on parliamentary issues in the dogana.

This final image of victory and defeat, advance and retreat, brings us back to the beginning of this chapter and the 1564 report of the clamoring shepherd army of "all the dogana and its *generalità* in Naples." The idea of comparing the sheep farmers (*masserie di pecore*) to a military army was another of Di Stefano's similes.[117] The *generalità* was like an army because both the shepherd and soldier carried arms. The right to bear arms was one of the *locati*'s oldest and dearest rights, which was granted by Alfonso in his 1447 foundation charter, confirmed by Charles V in 1536, and reaffirmed thereafter.[118] Such a right was highly unusual among commoners in early modern society for fear that they might cause disorder or rebellion. What better proof of the unique rationale governing state-pastoral relations? The shepherds' arms not only protected their sheep, but they defended the state as well.

Di Stefano's identification of shepherds as soldiers, however, did not stop there. Both a "sheep farm" and an army were on the move, and on the march, both were divided into their respective regiments and companies, both were preceded by horns, pipes, and drums, and both were trailed by camp followers and logistical staff of all kinds. Even the most eloquent poet of the pastoral, Virgil, compared the shepherd of Libya to the Roman legionnaire:

> All that he needs the African takes with him,
> His tent, gods, weapons, and at his heels his dog;
> Burdened like a steady soldier fighting for Rome
> Who can pitch camp after a forced march and stand ready
> For battle before the enemy knows he has come.[119]

The *generalità de' locati* could indeed be the equivalent of an army of soldiers!

The multiple analogies drawn between the *generalità* and the other institutions of society imbue the pastoral mode of production with a reality greater than the sum of these comparisons. That reality was essentially political, and, if we follow the military simile, it is what forged (in Machiavellian terms) good government; namely, good arms and good laws. For Di Stefano, the *generalità*'s unique ability to be army, commune, parliament, guild, city, religion, and Arcadia allowed the pastoral mode to transcend production and politics to become poetry. Although poetry may seem unrelated to the hard-headedness of the marketplace or the conspiracies of government, Di Stefano should not be dismissed for emphasizing the *ragion pastorale* in ideological terms consonant with eighteenth-century values on the state of nature and the nature of the state. Both of these concepts, like the *generalità,* were primitive and multiform, and they embodied the tensions between self and society. The pastoral mode, after all, holds its attraction for all of us still, because of the interplay between freedom and community and between innocence and cunning.

5 The Conflict between Rich and Poor

Equality under the law dominated the *generalità*'s concern for the king's justice and for the *locati*'s own rights. Moreover, this equality had special meaning for the poor *locati* in relationship to their powerful fellow *locati*. But how could a small-holding commoner be equal to someone like the Doria princes of Melfi with their 10,000 sheep?

Was the doganal reality like that of its Spanish Mesta cousin, where men of incredible wealth predominated? The existence of enormous flocks in the fifteenth century (the monastery of El Escorial, 40,000 head; Santa Maria del Paular, near Segovia, 30,000; the duke of Béjar, 25,000; the duke of Infantado, 20,000; not to mention those of the military orders) gave large holders extraordinary influence over Mesta offices and policies no matter how democratic the assemblies might appear.[1]

How did the egalitarian ideology in the dogana of Foggia rationalize the conflicting desires of different classes? Necessity demanded that poor sheepowners subordinate their personal interests to the common good and aggregate their wealth into an effective lobby against the rich. But was such solidarity enough? Untangling the contradictions between individualism and egalitarianism requires us to identify rich and poor and to analyze the changes in stratification and state policy over time. Who were these *ricchi* and who, the *poveri*?

Measuring Stratification: Sources

My measure of stratification will be the size of holdings as they were recorded in the annual tax rolls: the global tax lists (*squarciafogli*) and abbreviated tax lists (*squarciafoglietti*). After the 1553 introduction of the free bidding method of tax collection, as we have already seen, the global tax lists contained an estimation of flock size. Each individual grazier made his estimate during the month of November in private and secret audience before the doganiero and *credenziero* in order to register for pasture in the locations. The tax estimate of sheepowners entitled them to a certain amount of pasture and provided the base to calculate their tax share at the rate of 132 ducats per 1,000 sheep. There was little incentive to underestimate one's holdings and pay less tax because one's own herds would suffer most from insufficient fodder. On the contrary, it might often be in one's interest to overestimate one's holdings and pay more tax in order to receive grazing rights to more land. My calculations, therefore, are biased toward larger holding—exactly opposite to the kind of middling holding which, I am trying to demonstrate, predominated in the dogana.

The abbreviated tax lists, which were summary accounts compiled from the global tax lists, copied only one category of taxpayers (*locati*)—the *padroni* who made the tax declaration. The global tax lists, on the other hand, recorded three categories of *locati:* the *padroni* of the abbreviated tax lists, who can be divided into two groups—first, individual independent *padroni* who represented themselves alone, and second, *padroni* heads of "collectives" (*collettive*) representing themselves along with lesser holders (*padroncelli*)—and finally, the third group of lesser holders, the dependent *padroncelli*.[2] Membership in these three groups has already been summarized in my discussion of the *generalità*.

I have analyzed these tax lists by computer and base my conclusions about social stratification upon the declaration of *pecore reali fisse,* that is, an agreed upon number of "real, fixed sheep" as opposed to a second heading in the tax rolls for *pecore in alia tantum,* that is, sheep (often imaginary) declared for that year only. The figures derived from the real, fixed sheep do not reflect the actual number of sheep present in Puglia, nor do they give the actual wealth of investors, who may have been far richer than their pastoral "portfolio." The real, fixed sheep were fixed contracts between state administration and grazier which gave the dogana × amount of tax, and investors the right to corresponding pasture.[3] My analysis of the global tax lists, therefore, reflect an ideal view of the social structure as the state sanctioned or perceived it.

Defining Rich and Poor Before the Union of General and Particular Locations

The earliest evidence comes from one abbreviated tax list only, which has been preserved in Simancas as part of the investigation of the visitor general Gaspar de Quiroga (1559-64).[4] It provides a clear portrait of the rich and poor as they were defined in the dogana, that is, by pasture assignment in the general locations or locations of the poor versus the particular locations or locations of the rich. The best pastures, before the general locations and particular locations were united in 1585/86, were theoretically allocated to nobles, the wealthy, and the powerful.[5] In practice, however, the difference between *i ricchi* and *i poveri,* that is, the concession to them of pasture privileges, was not defined exclusively by blood or money.

The 259,987 sheep grazed in the twenty-three particular locations in 1559 comprised 19.8 percent of the total 1,314,961 head numbered in the locations at large. The 19.8 percent:80.2 percent ratio of 1559 compared favorably with the earlier 19.3 percent:80.7 percent ratio of the 1548 cadastral survey. Despite the 128 percent increase in locations from eighteen and the 148 percent increase in sheep from the 176,255 possible of 1548, the particular

THE CONFLICT BETWEEN RICH AND POOR   119

locations were growing proportionately with the general locations as a whole.

Among the forty-six cases (6.5 percent) listed in the locations of the rich, only thirty-nine individual *locati* or associations of sheepowners were named. The multiple listing of seven *locati* in two different locations was the normal means by which large holders found sufficient pasture and spread their risks of flock damage during harsh winters. Double listing was forbidden, however, because it could easily lead to abuses in pasture distribution, with the rich attempting to monopolize or resell at higher prices their assigned winter grazing. Some *locati* even set up dummy entities in the names of their wives, children, brothers, or relatives in as many as four or five locations in order to evade the law.[6]

Double listing, therefore, may not be easily detectable and could distort my analysis of the distribution of wealth. The fourteen cases from the 1559 particular locations demonstrate, however, that multiple professions do not necessarily skew the figures downward in favor of the middling holders. The largest holders were the ones most likely to double list, and an individual large holder could easily appear on the list as two large holders. If each case in 1559 is counted separately as an individual *locato,* seven extra, nonexistent *locati* would be created by the double listings. Four would be classified as large holders with more than 2,000 sheep and three as middling holders with 2,000 or fewer sheep. Statistically, in this instance, the differences should cancel each other out. The only distortion will be in the absolute number of increased *locati* and the lower percentage for small holders with 200 or fewer sheep.

The thirty-nine *locati* in the particular locations, then, can be compared according to wealth. Only five were middling holders (according to parameters which I will define presently) with 2,000 or fewer sheep, and two of these professed exactly 2,000 head. Another of these supposed middling holders, Giovanni Jacobo Leognano, professed a rather curious number of 1,941 sheep, as did two multiple listers in Correa Piccola, Ludovico di Carlo and Madonna Santia di Pasquale. Such an odd number, especially repeated three times in the same location, seems like an arbitrary code or fixed sum rather than a real number. We might expect to find Leognano professing sheep in some other location and, indeed, he claimed 1,159 other sheep in the general location of Castiglione for a round total of 3,100 head. The point is clear: even so-called middling holders in the particular locations were probably richer than their free bid indicates. In any case, we should expect to find that at least 90 percent of the *locati* in the particular locations were large holders; that is, wealth was a criterion for particular location privileges.

But was wealth a sufficient reason to be admitted to the particular location club? How did these rich *locati* in the particular locations compare to the *locati* in the locations at large? Were those rich *locati* in the particular locations the only large holders?

Counting the 709 cases only in the whole abbreviated tax list of 1559, we find that the particular locations claimed the eight wealthiest positions, all with more than 10,000 sheep. The general locations, however, also had their share of large holders. The large holders with 5,000 sheep or more included 41 cases (5.8 percent of the total). The general locations counted 19 cases and the particular locations, 22 (21 individuals, only 53.8 percent of the rich) to be at relative parity in numbers. In terms of controlling the 324,980 sheep or 24.7% of the professed total wealth which that 5.8 percent owned, we would expect the particular locations to dominate because of their skewing toward the top of the list. Thus, the general locations held only a little more than one-third— 122,700 sheep (37.9 percent)—to the particular locations' two-thirds— 202,280 (62.1 percent). Overall, however, those large holders in the general locations with flocks greater than 2,000 predominated. All owners in the particular locations with flocks larger than 2,000 head accounted for only 33.8 percent of the large holders' wealth in sheep and 23.6 percent of the cases. In other words, the very richest *locati* were assigned to the particular locations, but many *locati* in the general locations were richer than the other half in the particular locations. Among large holders themselves, those in the particular locations were a minority numbering only one-fourth and controlling only one-third of the wealth. Wealth alone did not determine classification in the particular locations.

Did another principle such as rank or social order determine privilege? Could the society of orders explain why some large holders did and others did not enjoy the privilege of particular location status? If clerical and noble holders are identified in the whole 1559 abbreviated tax list at large, 45.9 percent of these cases and 58.1 percent of their wealth appear in the particular locations. Obviously, not all members of the first two orders were assigned particular location privileges; nor were they even a majority among those who were. Among the particular locations the members of the first and second estate constituted only a little more than one-third of the individuals (fifteen *locati*, or 38.5 percent) and one-third of the wealth (89,373 sheep, or 34.4 percent). The commoners, who made up two-thirds of the particular locations (twenty-four *locati*, 62 percent with 170,614 sheep, or 66 percent) included the smallest holders with 1,330 and 1,500 head, but also the largest holder with 20,400. The mean holding for members of the third estate was 7,109 sheep, only slightly below the 7,190 mean for nobles. Rank was not the criterion for particular location preference.

What, then, did the doganal rich have in common besides their privilege to particular pastures? Wealth appears to be a necessary but not sufficient cause for particular location status. All large holders were not assigned to particular locations to graze their sheep in the locations of the rich. Rank seems to be all the more insignificant unless an individual was both a large holder and a member of one of the first two estates. Mean flock size for members of the first and second estate in particular locations compared to those in the general locations was more than three-fourths larger (5,257 to 2,928, or 180 percent). Equally important may have been familial and *nazione* connections. Ten of the thirty-nine *locati* (25.6 percent) were members of the same family. Could old patron-client networks have established the particular locations? Similarly, fifteen of the thirty *locati* with identifiable towns of origin came from the two trail head towns of Aquila (ten) and Sulmona (five). Could the major towns of the Abruzzi have been the recipients of particular locations privilege? In sum, an analysis of the *ricchi* in 1559 reveals that this dominant doganal "class" was not defined by the exclusive test of wealth or order, family, or place of origin. Its privileges to particular locations pasture were hereditary contracts which dated back to the foundation of the particular locations in 1470 and were held in perpetuity by *locati* who, in all probability, possessed some combination of all these traits.

Once the particular locations were abolished in 1586, however, what happened to the rich? The *ricchi* who were defined by pasture privilege between 1470 and 1586 were included with all other *locati* in the leveling of general pasture distribution. Who, then, became the "rich" of doganal complaint thereafter? It is to those rich after 1586—all large holders defined by flock size—that we must now turn.

The Structure of Stratification (1589–1788)

A complete serial record of global tax lists dating from soon after the 1585/86 unification of general and particular locations has been preserved in the doganal archive. I have chosen eleven random points for complete analysis from the serial record of global tax lists in Foggia: 1591, 1604, 1619, and every twenty years thereafter: 1639, 1659, 1979, 1699, 1719, 1739, 1759, and 1779. In order to control my sample ensuring that none of these years is anomalous, I have selected eight locations (one-third of the locations) and analyzed their social structure over the long term at 5-year intervals. that is, forty observation points over the 188-year period.[7] The composite portrait drawn from my eleven-point survey of 25,368 cases provides a definitive description of the distribution of wealth and stratification by status in the pastoral economy at the eleven discrete moments. By comparing these structures over time, the investment strategies employed by graziers and the policy of the doganal government in moving from one economic conjuncture to another comes into sharper focus.

First, for the long-term conjuncture, 13,352 *padroni* in the abbreviated tax lists or 25,368 *padroni* and *padroncelli* in the global tax lists professed 9,766,133 sheep in the eleven-year cross-section; that is, in mean terms, 1,223 *padroni* only or 2,306 total *locati,* who grazed sheep with mean flock sizes of 731 or 385 head respectively, had a total sheep wealth of 887,830 head in the general locations. Averages, however, falsify the data because of the incremental change in the economic conjuncture of the pastoral economy. Annual tax rolls conform to my earlier portrait of commercial demand in the dogana and should be analyzed according to its five periods:

1. 1447–94   positive (0 examples)
2. 1494–1550 negative (0 examples)
3. 1550–1612 positive (2 examples); mean wealth: 1,801,258 sheep
4. 1612–86   negative (4 examples); mean wealth: 633,116 sheep
5. 1686–1806 positive (5 examples); mean wealth: 726,230 sheep

Let us review the basis of this periodization in terms of the tax list data. Although periods 1 and 2 lie outside of the run of documentation, both were functions of political consolidation by the conquering Aragonese and Spanish respectively. The shift to greater investment in period 3 corresponded to the disparity between wheat and wool prices, to Philip II's fiscal needs at the time of his second bankruptcy in 1575, and to the Indian summer of the Italian economy. Periods 3 and 4, for their part, were dramatically divided by the great sheep mortality of 1612. But a closer look at the figures from the eight locations in this forty sample years suggests that the seventeenth-century crisis in Foggia was not that simple. If only 600,000 sheep survived that winter, one-half of that number (281,230 head) were grazing on one-third of the locations by 1614, and 347,975 head by 1619. Flock size was building up again. Other evidence confirms that another severe winter in 1622 and the general failure of credit in Italy in the 1620s turned a cyclical downturn into a long-term depression.[8] Recovery from the seventeenth-century crisis in period 4 was slow. The number of *locati* participating in doganal activity reflected the uncertain fortunes of pastoralism. During period 4, one of depression, *locati* numbers roughly doubled in the eight-location forty-year sample, from 392 to 774 inscribed *padroni*. With demographic, fiscal, and credit changes after 1660, the number of *locati* dropped back to its earlier levels. Although pastoral production totals did not return to the norm until the 1690s, the process of slow recovery among investors was underway, and it never fell back again after the infusion of *voce* credit in the 1680s. Period 5 *squarciafogli*, however, still record a relatively low number of total sheep because after 1686 the rich were again separated from the poor.

The distribution of wealth according to taxable sheep follows a predictable pattern. If only the *padroni* listed in the abbreviated tax lists are counted for the real, fixed sheep, the top 10 percent of the graziers professed 40.3 percent of the wealth. If we add the 18.0 percent held by the second decile, 20 percent of the sheepowners controlled almost 60 percent of the sheep. Including the *padroncelli*, that is, counting all *locati* in the global tax lists skews the distinction between rich and poor even more to the top: 10 percent of the graziers owned 52.3 percent of the wealth, and 20 percent held almost 70 percent.

Lorenz curves of this distribution in the eleven sample years vary slightly by time.9 In boom times more equality among sheepowners is exhibited, and in lean times, less. As the seventeenth-century crisis deepened, the inequality in wealth among graziers increased, and more wealth was concentrated in fewer hands by 1659. With recovery, the original pattern of slightly less inequality returned, but never to the same lower level as before the crisis. At all times, the basic inequality among sheep holders was evident.

Measurement of wealth by deciles of owners, however, distorts our understanding of social structure in the pastoral economy because it divides owners arbitrarily by a numerical ranking instead of some logical, internal category. Decile ranking does not take into account the significance of the gradient between ranks, that is, the size of the individual flock.

The assumption behind the division of holders into categories defined by flock size derives from anthropological studies of pastoral nomadism.[10] Because of ecological constraints, an equilibrium between variables of available pastures, animal numbers, and the human population working with or living off the animals must be maintained. Two sets of variables, which are both species specific, operate to determine minimum, maximum, and optimum herd size for viability and efficiency among pastoralists. First, herd size is a function of internal parameters which are set by animal behavior—the grazing needs of sheep; the relationship between intake and movement measured in distance and time; the quantity and quality of pasture with regard to both seasonal (climatic) and regional (topographical) variation; and finally, the comparative reproduction rates and life span which establish population growth and allelomimetic behavior (animal attachments important in herding). Second, herd size reflects the external agency of man and his decisions—the number of animals which one shepherd can handle effectively; the number needed for subsistence; or, if nonpastoral foods supplement the diet, the number which makes economic sense in the market.

Further, anthropologists tell us that, because of the close correlation between the numbers of animals and the numbers of shepherds, herd size influences the social structure of the herders. Thus, the social organization of pastoralists assumes a distinctive shape. The uncertainties of nature, animals, and man in a migratory livelihood system are counterbalanced by a rigidification of social structure and an elaboration of law or custom.

Pastoralism in the dogana of Foggia is no exception. If we recall the doganal practice outlined in part 1, the intricacies of doganal law, the distinctions between pastures (general locations and particular locations), the details of sheep demography and the fluctuations of the external market assume a far greater meaning than mere background information on material life. They point us toward a model of social organization which must take into account large-scale enterprise rather than subsistence herding, and the long-term variation rather than structural simplification. The only way to picture the *locati*'s social structure, then, would be to divide the *locati* into stratified categories according to wealth, as measured by flock size, over time.

Let us posit three categories:

1. Large holders professing more than 2,000 sheep
2. Middling holders professing 201–2,000 sheep
3. Small holders with 200 or fewer head

The idea of a tripartite division of society by wealth is not anachronistic theory. In 1764, in its attempt to collect unpaid *fida* debts at the end of the mid-eighteenth-century famine, the dogana "divided all the ranks (*tutto l'ordine*) of the *locati* into three different classes (*ceti*)" according to their ability to pay.[11] The first class comprised "barons, religious foundations, and other wealthy individuals who could pay independently of their income from pastoralism." The second class was made up of "persons of middle state who would not find it difficult to obtain credit to settle their debts." The third class was the "true poor" who possessed nothing more than the sheep which they wintered in Puglia. Special provisions were made for their debts to be postponed until the November following each spring fair, with their wool held on deposit by the dogana. My structural division of society into three groups thus conforms to doganal practice. But how does one determine the dividing lines between categories? How many sheep made an owner one of independent means, one who was credit worthy, or a subsistence herder?

The numerical basis of my categories is not arbitrary. For larger herds, 2,000 head defined the legal limit for *locati;* and for smaller herds, one shepherd was needed for every 200 sheep.[12] Anthropologists, geographers, historians, and demographers corroborate these maxima and minima in their research and agree upon a 200–500 optimum flock size for sheep.[13]

Here a reminder of the relationship between the productivity and the efficiency of work for small holders is important. It appears that small herds of 80–100 sheep were more profitable since they produced proportionately more milk, meat, and wool than large herds because hired help was unreliable and often unfaithful, whereas the self-employed shepherd increased his hours of labor and attentiveness.[14] Had the extensive sheepherding and grain-producing latifundia of southern Italy squeezed these smaller holders out of both pasture and markets by their capital alone? Delille argues that the relationship between rich and poor was not merely a balance of power defined by the size of their enterprise, but fundamentally an economic fact defined by the relationship between production and consumption.[15] First, the productivity advantage of smaller herds is canceled out by increased consumption costs. Since small holdings required more intensive labor, which, in turn, demanded more food, the increase in productivity did not necessarily compensate for the considerable difference in the proportion of that product consumed vis-à-vis the economies of scale that may have kept the consumption costs down for a larger work force.[16] Second, large holders hired employees in numbers equal to or less than the optimum rates for smaller flocks in order to raise productivity, especially for seasonal efficiency.[17]

Since the comparative advantage of large versus small holdings appears to be insoluble, we should not be content, therefore, to define optimum flocks theoretically by the variables of pasture fertility, seasonal variation, animal behavior, shepherd's ability to control so many sheep, economic constraints, or the testimony of expert informants like Gaudiani or Onorati. In addition to checking these sources, I have verified the consensus figures in an empirical analysis of the global tax lists. My three categories of large, middling, and small are constructed from even smaller subdivisions of the raw data. Sheep holders with flocks smaller than the 2,000 legal maximum for large holders were divided into six categories by flock size: 1–50, 51–100, 101–200, 201–500, 501–1,000, and 1,001–2,000.[18] Further, each of these categories has been compared over the long term in order to determine any common patterns of ownership and wealth for all *locati* and for *padroni* alone.

The number of *locati* in the global tax lists, which includes all *padroni* and *padroncelli*, reveals that flock size changed over time (appendix C.1). In period 3 before the 1611/12 sheep mortality disaster, few flocks (9.5 percent mean) numbered 50 sheep or less, whereas about one-third of the flocks (34.5 percent mean) were larger than 500 head. Thereafter, in periods 4 and 5, these categories were reversed: almost one-third of the flocks (32.6 percent mean) had 50 sheep or less, and few flocks (15.2 percent mean) numbered over 500 head (table 11 and fig. 7). The favorable investment climate for pastoralism in period 3 encouraged larger flocks during the late sixteenth-century recovery of the Italian economy. The slackening of international demand in periods 4 and 5, on the other hand, cut the ranks of large holders in half. The very smallest holders of flocks under 50 head, for their part, tripled because, even in hard times, doganal investment bought judicial privileges which were worth some sacrifice.[19] If the typical doganal investment in periods 4 and 5, then, were not made by holders of flocks greater than 500 sheep nor by the smallest herders with 50 sheep or less, middling *locati*, holding 51–500 sheep, must have made up the 52.2 percent difference.

The global tax lists of *padroni* only confirm and clarify this conclusion (app. C-2). By counting *padroni* only, I have eliminated the *padroncelli* from enumeration, and the results should be skewed toward larger holders.[20] The category with the most investors, holders of flocks with 201–500 sheep, accounted for more than one-fourth (26.0 percent) of all doganal *padroni* in periods 4 and 5. The adjacent categories provide a neat, statistical deviation with a ratio of 2:2:3:5:3:2:1 (fig. 8). Only the first category (1–50 sheep) is out of proportion because of the presence of some vassal *padroni* who sought special doganal jurisdiction. The 201–500 category emerges as the focus of the largest concentration of investors and, therefore, the optimum size of flocks in the seventeenth and eighteenth centuries.

The anthropological literature on optimum flock size for sheep is thus confirmed if we count only cases of *locati* registration in the global tax lists for real, fixed sheep during the period from the seventeenth-century crisis through

TABLE 11 Ownership and Wealth by Flock Size (1619–1779) (In *Reali Fisse*)

Sample	Total	1–50 Head	51–100 Head	101–200 Head	201–500 Head	501–1,000 Head	1,001–2,000 Head	>2,000 Head
All *locati*								
Cases	2,190	713	396	372	377	180	100	52
	(100.1%)	(32.6%)	(18.1%)	(17.0%)	(17.2%)	(8.2%)	(4.6%)	(2.4%)
Wealth in ducats	684,374	22,528	32,882	59,121	126,714	132,729	142,726	167,674
	(100.0)	(3.3)	(4.8)	(8.6)	(18.5)	(19.4)	(20.9)	(24.5)
Mean flock size	312	34	84	160	337	738	1,434	3,233
Padroni only								
Cases	1,202	163	141	196	313	200	127	62
	(100.0)	(13.6)	(11.7)	(16.3)	(26.0)	(16.6)	(10.6)	(5.2)
Wealth in ducats	684,845	5,690	12,048	31,530	107,433	147,255	180,474	200,415
	(100.1)	(0.8)	(1.8)	(4.6)	(15.7)	(21.5)	(26.4)	(29.3)
Mean flock size	570	39	88	162	345	736	1,426	3,218

Source: Mean of period 4 (1619–79) and period 5 (1699–1779) *Squarciafogli*, table 6.

Notes: Differences between totals are due to transcription, coding, and rounding errors. They are, however, insignificant at the ± 0.0025 level.

FIGURE 7 Ownership by All *Locati* in the Seventeenth and Eighteenth Centuries (*Pecore reali fisse*)

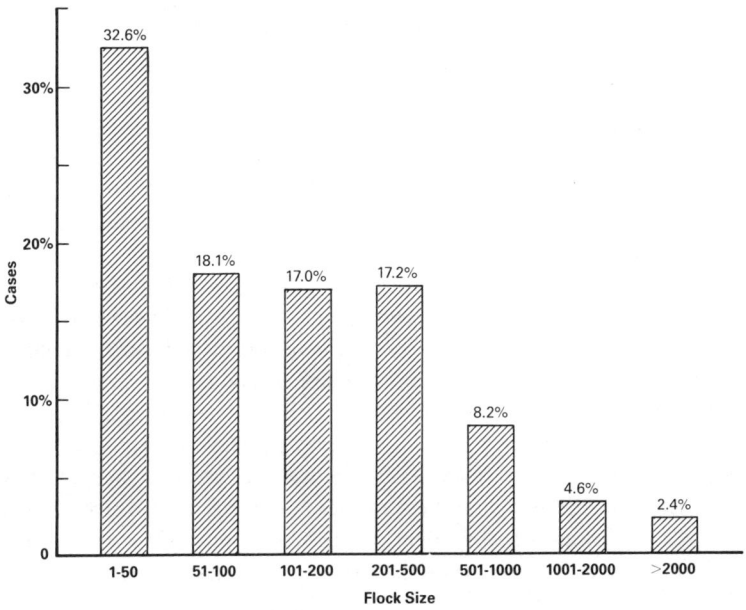

FIGURE 8 Ownership by *Padroni* Only in the Seventeenth and Eighteenth Centuries (*Pecore reali fisse*)

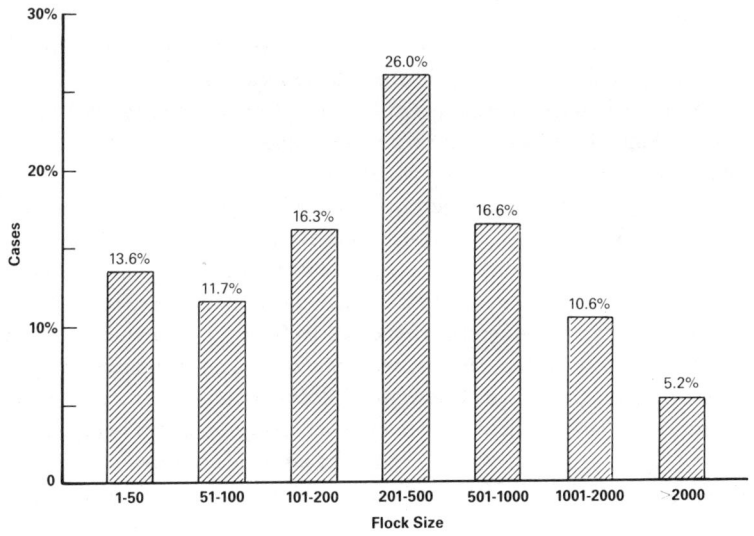

the eighteenth-century return to normalcy. By comparing anthropological theory and doganal practice, however, three important corollary conclusions should be emphasized. First, the economic fluctuations of the market caused optimum flock size to vary over the long term. Second, despite an ecologically optimum flock size, demand from the international market could still support cash cropping among a substantial number of large holders. Similarly, the benefits of doganal legal status tempted many to make token investments in pastoralism. Third, the numbers of *locati* with optimum flocks of 201–500 head did not necessarily ensure that they had power in the dogana. Since this was not a society of majority rule, only an examination of wealth will reveal who had economic clout (app. C-3).

The easiest categorization by wealth would be to follow the doganal distinction and divide holders into two groups—*i ricchi* and *i poveri*. But where was the poverty line drawn? If the criterion were optimum flock size, holders of more than 500 sheep—that is, those whose flocks needed more than one shepherd's full-time labor—would be the rich who held (depending on the counting of all *locati* or only *padroni*) 65 or 77 percent to the poor's 35 or 23 percent of the sheep. Many of these cases with more than 500 sheep, however, were owners with extended families or other unrelated *società* which combined their herds as a means of maximizing their labor input. They were certainly capital-intensive enterprises whose pastoralism was geared to the market, but whose fortune was entirely tied up in sheep. As far from the hard-core poor as a three-shepherd family with 600 sheep may have been, it was still even farther from the prince of Melfi and his eighty-seven-shepherd, 10,000-sheep investment. Only those owners with flocks greater than 2,000 sheep—that is, only owners who received special privileges to graze more sheep than the legal limit—should, therefore, be considered among the rich. Their number (62 cases) and their wealth (29 percent of the sheep) in the seventeenth and eighteenth centuries compare favorably with those of *padroni* in particular locations before the sixteenth-century unification of the locations.

I have used similar reasoning in conflating the remaining six categories into two. Among all *locati,* the wealth of holders with 1–200 sheep (16.7 percent) roughly equaled that of holders with 201–500 sheep (18.5 percent), with 501–1,000 sheep (19.4 percent), and with 1,001–2,000 sheep (20.9 percent) (fig. 9). This affinity of wealth, however, is misleading. An analysis of wealth of *padroni* only, which shakes out the *padroncelli* from our calculations, reveals a more graduated pyramid: 7.2, 15.7, 21.5, and 26.4 percent (almost a 1:2:3:4 ratio) for these four categories respectively (fig. 10). Owners with viable herds of 201–2,000 sheep, that is, with one to ten full time shepherds, had more in common than those whose small flocks required less than one shepherd's full-time labor. These owners of fewer than 200 sheep held extremely inefficient flocks unless they combined their animals under a single trail boss (*gargaro*), as the global tax lists often attest. Thus, by measuring the viability

FIGURE 9 Wealth of All *Locati* in the Seventeenth and Eighteenth Centuries (*Pecore reali fisse*)

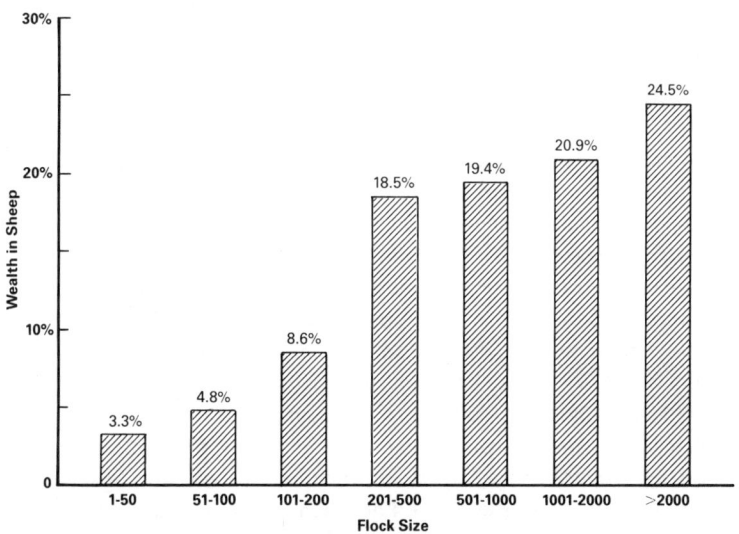

FIGURE 10 Wealth of *Padroni* Only in the Seventeenth and Eighteenth Centuries (*Pecore reali fisse*)

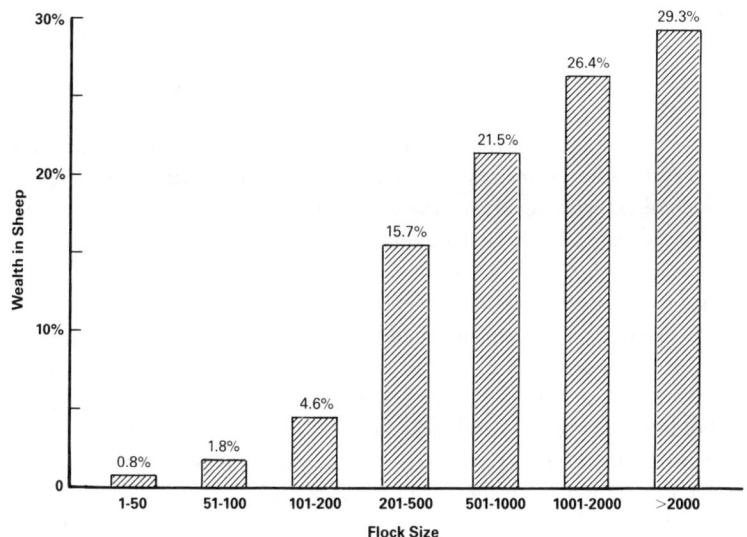

and efficiency of flocks, the truly small can be separated from middling holders.

Here an interesting comparison with the Spanish Mesta dramatizes the difference between the precarious existence of the subsistence grazier and the economic choices of the investment grazier counted among the smallest holders. If indeed, in 1561, 363 Spanish sheepowners had flocks under 50 sheep, with 32 percent of the total sheep wealth, Mesta wealth would contradict the mass of evidence on minimum flock size drawn from other transhumant settings around the Mediterranean. On the contrary, however, as Mickun's method of analyzing Mesta wealth in 1780 reveals, even higher percentages of small holders with flocks under 50 head (42.1 percent) controlled only 5.5 percent of total wealth in sheep.[21] The difference here is not just temporal, between sixteenth- and eighteenth-century sources. In the dogana the ownership profile is similar to that of Mickun: only 3.3 percent of the wealth was held by graziers or investors in nonviable flocks under 50 head. Subsistence graziers with minimum flocks of 50–200 head, on the other hand, held the majority of the wealth of small holders in Puglia (13.4 percent of total wealth) as in Castile (16.8 percent of total wealth). If 80–100 sheep formed the minimum viable flock worthy of one shepherd's energies, then many small-time Spanish investors with flocks under 50 sheep could not themselves have engaged in pastoral activity unless they amalgamated herds. The assumption that these smallest herders were subsistence shepherds must be nuanced. They were either impoverished pastoralists struggling *below* subsistence maintenance who had to rely upon their fellows to form larger, viable flocks; or vassals seeking to escape capricious baronial law courts; or wealthier owners who may have invested in the Mesta like a stock market which attracted small, capitalist-oriented speculators. The stakes many of these escaping vassals and small investors wagered may have been discretionary capital as opposed to the labor plus capital of middling holders or the substantial outlays of large holders. Hard times could force them to withdraw from the investment market and would make the wool supply even more sensitive to the secular curve. The existence of great numbers of the very smallest investors in Spain, thus, should alert us to three possibilities: the extreme poverty of the mass of Castilian graziers trying to attain the barest subsistence, the attractive appeal of regal rather than baronial justice, and the trickle-down effect of the international wool market which allowed for some small-time investments.

As I asserted at the beginning of the examination of the global tax lists, my categories are neither ideal nor imaginary but are derived from a statistical analysis of the data: the true small holders held flocks under 200 head, middling holders, 201–2,000, and large holders, over 2,000. With the structure of these three categories in place, then, we can examine them dynamically over time by comparing the percentage of holders in each category with the percentage of wealth they controlled over the three periods (app. C-4 and C-5; tables 12 and 13).

TABLE 12 *Squarciafogli* Social Stratification: *Padroni* Only

Period	Years	Small Holders 1–200	Middling Holders 201–2,000	Large Holders >2,000
3	1550–1611	7 percent owned 1 percent	72 percent owned 48 percent	21 percent owned 51 percent
4	1612–86	48 percent owned 11 percent	49 percent owned 67 percent	3 percent owned 23 percent
5	1686–1806	37 percent owned 7 percent	57 percent owned 60 percent	7 percent owned 33 percent

Sources: See appendix C-4.

TABLE 13 *Squarciafogli* Social Stratification: All *Locati*

Period	Years	Small Holders 1–200	Middling Holders 201–2,000	Large Holders >2,000
3	1550–1611	39 percent owned 6 percent	55 percent owned 58 percent	6 percent owned 36 percent
4	1612–86	73 percent owned 19 percent	26 percent owned 61 percent	2 percent owned 20 percent
5	1686–1806	63 percent owned 15 percent	34 percent owned 58 percent	3 percent owned 27 percent

Sources: See appendix C-5.

Changes in Structure (1589–1788)

A consistent pattern emerges from the *squarciafogli* tax lists in terms of wealth. Middling holders controlled about 60 percent of the wealth in all periods except period 3 of the abbreviated tax lists. Large holders held more wealth during the boom years of period 3 (54 percent or 36 percent, depending on how we count *locati*); thereafter, between one-fifth and one-third of the wealth. Small holders held more wealth during the lean years of period 4 (19 percent), roughly equivalent to the 20 percent held by large holders, according to the fullest accounting procedure, which includes the *padroncelli*.

Looking at the percentage of *locati* included in each of the three categories helps clarify these findings. Large holders numbered a mean 4 percent in all periods except period 3 of the abbreviated tax lists. Middling holders declined dramatically from period 3 to period 4, and then increased slightly with the better times of period 5. Small holders were at their peak during the seventeenth-century crisis described in period 4 but remain a significant majority (63 percent) of the total *locati* in period 5.

In other words, we might conclude that many new sheepowners invested in the dogana and that all graziers increased their herd size to maximum strength during the boom years of period 3. When crisis came in period 4, however, dominance shifted to the middling holders. The middling holders may have absorbed most of the sheep wealth lost by large holders, but the absolute number of owners in the middling categories remained relatively stable. Where did these rich investors go?

A core of large holders were wealthy enough to withstand any crisis, conservative enough not to change their heavy investments, or smart enough to diversify investments. Those other graziers falling down from large flock proprietorship may have had tenuous holdings to begin with. Either recently rising from middling status or belonging to a declining old family, some of these breeders slipped down a notch to become middling holders. The downward wave may have affected middling holders in the same way, some surviving and some dropping down to small holding. Others among the large holders may have liquidated their sheep wealth entirely and maintained only nominal existence in the dogana as small herders in order to receive the special judicial rights available to doganal inscribers.

During the period of boom, there was little need to maintain nominal membership in the dogana. If someone had money to invest in obtaining special doganal privileges, he had money to invest in sheep speculation. The falling off of the market after 1612, however, made profit taking more of a gamble. Maintaining special judicial privileges might be a safe investment, but economic speculation might not. Small holders who were keeping these judicial rights but decreasing their investment doubled both in absolute number and in percentage of participants.

There is no doubt, above all, that middling holders dominated the doganal institution. The *poveri locati* (small and middling holders) controlled at least one-half of doganal wealth in all periods and about three-fourths of wealth in the seventeenth and eighteenth centuries. The increase and influence of large holders was limited to period 3 of doganal growth. Although still controlling significant wealth in period 4 and on the increase in period 5, the finite number of large holders (a mean of 52) did not run the show. In fact, in terms of wealth, they were roughly equal to the vast army of the approximately 2,000 small holders annually inscribed in the dogana in period 4 (20 percent: 19 percent of the wealth), while only twice as wealthy as the yearly average of 1,300 small holders in period 5 (27 percent:15 percent). The collective wealth of the poor gave them their leverage against the rich.

Ownership status—the differences between independent *padroni, padroni* with dependents, and *padroncelli*—can also be analyzed as a social structural variable (table 14). Just as membership percentages in these three categories changed over time, wealth followed the same pattern. In period 3, wealth among the three categories of ownership status was distributed on a 2:1:1 ratio. The full impact of the seventeenth-century crisis had not struck in 1619, and owners had not yet realigned. For the body of period 4, however, *padroncelli* wealth declined to about 10 percent as ownership of sheep was concentrated in

TABLE 14 Ownership Status in the *Squarciafogli* (1591–1779) (In *Reali Fisse*)

Year	Padroni wealth/cases	Padroni *with* Padroncelli wealth/cases	Padroncelli wealth/cases
1591	814,391 (48.0%)	473,426 (27.9%)	408,508 (24.1%)
	610 (21.1)	515 (17.9)	1,760 (61.0)
1604	1,085,090 (56.7)	520,139 (27.2)	309,320 (24.1)
	959 (34.5)	536 (19.3)	1,284 (46.2)
1619	331,012 (37.4)	363,528 (41.1)	190,552 (21.5)
	487 (15.1)	646 (20.1)	2,085 (64.8)
1639	320,085 (53.1)	210,883 (35.0)	71,918 (11.9)
	712 (30.1)	453 (19.1)	1,203 (50.8)
1659	419,499 (71.2)	127,823 (21.7)	41,468 (7.0)
	1,696 (60.8)	387 (13.9)	707 (25.3)
1679	302,664 (66.3)	107,900 (23.6)	45,823 (10.0)
	483 (40.6)	274 (23.0)	433 (36.4)
1699	401,686 (55.5)	224,311 (31.0)	97,175 (13.4)
	627 (32.2)	430 (22.1)	893 (45.8)
1719	330,880 (41.7)	278,536 (35.1)	184,267 (23.2)
	505 (21.3)	483 (20.4)	1,382 (58.3)
1739	317,733 (46.8)	221,846 (32.7)	139,876 (20.6)
	574 (28.0)	380 (18.5)	1,097 (53.5)
1759	556,726 (78.6)	93,646 (13.2)	58,134 (8.2)
	932 (56.7)	204 (12.4)	508 (30.9)
1779	550,868 (76.4)	89,560 (12.4)	80,960 (11.2)
	1,333 (62.8)	226 (10.6)	564 (26.6)

Source: See table 6.
Note: Wealth in ducats.

the hands of *padroni*—about two-thirds for independent *padroni* and one-fourth for *padroni* heads of *collettive:* 13:5:2. The mid-eighteenth-century famine divided the long recovery of period 5 into an initial phase, with ownership rates of 5:3:2, followed by extreme concentration in the hands of independent *padroni* (75 percent) and only 10 percent in each of the other two categories: 15:2:2.

Unlike the previous analysis of wealth by flock size, in which we have seen that extreme wealth was concentrated into fewer hands and a larger middle sector eventually emerged, the seventeenth-century crisis of period 4 had only a temporary effect upon the structure of wealth by ownership status. *Padroncelli* declined during the crisis as independent *padroni* gained, but their original relationship returned at the beginning of the eighteenth century. What is dramatic here is the effect of the 1759–65 famine. Independent *padroni* captured the lion's share of wealth after that crisis and dominated the dogana until our documentation runs out.

TABLE 15 Relationship between *Padroni* Heads of *Collettive* and Their *Padroncelli* (1591–1779) (In *Reali Fisse*)

Year	Padroni *with* 0–24.9 *Percent of* Collettiva *Wealth*	Padroni *with* 25–49.9 *Percent of* Collettiva *Wealth*	Padroni *with* 50–74.9 *Percent of* Collettiva *Wealth*	Padroni *with* 75–100 *Percent of* Collettiva *Wealth*
1591	78 (15.1%)	156 (30.3%)	155 (30.1%)	126 (24.5%)
1604	43 (8.0)	127 (23.7)	198 (36.9)	168 (31.3)
1619	51 (7.9)	134 (20.7)	215 (33.3)	245 (37.9)
1639	24 (5.3)	66 (14.6)	129 (28.5)	227 (50.1)
1659	17 (4.4)	51 (13.2)	127 (32.8)	192 (49.6)
1679	14 (5.1)	57 (20.8)	95 (34.7)	108 (39.4)
1699	22 (5.1)	86 (20.0)	151 (35.1)	171 (39.8)
1719	58 (12.0)	139 (28.8)	156 (32.3)	129 (26.7)
1739	71 (18.7)	75 (19.7)	107 (28.2)	126 (33.2)
1759	35 (17.2)	48 (23.5)	50 (24.5)	70 (34.3)
1779	44 (19.5)	66 (29.2)	67 (29.6)	49 (21.7)
Mean	42 (10.2)	91 (22.1)	132 (32.1)	146 (35.5)

Source: See table 6.

The concentration of wealth in the hands of *padroni* only as a response to crises is demonstrated most clearly in the relationship between *padroni* heads of *collettive* and their *padroncelli* (table 15). If the *padroni* are divided into quartiles according to the percentage of *collettiva* wealth they controlled, *padroni* with less than 25 percent of the wealth numbered 10 percent of the cases; those with 25 percent and less than 50 percent of the wealth, 22 percent of the cases; those with 50 percent and less than 75 percent of the wealth, 32 percent of the cases; and those with 75 percent or more of the wealth, 36 percent of the cases. During the 1639 and 1659 low points of the seventeenth-century crisis, the 1:2:3:3 ratio was replaced by a 1:3:6:10 ratio (4.9, 14.0, 30.7, and 50.3 percent). *Padroni* with 75 percent or more of the wealth of their *collettiva* rose to over one-half the number counted. With 80 percent of the *padroni* heads of *collettive* owning 50 percent or more of the *collettiva* sheep, we can confirm the Lorenz curve findings that economic crisis concentrated wealth into fewer hands. Wealth fused in hard times and diffused in bad.

In individual terms, mean flock size of *padroni* with and without *collettive* was relatively equal (table 16). During periods 4 and 5, *padroni* flock size averaged 540 sheep for single owners and 477 for owners with dependents. In other words, mean size of *padroni* holdings conforms to the standard anthropological findings for flock size. The dependent *padroncelli*, on the other hand, at a mean of 105 head for periods 4 and 5, were primarily subsistence herders who were joining their flocks with others to create viable, economically pasturable units. Note also that comparing mean flock size according to

TABLE 16 Mean Flock Size by Ownership Status (1591–1779)

Year	Padroni	Padroni *with* Padroncelli	Padroncelli
1591	1,335	919	232
1604	1,131	970	241
1619	680	563	91
1639	450	466	60
1659	247	330	59
1679	627	394	106
1699	640	522	109
1719	655	577	133
1739	554	584	128
1759	597	459	114
1779	413	396	144

Source: See table 6.

Note: Mean for periods 4 and 5: *padroni*, 540; *padroni* with *padroncelli*, 477; *padroncelli*, 105.

ownership status also reveals change over time in three ways. First, mean flock size halved for all categories after the 1611/12 sheep death. Second, during the seventeenth-century crisis, mean flock size continued to decline from 1619 to 1659 before recovering. Third, at the bottom of the fall in 1659, we find a marked example of *padroni* with dependents having a higher mean flock size than single *padroni* (330:247). Crisis fostered cooperation as herds amalgamated.

An examination of wealth by social order from the global tax lists allows for further discrimination among large holders. Rank did not necessarily guarantee large holder status. Members of the first and second estates increased dramatically only in period 5, after the seventeenth-century crisis had been surmounted (table 17). Their resurgence went hand in hand with the reemergence of other large holders during the recovery in period 5 and was, therefore, tied to the secular trend, not their special status.

These two categories—clerical/noble holders and large holders—were exclusive and not necessarily overlapping realities. As late as 1659 investors from the higher orders of society comprised only a small percentage of the *locati* (less than 11 percent) and a little more than one-fourth of professed sheep wealth (27.1 percent). Large holders of flocks greater than 2,000 head who were members of the third estate, on the other hand, were important doganal members until the 1639 low point of the seventeenth-century crisis. Through the slow seventeenth-century recovery, religious institutions and members of the first and second estates increased their participation in the dogana by small increments. From 1659 they outnumbered the large holders approximately tenfold, thus making it obvious that most clerical and noble holders did not

TABLE 17 Large Holders and Social Orders in the Dogana (1591–1779)

Year	Large Holders >2,000		First and Second Estates	
	Cases	Wealth in Sheep	Cases	Wealth in Sheep
1591	181 (6.3%)	647,306 (38.2%)	221 (7.7%)	373,045 (22.0%)
1604	173 (6.2)	639,067 (33.4)	94 (3.4)	86,340 (4.5)
1619	56 (1.7)	162,720 (18.4)	143 (4.4)	92,919 (10.5)
1639	42 (1.7)	121,951 (20.2)	197 (8.3)	114,530 (12.9)
1659	35 (1.3)	124,017 (21.1)	305 (10.7)	159,655 (27.1)
1679	36 (3.0)	109,890 (24.1)	211 (17.7)	172,996 (37.9)
1699	59 (3.0)	186,230 (25.8)	425 (21.8)	319,995 (44.2)
1719	60 (2.5)	205,990 (26.0)	479 (20.2)	372,966 (47.0)
1739	61 (3.0)	214,604 (31.6)	487 (23.7)	337,589 (49.7)
1759	65 (4.0)	215,269 (30.4)	491 (29.9)	407,307 (57.5)
1779	52 (2.4)	168,394 (23.3)	822 (38.7)	475,163 (65.9)

Source: See table 6.

graze large flocks. They numbered about one-fourth of the *locati* (23.7 percent) and controlled only about one-half of the wealth (49.7 percent) by 1739. Their consolidation of doganal wealth, then, was effected only during the eighteenth century.

Despite the disproportionate wealth in the hands of some individual nobles and religious foundations, rank was not a prerequisite for invested wealth in the dogana. For every large holder like the prince of San Severo, with his 12,000 sheep in San Andrea, innumerable investors of the first and second estate (both *padroni* and *padroncelli*) were small holders with fewer than 200 sheep. The large holders, however, skewed mean holdings upward (table 18). As their mean wealth indicates, the average clerical and noble investor controlled about twice as much wealth as the average *locato*.

Another method of counting the sheep which were actually taxed emphasizes the conclusion that privilege, not wealth, determined social standing in the dogana. If we analyze all sheep professed in the global tax lists and reported in the abbreviated tax lists—that is, *pecore in alia tantum* in addition to the *pecore reali fisse*—we find that the total number of sheep jumps dramatically. There is no clear relationship, however, between the real, fixed sheep and those for this year only. Within each location, the rate of *professazione* of the *pecore in alia tantum* could vary greatly except during the time of fixed rates under the system of fixed agreement (1614–59). Thereafter. rates could vary among locations in the same year. We must remember, therefore, that the *pecore in alia tantum* bid was a reflection not of real sheep numbers, but of the need for pasture. Sheep were professed at N times their real number to bring the price of pasture to parity with that of arable. What these figures actually reflected, then, was

TABLE 18 Social Orders among All *Locati* (1591–1779) (First and Second Estates)

Year	Mean Wealth in Sheep	Percentage above Total Locati Mean
1591	1,688	287
1604	919	133
1619	650	236
1639	581	229
1659	523	248
1679	820	214
1699	753	203
1719	779	233
1739	693	209
1759	830	193
1779	578	170

Source: See table 6.

closed privileges to long-standing doganal participants who professed real, fixed sheep, and a modus vivendi for new investors who professed sheep for this year only to receive pasture.

If we compute our mathematically derived category of "adjusted sheep" (fixed, real and for this year only) from the global tax lists, we find that individual flock size is skewed even more toward larger holders than in the analysis of *padroni* only.[22] Nevertheless, the essential structure and conjuncture of holding in the dogana remains constant. Middling holders were the dominant group with about two-thirds of the cases and one-half of the wealth. Again, the economic shifts between periods accounted for the oscillation in the number of cases and the consolidation of wealth within the periods (appendix C.6).

Refeudalization? When and Why?

It would be easy to stop our story here and agree with Rosario Villari's refeudalization thesis, albeit for a later period and for different reasons.[23] The *ricchi* and eventually noble and ecclesiastical holders dominated in the dogana by the late eighteenth century, not the early and mid seventeenth. Thus, verifying their victory in the pastoral economy is not as important as determining when and why they arrived, as well as their staying power.

Ordona, the best predictor among our eight selected locations, provides a representative cross-section of doganal investors. I have charted the top ten owners in Ordona every five years through the seventeenth century. Only one large holder, the baronial family of the Marchesanos, held sheep before, during, and after the seventeenth-century crisis. Most large holders like the di Turris, Russos, Gallos, de Ferrarises, and di Sangros dropped out early in the century, with the 1611/12 sheep mortality again the main line of demarcation. The Collegio Romano of the Jesuits jumped in to fill the vacuum after 1614, as did the dukes of Ascoli (Ramamundo) after 1634, and the Chapel of the Most Holy Sacrament of Frattura after 1639. A second wave of investors joined Ordona after the mid-century plague and legal changes had fostered pastoral recovery: the Palmieros after 1665, the di Matteos after 1669, the Chapel of the Most Holy Annunciation of Cerciello after 1674, and the Mascitellos after 1680. The rise and fall of large and noble/ecclesiastical owners reflected an internal dynamic.

The longevity of the investments in Ordona is significant. Institutional investors like the Jesuits and religious chapels did not die out as did the lines of private families. These private families averaged only some twenty years in Ordona's top ten owners. The Marchesanos were exceptional in their ability to perpetuate their family.[24] And thus, the Marchesano and Palmiero families along with the religious institutions captured the leadership of the location as the dogana came out of its long crisis. One should conclude that the entrance of large holders into doganal membership resulted from the economic conjuncture and was not caused by their noble or ecclesiastical status.

In general terms, the doganal tax lists make clear that economic crisis fostered both greater differentiation between rich and poor and cooperation among the poor to stay the course. Hard times, especially the 1656 plague, and responsive changes in doganal law, such as the return to free bidding and the diffusion of *voce* pricing, encouraged investment in the sheep industry by those who could afford it. Rather than Villari's pre-Masaniello "baronial offensive" in the countryside, we should emphasize the post-1685 economic recovery as the rationale for baronial dominance.

Independent sources confirm these conclusions on investment strategies of large holders. Both the Certosa of San Martino in Naples and the Doria princes of Melfi increased the size of their herds in response to economic conditions. The Certosa of San Martino purchased a fief in Tressanti in 1598. Sheep numbers rose, as we have already noted, from around 2,000 head before the 1680s to more than double that thereafter.[25] Annual income from animal products averaged 14 percent of total Tressanti income in 1676/77 and rose to 31 percent by 1730.[26] The Dorias, for their part, grazed their sheep on the southern edge of the Tavoliere near their holdings in Melfi. Their account books trace sheep holdings on all their fiefs as princes of Melfi for ninety-two years from 1671/72 to 1763/64.[27] Before that date the Doria estates were primarily engaged in cereal agriculture. As we have seen, the 1656 plague precipitated a change in investment strategy. The preplague global tax lists in the location of Camarda (only one of the winter grazing locations pasturing Doria flocks) assigned 589 sheep to the Dorias, but immediately thereafter Doria sheep doubled to 1,200 head in 1657. By 1664 they professed 3,000 head, where they remained throughout Camarda's existence in the global tax lists. Overall, the Doria account books showed 7,000–9,000 head up to 1688, when the flocks began to increase dramatically, topping 10,000 by 1693. Numbers peaked in 1709 with 15,500 sheep and fell below 10,000 for only three years following the 1726 harsh winter, until the 1745 harsh winter halved the flocks down to the 6,000–7,000 level. Thereafter Doria sheep numbers leveled off, until the accounts cease in 1763/64 at the height of the great famine. Here is a perfect positive conjuncture of the pastoral over agricultural economy, from plague to famine (1656–1764).

Finally, the Jesuit farms in Puglia prove the rule. Four contiguous *masserie* were purchased in the early seventeenth century: Stornara and Stornarella in 1600, Ordona in 1604, and Orta in 1611.[28] All were speculative grain-producing investments purchased in the midst of a cyclical downturn. From the beginning, sheep were raised as a part of the balanced mix between agriculture and pastoral production. The global tax lists from Ordona portray a consistent level of pastoral investment reflected in budgetary income from the Jesuit archives. Animal products and animal breeding accounted for 16 percent of total income from 1644 to 1649, 19 percent for four years between 1683 and 1688, and 20 percent from 1694 to 1705.[29] Similarly, 31 percent of patrimonial income came from animals between 1683 and 1688 and 22 percent between 1697 and 1707.[30] The Jesuits held their agricultural/pastoral investments in Puglia in a steady state of balance between cash cropping for wheat and for wool on a 80 percent:20 percent ratio. They were not expanding at the expense of their smaller neighbors, but weathering the long seventeenth-century crisis on the strength of their diversified agricultural and pastoral holdings.

State Policy toward Rich and Poor

What conclusions can be drawn about doganal social structure? The oscillations of the economic curve sharpened the conflict between large holders and everyone else. In response to secular trends and social conflict, then, tax policy, *voce* pricing, and pasture distribution policy were the dogana's primary maintenance mechanisms to mediate tension. A detailed review of the seventeenth-century crisis in the dogana reveals the role of the state in attempting to stimulate recovery.

After the 1611/12 sheep mortality, the new viceroy, Lemos, initiated a new *modo di vivere* in 1615. This fixed agreement was initially accepted by the *locati* on a set of conditions which included a stable, unchanging group of high officers (doganiero, *auditore,* and two *credenzieri*) who would form an impartial tribunal in Foggia.[31] Unfortunately for the *locati*, the state's promise was not kept, and, although the sale of the office of doganiero was suspended, the other officers were changed annually. With the top officials in constant flux, the minor officers, who were far less concerned about affairs of state than about their own personal fortune, played an inordinate role in day-to-day management. By the end of the five-year term of the first fixed agreement contract, therefore, the small and poor *locati* "lamented" the *mal governo* which favored the rich and powerful.[32] With the change from voluntary to forced *professazione*, large holders were claiming fewer sheep than they actually held; for example, a 10,000-head flock was professed at 3,000 or 4,000 to avoid taxes. There was no threat of insufficient pasture because reduced sheep numbers removed the need to compete for scarce resources. These false declarations defrauded the poor, who would be required to make up the tax differential between real sheep and the fixed assessment. A numeration or certification of the true number of sheep was proposed.

In March 1624, then, the new doganal governor, Mattia Casanata, arranged for an immediate, accurate sheep census and a revised arrangement with the *locati*. Before the following autumn season could see the reforms put into effect, however, the needs of the state treasury forced the viceroy to sell the office of doganiero. Extortions multiplied under the new doganiero, Giuseppe Bernauda, to the extent that the 1625 governor, Fabio Capece Galeota, recommended the suspension of Bernauda's office. Galeota then negotiated a new three-year fixed agreement with the *locati* in 1626, which was renewed again in 1629.[33] When Bernauda was reinstated in 1630, he attempted a rapprochement with the *locati* and succeeded in persuading them to renew the fixed agreement contract in 1633.

In 1634 the doganal *credenziero* Gian Luigi Corcione forwarded an eight-point critique of the fixed agreement system's endemic abuses to the viceroy.[34] The abuse of poor *locati* by the rich constituted the first two items. In item 1 he described the unbearable burden of the "poor and middling *locati*," who were required to pay taxes on more sheep than they owned. Item 2 explained the problem in terms of the unequal weight imposed by such indirect taxation. Because the total tax obligation was fixed, tax rates and sheep numbers were gerrymandered according to that year's needs. In other words, when numbers rose five or six times above a *locati*'s real holdings, the tax for 500 or 600 rather than 100 head had to be paid. Corcione pointed out that such fixed taxes were actually regressive. The poor paid more than their fair share. "Contrary to the conventions of the world where expenses diverge among persons: Princes eat like Princes, Barons like Barons, private citizens like private citizens, and the Poor like the Poor, the poor *locato* is obliged to bear the same expenses for his sheep as the rich and powerful." Taxes on sheep were thus so high that the poor were required to sell their sheep capital just to pay taxes. Such a downward spiral helps explain the fall in the number of small investors and the overall decline in income as the seventeenth-century crisis worsened.

The official response prepared by the other doganal officers, however, countered Corcione's argument head on.[35] They claimed that no *locato* was burdened in the least. The number of real sheep in the account books was not diminishing, but increasing. My analysis of the eight locations in the global tax lists does not substantiate this assertion. On the contrary, after the initial rise in real, fixed sheep with the establishment of the fixed agreement tax, the number of sheep slowly eroded: 1614, 281,220 sheep; 1619, 347,975 sheep; 1624, 289,240 sheep; 1628, 201,293 sheep; 1634, 215,291 sheep.[36] Further, the fixed agreement apologists argued that the tax rates for the poor were of "just and equal weight." Again, this point was misleading and self-serving. The rate may have been proportional, but its impact was disproportionatelly absorbed by the poor.[37]

This seventeenth-century tax debate is reminiscent of the fairness issue in contemporary arguments over tax reform and graduated rates. Theoretical equality under the law may be appealing to the haves, but paying equal rates is not justice for the have-nots. If everyone paid at the same rate, the poor collectively would be paying a greater share of the overall tax burden. In terms of the individual *povero,* the squeeze is even more severe. His share is a much higher percentage of his disposable income and, therefore, keeps him at subsistence levels. On the other hand, equalizing tax rates necessarily favored the large holders with more assets because they could absorb their losses by cutting their conspicuous expenditures on luxury goods.

Despite the logical fallacies in the arguments of those opposed to changing the fixed agreement system, the need to collect revenues at all costs forced the Sommaria to shelve a *giunta* of investigation and reconfirm fixed agreement in the new contract of 1637.[38] In 1637, however, Bernauda died in office, and the new Genoese purchaser of the doganiero office, Agostino Managlia, under his deputy, Giambattista della Chiesa, reignited the controversy over frauds and favoritism by his overt disregard for *locati* equality. The Sommaria finally began to agree with the complaints of the poor and authorized another sheep numeration.[39] This *consulta* recognized that the mounting emergency demanded immediate action. "With more than a paternal eye," the Sommaria turned its attention to correcting the "frauds by the rich and powerful *locati*" against the "major part of the sheepowners' guild, the poor." The Sommaria presidents were convinced of the importance of "distributing the weight of the annual 190,000-ducat tax" more equitably. Their goal was clearly summarized in a 1639 follow-up *consulta:* "Each *locato,* whether rich or poor, whether weak or powerful, should pay the part which he takes."[40]

The depths of doganal decline, however, had not been fully appreciated until the sheep count had been completed. From the last numeration, during Berardino Montalvo's 1624 governance, to that of 1639, numbers had declined from 1.2 million to only 600,000, or, according to a 1644 account, from 1.5 million to 500,000 head.[41] That the dogana had shrunk to somewhere between one-half and one-third its normal size necessarily put undue burdens on all *locati* to pay the fixed agreement tax. Despite the inequities in the *modo di vivere* for the *locati,* the Sommaria became ever more concerned about maintaining its income base. The expedient of gaining the fixed agreement revenue, therefore, was renewed in 1639 and again in 1642, while the polemic on its prejudicial effects, both to state income and to *locati* justice, intensified.

Redressing the grievances of the poor was impractical as long as the doganal industry was so depressed. As much as the state wished to restore voluntary professions and regain higher revenues, according to regent Galeota's 1645 proposal, obstacles arose.[42] First, the fixed agreement tax, which was supposed to guarantee the state's annual income at a minimal level, could not be met. *Locati* fell into arrears and began to accumulate large debts in back taxes (*residui*). If paper credit and paper debits made the doganal system an illusory dream, abandoning fixed agreement would only confirm an even more disastrous reality. Further, as long as the demand of international buyers for wool declined, any hope of recovery seemed distant. Finally, the large and powerful holders opposed free bidding because they enjoyed unchecked success with the collusion of corrupt doganal officers.

One cause of the mounting grazier debt was the price paid for unused pasture.[43] In 1647 the deputies of the sheepowners' guild petitioned the Sommaria to exempt the *locati* from their tax payment on that portion of unused fodder which was assigned to agriculturists after the autumn distribution of pasture to the graziers. In their reduced condition, the pastoralists only requested a "just and proportionate *fida*" based upon land actually used. In the 1648/49 season, the new governor, Ettore Capecelatro, seconded these and other sheepowners' guild requests.[44] By 1655 the king's councils in Spain were debating remedies for the numerous abuses to the *poveri locati* in Foggia.[45] The memorial which they considered used extraordinarily vivid language to summarize the five grave abuses which had "killed . . . oppressed . . . annihilated . . . and reduced the poor almost totally to breathing corpses"! The poor were subject to extra, illegal taxes at various passes in and out of Puglia; unequal justice, even condemnation without defense; condemnation without appeal or review; suspension of grazing rights before assignment to winter pastures; and forceful confiscation of taxes without consent.

As the debate closed in on the question of the *modo di vivere* by 1661, the Spanish leadership and the Sommaria in Naples hoped to find the "causes of the dogana's deterioration and means for its restoration."[46] In order to prevent total ruin, return to the system of free bidding appeared to be the only alternative. Voluntary professions provided three advantages. First, tax underestimation could be prevented and an accurate numeration of sheep provided. Second, sheep which had been crossing over to the Papal States could be attracted once again to Puglia. Third, the problem of unpaid *fida*, the *residuos* in this Spanish document, would be resolved. Thus, the decree of 2 July 1661 formalized the long-awaited return to voluntary sheep estimation.[47]

In spite of the measures initiated by the state to stimulate the seventeenth-century doganal economy, it did not respond and continued to drift through the 1660s and 1670s. In a 1679 memorial, one Sigismundo della Joria of Chieti reported on pastoral affairs in the Doganella d'Abruzzo.[48] He argued that "the disorders of bad government," rather than bad weather or other accidents, were responsible for the continued decline in patrimonial income and impoverishment of the *locati*. "Extravagent tax burdens" and "particular privileges" were detrimental to "all poor vassals." Thus, as the poor were being overtaxed out of the pastoral economy, wealthy investors were realigning their holdings for the anticipated recovery. Social structural changes among owners were becoming apparent as two other factors, in addition to doganal reform, helped recharge the pastoral industry. First, the plague of 1656, which lowered population kingdomwide, made labor scarce and eased grain demand. Second, the infusion of credit, especially through the public price (*prezzo alla voce*). became more widespread in the 1680s. The Malthusian squeeze and merchant demand were conspiring to revive pastoral dominance. Finally, in 1685, with economic recovery sputtering in the dogana, the particular locations were restored as an expedient to stimulate the pastoral economy by putting more capital into the hands of the rich investors—a kind of supply-side tax incentive. Throughout the eighteenth century the rich, then, continued to squeeze the poor of money which would have otherwise gone to the state.

As the eighteenth-century recovery heated up, so did the conflict between rich and poor. In 1709 Governor Andrea Guerriero y Torres listed seventeen abuses and their remedies based upon his previous experience as governor eleven years earlier.[49] He found "the first and principal [abuse to be] the violence which the particular and poor *locati* suffer from the Powerful." In particular, Guerriero cited a fraud contrary to ancient doganal custom which was newly practiced by titled and powerful *locati* in the occupation of more than one (often four or five) locations. Similarly, in an undated list of five abuses and six extortions for which the *locati* sought redress, the new Austrian Habsburg governors were informed of doganal problems from before the time of President Vidman in 1698.[50] The first abuse emphasized the doganal tradition of just laws and how their circumvention was detrimental not only to the poor *locati*, but also to the *Real Patrimonio*. The four following items outlined how the poor suffered at the hands of rapacious Sommaria presidents; how their special tribunal had been so eroded that they suffered the same bad fortune as litigants in Naples; how the sale of offices to members of the same family in perpetuity was prejudicial to good government; and finally, how the office of general syndic had been demeaned, funds illegally expended, and favoritism in pasture distribution normalized. In another document of the Austrian period, circa 1721, the traditional doganal instructions were invoked for a precedent on favoritism to poor subjects who were no longer so well treated.[51] Charity wool which was given to the Franciscans should be taken from the big holders, not the small dependent sheepowners (*padroncelli*). *Locati* taxes were often dispersed among "relatives, servants, and dependents of doganal officials, in prejudice to the poor, and then they were noted as Secret Alms." The complaints of the poor against officers and the rich were "infinite," and we can conclude, as does this document, "To describe them all would make for a long story which would be tedious and horrible."

Evidence from another source, the number of particular syndics in the parliaments of the *generalità de' locati,* as we have already seen, suggests that the rich did not have such a sweeping victory. Although rich holders were the preferred representatives of the *locati* in the period of maximum doganal expansion before the 1611 sheep mortality, middling holders had replaced them by 1750, after the restructuring during the long seventeenth-century crisis. Some accommodation had been made for the poor to share power because their collective wealth could not be denied. Particular syndics' duties were not those of the rich, noble, or legal experts who served as general syndics.[52] Thus, in order to appease the great majority of middling and small holders whose wealth was hardly insignificant, the state became a partner with their democratic assembly--a legally defined commune, rather than a simple guild—and encouraged the replacement of rich parliamentary delegates with middling holders.

Special concern for the poor continued in three other areas in the last half of the eighteenth century. The state mediated relationships between the *locati* and the state, between the *locati* and state officers, and among the *locati* themselves. First, for the state, with regard to unpaid state taxes, the poor were given special payment extensions in the 1764 and 1791 decrees.[53] In 1790, for example, they could pay one-half their obligations immediately that spring and postpone the other half, making one payment in the following December and the rest at the next spring fair with that year's wool yield as collateral. Second, state officers, such as the *avvocato de' poveri,* were constantly monitored. Because of weak legal defense of the poor, Domenico Cimaglia was suspended from office by a state visit in 1802.[54] Third, with the competition for pasture intensifying as sheep numbers increased in the eighteenth century, rich and poor came into greater conflict. In 1785 the rules for distribution of the marginal pastures of the extraordinary pastures were reexamined.[55] Non-*locati* were forbidden access to these extraordinary pastures, and the principles of the free bidding were reaffirmed for their distribution.

In general, then, windfall profits, which came from the competitive price of pasture versus agricultural land, could be surrendered by the state to the rich in order to placate them for the erosion of their privileges and spur economic recovery, but the overwhelming economic participation of middling and small holders necessitated that they be compensated with political power in the *generalità,* provided economic concessions on tax obligations, and ensured competent legal counsel. The state, therefore, manipulated livelihood groups and the social and economic classes within them in a precarious balancing act in order to pacify the countryside and maintain good government.

Political policy balanced traditional privileges against the invisible hand of the market and the not-so-invisible hands of collective strength. The vaunted freedom of the shepherds was subject to the secular curve and the state's ability to enforce its power. Rich and poor did not rise and fall according to the mythology of proverbial wisdom, but by the dynamic of the market and the policy of the state. Rich versus poor and wheat versus wool were played off against one another to inhibit changes and to reinforce the status quo.

PART 3
La Ragion dello Stato

Reasons of state dictated self-maintenance, and the first rule of such a policy was "to conserve and increase" the royal patrimony. But money alone was never the sole goal of the absolutist state. As we have seen in the laws regulating space and time in the customhouse in part 1 and in the state's policy toward rich and poor sheepowners in part 2, the Neapolitan government sought to divide and conquer divergent interest groups and make them dependent upon the centralized state.

Part 3 explores state rationale more deeply, especially as it applied to the mediation between livelihood groups. Peace in the urban capital could be guaranteed only by sufficient grain supplies, a necessity which could only be procured by satisfying the needs of both agriculturists and pastoralists. If the sheepowners and their shepherds were not properly cared for, not only would the state treasury diminish, but violence in the countryside would threaten all rural production.

6 Royal Patrimony, Royal Justice, Royal Office

An Abruzzese folk tale of "One-Eye" (*Occhio-in-fronte*) retells Homer's story of Odysseus and Polyphemus. The numerous versions, collected in various places in 1883, transform Odysseus' sailing companions into friars, shepherds, students, or beggars.[1] All of the variants, thus, sing of marginal, traveling men in barren, alien climes who must confront fear and death with resourcefulness.

This popular tale of mountain shepherding culture emphasizes the cleverness of the two combatants and, in so doing, reminds us of the mentalities of the antagonistic groups sharing the pastoral landscape. The blinded giant cleverly inspects each sheep one by one in his attempt to catch his quarry, in the same way that the state monitored sheep numbers in the Foggian customhouse system to maintain its dominion. The ability of a trickster, like Odysseus-cum-friar/shepherd/student/beggar, to outsmart the one-eyed giant against all odds, on the other hand, recalls the sheepowners' self-image of self-reliance and freedom. Resident proprietor and traveler are at odds, just as the agriculturist and pastoralist are in competition.

Sheep Numbers and State Income

Numbering the sheep wintering in the Tavoliere and the income they generated for the royal patrimony is as problematic as the count of the blinded cyclops. Actual counting of sheep ended in 1553 with the establishment of the new *modo di vivere* for collecting taxes, voluntary bidding. The system changed twice more: fixed contracts or forced bidding, 1615–60; and the reestablishment of voluntary bidding, 1661–1806. In addition to numeration for tax purposes, sheep could also be counted after high mortalities in bad winters or during reforms and official visits. How can one distinguish between real sheep and tax-fiction sheep, between living sheep and dead ones? Any long-term series, therefore, runs the risk of comparing incompatible data.

Within the Tavoliere's ecological limit of 2.5 million head, sheep flocks grew and contracted with the economic conjuncture already outlined—three periods of growth separated by two of decline between 1447 and 1806:

1447–94   Growth to 1.7 million before the 1474 sheep mortality
           Mean: 1 million sheep and 100,000 ducats in income

FIGURE 11 Sheep in Foggia (1536–1805)

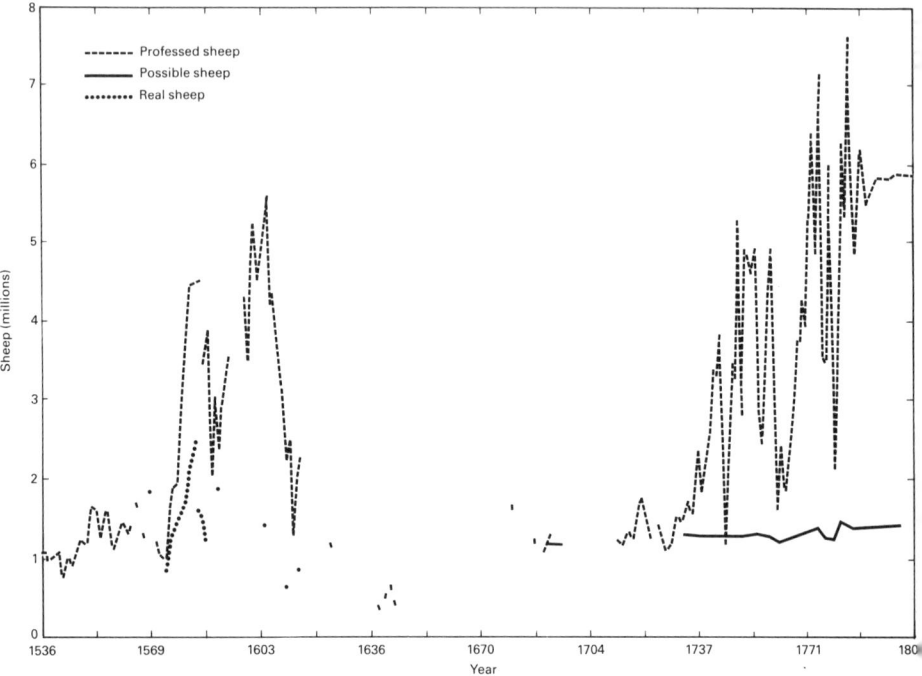

1494–1550	Decline to 600,000 sheep during the French invasions
	Mean: 1 million sheep and 100,000 ducats in income
1550–1612	Growth to 2.4 million sheep in the economic Indian summer
	Mean: 1.5 million sheep and 450,000 ducats in income
1612–86	Decline to 500,000 sheep after the 1611/12 sheep mortality
	Mean: 0.5–0.75 million sheep and 200,000 ducats in income
1686–1806	Growth to 1.7 million during the eighteenth-century boom
	Mean: 1.1 million sheep and 250,000 ducats in income

(See appendix D and fig. 11.) Even at the low point of grazier fortunes after 1.3 million sheep died in 1611/12, sheep never fell below one-half million. Such a decline was not a trivial matter for the Neapolitan treasury. The Kingdom had tied its very livelihood to the lives of sheep; state revenues depended heavily upon the pastoral economy.

A serial list of customhouse income replicates the same quantitative

FIGURE 12 Sheep Income in Foggia (1536–1805) (Ducats)

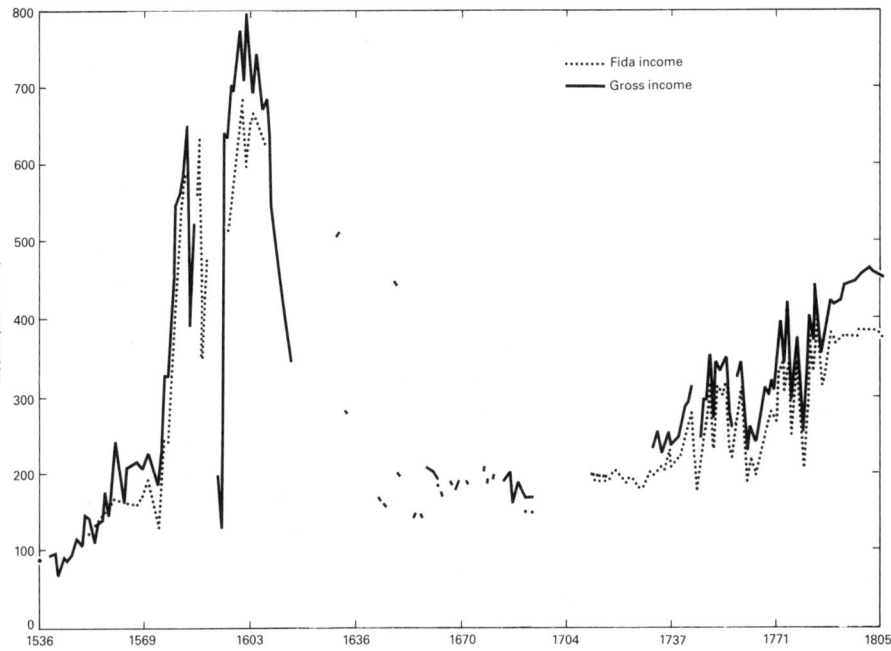

problems encountered in sheep numeration (app. D and fig. 12). Questions of when, how, and why the income was calculated, as well as what was included, make all our numbers problematic. Are the totals gross or net income? Do they include doganella and *terre salde* income? Are uncollected revenues owed but not yet paid (*residui*) included? Have overhead from salaries, pasture rents, or liens and concessions been subtracted? Who made the accounting, and when? Was it the customhouse officers or the budget office in Naples? Was it money actually collected or projected? Was it counted in the spring or when the yearly books were closed in August? Finally, how does one compare income collected at varying rates: the 50 percent tax rate increase of 1556, free bidding during the sixteenth-century inflation, the seventeenth-century fixed contracts, the 20 percent surtax after 1709? Numbers are not what they seem.

"Sheep in the Air"

One example illustrates the dilemma of counting sheep and income. As we have seen, the 5.5 million sheep professed in 1604/05 were highly fictitious, and the 700,000 ducats of annual income at the turn of the century were a kind of accounting legerdemain. Both of these anomalies in sheep and income

arose from the tax collection system of free bidding.[2] It took an emergency—
the budgetary crunch of Philip II's second bankruptcy of 1575—to transform
the sheep and income profile. Fabrizio di Sangro, doganiero from 7 February
1574 through December 1581, engineered the spectacular innovation of inflated sheep bids, and his eventual reward was promotion to higher office in the
Neapolitan capital.

The rise in sheep numbers and income was dramatic. A global balance
sheet of professed sheep with gross and net income during Fabrizio di Sangro's
tenure shows annual incremental growth from 1574 to 1581: from 1 million to
4 million sheep, from 200,000 to 600,000 ducats in gross income, and from
100,000 to 200,000 in net income.[3] Although the quadrupling of sheep
numbers in the late sixteenth century was an accounting method to compensate
for competitive land values, the actual doubling of net customhouse income
was not at all fictitious. Three-fourths of gross revenues were "rebated" or
credited to the sheepowners for "land not possessed," but the other one-fourth
stayed in the royal treasury. That one-fourth equaled the original income, thus
doubling the initial sum.

Evidence from the possible number of pasturable sheep in each of the
twenty-two divisions of the usual extraordinary pasture at Monteserico further
pinpoints the rise specifically to the year 1577/78.[4] The total increase in
possible sheep in Monteserico in 1578 was 7.9 times greater than in the
previous year. But the factor of increase was unique to each of the twenty-two
divisions and ranged from 7.55 in both Santo Pietro in Ulmo and Minerva to
4.11 in Gombarda, with a mean of 6.5 times the previous quotation.[5]

If we analyze all sheep professed in the global sheep tax rolls (*squarciafogli*)—that is, sheep in that year only (*pecore in alia tantum*) in addition to the
fixed, real sheep (*pecore reali fisse*)—we can see how the total number jumped
dramatically over the long term. These *alia* were equivalent to the imaginary
pecore in aerea. We must remember that the *alia* was not a measure of sheep, but
of the need for pasture. Sheep were professed at a factor of their real number to
bring the price of pasture into parity with that of the arable.[6] Sheep were a
fictive money of account. What the two kinds of bids actually reflected, then,
were closed privileges to long-standing doganal participants (the real, fixed
bids), and a modus vivendi for new investors (the *alia* bids).

The genius of the system of *pecore in aerea* was not that it doubled net
income, but how it did it. After 1577 the use of sheep in the air established an
economic formula to adjust for comparative land values between arable and
pasture. Given the immutable nature of agrarian contracts and the multiplicity
of privileges in early modern Europe, the Neapolitan accountants had figured
out a foolproof system to avoid wrangling over special interests and exemptions. They found a way to collect more tax without adjusting rates.[7] And they
let the free market—at a time of acute agricultural demand and high inflation—set the price.

The fraudulent manipulation of the free bidding system, however, undermined pasture allocation policy, especially at times of doganal expansion. The late sixteenth-century growth found its parallel in the positive conjuncture of the eighteenth century when the abuses of *pecore in aerea* can be clearly documented in the inflation of imaginary sheep after 1738. Only during the 1760–65 famine did bids decline, since there was less competition for pastoral land. But thereafter the precipitous rise of sheep bids above 5, 6, and even 7 million head reflected the power of the rich and their collusion with doganal officers.

Literary Evidence

The importance of differentiating between fact and fiction in sheep and income was not lost upon the great sixteenth-century historians of Italy, Guicciardini and Giovio, who establish the facts in their riveting narratives. In the destructive decade after the first French Invasion of 1494, the French-Spanish rivalry that determined the fate of Italy for two centuries dramatizes the significance and the wealth of the sheep customhouse. The economic importance of the dogana made Puglia a battleground during the initial struggle for dominance in the Kingdom. Guicciardini relied on hyperbole at one point in his narrative: at the location of Apricena there was an "almost infinite number of sheep and other animals."[8] Before joining battle, the Castilian horsemen stampeded this great flock to make the income of the dogana unobtainable for the French.

Fighting was suspended for almost two years, and the Kingdom was partitioned according to the Treaty of Granada on 11 November 1500. The French took the northern provinces and the Spanish the southern, with the revenues of the customhouse divided between them. Paolo Giovio provides a full and vivid account of the second phase of the battle for the dogana.[9] He claimed that more than 600,000 sheep and 200,000 other animals were present at San Severo when the Spanish light cavalry again thwarted French attempts to collect the doganal revenues. As heirs to their own pastoral tradition, the Spanish strategy was to attack the sheep. Firing into the immense flocks, they dismounted and began to shear the sheep that still lived and skin the dead ones. Guicciardini and Giovio drew grandiose literary descriptions only to suggest the order of magnitude of the customhouse. These large revenues eventually became part of the final settlement ending hostilities between Louis XII and Ferdinand the Catholic. The French withdrew and relinquished their claim to Naples in exchange for an annual indemnity of 50,000 ducats in gold (i.e., 57,500 ducats at 1.15 ducats per gold ducat) payable on the dogana of Foggia.[10]

Guicciardini's observation has become a truism for understanding the central government's interest in the customhouse at Foggia. He explains why the Spanish and French fought over the customhouse: it was "the most important source of income in the Kingdom of Naples because it brought in 80,000 ducats each year, all within the space of a month."[11] Using a phrase similar to

Guicciardini's, both Charles V and Philip II confirmed this judgment. In a "summary report of Naples" in 1532, the viceroy warned Charles of the "perdition and danger" to the Kingdom because its budget was running in the red by 40,000 ducats per year, even including the sheep customhouse, "the best and most certain income in the Kingdom."[12] In 1588, Philip wrote to his viceroy in Naples on matters of doganal reform and called the customhouse "the principal member of the royal treasury in the Kingdom."[13] The kings were not misinformed.

Antonio Calabria has studied the structure of Neapolitan state finances during Philip's reign in the second half of the sixteenth century.[14] Direct taxes collected on hearths (*fiscali*) make up the largest budget entry, 29 percent of net income. But they came from twelve provinces and eleven officers (*percetori*) in diverse payments. The sheep customhouse, on the other hand, provided a single source of income concentrated in time and place, 10 percent of net patrimonial income payable in Foggia at the time of the spring fair.[15]

Customhouse Budgets: Credits

The structure of customhouse income and expense clarifies the transhumance institution's budgetary importance for the Neapolitan treasury (tables 19 and 20). Income came to Foggia under five major rubrics. But taxes (*fida*) paid on the number of animals using pasture was the chief source of revenue.[16] Animals, both sheep and *grossi* (cattle and horses), brought in about 90 percent of customhouse income. Taxes on the larger animals (3 percent of income) and nonmigrating sheep (4 percent of income) contributed only a small fraction. The bulk of customhouse revenues (83 percent) came from transhumant sheep. Theoretically, the *fida* was due on 8 May, the closing day of the winter season and the feast of St. Michael that opened the spring fair. The state assumed that sheepowners received cash for their products during the fair and would pay their taxes with it before the sheep returned to summer pastures. No fines were levied on payments owed (*residui*) before 22 July when a 3 percent late fee was assessed. Evasion of taxes, especially this nonpayment, was a constant concern of doganal officials. The *cavallari*, who escorted the graziers to their posts before winter, now stood guard at the passes out of Capitanata in the spring to verify that the *locati* had paid their *fida*. By the late seventeenth century, wool in depositories stood security for *locati* taxes and the 3 percent fine was postponed until December.[17] At least nine different rate structures applied to these sheep, from 13.2 ducats per 100 head to 13.2 ducats per 1,000. The varying *fida* rates depended upon the quality of winter pasture (such as the poorer grasses in the location of Guardiola, and in the Saccione above, or Barletta below Puglia), on perpetual contracts signed to encourage certain regions to participate (such as Basilicata and Otranto), or privileges signed with particular towns (such as Piedimonte d'Alife, a wool-manufacturing town near Naples). One rate, above all, the 12 percent tax (12 *scudi* or 13.2 ducats per 100 sheep), collected upon

TABLE 19 The Foggian Customhouse Budget: Income

Credits		Percentage	
Animals			90
Sheep *fida*		83	
12 percent (13.2 ducats per 100 sheep)	80		
Other rates	3		
Larger animal *fida*		3	
Sheep not migrating to Puglia		4	
Shepherds' bread allowance			1
Land and property rental and sale of office			10
Summer pastures in Puglia		1	
Terre salde (former pasture for agriculture)		8	
Uso d'erba (fallow for grazing)		2	
Property rental and sale of office of *mastrodatti*		1	
Fines (*proventi*)			1
Doganella d'Abruzzo			1
		Total	103 (due to rounding error)

Sources: Budgets from four periods defined by changes in *modo di vivere*: 1) 1511, AGS, *Estado, Nápoles*, leg. 1004, f. 17; 2) 1549, AGS, *Visítas d'Italia*, leg. 348–18; 1573, AGS, *Estado, Nápoles*, leg. 1046, f. 146; 1608, ASFi, *Miscellanea Medicea*, f. 98, ins. 7; 1610, AGS, *Visítas d'Italia*, leg. 112-8; 1615, BNN, MS, Branc. V.D.14; 3) 1621, AGS, *Estado, Nápoles*, leg. 1884, f. 105; 4) 1673, ibid., leg. 3296, f. 141; 1701, AHN, *Estado*, lib. 450.

the great majority of sheep, brought in 80 percent of total revenue. It came from sheep wintered in Puglia and registered in the locations. The Tavoliere of Puglia, therefore, in extent of land and quantity of income remains our main focus.

The second source of customhouse income (about 11 percent) came from land and property rental, including the sale of the office of *mastrodatti*, or secretary. The renting of former pasture used as agricultural land (*terre salde*) and the renting of agricultural land in fallow (*uso d'erba*) amounted to 10 percent of total revenues.[18]

Renting of the customhouse pasture in summer (*fida della statonica*) brought in about 1 percent of revenue in fixed income of about 2,500 ducats.[19] Sometimes the income from the extraordinary usual pasture of Monteserico was included under this rubric, sometimes as a separate item; but its income was from pasture rental for sheep.[20] The buildings of the customhouse in Foggia could also be rented: commonly, the jail for about 100 ducats, the wool storage depositories in the doganal palace and even some houses for 452 ducats in 1621.[21] Finally, in the early seventeenth century, the office of *mastrodatti* was

TABLE 20   The Foggian Customhouse Budget: Expense

Debits	Percentage
Ordinary overhead	30–20
Salaries	3
Charity and gifts	1
Sheep numeration	1
Pasture	25–15
Ordinary	
Extraordinary usual	
Extraordinary unusual	
Reimbursement for *pecore in aerea*	
paid to *locati*	
paid to landowners	
Assigned or extraordinary expenses	70–80
Payments and concessions	30–70
Consigned *in feudum*	
Consigned *in burgensaticum*	
Gifts for life	
Military treasurer	10–50
Miscellaneous	
Daily expenses	
Remainder for court in Naples	

Source: See table 19.

sold every three years for about 8,000–12,000 ducats, until it was assigned to a dependent of a large holder.[22]

Because the value of agricultural land could fluctuate over time, most of this income depended upon the economic conjuncture. For example, in the six years during the famine between 1605 and 1610, *terre salde* rents averaged 100,000 ducats per year.[23] Such extraordinary windfall income skewed planning for the fixed contract (*transazione*) taxes after the 1611/12 sheep death. A model budget of expected income under the new system projects 103,416 ducats from *terre salde* rents.[24] In the four years thereafter, 1611–14, *terre salde* plots actually accounted for only 20,000 ducats annually. Over the long term of the seventeenth and eighteenth centuries, *terre salde* income averaged close to that 20,000-ducat figure, and fallow renting brought in about 5,000 additional ducats.[25]

Three other sources of income rounded out the total. Sheepowners in some locations paid a minimal tax of 4.4 ducats per 100 sheep beyond the *fida* for the distribution of bread (*utilità del pane*).[26] A fixed sum of 4,000.37 ducats was established no matter how many sheep were in transhumance and applied only to those *locati* who depended upon the government-run bakeries in the Tavoliere. In other words, the *locati* did help to defray the costs of their subsistence at the nominal rate of 4.4 ducats per man, although the state still subsidized the bread monopoly, which maintained some thirty-three bakeries in the Tavoliere countryside and thirteen in its towns in the mid-eighteenth century.[27]

Next, fines (*proventi*) were assessed for civil permissions such as renting privately owned pasture (*dispensazione*) and numerous criminal offenses such as grazing on private lands without doganal approval (*contravenzione*), grazing on doganal land leased before the official opening or on land assigned to others (*scommissione*), and illegal cultivation of land reserved for pasture or sheepwalks (*disordine*).[28] Such fines accounted for only about 1 percent of income.

Finally, the Doganella d'Abruzzo, which controlled nontranshumant sheep grazing for certain areas in the Abruzzi, could be included in the Foggian totals or listed as a separate entry. Its income ranged from 3,000 to 10,000 ducats, little more than 1 percent of total income. In sum, almost all doganal income came from two sources: annual pasture taxes (*fida*)—90 percent; and land rental for planting in pasture—10 percent.

Customhouse Budgets: Debits

Customhouse expenses are much more complicated to assess because of the inflationary escalator of *pecore in aerea*. Most simply, two kinds of expenses are accounted for—ordinary or overhead expenses and extraordinary or assigned expenses. The ordinary debits included salaries to officers, charity and gifts, pasture payments, and reimbursements. The extraordinary outlays went for special projects, usually military emergencies plus annuity payments to pensioners and the like.

The ordinary expenses seem to have taken a larger bite out of the doganal budget before the 50 percent tax increase of 1556—close to 30 percent. After the increase, since revenues increased although fixed overhead costs remained the same, overhead expenses amounted to only about 20 percent of the total. Bianchini, citing Mazzella's 1592 figures, claims that the customhouse netted only a 40 percent return.[29] This complaint of high overhead, as much as 60 percent, has often been repeated by customhouse critics. It points out the difficulties in determining effective net revenues during the convoluted accounting tricks of sheep in the air and "reimbursement of land not occupied." My 20 percent figure comes from later budgets of 1621, 1673, and 1701, 1702, and 1703, when *pecore in aerea* were no longer an important bookkeeping subterfuge. In fact, if such paper transfers are removed from the calculations of these late sixteenth- and early seventeenth-century budgets—that is, if *pecore in aerea* monies are simply not counted as either overhead or revenue—effective overhead in these budgets approximates the 20 percent mark. Overhead payments, then, included about 1–3 percent for salaries, 2 percent for sheep numeration before 1553, and about 15–25 percent for pasture payments to private individuals.

The big money, 70–80 percent, was assigned to extraordinary expenses.

Let us look at a few examples. In 1535 the war of Corfu raged, and the imperial troops were owed "at least 30,000 *scudi*." The viceroy wrote to the Emperor Charles, "I have been waiting since this morning for the payment from the customhouse . . . expecting the resolution [of the crisis] from hour to hour. . . Without the payment from the customhouse, I do not see how the soldiers' payroll can be met."[30] In 1589/90, the year after the defeat of the Armada, 76,467 ducats of customhouse income were expended upon twenty-eight galleys of the Kingdom's fleet.[31] In 1602, sixteen galleys were outfitted by means of three equal budget payments: one from the customhouse in May, one from the "new impost" on olive oil in August, and one from the customhouse's *terre salde* income and the silk tax in December. The dogana of Foggia thus contributed 49 percent of the bill, 78,333.33 ducats.[32] In 1621, 144,129 ducats (39 percent of revenue) and in 1673, 92,109 ducats (52 percent of revenue) went directly to the military fund.[33] In 1701, 120,000 ducats of customhouse revenue were diverted to feed the Spanish army in Milan.[34] In modern accounting terms, the sheep customhouse was a "cash cow." Its guaranteed revenues could underwrite specific, immediate needs like galley construction or, as in 1621, provide 27,000 ducats for "the purchase of grain at the service of the Royal Court" and 1,668 ducats for the grain's transport. Every spring the dogana's concentrated revenues provided extraordinary opportunities for the royal treasury.

In addition to military expenditures, doganal revenues were used for a variety of dynastic or local Neapolitan disbursements. In the early sixteenth-century budgets (1511 and 1515), doganal revenues gave 7,000 ducats for the "provision" of the queen, Juana La Loca.[35] In 1549/50, the viceroy received one-third of his 10,000-ducat salary from the dogana plus another 15,000 ducats for operating expenses (*conto continuo*).[36] Similarly, in that same year, fortifications and galleys as well as numerous other nobles and royal family members (Margarita of Austria, the emperor's daughter) received provisions drawn from the sheep customhouse income. These payments included 1,022 ducats for the ambassador in Rome and 954 for the ambassador in Genoa. In Genoa, Juan de Figueroa, the ex-doganiero and still a regent of the Kingdom, was also able to draw a salary of 36 ducats for his personal servant. Such prebends certainly should not be considered customhouse expenses to be met before net revenues were turned over to the royal treasurer. In the same category should be included about 70,000 ducats annually assigned or conceded to various individuals "in fiefdom," "in burgensaticum," and as "gifts for life."

Further, because the doganal revenues were so regular, they provided perfect collateral for innumerable expenditures of a dynastic or political nature. The king of Poland and the Elector Palatine received doganal annuities of 43,000 ducats as heirs of the large dowry given in 1556 to Bona Sforza upon her marriage to the king of Poland, and the duke of Modena received 49,867 ducats from a similar dowry given in 1585 to the *infanta* Caterina, the daughter of Philip II, upon her marriage to Carlo Emanuele I, duke of Savoy.[37] In 1608 the grand duke of Tuscany, Cosimo II, enjoyed two credits yielding 36,573 ducats on *terre salde*.[38] These were all 8 and 9 percent annuities paid on the best revenues. Such secured monetary commitments mortgaged the dogana of Foggia and eventually consumed its income before it was even collected. For Spanish fiscal practice, this alienation of revenues was not unusual, but part of the continuing crisis of Spanish rule.[39]

Finally, the viceregal budgets included two categories of charity. Outrights gifts were rather small (less than 1 percent), but black wool donations could be valued up to the tithing level of one-tenth. Black wool gifts began in 1536 when Charles V granted special price considerations to the "poor men and dependent holders (*padroncelli*) in the customhouse."[40] He guaranteed the sale of wool up to 10,000 ducats at subsidized public (*voce*) prices. The purpose of this concession was to prevent the smallest holders from being shut out of the market by their larger competitors and thus not being able to pay customhouse taxes. These sales amounted to about 5 percent of total wool sales.[41] The wool was then turned over to the mendicant friars for their religious habits.

In the case of the black wool gift giving, Counter Reformation spirituality guided economic rationale. It was an act of personal piety to clothe the "naked" begging friars. Good works of this kind were performed because the state was not only the collective embodiment of the personal wealth and prestige of the sovereign. Someone like Philip II did not just own the royal demesne in Puglia on his own account. He owed his continued ownership and rule to the benevolence of heaven. He therefore had the obligation to dispose of his goods as a responsible Christian—providing for the dowries of his daughters and his 10 percent tithe to the Church. The Christian image of the Good Shepherd and the manifestation of the Infant Jesus before adoring shepherds provided a readily understandable ideology which marked the simpler, pastoral economy as a special favorite of the Lord. Good government derived ultimately from the personal righteousness of its rulers. Man's law was proclaimed to be copied from God's; man's collective policies in government were consciously striving to live up to their divine counterpart.

The Rationale of Good Government

Collecting such revenues depended upon good government of the customhouse, and a formulaic opening graced most high-level correspondence about its rule: "for the maintenance and increase of its revenues." An anonymous seventeenth-century document expresses the government's responsibility more fully. "The patrimony's most certain, secure, and the greatest income that the Royal Court holds in the Kingdom is that of the Customhouse at Foggia. It is none other than a true industry. Like [all] industries, it is necessary that it be governed with diligence, zeal, and vigilance for its maintenance and increase. When they are lacking, it falls easily into collapse, as is seen."[42] Good government, then, was not altruistic justice, but self-interested common sense on the part of the state.[43] The delegated government of an absentee monarch looked to increase its revenues and to maintain its hold upon Naples.

Any number of Spanish vistors' reports or reform documents sent to the Sommaria in Naples or the king in Spain in the sixteenth century concerning the *dogana delle pecore* attest to pervasive themes of good government. Good government meant that doganal officers should enforce the laws by obeying them themselves, by applying them impartially, by dispensing equal justice, by maintaining order, and by prosecuting thieves. Over the long term, neither frauds nor reforming reports ceased. We have already seen, for example, how the problems of the Foggian customhouse in the sixteenth century were repeated in one official report after another: Figueroa in 1539, Quiroga in 1560, Enriquez in 1578, Guzmán in 1581, Fornaro in 1588, and Saluzzo in 1608. Official mismanagement and agricultural usurpation continually threatened fiscal revenues and pastoral privileges.

The Meaning of Continual Reforms

How can we interpret the continuing frauds and calls for reform? Officials were extorting bribes from individual herders and renters while at the same time circumventing doganal law. But the Sommaria administration in Naples was not deceived by these irregularities. Why did it not institute wide-ranging reforms rather than merely replacing or fining corrupt officials? The ideological polemics against central authority, economic mismanagement, and social unrest grow out of this illicit behavior. Condemnation after the fact misses the differences that distinguish the system of expedience that characterized Spanish administration from our modern concerns about capital formation and rationalization.

In their attempts to explain the structure of the dogana or its early modern growth and decline, modern interpretive models have placed the dogana in the competing historiographical traditions of the Kingdom of Naples. The work of Coniglio presents the customhouse at Foggia as further evidence of institutional abuse and government decline under the Spanish viceroyalty. He builds upon Croce's description of a sick society which awaited enlightened, liberal remedies. Colapietra's doganal descriptions develop the themes of these same enlightened reformers without correlating economic reality to their rhetorical and theoretical reasoning. His analysis merely restates the problem of the customhouse from eighteenth-century concerns about monopolistic sanctions and archaic livelihood. Villari uses the dogana as an important example in his social portrait of refeudalization in the countryside during the years preceding the 1647 revolt. But none of these proposals gets at the geographic, demographic, and economic structure that underlies the operation of the dogana.

Coniglio's model suffers from the same circular assumptions that were revealed by the outmoded debate on Spanish dominance. His conclusions are skewed by his evidence—official reports by Spanish visitors sent to examine abuses. If we were to adopt Coniglio's interpretation, the dogana would have been in constant decline from the very moment of its conception. This is a circular theory—the ever-widening vortex of Spanish abuse. It discounts the internal dynamic of the customhouse—the tension between pastoralism and agriculture and between large holders and small. Instead of arguing from the structural foundation of the institution, Coniglio can offer no rationale for the constant reformation of the dogana other than the natural greed of its officials and the preferential justice of the crown. It is as if he were describing someone fallen from grace, always repentant and forgiven by an omnipotent, external God. Spanish administration, however external, was in no way omnipotent. At best it loosely covered the diverse contradictions of Neapolitan society. To claim that endemic corruption within the administration of the dogana (or the Spanish government throughout the Kingdom for that matter) caused seventeenth-century decline is to be content with a model of extrinsic rather than intrinsic causality.[44] Crisis in society did not derive from the abuse, but from the structure of government.

Villari, on the other hand, sees the dogana of Foggia as "perhaps the most typical" of feudal reactions in the countryside.[45] Baronial usurpation and enclosure of public lands after 1637 were indications of the growth of provincial power. The state could neither maintain control of pasture nor ensure freedom of the market. The crisis in the dogana of Foggia, then, was caused by the success of the baronial offensive and the crisis of credit.

Villari is interpreting the objective facts of the seventeenth century—the failing power of the centralizing state, the depression in the economy, and the baronial offensive—as causally linked phenomena. As a superstructural formula, this paradigm is attractive. Villari, however, has not consulted the archives of the dogana, and his explanation rests on the impressions of secondary sources. His interpretation does not fit the data and conjunctures of the dogana.

In the early seventeenth century, right of eminent domain and direct involvement of the government in land reallocation were premature attempts at manipulating the economy in an entrenched, feudal environment. The unique concurrence of low population and strong ruler that had marked Alfonso's fifteenth-century foundation of a transhumant customhouse agency in Puglia had long passed. Large, short-term expenditures, spent as seed money to stimulate steady income, could not be justified when what was needed were immediate, large revenues. Good government also had external constraints imposed by powerful baronial interests, as well as its own insatiable internal need for revenues. Good government did not only mean fiscal expediency, however. It also had to conform to the political exigencies of the Spanish Empire. Dividing and conquering in a regional balancing act could often mean that a rational economic policy was impolitic.

Maximization of revenues, therefore, was not the only concern of the Spanish administration in Naples. Larger political realities often determined policy. Whether it was the horse-raising customhouse in Terra d'Otranto, the provisioning of galleys, or the venality of offices, Neapolitan economic policy was dictated by Spanish political necessity. Such economic transfers in the forms of taxes and political duties have an understandable logic, if not a beneficial effect.

Sale of Offices

Especially in the appointment of state officials, fiscal expediency dictated a policy of the sale of offices. Good Shepherds, in the Christian sense, were hard to find.

The sale of offices throughout the Spanish Empire has often been examined.[46] Parry divides the sale of colonial offices in the Indies into three periods. Under Charles V, fee-earning offices were given as rewards for service. Offices could be sold by private persons, some court favorites engaging in large-scale activities, but the crown per se did not sell them. Under Philip II and Philip III, fee-earning and honorific offices were sold by the crown itself. Restrictions were placed on private sales—the state had to receive its cut. Judicial posts and senior administrative and financial posts were not subject to sale. Later, however, as the Spanish fiscal profile worsened, Philip IV and Charles II sold almost any office whenever they could find someone interested in buying.[47] The general pattern of increased sales and relaxed rules holds true, despite variation in specifics, throughout the empire. As fiscal pressures increased, more and more offices were sold. By 1630, Antonio de Léon-Pineolo's treatise on the legislation, sale, and confirmation of offices estimated that the total capital value of salable offices in the Indies was 771,738 ducats—an average annual income of about 38,000 ducats for the state.[48] The 1636 budget of Naples counted 55,484.84 ducats from the sale and increase of offices.[49] In 1670, Villari found that 34 general offices, 30 provincial offices, and 65 local offices were vendible.[50] Most of these offices attracted nobles. Only 16 out of 50 local officials were nonaristocrats in 1670.[51] The rationale behind office holding was not service, but self-aggrandizement.

The abuses deriving from the sale of public offices did not come from the incompetence of the officeholders, but from their greed.[52] The system was organized to obtain an initial large sum of money for the state treasury. The salaries of officers were meager. The state treasury was in business to collect revenues, not to pay out salaries. The system itself encouraged officeholders to make back their intial investment, maintain themselves in office comfortably, and then some.[53] Any good intentions for reform from above were always shortcircuited by the administrator's personal finances and by his desire to receive reimbursement for his capital outlay with interest.

This is not to suggest that corruption among officeholders was not perceived as a crime. The terms of their tenure, however, assumed that they would be rapacious. Their own self-image supported the consequent abuses. Of-

ROYAL PATRIMONY, ROYAL JUSTICE, ROYAL OFFICE 163

ficeholders had the mentality of "cavaliers," not of bureaucratic functionaries.[54] The higher officials were in fact nobles, but the average "civil servant" (notary or lawyer) typically came from the urban lower classes, sometimes from the peasantry.[55] Often claiming descent from *hidalgo* families, these social and economic climbers were interested in career advancement. Their goal was to gather enough money to invest in land or to obtain a royal pension.[56] It should come as no surprise, therefore, that the primary interest of officers in an institution like the *dogana delle pecore* was for their own immediate gain.[57] Thus state officials took their separate place among the other interest groups. Competition between agriculturist and pastoralist, and between state and subject, was complicated by these intervening middlemen in their attempts to get rich at the expense of both ruler and subjects.

Equal Justice

In the dogana of Foggia, unequal distribution of justice and of land were the commonest abuses of office. Only civil cases have been preserved before 1758. They concern land transfers, sales, wills, dowries. inheritance, nonpayment of debts, and the like.[58] These were the cases which provided most temptation to judges and litigants. But frauds in the forms of kickbacks and collusion on pasture rental, tax assessment, wool weighing and shipping are endless.

Raffaelo Ajello has investigated the judicial system of the customhouse in the context of the larger issue of judicial and legislative reform in the eighteenth century. Ajello focuses on the "fictitious" *locati* who had paid customhouse taxes in order to "buy" justice in its court.[59] The doganal judicial system had become one of the major forms of protection for doganal taxpayers. The doganal tribunal superseded other jurisdictions, royal, feudal, general, or personal. In order to escape feudal control, it had become the practice to inscribe in the dogana. Sheepowners listed in the *squarciafogli* tax lists claiming seven sheep are common. This may have been the minimum yearly tax necessary to subscribe to customhouse justice.

While there were numbers of such fictitious *locati* seeking to avoid the feudal courts of their local barons, doganal justice did not come cheaply. I have already argued that the baronial complaints against the dogana in 1589, 1593, 1617, and 1621 were often more economic than judicial. Landowning nobility opposed sheepowning commoners; as agriculturists, the barons wanted more land for cultivation. The doganal judicial system was not antibaronial, only extrabaronial. Good government tried to balance off rival interest groups by encouraging internecine antagonisms which prevented concerted, antistate uprisings. By 1657, Di Stefano claims that the barons had scored a victory. *Locati* who were not within the doganal jurisdiction needed to register 400 sheep, that is, pay 52.8 ducats in tax—not an insignificant sum.[60] It does appear, nevertheless, that the numbers of fictitious *locati* began to grow as the positive, eighteenth-century economic climate matured. The extraordinary jurisdiction of the customhouse court explains the motive. Doganal justice applied in both winter and summer, in both civil and criminal cases, in all matters, not just those depending upon the sheep industry.[61]

Although the seventeenth century may have seen a different intensity of favoritism, it probably did not experience a different kind of judicial abuse. The qualitative description of abuse must emphasize the problem of the venality of offices. Underpaid, growing in numbers as functions were split up to bring in more revenue, the notaries and lawyers in lower administrative offices depended upon private relationships with their superiors—and their subordinates. Advancement was based on patronage—an exchange of services. Extortion and illegal kickbacks were the norm.[62]

The unfair assignment of land to large landholders instead of pastoralists documents a typical abuse. Small sheepowners complained about discrimination to the doganiero, to royal visitors, to viceroys, and even directly to the king in the person of Charles V when he visited Naples. Similarly, I have emphasized that voluntary bidding was sometimes an elaborate ruse to plant land with grain, land that was legally designated for grazing.

Often through collusion with doganal officers, voluntary bids were inflated so that marginal landowners might reap profits by renting their otherwise worthless land. Some large agricultural holders maintained doganal connections in order to plant illegal grain on prime land, and then rent their marginal land to the dogana for the sheep they had displaced. The inequality in land ownership between large and small holders underscored the temptations undermining good government. In general, 10 percent of landowners received more than 50 percent of doganal rental payments, while more than 50 percent of the holders received less than 10 percent of the payments.[63]

Visual Evidence

Antonio de Michele's 1686 map of the "location of San Andrea" (fig. 13) offers a graphic visualization of the contemporary meaning of good government.[64] The year 1686 is significant because it marks the return to special locations for large sheepowners and the victory of the viceroy marchese del Carpio in his offensive against Abruzzesi banditry. Both pacification of the countryside leading into Puglia and separation of large from small holders coincided with the successful restarting of the pastoral economy.

In scale with the geography of the countryside, the town of San Severo lies just outside the location in the lower left-hand corner of the map. To balance the city and its surrounding agricultural plots, a most peculiar drawing fills the upper right-hand corner (fig. 14). Two roebucks upon a hillock face each other, rearing back on their hind legs. Below them is a flock of sheep and horses (?) flanked by dogs and guarded by a crozier-carrying wolf! Across the clearly marked boundary of the location, another flock grazes, watched by a dog and a

FIGURE 13 The Location of San Andrea from Antonio de Michele's Maps (1686)

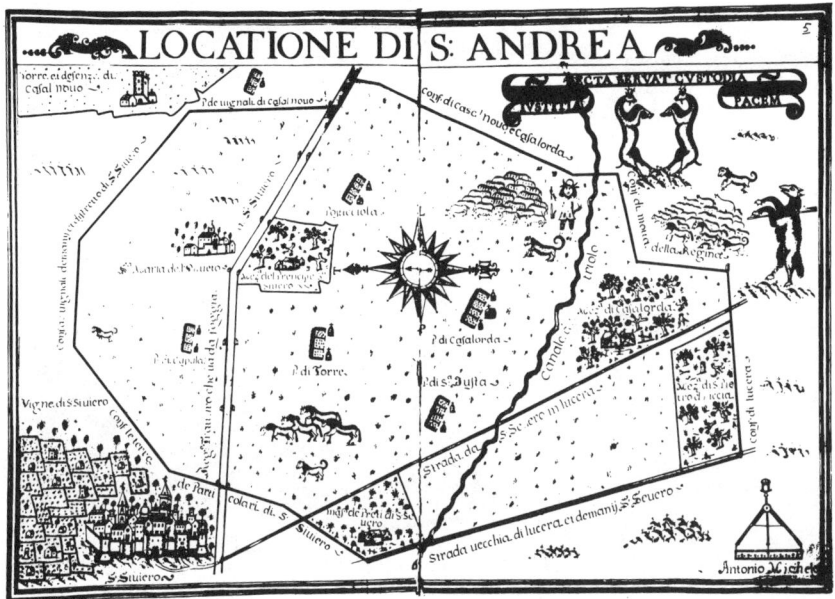

Source: Antonio de Michele's Maps (1686), ASFg, *Dogana,* serie I, vol. 20, 5r. Reprinted by permission.

normal shepherd, who gazes out at the viewer. Above the whole scene is a Latin scroll, "Good custodianship conserves peace through justice" (*Recta servat custodia justitia pacem*).

The inscription makes the meaning deceptively obvious. The justice of good laws and good government maintained peace and harmony. The contrast between the city and its farms with the countryside and its animals emphasizes the compatibility of civilization and cultivation with wilderness and pasturage. Even outside of the location, in the two extremes of nature and culture, such law had its peaceful effect beyond simply "law and order." Even within nature itself, an inexplicable harmony reigns. The two wild roebucks have been tamed by the scroll's justice. Their ritual combat and conflict are frozen at a moment of equal power and majesty, while the wolf lies down with his lambs.

But why the wolf, such an inconceivable shepherd? Are we perhaps reminded of Cervantes' "Colloquy of the Dogs," where the shepherds are themselves more dangerous to the flocks than the wolves? Maybe the real shepherds must be as crafty or powerful as wolves. In contrast to the realistic drawing of the shepherd across the confines of the location and the numerous other cane-carrying and gun-toting shepherds in other Michele maps,[65] the big, good wolf seems completely out of place. In contrast to the two wild roebucks, the

FIGURE 14 Detail from Antonio de Michele's Map of the Location of San Andrea

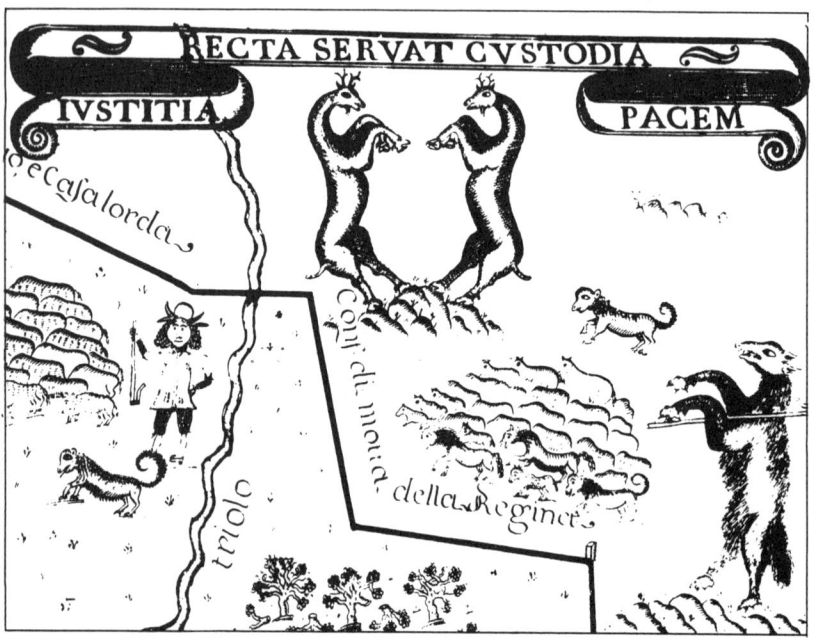

Source: See figure 13. Reprinted by permission.

wolf, also on his hind legs, is not rearing back, but almost walking erect like a man. Further, the wolf is larger than the two roebucks, and almost twice as large as the shepherd guarding sheep of the same size. Yet untamed nature seems to become civilized. The wolf seems to have a smile on his face, content in the harmony of his labors. No, this strange shepherd is not necessarily a sheep in wolf's clothing. He seems tame, but his teeth and claws are still quite apparent. This is not simply caprice, or a subtle joke. The wolf need not specifically refer to the "armed knights" (*cavallari*) whose abuse of office made them the dogana's "wolves."[66] It is enough to remind us that unequals are equals, outcasts find their place, and sworn enemies work together in the pastoral harmony and "good custodianship" of the customhouse system.[67]

The Office of Doganiero

The one person entrusted to guarantee justice in the system was the doganiero, the chief administrative and political officer of the dogana.[68] He was an authority unto himself, having "the power of sovereignty"; "the motor (or mover) and rector of this whole government."[69] He reported directly to the Sommaria and was subject only to the viceroy and the king. After 1550 his annual stipend was 1,000 ducats. In addition, he received another 200 ducats annually for the Doganella d'Abruzzo, until it was separated from the dogana in 1590. The responsibility of being in charge of prisoners (*postello delle carcere*) brought in another 200 ducats.[70]

A brief prepared for the 1560 general visit of Quiroga outlined the principal duties of the doganiero:

To make a list and accounting of animals on which the *fida* was paid
To assign sheep to ordinary pastures and, when these were filled, to extraordinary pastures
To collect the *fida* in April and submit a budget to the royal court
To administer justice in the doganal tribunal[71]

In addition to overseeing the pastoral industry and collecting its taxes, the doganiero was chief judge of the customhouse's unique court. He also oversaw the renting of agricultural land,[72] thus maintaining control of both arable and pasture.

After 1646 the office was abolished and a biennially appointed governor or president of the Sommaria acted as chief officer. These new governors were proven legal experts and nobles of the robe. Previously, from the first doganiero, Montluber, the doganieri had not been learned "doctors, but soldiers, knights and nobles" who were at first favorites of the king, then purchasers of the office.[73]

Venality of the office was meant to bolster the central treasury. When the sheepowners paid 10,000 ducats to purchase the office of doganiero for Juan de Figueroa in 1538, they were breaking precedent in two ways.[74] First, a royal favorite was not trying to further his career by buying his way into more money and power. Instead, the graziers were attempting to select an impartial governor and judge. Second, they were unseating a duly commissioned doganiero, Francesco Carroz, albeit he had only purchased the office the previous August for the same price. If the "normal" purchase price for venal offices in the Spanish Empire was about ten times salary, the 10,000-ducat price of 1538 was on the mark.[75] But, if the doganiero's stipend did not increase after 1550, some other variable inflated its value by the end of the century. Five bids recorded between 1581 and 1637 averaged 40,000 ducats.[76] The 40,000 ducats spent to buy the office after 1581, then, did not reflect budgetary needs or stipend expectations. The aspirant doganiero was not patriotically pledging an inflated *donativo*, nor was he interested in reaping small rewards. There was keen competition for the office; the high bid of the Monsorio purchase in 1602 came from a candle auction. The doganiero's office was a prize that went to the highest bidder. There was power to be exercised and bigger money to be made. The doganiero might expect to make 8,000–10,000 ducats per year beyond his salary![77]

The di Sangro Family

During the mid sixteenth century, the office of doganiero began to assume the character of a hereditary fief in the hands of an aristocratic Neapolitan family, the di Sangros of the district of Nido. Where did this branch of the family come from and how did they perform in office? The family history makes an exemplary group biography of a Neapolitan family loyal to their Aragonese and Spanish lords.[78]

The di Sangros claimed descent from Charlemagne in the person of a count of the Marsi (the Abruzzese territory around Lake Fucino) from the year 930. The true identification of the founder of the line is insignificant save for the connection with the Abruzzi, where they were eventually to enjoy good fortune. Family documentation really begins in the fifteenth century as an elder branch distinguished itself in its loyalty to the Aragonese dynasty. In the mid fifteenth century, one Paolo di Sangro, whom we have already met with an exemption for 10,000 sheep, followed Alfonso the Magnanimous and was captain general in Florence. His son Carlo di Sangro remained loyal to Ferdinand, and, although Carlo's son Gianfrancesco died young, a grandson Paolo distinguished himself in battle and was killed in the service of Charles V. It is this Paolo di Sangro, marchese of Torremaggiore (d. ca. 1530) and his son, also Gianfrancesco, in 1533 created princes of San Severo, who are important cousins and in-laws for the cadet branch of the family that produced our doganieri in Foggia.[79]

The cadet branch descends from Lucido di Sangro, who remained close to the Neapolitan kings during the crisis of the 1490s. His son Giovanni, further, provided the basis for the family's prestige and wealth from his service and loyalty as an officer under Alfonso II and the defeated Neapolitan Aragonese. This Giovanni di Sangro, whose eldest son became the first di Sangro doganiero in Foggia, was responsible for assembling quite a fortune in the Abruzzi and Puglia. He received 1,000 sheep, 100 cows, 200 ducats, and other gifts in 1494 for his services as majordomo to Alfonso II. Ferdinand the Catholic made him castelan of Capua (shared with another di Sangro cousin) in 1507 and gave him a 1,000-ducat stipend in perpetuity. In addition, Giovanni married well. His wife came from the wealthy, noble Dentice family and brought in dowry the fiefs of Ischitella and Peschici in Capitanata, and Barano in the Abruzzi near Aquila. His children were well situated to make their move in the newly conquered Spanish kingdom ruled by the young prince Charles in the 1520s and 1530s.

Above all, these early di Sangros were military men, and their rewards, recompense for loyalty and service. Charles V's concessions to partisans at the expense of the rebels in 1528 are indicative of the kinds of rewards and punishments to be meted out. In the dogana of Foggia, for example, Charles replaced officers who were not faithful to Spain against the invading French Lautrec: the two *credenzieri* and two of the *cavallari,* as well as the *credenziero* of the doganella.⁸⁰ Mixed and changing loyalties cursed the Neopolitan baronial class in the long Angevin-Aragonese, French-Spanish struggle to control the Kingdom.

Ferrante di Sangro, then, Giovanni's eldest son, purchased the office of doganiero in 1542 when the Spanish troubleshooter Juan de Figueroa, was recalled to Spain. During the War of Siena (1552–57), Ferrante distinguished himself as general provisioning officer in the army. Presumably, his connections with the lamb and meat market in Foggia were important here. Later he served on numerous ambassadorial missions to Rome because of his family relationship to Paul IV (1555–59). Ferrante's younger siblings also had noteworthy careers which crisscrossed Charles V's beneficient attention. Geronimo di Sangro was a colonel in the Italian army;⁸¹ Giammatista was a gentleman of Charles' court.⁸² A sister, Violante, married Paolo di Sangro from the senior branch with a dowry of 11,000 ducats, and their son became Charles V's newly created prince of San Severo. This Paolo, followed by his son Gianfrancesco, served as a member of the Collateral Council in Naples and must have looked with favor upon his in-law cousins.

Ferrante di Sangro was succeeded as doganiero of the Foggian customhouse by his two sons, Gian Luigi (who died young while in office) and Fabrizio (who had initially taken orders before being called to replace his elder brother). The latter is the extraordinary centerpiece of the story. Born in 1532, Fabrizio served as a lieutenant to his father in the first War of Siena, with further military service in the galleys under Andrea Doria in a company of three hundred infantry and as lieutenant under his uncle Geronimo. His upkeep, as well as that of other di Sangros, often depended upon the sheep customhouse. He was listed as cashier in 1550, and another of his father's brothers, Alfonso, collected a 200-ducat perpetual annuity.⁸³ Because Paul IV was a relative (Fabrizio calls him an "uncle"),⁸⁴ Fabrizio had pretensions to a clerical career and even to being created a cardinal during his seven embassies between Naples and Rome, until he took the emperor's side in the Carafa War (1555–57) and broke with his "uncle." He followed Charles about Europe and for five months in 1560 assisted the Neapolitan delegation at the papal consistory that elected Pius IV. After returning to Foggia in 1574 to become doganiero, this forty-two-year-old ex-military man, ex-cleric, and royal ambassador proved to be an extraordinary administrator by raising customhouse income in seven years, according to his own accounting, from 184,000 ducats to 601,879 ducats. Fabrizio renounced the office in 1580 for an 8,000-ducat reimbursement, an 800-ducat annual pension for five years, and a 4,000-ducat flat payment.⁸⁵ Fabrizio claims to have received only one installment and from 1582–85 served in the important post of *scrivania di razione* (chief military disbursement officer) in Naples. Soon thereafter, in 1588, the Guzmán general visit convicted Fabrizio of abuses in his office of doganiero and fined him 10,000 ducats. Possibly to pay this debt, he entered the private service of the prince of Bisignano, serving for one year as governor of estates and for five as curator. In a bitter quarrel with the new doganiero (Giovan Antonio Carbone, marchese di Padula), Fabrizio was imprisoned in the Casalnuovo for several months upon the arrival of the new viceroy, conte de Olivares, around 1595 but then was made a duke in December of that year with a purchase price of 4,000 Castilian ducats.[86] The new king, Philip III, called upon the then seventy-year-old duke of Vietri, as a trusted and experienced administrator, to serve once again as *scrivania di razione*.[87] In 1606, Fabrizio assisted in important treaty negotiations with the Venetians for eight months and was renewed as *scrivania di razione* in 1608. In 1612, we know, he was recalled to Foggia as doganiero to oversee what was left after the disastrous winter when 1.3 million sheep were killed. In 1613, at eighty, he was named as councillor without stipend to the Collateral Council in Naples.[88]

The di Sangro story should not end here. Did Fabrizio have any influence in the customhouse after his departure in 1580? Despite momentary conviction for fraud, he was still working in fiscal politics in Naples for the next thirty years. First, his successor, Alfonso Caracciolo, may not have been a chance appointment. Fabrizio's second wife, Laura Caracciolo, may have been the new doganiero's sister.[89] Second, Fabrizio's first wife, Violante di Sangro, was his first cousin, one of Giammatista's daughters. Her sister Adriana married into the Monsorio family, and it could well be that the 1603 doganiero, her brother-in-law Ferrante Monsorio, made a successful bid to office through this family connection.

Why did the three di Sangro administrations, in the course of royal visitors' investigation, all fall far short of meeting the ideal of good government? In each case, the visitors general found them guilty of frauds, and the penalty was loss of office. The actual verdicts against Ferrante and Gian Luigi are problematic, probably because they died in office.[90] The charges and verdict against Fabrizio are more easily accessible.[91] The nine counts of fraud bear witness to the punishment of loss of office and 10,000 ducats fine. Fabrizio had accepted innumerable bribes and kickbacks in his own and his wife's name: at least three horses, wine, clothes, jewelry, and more. Worse, he illegally kept the enclosure of Sierra Cimino in Monteserico, valued at 700 ducats per year, for himself. He enrolled fictitious *locati* knowingly for a consideration, and he even enrolled some of his own sheep hidden under his wife's and daughter's names. But loss of office was hardly a disgrace. Within a short time, he was again in royal service with an even more sensitive fiscal charge. And a similar fate awaited many of his successor doganieri. For Fabrizio's part, he could always boast of his service in raising state revenues.

Alfonso Caracciolo's rule was more corrupt than his predecessors', and, with his death in 1588, the Sommaria reorganized the office. It separated the Doganella d'Abruzzo from the dogana of Foggia and appointed one of the ten Sommaria presidents annually to oversee the doganal operation. Customhouse revenues shrank under the careful scrutiny of the Sommaria presidents as they weeded out abuses. Ferrante Fornaro's official investigation recommended suspension of sale of the office of doganiero. Financial necessity, however, outweighed good management, and the office of doganiero was again sold in 1593.

The new doganiero, the marchese di Padula, was placed under some restriction, however, and this may have been the basis for his feud with Fabrizio di Sangro. In order to ensure the impartiality of justice, the revenues of the *mastrodatti* were passed directly to the treasury.[92] But by 1603, Padula was prosecuted and acquitted for abuses and embezzlement. This same fate awaited his successor, Ferrante Monsorio, who was tried and acquitted two years later. Official inquiries assumed a repetitive pattern—complaints of abuse, investigation, trial, and acquittal. Such an administrative history helps us to understand, above all, the meteoric rise in doganal revenues and sheep numbers in the voluntary bidding and *pecore in aerea* system from 1575 to 1610. Abuses were tolerated because customhouse officials were enriching not only themselves, but also the state treasury.

When the Foggian fair saw total pastoral sales of some 400,000 ducats around 1600 and the customhouse collecting 600,000 ducats to pass on 200,000 ducats to the royal treasury, we can be sure that agriculturists, pastoralists, and bureaucrats were all taking their cut. This visible market exchange does not begin to account for the sub rosa transfers, illegal production, contraband, and fraud that was a part of the day-to-day economic system. If good government meant fiscal responsibility, it was circumscribed by the personal interest of both doganal officers and doganal members. The large amounts of capital present in the rural economy of Capitanata were invested in a rational market but often extracted in an extralegal manner.[93] There is no accounting for how much wealth escaped the doganal mechanism. It was not inconsiderable. But even without hard data on contraband, the taxes accruing to the state and the sales estimated as entering the legal market are quite formidable in themselves.

Other Offices

Because of his noble blood and high connections, the doganiero himself was often able to escape personal censure. Reforms were aimed at the office instead, by splitting its functions and discontinuing its sale. Lower officers, however, were not always as immune from punishment as the "magnificent doganiero." In 1581, for example, the visitor's report of Lope de Guzmán includes a detailed review of customhouse abuses and penalties imposed office by office. During this period of maximum institutional development at the end of the sixteenth century, the doganiero shaped major responsibilities with an auditor (*auditore*) and two accountants (*credenzieri*). It was these commoner bureaucrats rather than the noble doganiero who were more subject to censure—the scapegoats sacrificed for good government.

The *auditore* along with his colleagues formed the special tribunal for the *locati*.[94] The *auditore* was a judge ordinary, civil and criminal, on doganal matters that did not touch on direct fiscal affairs. He was named by the viceroy for a two- or three-year term and received an annual stipend of 300 ducats.

The office of *credenziero*, appointed by the king, was divided in two in 1536 because of growing responsibilities. One *credenziero* was assigned to economic questions and another to judicial issues. The *credenziero* for economic affairs was responsible for the official register of taxation (*squarciafoglio*), determined the exaction of pasture tax (*fida*), and oversaw budgets and accounts. He played an important role, therefore, in the distribution and assignment of pasture. His annual stipend was 200 ducats. The other *credenziero* sat on the special tribunal for the *locati* along with the doganiero and *auditore*. He was *avvocato* and *procuratore* for fiscal affairs. His annual stipend was 300 ducats.[95] In 1721 both offices were subordinated to an *avvocato fiscale*, who collected an annual stipend of 1,200 ducats.[96]

Three families dominated the office of *credenziero* in the late sixteenth and the seventeenth and eighteenth centuries—the Corcione, the Freda, and the Giordano families. Longevity seems to mark the officeholders' tenure, and it was a stepping stone on the bureaucracy's *cursus honorum*. In 1607, for example, Miguel Salla retired as *credenziero* after twelve years of service in Foggia, but with fifty years overall in various offices in the Kingdom.[97] Gian Luigi Corcione, on the other hand, did not want to make Foggia his last stop. His father, Sigismondo, had been *credenziero* before him for almost thirty-three years, from 1573 to his death in 1605. Gian Luigi succeeded him and served for twenty years before becoming *auditore* for the next six. Then, in 1631, he wrote to the court in Naples seeking some higher position in the capital itself—as a judge in the Vicaria, a member of the Council of Santa Clara, or a president of the Sommaria.[98]

Minor offices were also important. The cashier (*cassiere* or *percettore*) collected the tax from the sheepowners and kept an account of it for the Sommaria.[99] This office was totally dependent upon the doganiero and provided infinite opportunities for greed or collusion with merchant bankers to siphon capital out of the dogana. In 1575 he was paid 150 ducats annually but eventually received 500 ducats per year. The "head bookkeeper" (*libro maggiore*) kept the official register of accounts.[100] He stood in front of the large book (*libro maggiore*) recording daily debits and credits. He issued "invoices" to the graziers. Similarly, no monies could be paid without his receipt. In 1666 the *libro maggiore* received a 300-ducat annual stipend, plus fees. The *mastrodatti* was secretary of all records.[101] His annual stipend was 20 ducats, plus piece rates for every document registered. With the ton of paper passing through his hands, some additional 3,000 ducats amounted to no mean income. The doganiero originally appointed all three of these officers for life, but in the eighteenth century the *mastrodatti*'s term was reduced to three years, and both his office and that of *libro maggiore* became vendible. Finally, an *archivario*, appointed for life by the Sommaria, tended the archive for a 120-ducat annual stipend.

The *cavallari* were mounted horsemen who formed a squadron of armed knights.[102] They were the "wolves" of the dogana who patrolled sheepwalks and passes, escorted the *locati* to their posts, protected sheep and shepherds from assault and theft, and prevented *locati* from leaving Puglia before paying their pasture tax. There were originally twenty-four "ordinary horsemen"; later they were increased by ten "extraordinary horsemen." The total number of *cavallari* was eventually limited to thirty. The office was sold or conceded to heirs for life. By the mid seventeenth century, *consulte* of the Collateral Council report that the mean price paid for the office was 297 ducats.[103] The annual stipend for each *cavallaro* varied according to rank. The budgets of 1575, 1603, 1604, and 1605 allocated 90 ducats to their captain; 72 ducats to each of 8 *cavallari;* 60 ducats to each of 3; 50 ducats to each of 3; and 45 ducats to each of 9. By 1666, Coda's "Brief Discourse" lists 30 *cavallari* at 45 ducats per year and a separate squadron of 24 soldiers (*soldati di compagni*) at 8 ducats per month, with their own lieutenant at 10 ducats per month.

The lowest officers were the jailers and the messengers, who served or posted public banns and decrees (*alguzzini* or *banditori*). Five *alguzzini* received 17.5 ducats each.[104] Two other offices were intimately tied to doganal activities but remained outside of the official state organization. The "weighers of wool" (*pesatori di lana*), whom we will meet soon, were not paid by the state but by buyers and sellers at the fair. They oversaw weights and measures as wool was weighed in and out of deposit. The royal surveyors (*compassatori* or *regi agrimensori*) were nominated by the doganiero. They measured doganal territories, geographically regularized the locations, and determined the boundaries of pasture.

The use of space in the doganal palace gives a visual understanding of the function and pecking order of customhouse officers. In the original doganal palace used until damaged in the 1731 earthquake, floor plans for its three floors reveal six major customhouse functions.[105] The ground floor consisted of a jail, with space for a guardroom, storerooms for provisions, and a few storerooms with street access for wool depositories. The first floor contained the customhouse tribunal, a large meeting room for the *locati,* and offices for various officials—secretary, *libro maggiore,* and *percettore*. The small second floor housed the customhouse archive.

After the earthquake, the government purchased the new Jesuit college, which was already under construction outside the historic center, and made it the new seat of customhouse administration. It provided three full floors built around an internal courtyard. A 1762 description allows for a reconstruction of the floor plan.[106] The ground floor again housed the jail, now with ample barracks for the guards, plus the storerooms and wool depositories. Instead of four rooms available for wool depositories, the new palace offered at least ten. The first floor had enlarged meeting rooms and tribunal. It contained the archive and various administrative offices, including new ones for agriculturists renting *terre salde* and pastoralists getting their *passate* (tax receipts for exit visas). In addition, a living area, with private entrance, for the customhouse governor took up more than one-quarter of the whole floor. The second floor was all given over to apartments: three large ones, for the *auditore, avvocato fiscale,* and one unfinished, with a fourth, much smaller apartment at the doganal governor's disposition. By 1788 this top floor had been redesigned and filled up.[107] The governor's small extra apartment disappeared, and a large balcony was enclosed to allow for the division of the south wing into two separate apartments for two *auditori.* The *avvocato fiscale's* apartment in the north wing lost a few rooms to allow them to be joined with the previously undetermined area for new office space for the scribes and an additional floor for the archives.[108]

Two trends are noteworthy in comparing the old and new customhouse seat. First, the most important officers now resided in the palace and made it the focal point of the secular life of Foggia day and night. Second, the growth of the economy and the accumulation of paper by the late eighteenth century made it necessary to provide for a second *auditore,* the expanded archive, and more office space for the growing bureaucracy. The bustle of activity can be inferred from a 1723 royal order which set down the working hours for the *libro maggiore* and *percettore:* 6:00 A.M. to 12:00 noon and vespers to *vimmaria* (one evening prayer to another) in summer; 9:00 A.M. to 12:00 noon and 3:00 P.M. to evening in winter.[109]

The amount of the stipend gives some idea of the importance attached to these offices. Braudel has estimated general wages for the age of Philip II to run far below the 200-, 300-, and 1,000-ducat salary of the major doganal offices. From the Sommaria, Braudel calculates per capita income of peasants in the Kingdom to be about 10 ducats per year by the end of the sixteenth century. For the Mediterranean in general he offers "a rough classification." Income below 20 ducats was a subsistence wage; between 20 and 40 ducats, "small"; and between 40 and 150 ducats, "reasonable."[110] On Braudel's scale, even minor doganal officers were paid reasonable wages.

The problem with doganal officers' salaries, however, was that they were fixed stipends from the mid sixteenth century. Since wages did not keep pace with rising prices—wool alone, we shall see, doubled from 30 ducats per *rubbio* in the 1580s to 60 ducats per *rubbio* in the 1780s—doganal officers had to make up this cost of living differential somewhere. Abuse of office was the inevitable result.

Thus, although all of these officers shared in the pastoral rhetoric of the Good Shepherd and his sheep, such an ideal was more rhetoric than reality. In practice, everyone knew that sheep were the most silly and foolish animals in the world which would lead one another to the slaughter. Rabelais relates a well-known story about Panurge and the sheep merchant, Didenault, aboard ship. Panurge haggles over the price of one sheep, then throws it overboard. All the other sheep follow, and the shepherds too are drowned in their attempt to save the sheep.[111]

Everyone knew that the shepherds were a rude and dull lot. Did the state believe that it was any more efficient an overseer of its sheep than the shepherd was of his? The state could easily be substituted for the shepherd in the Foggian proverb: "The sheep have ninety-nine faults, and with the shepherd, one hundred" (*pecure tene nuvantanove difette e ne fá ciente cu i pecurare*).[112] Reminiscent of the Good Shepherd, who left the ninety-nine in his flock to search for the one lost sheep, the proverb turns the gospel story upside down and here makes the shepherds as wayward as the sheep. Governmental abuse and mismanagement brought that last fatal flaw, a stagnant intransigence, to bear upon the rural economy of the Kingdom. Just as the shepherd's fault could greatly affect the sheep, so too could the state's. Official abuse and intervention added another dimension to the dogana's already complicated internal problematic. In addition to the conflicts between wheat and wool and rich and poor for the domination of the fertile plain of Puglia, now state administrators bearing justice or favoritism could swing the balance to one side or another, enrich themselves, or, indeed, even maintain good government.

The dogana of Foggia, however, was only one part of the larger puzzle of centralized rule in Naples. Andrea Doria's 1536 candid memorial to Charles V on the internal affairs of Naples and the international situation in Italy gives an incisive evaluation of the problems facing the Kingdom as the emperor came to winter there after his victory in Tunis.[113] In addition to the grave questions of war and peace from Algeria to Milan, two domestic concerns threatened to bring the Kingdom to ruin. First, the viceroy Pedro de Toledo, who is judged to be of good will, "does not know how to form a good government." Doria's analysis rejects the policy of divide and conquer for it only "creates divisions in time of peace" that "will cause [us] to lose in every small war." For Doria, fission brings eventual collapse, not a stronger, unified state. This misguided viceregal policy is expressed in two dangerous antagonisms—that between the viceroy and the barons, and that between the barons and the poor. In other words, the problem of good government from above was to remedy conflict between the person of the viceroy or the central administration and the dominant class, as well as between classes, the haves and have-nots. Doria's second concern linked this analysis to the specifics of state finance. Extortionist taxation was robbing the Kingdom and leading to its destruction, "consuming even the blood of the poor." "The officials, treasurers, tax collectors, doganieri, commissars, and judges of this Kingdom are all guilty of these extortions." Royal income, royal justice, and royal office operated between the person of the monarch and his subjects. As these royal functions implemented the state's reason, they often undermined its being.

7 The Competition between Wheat and Wool

The Kingdom's Demographic Profile

On 29 April 1550 the *Vicaria* and the chief justice of the Kingdom, in the name of the viceroy Pedro de Toledo, disseminated a printed proclamation on law and order—"grave and enormous crimes like murder and theft"—in the city of Naples.[1] The decree linked urban violence to "the multitude of unemployed continually flowing into the city" from the countryside. Provincials, in their flight from starvation after the famine of 1547, continued to seek refuge in the city but found few prospects save vagrancy and delinquency. In fact, comparing a special census conducted in 1547 to facilitate the distribution of bread with the 1528 fiscal census, Naples had grown 37 percent in twenty years, from 155,000 to over 212,203 inhabitants.[2] The decree, therefore, ordered that vagabonds and delinquents be expelled from the city and condemned to up to five years in the galleys, that labor permits be issued to identify bona fide workers, and that gun control be enforced.

Violence, unemployment, population growth, and famine were inextricably connected in the mid sixteenth century as the dangers of urban massing became a part of the day-to-day anxieties of the viceregal administration. Because the interrelationship between demographic pressure, grain supply, and grain prices made famine and riot an ever-increasing probability, in 1560 the viceroy Alcala in Naples exchanged letters with Philip II in Spain on the city's growth and the need to procure more bread.[3] One of the solutions proposed to the king was to rent more pastoral land of the *dogana delle pecore* for grain production in order to ensure bread for the capital.

In addition to its guaranteed bread supplies, the city of Naples offered fiscal immunities to its inhabitants. As hearth taxes put tighter constraints upon provincial taxpayers after the reorganization of the Kingdom by Spain, only the tax-exempt status of the Neapolitan capital promised relief. Unemployment in the city, however, made migration an illusory solution. As the Neapolitan capital continued to grow in the second half of the sixteenth century, it urbanized without development.

By 1600 its 250,000 inhabitants made Naples the largest city in Western Europe, second in Europe only to Istanbul. By the mid seventeenth century, the Neapolitan capital held its high ranking with a population of 360,000. Even the catastrophic plague of 1656, which killed almost two-thirds of these inhabitants, leaving only some 100,000 survivors, could not curtail the long-term population explosion.[4] By 1707 city population was up to 215,000; by 1742, 315,000; and by the beginning of the nineteenth century, over 400,000 inhabitants placed Naples among the top five European cities: ahead of Madrid, behind London, Paris, and Istanbul.

The capital's population (roughly 10 percent of the Kingdom's) mirrored demographic change outside the city. According to the counting of hearths, population in the Kingdom doubled from 1.15 million in 1505 to 2.43 million in 1595 (+112 percent) and declined to 1.78 million after the 1656 plague (−27 percent by 1669). Recovery after the seventeenth-century crisis brought takeoff—3.0 million in 1700, 3.8 million in 1750, and 5.0 million in 1800.

Population density in the countryside is another measure of this urban-rural continuum. Capitanata's 8,364 square kilometers, for example, ranked it second in size among the twelve provinces of the Kingdom of Naples with 9 percent of the Kingdom's total area.[5] In total population, however, Capitanata ranked eleventh or twelfth in the Kingdom throughout the early modern period and was, most appropriately for its pastoral economy, the Kingdom's most sparsely populated province.

Neither the city's ills nor possible remedies could be separated from a discussion of the countryside. Social and economic stratification exacerbated the contradictions between city and country and between townsman, farmer, and shepherd. The differences between urban and rural fortunes underlined the demeaning options open to individuals in the Kingdom: provincial taxation and starvation or urban pauperism and parasitism.[6]

Feeding the People

How did this growing population feed itself? From 1560 to 1641, Coniglio estimates that the chief single source of grain imported into the city of Naples (21 percent) was Puglia.[7] Manfredonia and Barletta were the chief ports for grain embarcation. In 1539–40 they shipped 95,350 *tomoli* of wheat and 38,757 *tomoli* of barley to Naples.[8] They were named first in the 1586 *consulta* which investigated ship loading irregularities.[9]

In addition, the Kingdom imported grain from the autonomous Spanish viceroyalty in Sicily for the Neapolitan capital and often exported fixed quantities of grain from the Abruzzi, Puglia, and Basilicata to Venice.[10] Although the quality of Adriatic wheat was inferior to that of Sicily and the shipping route to Naples was longer and more dangerous,[11] its exportation was made illegal unless there was a surplus in Naples. Even in normal years, more grain was imported into the Kingdom than was exported out of it. From 1560 to 1641 the capital consumed between 32–36 percent domestic grains, 38–45 percent foreign grains, while 23–26 percent are unidentifiable.[12] Guaranteeing grain supplies was far and away the state's major responsibility.

Extracommercial activity, nevertheless, circumvented official scrutiny as piracy, brigandage, contraband, and frauds of all kinds played their part in thwarting the central government's attempt to control grain production and distribution. A *consulta* of 1569 recorded negotiations for reimbursement for Venetian piracy. Venetian galleys seized two ships bound for Naples from Puglia with 200 *carra* (7,200 *tomoli*) of grain. The settlement referred to two previous incidents, 1560 and 1563, as precedents.[13] Fear of Venetian or Maltese piracy lasted throughout the century. A document from 1591 reflected the tense anxiety and fearful anticipation of the citizens of Naples who awaited the Puglian grain ships. Galleys had been sent to escort and defend the grain ships from attack. How much good would come if their prayers were answered and the ships arrived safely![14] Similarly, in 1575, one Pietro de Franchi was caught trafficking in cereals. He was fined 3 ducats per *carro* for 3,000 *carra* and was required personally to oversee the transport of an equal quantity of wheat to the city of Naples from the Kingdom of Sicily.[15]

Two other *consulte*, dated 1573 and 1574, discussed "the infinite contrabands made in extracting wheat from the Kingdom by way of Santa Maria di Tremiti."[16] An unknown informer disclosed extensive contraband operations which had extracted grain from the Kingdom during the famine of 1570. The Tremiti islands, just off the coast of the Lago di Lesina, were the first step in a network that extended to Ancona, Piacenza, and finally the Venetian market.

Thus, even foreign policy was tied to agricultural products. More serious than Venetian piracy in the Adriatic was the Ottoman threat. While religious fervor and strategic protection from the Ottoman Empire was the rationale for Spanish activities along the Illyrian coast, the tribute payments of the Adriatic enclaves underline provisioning needs. In 1608, five five-year agreements were reached between the Sommaria and 53 Franciscan monasteries. The monasteries granted agricultural concessions in return for protection. There were 9 in the territory of Ragusa, 20 in Dalmatia, 16 in Croatia, 6 in Albania, and 2 in Bosnia Argentina in Illyria. The agreements were renewed throughout the seventeenth century.[17] Grain demand was one of the chief motives for Spanish interest in the Balkans.

Political disasters exacerbated the problem. When the Turks sacked Manfredonia in 1620, the previous century of Spanish policy in the Kingdom began to crumble.[18] A Turkish fleet of fifty-six galleys landed "without doubts or fear of the fortress." But it was not only the port of Manfredonia that was in danger. The marketplace of the dogana was only thirty-eight kilometers inland on the plain. The short journey from Foggia to the sea was no longer an advantage as the Turks "ran through the countryside up to Foggia." The waning wool and grain markets during the seventeenth-century crisis suffered continued damage as the Ottomans made the entire coast of Puglia more dangerous for commercial activity.

The Organization of Production

Grain for Naples was not bought on the open markets but contracted for by a state monopoly.[19] The result was a hierarchical, bureaucratic system that maximized profit and minimized risk for the three parties involved—state, foreign merchants, and large landholders. The capital city funneled provincial resources into its coffers. Absentee landlords drew rents; merchants, profits; and the state, taxes.

Land tenure in a province like Capitanata was organized from the Neapolitan capital like a colonial monopoly. Cash cropping made the large farms of Puglia not an element or even the foundation of a complex, agrarian economy, but instead the most important and, in fact, the exclusive production unit in Capitanata.

In Capitanta the last decades of the sixteenth century were an especially active period of investment in grain cultivation. In Aurelio Lepre's study of land tenure in the Abruzzi and Puglia, he examined three large landholders and their farms in Capitanata.[20] The duke of Seripando and Muscettola di Leporano purchased his holdings at Castiglione in 1580 and 1584. The Jesuits of the Collegio Romano and Noviziato Romano held Stornara and Stornarella (1600), Ordona (1604), and Orta (1611). The farms of Tressanti were purchased by the Certosa di San Martino of Naples in 1598. All holdings were within locations of the Tavoliere di Puglia administered by the dogana. They were independent of customhouse jurisdiction while subject to the same economic rhythm and pressure.

In the seventeenth century, 84.13, 87.83, and 74.45 percent of the revenues of the three holdings respectively came from agricultural production. Only 8.32, 5.66, and 17.56 percent came from grazing. While the average purchase price for the Jesuit farms was about 51,500 ducats, annual profits were about 15,000 ducats; that is, a 29.13 percent annual rate of return. Big money was invested for exceptional returns.

The crash of the early seventeenth century emphasized the staying power of agricultural investment and production units in Puglia. The economic downturn that was first felt in Capitanata in 1609/10 and only bottomed out in the 1620s was marked by sharply falling grain prices. By 1616 the Jesuits began to consider selling all or part of their holdings. Despite the gravity of the crisis, however, the great farms resisted and emerged intact. Despite the violence of the crash, the existence of the system was not put up for discussion. The internal structure of the farms of Puglia and its relationship to the Kingdom remained unchanged. The social crisis of revolt in 1647 and plague in 1656 are further proofs of the permanence of agricultural structures in Capitanata. In these agricultural enclaves, in opposition to the general trend, pastoral income actually declined. The Jesuits, for their part, expanded their agricultural holdings to Troia and maintained their investment in Capitanata until 1767, when the order was expelled from the Kingdom and its property confiscated.

Regional Markets

The regional particularism of the Kingdom's twelve provinces is a critical variable to keep in mind as we try to understand how the southern Italian economy developed and how its social structure rigidified. The provinces did not form an articulated, interdependent unit. Instead, rural antagonism intensified between feudal and communal powers as the economy improved.[21] Large absentee landlords (baronial and ecclessiastical latifundia which together comprised eight-ninths of the landed property) and local communes (towns with cheap labor and provincial crafts) vied with one another for domination of the countryside. Cash crops—grain, vines, olives, fruits, wool, and livestock— were financed by foreign capital and were produced on the large estates for nonlocal consumption. Fairs at Salerno, Barletta, Lanciano, Aversa, and Foggia siphoned off the surplus to the wealthy minority resident in the Neapolitan capital or the Italian North. The countryside was left with provincial foci at Aquila, Foggia, Bari, Lecce, Taranto, Reggio di Calabria, Salerno, etc. which did not look to the same center. Venice, Milan, Ragusa, and above all, Genoa developed their own spheres of influence and investment. Regional compartmentalization and discontinuity created isolated pockets of competing interest. In the struggle to preserve their traditional provincial power, baronial factions were allied with foreign merchants to maintain their economic stranglehold on the land. Profits were concentrated in the hands of those landholders already rich and those foreign merchants who reinvested their money outside the Kingdom.

Thus, demand for food, prices of grain, fiscal pressure, baronial offensive, and urban migration were linked with the growing numbers of people.[22] Because the expanding population was distributed unevenly by region and unevenly by time, the cumulative effects of demographic change had profound consequences for the social and economic profile of the Kingdom. Cultivation of cereals was increased, and land-use patterns were reorganized. Agricultural productivity, in turn, stimulated further population growth and redistribution. The rural and urban landscape were in constant flux.

Understanding the growth of the capital and the articulation of the provinces helps to explain the development of large-scale, cash-cropping "industries" in the countryside—especially counterproductive, "man-eating" ones like sheep farming. The countryside of provincial Capitanata, for example, embodied the contradictions so obviously magnified in the city as political expediency gerrymandered economic viability. The political rivalry and socioeconomic upheaval that accompanied population growth and decline only becomes intelligible when one examines the relative size, rate, and density of population growth, as well as the relationship between demography and livelihood in the discrete regions and environments of the Kingdom.

This model of regional economy fostered by the Spanish administration elevated the Neapolitan capital to the first rank. It became an international city, the focal point for regional economy, society, and values. In turn, it reflected the broader policy of the Spanish Empire: a great base for the political and military operations of Spain in Italy and the Mediterranean.[23] The provinces, on the other hand, remained involved in petty rivalries. Interregional commerce was discouraged in favor of the Neapolitan capital city and the larger enterprises of Genoese and other foreigners.

Correcting Misguided Government Grain Policy in the Sixteenth Century

Let us examine how this regional model worked in practice by reviewing government pastoral and agricultural policy. The 1548 cadastral survey reordering Capitanata measured and reassigned 2,060 *carra* to the pastoralists. Pastoralism was favored because controlling the migratory shepherd industry kept violence in the countryside at a minimum and royal revenues at a maximum.

With the burgeoning population in both the Neapolitan capital and the provincial hinterland, however, the 1548 general reintegration would prove to be a grave political and economic blunder. In arguing the agriculturists' point of view in a letter addressed to Philip II soon after his ascension to the throne, a Genoese landholder near Taranto, Giovan Battista Alliata, expressed consternation at the misguided fiscal policy employed by the king's Neapolitan ministers to favor the pastoralists in the reintegration.[24] Short-term advantages gained from increased revenue could not offset what was inevitably going to offend the people. The cadastral survey had allowed pastoralism to displace agriculture in the Kingdom's most fertile grain-producing region. The common people did not eat meat from livestock which was, in any case, shipped out of the Kingdom. Famine was caused by an absence of grain. The people would necessarily riot when no bread could be found.[25] Alliata's train of reasoning continued: sheep had been allowed to eat men in Puglia and the consequences for the Kingdom were already becoming apparent. Every year there was a new famine scare. Moreover, increased revenues were illusory because the pastoralists were retrograde capitalists who raised 10,000, 15,000, 20,000, or 30,000 sheep for wool and meat production so that they could hoard the profits, burying them in the ground without reinvesting in productive enterprises. Arable land should be returned to cultivation and the *dogana delle pecore* curtailed. Agriculture could not only feed the Kingdom but make it rich through grain sales to Genoese, Venetians, and other foreigners. Of course, the grain-growing Genoese Alliata had some interest in such a solution.

The severe famine of 1555 persuaded the viceregal administration to reverse the short-lived land allocation of 1548 even before Alliata's antipastoral polemic was composed. Virgin land for cultivation (*terre salde a coltura*) was taken out of doganal pasture, and 1,000 *carra* were to be rented on a short-term basis. Again in 1560, 500 *carra* were made *terre salde,* and thereafter the terms of rented land were renewed: in 1562, 1,000 *carra;* in 1567, only 500; in 1577, only 230; in 1584, only 400; and in 1591, two separate reassignments, one for 600, and one for 1,000.[26]

The banns promulgating *terre salde* rental in 1560 explained that arable land was taken out of pasture as an expedient to combat famine.[27] Despite the best efforts of agriculturists, they could not produce enough grain. The principal reason for poor harvests was soil exhaustion. Because loss of fertility meant lower yields, new fields had to be sown. Administrative rationale gave no hint of past bureaucratic errors in extending too much land to pastoralists. Instead, the Neapolitan reports lauded the phenomenal results obtained from planting *terre salde* formerly in pasture: 10,000 *carra* of wheat from 500 *carra* of land for a 1:20 land/yield ratio.[28] Only in 1591 did the Sommaria expand its explanation for *terre salde* renting beyond crop failure to include extraordinary famine and population growth—never any mention of a misguided policy in terms of the pastoral/agricultural ratio.[29]

As early as 1562 the king's councillors in Spain were discussing a proposal of Julio Cinugui to establish a permanent agricultural system which would return the Tavoliere to its prereintegration level of cereal production.[30] From the 12,000 *carra* of royal demesne at the pastoralists' disposition, the court would initiate a twenty-four-year rotation cycle in which four plots of 3,000 *carra* (where each *carro* was measured at 15 *versure*) would be planted for six-year periods. At 15 ducats per *carro,* the cultivated land would provide an income of 45,000 ducats and produce enough grain not only for the Kingdom but also for export. No harm would come to the dogana's sheep market according to the meticulous accounting which makes up the bulk of the *consulta.* The proposal would not bring "total ruin to the dogana" because 3,000 *carra* at 15 *versure* were roughly equal to 2,000 *carra* at 20 *versure*—the amount of land added to pasture after the 1548 cadastral survey. In other words, the dogana could operate its transhumant activities with the same amount of pasture as before the survey (grazing extra sheep on the extraordinary pasture) and in addition collect rent on virgin land used for planting of 2,000 *carra* for the "universal benefit of the whole Kingdom."

No such plan was adopted. Renting *terre salde,* however, remained a permanent part of the doganal institution and provided a fixed income of some 20,000 ducats annually. But neither the increased income nor the increased grain satisfied demand.

The big money was being made not by the state, but by land speculators. Cereal prices rose 153 percent from 1501 to 1614.[31] Price movement for wheat varied by region in the Kingdom as follows:

1500	1 *carlino* per *tomolo*
1520–40	2–5 *carlini* per *tomolo*
1540–60	3–7 *carlini* per *tomolo*
1560–85	4–9 *carlini* per *tomolo*
1585–94	9–18 *carlini* per *tomolo*
1595–1603	6–16 *carlini* per *tomolo*[32]

Between 1550 and 1600 median prices increased by 70 percent for grain, 85 percent for oil, 105 percent for cheese, and 70 percent for pork.[33] Wine, beans, silk—all commodities were up. Salaries, however, rose only 21 percent. Inflation and the growing differential between prices and wages contributed to the scarcity of foodstuffs and the squeeze on consumers.

For the royal treasury, revenues began to decline despite the 1556 increased tax rates on pastoral products. Gabelles on silk, iron,[34] wine, oil, soap, salt, and even playing cards were instituted. All products subject to weights and measures were taxed at higher rates during the second half of the sixteenth century.[35] Under the weight of Philip II's foreign policy in Europe and America, expenditures and inflation were eating up both revenue and credit throughout the empire. By 1580 a plan was under consideration to close seven of the eleven Neapolitan banks.[36] Between 1593 and 1597 the situation became critical. The viceregal budget could only be balanced by large *donativi* (levies granted by communes, institutions like the Foggian customs, and individuals), a situation that only deepened the crisis of credit.[37] And the solution—royal bankruptcy (Philip's third was declared on 29 November 1596)—only put off the final reckoning.

In 1600, then, Capitanata was the center of extensive wool and grain production. Investment was heavy despite mounting inflation and weakening credit. Competition for land use between sheep and wheat interests was fierce. Sheepherding profits provided one of the largest single sources of income to balance Neapolitan foreign payments as one-third of production was exported to northern Italian markets. Grain may have fed the Kingdom, but wool paid the bills. The history of the dogana of Foggia in this epoch is a governmental balancing act offering privileges and subterfuge to irreconcilable rivals.[38] The social and economic structure of Capitanata was built on this structure of conflict and antagonism, the unstable relationship between cereal agriculture and sheep pastoralism.

The economic florescence was only a brief moment for Capitanata, the Kingdom of Naples, and Italy in general. The economic downturn had already begun with the grain crises of the first decade of the seventeenth century. Then the dogana of Foggia was particularly hard hit in a single blow. The severe winter of 1611/12 caused enormous sheep deaths. Flocks were reduced to about 500,000 head, a 69 percent reduction. With the loss of their profits and ready cash from that year's sales, the loss of their capital investment in dead sheep, and the tightening credit, innumerable small holders were wiped out. No wonder the viceregal reform of state finances administered by Lemos substituted fixed agreements for free bidding taxation in 1615. The Lemos reform was far-reaching. The entire structure of viceregal income had to be reeexamined and redefined.

Simultaneously in Naples, money (with respect to 1610) was devalued 8.4 percent in 1611, 15.9 percent in 1617, 20.31 percent in 1618, and 33.1 percent in 1620.[39] Thus, the general crisis in Italy has been identified in two expanding phases, 1609–13 and 1619–22.[40] The crash of currency and credit developed out of a normal cyclical crisis when these short-term crises became a structural one.

Successful Government Market Policy in the Sixteenth Century

Let us return to 1548, before the definitive Spanish reorganization of the Kingdom under the viceroy Pedro de Toledo, and look at a more successful government economic policy. The Spanish found two fairs in Lucera and three in Foggia. They consolidated those in Foggia into one month-long spring fair and subordinated all other fairs to it.

Lucera's ancient summer fair from 24 June to 8 July was the oldest in the region.[41] No archival evidence of this fair has been found for the Aragonese period save two notarial contracts for a March and a November fair in Lucera in 1474 and 1477 respectively.[42] Some sixteenth-century evidence exists. In February 1583, when a Turkish ship was wrecked off the coast of nearby Rodi, the doganiero of the sheep customhouse at Foggia, Alfonso Caracciolo, was instructed to salvage its cargo and sell its personnel and merchandise at the upcoming March fair at Lucera.[43] Three years later, because of the rain, snow, and extreme cold in 1586, poor attendance at the twenty-day March fair led to its extension. In similar compensation for the previous year's bad weather, the following November fair was extended even before it opened.[44] The Sommaria continued to issue banns announcing both the March and November Lucera fairs as late as 1600.[45]

Foggia, for its part, had fairs from "the most ancient times that anyone can remember" on the four days before and after 11 October, 21 March, and 21 August.[46] With Spanish pacification in force throughout Italy by the mid sixteenth century, the 40,000 *rubbi* of wool harvested in Foggia in 1535 began to rise.[47] In 1536, Charles V's refoundation of the customhouse concerned itself with strengthening bureaucratic centralization of the pastoral industry at Foggia. His instructions provided that the Foggian fair alone could sell pastoral products and that only pastoralists enrolled in the customhouse system could sell their products at the Foggian fair, under penalty of confiscation of their goods.[48] As increased sheep transhumance concentrated more and more activity in the spring shearing season at Foggia, some regulation was needed in order to control the increased goods and participants.[49] In 1541 the first of some nine concessions requested by the commune and citizens of Foggia from the viceroy Pedro de Toledo urged that a unified spring fair be established in April. The Sommaria referred the matter to the Foggian customhouse.[50] At the end of the March 1549 fair, then, Charles V ordered that one free spring fair be established in April to replace the other three.[51] By 1561 wool sales in Foggia had doubled to 80,000 *rubbi*.[52]

The Organization of the Foggian Fair

The fair opened on 1 April with a solemn procesession of citizens, foreigners, customhouse magistrates, elected representatives, and soldiers carrying an official flag to a place of public display in the window of the palace of justice. The captain of the town's militia consigned the scepter of justice to the chief judge (*mastro iurato*) of the customhouse court who presided for the duration of the fair.[53] Another such solemn occasion marked the beginning of sales at the fair. On an appointed morning the graziers paraded their meat animals in the "showing of the castrated lambs" (*mostra dei castrati*) before the assembled buyers and in the presence of the doganiero and other customhouse officers.[54]

The *mostra* of animals was not just given symbolic priority. Income from the sale of meat animals (lambs and castrated rams) was initially used as payment to the customhouse for pasture taxes (*fida*).[55] But laws prevented sheep from being sequestered for taxes or any other kind of debt.[56] When pasture taxes were raised 50 percent in 1556, animal income alone could not meet this obligation. Voluntary bids, inflated by the competition between sheepowners for good pasture, made up part of the difference. Promoting the wool trade was the best way to ensure the state's revenues.[57]

Charles' new Foggian fair lasted for the entire month of April, while sheepowners placed their wool in depositories. The whole range of pastoral products—wool, lambs and castrated rams for meat, cheese, goat kids, calves, skins, leather goods—were bought and sold. Approximate percentages of a sheepowner's income in the seventeenth and eighteenth centuries offer a rough guide to the relative value of pastoral products—about one-half wool, one-fourth to two-fifths meat, and one-tenth to one-fifth cheese.[58] As we shall see, however, not all this income matured in the spring. August wool (16 percent of total income) as well as lambs born in August and cheese cured over the summer (about one-half of their respective totals) were marketed in Abruzzesi fall fairs. Pastoral products sold in the unified spring fair at Foggia accounted for slightly more than one-half of a sheepowner's annual gross income—one-third wool, one-tenth meat, and less than one-tenth cheese.

The fair's celebration culminated on 26 April, the principal feast of St. Guglielmo and St. Pellegrino, with two palios, one a horse race and the other a foot race, which had previously been run on the Annunciation at the end of the March fair.[59] Di Stefano emphasized that shearing time was a season of "festival, joyfulness, and merrymaking" like that of the grain harvest and the *vendemmia.* "The shepherds congregated together among themselves and with friends and relatives" to engage in drinking bouts and excesses just as they had from biblical times.60 By the eighteenth century the population of Foggia swelled during the spring fair. Housing, which was already scarce during the winter season because of the presence of powerful sheepowners, became difficult to find, even for citizens of Foggia.61

The Foggian Fair's Privileges: Justice and Tax-Exemption

In the midst of the month-long festivities, then, police powers to maintain public order were transferred to customhouse jurisdiction without, however, relieving the Foggian captain of the responsibilities of his office.62 The unified April fair, like its predecessor fairs, provided special judicial guarantees and protection for participants.63 In addition, the privileged status of a free fair, exempt from import and export duties, made the new Foggian fair one of the Kingdom's four elite fairs, along with Salerno, Aversa, and Lanciano. "We also order and command that when castrated animals, wool, cheese, and other merchandise of these *locati* is sold in said Fair of Foggia, they are to be free and immune, even though they are exported from the Kingdom, *even* if the buyers are men unenrolled in the Dogana and from outside the Kingdom."64 De Dominicis explained that the purpose of this privilege was to ensure the continued participation of foreign merchants, especially the Venetians, who had an ancient tradition of buying wool from Foggia.65

Taxes levied on citizens and foreign merchants were much lower than those paid through the normal customs of the Kingdom. The Foggian fair exempted imposts on internal goods (*dazio della contrattazione* or *della Piazza*) at 18 *grana* for every *oncia* (6 ducats) worth of merchandise (i.e., a tax at the rate of 3 percent); imposts on exports between provinces or outside the Kingdom (*diritto di Fondaco*) at 15 *grana* per *oncia* (i.e., at 2.5 percent); the new gabelle of Charles III of Anjou at 6 *grana* per *oncia* (i.e., at 1 percent). Doganal sheep were even exempted from the Church's one-tenth (*decima* at 10 percent).66 Instead of these accumulated taxes on goods, the 1551 decree of Charles V fixed taxes at the Foggian fair as a license fee of only one *carlino* per man. Fines for noncompliance—that is, selling goods without a license—were 5 *carlini* for each offense.67

The fair at Foggia soon became the Kingdom's largest wool and animal fair. Its preeminence in raw material exchange complemented the other three free fairs, where finished products were sold. Aversa stands near the Neapolitan capital, while Lanciano and Salerno were the focal points where the Kingdom's wool-manufacturing centers in the Abruzzi and Principato Citra sold their cloths.68 At Foggia, in exchange for pastoral products, foreign merchants also sold manufactured goods for urban consumption, luxury goods for the large landlords and state officials, and utilitarian manufactures like tools and firearms for shepherds and peasants.69 By the eighteenth century, De Dominicis claimed that, in order to attract manufactures and other goods, such as spices, these free fairs imposed duties of less than one-half those generally placed on imported and exported goods.[70]

Much customhouse adjudication focused on these tax immunities. In 1649, for example, when the merchant Pietro Zanetti, resident in Foggia, dragged his exports on into the summer, as was common, the port of Manfredonia attempted to collect duty on 1,000 *cantara* of cheese bound for Naples.[71] The disputed taxes were hardly insignificant: 10.3 percent of the value of the merchandise, plus another 250 ducats assessed on its weight. The courts were forced to clarify that this customhouse exemption did not depend upon the time of their sale or shipment, but upon the origins of the products. Both sellers and buyers were free from taxation whenever they shipped their goods.

In 1665 an accusation of fraud against Marino Blasi, Michele de Marco, and other dealers in lambskins and hides from Ragusa turned on this same point of law—the origin of the goods.[72] The port of Barletta claimed that their merchandise had been prepared "for export with many errors," that it had not all been bought at the Foggian fair, but "in some other place in the Kingdom," and that it was, therefore, liable to normal duties despite their fraudulent claims.

From Charles V's 1536 concession to graziers, sale of pastoral products outside Foggia had been forbidden, as had sales in Foggia of pastoral products by unenrolled sheepowners. By the mid seventeenth century, fixed contract taxes had become so burdensome that sheepowners sought to avoid them by fraudulently circumventing the Foggian fair. The prince of Altamura even claimed an indemnity because Foggia's monopoly prevented his town's ancient fair from functioning.[73] The state responded swiftly with an edict reaffirming the illegality of fairs outside Foggia.[74] Sheepowners who persisted in seeking markets at the 25 April fair in Altamura or Gravina in nearby Basilicata received harsh punishments. Not only would sellers' animals be confiscated, but buyers would have to pay a 1,000-ducat fine. Two-thirds of the fine would go to the viceregal treasury, and the other one-third to the denouncer.[75] Thus, although the animal and pastoral products fairs of Gravina and Altamura continued through the eighteenth century, only those graziers with special licenses could participate, as these fairs were considered an adjunct to the Foggian fair.[76] These Ragusans in 1665, then, were acquitted because the extraction of all pastoral products fell under customhouse jurisdiction wherever they were purchased.

Similarly, customhouse tax exemptions applied wherever the goods were exported, even if transported overland to Naples and exported from there. The earliest legal precedent for the exemption of wool exports from the Neapolitan capital dated from 25 August 1730. The practice of shipping wool west derived from the decline of Venice and the increase of French, Dutch, and English shipping in the Mediterranean. When Manfredonia, which served as the Adriatic outlet for Foggian wool,[77] began to accumulate 20,000 *rubbi* of surplus unsold wool (17,618 *rubbi* from 1759 and 21,816 *rubbi* from 1760),[78] the sellers sought to accommodate the French and northern European buyers who wished to avoid the perils of navigation in the Adriatic. In 1759, because no wool exports had been registered in Naples since 1742, the port of Naples raised new pretensions to assess a tax of 36 *carlini* per *cantara* on wool exports. The state reduced the tax claims to 15 *carlini* per *cantara* of raw wool; and in 1760 it lowered them to only 33 *grana* (3.3 *carlini*) per *cantara* thereafter.[79] Wool taxes were to be levied in Naples at the same rate as in Manfredonia; profit margins on wool sales to foreigners could not be increased beyond the wool's "intrinsic price and the high cost of transport from Foggia."

By the late eighteenth century, these exemptions were so attractive that "many individuals who were not wool merchants, but only present to cultivate the countryside" attempted to gain the status of "firsthand wool buyers." These "fictitious merchants" defrauded the state of 24 *carlini* each by paying a merchant license fee instead of rent for virgin land.[80] Just like the phantom sheepowners who enrolled in the customhouse for its judicial privileges,[81] these fictitious merchants fraudulently sought special customhouse tax exemptions; or like speculators, they bought agricultural products to resell them illegally at higher prices.[82] Eventually the customhouse archive was called in to resolve such disputes by preserving merchant registrations and certifications as firsthand wool buyers.[83]

The Foggian Fair Restructured

Charles V's 1551 memorial confirming the unified Foggian fair thus emphasized three points: the fair's consolidated April date, judicial privileges, and tax exemptions. The main innovation, a one-month concentration of activity in April, however, soon gave way to economic expediency. In 1577, plague in northern Italy delayed the showing of the castrated lambs until a special exemption could be obtained from the viceroy to allow merchants no farther north than Bologna to attend the fair. The solemn opening took place on 16 April.[84] Even as a one-time emergency measure, a precedent had been set. In the decades following the 1611/12 depletion of flocks, moving the fair's date became an experimental means to increase buyer participation. After the 1611/12 sheep death, greater demand put stress on the lowered supply of pastoral products. Since the Kingdom's laws gave priority to domestic consumption, the meat needs of the Neapolitan capital were squeezing out the important foreign buyers of lambs and castrated animals. Further, in 1617 war between Naples and Venice kept many other merchants away from the fair, and lower demand deflated prices.[85] To facilitate the arrival of more buyers, the *mostra* was put off until 1 May. In 1619, in order to stimulate merchant participation, Jews were even given special exemptions to attend the fair without wearing their customary hat-badges.[86] By the 1620s the April date of the spring fair did not correspond to recorded wool sales. While wool was still shorn and placed in deposit in the early spring, overall the bulk of the wool was taken out of deposit and sold in a five-week period between May and June.[87] In the *transazione* contracts between 1626 and 1636, a compromise dating of the fair (*mostra* on 25 April, with wool sales extending to 25 May) was set to placate sellers and attract buyers.[88] Neither sellers nor buyers responded favorably since the fair's date was not the critical variable for economic recovery.

Data from six random seventeenth-century fairs verify that no definitive pattern was established during the downturn.[89] Wool sales continued in either May or June, with two-thirds to three-fourths of wool transactions recorded and wool quantity sold between them (table 21). The fluctuations of the Easter calendar make as good a hypothesis as any to explain changes in the fair's dates. When Easter fell early, the feasts of the Ascension and Pentecost, forty and fifty days later, could shift the start of the fair. In 1641, since Ascension Thursday fell on 9 May and Pentecost Sunday on 19 May, the fair got into full swing the following weekend, Friday 24 May. In 1670, with the Ascension on 15 May and Pentecost on 25 May, the fair began on 27 May. In both cases, early Easters delayed the start of the Foggian fair until late in May, after Penteost, and the majority of wool sales were pushed back into June. If Easter were really early, however, as in 1655, with the Ascension on 6 May and Pentecost on 16 May, the delayed start of the fair would cause minimal disruptions. Wool sales began in earnest on 16 May, only a week late. Sales data from 1625 proves this hypothetical rule. When Ascension fell on St. Michael's Day, 8 May itself, both feasts were celebrated simultaneously, a long holiday declared, and wool sales begun on Sunday 11 May. The characteristic May dating of the fair appears to have become uniform only in the 1680s after the new *voce* price credit system was put in place.

The ideal structure, as it appeared in the 1685 and 1700 fairs, allowed for the fair to begin with the celebrations on 8 May for the Feast of the Apparition of St. Michael in the Gargano, the official closing of the winter season. Some small quantities of wool were sold before the feast and none sold on the day itself. Sales were concentrated in the weeks immediately following. No one day of the week was favored, although highest totals (about 10 percent of total wool in a single day) were often recorded on Saturdays. Sundays were market days like every other.[90]

Why was the original March fair pushed further back to May? One long, unified May/June fair worked for the convenience of both state and buyers. The mechanism of the fair could equally serve the buyers of spring wool and the buyers of summer wheat, because as May's pastoral fair wound down in late June, the wheat harvest came in. Further, since these same buyers were also advancing credit to fuel production, they began to assume a larger role in the government's decision-making process. This confluence between buyer and bureaucratic interests forged an alliance characteristic of mercantile-en-

TABLE 21 Wool Quantity and Sales at Foggia by Month (In *Rubbi*)

| | | May | | |
Year	Paranza	Transactions	Wool Sold	Mean Quantity per Transaction
1625	Sulmona	125 (55.6%)	9,793 (67.7%)	78
1641	Sulmona	86 (31.3)	4,329 (24.8)	50
1655	Sulmona	226 (80.4)	10,811 (70.0)	48
1670	Sulmona	49 (25.8)	3,489 (22.7)	71
	All	91 (15.3)	8,538 (15.8)	94
1685	Sulmona	94 (83.2)	16,712 (82.5)	178
	All	333 (74.5)	43,174 (72.0)	130
1700	Sulmona	135 (79.4)	16,120 (71.5)	119
	All	547 (76.3)	68,592 (75.2)	125

Sources: ASFg, *Dogana,* serie V, regg. 2001 (1625), 2017 (1641), 2029 (1655), 2057–2060 (1670), 2114–2117 (1685), and 2167–2170 (1700).

Note: Account books in 1625 and 1685 record a few cases without dates. Account books in 1625 record sales in April; 1670 in April, July, August, September, October, and the following spring; 1685 in July.

trepreneurial relationships with the state and underlines the complex capitalist underpinning of the pastoral economy.

In practice, then, the Foggian fair continued through the summer, from April through August, because of climate, transport, products, and buyers.[91] Thus, since the port of Manfredonia was within one or two carting days on the plain, the large supply of raw wool in deposit at Foggia was transported and exported commodiously over the summer without creating bottlenecks.[92] In the four years 1714 through 1717, for example, the Venetian consul for Capitanata recorded that some 118 ships sailed from Manfredonia, about 30 per year. The bulk of traffic, 70 percent of the ships, operated between May and September, that is, about one ship per week. No ships sailed in December and January, and only 12 percent in the long winter season, November through March. The Venetian consul also recorded 85 sailings, about 21 per year, from Barletta in the same period. Only one of these ships carried wool, and it had previously stopped at Manfredonia for cargo. Almost one-half (48 percent) of Barletta's traffic in comparison to less than one-third (31 percent) of Manfredonia's was concentrated in May and June at the peak of fair activity.[93]

In the meantime, wheat matured and was harvested in late June and July. Cereal cash crops were stored and exported on demand and, in turn, reinforced the mercantile concentration in the Tavoliere. The dovetailing of wool and wheat harvests and their storage in the depositories of Foggia gradually transformed the out of town buyers into resident merchants.

| | June | Mean Quantity | Annual |
Transactions	Wool Sold	per Transaction	Mean
84 (37.3%)	3,884 (26.9%)	46	64
189 (68.7)	13,096 (75.2)	69	63
55 (19.6)	4,639 (30.0)	84	55
128 (67.4)	10,509 (68.5)	82	80
373 (62.6)	34,509 (63.9)	93	91
19 (16.8)	3,537 (17.5)	186	179
70 (15.7)	13,222 (22.0)	189	134
35 (20.6)	6,433 (28.5)	184	133
170 (23.7)	22,659 (24.8)	133	127

Cyclical Crises

The portrait of economy and society in Capitanata and the Kingdom in 1600 is well delineated. The exportation of capital by foreign merchants, the growing crisis of credit, increasing fiscal pressures from the state, the resultant control of finances and political power in the hands of fewer and fewer aristocrats, and class polarization have been described by many students of seventeenth-century Naples.[94] The end of demographic growth, the closing of the communes by oligarchic prerogative, the decline of cereal prices, and the drying up of the wool market moved southern society closer and closer to what Galasso calls the "debacle." The weak "industries" of the South soon shriveled up. The wool guild at Naples suffered near extinction, while the silk guild in Calabria fared no better.[95] The monetary crisis and bank failures of 1622 were the final blow.[96] Viceregal currency reforms proved ineffective, and all public banks failed except one, *il Banco dei Poveri*. Its peculiar administrative structure, a bureaucracy that crisscrossed the Neapolitan elite, prevented its fall.

The collapse of the Neapolitan economy and the solidification of southern social structure were not caused by outside forces alone. Their endemic weaknesses are obvious. At the same time, the seventeenth-century crisis of Naples was not an isolated phenomenon. As part of the quixotic illusions of the decaying Spanish Empire, and as the raw material supplier for a declining northern Italy, the Kingdom was responsive to the general economic downturn in Europe.[97] Explanations of Neapolitan decline must balance both internal and external pressures. As the external crisis deepened, internal reform only seemed to worsen the situation. It was not the errors of the viceregal administration nor the corruption of its officials which caused the disorders of the seventeenth century in Naples.⁹⁸ Rather, the cumulative effects of decades of overextended expenditures and overestimated resources; the precarious balance of regional economies; the erosion of its imperial framework; the supersaturation of older markets; its colonial relationship to the fully matured economy of the North; and the contradictory nature of internal institutional structures marked the end of the Indian summer economic boom for Naples and Italy.⁹⁹

In the seventeenth, eighteenth, and nineteenth centuries, the dogana and the Kingdom lived through cyclical repetitions of this crisis. The slow economic recovery after 1680 stalled with the War of the Spanish Succession in the first decade of the new century. The stabilization and growth after the Bourbon ascendancy in 1734 aborted with the famine of 1763/64. Population pressure in the last quarter of the eighteenth century demanded a land reform census (*censuazione*) and manumission (*affrancazione*) in the early nineteenth. Thus, the wheat and wool markets of the Tavoliere di Puglia reflected secular economic trends. Structures did not change but modified themselves to the changing economic circumstances that determined the needs of a dual economy of international trade and local subsistence.

PART 4

La Ragion del Mercato

The doganal administration's search to find some way out of the long seventeenth-century crisis and the state's decisive establishment of the unified spring fair of Foggia, as described in parts 2 and 3, prepared the way for further state intervention in the market. Once recovery was underway, the customhouse continued to oversee the conflictual relationship between buyers and sellers. Seller solidarity in the face of recurrent buyer attempts to create unfair monopolies received responsive treatment from the doganal bureaucracy. The buyers, for their part, continued to enjoy wool tax exemptions and government encouragement for wool manufacturing in the Neapolitan capital. The effect of low taxes and the promotion of home industry thus helped sustain a healthy balance between the foreign and domestic woolen markets. The interplay between the structures of production and demand at the Foggian fair reflected a constant tension in need of resolution.

8 The Fair of Foggia: Production and Prices

Wool-Weighing Sources

Can we move from our social structural and political analysis to an understanding of the Foggian economy? What do we know about the structure of the market at the Foggian fair? How did it change over time?

The best source for production and purchase of wool at the fair of Foggia is an extraordinary run of serial documentation, the account books of the "weighers of wool" (*pesatori di lana*).[1] The account books were divided into two parts, wool put into deposit (*infondacatura*) and wool taken out of deposit (*sfondacatura*). Entries registered wool owners by transactions. Thus, the sales accounts provide information on dates, transactions, names and origins of buyers and sellers, wool quantities, and prices.

The weighers of wool oversaw weights and measures at the fair.[2] In exchange the weighers originally received one *grano* per *rubbio* of wool weighed, a stipend increased in the seventeenth century to two *grani* for white wool and three for black.[3] By 1584, Aquila, the largest "weighing station" (*paranza*), employed six regular weighers, three for white and three for black wool; Sulmona and Castel di Sangro, three weighers each. Including these twelve official wool weighers, some forty persons participated in the weighing, and each received 10–30 ducats annually.[4] Sellers and buyers shared equally in paying wages; thus weighers were not customhouse or government officers, but salaried representatives of the sheepowners from the graziers' trail-head towns of Aquila, Sulmona, and Castel di Sangro, who were confirmed by the state.[5]

Wool weighers were licensed to prevent frauds. They were especially alert to foreign impurities mixed into the wool or wool soaked in water to increase its weight.[6] The weighers themselves, however, could be corrupted into favoring their compatriot sellers by putting their thumbs on the scales. In 1583 all the customhouse weighers were jailed because of fraudulent scales. Weighers from the royal mint took their place.[7] In 1711 the weighers from Castel di Sangro committed fraud against the state customhouse by double accounting. They sent customhouse tax officers different weight information from that registered in their account books.[8] A similar charge of tax evasion by double bookkeeping was levied against all the weighers in 1725.[9] The possibilities for wool weighers' frauds seemed endless. They could be agents for themselves between the market and the state, or suborned partners of buyers, sellers, or state.

The Foggian archive preserves the registers of the weighing station of Sulmona alone from 1623.[10] One lone account book of black wool from Aquila is extant for 1651, and then a series from 1663. A complete serial record of the four account books (Aquila white and black wool, Sulmona, and Castel di Sangro) begins in 1666 and extends to 1791 with occasional lacunae.[11] The Aquila account books continue until 1801.

Can anything be said about the early seventeenth-century Foggian fair before all the account books become extant in 1666? If we construct a linear regression from the twenty-seven valid cases of complete sales from the late seventeenth century, the weighing station of Sulmona comes into clearer focus. Its reliability as a predictor of total wool between 1666 and 1700 is about 71 percent.[12] We can then proceed confidently to define the fair's structure from its earliest sources in the Sulmona account books and point to the town's pride of place remembered by the Ovidian couplet copied on the cover of the 1701 account book:

Sulmona is my hometown, a land rich in ice-cold streams,
Thrice thirty miles from the city.[13]

I have selected sample account books from the seventeenth century at fifteen-year intervals—1625, 1641, 1655, 1670, 1685, and 1700.[14] My detailed analysis is limited to the seventeenth-century account books because, as I mentioned earlier, the *voce* pricing system replaced market prices after 1680. Data from these books alone, however, should be sufficient to define the structure of the Foggian fair. All six years yield information from Sulmona; the last three provide a global analysis from all four account books of the three weighing stations.

While the account book variables draw a portrait of production and exchange in the pastoral industries, both structurally and dynamically, two other serial sources aid analysis. The Doria account books from Melfi offer animal production and price information for a flock of some 10,000 sheep from 1672 to 1763. Although they do not provide comparable production totals, the Doria data supplement our knowledge of prices, contracts and price-setting mechanisms, and other pastoral products. Secondly, the *voce* prices for wool, cheese, and grain were recorded in Foggia from 1731.[15] They allow for both quantitative and qualitative comparisons. The seventeenth- and eighteenth-century Foggian fair, then, can be reconstructed in static approximation and in its long-term trends.

Wool Production

General statistics suggest the rough correlation that, in the seventeenth century, Sulmona accounted for some one-fourth to one-third of total wool (table 22). Annual number of transactions at Sulmona in the seventeenth century averaged 209. At Sulmona, sellers averaged 76 sheepowners, and

THE FAIR OF FOGGIA: PRODUCTION AND PRICES   197

TABLE 22 General Statistics from the Seventeenth-Century Foggian Fair

Year	Paranza	Transactions	Sellers	Buyers	Wool Sold (In Rubbi)
1625	Sulmona	225	85	245	14,460
1641	Sulmona	275	91	179	17,425
1655	Sulmona	281	71	150	15,451
1670	Aquila *bianca*	162	79	66	17,858
	Aquila *nera*	94	50	63	7,590
	Sulmona	190	66	90	15,340
	Castel di Sangro	150	59	71	13,192
	All	596	253	225	53,980
1685	Aquila *bianca*	159	77	64	19,155
	Aquila *nera*	82	52	50	6,968
	Sulmona	113	57	36	20,249
	Castel di Sangro	93	46	30	13,595
	All	447	232	133	59,967
1700	Aquila *bianca*	189	105	55	29,943
	Aquila *nera*	135	108	72	11,904
	Sulmona	170	84	66	22,553
	Castel di Sangro	223	107	75	26,850
	All	717	406	184	91,251

Source: See table 21.

buyers averaged 111 merchants. While sellers remained relatively constant in Sulmona across the century, the number of buyers and transactions declined from 1670, with a low point in 1685. Fewer merchants were buying larger quantities of wool in the last third of the century. Thus, the seventeenth-century crisis concentrated capital into the fewer hands capable of reaping the profits of rising production.

Over the long term, 1623–1801, some 107 complete sales totals were preserved (app. E-1). From these 107 cases, we can compare the relative size of the three weighing stations and the predictability value of their account books. Thus, the mean total of wool sold at Foggia from 1667 to 1791 was 80,440 *rubbi,* that is, about the amount of wool produced by one million sheep. The three weighing stations sold wool in these proportions: 48.3, 30.9 (a further confirmation of the validity of the seventeenth-century extrapolation), and 20.7 percent respectively—30,417 *rubbi* of white wool in Aquila, 8,451 *rubbi* of black wool in Aquila, 24,874 *rubbi* in Sulmona, and 16,686 *rubbi* in Castel di Sangro. The difference between high and low amounts of wool taken out of deposit in any one year was enormous—44,397 *rubbi* in 1709 and more than three times that, 135,726 *rubbi,* in 1783.[16] So great were these fluctuations among the account books that a linear regression does not allow firm conclusions to be drawn for three of the account books. The account book for white wool from Aquila alone predicts about 73 percent of total wool variation.[17] In other words, rise and fall of white wool production in Aquila provides the only source which more often than not reflects the general trend in total wool production. The Aquila black wool account book, on the other hand, is the worst predictor. Aquila black wool production remained relatively stable since black wool had a fixed market in uniforms for the Kingdom's army and in religious habits for its clergy.[18]

If we add some 65 estimates to the 107 complete sales records, we can draw a 172-point long-term curve for wool sales in Foggia from 1623 to 1801 (fig. 15). The data lead us to two important conclusions—one explaining short-term fluctuations; the other, long-term trends. First, the lows in 1648, 1649, 1657, 1709, 1726, 1732, 1745, 1761, and 1764 all came as sharp declines because of some precipitating external factor, either political or climatological crisis. Second, evening out these sharp fluctuations by five-year weighted moving averages (app. E-2) reveals two clear production periods: one, from 1623 to 1691, corresponded to the general crisis of the seventeenth century; and the second, from 1691 to 1801, reestablished the dogana at its earlier, sixteenth-century norm.[19] Simple generalizations on the whole curve distort the real picture of equilibrium and change.

First, as we have seen in our earlier schematization of doganal periodization, short-term fluctuations were often caused by human and animal mortality. The plagues of 1656 and 1764 and the famine of 1761 caused blips in the wool production curve. Likewise, we have already examined the effects of sheep deaths after harsh winters, as in 1726 and 1745. My earlier general model of sheepography would predict residual effects for three years. In these two cases, however, sheep replacement is completed within two years, probably because of the limited damage to total flock size, the uneven distribution of flock damage, and the overall climate of economic boom in the eighteenth century. Political effects, on the other hand, show strong residual effects, as in the revolt of 1647/48 and the War of the Spanish Succession in 1709. The 1731 Foggian earthquake, which disrupted the bureaucracy and the city more than the sheep in the countryside, makes a good test case in the following year's decline. Coupled with the War of the Polish Succession, whose first phase saw Austria's Italian possessions—Milan, Naples, and Sicily—conquered by Spain, such events precipitated low wool sales because the customhouse system of centralized transhumance and the primacy given to the fair in Foggia were essentially political innovations maintained by special privileges and were geared to international wool demand. Not surprisingly, all of these poor production years left physical marks in the account books in the form of smaller ledgers, changed formats, and different accounting methods.[20] In such cases, the relationship between domestic and foreign buyers changed.

Smoothing our curve, secondly, highlights the two periods. Mean wool production from 1623 to 1691 was 55,000 *rubbi* and from 1692 to 1801,

FIGURE 15 Total Wool Sold at Foggia (1623-1806) (*Rubbi*)

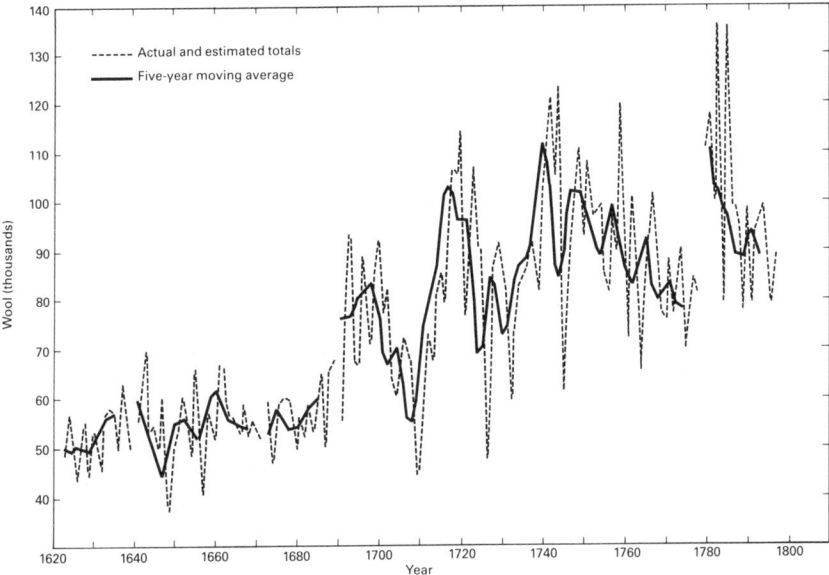

87,000 *rubbi*, that is, an increase of 158 percent. Wool production of 40,000–60,000 *rubbi* in this first period corresponded to a total sheep count of 500,000–750,000 head. The pastoral industry looked as though it might break out of its long crisis on numerous occasions like 1643 and 1661 with the hopes of a return to the free bidding system of tax collection. Sustained growth only began, however, in the 1680s with the concerted infusion of credit into the market by means of the public pricing system and the renewed separation of large and small holders. The last years of Spanish rule in Naples witnessed a transitional growth in production from 1692 to 1713 with a mean of 72,000 *rubbi* of wool shorn from some 750,000–1 million sheep. Amidst the anxieties of the Spanish succession, Neapolitan wool production may have gained some independent impetus. The rising production figures were not lost on contemporary witnesses. Di Stefano noted that the fall in production in 1704 and 1705 was in sharp contrast to the 85,000-*rubbi* norm.[21] Thereafter, the long period of sustained production only began with the stabilization of the Austrian succession in Naples. From 1713 to 1801 sales averaged 90,000 *rubbi* of wool from 1–1.3 million sheep. Three minibooms were recorded within this eighteenth-century production period: 1717–25, with a mean of 98,000 *rubbi;* 1740–67, with a mean of 95,000 *rubbi;* and 1780–97, with a mean of 97,000 *rubbi*. Eighteenth-century flocks peaked, then, at 1.7 million head, with a mean of 1.1 million.

Wool Demand

Big buyers for the textile manufacturers from northern Italy dominated the international wool market. Contrary to what we might expect from this large international market, however, the average size of transactions was often slightly lower during the times of peak sales than the annual mean (see table 21). Wool was not all bought up by a few large buyers in a few big transactions. Many small buyers and small sellers participated in the fair. Some larger buyers stayed for weeks and bought wool piecemeal from numerous sellers. Larger quantities of wool were purchased later in the season to close out inventories, but lower prices were not offered until immediately before the following year's fair.[22] Thus, wool continued to be sold from the depositories through November to merchants who might participate in the fairs of Salerno and Benevento.[23]

Foreign merchants, according to received wisdom, dominated the economy of the Kingdom. The importance of Catalan, Genoese, Florentine, and Milanese capital has been a truism of Neapolitan historiography.[24] But these large-scale international merchants, in fact, seem only to have controlled about one-third of Neapolitan trade. From the accounts of ten fairs at Lanciano (1447, 1453, 1454, 1456, 1457, and 1470), the Sommaria in Naples documented that there were over 1,800 merchants present, about 500 (38 percent) foreigners from more than 100 different places.[25] The notarial records of 102 transactions registered by Petruccio Pisano at the fair at Salerno from 18 to 24 September 1478 show that 75 out of 286 merchants (26 percent) were foreigners who bought 38 percent and sold 61 percent of the total merchandise.[26] This foreign merchant ratio, approximating one-third of goods sold, conformed to the Kingdom's statutes on exports.[27]

Although international trade often captures the economic historian's attention, the greater part of the Foggian market was involved in trade within the Kingdom. About two-thirds of production was sold to local manufacturers in the Abruzzi and Principato Citra, meats and cheeses were food supplements for domestic as well as international consumption, and these domestic markets were serviced by a large body of local merchants who often escape detection. Similarly, grain, wool's complementary cash crop in the Tavoliere of Puglia, was shipped to the Neapolitan capital. It was illegal to export wheat from the Kingdom without special authorization. Emphasis on entrepreneurial history or the Kingdom's dependency upon foreign mercantile exploitation and international money markets should not blind us to the vibrant domestic network among local merchants trading at the Foggian fair.

Wool Supply versus Wool Demand

Wool production as compared to wool sales can be examined in the two halves of the wool weighers' account books, wool placed in and taken out of depositories. Logically, we would expect more wool to be weighed in than out because some production might not be sold, and, obviously, what does not go in cannot come out. But here the wool weighers' accounts are deceptive. Moisture accumulated by wool in storage could add to its weight.[28] Wool not weighed into storage could be counted in the sold ledger, especially for the mid eighteenth century, when "revealed" wool (*rivelata*), that is, claimed or owned by sellers who made previous arrangements with buyers, was listed as a separate category. Consequently, in the 96 cases where both *infondacatura* and *sfondacatura* figures are available, more than one-half, 53 cases, show more wool taken out of deposit.[29] What is significant, then, are those 43 other years. When wool production totals outdistanced wool sales totals by more than 10 percent, these differences corresponded to real crises in the relationship between oversupply or slackened demand. Some 15 cases stand out in six groups: (1) 1667, 1670; (2) 1710; (3) 1732, 1735, 1739; (4) 1757, 1758; (5) 1775, 1776, 1777, 1779, 1784; and (6) 1796, 1801. The margin of difference ranges between 10 and 20 percent in all these cases, save 1710, where an extraordinarily high 31 percent difference can be measured. The *voce* price quotations also listed unsold wool from the previous year for 70 consecutive years, 1737–1806.[30] Here 48 cases (69 percent) recorded unsold wool. But only three cases, 1759, 1760, and 1764, reached 10 percent of production; and only twelve cases 1748, 1753, 1754, 1759, 1760, 1764, 1774, 1775, 1794, 1795, 1803, and 1806, reached 5 percent of production.

The 1710 anomaly coincided with the disruption of the international market during the War of the Spanish Succession and the change in the ruling dynasty of Naples from Spanish to Austrian Habsburgs. The difference between supply and demand rose so high because the new rulers introduced a 20 percent surtax on pasture. Since prices followed the principle of supply and demand, wool prices fell 25 percent, some 10 *carlini*. The 1732, 1735, and 1739 episodes also corresponded to another war and dynastic succession, the War of the Polish Succession and the Spanish Bourbon replacement of the Austrian Habsburgs in Naples. Although demand fell 15–18%, prices fell only two *carlini*. The new Bourbon monarchs brought less disturbance to the market because they could encourage more western exports to France, which had begun from Naples only a few years before,[31] since the second phase of the hostilities in the War of the Polish Succession shifted from Italy to the Upper Rhine. Further, they stabilized the *voce* system, established archivally kept accounts from their accession, and raised prices dramatically by 8 *carlini* (22 percent) in 1735.[32] The 1779 cases were also political. War between France and England kept the French buyers away during the May fair. But in the lengthy controversy which ensued, later evidence suggests that the French made their purchases eventually and the discrepancy lay more in reporting techniques than in fact.[33]

Two of the other three cases were more economic than political. In the 1660s the reinstatement of voluntary bidding tax assessments was meant to restimulate the wool market. Production increased, but no buyers appeared to pick up the slack, and the 1670s witnessed larger supplies than demand. This tax break began a false recovery because no real money was infused into the system. Again, the end of the seventeenth century crisis had to wait for the credit mechanisms of the 1680s. Secondly, the mid-eighteenth-century cases of production/sales discrepancies depended on the relationship between wool and wheat. Famines in the late 1750s put pressure on the agrarian economy for cereals.[34] Here again the wool buyers attempted to set up monopolies by buying wool below current prices and by delaying purchases until after the season. Balance sheets from 1760 and 1761 claim that the sellers lost 160,000 ducats as wool was undersold by 6.5–13 ducats.[35] This unsold wool in Foggia stimulated overland transport and export from Naples. Finally, the late 1790s and the turn of the century saw a combination of politics and famines. The Napoleonic Wars, projects for reform, and failed harvests (1802/03) enforced another price squeeze. The precarious relationship between supply and demand thus provides insight into price fluctuations, helps pinpoint critical junctures in the economy, and aids in the discrimination between internal and external economic impediments.

Wool Quality

Wool qualities, for their part, remained in relatively stable proportion across the seventeenth century. The Sulmona account book records a slight increase in black and castrated sheep's wool (from 2.5 percent in 1625 to 8.5 percent in 1700), but the white wool of May (*maggiorina*) always predominated, with some 85 percent. The four account books of the three weighing stations confirm this stability for wool taken out of deposit in the last third of the century: white wool, 71 percent; lambswool, 11 percent; black wool, 13 percent; and castrated sheep's wool, 4 percent. White wool was the chief cash crop, with lambswool and black wool in approximate parity at about 10 percent of production. Wool from castrated sheep was relatively insignificant, and if it is excluded, the percentages are adjusted to 75 percent, 12 percent, and 14 percent for white, lambs', and black wool respectively.

Wool quality was also recorded for wool placed into depositories. Eighteenth-century public price quotations were partly based upon wool supply, and consequently annual wool quantities were recorded. For the 88 cases listed from 1670 to 1805, only three wool qualities are recorded: May white, lambs', and black. They were divided in the following mean proportions: May white wool, 68,658 *rubbi* (79 percent); lambswool, 9,084 *rubbi* (10 percent); black wool, 8,864 *rubbi* (10 percent); for total wool, 87,050 *rubbi*. Figures for wool qualities taken out and put into depositories are structurally similar, with the lone difference in the relationship between lambswool and black wool. Black wool production was slightly greater than lambswool production in the seventeenth century until about 1734. Totals parallel each other thereafter until about 1757, when lambswool production slightly outpaced that of black.

Simply, black wool was somewhat more important in the seventeenth century and the first quarter of the eighteenth, lambswool in the second half of the eighteenth because black wool was consumed nationally whereas lambswool had an international market. Production of both wools, however, remained relatively uniform, at close parity, with minor fluctuations. May white wool, which accounted for about three-fourths of production, was the chief crop.

The Foggian account books, it should be emphasized again, do not record summer wool, which was shorn and sold in the mountains in August before the descent to winter grazing. The Doria account books, however, list August wool along with May white and lambswool. Here May white predominates, with 55.7 percent of production, while August white provides 22.8 percent and lambswool, 8.7 percent. The August white mean was 40.9 percent that of the May white. In other words, summer shearing usually produced somewhat less than one-half as much wool as in the spring. The mean price of 90 Doria quotations of August white and 89 Doria quotations of lambswool were practically equivalent, 28.39 and 27.81 *carlini* per *rubbio* respectively. But both lagged behind the mean price for 91 quotations of May white at 37.69 *carlini* per *rubbio* by some 10 *carlini*. This differential corresponded to the paradigm for lambswool versus May wool prices in the seventeenth century, that is, a fixed increment rather than a percentage formula.

When spring wool harvests were low for any reason, whether climatic, economic, or political, however, August wool production could be proportionately higher. Such was the case in Marcantonio Coda's 1666 estimate of an individual sheepowner's budget. Coda gives income from August wool as 50 percent that of May wool, a fact that could be true only if August wool production were higher or May wool lower than normal. If the 1667 *voce* prices for second-condition white (27 *carlini*) and for lambswool (22 *carlini*), being equivalent to August wool, are plugged into the Coda budget, then the 187.2 ducats income for spring wool would have come from 69.3 *rubbi* and the 93.5 ducats of summer wool from 42.5 *rubbi,* that is, a ratio of 61 percent, August/May. Evidence from the Doria estates in the 1670s documents this atypically high relationship as August wool production was also 61 percent that of May white. Here again is further confirmation of the general sheepowner rationale. Poor markets in Foggia channeled wool production into other markets. If, then, about 70,000 *rubbi* of May white were produced annually in Foggia, some 30,000–40,000 *rubbi* of August white should have been sold somewhere else in the fall.[36]

Wool Price

The selling price of the four spring wool qualities was not fixed in the seventeenth-century account books until the establishment of the public price. Quoted rates in the Sulmona account books varied widely, within a median range of 7 *carlini* per *rubbio,* for lambs' and white wool. White wool rates offer the best evidence since we already know that after the institutionalization of the *voce* system, the white wool of May was divided into three conditions. Even if white wool grades were not introduced in Foggia until 1667, large quantities of white wool were sold at varying rates long before that date. In 1625, 1641, and 1655, for example, three dominant selling prices corresponded to high grade (23 percent of white wool), medium (14 percent), and low (14 percent), while the remaining 49 percent of white wool was sold at other prices. Further, no paradigm separated high, medium, and low prices, although 1 *carlino* per *rubbio* was most common. No one grade of white wool predominated, but the quantity of grades fluctuated from year to year; for example, 1670 was a poor year with very little high-quality (7 percent) and much more low-quality (40 percent) white wool. Prices of the same grades thus also diverged widely between years, by almost 50 percent between 1655 and 1670.

Wool price data is sporadic for the sixteenth and early seventeenth centuries. The four quotations—1526, 1581, 1582, and 1606—suggest a stable mean of about 32 *carlini* per *rubbio* in normal times.[37] From 1623 a price series can be constructed up to 1845 (app. E-1). Serial prices conform to the rough parameters of 30–40 *carlini* until the grave difficulties in the late 1630s, when prices fell to the 20–30-*carlini* level. Prices returned to the 30–40-*carlini* level after the 1680s introduction of the *voce* system and remained there until the 1690s boom. From 1693 until the 1710 crash, prices pushed at the upward limit of that threshold. After the 1710 fall, prices only reach the 40-*carlini* level again with lowered supply in the sheep death of 1726. Finally, a discrete price increase was engineered in 1734 with the stablization of the *voce* pricing system.[38] A gradual rise followed: 1734–67 in the 40–50-*carlini* level; 1768–85 in the 50–60-*carlini* level; 1786–97 in the 60–70-*carlini* level; 1798–1819 (with an 1808–15 lacuna) in the 70–80-ducat level; thereafter, 1820–45 back down in the 60–70-ducat range. If we take 30 *carlini* as the starting norm, then, prices were stable through the sixteenth and seventeenth centuries, were depressed by 30 percent during the seventeenth-century crisis, and rose slightly more than 230 percent in the eighteenth century before the extraordinary fluctuations during the Napoleonic Wars.

Product Value

Price quotations alone are deceiving unless correlated with the quantity of wool sold. The product value (production × price) points out an inverse correlation between prices and supply. In the sample weigher's accounts with market prices, the mean product value in 1625 (131,000 ducats), 1641 (143,000 ducats), and 1655 (169,000 ducats) fluctuated around an equilibrium of 140,000 ducats. As production rose in 1641, prices fell from 30 to 26 *carlini* per *rubbio;* as production fell in 1655, prices rose to 35 *carlini* per *rubbio*. Product value in 1670 (110,000 ducats), however, fell most precipitously below the established equilibrium since falling prices (to 21 *carlini* per *rubbio*) met no resistence in the face of greatly increased production. To understand the 1670 anomaly, let us examine the overall product value curve (app. E-1).

During the downturn from 1625 to 1684, product value of wool sold at Foggia averaged about 140,000 ducats. Afterward, with recovery between 1685 and 1797, it averaged more than 375,000 ducats. Two important conclusions emerge from the long-term series of wool product values. First, slumps were tied directly to slackening demand. In the 1640s the fiscal and economic crisis in the Kingdom continued to worsen and the story of credit brokers themselves going under is well known.[39] The fall in wool production in 1644, then, found no eager buyers, and prices fell rather than rose. The depressed prices continued through the revolt until 1651. The return to free bidding in 1660 had a similar effect on supply and demand curves. Sheepowners brought in more wool to market, but there were fewer buyers to sustain prices. The false start of this tax incentive recovery underlines the determinitive character of demand in the wool trade. Sellers' efforts depended on that capital income. Rural credit was a function of merchant input. Second, upward income curves were inflation driven. The slow rise of wool product values, once recovery was underway, corresponded to similar rises in other commodities.

Rural Credit

A corollary of these two principles is that credit operations at the Foggian fair fueled the rural economy and are a barometer of demand. Four kinds of credit arrangements were used by notaries operating at the Foggian fair in the early seventeenth century.[40] Letters of exchange facilitated monetary transfers, *censi* served transfers of real property and dowries, *voce* contracts were common for sales of cash crops such as olive oil and grain, and finally, joint-stock companies (*societas*) on the *commenda* model, with silent capital investors and active merchant factors, participated in all kinds of artisanal and commercial affairs.

Credit arrangements were defined not only by the kind of property exchanged, but also by the relationship between lender and borrower. The eighteenth-century olive oil market offers the best-known evidence.[41] Borrower need determined three classes of sellers. The most needy employed *voce* contracts, where the terms lay in the hands of lenders, that is, mercantile capital and central authority. Better-off borrowers put down cash themselves and sold products at market prices. But the best-off borrowers used *contratti a liquidazione,* in which their produce could be sold at optimum market prices even after being delivered to the middleman merchants. In other words, sellers were either dependent upon buyers to sustain them through the long production season, rich enough to finance themselves, or so rich as to receive concessions from buyers.

A joint-stock company contract notarized in Naples on 7 June 1582 exemplifies how the richest sellers operated in the market.[42] Three partners—financiers, middlemen wool merchants, and wool sellers—bound themselves together for a fixed term of two years in order to market Foggian wool in northern Italy. Two Neapolitan public bankers, Carolo Marocco and Giovan Giacobo Casola, put up the capital, while Cesare de Cesare of Sancte Anatolie and his brothers Petro Paulo, Geronimo, and Lucantonio acted as procurators. De Cesare bought 4,833.27 *rubbi* of May white wool in Foggia on 12 May from Giovan Maria Pascale of Bugnara (Abruzzo Citra) for 9,819.9 ducats. Five percent was added to the purchase price for Pascale to prepare the wool for storage and exportation. Total paid to Pascale: 10,353 ducats. De Cesare received 2,400 ducats, that is, 9 percent compound interest on the total purchase price, for services and promises to ship the wool "to Senigallia or another port in the Gulf of Venice in order to sell it at the best possible price." After repayment of the total 12,753 ducats of capital outlay by Marocco and Casola, the partners agreed to share profits or losses in fifths: two shares each to financiers and procurators, one share to seller. A few other stipulations on repayment are noteworthy. The De Cesares could exchange raw wool for cloth from the Marches and Umbria, but risks were lowered because they were forbidden to ship it back to Naples by sea. If the raw wool was unsold by the 30 April 1584 contract termination, the De Cesares could make one last effort at the Salerno fair of September 1584.

The contract's purpose and division of capital and labor is clear. A big seller like Pascale, whose wool sales corresponded to a flock of some 60,000 sheep, had leverage with buyers and could share in profits above the market price of wool at harvest. He would gain from selling at times other than at supply's peak and from selling directly to manufacturers at their home workshops. Note again the port of entry, Senigallia. The market was not Venice itself, but the Terraferma manufactureres who specialized in lower-quality cloth. The 20.3 *carlini* per *rubbio* market price received in Foggia (note this was already at the top end of the 15–20 *carlini* average for 1582) was increased by 5 percent to 21.4 *carlini* per *rubbio* for export preparation. Any resale above the financiers' break-even point of 26.4 *carlini* per *rubbio* (that is, adding in the 9 percent procurator commission) would be shared 40 percent, 40 percent, 20 percent. But all partners were liable for loss, albeit for the seller at his lower, 20 percent rate.

Sellers who marketed their own wool usually appeared at the beginning of the *sfondacatura* ledger in the wool weighers' accounts. In 1670, for example, six sellers received wool averaging 391 *rubbi* for themselves.[43] The prince of Melfi was already placing 490 *rubbi* of wool on his own account in Venice. One Duke Antonio placed 1,025 *rubbi* and Isabella Caracciolo placed 430 *rubbi* on their accounts in Venice. Ettore Carafa put 159 *rubbi* on his account at Cusano. Two nonnoble sellers placed 94 and 147 *rubbi* of wool on their own account, the former at San Severino, the latter unspecified. Similarly, the Jesuits at Orta and

Ordona maintained close ties with merchants at the Salerno fair. They kept a correspondent there who bought and sold their goods.[44]

Later in the eighteenth century, an individual big owner of 10,000 sheep like the prince of Melfi might settle for direct cash exchange at market prices. In the mid eighteenth century, for example, the Doria estates at Melfi contracted purchase agreements with specific merchants. Mean wool quantity sold by the Dorias amounted to 120 *rubbi*. Michele de Luzio of Montorio in 1750 and 1752 and Francesco Barone of Salerno in 1754 purchased all wool grades for two years each at a fixed price set by May white second-condition *voce* rates.[45] Two cash payments were made; one at purchase, one in the autumn. Thereafter, contracts tended to be on an annual basis until the end of the century, when two multiyear contracts sold August wool in 1797–1803 and 1804–09.[46]

The Dorias appear to have preferred to minimize risks by accepting a flat payment in the eighteenth century. For their Melfi estates, sheep farming was a blue-chip investment with a consciously planned rate of return, not a speculative enterprise to make extraordinary profits. The security of relying on their own credit and accepting the market price at harvest is what separated such big sellers from the majority of smaller holders.

For those smaller sellers in the third category of credit arrangements, buyer demand and buyer credit determined participation in the wool trade. As we have already seen, the peculiar calculation of the *voce* price system placed these sellers at a disadvantage to buyers.

Meat and Cheese

If wool income has been our primary focus, we should not neglect meat and cheese sales. How much was sold and how did production change over time?

Lambing and cheese making were closely related functions of the fecundity rate. If our estimate of 0.5 lambs per female sheep is accurate, then, 1 million sheep should have netted 450,000 lambs—150,000 as replacement animals and 300,000 divided between spring and fall markets. Demand came for meat and cheese as dietary supplements for urban populations; thus the interest of Florence, Venice, and Naples in such produce. Meat from *castrati* had a strong export market, whereas cheese was almost exclusively used in domestic consumption.[47]

The only global series on meat animal production at Foggia is rather late, 1766–94 (appendix E.3). In these 28 years, lambs far exceeded *castrati*, two to one. Mean number of animals was about 75,000, with 50,000 lambs to 25,000 *castrati*. Of these 75,000 animals, three-eighths were exported in about equal proportions, 14,463 lambs/ 15,813 *castrati* annually. The five-eighths kept in the Kingdom were predominantly lambs, 35,000 versus 11,000 *castrati*.

Why such low production figures in comparison to our estimates? First, these births must have been *vernarecci* and *cordeschi* lambs, that is, those born during winter or spring on the Tavoliere.[48] More animals and cheese were probably sold at the Abruzzi autumn fairs, where animals brought higher prices. The Dorias, for example, in their seventeenth- and eighteenth-century account books sold spring lambs at a mean of 8 *carlini* versus 12 *carlini* in fall (app. E-4). The Dorias averaged 372 of these spring lambs as opposed to 1,233 autumn lambs.[49] This 30 percent differential would make our estimate of about 90,000 spring animals for sale at Foggia compare favorably with the observed data.

Cheese predictions follow this same paradigm. We would predict 82,000 *pesa* from 1 million sheep. Serial data for cheese comes from the *voce* price lists (1730–1826) (app. E-5). For the 87 reported years, mean cheese production at Foggia was 60,000 *pesa*. About three-fourths of possible cheese production, then, was marketed in Foggia, with the other one-fourth probably consumed along the way or sold at Abruzzi fairs.

Other Fairs

Sheepherding thus had two seasonal foci. The spring market had been consolidated at Foggia by the central government in the sixteenth century, but the autumnal markets continued in the mountain valleys ringing the plain of Puglia. By the late eighteenth century, for example, only eleven fairs remained in Capitanata, seven in Molise, eleven in Abruzzo Citra, but seventy-four in Abruzzo Ultra.[50] Obviously, the greater isolation and farther distances from the capital multiplied fairs in the peripheral provinces. More to the point, Abruzzo Ultra's high pastoral profile required frequent exchange between pastoralists and agriculturists.

The fair of Lanciano in particular was linked to the pastoral season since its celebration in late August marked the beginning of the descent from the mountains. Officials circulated through the small Abruzzi villages counting sheep and preparing for the winter migrations.[51] Lanciano also celebrated a May fair at the beginning of the summer as sheep returned from winter pasture. In the mid fifteenth century more *castrati* were actually sold in the spring. Six fairs, in both May and August between 1447 and 1457, counted a mean of 3,500 *castrati* sold, 75 percent of them exported outside the Kingdom.[52] Castel di Sangro likewise celebrated two fairs, one in July and the other in November. They accounted for about 4,800 *castrati* sold and 57 percent exported, in the same period.[53] In addition, four other Abruzzi fairs specialized in animals and their products—Albe, Celano, Pescara, and Tagliacozzo.[54] As the round of fairs multiplied, pastoral products were dispersed through the mountain countryside.

THE FAIR OF FOGGIA: PRODUCTION AND PRICES 209

FIGURE 16   *Voce* Prices of Staples (1731-1845) (*Carlini*)

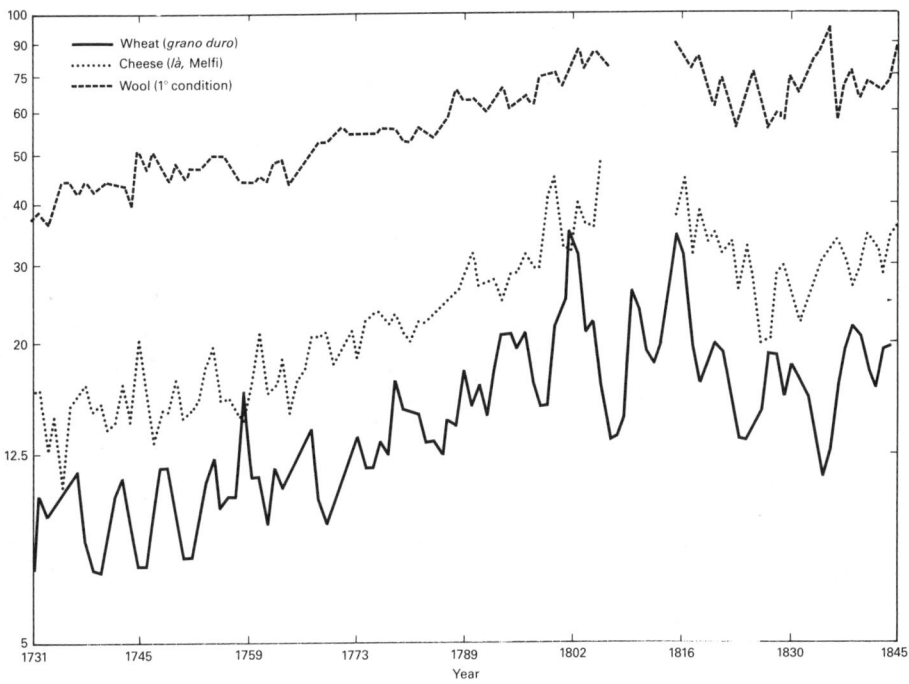

Comparative Prices

In general, the three pastoral price curves of wool, meat, and cheese followed the same trajectory as other agricultural products. The corresponding rise in the rate of wheat prices, in particular, versus the rate of wool, meat, and cheese price increases defined the equilibrium maintained between agriculture and pastoralism in the eighteenth century (figs. 16 and 17).[55] Grain prices and salaries also conformed neatly across the century, except during the famine of 1759–64.[56]

Only after 1788—when grain doubled its 1731–58 price, then tripled and quadrupled in the first five years of the new century while wool prices remained stable at 1.5–1.75 times their 1731–58 price—did the pressure for reform of the doganal system become intense.[57] Over the long term, however, this crisis from the 1790s to the decade of French rule was only a momentary disturbance in the relationship between wheat and wool, for after 1815 agricultural price differentials returned to their former levels. The abnormally high wheat prices distorted by the Napoleonic Wars evened out and, despite a reorganized pastoral institution and the dissolution of the customhouse system,

FIGURE 17 *Voce* Prices of Staples, Base Year Comparisons (1731-1845)

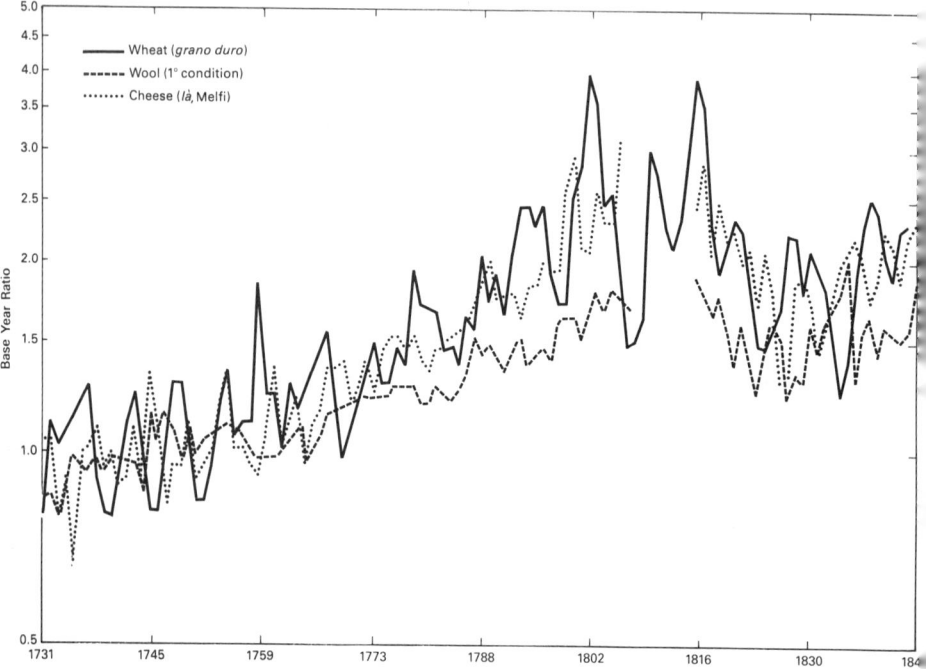

nineteenth-century pastoral production at Foggia returned to a mean of 75,000 *rubbi* of wool between 1815 and 1832.

Far from collapsing, the Foggian market recovered, and the city of Foggia itself grew spectacularly. By 1732, Foggia exchanged places with Lucera, 1,545 to 1,069 hearths (about 7,725 to 5,345 inhabitants), and ranked as the largest town in the province of Capitanata. Still Foggia ranked only twentieth among the Kingdom's provincial towns, all an order of magnitude behind the Neapolitan capital's 315,000 inhabitants, as measured in 1742. At the Kingdom's first actual head count in 1767, Foggia numbered 13,401 inhabitants. By 1816 it had emerged as the second largest town in the Kingdom; and by 1825 the most important provincial capital on the mainland. By Unification in 1860 only Naples and Palermo were larger.[58]

Such continuity in the pastoral economy emphasizes the cyclical nature of the market. Demography, animal husbandry, climate, and political policy set parameters on production, while the market defined demand and often financed production through credit mechanisms. The market reflected the international economic conjuncture quite closely, even though domestic demand accounted for almost two-thirds of production. This strong domestic demand established a minimum threshold upon which solid investments depended. As the international economic climate fluctuated, internal fortunes ebbed and flowed, internal tensions calmed or intensified. The structure of exchange at the Foggian fair thus only points to the real problem of exchange, who gets the better of a transaction—that is, the contention and accommodation in pastoral economics.

9 Sellers and Buyers at the Fair of Foggia

Monopoly Price Fixing

At the Foggian fair, a multitude of individual interests collided and contended. One party's advantage was another's disadvantage; large sellers could undersell small ones; sellers of different products competed with one another; both sellers and buyers wished to buy cheap and sell dear. Successful exchange had to balance the fear of untoward maximization with some kind of reciprocity, competition, or regulation.

The inequality of exchange is highlighted all the more in a seasonal market like Foggia's where time and money were the key variables. Pastoral products flooded the market in the spring, at the very moment when the pastoral owners had to abandon their produce in order to transport their stock back up the mountains for summer pasture.[1] As a further constraint, the state customhouse was a third player in the game between buyers and sellers. First, its annual winter pasturing tax was due upon the sale of pastoral products. Second, large capital transfers from the foreign wool buyers helped to offset the Kingdom's balance of payments.[2] Increased supply, the migration imperative, and cash for employees' wages, for state taxes, and the international balance of payments all gave buyers, who represented capital and manufacturing interests, the distinct edge in setting prices.

Monopolistic attempts by buyers to distort prices can be documented from the earliest customhouse records. The first sheepowners' requests to Ferrante in 1470 complained of mercantile capital's manipulation of prices. "Item, that your Majesty, upon good counsel, ought to make certain good provisions that wool prices be maintained; contrary to the merchant buyers of wool who are joining together to lower prices, which will be the undoing of such [doganal] income, but so that as many men as strive to increase their flocks can do so successfully."[3] The king granted this request because the royal treasury depended on the sellers' profits for its taxes, not because he believed in free enterprise or upward mobility.

Upon Charles V's refoundation of the doganal system in 1536, the graziers requested and were granted some kind of price supports for their poorest members. When wool and meat prices fell to low levels, the doganiero was to protect both the poor independent and the poor dependent, small-time sheepowners by guaranteeing the purchase of up to 10,000 ducats of their production at the public (*voce*) price.⁴ Here again, the state's intent was not economic equality, but economic viability so that the smallest members could pay their taxes. Similarly, in 1581, after a short absence of strong state administrative presence in Foggia, the new doganiero Alfonso Caracciolo reported that wool buyers had been in league with one another during the past few years. His diligence was stopping "in every way and manner possible those conventicles" whose frauds had damaged both sellers and state.⁵

The state's attempt to reignite the pastoral economy at the end of the seventeenth-century crisis offers another example of how government imposed its political power in order to curb the merchants' economic clout. In 1667, when the number of buyers had so declined that the remaining few threatened to corner the market, the president of the dogana, Don Melchior de Navarra, intervened on the side of the wool sellers. He initiated the state oversight of prices *alla voce*. Prices of cheese were also regulated, buyers' monopolies impeded, and the squeeze upon sellers curtailed.⁶ The 1668 *Pramatica LXXIX de officio Procuratoris Caesaris* continued the state's initiative to guarantee its income by overseeing both buyers and sellers. The viceroy's instructions included provisions which restricted the merchants' ability to set prices, reformed the office of wool weigher, obligated sellers to place their wool into depositories in Foggia, allowed sellers who paid their taxes in advance to lead unshorn sheep out of Puglia, and required final tax payments from the others by 22 July.⁷ The sheepowners' guild continued to complain about the "union" among wool merchants which created a "monopoly" to keep prices low. They argued that harm came to both themselves and the state because the big merchants from Venice, Florence, Cerreto, and Piedimonte d'Alife constrained middling merchants from buying wool at "convenient prices."⁸ In response, actual prices were no longer recorded in the wool weighers' account books after 1680, when the weighers merely adopted the shorthand of recording "at the public price."⁹

In 1704 another merchant monopoly was uncovered and six buyers named. They had formed a company to buy wool below market prices, "not because that price was not just, but only because they intended to take advantage of the small sellers." The 1703 *voce* price of 50 *carlini* had fallen to 46 *carlini* in 1704, but these foreign merchants wanted to pay 1 *carlino* less.¹⁰

As the eighteenth-century legal commentators reflected upon this kind of fraud and corrective customhouse legislation, they began to forge an economic theory which rationalized the state's right to intervene in the pastoral economy. In his 1715 review of the dogana, Gaudiani explained the state's role in setting prices in this way: "all the rationale of good administration" demanded that the pastoralists be guaranteed just prices for the bread they bought while they wintered in Puglia and for the goods they sold there in the spring. If not, they "would be suffocated by the intense greed of the buyers who would easily gorge themselves on the weakness of others' necessities."¹¹ Di Stefano argued in 1731 that "the diligence and authority of magistrates places brakes on the avarice of merchants; [there is] no kind of man [who] is more fallacious and insidious."

He cited "the eruditions and doctrines noted by the governor of the Foggian customhouse in 1669, Regent de Filippo, who experienced the mercenariness and maliciousness of foreign and domestic merchants. For every small and vile gain, they perjure themselves and plot a thousand frauds and monopolies which are forbidden to private parties."[12] De Dominicis' rhetoric in 1781 expressed the same need for the "efficacious expedients" of the customhouse government "to impede the depression of prices . . . and the prejudicial union of buyers."[13] Good government's self-interest demanded that its revenues be maintained and increased. Only inadvertently did its policies provide foundation for a theory of exchange which ensured justice to the sellers, freedom in the market, and favored public order over private profits.

Sellers and Buyers from Crisis to Recovery

The wool weighers' account books, in differentiating sellers and buyers by place of origin, social order, and the amount of wealth (in wool) they controlled, give us a quantifiable description of supply and demand. We can refine the portrait by comparing three different variables in each category—the number of sellers or buyers, the number of their transactions, and the quantity of wool sold. The decline and recovery of the seventeenth-century economy is again the litmus test to judge the presence and resolution of conflict in the customhouse. How did individual sheepowners adjust to the changing economic conjuncture which saw a 69 percent increase in wool sold between 1670 and 1700, from 53,980 to 91,251 *rubbi?*

By 1700 sellers had almost doubled from their 1670 and 1685 numbers, from 253 and 232 to 406. Rich individual sellers like the prince of Troia increased their wool sales fourfold, from 728 *rubbi* in 1670 to 2,940 *rubbi* in 1700. The improved economic climate encouraged more investment in sheep farming on the part of rich and poor alike and pushed pastoral livelihood ever further into marginal mountain zones. Rocca del Raso, a community already heavily pastoral, for example, sold some 56 percent more wool—4,904 *rubbi* in 1700 as opposed to 3,145 *rubbi* in 1670.

Likewise, new buyers entered the market. From no representatives on the Venetian Terraferma in 1670, seven Bergamaschi merchants bought 26,693 *rubbi* of wool in 1700, while the eight Venetians who had purchased 10,708 *rubbi* disappeared. Further, natives of the Kingdom intensified their participation between 1670 and 1700. Merchants from Naples and San Severino, for example, doubled their purchases from 10,000 and 8,000 *rubbi* to 20,000 and 16,000 *rubbi* respectively.

The large sellers like the Santissima Annunziata of Sulmona or the prince of Melfi, however, are far removed from the rude shepherds inhabiting our pastoral literary consciousness. The great merchants from Venice or Bergamo and those resident in Foggia likewise are a far cry from the fourteenth-century merchant-trickster priest Dom Gianni and his cuckolded fellow merchant

Pietro, who worked "the round of Apulian fairs, buying and selling merchandise" along the southern edge of the Tavoliere in Boccaccio's tenth *novella* of Day Nine.[14] Thus, the contrast between the sheepowner "industries" of princes or religious foundations and the inarticulate, stunned shepherds attending Neapolitan Christmas cribs, or between the large, international merchant-financier and the petty itinerant merchants highlight the give-and-take between rich and poor, between buyers and sellers, between times of boom and times of bust, between the market and "natural" economy, and between the foreign and domestic markets operative at the Foggian fair.

Sellers' Origins

The geography of sellers can be measured in various ways—by province, by account book (which should correspond to specific sheepwalks and, thus, cut through a number of provinces), and by individual town. The high number of unnamed or unidentifiable places often makes firm conclusions difficult. In two of the three years with complete records, for example, missing places accounted for almost one-third of the wealth—in 1670, 30.9 percent and in 1700, 31.2 percent.

Assuming that the absolute percentages would continue to be evenly distributed in these missing cases, however, we can approximate the sellers' provincial origins in relative, adjusted percentages (table 23). The profile of sellers' origins in the last third of the seventeenth century, then, confirms the overwhelming presence of Abruzzesi: 44 percent of wool wealth from Abruzzi Citra and 28 percent from Abruzzi Ultra. With two-thirds of the wealth concentrated in the Abruzzi, the other provinces—Molise (11 percent), Capitanata (8 percent), Terra di Bari and Otranto (5 percent), and the rest (4 percent)—made up only between one-third and one-fourth of sheepowners' wealth. In addition to wealth, both the percentages of sellers and of their transactions conform to this general pattern. Clearly flock ownership by mountain dwellers (inverse transhumance) was the norm among wool sellers, and Abruzzo Citra was the most important center of sheep ownership.

We might recall that wool quality was defined by its origins in the two Abruzzi provinces—first-condition from Lucoli in Abruzzo Ultra and second-condition from Celano in Abruzzo Citra.[15] A 1722 Venetian survey of wool in merchant depositories confirms the differentiation by quality and quantity.[16] Out of 188 bales (*balle*) of Puglia wool, 12 *balle* (6 percent) came from Lucoli, 113 (60 percent) came from Celano, 38 (20 percent) were *matricina* sacks, 9 (5 percent) were lambswool, and 16 (9 percent) August white. Abruzzo Citra white wool of the second condition was the big seller.

The wool weighers' account books allow us to be more discriminate than merely identifying provincial origins. Allegiance to the three weighing stations should, theoretically, be determined by use of the trails emanating from the respective trail heads. Thus, the two Aquila accounts find most of their

TABLE 23 Wool Sellers' Origins: Quantity of Wool by Province (1670–1700) (In Absolute and Relative Percentages)

Year	Abruzzo Ultra	Abruzzo Citra	Capitanata	Molise	Bari and Otranto
1670	20.9 (30)	27.4 (40)	5.3 (8)	9.2 (13)	3.9 (6)
1685	26.0 (31)	40.0 (48)	4.2 (5)	6.9 (8)	4.0 (5)
1700	15.8 (23)	30.7 (45)	8.4 (12)	7.1 (10)	1.4 (2)
Mean	(28)	(44)	(8)	(11)	(5)

Source: See table 21.

Note: Relative percentage in parentheses is calculated without missing values.

TABLE 24 Top Ten Wool Sellers' Towns of Origin (1670–1700) (In *Rubbi*)

1670			1685		
Town	Wool	Sellers	Town	Wool	Sellers
Lucoli	3,637	13	Lucoli	5,678	25
Rocca del Raso	3,145	19	Rocca del Raso	4,013	13
Pesco Costanzo	2,418	11	Scanno	3,131	32
Capracotta	2,111	11	Pesco Costanzo	2,928	12
Rocca di Calascio	1,894	8	Pacentro	2,511	9
Scanno	1,757	15	Pesco Asseroli	2,378	5
Santo Stefano	1,405	6	Capracotta	2,325	7
Peschio Pignataro	1,265	6	Ovindoli	1,909	8
Campo di Giove	1,216	7	Castel del Monte	1,666	5
Troia	1,013	3	Campo di Giove	1,615	7

Source: See table 21.

sheepowners drawn from Abruzzo Ultra. In the Aquila *bianca* account, 47 percent of the owners originated in Abruzzo Ultra; in Aquila *nera,* 56 percent. The Sulmona and Castel di Sangro accounts, on the other hand, had 58 percent and 55 percent respectively of their owners originating in Abruzzo Citra. Similarly, by this geographic principle, Castel di Sangro boasted a majority of the Molise and Capitanata owners.

Not all membership in the weighing stations, however, was determined by geography. Miscellaneous provincial origins were listed in all weighing stations save the account book of Aquila *nera* where only black wool, almost exclusively from the Abruzzi, was registered. Sheepowners from the same town could even list themselves in different weighing stations. In each of the complete reporting years, 1670, 1685, and 1700, at least nine towns were represented in more than one account book. But each of these towns had a definite orientation to one weighing station above the others. These exceptions, one or

Basilicata	Terra di Lavoro	Principato Citra and Ultra	Royal Court	Unverified or Not Given
0.9	1.4	0.1	—	30.9
1.0	0.7	0.4	—	17.2
0.6	1.2	3.6	—	31.2

	1700	
Town	Wool	Sellers
Rocca del Raso	4,904	25
Troia	2,940	1
Campo di Giove	2,721	12
Capracotta	2,344	11
Rivisondoli	2,064	7
Pesco Asseroli	1,945	14
Ovindoli	1,822	7
San Severo	1,607	1
Barrea	1,513	4
Castel di Sangro	1,425	4

two lone sellers among a town's majority, make it clear that the account books are accurate indicators of geographical migrations. Further, such double accounting reveals only five towns where both black wool and white wool were raised. Thus, towns generally specialized by quality and enjoyed some hierarchical differentiation by quantity.

Ranking of towns by number of sellers and by their collective wealth provides two different hierarchical principles to judge a town's role in the Foggian fair (table 24). Some towns were more pastorally oriented than others. Since the mean population of the top ten wool sellers' towns in 1670 (computed by the 1669 hearth count) was about 1,000 individuals, sheepowner power in places like Rocca del Raso, with a mean of 19 wool sellers in the fourth quarter of the seventeenth century, would have been considerable at about 10 percent of the towns' families. Similarly, other mountain towns such as Scanno, Lucoli, Pesco Costanzo, and Capracotta had large pastoral contingents. Large numbers of sellers, however, did not guarantee large amounts of wool produced and sold. In 1670, Scanno ranked second in sellers but sixth in wool sold; in 1685, first in sellers but third in production; in 1700, fifth in sellers with ten, but only thirteenth in production with 1,299 *rubbi*. Scanno's numerous sellers, as did those of Castel del Monte and Calascio, dealt exclusively in black wool, which was produced in smaller quantities and sold at lower prices. A sharp dichotomy existed between the many small holders from one town and the few larger holders from another. Some towns, such as the Tavoliere plain towns of Troia and San Severo, had high pastoral profiles in the 1700 accounts only because one very large seller had invested in sheep. The differences between agricultural and pastoral livelihood and between large and small owners cut through local economies. Did numbers alone or wealth alone rule? Was there harmony or conflict among those sellers with opposing interests? Such tension remained open and unresolved.

Sellers' Wealth

In order to visualize this cleavage, let us rank the sellers from smallest to largest by wealth. A characteristic spread emerges between rich and poor. Among the three years with all account books reporting, 20 percent of the sellers controlled about 50 percent of the wealth, while the bottom 50 percent of the sellers controlled less than 20 percent of the wealth. Although the Sulmona account book appears to reflect a greater degree of equality among sellers, with fewer big owners, it still demonstrates a marked concentration of wealth at the top. Further, the Sulmona account book alone helps us chart change over time. After a decline in the wealth of the owners in the 90th percentile during the depths of the seventeenth-century crisis, holders in both the 80th and 90th percentiles increased their wealth after 1670.

Further statistics on the distribution of sellers, however, indicate that their variation by wealth was relatively uniform. For the three complete years, 1670, 1685, and 1700, an examination of their top ten sellers suggests how skewing distorted the overall smoothness of the distribution curve (table 25). The variation in the top five or six sellers, as above, soon gives way to a smooth descent. Standard deviations within the deciles measure this graduated uniformity.[17] It is important to note that the standard deviation of the wealth of all sellers varies less than 30 *rubbi* from the mean in each decile except for those sellers above the 90th percentile. There the large size of the standard deviation (204, 225, and 418 *rubbi* in 1670, 1685, and 1700) points to the high variation among the largest sellers' wealth. Further, in 1700 this tendency of increased size of standard deviation has entered the ranks above the 80th percentile (52 *rubbi*). As the wool market recovered, more large holders were drawn into it. This statistical observation has extraordinary importance because it nuances the separation between rich and poor sellers. Instead of focusing exclusively on the gulf between large and small, the standard deviations point out the co-

SELLERS AND BUYERS AT THE FAIR OF FOGGIA   219

TABLE 25   Top Ten Wool Sellers (1670–1700) (In *Rubbi*)

1670		1685		1700	
Seller	Wool	Seller	Wool	Seller	Wool
Duca Antonio	1,181	Principe di Troia	1,246	Principe di Troia	2,940
Ill. Sr. Ettore Carafa (Naples)	1,167	Rosino Rossi (Opi)	1,206	Principe di San Severo	1,607
Ill. Marchese di Vasto	825	Cappella di Santissimo Pescasseroli)	1,078	Donato Antonio Gayari & comp.	1,189
GianBat & Ventura Marinanza & Manlio Ciccozzi (Lucoli)	797	Duca di Casoli	990	Principe della Riccia	1,111
Ill. Sr. Francesco Giudice (Naples)	778	Duca d'Andria	945	Conte & Contessa di Poderira	1,104
Principe di Troia	728	Duca di Bovino	818	Emin. Cardinal del Giudice & Ill. Duchessa di Basaccie (Naples)	1,029
Madonna dell'Ospitale (Rivisondoli)	595	Sig. Angelo Alfieri	800	Cappella di S. Giovanni (Campo di Giove)	954
Angelo di Fulvio di Rosato (Lecce)	593	Santo di Sulputio Majcitelli (Gioia)	722	Principe di S. Buono	939
Donato Vespa (Calascio)	588	Leone Andria (Capracotta)	693	Ill. Duca di Calabritto	873
Cappella di Santissimo Santo (Rivisondoli)	584	Santissima Annunziata (Sulmona)	692	Abba di S. Leonardo (Siponto)	858

Source: See table 21.

hesiveness within the two distinct groups at Foggia—a handful of extremely large sellers and a mass of relatively equal middling and small sellers in an unbroken continuum.

The bifurcation between rich and middling sellers does not reflect a difference between market-oriented and subsistence graziers. Early modern transhumant systems were predicated upon a market economy, and the Foggian fair aptly demonstrates its operation. Instead, the dual profile of sellers' wealth emphasizes the exceptional equilibrium maintained by the customhouse of Foggia. Here large conglomerates coexisted with the smallest of sheepowners without monopolizing production and eliminating individual private enterprise. As in agricultural land ownership, the economic conjuncture determined the trend for consolidation or dispersion of holdings.[18] But the state customhouse protected small holders against the trend.

A marked chronological trend to concentrate wealth into the hands of large owners during the seventeenth-century crisis can be documented even more graphically by examining their social order. In the Sulmona account books the prince of San Severo, who could presumably finance himself, sold large quantities of wool throughout the lean years between the 1620s and 1640s: 845; 859, and 973 *rubbi* in 1626, 1627, and 1628 respectively, all to Bergamaschi buyers; 1,118, 1,161, and 1,089 *rubbi* in 1642, 1643, and 1645 respectively to native manufacturers; but only 135 *rubbi* in 1648.[19] Similarly, the prince of Minervino sold 527 and 791 *rubbi* of wool in 1630 and 1635 respectively; Geronimo Pignatelli, a noble of Naples, 476 *rubbi* in 1641; and the Santissima Annunziata of Sulmona maintained a constant presence with about 500 *rubbi* of wool sold annually between 1625 and 1655.[20]

Dividing the sellers into religious, nobles, and commoners, we note that the mean size of wool sales among nobles for the three years with complete records (485 *rubbi*) was almost two and one-half times that of commoners (197 *rubbi*), with that of the first estate (306 *rubbi*) in between (table 26). Again the Sulmona account book dramatizes the rise in all sheep wealth, but especially that of nobles, after 1670. The complete records focus our attention on that rise after 1685. The Certosa of San Martino in Naples offers a perfect example. The monastery owned an estate in the location of Tressanti, where it maintained a stable flock of 2,000 sheep throughout most of the seventeenth century but doubled its size to 4,000 in 1688.[21]

TABLE 26 Sellers and Sellers' Wealth by Social Order

		First Estate		
Year	Paranza	Sellers	Wealth	Mean Wealth[a]
1625	Sulmona	—	—	—
1641	Sulmona	15.4%	17.0%	211
1655	Sulmona	18.5	16.4	282
1670	Sulmona	15.2	17.6	269
	All	12.6	14.2	240
1685	Sulmona	28.1	28.4	359
	All	14.2	18.5	335
1700	Sulmona	19.1	24.9	353
	All	11.8	18.0	342
Mean	Sulmona	19.3[b]	20.9[b]	295[b]
	All	13.0	16.9	306

Source: See table 21.
[a]Mean wealth in *rubbi*.
[b]Excludes 1625.

SELLERS AND BUYERS AT THE FAIR OF FOGGIA

But despite the increase in the mean size of wealth among individual members of the first two estates, their collective wealth still paled in comparison to commoners. Commoners numbered 80 percent of the sellers, and two-thirds of the collective wealth still remained in their hands. Members of the first estate (13.0 percent) were almost double those of the second estate (7.4 percent), but together they each sold about the same percentage of wool (16.9 percent and 15.7 percent). The increase of wealth in their hands after 1685 is significant. As the seventeenth-century crisis was surmounted, sellers were richer and religious and nobles joined their numbers. But religious and nobles still numbered only about one-fifth of the sellers and sold only about one-third of the wool.

This portrait is, however, only an approximation because wool sellers in the weighers' account books number only about one-fifth of all sheepowners. The whole sheepowner population has already been analyzed in more detail from the animal tax lists in order to understand the owners' rationale. The presence of diverse groups with diverse interests, let me reiterate, is a general conclusion that remains constant at every level of abstraction.

Sellers' Budgets

A review of a middling holder's budget should clarify both his economic status and rationale. Maintaining flocks in transhumance demanded a substan-

Second Estate			Third Estate		
Sellers	Wealth	Mean Wealth[a]	Sellers	Wealth	Mean Wealth[a]
5.9%	8.5%	245	94.1%	91.5%	166
7.7	8.9	223	74.4	73.3	188
5.0	4.4	227	73.3	75.6	205
7.6	10.2	913	77.3	72.2	217
8.7	17.2	423	78.7	68.5	186
10.5	18.7	631	61.4	52.9	306
4.7	9.4	513	81.0	72.0	229
7.1	14.1	531	73.8	60.9	221
8.9	20.5	519	79.3	61.6	175
7.3	10.8	462	75.7	71.0	217
7.4	15.7	485	79.7	67.4	197

tial capital outlay in sheep. Sheepowners expected a relatively high rate of return with minor risks. In 1666, Coda documents that a middling grazier with 1,000 sheep would spend some 540 ducats for an income of 585 ducats, that is, 45 ducats' profit, an 8 percent return on investment. In comparison to his ordinary shepherds, who were paid 20 ducats annual salary plus a bread allowance of 11 ducats, the chief shepherd, who received an extra 5 ducats, and the wool weighers, who received 10–30 ducats, the profit of an independent sheepowner gave him an annual income about 50 percent greater than that of his employees. But that 8 percent profit margin comes to us from the tail end of the seventeenth-century downturn, when wool prices were depressed and few foreign buyers present. No other middling holder budgets survive, although Cimaglia's incomplete 1783 approximation based upon cost-benefit analysis of one sheep gives a 6 percent profit margin, and Silla's 1783 budget for a 2,000 sheep flock gives a 12 percent profit margin.[22]

A large holder's account books, however, survive for the Doria estates. An examination of income and expenses of the Doria pastoral enterprise in the twelve years from 1752 to 1763—that is, the tail end of the eighteenth-century upturn—provides a strikingly similar structure to the Coda model budget, despite their difference in economies of size—10,000 to 1,000 sheep (tables 27 and 28). Income derives from the same three main sources in relatively equal proportions: wool, 48 percent in Coda and 49 percent in Doria; animals (meat and skins), 33 percent in Coda and 38 percent in Doria; cheese, 19 percent in Coda and 9 percent in Doria. (Note the 10 percent cheese differential; it will become significant shortly.) Likewise, the same expenditures were encountered proportionately: salaries, 22 percent in both Coda and Doria; pasture and taxes, 45 percent in both Coda and Doria; provisions and capital outlays, 18 percent in Coda and 21 percent in Doria; miscellaneous, 15 percent in Coda and 12 percent in Doria. Income from wool, meat, and cheese, and expenses for salaries, pasture and taxes, provisions and equipment, and miscellaneous defined the pastoral budget, whether large or small.

The Doria bottom line, 7,055 minus 5,561 ducats (a 21 percent profit margin), however, is vastly different from Coda's account. Doria income for 76 cases over the 1672–1763 span—roughly the favorable pastoral conjuncture from sheep investment after the 1667 plague to the famine crises of the 1760s—averaged 8,315 ducats. Income ranged from a high of 11,816 to a low of 3,099 ducats. Expenses ranged from 1,940 to 7,029 ducats with a 4,829 ducat mean. Only 66 valid observations of their difference can be computed. The range from −6,193 to 6,727 ducats averaged to a positive mean of 1,763. The profit margin for the Doria pastoral industry, then, was 21 percent over the long term, exactly equivalent to that of the twelve years examined in detail above. In other words, the Dorias expected a profit almost three times greater than Coda's seventeenth-century investor.

This dramatic difference cannot be explained by the relative size of their holdings since the structure of both income and expense accounts are the same.

Further, the debit ledger not only is structurally equivalent but remained constant—about 20 ducats annually for shepherds' wages, 13.2 ducats per *carro* for pasture, and 10 ducats annually per employee for bread.[23] Income was what changed. The meat/wool ratio in Coda was 69 percent versus 78 percent for the Doria budgets; the cheese/wool ratio was 40 percent in Coda versus 18 percent for Doria. Prices alone—the positive versus the negative conjuncture—are what made pastoral livelihood so profitable in the eighteenth century. The cheese income differential provides the clue. Whereas cheese prices stood static at 16–18 *carlini* per *pesa* in 1666 and 16.75 *carlini* per *pesa* for the 1752–63 mean, May wool prices rose from about 27 *carlini* per *rubbio* in 1666 to 46 *carlini* per *rubbio* for the twelve-year mean, and summer meat prices from about 8 to 15 *carlini*. The mean product value ratio between cheese and May wool in the eighteenth century was 24.6 percent versus the seventeenth-century Coda reading of twice that, 59.8 percent. Note that supply would also change up or down to meet demand: more May and less August wool, more spring lambs, and so forth in boom times. Cheese sold for domestic consumption was in less demand than wool and meat, part of which were intended for international buyers. Thus, higher prices fueled pastoral profits. And what a profit—21 percent! Such profits approximated the 29 percent return reaped by the Jesuits in their agricultural enterprise. Need one say more about investor rationale?

One other observation gleaned from the Doria budgets emphasizes that very low pastoral risk encouraged graziers to reap such returns. With expenditures constant for wages to an unskilled, abundant labor force, for pasture taxes fixed by the state in 1556, and for victuals and equipment regulated by the state, internal economic risks were minimal. When did the Doria encounter losses in the eighteenth century? They spilled red ink only eight times: 1710, 1711, 1716, 1726, 1732, 1733, and 1763. By now the dates should give the answer away—either political change, which disrupted the international market, or natural disasters, which affected flock size. In general, short-term fluctuations came from external forces outside owners' control, and they were rare. Profits were normally so large that one could expect to survive such short-term disasters.

Business as usual, then, saw sellers place their raw wool in depositories (*fondaci*) in Foggia. A partial list of some 61 depositories in the seventeenth century gives a cross-section of Foggia's elite families—Brancia, Coda, Scarnera, Petrea, Calvanese, Sacchetti, Saggese, Di Pila, Calabria.[24] Not only men, but four women proprietors are included. The Santissima Annunziata of Sulmona, one of the large sheepowners, numbered among some seven religious foundations owning depositories. Other wool sellers such as Liberatore di Camillo (Rocca del Raso), Andrea Marinanza (Lucoli), and Giuseppe Pietrantonio (Rovere), owned their own depositories. Not all depository owners ran the business; seven different landlords rented to eight tenants. Seven proprietors owned and one renter occupied two depositories. In all, fifty-three of the sixty-one depositories were separately owned or operated. In a city of some

TABLE 27 Budgets of the Doria Sheep Industry at Melfi (1752–1763): Income (In Ducats)

Year	Total Income	Cheese	Animals, Meat, and Skins	Wool	Pasture and Taxes	Bread, Wine, and Barley
1751/52	7,379.94	634 (8.6%)	2,929 (39.7%)	3,494 (47.3%)	306 (4.1%)	18 (0.2%)
1752/53	7,392.73	943 (12.8)	2,325 (31.5)	3,905 (52.8)	211 (2.9)	9 (0.1)
1753/54	6,945.32	413 (6.0)	2,748 (39.6)	3,564 (51.3)	216 (3.1)	4 (0.1)
1754/55	6,289.04	498 (7.9)	2,774 (44.1)	2,814 (44.7)	196 (3.1)	8 (0.1)
1755/56	6,868.03	641 (9.3)	2,526 (36.8)	2,942 (42.8)	748 (10.9)	11 (0.2)
1756/57	7,482.01	983 (13.1)	2,379 (31.8)	3,636 (48.6)	484 (6.5)	1 (0.1)
1757/58	6,627.12	490 (7.4)	2,349 (35.4)	3,542 (53.4)	244 (3.7)	3 (0.1)
1758/59	6,936.58	548 (7.9)	2,537 (36.6)	3,588 (51.7)	251 (3.6)	13 (0.2)
1759/60	6,643.87	454 (6.8)	2,814 (42.4)	3,197 (48.1)	177 (2.7)	2 (0.1)
1760/61	6,534.18	750 (11.5)	2,579 (39.5)	3,019 (46.2)	179 (2.7)	9 (0.1)
1761/62	7,729.40	995 (12.9)	2,827 (36.6)	3,735 (48.3)	172 (2.2)	1 (0.1)
1762/63	7,826.89	712 (9.2)	2,975 (38.5)	3,754 (48.6)	281 (3.6)	8 (0.1)
Mean	7,055	(9.4)	(37.7)	(48.7)	(4.1)	(1.3)

Source: ADLPR, scaf. 16/56, "Industrie nello stato di Melfi (1707 a 1784). Conti delli Massari delle Pecore."

Note: The Doria account books were kept from May to May in 1753 and 1754, and from September through August thereafter.

TABLE 28 Budgets of the Doria Sheep Industry at Melfi (1752–1763): Expense (In Ducats)

Year	Total Expenses	Salaries	Pasture and Taxes	Provisions and Equipment	Foggian Expenses	Miscellaneous
1751/52	5,437.11	1,259 (23.1%)	2,348 (43.2%)	1,133 (20.9%)	338 (6.2%)	359 (6.6%)
1752/53	5,101.66	1,258 (24.7)	2,069 (40.6)	886 (17.4)	345 (6.8)	543 (10.7)
1753/54	6,811.53	1,325 (19.5)	3,495 (51.3)	1,190 (17.5)	346 (5.1)	456 (6.7)
1754/55	5,755.50	1,199 (20.8)	2,245 (39.0)	1,375 (23.9)	247 (4.3)	691 (12.0)
1755/56	5,272.18	1,090 (20.7)	2,383 (45.2)	1,267 (24.0)	233 (4.4)	298 (5.7)
1756/57	5,034.54	1,149 (22.8)	2,283 (45.3)	999 (19.8)	255 (5.1)	349 (6.9)
1757/58	5,193.65	1,191 (22.9)	2,246 (43.3)	1,124 (21.6)	233 (4.5)	400 (7.7)
1758/59	5,274.22	1,139 (21.6)	2,330 (44.2)	1,159 (22.0)	231 (4.4)	416 (7.9)
1759/60	6,009.25	1,147 (19.1)	2,824 (47.0)	1,489 (24.8)	209 (3.4)	341 (5.7)
1760/61	5,523.80	1,176 (21.3)	2,605 (47.2)	1,164 (21.1)	204 (3.7)	375 (6.8)
1761/62	5,332.61	1,159 (21.7)	2,506 (47.0)	1,056 (19.8)	176 (3.3)	437 (8.2)
1762/63	5,990.50	1,260 (21.0)	2,810 (46.9)	1,201 (20.0)	157 (2.6)	562 (9.4)
Mean	5,561	(21.6)	(45.0)	(21.1)	(4.5)	(7.9)

Source: See table 27.

Note: The Doria account books were kept from May to May in 1753 and 1754, and from September through August thereafter.

1,000 hearths, more than 5 percent of Foggia's families owned wool warehouses. Such investments were highly contested. In 1773 candlestick auctions began the bidding for depository proprietorship at 16 ducats per year but required three candles before the final bid went to Emilio Guadagno for 25 ducats.[25] The market streets of Foggia were indeed lined with wool depositories inside the city gates just as the subterranean grain depositories were mined under the plaza outside the gates. Everyone awaited the buyers.

Identifying the Buyers

Buyers can be examined in the same way as sellers, by origin and by wealth. Defining how much they bought and where they were taking their purchases will help us understand who these buyers were. Here the presence of large and small buyers defines a dual economy of domestic and foreign demand. Again the shifts in quantity as well as origin draw a portrait of structure and change in the wool market.

What can we say about geography? Overall, the seventeenth-century weighers' account books provides a clear, if not definitive, picture of buyers' origins. Buyers acted directly as factors for cloth manufacturers or as independent middlemen who hoped to transport and sell the raw Foggian wool to those manufacturers for a profit. In both cases, their towns of origin—either within or without the Kingdom—generally indicate the destinations of their wool purchases.

The first problem we must solve, however, is correct identification of the buyers' provenances. The account books are often silent. In 1655, for example, the fourth largest buyers, Giovanni Galiti and Giovanni Basiletti, who purchased 602 *rubbi* of Sulmona wool in partnership, appear without Christian names or towns of origin. Perhaps they were too well known. The 1654 account book, however, identifies them more completely and lists them as Venetians.[26] Next, there is no guarantee that a buyer purchased wool only for his own town of origin. Did Francesco Antonio Zimma send all of his 1,245 *rubbi* to Aquila in 1655?[27] Couldn't he have been plying the old Abruzzi road up to Florence or into the Marches? Worse, sometimes the account books identify the same individual with two different provenances. Pietro Zanetti, a resident of Foggia we have already met shipping cheese to Naples, shipped wool to Venice in 1670 and, with one Federico Zanetti, to Sulmona in 1685; Giovanni Zenucchi shipped wool to Chieti in 1697 and Bergamo in 1700; and Giovanni Battista Mazza shipped wool to Venice and Bari in 1704.[28] Large merchant middlemen were probably making specific purchases for different buyers from different places. More complicated, still, some buyers became prosperous residents of Foggia, and local palaces bear their family names: Rosati, Filiasi, Siniscalchi, Ricciardi, and De Luca.[29] They could buy wool on commission for foreign buyers from their hometown or any other, but they should certainly not all be called Foggian buyers.[30]

SELLERS AND BUYERS AT THE FAIR OF FOGGIA 227

Misidentifying buyers, therefore, is always possible given the hundreds of transactions per year. I have tried to link registers, but by no means do I claim infallibility. The unidentified origins of 27 percent of the buyers in 1685, for example, hinge on only a few individuals. The third, fourth, and sixth largest buyers—that is, 19 percent of total wool wealth—have no identifiable place of origin. Is Angelo Alfieri, the third largest buyer, a descendent of the Milanese Alfieros present at Foggia in 1626? This seems too problematic a guess. Similarly, are the Marchettis, Foggian residents and rarely identified by place, really from Foggia? I have chosen to list them as Venetian, rather than Neapolitan according to some ten sales in the 1685 Sulmona account book.[31] Thus identified as Venetians, the Marchettis, who were far and away the single largest buyers in the three sample years with full reporting (17 percent of all wool sold in 1670, 25 percent in 1685, and 15 percent in 1700), confirm literary sources with quantitative certainty on the importance of the northern Italian market.

Another word of caution is in order. General statistics and breakdowns of wool buyers' origins by trail heads show why the Sulmona account books alone do not provide sufficient information on buyers. Buyers did not spread their purchases out evenly over the three weighing stations. Sulmona buyers accounted for only 35 percent of all buyers in the last quarter of the century. On the contrary, wool buyers tended to localize their purchases by the quality and distance variables encoded in the different weighing stations. In 1670 foreign buyers, for example, bought most of their second-condition white wool from Sulmona (37 percent of that *paranza*'s wool) and Castel di Sangro (26 percent of that *paranza*'s wool), and 48 percent of the best first-condition white wool from Aquila. Principato purchases, on the other hand, were fairly evenly distributed among the three weighing stations, with a marked tendency to favor the better-quality Aquila wool by the end of the century because the improved economic conjuncture probably allowed the manufacturers around Salerno to increase production of higher-quality woolens (*panni alti*). Abruzzi wool purchases were small and limited to the two weighing stations from their home provinces, Aquila and Sulmona. Aquila black wool was the lone quality purchased (often given as mendicant charity) in heavy quantities by local consumers in Molise and Capitanata. Here again, Terra di Lavoro (especially the military uniform works at Cerreto)[32] dominated the black wool purchases. Little black wool seems to have been destined for cloth production in Venice or Salerno. On the other hand, castrated sheeps' wool was of high quality, and Venetians purchased all of it in 1668.[33]

Buyers' Wealth

It should already be apparent that large wool buyers played an inordinate role in the market (table 29). Note the sharp drop-off, a mean of about 40 percent, in quantity of wool purchased by the fourth and fifth buyers in the sample years. The top four buyers alone accounted for a mean of 21 percent (23,

TABLE 29 Top Five Wool Buyers (1625–1700) (In *Rubbi*)

Sulmona, 1625		Sulmona, 1641		Sulmona, 1655	
Buyer	Wool	Buyer	Wool	Buyer	Wool
Alessio Gualdo (Bergamo)	1,190	Pietro Zanetti (Venice)	1,180	Francesco Antonio Zimma (Aquila)	1,246
Francesco & GianBattista Moroni (Bergamo)	863	Felippo Tauro (Naples)	584	Burtolo Boricelli (Bergamo)[a]	961
Gerolomo Perini (Bergamo)	689	Ludovico Colantonio (Aquila)	550	Giovanni Paganese (Bergamo)[a]	890
GianDomenico Buffane (Milan)	576	Anello Battinello (Costa d'Amalfi)	546	Giovanni Galiti & Giovanni Basiletti (Venice)	602
Giorgio Sanino [not given]	380	Cav. Mutio Gamielli (Piedimonte d'Alife)	430	Michelangelo Vallano (Costa d'Amalfi)	482

Source: See table 21.
[a]Paganese and Boricelli bought 144 *rubbi* in partnership, divided evenly.
[b]Antonio Greppi purchased 2,182 *rubbi* in partnership with Marco Greppi, included here.

16, and 24 percent respectively) for all wool sold in the Sulmona weighers' books for 1625, 1641, and 1655, up to a mean of 44 percent (38, 48, and 45 percent respectively) in all weighers' books for 1670, 1685, and 1700.

Dividing buyers into deciles further confirms the dichotomy between rich and poor. In the complete account books of 1670, 1685, and 1700, the top ten percent of the buyers bought more than two-thirds (71 percent) of the wool sold in Foggia. In other words, fewer than 20 out of 200 buyers dominated the market. The chasm between them and the 80th decile was enormous, more than a 60 percent difference. The continuity between the lower 90 percent of the buyers is highlighted in a table of standard deviations within deciles. Again, as in the case of sellers, a marked chronological trend toward the spreading out of buyers accompanied the late seventeenth-century recovery as greater wealth trickled down the hierarchical scale.

Buyers' Origins

The reason for this dichotomy between the very few large merchants and everyone else comes into greater focus when we examine towns of origin (tables 30 and 31). The top five towns in the Sulmona account books bought 67 percent of the wool in 1625, 69 percent in 1641, and 57 percent in 1655; and in the complete account books, 57 percent in 1670, 58 percent in 1685, and 77 percent in 1700. The richest buyers thus came from a handful of towns which maintained their importance across the century as buyers of almost two-thirds

SELLERS AND BUYERS AT THE FAIR OF FOGGIA   229

All, 1670		All, 1685		All, 1700	
Buyer	Wool	Buyer	Wool	Buyer	Wool
Pietro Marchetti (Venice)	9,162	Pietro Marchetti (Venice)	15,227	Giovanni Marchetti (Venice)	14,104
Giovanni Galiti (Venice)	6,650	Pietro Zanetti (Venice)	5,168	Antonio Greppi (Bergamo)[b]	12,923
Rocco Gelmi (Chieti)	2,481	Angelo Alfieri [not given]	4,542	Dominico Farina (San Severino)	8,294
Andrea Vignano [not given]	2,346	Giuseppe Ricciardi [not given]	4,051	Giovanni Zenucchi (Bergamo)	7,889
Pietro Zanetti (Venice)	1,705	Giuseppe Zenucchi (Venice)	2,706	Giovanni Vitale (Bergamo)	4,000

TABLE 30 Top Ten Wool Buyers' Towns of Origin (1625–1655) (In *Rubbi*)

1625			1641			1655		
Town	Wool	Buyers	Town	Wool	Buyers	Town	Wool	Buyers
Bergamo	3,820	18	Piedimonte d'Alife	3,207	34	Costa d'Amalfi	3,179	72
San Severino	2,310	47	San Severino	2,954	60	Bergamo	1,852	11
Costa d'Amalfi	1,287	33	Costa d'Amalfi	2,641	44	San Severino	1,424	41
Piedimonte d'Alife	1,148	12	Naples	2,001	44	Aquila	1,246	5
Castiglione	1,125	18	Venice	1,180	7	Naples	1,088	26
Naples	945	35	Aquila	906	9	Venice	878	5
Milan	576	18	Foggia	708	13	Gifoni	697	27
Lama	421	10	Castiglione	496	13	Piedimonte d'Alife	651	13
Venice	332	3	Salerno	473	11	Cusano	164	1
Costa del Aquila	312	3	Bergamo	293	2	Peschio	162	2

Source: See table 21.

TABLE 31 Top Ten Wool Buyers' Towns of Origin (1670–1700) (In *Rubbi*)

1670			1685			1700		
Town	Wool	Buyers	Town	Wool	Buyers	Town	Wool	Buyer
Venice	19,870	9	Venice	20,395	2	Bergamo	26,693	7
San Severino	8,156	50	San Severino	5,280	14	San Severino	16,085	33
Costa d'Amalfi	3,993	6	Naples	3,989	15	Venice	14,299	2
Piedimonte d'Alife	2,876	10	Bergamo	2,706	1	Naples	6,121	19
Chieti	2,507	2	Piedimonte d'Alife	2,324	10	Piedimonte d'Alife	3,811	20
Cerreto	1,651	6	Chieti	1,994	1	Cerreto	3,318	14
Gifoni	1,377	9	Cerreto	1,301	10	Morcone	3,196	13
Morcone	866	11	Morcone	1,208	12	Brescia	2,262	1
Cusano[a]	627	4	Melfi	1,150	2	Costa d'Amalfi	1,628	4
Naples	515	11	Cusano	923	8	Salerno	966	8

Source: See table 21.

[a]Cusano is the ninth town by buyers' wealth, but six individual buyers, whose provenance was listed as the procurator of the royal court, purchased 795 *rubbi* of wool to rank ahead of it.

TABLE 32 Wool Buyers' Origins: Quantity of Wool by Province (1625–1700) (In *Rubbi* and Absolute and Relative Percentages)

	Italy outside Kingdom		Terra di Lavoro		Principato Citra and Ultra	
Year	Wool	Percentage	Wool	Percentage	Wool	Percentage
Sulmona						
1625	4,728	32.7 (35)	3,296	22.8 (25)	3,771	26.1 (28)
1641	1,993	11.4 (12)	5,995	34.4 (36)	6,744	38.7 (40)
1655	3,332	21.6 (26)	2,009	13.0 (16)	5,447	35.8 (44)
1670	4,104	26.8 (32)	854	5.6 (7)	6,598	43.0 (51)
1685	10,065	50.0 (56)	2,760	13.6 (16)	1,965	9.7 (11)
1700	13,278	58.9 (63)	2,845	12.6 (13)	5,004	22.2 (24)
Mean		(37)		(19)		(33)
All						
1670	19,870	36.1 (43)	7,584	13.8 (16)	14,068	25.6 (30)
1685	22,694	37.8 (52)	8,539	14.2 (20)	7,381	12.3 (17)
1700	43,255	47.4 (52)	14,105	15.5 (17)	20,609	22.6 (25)
Mean		(49)		(18)		(24)

Source: See table 21.

Note: Relative percentages in parentheses are calculated without missing values.

of Foggia's wool (64 percent mean). San Severino is named among the top five towns in all six sample years, Piedimonte d'Alife five times, the Amalfi Coast towns, Naples, Venice, and Bergamo four times, and three other towns once each. The big buyers, then, all came from important centers of wool manufacturing around the Salerno fair, the Neapolitan capital, and the state of Venice. Further, since the number of buyers in these towns for the three complete years compares favorably with the 90th decile by wealth, it is clear that the Foggian fair exemplified a classic dual economy.

We had best differentiate the provincial destinations and their local wool industries (table 32). Three provincial foci stand out: Principato Citra around Salerno, Terra di Lavoro around Naples, and Abruzzo Ultra around Aquila and the Lanciano fair. In the 1620s, Principato accounted for 40 percent of acquisitions, Terra di Lavoro for 30 percent, and the Abruzzi for 10 percent.[34] My global statistics from 1670, 1685, and 1700 show a return of the international buyers to the market, but Principato still in the lead among domestic buyers with 24 percent, Terra di Lavoro with 18 percent, and the Abruzzi with 3 percent.

The Domestic Market

These national wool industries did not grow up in isolation; their foundation and development parallel that of raw material production in Puglia. The

Abruzzo Citra and Ultra		Other Kingdom		Not Given or Unverified	
Wool	Percentage	Wool	Percentage		
1,446	10.0 (11)	165	1.1	1,053	7.3
1,234	7.1 (7)	708	4.1	750	4.3
1,590	10.3 (13)	271	1.8	2,801	18.1
1,185	7.7 (9)	110	0.7	2,490	16.2
1,637	8.1 (9)	1,051	5.2	2,772	13.7
—	—	52	0.2	1,374	6.1
	(8)				
2,851	5.3 (6)	2,294	4.2	8,314	15.4
1,713	2.9 (4)	3,441	5.7	16,199	27.0
135	0.1	4,297	4.7	8,849	9.7
	(3)				

TABLE 33 Top Four National Consumers of Foggian Wool (1625–1700) (In *Rubbi*)

Town	Paranza	1625	1641
Piedimonte d'Alife	Sulmona All	1,148 (100)	3,207 (279)
San Severino	Sulmona All	2,310 (100)	2,954 (128)
Costa d'Amalfi	Sulmona All	1,287 (100)	2,641 (205)
Naples	Sulmona All	945 (100)	2,001 (212)

Source: See table 21.
Note: The 1625 index is given in parentheses.

Neapolitan wool guild and the provincial manufacturers around Salerno date from the thirteenth century. Coniglio finds first evidence in 1269, the dyeing of cloth at Amalfi in 1271 and 1272, and, with strong Florentine connections, manufactures in the capital from 1308.[35] Obviously, the Neapolitans could have imported raw foreign wool as the Florentines did, but the foundation of the *dogana delle pecore* in Puglia by the mid thirteenth century fits neatly with native manufacturing. Ferrante's 1463 prohibition on foreign cloth and 1480 concessions to foreign merchants and artisans who wished to establish themselves in Naples are well known in the larger context of Florentine-Neapolitan relations and again coincide with a period of customhouse growth.[36] Charles V's 1536 confirmation of the wool guild's statutes comes at the same time that he reaffirms the pastoral industries in Foggia. Similarly, the industries declined in the seventeenth century and reasserted themselves in the eighteenth.[37]

The production of woolens was closely articulated with the Neapolitan silk industry, and Coniglio hints at a grand design in Habsburg imperial politics to coordinate the various textile industries in its domains.[38] Certainly, the production and exportation of raw Calabrian silk grew in the sixteenth century, as did the numbers of silk guild members in the guild matriculation lists in Naples.[39] Heretofore, silk has gotten the headlines among the capital's manufactures. But if the wool coming into Naples had not all been exported to Florence,[40] that native Neapolitan industry would also have been booming.

With the restarting of the pastoral economy by the late seventeenth century, native manufacturing also prospered. For the complete accounting years, 1670, 1685, and 1700, Principato buyers numbered 77, 20, and 59, with 260, 62, and 185 transactions respectively at the Foggian fair. They represented manufacturers who produced cloth to be vented at the September Salerno fair.[41] In San Cipriano Picentino woolens were manufactured from the fifteenth into the nineteenth century.[42] Gifoni had a long-established cloth

1655	1670	1685	1700
651 (57)	614 (53)	856 (75)	784 (68)
	2,876	2,324	3,811
1,424 (62)	3,378 (146)	1,451 (63)	3,020 (131)
	8,156	5,280	16,085
3,179 (247)	2,510 (195)	513 (40)	861 (67)
	3,993	704	1,628
1,088 (115)	791 (84)	6,772 (717)	5,301 (561)
	515	3,989	6,121

industry which began to develop after the 1530 end of the French Wars.[43] Marino Caracciolo, prince of Avellino, introduced the production of woolens there between 1581 and 1591.[44] In addition, among others, the seventeenth-century weighers' accounts attest to wool industries in Cava, the Amalfi Coast towns, Salerno itself, and, by far the largest, San Severino. Similarly, Terra di Lavoro towns claimed 45, 42, and 53 buyers who made 71, 105, and 141 transactions in 1670, 1685, and 1700 respectively. By the late eighteenth century, the Kingdom produced more than 50,000 cloths (almost twice as many as Venice, Bergamo, or Florence in their late sixteenth-century heyday), with an export income of almost 725,000 ducats.[45] Production centered in the three provincial foci: Principato Citra (47 percent), Terra di Lavoro (32 percent), and the Abruzzi (11 percent).

Note especially that as the conjuncture again becomes positive in 1700, the growth in international purchases comes at the expense of total percentage, not absolute weight, of wool purchased by Principato, Terra di Lavoro, and the Abruzzi. Why? First, the Salerno market also increased its consumption of raw wool for cloths to be sold at its fair because it too was involved in the international market exporting finished woolens. Second, the Neapolitan capital's wool guild proved to be elastic in its ability to rebound from the crisis. Third, depressed wool sales in Foggia increased August wool sales in the Abruzzi, whereas increased sales in Foggia lessened internal mountain demand. Flocks were increased, and the increased number of sheep bearing August fleece may have satisfied Abruzzi demand. Thus, it is important that wool purchases around Salerno and Naples nearly doubled if we compare 1625 and 1700, the two points outside the negative conjuncture.

Absolute values are significant because they explain that the domestic markets continued to purchase raw wool at consistent levels before, during, and after the crisis. The indexed change in wool purchases for the four largest national manufacturing centers across the six sample years clarifies the problem (table 33). Remembering the difficulty in comparing the Sulmona only account books, we can still get a rough idea of the stability in domestic consumption through the seventeenth-century crisis. Let us take the 1625 figure as our index. In 1641 national buyers appear to have taken up some of the slack from the disappearing international buyers and nearly doubled their wool purchases. But by 1655, Piedimonte and San Severino, with a decline to about 60 percent of normal purchases had altered their buying program to purchase wool in a *paranza* other than Sulmona. The Amalfi Coast towns' consumption alone gives some idea of the slackened growth curve in Sulmona. From 1670 to 1700, Piedimonte and San Severino purchased only 26 percent of their wool in Sulmona, whereas the Amalfi Coast towns purchased 63 percent. Note that 1685 appears to have been a poor year that shook out weak performers before the takeoff, for all save Naples. Finally, the late-century recovery may have allowed the big consumers like Naples to grow apace and smaller ones like the Amalfi Coast towns to decline in the face of increased competition, whereas the solidly based industries in Piedimonte and San Severino held their own or grew slightly.

International Demand

As we look at provincial origins of buyers, the important distinction here is between exported and national wool. For the full reporting of the last quarter of the seventeenth century, wool exports to other Italian towns averaged 49 percent compared to the Kingdom's 51 percent native consumption. But this mean figure is extremely misleading because of the poor reporting (27 percent of origins not given).[46] Again we must remember the effects of economic trends. If one looks over the long-term conjuncture of the seventeenth-century downturn, foreign demand appears to have been about one-third to one-half of sales before the crisis, dropped down to one-fourth or below during it, and moved back up to one-third to one half after it. Thus, in the Sulmona account books foreign buyers dropped out of the Foggian market after 1628, and overall from 1623 to 1642 foreign buyers purchased only 12 percent of the wool.[47] In 1631, for example, plague kept most of the foreign merchants away, and there was a scarcity of money. Prices fell "because the majority of the buyers of wool came from Venice, Bergamo, Milan and other places outside of the Kingdom."[48] The norm in good times, however, saw one-third to one-half of the buyers as international.

Domenico Sella's description of the seventeenth-century economy of Spanish Lombardy as crisis and continuity aptly describes northern Italian wool manufacturing in the states of both Milan and Venice. In Lombardy sharp declines in major production centers like Como, Milan, and Cremona, as well as production of coarser goods in small towns like Brianza and Monza, shook the woolen industry by the 1630s and 1640s.[49] By late century, woolen production was almost extinct: Como, from 400 cloths in 1650 to none by 1700; Milan, from 3,000 cloths in 1640 to about 1,000 per year in the 1660s, to some 100 by 1705.[50] In Venetian territory, Venice itself produced only 9,975 cloths in 1665 and 2,803 in 1701.[51]

In Bergamo alone the woolen industry revived. Here crisis brought reorientation of industry to the countryside.[52] And the revival of Bergamo was reflected in Foggia because the cost of raw materials was a critical component of the wool manufacturers' balance sheet, some one-third of expenses.[53]

Since keeping input costs down ensured higher profits, a 1596 report on "how woolen cloth is made" in Bergamo explained the source and expense of raw materials. "The wool is brought from Milan and from Florence. The greater part is Spanish wool, and some is from Puglia, but only a little. Because it must be conducted by way of Venice, it incurs great expense."[54] Where wool came from and how it got there determined not only cost, but also quality. This 1596 description further points out the distinction between high- and low-quality cloths: 8,500 pieces of *panni alti* and 18,000 of *panni bassi*, for a total of 26,500 cloths. By the late seventeenth century, Bergamo was exceeding these numbers with a mean of 34,619 pieces in the 17 years between 1685 and 1710. A sharp downturn of 23 percent, which coincided with the War of the Spanish Succession, left a mean approaching the sixteenth-century figure, 26,677 pieces for the three years 1708 to 1710.[55] Significantly, higher-quality woolens declined at a rate almost twice that of the low-quality woolens, 32 percent to 17 percent, although relative proportions of high to low quality had only declined three points below the mean, to 36 percent at its low in 1708 and 1709. The significant difference between the late sixteenth- and late seventeenth-century woolen industry at Bergamo had, in fact, been the rise in the proportion of high-quality cloths from 32 percent and 30 percent of production in 1596 and 1685 to 41 percent between 1701 and 1707. Bergamo was replacing some of the older manufacturing centers in the high-quality market (most notably Venice itself), but, at the same time, that high-quality market was the one most susceptible to decline during the downturn.

This quality comparison can be linked to raw wool. High-quality cloths were actually made in a variety of grades. In 1686 three kinds of wool were differentiated by origin: Venice, Foggia, and Rome. While local Venetian wool made low-quality goods, the similar fibers from Foggia and Rome made high-quality goods.[56] Among the "four or five grades" attested to in Bergamo in 1697, "wool from the customhouse of Naples which is bought in the fair of Foggia" stood right below Spanish wools. The cloths of Foggian wool were high quality but brought a lower price than those of highest-quality Spanish wools.[57]

How much of the raw wool in Bergamo was from Foggia? In 1767 a questionnaire to 26 manufactuers in Bergamo who each averaged 85 cloths per year found that 24 bought both "fine" and "ordinary wool."[58] The fine wool was called Puglian or Foggian and was bought in Brescia, Bergamo, Venice, or

Foggia according to the *voce* of the Kingdom. The price of ordinary wool, called Levantine, Turkish, or Ragusan, corresponded to its quality. The two non-respondents claimed they bought their wool only in Venice.

But what proportion of the fine and ordinary wool was consumed in Bergamo? Five factories surveyed between 1788 and 1792 expended 92,214 ducats on Puglian wool out of a total of 188,520 ducats, that is, 49 percent.[59] By the late eighteenth century, then, 50 percent of Bergamaschi cloth production depended on Foggian raw wool.

The Venetian dominance of Foggia's foreign wool market, whether to Venice itself or the Terraferma, was a constant from the fifteenth century.[60] When the Venetian merchants were not physically present in Foggia, native Neapolitans, as in the joint-stock company of 1582, were making deals to ship raw wool to them.[61] In exchange, the Neapolitans might import Venetian woolens or cheaper goods from the Marches and Umbria. The decline in Venetian wool production during the early seventeenth century paralleled the crisis in the supply from Foggia.[62] As the seventeenth-century crisis developed, the absence of foreign buyers lowered and reoriented production in the Foggian market toward national buyers. Not only lessened demand and credit, but a new monopoly of native merchants, who profited from the accumulated hatred for the Venetians and the restrictive tax system of fixed rates imposed on sheepowners, maintained prices at depressed levels between the 1620s and 1680s.[63] As woolen manufacturing reestablished itself in the northern Italian countryside in the late seventeenth century, foreign demand again hit Foggia.

When in 1679 the Sommaria spoke of the leading merchant towns at the Foggian fair as Venice, Florence, Cerreto, and Piedimonte d'Alife,[64] it is clear that it knew what it was talking about. Venetians from the island or inland were, and continued to be, the chief foreign buyers at the Foggian fair. The Kingdom's natives from the town of Piedimonte continually consumed the most white wool internally, and those from Cerreto the most black wool. But who were these elusive Florentines who have left only passing reference?

We do know that the Florentines were very active in the meat and animal market at Foggia. Along with foreign merchants from Umbria and the March of Ancona, Tuscan merchants purchased 20,424 castrated sheep, more than 90 percent of those for sale, at the 1577 fair.[65] In letters from Naples between 1621 and 1624, Vincenzio Vettori, a name with an old Florentine aristocratic ring, wrote that he had purchased castrated sheep worth 10,000 ducats in 1624.[66] Whether these *castrati* sold at 1 ducat or 15 *carlini* per head, the exact number of castrated animals does not diminish the size of this extraordinary expenditure. Note that Vettori's letter is dated in the midst of the spring Foggian fair, as were earlier letters in 1622 and 1623.[67] Further, he makes a reference to an accounting of the last fourteen years, presumably 1611–24, that is, commencing with the great sheep death of 1611/12. Three earlier random letters from Naples dated July and August 1606 reported on affairs in the

Foggian customhouse.⁶⁸ The sale of the office of doganiero to the marchese of Corato for 30,000 ducats was noted, and one Vincenzo Aquilani of Pisa (does his name give a hint of the overland route via Aquila?) was given some kind of book of a Sommaria president, presumably a Foggian account book compiled by one of its annual overseers. The book had been consigned to Ferrante Brancio, "who is the leading lawyer of the city."

My best guess is that the Florentines contracted Foggian products from their resident factors in the Neapolitan capital. Buyers like Vettori would attend the Foggian fair and have dealings with the best corporate lawyers in the capital. In addition, residents of Foggia such as Pietro Marchetti may have made wool shipments to the Florentine factors. If most of Marchetti's wool purchases were indeed going to Naples, some of the wool may have been going on to Tuscany.⁶⁹

The dramatic shift in the Foggian market came with the 1730 exemption given to wool exports from Naples.⁷⁰ Opening up of this western route, especially after 1760, redirected a great percentage of foreign-bound wool. Once the Venetian shipping monopoly from Manfredonia was broken, new markets could develop. But the overland transport from Foggia for export from Naples could be prohibitively expensive. In 1767 a Frenchman named Stefano Brunel, who rented land in Cerignola and Bisaccia, contracted for two wool shipments from Barletta to Marseilles. The *Matricana*, under the French captain Giovanni Giuseppe Bonare, carried 60 *balle* (1,800 *rubbi*) of wool, and the *Marsigliana*, under the French captain Luigi Severante, carried 65 *balle* (1,950 *rubbi*).⁷¹ In 1770 the customhouse president, Angelo Granito, wrote to his superiors in Naples that the expense of overland transportation for export from Naples was well known, and the perils of sea transport from Puglia via other than Venetian carriers, but especially national ones, brought considerable dangers from pirates and from the differences in the technology of their fleets (the Venetians used square rigging, the Neapolitans lateen rigging).⁷² Further, the Venetians brought needed finished goods to the Foggian fair in exchange, which reduced their carrying charges on the return trip to about 0.36 *carlini* per *rubbio* of wool.⁷³ National carriers, on the other hand, not only had to adopt much higher transportation charges, but, as non-Venetian importers, they were also subject to port fees in Venice at a 10 percent rate, a price which amounted to a little more than 0.5 *carlini* per *rubbio* of wool in 1770.⁷⁴ For an average shipment of 60 *balle*, then, these charges would mount up: Manfredonia to Venice via Venetian lines, 192.6 ducats; via Neapolitan lines, at least 192.6 ducats for shipment (but probably much more) + 960 ducats for taxes = 1,152.6 ducats. Who wouldn't ship Venetian? But such leverage given to Venetian buyers caused the sheepowners to clamor for more national lines to combat the Venetian monopoly.

Sommaria president Granito continued that national buyers consumed about 35,000 *rubbi* of wool annually, the same amount that Venetian merchants bought, and neither alone came near consuming the supply of 84,000 *rubbi* and "much more not placed in deposit."[75] What was to be done with the unsold excess of more than 14,000 *rubbi?* Enter the western market.

When the disruptions of the French-English wars delayed wool purchases in the spring of 1779, the setters of the *voce* price checked back over the past few years' wool sales.[76] In 1777, 90,411 *rubbi* were sold: 44,192 (49 percent) was exported, and 46,219 (51 percent) stayed in the Kingdom; in 1778, 81,109 *rubbi* were sold: 38,191 (47 percent) was exported, and 42,918 (53 percent) stayed in the Kingdom. The previous year was judged to be a normal year: one-half of production stayed in the Kingdom, one-fourth was exported to the state of Venice, and one-fourth to France.[77] Wool exports to France and Venice in the 1770s and 1780s confirm this increased western profile.[78] In 1765, 43,000 *rubbi* still went to Venice alone, whereas the 1771–90 mean was 17,000 *rubbi* to Venice with another 19,000 *rubbi* shipped annually to France between 1775 and 1787. French shipments all went to Marseilles and the southern French textile manufacturers.[79] From complete dominance of exported wool amounting to about one-half of Foggia's production, the Venetian market was forced to divide its share evenly with France from the 1770s. The Venetian wool monopoly had, in fact, been reduced by more than one-third at the same time that high production figures had been maintained in Foggia.

The Changing Structure of the Wool Trade

To recapitulate, the seventeenth-century crisis applies to international trade and credit, not domestic manufacture. The traditional method of talking about the dual economy is to argue that subsistence as compared to market production defined investment strategies. But in the cash cropping of wool, almost all production was destined to be manufactured into cloth via markets. If producers were not consuming their own wool, who was?

Immanuel Wallerstein proposes a simple mechanism of explanation for producer maximization and the resilience of regional markets in hard times.[80] His examples are drawn from eastern and central European grain producers and focus on the relationship between the concentration of land through confiscation of peasant or small holdings and the extraction of forced labor from the newly underemployed peasant. The peasants presumably still held enough land for subsistence while their extra labor went to expand their lord's cash-crop production. The same argument has been proposed for seventeenth-century Sicilian grain production, "a short-lived 'triumph' [of the internal markets] over the external one."[81]

Both of these examples focus on the supply side of the equation, whereas my wool evidence here has examined the demand side. While it is true from evidence about wool sellers that some trend toward concentration and re-feudalization is under way during the seventeenth-century crisis, I find that the reconstitution of the producer profile really takes place much later, when the eighteenth-century wool boom picks up. For the seventeenth-century crisis instead, I see weak market demand as the critical variable that depressed prices and halved supply.

Amidst this depression, why does the national market have sustaining power? It is not that the international credit crisis did not affect the national markets, but that, in the dual economy, the credit disadvantages of the national producers vis-à-vis the foreign monopolists could be overcome. With foreign textiles too expensive for purchase in the Kingdom and other peripheral markets, the foreign raw wool buyers cut back on production. As production and prices fell, national buyers had a competitive advantage and could maintain their absolute level of consumption with lower capital requirements.[82] If money and credit were the key to a wool boom, the absence of their international exponents in the seventeenth-century crisis did not kill the national market of barter and self-sufficiency, rural indebtedness, and domestic textiles.

The stability or constancy of the national textile industry provides a benchmark to evaluate the unchanging demand within the Kingdom—the 45,000 *rubbi* (52 percent) of wool consumed internally in 1777 and 1778 match neatly with the 55,000 *rubbi* total production mean from 1623 to 1691. Quite simply, wool, unlike grain, was not solely a product with subsistence value. Its supply and demand were much more elastic since clothing, more than food, was governed by discretionary choices.[83] But here, too, there is a point below which one cannot descend, and the Kingdom's internal wool manufacturers maintained their production to meet that minimal need through good times and bad.

The new positive wool conjuncture in the eighteenth century also witnessed a restructuring of the buyers' profile. My examination of the eighteenth-century weighers' account books is only impressionistic, but few buyers of larger size seemed to be named. Neapolitans like Ignazio Paliotti, Giuseppe Bambino, Ignazio Cruscole, Gennaro Pascha, and Ignazio Forte are present in addition to Venetians and Foggian residents with palaces. Especially after 1760, something like an age of great merchants—Rosati, Filiasi, and De Luca—emerges at the fair.

The Kingdom's Trade Budget

Finally, the best way to evaluate the commercial activity at Foggia is to assess the place of wool in the Kingdom's international balance of payments. In 1751, Galiani already taught that "exchange could be justly considered the pulse of the civil body of society," and that sovereigns should keep track of international credits and debits. In the Kingdom, "the fair of Foggia was almost our heart where money was absorbed to restrengthen us."[84] With about 600,000 ducats' worth of pastoral products sold annually at Foggia in the eighteenth century,[85] Galiani's common metaphor was common sense. Let us compare the profile of imports and exports before and after the seventeenth-century crisis.

The precrisis balance of payments leaves little doubt that the Kingdom of Naples was a peripheral raw material producer. In 1520, for example, three products alone accounted for almost three-fourths of exports: grain, 28 percent; olive oil, 25 percent; and silk, 19 percent.[86] In his reconstruction of late sixteenth-century trade budgets, Galasso reviews these individual agricultural products and includes finished silk cloths. He estimates an imbalance of 10:1 in favor of exports about 1580, and about 5:1 in 1622: "the typical trade of a country that we would call today, 'underdeveloped.'"[87] Aymard refines this "optimistic" calculation and divides the long-term conjuncture into three periods: "a fifteenth century of cheap wheat and very favorable to 'industrial' countries, a sixteenth century filled with wheat producers, a seventeenth century characterized by a general winding down of exchange." For Naples, he contrasts, "two economies: wheat and silk, wool and oil against textiles and metals; and two societies": large agricultural producers and small.[88]

After the seventeenth-century crisis, the character of products imported and exported by the Kingdom did not change. A 1771 budget confirms that chief imports were still textiles, leather and metal goods (60 percent), whereas exports were still olive oil, wheat, wool, and silk (82 percent).[89] The Kingdom continued to be an exporter of raw materials for finished products, but the price differential between industrial goods and agricultural products had shifted dramatically to give the Kingdom a trade deficit. By 1771 agricultural products no longer paid for imports. Naples had become a debtor nation and, already in her eighteenth-century splendor, had begun the long slide down to commercial impoverishment.

More specific analysis of the eighteenth-century trade budget, however, convinces us that this stereotyped portrait of inevitable decline, underdevelopment, and antipathy to change may not be completely accurate. The wool entry is deceiving because 92 percent of export income comes from finished goods, not raw wool. Thus, the 810,000 ducats in woolen cloth exports nearly match the 885,000 ducats in woolen imports. If, in fact, other textile manufacturers had been able to follow the wool guild's model, the more than 2:1 discrepancy between silk imports and exports, the 4:1 discrepancy for cotton, and the 15:1 discrepancy for linen would have been reversed, and Naples would have run a surplus as an industrial nation. If a national wool textile industry could flourish in a pastoral society like Naples, why couldn't the others? The absence of these other textile industries does not seem to be predetermined by the agricultural economy, dependency theory, or the dual economy. The coordination of native raw material and industrial production in the wool sector gives us reason to pause. A whole line of modern historical research may be misdirected and misfocused. Neapolitan involution and inertia may not be what it seems.

The concentration of activity at the Foggian fair did not merely offer buyers and sellers the opportunity to exchange pastoral products in the spring. Monopolist prices, class conflict, and the international balance of payments were reason enough for the state to be interested in controlling the fair. Big buyers had to be placated if the sellers and the state expected to satisfy their rationale to reap profits and collect taxes. Taking into consideration also the equally important production of grain, which made Capitanata the Kingdom's breadbasket, one readily understands why Foggia grew from a dusty crossroads town to become the most important provincial capital in the country, and why the shepherds' economy became a school for scholars of political economy.

PART 5
La Ragion Pastorale

What place did pastoralism hold in the ideology of the Old Regime? How was its presence intellectually justified in far-off urban capitals? From pastoralism's late medieval foundations as a rational means to exploit marginal land during times of low population density, the monarchical state clothed the pastoral industries in a typical Renaissance marriage between classical and Christian tradition. God's favorite, the good shepherd Abel, had been killed by his jealous farmer-brother, Cain. But now the central state was acting like Christ the Good Shepherd and restoring good government between agriculture and pasturage. Di Stefano's Arcadian mumbo jumbo only echoed the persistent invocation of pagan and Christian texts tying modern practice to ancient tradition. Such arcane ideology is not inconsistent with what became the modern mode of discourse in the birth of political economy in the late eighteenth century. For someone so schooled like De Dominicis, Renaissance *buon governo* and Di Stefano's Arcadianism became balanced sectoral analysis between pastoralism, agriculture, and manufacturing.

The Neapolitan famine of 1764 decisively shifted majority opinion, however. Just as Renaissance humanists transformed Brutus and Cassius from assassins of Caesar and the state into heroic defenders of public liberty, so too Enlightenment economists made Cain the hero over Abel. Agriculture and the noble agrarian state became the model for thinkers everywhere—in Glasgow and Edinburgh, Paris, Madrid, Naples, and Monticello. Enlightenment ideology and the Napoleonic occupation of Naples killed the sheep customhouse, but not pastoralism. Transhumance continued to thrive in the Tavoliere of Puglia because it expediently exploited the marginal zone. But if both its time and space were at hand, the meaning of pastoralism and its place in schemes of universal history and economic development lived on.

10 *From Pastoral Models to Political Economy*

The Enlightenment Critique

Ferdinando Galiani was one of the first reformers to pinpoint the errors of Neapolitan agriculture according to the theories of the new, eighteenth-century school of political economy. In an addendum to the second edition of *Della moneta* in 1780, he summarized his conclusions on the impediments to agricultural growth in the Kingdom: (1) the unequal tax burden levied on the countryside vis-à-vis the Neapolitan capital; (2) the impossibility of cultivating arable land which was encumbered by feudal customs and communal services; and (3) the state's support of a pastoral economy in the fertile plain of Puglia.[1] Each point emphasized a common-sense contradiction of rational maximization. In this oft cited passage, although not the first reexamination of the dogana of Foggia, Galiani denounced the pastoral system at Foggia because it favored pastoralism over agriculture, against the logic of alimentary demand. Galiani argues that "this province [Capitanata] is inhabited by 100,000 people when it could feed and make rich and happy 300,000." The state preferred to fill its coffers with short-term tax profits instead of its subjects' stomachs with bread. "No other similar example [exists] in civilized Europe, but only in the African desert and in barbarous Tartary."

The first edition of Galiani's *Della moneta* thirty years earlier[2] did not include his antipastoral critique—not, as he retells it, because of his immaturity as an economic thinker, but because at that early date the disparity between population and production had not yet reached an alarming state. Moreover, as the son of a judge (*auditore*) of the customhouse, Galiani was born in Chieti in the Abruzzi domains of the pastoral system. His education had been anything but provincial, but the importance of provincial economic activities like those at Foggia weighed heavily in *Della moneta*'s concern for international monetary policy. Only the dramatic catastrophe of the 1764 famine forced a rethinking of the pastoral-agricultural relationship and an examination of the effects of population pressure upon production.

Galiani's precocious, anonymous publication of *Della moneta* in 1751 at the age of twenty-one catapulted him into the front rank of European economic thinkers, and this work became one of the cornerstones of the new academic discipline of political economy. Naples further distinguished itself with the foundation of the first European chair in political economy in 1754. Just as the installation of an independent Bourbon monarchy in Naples in 1734 is considered to be a new beginning in Neapolitan political history, the establishment of the science of political economy in the university curriculum marked a new birth for the practical affairs of economics and government.

Antonio Genovesi, the dynamic holder of the chair from 1754 to 1769, became the teacher of a generation of enlightened economic thinkers and reformers.[3] In their attempt to create local agrarian societies, to improve production of specific commodities such as oil, silk, grain, or wool, and to establish a scholarly exchange with the Georgofili Academy in Florence and Venetian agrarian societies, Genovesi's school formulated a vision of political economy based upon the facts, instead of the myths, of the Kingdom's economic activity. The whole program took its critical direction from the disastrous famine of 1764. Ideas on free trade in cereals, population as the wealth of nations, and agricultural and commercial progress predominated inquiry.

The acute experience of 1764 thus forged an economic consciousness intent upon solving the problem of hunger. Nicola Fortunato's 1767 *Discovery of the antique Kingdom of Naples to its present state, both its sovereignty and its People* typified the reforming mentality.[4] Fortunato's prefamine *Reflections upon commerce ancient and modern in the Kingdom of Naples* (1760), which Genovesi had sponsored, was a descriptive survey of the Kingdom's resources.[5] The new 1767 *Discovery*, written after the worst of the famine, on the other hand, explored a relationship dear to the professor of political economy—the problem of population and agriculture.

The centerpiece of Fortunato's *Discovery* was a "Remonstrance touching the Provisioning of the City and Kingdom," with about half of its forty-five pages taken up by a "Digression on the Royal Tavoliere of Puglia."[6] Fortunato focused on the 1548 *reintegra* as a disaster that incorrectly sanctioned pasturage over agriculture and rich holders (*Opulenti* and *Magnati*) to the disadvantage of the poor. He argued that the Tavoliere's income could be quadrupled if turned over to farming and that all the grain would stabilize the Kingdom's cereal needs. After analyzing the intricacies of the customhouse system, he included a note near the end of his text which was to launch a polemic that would not die until the sheep customhouse was dismantled.

> In such manner all the Tavoliere of Puglia, which according to the present system necessarily remains even more depopulated and deserted than impoverished, would come to be populated and so many new towns would spring up as in its antique state. [It would bring] other significant advantages to the Royal Treasury and the Kingdom. At the same time, it would accommodate so many families who now live miserably in the inhospitable mountains of the two Abruzzi, Basilicata, and in other incommodious and unfortunate places in the Kingdom where, for the absence of sustenance, the population decreases every hour and becomes notably diminished. Whence from the great fertility of the soil of the Tavoliere and the advantages of its

location, it would significantly increase the population in proportion to its sustenance.[7]

In the context of Genovesi's school in Naples and the pan-European interest in political economy, Galiani's posting as secretary to the Kingdom's ambassador to France between 1759 and 1769 allowed him to make direct contacts with the French physiocrats and encyclopedists and gave him firsthand knowledge of the crisis of the Old Regime in France. With the 1764 Neapolitan famine and bread crises in general keenly on the public mind, Galiani's *Dialogues sur le commerce des bleds* (1770) rethought the physiocratic arguments on the free trade in cereals, rejected them in support of controls, and defended commerce and industry over agriculture.[8] His later research and the problem of famine dictated the 1780 addendum against pastoralism in the new edition of *Della moneta*.

Another work in 1780 emphasizes the depth of the polemic on pastoral livelihood and the sheep customhouse. For Filippo Briganti in his chapter on pastoralism in the *Economic examination of the civil system* (1780), the pasturage of animals from bees to elephants and from the first peoples to the present concludes with the same theory of sustenance as Fortunato and Galiani propounded.[9] "To satiate a family of cultivators, a small field is enough; to nourish a pastoral family an immense tract of prairie unoccupied by any other inhabitants is necessary. The great problem of rural philosophy is to find the easiest way to feed the greatest number of human mouths in the smallest expanse of land."[10] Closely related to agricultural sustenance, Briganti's hostility to pasturage is expressed in a violent vocabulary which finds pastoralism the aggressor: "the brutal voracity of quadrupeds . . . who would run about avidly to bring an end to the treasures of vegetation by digging it up from human industry and diligence . . . Peaceful agriculture, which had to arm for the first war against pasturage, bathed its innocent hands in blood."[11] Briganti's argument is arranged chronologically and emphasizes the place pastoral society holds in the four-stage theory of evolutionary development.[12] "The Romans were born shepherds, but man does not become such overnight. He passed gradually from the wild life to the pasturing life, from the pasturing life to the cultivating life." Briganti employs ideas like man's "perfectability," "the progressive action of the second stage," "the first epoch of the nation."[13]

In addition to the commonplace idea of progress in the four-stage theory, Briganti outlines a similarly common three-point explanation of the relationship of the arts, rather than nature, to "civil prosperity." Arts are, namely, necessary, useful, and decorative.[14] But the art "most worthy of preference," "the basis and foundation of everything," is agriculture. Pasturage is "subsidiary," "a continuation, not the principle object of the rustic economy." "A people who work with their own hands can live. A people who add to their own work that of domesticated animals ('docile quadrupeds') can live well. A people who squander all the vegetation of a vast horizon on beasts are very close to ceasing to live." Nature does not allow the arts to reverse their order of priority. In fact, nature establishes environmental limits for economic practice in particular regions. It is not that God proposes and man disposes, rather that man's "art can do anything, but nature is a great teacher."[15] In fact, for Briganti, nature established environmental limits for economic practice in particular regions. Thus, his last sentence combines pastoralism as an art with the demands of sustenance. "Pastoralism is, therefore, equal to all the subaltern arts; it is accessory, not the principle object of every nation which wishes to procure a *copious sustenance*."[16] All this nature-culture argument is similar to Galiani's comparison between "civilized Europe" and "barbarous Tartary," or, in the invective of Briganti: "The Tartars, Arabs, Kurds, and Bedouins are pastoral people and for a long time have prospered on the multiplication of animals. They devastate the solitudes of Africa and the most beautiful provinces of Asia."[17]

Thus, the antipastoral polemic began in the new key of political economy only after the 1764 famine. Late eighteenth-century witnesses criticized and maligned sheepherding in Spain and Italy for retarding agricultural and commercial development in favor of retrograde, pastoral privileges. Sheep ate men because sheepowners had the political clout and enjoyed exorbitant economic advantages to maintain their large-scale enterprises in the face of demographic growth, agricultural shortfall, and commercial and industrial decline. The antipastoral polemics of Enlightened economists and political reformers such as Galiani and Campomanes focused upon conflict rather than cooperation.[18] The structural opposition between the centralized state and provincial interests, between the agricultural and pastoral lobby, between large and small proprietors, and between city (often foreign) merchant entrepreneurs and rural producers prevented pastoral harmony. Whereas such antitheses and antagonisms had ushered in change for former pastoral economies such as England, they only strengthened the intransigence in Italy and Spain.[19]

The Enlightened critique remains close to the conclusions of modern economic historians. Pastoralism significantly impeded economic takeoff as it fostered agricultural involution, rural refeudalization, and commercial and industrial underdevelopment. Its roots lie in two contradictions: the precocious, bureaucratic centralization of the Mediterranean's medieval kingdoms and the dynamism of its towns versus their stranglehold on the countryside. Such a legacy describes a kind of recidivism characteristic of the Mediterranean's slow, unique path in the transition from feudalism to capitalism.[20]

The Pastoral Mode Defined and Defended

In a meticulous analysis of the sixteenth- and seventeenth-century Mesta account books, Jean Paul Le Flem, more than anyone else, has demonstrated the anachronistic fallacy of applying wholesale the perceptions and preconceptions of eighteenth-century political economy as well as those of modern economics to five centuries of pastoral activity.[21] There are many paths to capitalism and many versions of the pastoral.

Late medieval and early modern pastoral institutions—the Mesta in Castile, the Casa de Ganaderos of Saragossa in Aragon, the *dogana delle pecore* in Puglia, the Patrimonio di San Pietro in Tuscia at Rome—demonstrate the importance of four elements: monarchical centralization, crown revenues, rural pacification, and foreign exchange. Royal government encouraged and ensured their success by providing political stability, freedom from local tolls and bandits, expeditious justice, and free markets. Pastoral economy in the Mediterranean encompassed the favorable, long-term, secular curve which extended from the medieval foundation of state-chartered transhumant institutions in the early thirteenth century to their dissolution in the early nineteenth.

The Neapolitan state's continuing interest in maintaining its revenues and the viability of its patrimonial institutions encouraged legal and economic thinkers to reflect upon the day-to-day realities of pastoral livelihood with a view to reform and improvement. Their analysis attempted to explain the meaning of the Foggian customhouse and its place in society. Their economic idylls, varying with emergencies and long-term trends, changed over time. They described the royal sheep customs as everything from a reflection of some classical model to a Spanish barbarism, from the linchpin of the Neapolitan economy to an impediment to its growth. Different accounts inspired different programs of pastoral reform. Politics, poetics, law, and economics provided theoretical rationalization for the material realities of pastoral management. Untangling these arguments in their historical context clarifies how assumptions about pastoral society influenced the invention of political economy and the strong Enlightenment attack upon the pastoral mode of production.

The earliest reformers wrote internal administrative reports, like the Enriquez, "Compendio breve" of 1578. They placed the pastoral economy of the Foggian sheep customhouse in an unbroken tradition from the ancients in order to emphasize the Aragonese foundation and Spanish legitimacy in the Kingdom of Naples. The three earliest printed works on the dogana of Foggia—those of Coda (1666), Moles (1670), and Ageta (1692) on the other hand—were compendia of laws. Narrative exposition and authorial intrusion were limited. Transcribed documents, decrees, and instructions carried the weight of the argument to provide the information to pull the pastoral industry out of the seventeenth-century crisis.

The three eighteenth-century lawyers, Gaudiani (1715), Di Stefano (1731), and De Dominicis (1781), for their part, subordinated these two earlier trends to three distinct ideological apologies. Although each began with practical legal experience, cited classical authorities, assembled legal opinions of doganal commentators, and transcribed doganal archival documents, different theoretical frameworks guided their analysis. Gaudiani's good government, Di Stefano's Arcadian rationale, and De Dominicis' political economy, nevertheless, arrived at the same end. All three envisioned a just and harmonious society. Pastoral livelihood was judged to be a necessary component of such a balanced world. Despite the customhouse's faults, intelligent reform could restore rural society to its flowering state.

Andrea Gaudiani (1652–1716) used Tacitus as his exemplar of good government and argued for a legalist model of statecraft in its administration. In the preface to his manuscript, *Information for the Good Government of the Royal Sheep Customhouse in Puglia*,[22] Gaudiani tells his "most kindly reader" that "from the confusion of the laws is born the disharmony of government."[23] Thus he intends to expose the true purpose of the dogana in its laws in order to contrast current decadent practice with the institution's just purpose. "There will not be a man of sane mind who will not confess this truth: that this royal patrimony is being ruined. Because its laws have been placed in a corner, it is governed by caprice and with practices totally contrary to its own institutes."[24] Gaudiani concludes his treatise as he began it, with a denunciation of capriciousness. The customhouse would be a healthier institution if administered according to its good laws; but, governed as it is by "caprice and ambition," everything "is found to be in confusion and disharmony."[25] The repeated words *confusion, disharmony,* and *caprice* frame Gaudiani's narrative.

Among Gaudiani's innumerable classical and modern sources bearing witness to pastoral and agricultural law and practice, Tacitus alone had nothing to say about sheep; yet he is cited more than twice as often as any other ancient author. Ten references to Tacitus make him the authoritative model for Gaudiani's conception of law and politics at Foggia.[26]

All ten citations of Tacitus are related to good government, Gaudiani's organizing principle. All comment upon the confusion and corruption of the laws and the consequences of disharmony and offer "the lost guide of light to walk gropingly and meet danger easily."[27] The two Gaudiani quotations from Tacitus' history of Roman law are perfect examples of his techniques.[28] In Gaudiani's chapter on doganal laws, he does not praise laws for their existence but condemns the society that spawned them and repeated them over and over again. "It is enough to say with Tacitus, 'And now bills began to pass, not only of national but of purely individual application, and when the state was most corrupt, laws were most abundant'" (*Annals,* II, 27). Here Tacitus' insight states Gaudiani's conclusion. Gaudiani draws his own lesson that the inobservance of law only leads to even greater abuse and derision of that law. Again Tacitus offers a pithy exemplum: "and with remedies more disastrous than the abuses, [Pompey] this maker and breaker of his own enactments" (*Annals,* III, 28).

Gaudiani, like Tacitus, believes that government and law cannot force men to be just, honest, and good, to renounce ambition, cupidity, greed, and caprice. The problems of "intolerable extorsions" (p. 36), of "private interest as a sworn enemy of justice" (p. 259), of the abuse of offices, of the oppression of the minority by the rich, and of the quarrels among the *locati* cannot be legislated away.

At the same time, "no one spends to lose."²⁹ Gaudiani understands that the business of the customhouse is to make money, and he knows how it is made. The laws of supply and demand operate in the rural economy. "This is the difference between an abundant harvest with low prices, and a sparse harvest at high prices; the first will be more profitable than the second because there is more harvest to sell."³⁰ For the pastoral industry, "the advance of prices does not cause an increase in revenues but decreases them more quickly."³¹ From the first page of chapter 1, Gaudiani makes it clear that "the unique capital of this customhouse" is the sheep. "When sheep multiply, revenues increase." The state's income is, therefore, tied to the success of the sheepowners. With the increase of the fruits of pasturage, both individual owners and the state will advance their capital.³²

In addition to profit, Gaudiani emphasizes the freedom and equality of the pastoral industries under the customhouse system. Liberty or freedom to make contracts at just prices derives from the natural law.³³ Gaudiani's antimonopolist arguments, as we have seen, are in the long tradition of the scholastics and jurists. Gaudiani's arguments against forced bidding and the "voluntary" nature of sheepowner participation in the customhouse system combine with the antimonopolist theory to create a unique status for sheepowners.³⁴ Thus, the customhouse laws, which gave the graziers' special privileges and immunities, are based on this freedom, while "the fundamental principle of the customhouse is the equality" given to the graziers.³⁵ They bear royal tax burdens equally, and they have the right to equitable distribution of pasture. The whole system depends upon a meticulous concern for justice. Limited pastures of unequal quality must be evaluated and assigned justly. "Private interest [is] the sworn enemy of justice."³⁶ Harmony, then, must bind shepherd and farmer. For "from these two sole, most ancient arts [agriculture and pasturage], although rustic, depends all the assistance of whatever is necessary for the sustenance of the people."³⁷ From this harmony comes the model of good government, the binding together of the rustic economy and the state's governance.

Stefano Di Stefano (1665–1737), a younger contemporary of Gaudiani, extended that legal legacy into classical poetics and constructed a model based on the literary ideal of the pastoral as preached by the eighteenth-century Arcadian Academy. He organizes his work, *Pastoral Rationale,* into two volumes according to his subtitle, *Commentary on Pragmatic LXXIX, De Officio Procuratoris Caesaris.*³⁸ After nineteen pages of dedicatory paraphernalia and twenty-four pages of introduction, Di Stefano begins with an explication of the pragmatic's proem, followed by forty-nine chapters, one on each of the pragmatic's items. But his method of exposition is hardly straightforward. Every chapter has countless digressions, meanderings, nested footnotes, and references. The pragmatic of 1669 often seems only a touchstone to get at the real, underlying principle of doganal organization, pastoral poetry.

Di Stefano models his work on Gian Vincenzo Gravina's *Della ragion poetica* and its Arcadian aesthetic—a work is to a rule as a rule is to a rationale.[39] If Di Stefano is read as a member of the Accademia degli Arcadi who was writing a self-conscious Arcadian treatise, then, his seemingly diffuse analysis of Pragmatic LXXIX does indeed become clear. Di Stefano wishes to explain more than the surface institution and its laws; he wishes to explain them in terms of their fundamental rationale. That rationale is pastoral poetry. Its pristine harmony is meant to be the model for both the customhouse law and the customhouse institution. That ideological harmony is meant to be the organizing principle for both his book and the real countryside it describes. The rationale behind the laws of the institution of the dogana of Foggia points to a membership composed of "an exalted, noble, full, and powerful class (*ordine*) . . . not inferior to other communities" and a set of instructions which are "reasonable, humane, and uniform with the natural law."[40]

Di Stefano's introduction emphasizes that the justification for all this high-toned pastoral fervor is the "antiquity, nobility, utility, and necessity of Pastoralism."[41] He summarized the biblical stories of Cain and Abel, King David, Solomon's Song of Songs as a pastoral drama, the Nativity, the Good Shepherd, and the Paschal Lamb. He recalled Homer's cyclops, Varro's lines on sheep in Apulia from *De re rustica,* and Virgil's countless allusions in the *Georgics.* Amassing every possible reference to sheep and shepherds in vulgar literature from Dante, Petrarch, Sannazaro, Tasso, and Guarini to the Accademia degli Arcadi, he had no doubts about the relationship between the poetic pastoral image and the realities of pastoral life.

Tradition has elevated pastoralism to be "the most ancient, the most useful, the most noble and honest subject that could be."[42] "The pastoral art [with the double meaning of guild in Italian] is so ancient, that it was born even before the earth was created in those fortunate times *when milk was the food of the little, bitty world and the woods its cradle.*"[43] Need I continue Di Stefano's tortured demonstration from Varro and Genesis that "rustic practices and pastoralism precede the state of citizens and civil life"?

Di Stefano emphasizes, above all, the rights and freedoms of the members of the sheepowners' guild. Its independent origins and self-governance exemplified his pastoral ideal. Further, the shepherds were not alone, but linked to farming and manufacturing. The harmonious interconnection of all levels and livelihoods in society is what made pastoralism such a perfect state worthy of serving as a model for society at large. Finally, the customhouse officers were also an integral part of the whole, for their oversight and impartial justice maintained the climate for pastoralism to flourish. Pastoralism was a self-generating system, and the customhouse a self-regulating institution to keep men on that right path. Poetry, law, and institution were the foundations of rural society and economy. As expressed in the motto above the laurel wreath with crossed shepherd's flute and cane, "Either to delight or to be useful" (*aut delectare, aut prodesse*), the customhouse, like Di Stefano's pastoral book, was meant to charm and to teach, to civilize the world.[44] His work was so successful and the customhouse so productive that no new published work on the dogana appeared for thirty-seven years, until after the famine, when Fortunato wrote his critique.

After the 1764 famine, in response to the early doganal critics, Francesco Nicola De Dominicis (1734–?), who was a student of Antonio Genovesi's new school of political economy, defended the pastoral tradition in the context of this emerging new discipline. He begins his treatise, *The Political and Economic State of the Sheep Customhouse of Foggia*, with five introductory chapters organized according to the "sublime science of public economy,"[45] that is, the four-stage theory and the population-prosperity theory. After the general introduction, the three stages of civilized production are examined: chapter 2, on pastoralism; chapters 3 and 4, on agriculture (farming and arborial culture); and chapter 5, on industries. The Enlightenment economic variable is population. "There is no doubt that the number of inhabitants is always proportional to the greater or lesser cultivation of the Earth, to the dissemination of Arts and Crafts, and to the amplitude of Commerce."[46] De Dominicis argues that "primitive livelihoods" (*applicazioni*) such as hunting and sheepherding cannot sustain the same population as agriculture, the arts, and commerce. He even develops a kind of incipient population theory linked to various productive systems in different geographic zones.[47]

De Dominicis diverges from his fellow Neapolitan political economists in his evaluation of pastoralism. If practiced alone and allowed to become the principal endeavor of a population, this "excess" will "reduce the nation ... to a barbarous state of nature." If an accurate assessment of climate and soils is made, however, a "just equilibrium among the primitive arts" would create civil society. For De Dominicis, the four-stage theory does not constitute an evolutionary model, but an equilibrium model. This judgment makes pastoralism a positive component among the arts of civilization.

The equilibrium model, then, is further linked to the debate on luxury and "politeness."[48] In De Dominicis' discussion of the arts and crafts, silk and woolen cloth manufacturing provide perfect examples of a nation's civility and progress. Native industries are the best safeguards against "the prejudices of luxury by foreign manufactures." But at the same time, these industries cannot exist without the continuum between raw material production and finished goods. Civil life therefore depends upon a growing industrial sector founded upon progress in pasturage and agriculture. The dogana of Foggia offers institutional embodiment of good laws and good economics in its goal of a just equilibrium among all productive sectors.

In the same way, De Dominicis argues for free trade and against monopolies.[49] He demonstrates that "the principles of economic science" have been incorrect in enforcing protectionism and special privileges in the pastoral economy. The results have been to keep the Kingdom's provinces underpopulated and foreign merchants in charge of the purse strings. He was actively involved, therefore, in the development of the wool trade via the land route to

Naples after 1780. Here he argues that a just equilibrium between manufactures in the capital and raw material production in the countryside could break foreign domination. Native woolen manufactures around Naples and Salerno as well as the growth of the French market proved him right, but even they, he complained, only consumed about 50 percent of the nation's raw wool.

Thus, De Dominicis could look back to the Roman foundation of pastoralism in Puglia and praise the ancient shepherds of the Roman Republic for finding security and independence in pastoral life.[50] Pastoral life was a form of livelihood ecologically in tune with nature and with agriculturists: pasturage and agriculture were "two loving sisters" who, harmoniously joined together, satisfied "all the natural needs of life." Pastoralism, moreover, helped to maintain the population, sustain agriculture, facilitate the arts and crafts, and develop commerce. It was one part of an indissoluble whole that "constitued the true power and characteristic happiness of a polite nation."[51]

The Pastoral Mode Disapproved

De Dominicis' 1781 translation of the pastoral economy into the ideology of the new school of political economy was a lone voice in response to Fortunato and Galiani. In the 1780s, when Enlightened political economists concluded high-level investigations of the Kingdom of Naples' economic problems in order to implement reform from above, glaring abuses convinced most customhouse critics that the dogana could not be easily reformed on any model—legal, poetic, or Enlightened.

By the 1780s the provincial critics, closer to the anomalies of agrarian life, had begun to diverge from the group of reformers writing from the Neapolitan capital. Although both had grown out of Genovesi's school, a slightly more philosophical, utopian orientation marked the movement in the capital.[52] From the city's perspective, pastoralism had been an important civilizing art in mankind's infancy, but now it was a "sickly body enervated and destructive of a healthy one."[53] In the provinces more severe critics noted the impediments to reform and proposed technical, immediate remedies. For them, pastoralism should not cease, but with its contradictions thus removed, it should adopt modern methods.[54] Both groups took exception to the uneconomic foundations of the customhouse on the Enlightened principles of political economy. The tension between city and country in the Kingdom was an enduring theme in all aspects of social, economic, political, and even intellectual life.

All of these reformist polemics recognized the crisis in the countryside, and all demanded some kind of reorganization of the customhouse structure. The investigation of the dogana reflected interest in solving the problem of the population and prosperity of the Kingdom. The Enlightenment controversy focused on crucial economic issues: public policy, private enterprise, and economic development. Disagreement existed over what constituted an advanced economy and the relationship between raw materials and manufacturing within it. How could the modern state continue to own royal demesne into the nineteenth century? What was the proper sphere for governmental initiative? What was the place of free enterprise and private property? Could technological change revitalize and transform the stagnant economy?[55]

Giuseppe Maria Galanti was the pivotal figure, reformer–cum–state minister.[56] He had been sent from his native Molise to study in the Neapolitan capital in 1753 at the age of nine years and became another of the young intellectuals of provincial origin who gravitated to Antonio Genovesi. In 1782, Ferdinand I commissioned Galanti to proceed with a program of investigation into each of the twelve provinces in order to arrive at the "true state of the provinces and the commerce that exists there."[57] For thirteen years, Galanti conducted a meticulous examination of the intricate network of provincial life. Thus was born his masterpiece, *The New Historical and Geographical Description of the Sicilies* (1786–94).

For Galanti the sheep customhouse at Foggia was one of the Kingdom's many self-contradictory, decadent institutions that had to be abolished. He described the customhouse system as a "bizarre economy," a "singular economy," a "barbarous system." "The Tartar-Spanish system of the Tavoliere has already put in place the maximum deformity in the public economy by occupying such land with few proprietors... Its net income is a mere trifle ['a true bagatelle'] for so vast and pleasant a region."[58]

Galanti's condemnation follows the checklist of Enlightenment assumptions expressed in the earlier analyses. First, he believes that population is wealth, "the most precious thing."[59] Second, he identifies the customhouse system with barbarism: "its rules tend to make our province nothing less than a desert like that of Tartary."[60] Pastoralism itself is a low stage of civilization, with "a wandering people, little civilized."[61] Third, agriculture should have priority over pastoralism because farming provides a people's sustenance. The determination to favor the sheep customhouse system "put shepherds and farmers in perpetual war... It does not seem to me that the wise Alfonso rendered agriculture and pasturage truly *sisters,* as is said."[62] Fourth, the customhouse's only purpose is fiscal, but even that is far below what could be gleaned from such a territory. "The fisc remains always prejudicial, and the people oppressed."[63] Fifth, the customhouse system points out the weaknesses of the Kingdom's internal structure. Foreigners are required to buy pastoral products, and even they need special protection and privileges.[64] Finally, Galanti argues that deregulation would allow the freedom of the market, rather than monopolies which were usually in the hands of foreign capitalists, to dictate economic practice. "Give men liberty to act in their own way and according to their own interests, which together forms the public interest."[65]

Galanti's point is that the migratory pastoralism of the customhouse system had caused great damage to land and economy in the Kingdom. If it once was expedient during low population periods, that was no longer the case. The system was now artificially maintained by restrictive laws and counterproductive rights. A curious historical inversion proves the case. Whereas the fifteenth-century foundation of pastoralism in the Tavoliere found resistance from large holders of agricultural lands, now reform of the Tavoliere to restore agricultural products finds the large holders invested in pastoral wealth and opposed to the few engaged in agriculture.[66] If all these government obstacles and "barbarous laws" were removed, Galanti believed it would be easy to reorder the Tavoliere. His plan called for a reclaiming of the Tavoliere, like the draining of the Pontine marshes in the Papal States.[67]

Thus, after 1780 the critics ground their indictment of doganal barbarism in a profound commitment to eradicate the Kingdom's contradictions, such as a pastoral economy in the face of agricultural necessity, and to remove state intervention in the economy, such as the support of special privileges contrary to the common good. Population pressure, grain demand, the evolutionary rules of civilization, even fiscal needs could not allow such backwardness. Pastoralism was simply disapproved because it had outlived mankind's present "stage" of development.

The Pastoral Mode in Perspective

If pastoralism was disapproved by the Neapolitan school of political economy in the 1780s, was it disproved? Even more to the point, why did it continue for another one hundred years? Twenty-five authors (plus two anonymous ones) composed thirty-six treatises which commented upon the Foggian customhouse between the 1764 famine and the 1806 abolition of the dogana (app. F). At least thirty of these works were published in Naples, the center of a lively economic movement. The major arguments can be classified into two categories, internal and external to the customhouse institution itself.

First, there was no dispute over the need to reform a frail, human institution. Abuses came naturally from internal contradictions in the customhouse system. Monopolies in production, from the dominance of large holders, or in consumption, by foreign merchants, could skew pasture distribution or prices. The original laws of the dogana attempted to create a just equality among all parties. Implementation of eighteenth-century ideas on free trade and deregulation were often seen to be the cure for the institutions's ills. In addition, lack of skill or diligence by sheepowners had caused a degeneration in wool quality. Only a revival of pastoral practice with modern "scientific" methods could restore the institution to its best state.

Second, the assumptions of political economy provided external arguments to reevaluate pastoral livelihood systems. The population-prosperity theory blamed the pastoral economy for the curtailment of agriculture and the consequent restrictions upon population growth. Further, the four-stage theory of evolutionary progress placed pastoralism on the second stage of civilization's development. As a barbaric art of uncivilized peoples, pastoralism became the target for reformers wishing to eradicate retrograde industries. In this context, the theoretical discussion between proponents and opponents of pastoralism centered upon either an evolutionary or equilibrium model of society. Were agriculture and pasturage the "loving sisters" of De Dominicis, or were they not, as a skeptical Galanti sneered? If progress came with increased agricultural production and population growth, pastoralism should be abolished. If pastoralism reflected the harmonious way in which diverse components of society worked together, it should be encouraged.

The critical issue here was the creation of wealth. Equilibrium models were good mercantalist theory. Wealth could not be created; it was some fixed resource which could be lost, gained, or divided. But proponents of customhouse reform need not subscribe to the idea that the Old Regime economy was held together by the recognition of special rights and privileges, regulation, and protectionism. De Dominicis argued, on the contrary, for free trade and deregulation with the belief that exchange was the cement of society. Exchange created just and equitable harmony. Pastoralism, therefore, was an integral part of balanced sectoral economies.[68] With the gradual triumph of the maximizing market mentalities of classical economics, however, models of balanced harmony and the just price gave way to the justification of self-interest, and progressive models argued for large populations because more people created more wealth.

It is easy to misread the Enlightenment critics in their condemnation of the pastoral-agricultural economy. Their "reforms" come at the end of two centuries of slow economic and demographic recovery, at the moment when further agricultural growth had run up against the twin barriers of population growth and technological impasse. The structural imbalance of the dogana had profound effects not only on declining fiscal revenues but on declining food supplies as well. Ecological balance could not maintain itself in the face of an antagonistic state policy. Like Spain from the time of the Mesta in the sixteenth century, late eighteenth-century Naples suffered from the consequences of a short-sighted policy toward the agricultural interest at a time of rapid population increase.[69] The interrelationship of population growth and grain shortage in Spain and Naples were analogous. While the Enlightenment analysis was accurate for the end of the eighteenth century, the internal economic dilemma of the Kingdom of Naples cannot be explained by ex post facto criticism or a flawed anthropology of ascending stages of civilization. Further, one should not just look back, but also forward. Population growth slowed down in the nineteenth century, and the acute food shortages of a Malthusian catastrophe never materialized as emigration provided an outlet from the Kingdom.[70]

Fortunato's and Galiani's anticipation of the Malthusian squeeze does nothing more than bring into focus the outlines of the secular curve, not the classes contending in the system.[71] Charting the oscillation between agricultural and pastoral ascendancy merely confirms the relationships between supply and demand, between population and prices. Rivalries between agriculture and pastoralism, for their part, did not determine land use. Large holders moved interchangeably from one form of production to another, according to their economic advantage and political interest. The question should rather be, What determined that advantage and interest? Thus, market forces such as labor supply, interest rates, purchase contracts, and international demand, as well as government policies such as tax rates, pasture assignment, and price fixing come to the fore as determinant variables.

Similarly, no agrarian revolution in methods and technology could alleviate the social structural inequities which derived from differences in farm size or land tenure practices. Hitherto unknown technological solutions more than likely made the rich richer, and the poor poorer. The economic effect of the postunification drainage of the Abruzzese Lago di Fucino, for example, dramatized that such innovation enriched only its baronial patron, not the region.[72] External remedies do not necessarily reorder society but often allow old, ingrained structures to dominate or to inhibit the new technological overlay.

Thus, although the enlightened examination of pastoralism led to the 1806 doganal reform, it did not lead to agrarian change. Although the reform ostensibly reassigned the ownership of the means of production from public to private hands, the administrative reorganization of juridical and proprietary rights in the Tavoliere of Puglia had no immediate debilitating effect upon the pastoral livelihood system.[73] Wool production continued at its normal rate through the 1840s. Land divested from the royal patrimony was merely divided up into vast latifundia. With hindsight on the eve of Unification in 1859, Carlo de Cesare judged the 1806 reform to be a "profound economic error" because of the emergence of a new breed of unproductive large holders. The entire area of 12,344 *carra*, 9 *versure*, and 8 *catene* (about 4,000 sq. km) was divided among 500 landowners (merchants, speculators, and gentlemen farmers ["uomini del dolce far niente"]) who were, in their ignorance and haughtiness, hostile to agriculture.[74] Pastoral livelihood only retreated from the plain of Puglia after Italian Unification, when Australian wool began to dominate the international wool trade and the technology of artesian wells, which provided ground water for irrigating wheat fields, washed the sheep out of the arable.[75]

Why was the enthusiasm of the Neapolitan intellecutal reawakening a barren enterprise? Like the cooption of individual spiritual experimentation and the routinization of grass-roots reforms by the Council of Trent, reform from above in the Kingdom of Naples was an attempt to encourage and control an economic revolution without disrupting the social order. Palmieri, for example, proposed a reform program whereby the government would inject capital, in the form of credit, into the provinces; provincial landowners would transform themselves into entrepreneurs; and "maximum employment" would stabilize the agricultural labor market.[76] Hardly a revolutionary manifesto; yet why did even moderate reform like Palmieri's not take hold? Was the system too far gone? Was the time not yet ripe? Was opposition too strong? Was it mere chance that the anti-Jacobin reaction was victorious and reformers hanged in 1799? Were the intellectuals important, if impotent, only because the economy and society were stagnant?

Reform from above was doomed to fail in southern Italy because of the unique composition of Neapolitan social and economic structure. It was not the will of the reformers which failed. It was not the incompetence or disinterest of the government. It was not the powerful interest groups who opposed reform that were decisive. The flaw was within the structure of the system.[77] Reform from above only confirmed the hierarchical nature of the age-old patronage system. This hierarchical structure was reflected in all institutions and ideologies, Church and state. A change in direction from above had little effect on the organization of the deep structure. Some greater power was necessary to dismantle and reconstitute it. If that power could not be generated internally, organically from below, rural reform would have to wait for the intervention from without—the victorious Napoleonic armies and Joseph Bonaparte's land reform of 1806 abolished the doganal system. And the proof is that these reforms reordered but did not change economy or society.

As a whole, the criticism of the *illuministi* pinpointed the archaism of the dogana by focusing on the balance of nature, the limited returns of a pastoral economy, and the abuses of the system. What they did not see were the long-term fluctuations of wool and wheat production as reflections of the international market. Trying to make Capitanata conform to the Enlightened blueprint for a "civilized" state meant the imposition of an external, "colonial" ideology upon a provincial rural economy. Reform could not come from above without fundamental change below.

Herein lies the crux of the problem of southern Italy. The backwardness of the Kingdom did not depend upon resistance to sorely overdue land reform or exploitation by foreign merchants. The backwardness of provincial life did not depend upon who controlled the means of production or even what products were produced. Instead, geography, livelihood, wealth, nobility, government, and markets created a system of overlapping and intertwining patron-client relationships. The irreconcilable contradictions of these antagonistic interest groups generated an internal structure in which each component part reinforced and supported the others, while at the same time undermining and opposing them. This internal, multidimensional dialectic institutionalized reality into an ideology of conflict without change.

Change from above, therefore, is not change at all. It is only a shifting of advantage from one group to another. Various great traditions, competing wool and grain markets, and state centralizaion vied for allegiance and attention. Yet all external stimuli, whether emanating from the rich, the state bureaucrats, or merchant capitalists, were translated by a consistent provincial ideology into the pervasive terms of the clientele system. The rural life of peasants and shepherds stood outside time, morality, and change. The rural world of the Mezzogiorno imposes its patron-client rationale upon outsiders rather than conforming to theirs.[78]

Despite, therefore, the internal struggles among the customhouse interest groups, there was a kind of chaotic continuity. The dialectic among the doganal factions did not produce change, but stagnation. Only the strength of the institution was undermined. Post–World War II Italian politics may serve as a good comparative example. A seemingly infinite array of governments may give the impression of instability. Christian Democracy and its many alliances, however, have dominated and continue to dominate government without interruption, with little view toward finding some path toward compromise. Such chaotic stability vitiates the foundation of government and irresponsibly ignores outside challenges. The sheep customhouse structure does not appear to have been a unique kind of Italian institution.

It is from material life, above all, that the realities of Neapolitan society derive. Agricultural and regional history and the development of capitalist markets in the provinces point to a vibrant economic activity before the French invasions in the fifteenth century, and after them in the sixteenth century. Similarly, the crisis of the seventeenth century was only a short-term fluctuation within the colonial economy of the Kingdom. Southern capital was reinvested in other sectors during the eclipse of northern Italian producing centers like Venice. By the 1680s, however, new textile centers such as Bergamo demanded more and more raw wool. Sheep investment once again became profitable, and the dogana flourished during its third positive conjuncture in the eighteenth century.

In the provinces of the Abruzzi and Capitanata, the "natural history" or internal organization of the sheep customhouse of Foggia determined investment strategies and gratified the insatiable demand for state finances. It was a natural history founded on competition for land and fostered by the competition of the market. Bureaucratic intrusion attempted to mediate agricultural and pastoral rivalries and the socioeconomic inequalities of rural life. Land reforms and provisioning plans thus far outweighed the countless petty administrative abuses. And through it all, hard-headed business sense judged a guaranteed 8 percent income in bad times and a 21 percent income in good times to be a sound investment.

In addition to security and profit, land investment in the bucolic industries of Puglia was buttressed by the pervasive literary ideology of the pastoral. Biblical and classical literature "verified" the importance of the pastoral economy. Thus, both the subtleties of economic thought and the sublimities of literary invention defined a rationale for economic realities. Rural society and economy in Capitanata and the Abruzzi in the early modern period remained that of some backwater, colonial world. But, looking at the quantity and velocity of its economic activity and the voluminous writings of the men it produced provides a model of integration and articulation whose significance extends far beyond that world.

CONCLUSION

The old Kingdom of Naples and the contemporary problems of southern Italy may be one of the most dramatic and persistent political specimens, or regional examples, of the failure of modernization. In the Kingdom of Naples, the more things changed, the more they remained the same: eighteenth-century enlightenment without reform, nineteenth-century unification without integration, and twentieth-century industrialization without development. Such oxymora, thus, express proverbial wisdom in terms of an anachronistic model. Naples, past and present, embodies the archeological remains of a fossilized world, the institutional inertia of inescapable decadence, and the personal ideology of an omnipresent *miseria*.

On its own terms, the Kingdom of Naples, hardly the model of good government in the Old Regime, had, nevertheless, managed to maintain its social and economic structures fairly intact as it joined the new, unified Italian state in 1860.[1] How had the Old Regime maintained itself? How had the economic advantage of the few been sustained in the face of the many? Despite urban masses in need of bread, why had wool continued to dominate wheat well into the nineteenth century? What pact had the Neapolitan government struck, and with whom, to ensure social cohesion and defuse conflict between rich and poor, farmers and shepherds, merchants and producers.

The best answer invariably takes us back to the countryside, where the little tradition played a formative role in forging social relations into a particular pattern of cohesion and confrontation. Received wisdom teaches that the gulf between city and countryside in the Italian South mirrored the exploitive extraction of southern raw materials by the commercial and industrial North. This traditional interpretation claims that the Neapolitan state joined with foreign merchants to link raw material production in the southern countryside with urban markets in northern Italy, to thwart the formation of native industries, and to inhibit the development of an indigenous, entrepreneurial class. Economic transformation, in this standard view, was held in check from above, through the complicity of the state, privileged interests, and foreign capital. As absentee merchant creditors began to finance an agrarian system and a state bureaucracy, both of which fell into ever-increasing debt, the state found itself paying the price for its short-term profits, for its ignorance of agrarian economics, and for the concentration of property in the hands of a few. In this headlong rush to maximize their immediate economic advantage, then, all partners in this politico-economic coalition found themselves subsidizing a parasitic society and sinking into an ever-deepening vortex of poverty.

The broad outlines of this widely diffused economic paradigm of underdevelopment and dependency make the early modern Neapolitan state itself an impediment to change, conspirator with the feudal aristocracy, large landowners, and merchant-capitalists to live off the exploitation of everyone else. Explaining the economic transition that failed or the test case of refeudalization in such terms, however, condemns government's irrationality without understanding its rationale.

In fact, in the pastoral economy of the Adriatic provinces, a somewhat different kind of ideology was at work. Population pressure, fiscal demands, and market profits were not the only concerns of early modern European states. The economic dilemma facing pastoral and agricultural production in preindustrial society was not perceived as one which required a breakthrough to higher yields or streamlined management. Rather, it was a problem of keeping the peace, given the limits of growth and marginal utility. How does an economic system operate within defined parameters? How does it arrive at an equilibrium with competing enterprises? How does it divide finite resources? Hence, practical experience reinforced mercantilist theory which perceived money, especially wealth in land, as a fixed resource that could not be created, but only exchanged.[2]

We cannot fault these states for not acting according to the yet undiscovered principles of economic takeoff to sustained growth. Agricultural economies as primary sector producers could not alchemically create wealth out of nothing or free themselves from the vicissitudes of climate, war and peace, or demand. Industrialization, likewise, was not the inevitable or unambiguous success we would like to believe.[3] In 1800 manufacturing accounted for only about one-fourth versus agriculture's three-fourths of continental production.[4] Further, the social dislocation caused by ever-growing and expanding economic systems threatened to levy too high a price for the privileged bodies enjoying traditional good government in kingdoms like Naples.

Good government in late medieval and early modern Italy was the catch phrase for a golden mean of sound politics. The conquering Aragonese who newly chartered the sheep customhouse in 1447 had not borrowed an Iberian institution but elaborated a native Neapolitan one. The state did indeed seek expedient economic self-interest in the fiscal advantages of the sheep customhouse system—10 percent of net income collected in cash within a single month at one place. But since the state had no interest in depriving itself of its guaranteed revenues, it attempted to balance the divergent interests of livelihood systems, social orders, and economic classes in order to resolve conflict and maintain the status quo. The state acted as a deft middleman by creating stability in an ecologically limited system, by manipulating vested

CONCLUSION 263

interests without alienation, and by sanctioning the power of corporate bodies without depleting the wealth of the few. As such good government prevented things from getting better, however, it ensured that they would get worse.

For the bureaucratic administration of the agrarian countryside, pastoral economics were subordinated to the urgency of state finances, administered according to the politics of pacification, and rationalized by the ideology of the literary pastoral. Translated into the practicalities of the sheep customhouse system of extreme social stratification, *buon governo* meant catering to the interests of the elite and meeting the subsistence needs of the many, while reaping state profits off the top. City and country, exploiters and exploited, privileged and underprivileged, rich and poor could thus coexist in Naples as a result of a conscious policy of good government.[5] With this pastoral reverie, Old Regime Naples rationalized its dilemma between patriarchy and patronage, balanced its policy between economic inequality and Arcadian democracy, maintained its position between city and country, and never dreamed that its world would change.

The pattern of investment in the pastoral economy, similarly, followed simple economic logic. Demand fueled raw wool production, and northern Italian production centers like Venice linked rural sheep farming to the international market. Foggian wool sellers and northern Italian wool manufacturers experienced three boom periods—1447–94, 1548–1612, and 1685–1806. In between, two crises associated with wars—the French Invasions and the Thirty Years' War—depressed production and prices in the Italian wool trade from 1494 to 1548 and from 1612 to 1685. The seventeenth-century crisis is particularly instructive. With the decline of manufacturing centers in the North, the South experienced the same long-term recession. Money that had sought short-term advantages in wool now sought long-term security in land. This was not refeudalization, or a baronial offensive, in the countryside. No real structural change had realigned Neapolitan wealth and power, but rather the vicissitudes of the secular trend had elicited a rational economic response.[6] After the 1656 plague in the Kingdom, monied agriculturists took advantage of a reduced labor force to shift investments from wheat to wool. Big landowners like the Dorias became big sheepowners. But small-time producers never disappeared. As production picked up in the 1680s with the demand of new manufacturing centers in places like Bergamo, the raw wool market in the dogana of Foggia also recovered, benefiting rich and poor alike. As a response to market demand, raw material supply was not subject to the caprice of noble entrenchment and privilege.

Decline and growth in the southern raw material market corresponded to the fluctuations in industrial production per se, wherever such manufacturing centers might appear. The growth of the domestic woolen cloth industry is a case in point. It strengthened its infrastructure during the long seventeenth-century downturn and built upon that foundation during the eighteenth-century expansion. Internal production centers around Naples and Salerno, which consumed about one-half of Foggia's raw wool, made the wool trade multisectoral in defiance of the "colonial" profile characterizing the Kingdom's overall international trade balance.

By the late eighteenth century, population growth within the Kingdom and fear of recurrent famine prejudiced production in favor of wheat. With the twenty-five years of war and revolution from the 1790s, the growing divergence between the prices of commodities reflected the short-term victory of wheat over wool. Advocates of change of the customhouse system had their day, but sheep transhumance did not decay. The sheep customhouse system alone was disbanded; in 1860, 750,000 sheep still filled the Tavoliere in winter. With the legal dissolution of feudalism in 1806, the means of production had not changed; its ownership had only become more consolidated among a few large holders. No new grain supply had been guaranteed; no shortcut to economic development had been achieved.

In its nineteenth-century attempts to modernize the Kingdom's economy by ascending from one stage of growth or mode of production to another, the central government was repeating what it had always done vis-à-vis the countryside. It imposed urban values upon rural production. Whether those values were the Renaissance ideal of good government, the literary illusion of pastoral harmony, the enlightened rationalism of political economy, or even twentieth-century theories of economic development, the results amounted to more of the same. The circle remained closed. Interconnections prevented escape, except through migration out of the system.

Involution rather than evolution was a product of millennia of pastoral-agricultural antagonism. Instead of fostering change, the competition for circumscribed resources between livelihood systems, social orders, and economic classes engendered accommodation, which fluctuated along a scale from outright exploitation by one party or another to harmonious cooperation.[7] The particularism and fragmentation characteristic of southern Italian peasant society does not stem from some undefined Mediterranean machismo or the vestigial consciousness of the shepherds' vaunted liberty and egalitarianism. Rather, in their struggle among themselves and in their conflict with external domination from urban, bureaucratic, and merchant-capitalist forces, social structural relationships solidified into a mentality that has persisted and been reinforced by the continuing incursion of the center into the periphery.

Reform from above is not change, but imposition of external will and alien categories upon the many foreign cultures below. No monolithic hegemony, material or cultural, can succeed in annihilating the little tradition and the little individuals who inhabit its many worlds. Backwardness may spawn a broad spectrum of responses from despair and escapism, cooptation and false consciousness, to revolutionary zeal and resistance. All such strategies derive from the unresolved tension of deep structural oppositions and a common world view of fate. Fate, as the inevitable order of things, can be conquered only when reality is denied, when individuals defy fate's reign and seize its domain for themselves in order to break out of their circular or cyclical confinement.

APPENDIX A
Weights and Measures

Money

Grano = (money of account coined in silver until 1572; from 1630 coined in copper)
Carlino = 10 grana
Tarì = 2 carlini; 20 grana
Ducat = 10 carlini; 5 tarì; 100 grana
Oncia = 6 ducats

Exchange

Castilian ducat = 1.20 Neapolitan ducats (before 1611)
                 = 1.44 Neapolitan ducats (after 1611)
Venetian scudo = 1.10 Neapolitan ducats
Roman scudo = 0.94 Neapolitan ducat (1671)

Length

Palma = 0.26 mile
Passo or Trapasso = 7 palmi
                  = 1.85 miles

Surface

Tomolo = 24 misure; 20 passi squared
       = 0.4089 hectare
Vesura = 3 tomoli; 60 passi squared
       = 1.2269 hectare
Carro = 20 versure; 60 tomoli
       = 24.5 hectares; ca. 60 acres

Capacity

Tomolo = 0.555 hectoliter; 40 kilograms
Salma = 8 tomoli
      = ca. 320 kilograms
Carro = 36 tomoli (wheat)
      = 1,440 kilograms; 19 hectoliters
      = 48 tomoli (barley)
      = 50 tomoli (oats)

Weight

Cheese:	Rotolo	=	ca. 891 grams
	Pesa	=	22 rotola
		=	19.601 kilograms
	Cantaro	=	5 pesa = 100 rotola
Wool:	Libbra	=	ca. 343 grams
	Rubbio	=	26 libbre
		=	8.91 kilograms
	Cantaro	=	10 rubbi
		=	89.1 kilograms

APPENDIX B
Locazioni *and* Nazioni *in the Dogana*

Locazioni	Nazioni	Province
Lesina	Opi, Pacentro (until 1679)	Abruzzo Citra
Procina	Campo di Giove, Canzano, Piedimonte	Abruzzo Citra
Arignano	Valle Aventina, Peligni	Abruzzo Citra
San Andrea	Pesco Costanzo (in 1679 to prince of San Severo)	Abruzzo Citra
Casalnuovo	Carapella River Valley, Calascio, Santo Stephano, San Demetro	Abruzzo Ultra
Candelaro	Rocca del Raso, Rivisondoli, Barrea	Abruzzo Citra
Castiglione	Lucoli	Abruzzo Ultra
Tressanti	Montereale, Lucoli	Abruzzo Ultra
Pontalbanito	Rocca Valle Scura, Pettorano	Abruzzo Citra
Cave	San Pietro d'Avellena, Pesco Pignataro	Contado di Molise
Orta	Ovindoli, Pesco Costanzo, Rovere	Abruzzo Ultra
Ordona	Frattura, Introdacqua, Colle Longo, Opi	Abruzzo Citra
Feudo	Albe, Valle del Lago, Cucolo, Marsi	Abruzzo Ultra
Corleto	Montella, Bagnoli, San Angelo Lombardo	Principato Ultra
Vallecannella	Amatrice, Pesco Lanciano, Vasto Girardo	Abruzzo Ultra
Salsola	Barisciano	Abruzzo Ultra
San Giuliano	Castel del Monte	Abruzzo Ultra
Salpi	Scanno, Sergi, Pescasseroli	Abruzzo Citra
Trinità	Agnone, Pesco Costanzo	Abruzzo Citra
Canosa	Vasto Girardo, Capracotta, Rosito	Contado di Molise
Camarda	Nusco, Melfi	Principato Ultra, Basilicata
Andria	Carapella River Valley, Calascio, Santo Stephano, San Demetro	Abruzzo Ultra
Guardiola	Rocca Mandolfi, Frosilone	Cantado di Molise

Sources: ASFg, *Dogana*, serie V, regg. 745–1100, "Libri di Squarciafogli" (1589–1788); Annibale Moles, *Decisiones Supremi Tribunalis Camerae Summariae Regni Neapolis* (Naples: Egidio Longo, 1670), pp. 175–78.

APPENDIX C
Doganal Social Structure

TABLE C-1 Ownership: All *Locati* by Flock Size in the *Squarciafogli* (In *Reali Fisse*)

Year	1–50 Head	51–100 Head	101–200 Head
Period 3			
1591	311 (10.8%)	402 (13.9%)	553 (19.2%)
1604	228 (8.2)	304 (10.9)	425 (15.3)
Period 4			
1619	1,001 (31.1)	660 (20.5)	590 (18.3)
1639	979 (41.3)	353 (14.9)	359 (15.2)
1659	1,238 (44.4)	498 (17.8)	414 (14.8)
1679	251 (21.1)	230 (19.3)	263 (22.1)
Period 5			
1699	500 (25.6)	387 (19.8)	343 (17.6)
1719	791 (33.4)	422 (17.8)	382 (16.1)
1739	761 (37.1)	362 (17.6)	301 (14.7)
1759	415 (25.2)	256 (15.6)	278 (16.9)
1779	479 (22.6)	396 (18.7)	421 (19.8)
Mean Flock Size	34	84	159

Source: ASFg, *Dogana*, serie V, regg. 745–1100, "Libri di squarciafogli" (1589–1788); see also table 6.

201–500 *Head*	501–1,000 *Head*	1,001–2,000 *Head*	>2,000 *Head*
754 (26.1%)	422 (14.6%)	262 (9.1%)	181 (6.3%)
731 (26.3)	553 (19.9)	365 (13.1)	173 (6.2)
514 (16.0)	268 (8.3)	129 (4.0)	56 (1.7)
346 (14.6)	191 (8.1)	98 (4.1)	42 (1.7)
359 (12.9)	170 (6.1)	76 (2.7)	35 (1.3)
219 (18.4)	123 (10.3)	68 (5.7)	36 (3.0)
382 (19.6)	179 (9.2)	100 (5.1)	59 (3.0)
408 (17.2)	191 (8.1)	116 (4.9)	60 (2.5)
309 (15.1)	166 (8.1)	91 (4.4)	61 (3.0)
331 (20.1)	182 (11.1)	117 (7.1)	65 (4.0)
524 (24.7)	150 (7.1)	101 (4.8)	52 (2.4)
337	736	1,428	3,307

TABLE C-2 Ownership: *Padroni* Only by Flock Size in the *Squarciafogli* (In *Reali Fisse*)

Year	1–50 Head	51–100 Head	101–200 Head
Period 3			
1591	1 (0.1%)	10 (0.9%)	64 (5.7%)
1604	0 —	36 (2.4)	79 (5.3)
Period 4			
1619	0 —	48 (4.2)	157 (13.9)
1639	145 (12.5)	123 (10.6)	210 (18.1)
1659	689 (33.1)	381 (18.3)	350 (16.8)
1679	32 (4.2)	71 (9.4)	154 (20.3)
Period 5			
1699	53 (5.0)	96 (9.1)	162 (15.3)
1719	70 (7.1)	91 (9.2)	114 (11.6)
1739	143 (15.0)	98 (10.3)	126 (13.2)
1759	136 (12.0)	124 (10.9)	189 (16.7)
1779	200 (12.8)	241 (15.5)	300 (19.2)
Mean Flock Size	33	90	166

Source: See table C-1.

TABLE C-3 Wealth of All *Locati* by Flock Size in the *Squarciafogli* (In *Reali Fisse*)

Year	1–50 Head	51–100 Head	101–200 Head
Period 3			
1591	10,325 (0.6%)	32,263 (1.9%)	85,138 (5.0%)
1604	9,164 (0.5)	27,161 (1.4)	69,289 (3.6)
Period 4			
1619	30,827 (3.5)	51,987 (5.9)	89,512 (10.1)
1639	22,395 (3.7)	26,218 (4.3)	52,808 (8.8)
1659	33,216 (5.6)	36,771 (6.2)	59,662 (10.1)
1679	9,495 (2.1)	20,246 (4.4)	43,605 (9.6)
Period 5			
1699	18,450 (2.6)	34,580 (4.8)	57,711 (8.0)
1719	28,998 (3.7)	36,967 (4.7)	63,163 (8.0)
1739	26,392 (5.4)	32,013 (4.7)	49,747 (7.3)
1759	15,336 (2.2)	21,650 (3.1)	44,422 (6.3)
1779	17,640 (2.4)	35,510 (4.9)	71,455 (9.9)
Mean	(2.9)	(4.2)	(7.9)

Source: See table C-1.

DOGANAL SOCIAL STRUCTURE

201–500 Head	501–1,000 Head	1,001–2,000 Head	>2,000 Head
192 (17.1%)	290 (25.8%)	291 (25.9%)	277 (24.6%)
286 (19.1)	426 (28.5)	422 (28.3)	246 (16.5)
318 (28.1)	335 (29.6)	197 (17.4)	77 (6.8)
288 (24.9)	226 (19.5)	122 (10.5)	44 (3.8)
362 (17.4)	176 (8.4)	89 (4.3)	36 (1.7)
254 (33.6)	124 (16.4)	86 (11.4)	36 (4.8)
336 (31.8)	212 (20.1)	126 (11.9)	72 (6.8)
274 (27.8)	191 (19.4)	163 (16.5)	84 (8.5)
229 (24.0)	164 (17.2)	117 (12.3)	76 (8.0)
285 (25.1)	199 (17.5)	130 (11.5)	72 (6.3)
470 (30.1)	175 (11.2)	110 (7.1)	63 (4.0)
350	742	1,425	3,269

Source: See table C-1.

201–500 Head	501–1,000 Head	1,001–2,000 Head	>2,000 Head
248,024 (14.6%)	304,586 (18.0%)	368,683 (21.7%)	647,306 (38.2%)
255,291 (13.3)	404,890 (21.1)	509,649 (26.6)	639,067 (33.4)
170,727 (19.3)	195,269 (22.1)	184,050 (20.8)	162,720 (18.4)
110,581 (18.3)	134,708 (22.3)	134,226 (22.3)	121,951 (20.2)
112,470 (19.1)	119,342 (20.3)	103,312 (17.5)	124,017 (21.1)
76,856 (16.8)	92,320 (20.2)	150,330 (20.8)	109,890 (24.1)
134,230 (18.6)	141,641 (19.6)	150,330 (20.8)	186,230 (25.8)
145,400 (18.3)	144,209 (18.2)	168,956 (12.3)	205,990 (26.0)
105,978 (15.6)	124,437 (18.3)	126,284 (18.6)	214,604 (31.6)
112,339 (15.9)	131,764 (18.6)	167,726 (23.3)	215,269 (30.4)
171,842 (23.8)	110,875 (15.4)	145,672 (20.2)	168,394 (23.3)
(17.6)	(19.5)	(21.4)	(26.6)

TABLE C-4 Distribution of Ownership and Wealth among *Squarciafogli Padroni* Only (In *Reali Fisse*)

Year	Total Cases/Wealth	Small Holders 1–200 Cases/Wealth	Middling Holders 201–2,000 Cases/Wealth	Large Holders >2,000 Cases/Wealth
1559	709 1,314,961	16 (2.3%) 2,690 (0.2)	498 (70.2%) 543,038 (41.3)	195 (27.5%) 769,233 (58.5)
1591	1,125 1,692,076	75 (6.7) 12,300 (0.7)	773 (68.7) 709,274 (41.9)	277 (24.6) 970,502 (57.4)
1604	1,495 1,910,440	115 (7.7) 18,139 (1.0)	1,134 (75.9) 1,033,620 (54.1)	246 (16.5) 858,681 (44.9)
1619	1,133 885,375	205 (18.1) 29,328 (3.3)	850 (75.0) 633,007 (71.5)	77 (6.8) 223,040 (25.2)
1639	1,165 602,806	478 (41.0) 46,298 (7.7)	636 (54.6) 426,978 (70.8)	44 (3.8) 129,530 (21.5)
1659	2,083 587,939	1,420 (68.2) 99,998 (17.0)	627 (30.1) 359,792 (61.2)	36 (1.7) 128,149 (21.8)
1679	757 456,347	257 (33.9) 33,674 (7.4)	464 (61.3) 310,583 (68.1)	36 (4.8) 112,090 (24.6)
1699	1,057 723,212	311 (29.4) 37,945 (5.2)	674 (63.8) 462,827 (64.0)	72 (6.8) 222,440 (30.8)
1719	988 795,003	275 (27.8) 29,889 (3.8)	628 (63.6) 480,109 (60.4)	84 (8.5) 285,005 (35.8)
1739	954 680,892	367 (38.5) 35,143 (5.2)	510 (53.5) 375,386 (55.1)	76 (8.0) 270,363 (39.7)
1759	1,136 709,235	449 (39.5) 48,247 (6.8)	614 (54.0) 426,985 (60.2)	72 (6.3) 234,003 (33.0)
1779	1,559 722,808	741 (47.5) 82,895 (11.5)	755 (48.4) 440,799 (61.0)	63 (4.0) 199,114 (27.5)

Sources: AGS, *Visítas de Italia, Nápoles*, leg. 15:15 (1559); ASFg, *Dogana*, serie V, regg. 745–1100, "Libri di squarciafogli" (1589–1788); see also table 6.

TABLE C-5 Distribution of Ownership and Wealth among All *Locati* in *Squarciafogli* (In *Reali Fisse*)

Year	Total Cases/Wealth	Small Holders 1–200 Cases/Wealth	Middling Holders 201–2,000 Cases/Wealth	Large Holders >2,000 Cases/Wealth
1591	2,885	1,266 (43.9%)	1,438 (49.8%)	181 (6.3%)
	1,696,325	127,726 (7.5)	921,293 (54.3)	647,306 (38.2)
1604	2,779	957 (34.4)	1,649 (59.3)	173 (6.2)
	1,914,549	105,614 (5.5)	1,169,830 (61.1)	639,067 (33.4)
1619	3,218	2,251 (70.0)	911 (28.3)	56 (1.7)
	885,092	172,326 (19.5)	550,046 (62.1)	162,720 (18.4)
1639	2,368	1,691 (71.4)	635 (26.8)	42 (1.7)
	602,886	101,420 (16.8)	379,515 (62.9)	121,951 (20.2)
1659	2,790	2,150 (77.1)	605 (21.7)	35 (1.3)
	588,790	129,649 (22.0)	335,124 (56.9)	124,017 (21.1)
1679	1,190	744 (62.5)	410 (34.5)	36 (3.0)
	456,387	73,346 (16.1)	273,151 (59.9)	109,890 (24.1)
1699	1,950	1,230 (63.0)	661 (33.9)	59 (3.0)
	723,172	110,741 (15.3)	426,201 (58.9)	186,230 (25.8)
1719	2,370	1,595 (67.3)	715 (30.2)	60 (2.5)
	793,683	129,128 (16.3)	458,565 (57.8)	205,990 (26.0)
1739	2,051	1,424 (69.4)	566 (27.6)	61 (3.0)
	679,455	108,152 (15.9)	356,699 (52.5)	214,604 (31.6)
1759	1,644	949 (57.5)	630 (38.3)	65 (4.0)
	708,506	81,408 (11.5)	411,829 (58.1)	215,269 (30.4)
1779	2,123	1,296 (61.0)	775 (36.5)	52 (2.4)
	721,388	124,605 (17.3)	428,389 (59.4)	168,394 (23.3)

Source: ASFg, *Dogana,* serie V, regg. 745–1100, "Libri di squarciafogli" (1589–1788); see also table 6.

Note: The difference between totals of *padroni* only and all *locati* are due to transcription and coding errors. They are, however, insignificant at the ± 0.0025 level.

TABLE C-6 Distribution of Ownership and Wealth among *Squarciafogli Padroni* only (In Adjusted Sheep)

Year	Total Cases/Wealth	Small Holders 1–200 Cases/Wealth	Middling Holders 201–2,000 Cases/Wealth	Large Holders >2,000 Cases/Wealth
1591	1,126	65 (5.8%)	745 (66.2%)	316 (28.1%)
	1,839,176	10,571 (0.6)	697,321 (37.9)	1,131,284 (61.5)
1604	1,587	85 (5.4)	1,112 (70.1)	390 (24.6)
	2,576,117	13,425 (0.5)	1,093,656 (42.5)	1,469,036 (57.0)
1619	1,132	70 (6.2)	867 (76.6)	195 (17.2)
	1,375,044	11,359 (0.8)	729,000 (53.0)	634,685 (46.2)
1639	1,210	278 (23.0)	771 (63.7)	161 (13.3)
	1,192,509	28,067 (2.4)	606,559 (50.9)	567,883 (47.6)
1659	2,083	1,301 (62.5)	726 (34.9)	56 (2.7)
	739,435	98,845 (13.4)	433,886 (58.7)	206,704 (28.0)
1679	757	184 (24.3)	511 (67.5)	62 (8.2)
	554,696	23,173 (4.2)	336,568 (60.7)	194,954 (35.1)
1699	1,057	244 (23.1)	682 (64.5)	131 (12.4)
	1,485,153	15,751 (1.1)	556,157 (37.4)	913,245 (61.5)
1719	987	196 (19.9)	667 (67.6)	124 (12.6)
	983,490	20,198 (2.1)	519,012 (52.8)	444,280 (45.2)
1739	953	242 (25.4)	572 (60.0)	139 (14.6)
	991,519	24,055 (2.4)	471,528 (47.6)	495,937 (50.0)
1759	1,135	167 (14.7)	721 (63.5)	247 (21.8)
	1,671,910	18,979 (1.1)	615,122 (36.8)	1,037,811 (62.1)
1779	1,559	447 (28.7)	1,007 (64.6)	105 (6.7)
	1,040,132	50,647 (4.9)	665,536 (64.0)	323,948 (31.1)

Sources: ASFg, *Dogana*, serie V, regg. 745–1100, "Libri di squarciafogli" (1589–1788); see also table 6.

APPENDIX D
Sheep and Income in the Dogana (1443–1806)

| | | Income (In Ducats) | | |
Year	Sheep	Gross	Fida	Net
1443			18,168	
1445	424,642	38,516		
1449	925,286	92,972		
1450	1,019,821	103,011		
1451	855,731	85,798		
1465	600,000			
1474	1,700,000 but 700,000 winter death			
1483		136,000		
1496		100,000		
1501		83,280		
1507		89,000		
1508		109,000		
1511	1,340,257	109,949		
1515		109,000		
1519	1,800,000			
1521	2,000,000	100,000		72,000
1531		40,000		
1532	550,000			
1533	722,000			
1534	800,000			
1535	700,000	87,026		57,000
1536	1,048,396		90,827	72,604

| | | | Income (In Ducats) | |
Year	Sheep	Gross	Fida	Net
1537				45,151
1538	961,053			
1540	1,026,573	95,617		
1541	1,066,317	98,890	93,264	72,768
1542	738,369	69,577		
1543	836,944	78,454		
1544	1,003,493	92,458		
1545	888,392	86,549		
1546	1,003,493	92,802		
1547	1,142,401	105,657		
1548	1,228,636	112,261		
1549	1,149,021	104,986	100,415	77,943
1550	1,201,095	109,808		
1551	1,616,401	145,962		
1552	1,575,988	141,387		
1553	1,450,848	130,563	124,507	96,615
1554	1,249,378	111,388		
1555	1,513,156	134,627		
1556	1,564,203	137,257		
1557	1,323,369	174,676		103,359
1558	1,107,541	145,717		−1,239
1559	1,236,030	172,784		
1560	1,325,000	237,300	167,464	
1561	1,385,000			
1562	1,306,000			
1563	1,374,000	164,067		
1564		207,474		
1565	1,660,000			170,000
1567	1,267,637	213,565	158,137	
1569		205,477	170,189	
1570			185,118	
1571	1,163,507	224,534	193,352	96,089
1572	1,023,414			
1574	969,144[a]	184,774	131,067	87,483
1575	1,622,819[a]	225,766	202,882	99,786
1576	1,878,378[a]	324,912	238,748	99,686
1577	1,912,120[a]	325,117	241,772	94,729
1578	2,522,614[a]	393,569		172,297
1579	2,978,811[a]	454,729		189,852
1580	3,723,372[a]	546,256		220,424

SHEEP AND INCOME IN THE DOGANA

Year	Sheep	Income (In Ducats)		
		Gross	Fida	Net
1581	4,294,822[a]	561,105	548,084	199,635
1582	4,471,492[a]	585,930	571,289	185,559
1583	4,479,128[a]	642,944	591,461	218,314
1584		388,202		155,904
1585	3,446,811	516,705		299,133
1586	3,446,863		524,081	281,788
1587	3,869,045[a]		629,186	
1588	2,045,000[a]	317,854	354,398	
1589	3,018,000		472,399	
1590	2,399,042			107,578
1591	2,881,217[a]			75,292
1592	3,057,430			71,636
1593	3,502,627	196,868		129,546
1594		128,846		71,442
1595		639,063	514,865	151,867
1596		633,465	510,447	115,176
1597		693,672		170,015
1598	4,286,380	692,535		174,851
1599	3,535,145			
1600	4,708,029	769,527	661,855	
1601	5,177,634	708,506	680,394	
1602	4,521,687	792,399	593,898	63,243
1603	4,803,460	703,202	649,082	
1604	4,958,071	592,368	661,776	
1605	5,552,305	737,642		259,045
1606	4,202,701	712,337		214,624
1607	4,372,603[a]	668,329		213,858
1608	3,937,370	680,783	626,662	98,856
1609	3,179,472	635,637		132,726
1610	3,073,489	544,284		171,324
1611	2,262,512			175,287
1612	2,486,698[a]			162,974
1613	1,310,193			142,525
1614	1,976,542			163,067
1615	2,212,513[a]			164,717
1616		342,068		314,178
1624	1,200,000			
1630		498,528		
1633		275,538		
1638	400,000			

APPENDIX D

| | | \multicolumn{3}{c}{Income (In Ducats)} |
Year	Sheep	Gross	Fida	Net
1639	610,000			
1640	700,000			
1644	522,000	163,730		
1645		159,178		
1648		424,046		
1651		196,577		
1654		146,544		
1657		146,669		
1659		204,170		
1661		202,056		
1662		192,423	170,012	
1664		160,747		
1670		179,439		
1672		168,611		
1673		193,177		
1675		189,511		
1680	1,607,000	200,000		
1682		172,428		
1683		172,428		
1687	1,297,488	173,256		
1688		183,068		
1689	1,208,973	162,106		
1690	1,310,514	172,315		
1691		166,523	148,229	
1693		166,703	147,255	
1713	1,202,468	193,647	189,276	
1714	1,188,111	192,215	187,845	
1715	1,251,778	190,321	186,064	

SHEEP AND INCOME IN THE DOGANA

			Income (In Ducats)	
Year	Sheep	Gross	Fida	Net
1716	1,321,468	192,226	187,969	
1717	1,254,537	190,185	185,974	
1718	1,353,640		188,223	
1719	1,662,350		197,570	
1720	1,742,878		200,542	
1721	1,493,358		192,189	
1722	1,265,307			
1723	1,287,812		185,189	
1724	1,398,633		191,032	
1725	1,418,150		190,427	
1726	1,345,171		188,736	
1727	1,087,344		177,282	
1728	1,163,816		178,441	
1729	1,164,865		180,792	
1730	1,294,497		187,244	
1731	1,509,974		197,000	
1732	1,456,667	230,439	195,406	
1733	1,537,599	250,121	199,306	
1734	1,669,958	230,585	202,456	
1735	1,571,227	225,109	199,134	
1736	2,024,385	238,807	213,280	
1737	2,375,038	249,474	224,162	
1738	1,831,648	234,366	207,407	
1739	2,079,762	241,903	214,591	
1740	2,168,241	243,537	217,093	
1741	2,555,714	254,785	228,504	
1742	3,404,185	283,187	255,089	
1743	3,353,872	287,411	252,612	
1744	3,806,990	305,428	273,753	
1745	2,138,439		222,958	
1746	1,216,050		181,019	
1747	2,052,735	243,816	211,161	
1748	3,422,988	291,385	257,705	
1749	3,274,722	290,909	252,519	
1750	5,266,059	348,414	315,384	
1751	2,862,589	270,138	236,049	
1752	4,918,740	338,656	305,118	
1753	4,668,137	330,303	294,807	
1754	4,615,697	332,205	295,769	
1755	4,873,237	345,016	309,050	
1756	2,938,699	276,712	235,124	
1757	2,497,111	257,115	217,172	
1758	3,068,995		237,497	
1759	4,349,802	320,207	282,636	

| | | Income (In Ducats) | | |
Year	Sheep	Gross	Fida	Net
1760	4,868,147	337,900		301,238
1761	2,834,324	272,944		233,957
1762	1,647,352	229,121		188,107
1763	2,396,045	254,232		214,702
1764	1,882,915	242,825		200,912
1765	1,943,891	238,140		197,934
1766	2,366,934	260,012		220,675
1767	2,985,030	276,850		237,556
1768	3,782,501	305,444		268,298
1769	3,777,512	299,568		262,452
1770	4,217,763	315,555		277,756
1771	3,927,720	304,603		266,489
1772	5,261,743	360,090		323,228
1773	6,356,665	390,116		353,400
1774	4,892,370	339,652		304,288
1775	7,089,310	417,284		382,087
1776	3,584,901	292,610		254,217
1777	3,472,928	294,870		257,964
1778	5,954,157	371,674		336,537
1779	3,598,881	297,479		253,916
1780	2,168,315	250,753		208,068
1781	3,536,755	302,952		262,641
1782	6,217,039	398,347		361,585
1783	5,356,560	369,316		329,766
1784	7,558,798	440,512		403,257
1785	5,828,261	377,225		337,430
1786	4,831,279	352,319		311,345
1787	5,832,738	376,065		336,846
1788	6,149,354	390,405		351,011
1789	5,910,857	418,390		375,387
1790	5,484,799	412,800		362,618
1791	5,584,802	417,491		365,826
1792	5,684,714	418,936		369,018
1793	5,784,718	437,038		372,194
1794	5,784,718	440,566		372,194
1795	5,784,718	442,413		372,278
1796	5,784,143	441,909		372,207
1797	5,784,143	444,097		372,207
1798	5,830,787	449,438		379,499
1799	5,830,787	455,313		379,499
1800	5,830,787	454,126		379,499
1801	5,830,787	460,119		379,499
1802	5,830,787	462,011		379,499

SHEEP AND INCOME IN THE DOGANA

Year	Sheep	Income (In Ducats)		
		Gross	Fida	Net
1803	5,830,579	455,617	379,488	
1804	5,830,014	454,055	379,459	
1805	5,830,014	450,981	374,791	

Sources: Dozens of manuscript and printed sources, often conflicting, have been consulted. I have prepared this appendix as one might edit a text by tediously sorting variants and sources.

[a]During the inflated rise of sheep numbers under the *professazione voluntaria* system, the number of real sheep was sometimes counted or calculated: 1574, 805,999; 1575, 1,204,910; 1576, 1,273,649; 1577, 1,352,102; 1578, 1,545,112; 1579, 1,700,062; 1580, 1,914,186; 1581, 2,147,599; 1582, 2,303,029; 1583, 2,440,491; 1587, 1,528,605; 1588, ca. 1,000,000; 1591, 1,785,158; 1607, 1,137,960; 1612, 570,000; 1615, ca. 700,000.

APPENDIX E
Production, Prices, and Product Value

TABLE E-1   Wool Production, Prices, and Product Value at Foggia
(In *Rubbi, Carlini* per *Rubbio*, and Ducats respectively)

Year	Wool in Deposit	Wool out of Deposit	Price	Product Value
1562			33–34	
1581			26–33	
1582			15–20	
1606			30–32	
1623		48,696[a]	18.78	91,451
1624		56,630[a]	20.92	118,450
1625		49,977[a]	28.75	143,840
1626		43,621[a]	34.69	151,321
1627		50,991[a]	34.74	177,143
1628		55,189[a]	37.20	205,303
1629		44,319[a]	38.17	169,166
1630		52,681[a]	30.30	159,623
1631		50,074[a]	28.39	142,160
1632		45,398[a]	30.25	137,329
1633		56,040[a]	33.46	187,510
1634		57,629[a]	36.77	211,902
1635		56,807[a]	33.53	190,474
1636		49,998[a]	32.24	161,194
1637		63,092[a]	24.33	153,503
1638		57,636[a]	29.22	168,412
1639		49,891[a]	33.57	167,484
1641		55,732[a]	26.08	144,903
1642		57,689[a]	30.03	173,240
1643		69,347[a]	27–31	201,107
1644		52,785[a]	20–23.75	115,467
1645		54,404[a]	21.5–27	131,930
1646		49,254[a]	25–30	135,449
1647		60,215	27.75–30	137,743

Year	Wool in Deposit	Wool out of Deposit	Price	Product Value
1648		37,018[a]	23–26	90,694
1649		36,758	23–26	90,056
1650		49,959[a]	24–28	129,893
1651		53,325[a]	34–39	194,636
1652		60,367	26–29	166,009
1653		54,484[a]	31.5–34	178,435
1654		48,920[a]	32.5–35	165,105
1655		65,519	35.0	229,315
1656		54,463	33–36.5	189,260
1657		40,811[a]	21.25–24	92,335
1658		57,578[a]	20–24	126,672
1659		55,898[a]	24–27.5	143,937
1660		51,423[a]	32–34	169,696
1661		66,652[a]	27.25–31	194,124
1662		64,613[a]	22–30	167,994
1663		59,078[a]	22.5–25.5	141,787
1664		57,622[a]	25–30	158,461
1665		54,701	29–31.5	165,469
1666	56,593	53,535	29.75–31.25	162,977
1667	66,380	58,651	23.75–28	151,907
1668	56,259	52,366	25–30	144,007
1669	55,639	55,344	22–26	132,825
1670	63,858	53,059	21.0	111,425
1671		52,271	21–23.5	116,302
1672			25.0	
1673		58,977[b]	21–24.5	143,019
1674		47,282	21–23	96,927
1675	51,334	48,754	22–26	118,229
1676		58,533	25–27.5	158,039
1677		60,310	22.5–30	158,312
1678		59,663	23–28.75	143,191
1679		54,998	23–25	120,995
1680	49,164	49,788	21.5–23	109,533
1681		55,834	22–28	132,605
1682		52,461	24.75–27.5	136,399
1683		58,476	29–32	169,581
1684		53,655	24–35	166,332
1685	62,151	59,773	35.0	209,206
1686		64,242	32–33	200,757
1687		50,616[b]	30.5–31.5	156,910
1688		65,222	31	208,712
1689		67,087	36–37	241,514
1690	58,484		32.5	
1691		55,699[b]	32.0	178,237

TABLE E-I (continued)

Year	Wool in Deposit	Wool out of Deposit	Price	Product Value
1692		80,466[b]	31.25–39	282,637
1693		92,449[b]	45.5	388,286
1694		67,886[b]	40.5	274,938
1695	68,484	66,491	43.5	289,236
1696	89,711	88,730	44.5	394,850
1697	85,558	84,330	45.5	383,701
1698	68,151	70,784	45.5	322,069
1699	81,648	84,962	47.5	403,570
1700	86,501	91,777	54.5	500,182
1701		77,463	40.0	309,851
1702		82,165	34.0	279,362
1703		64,482	48.5	321,739
1704		60,541	40.0	242,165
1705	73,686	68,106[b]	41.0	279,235
1706		71,954	40.0	287,818
1707		67,767	40.0	271,067
1708		68,128	39.0	265,700
1709		44,397	40.0	177,588
1710	69,493	47,991	30.5	146,372
1711		58,438	30.5	178,235
1712		73,582	31.0	228,105
1713		67,116	31.0	208,061
1714		80,595	31.0	249,843
1715	79,323[c]	84,763	35.0	296,670
1716		79,470[b]	36.0	286,091
1717		92,759	32.0	296,830
1718		106,752	36.25	386,976
1719		105,586	35.5	374,831
1720	107,210	114,050	35.5	404,876
1721		76,764	30.0	230,292
1722		97,997	30.0	293,992
1723		106,949	35.5	379,668
1724		90,538	33.5	303,303
1725	93,687	89,813	35.17	315,874
1726		47,818	41.0	196,055
1727		61,058	43.5	265,603
1728		86,807	41.5	360,250
1729		91,361[b]	32.5	296,923
1730	88,633	85,462	31.0	264,931
1731		82,036	38–35	299,430
1732	72,955	59,163[b]	39–36	221,863
1733	75,623	73,241	37–34	260,005
1734	84,079	82,296	37.0	304,494

PRODUCTION, PRICES, AND PRODUCT VALUE 287

Year	Wool in Deposit	Wool out of Deposit	Price	Product Value
1735	97,283	84,135	45–42	365,987
1736	87,684	85,795	45–42	373,208
1737	97,687	92,519	42.5–39.5	379,327
1738	87,684	86,854	45–42	377,814
1739	95,938	81,784	43–40	339,405
1740	95,393	102,673	44–41	436,362
1741	100,784	103,092	45–42	448,449
1742	116,962	120,813	44.5–41.5	519,496
1743	101,289	105,152	44–41	446,897
1744	127,870	123,081	40–37	473,861
1745	57,985	61,652	52–49	311,345
1746	76,109	77,658	48–45	361,110
1747	86,686	91,645	52–49	462,808
1748	96,812	99,899	49–46	474,520
1749	108,558	110,793	45–42	478,845
1750	90,176	93,114	49–46	442,290
1751	102,300	107,874	46–43	480,040
1752	95,432	97,602	48–45	453,848
1753	95,506	98,291	48–45	457,052
1754	93,591[d]	99,004	49.5–46.5	475,218
1755	78,552[d]	85,711	51–48	424,272
1756	81,337	81,511[b]	51–48	403,480
1757	107,399	96,935[b]	49–46	460,441
1758	109,151	90,080[b]	46–43	400,856
1759	116,245	120,319	45–42	523,387
1760	84,758	90,088	45–42	391,884
1761	69,092	72,152	46–43	321,078
1762	93,332	100,606	45–42	437,638
1763	83,750	87,984	49–46	417,923
1764	64,375	65,904	50–47	319,634
1765	87,830	90,290	44.5–41.5	388,247
1766	93,277	93,178	47–44	423,962
1767	97,407	101,330	48–45	471,185
1768	77,821	84,750	52–49	427,987
1769	79,635	77,644	54–51	407,632
1770	76,863	75,640	54–51	397,112
1771	88,328	88,271	56–53	481,078
1772	73,286	76,783	57.5–54.5	429,987
1773	84,180	84,492	56.5–53.5	464,707
1774	84,180	90,577	56–53	493,646
1775	78,819	70,151	56.5–53.5	385,832
1776	82,871	74,173	56.5–53.5	407,953
1777	94,133	84,782	58–55	479,019

TABLE E-1 (*continued*)

Year	Wool in Deposit	Wool out of Deposit	Price	Product Value
1778	84,905	81,332	58–55	459,524
1779	92,532		58–55	
1780	101,380	111,319[e]	55–52	595,557
1781	113,632	117,885	55–52	630,684
1782	96,415	99,935	58–55	564,635
1783	114,148	135,726	56.5–53.5	746,492
1784	92,200	79,340[b]	55.5–52.5	428,436
1785	90,488	135,726	57.5–53.5	607,360
1786	80,933	98,996	61–58	589,029
1787	78,181	99,264[f]	69–66	670,032
1788	82,947	95,232[f]	66–63	614,246
1789	68,547	78,364[f]	67–64	513,284
1790	89,540	98,540[f]	64–61	615,875
1791	65,871	78,927	62.5–59.5	481,453
1792	84,736	94,486[e]	65.5–62.5	604,710
1793	88,824	97,719[e]	69.5–66.5	664,489
1794	89,047	99,363[e]	63–60	611,083
1795	89,047	85,122[e]	65–62	546,525
1796	89,257	79,410[e]	66.5–63.5	504,254
1797	92,566	88,952[e]	65–62	564,845
1798	93,634		73–70	
1799	67,486		75–72	
1800	73,541		75–72	
1801	82,667	67,106[e]	70–67	459,676
1802	79,520		76–73	
1803	93,497		82–79	
1804	110,764		77.5–74.5	
1805	112,713		82.5–81.0	
1806			82.8–79.8	
1807			77.5–74.5	
1815	77,036			*Inventory Value*
1816	74,142		86.2	627,983
1817	83,599		80.8	662,936
1818	98,097		76.0	730,824
1819	96,260		81.0	765,268
1820	93,393		71.3–68.3	651,886
1821	73,797		63.5–60.5	457,542
1822	65,360		72.5–69.5	464,057
1823	64,692		64–61	404,323
1824	67,741		58–55	382,735
1825	62,221		66.5–63.5	404,438
1826	65,846		74–71	477,382

Year	Wool in Deposit	Wool out of Deposit	Price	Inventory Value
1827	72,624		68–65	482,947
1828	83,174		57–54	461,615
1829	69,098		61–58	411,135
1830	65,711		59.8–56.8	383,095
1831	67,572		72.8–69.8	481,787
1832	65,556		67.8–64.8	434,635
1833			72.8	
1834			80.0	
1835	67,627		83.0	551,161
1836	79,734		93.0	729,567
1837			60.0	
1838			71.0	
1839			74.0	
1840			65.8	
1841			71.3	
1842			70.5	
1843			69.0	
1844			71.5	
1845	100,896		84.3	469,162
1846	106,848			

Sources: Wool in deposit: ASFg, *Dogana,* serie V, regg. 1991–2551, "Libri di pesatori di lana," as computed by Antonio Massenzio, "Il mercato della lana in Foggia dal 1600 al 1800," Tesi di Laurea, Università degli Studi di Bari, 1963/64; and Pasquale di Cicco, "Produzione della lana nella R. Dogana di Foggia e relativo commercio con Terra di Lavoro nella seconda metà del Seicento," *Archivio Storico Pugliese* 24(1971):3–59. ASFg, *Dogana,* serie I, fas. 355, 356, "Atti della voce della lana." ASFg, *Amministrazione del Tavoliere, Scritture dell'Ufficio,* fas. 22.

Wool out of deposit: ASFg, *Dogana,* serie V, regg. 1999–2551 (1623–1801), "Libri di pesatori di lana."

Prices: All of the above; ADLPR (cited in full in chap. 1, n.116); Maria C. Nardella, "Attività creditizie e commerciali a Foggia nella prima metà del XVII secolo," in *Produzione, mercato e classi sociali nella Capitanata moderna e contemporanea,* ed. Angelo Massafra (Foggia: Amministrazione Provinciale di Capitanata, 1984), pp. 57–131 for 1623–42.

Note: Italics indicate extrapolated total.
[a]Total calculated from linear regression on Sulmona accounts (1623–1700).
[b]Total calculated by interpolating missing account book total from previous and following citations, then adding estimate to given quantities.
[c]No register for Castel di Sangro.
[d]*Infondacatura* totals taken before all wool was placed in deposit: 1754, another 6,071 *rubbi,* total=100,427; 1755, 5,634 *rubbi,* total=85,310.
[e]Totals are addition of extant account books only, with the assumption that missing accounts may not have recorded any wool for that year.
[f]Castel di Sangro *infondacatura* exists for these years. Totals for wool in deposit at Castel di Sango added to totals for wool out of deposit from other *paranze.*

TABLE E-2 Five-year Weighted Moving Average for Wool Sold in Foggia (1625–1795) (In *Rubbi*)

Year	Wool	Year	Wool	Year	Wool	Year	Wool
1625	50,013	1677	57,896	1725	79,350	1769	82,589
1626	49,401	1678	57,546	1726	69,170	1770	80,031
1627	49,431	1679	55,558	1727	70,399	1771	81,309
1628	50,276	1680	53,682	1728	77,614	1772	82,454
1629	49,973	1681	53,940	1729	84,634	1773	82,951
1630	49,524	1682	54,381	1730	83,238	1774	81,330
1631	49,304	1683	55,917	1731	77,772	1775	78,802
1632	50,970	1684	57,129	1732	72,866	1776	78,254
1633	53,450	1685	58,244	1733	74,311		
1634	54,886	1686	59,153	1734	78,509	1782	111,136
1635	56,089	1687	59,737	1735	83,815	1783	110,229
1636	56,117			1736	86,648	1784	102,812
1637	56,804	1693	76,359	1737	87,640	1785	101,892
		1694	76,747	1738	88,625	1786	98,555
1643	59,902	1695	76,608	1739	91,112	1787	97,007
1644	56,977	1696	78,499	1740	98,381	1788	93,165
1645	55,205	1697	80,385	1741	104,797	1789	88,980
1646	51,866	1698	81,271	1742	111,630	1790	88,879
1647	49,372	1699	82,421	1743	107,553	1791	88,767
1648	44,912	1700	83,680	1744	100,146	1792	92,738
1649	44,195	1701	81,079	1745	87,025	1793	93,878
1650	47,491	1702	75,855	1746	84,727	1794	93,074
1651	52,429	1703	69,380	1747	90,165	1795	88,842
1652	55,066	1704	66,768	1748	97,259		
1653	55,651	1705	67,304	1749	101,990		
1654	55,732	1706	69,830	1750	101,574	Wool Production	
1655	55,401	1707	68,464	1751	101,570	Five-Year Weighted	
1656	53,615	1708	63,167	1752	99,694	Moving Average	
1657	51,992	1709	55,940	1753	97,962	(1817–30)	
1658	52,448	1710	55,019	1754	93,791		
1659	54,795	1711	59,603	1755	90,375	1817	85,410
1660	57,951	1712	68,153	1756	88,767	1818	91,283
1661	60,778	1713	74,699	1757	93,334	1819	92,129
1662	61,593	1714	79,057	1758	97,371	1820	87,084
1663	60,440	1715	82,305	1759	98,930	1821	77,761
1664	57,607	1716	86,754	1760	93,987	1822	70,466
1665	55,993	1717	93,451	1761	89,571	1823	66,868
1666	55,221	1718	101,273	1762	86,452	1824	65,846
1667	55,288	1719	103,208	1763	84,378	1825	66,168
1668	54,619	1720	101,399	1764	83,114	1826	68,554
1669	54,199	1721	96,324	1765	86,482	1827	71,914
		1722	96,222	1766	90,380	1828	73,836
1675	53,019	1723	96,054	1767	91,974	1829	71,695
1676	55,629	1724	90,105	1768	86,778	1830	68,800

Source: See table E-1.

TABLE E-3 Animals Sold for Meat at the Foggian Fair

Year	Animals Exported		Animals Kept in Kingdom		Total		All Animals
	Lambs	Castrati	Lambs	Castrati	Lambs	Castrati	
1766	17,126	9,458	26,154	2,735	43,280	12,193	55,473
1767	9,888	5,036	29,132	7,070	39,020	12,106	51,126
1768	7,075	18,779	25,259	7,560	32,334	26,339	58,673
1769	7,938	19,050	30,473	2,971	38,411	22,021	60,432
1770	4,795[a]	23,011	25,447	2,802	30,242[a]	25,813	56,055[a]
1771	12,155	17,507	50,279	6,184	62,434	23,691	86,125
1772	9,150	22,219	16,333	5,220	25,483	27,439	52,922
1773	10,580	15,879	31,928	9,141	42,508	25,020	67,528
1774	27,739	23,548	53,046	14,218	80,785	37,766	118,551
1775	700[a]	14,689	25,818	11,168	26,518[a]	25,857	52,375[a]
1776	15,102	18,154	38,310	16,004	53,412	34,158	87,570
1777	16,998	18,593	39,274	13,758	56,272	32,351	88,623
1778	11,835	17,975	30,226	5,797	42,061	23,772	65,833
1779	27,262	17,170	36,939	14,449	64,201	31,619	95,820
1780	20,588	17,901	44,552	14,344	65,140	32,245	97,385
1781	27,700	15,740	56,753	15,821	84,453	31,561	116,014
1782	45,031	22,847	51,482	15,567	96,513	38,414	134,927
1783	22,300	20,806	38,156	16,957	61,456	37,763	99,219
1785	31,802	22,630	45,254	18,720	77,056	41,350	118,406
1786	16,600	13,348	39,916	12,763	56,516	26,111	82,627
1787	15,507	16,320	42,279	7,736	57,786	24,056	81,842
1788	12,520	16,826	45,863	35,891	58,383	52,717	111,100
1789	4,164	10,164	9,295	12,519	13,459	22,683	36,142
1790	2,570	6,972	53,927	9,678	56,497	16,650	73,147
1791	—	—	29,025	5,611	29,025[a]	5,611[a]	34,636[a]
1792	5,210	5,650	27,204	10,495	32,414	16,145	48,659
1793	4,650	873	36,088	12,420	40,738	13,293	54,032
1794	—	—	24,130	7,570	24,130[a]	7,570[a]	31,700[a]
1795	3,505	—	28,846	—	32,351		

Sources: ASFg, *Dogana*, serie I, fas. 1053–1055 (nn. 19306–19340), "Volume diverse providenze per il reparo degli agnelli, ed altri animali di fiera."

[a] Incomplete record.

TABLE E-4 Meat Prices at Foggia (In *Carlini* per Animal)

Year	Vernarecci	Primaticci	Year	Vernarecci	Primaticci
1654	11	13	1714	7.25	13.0
			1715	7.25	13.0
1672		7	1716	7.0	14.0
			1717	6.5	12.0
1674	3		1718	7.5	13.0
1675	4	8.3	1719	8.0	13.0
1676	4.5	8.0	1720	8.0	13.0
			1721	8.0	13.0
1678		7.5	1722	6.75	11.5
1679		8.75	1723	7.5	12.0
1680		8.1	1724	6.75	12.25
1681		9.0	1725	7.0	13.0
1682		9.0	1726	7.0	14.0
			1727	8.25	12.0
1684		9.5	1728	7.5	12.0
1685		9.0	1729	7.25	13.0
1686		9.0	1730	8.5	11.0
1687		11.5	1731	8.0	12.5
1688		9.75	1732	6.0	12.0
1689		10.25	1733	6.5	13.0
1690		10.25	1734	7.0	12.0
			1735	7.5	12.5
1692	8.75	9.5	1736	8.0	12.0
1693		10.0	1737	8.0	14.0
1694		13.0	1738	10.0	14.5
1695	10.5	12.5	1739	9.0	12.0
1696		13.0	1740	8.0	15.0
1697		13.25	1741	10.0	13.5
1698		13.0	1742	10.0	14.5
1699		13.0	1743	8.0	11.0
1700		14.0	1744		18.0
1701		13.0	1745		15.0
1702		9.5	1746		15.5
1703	6.0 and 7.5	11.0 and 13.0	1747		14.5
1704	6.0	12.5	1748		15.0
1705		12.0	1749	10.375	14.5
1706	7.0	11.5	1750	10.5	14.0
1707	6.0	10.5	1751	11.0	15.25
1708	6.5	11.0	1752	11.5	15.25
1709	6.0	11.75	1753	11.25	14.0
1710	6.0	11.0	1754	10.0	15.0
1711	6.5	11.0	1755	11.0	14.0
1712	6.5	11.5	1756	11.0	15.0
1713	7.25	12.5	1757	10.5	14.5

Year	Vernarecci	Primaticci
1758	12.75	15.5
1759	11.0	14.0
1760	7.5	15.125
1761	10.0	12.5
1762	9.0	14.0
1763	8.0	13.5

Sources: Doria statistics from ADLPR (cited in full in chap. 1, n. 116).

TABLE E-5   Cheese Production, Prices, and Product Value at Foggia
(In *Pesa, Carlini* per *Pesa,* and Ducats Respectively)

Year	New Cheese Production	Price	Percentage Unsold	Product Value
1672		16 and 18		
1673		17 and 18		
1676		16.4		
1681		10.0		
1682		10.0		
1684		10.0		
1685		10.0		
1687		8.0		
1688		9.0		
1689		12.0		
1690		12.0		
1691		11.0		
1692		9.25		
1693		11.25		
1694		16.0		
1695		13.25		
1696		11.0		
1697		12.88		
1698		16.75		
1699		16.38		
1700		16.4		
1701		15.25		
1702		16.88		
1703		13.5		
1704		12.0		
1705		13.5		
1706		14.5		
1707		13.0		
1708		11.5		
1709		13.0		
1710		14.0		
1711		15.0		
1712		13.25		
1713		13.0		
1714		15.0		
1715		13.5		
1716		17.5		
1717		15.0		

PRODUCTION, PRICES, AND PRODUCT VALUE   295

Year	New Cheese Production	Price	Percentage Unsold	Product Value
1718		12.5		
1719		12.0		
1720		14.75		
1721		15.25		
1722		11.5		
1723		9.5		
1724		11.0		
1725		14.0		
1726		17.0		
1727		9.0		
1728		9.5		
1729		11.0		
1730	67,646	13.5	15.7	79,836
1731	40,312	15.5	0	64,499
1732	38,967	15.5	21.2	49,098
1733	57,307	11.5	14.1	59,060
1734	59,306	13.5	10.0	74,733
1735	81,846	9.5	26.4	60,226
1736	47,537	14.5	23.6	54,506
1737	50,144	15.0	6.9	72,415
1738	68,104	16.0	19.5	90,410
1739	62,696	14.0	18.6	74,038
1740	63,155	14.5	10.0	85,233
1741	86,075	13.0	11.2	103,160
1742	74,592	13.5	13.3	90,513
1743	69,022	16.0	23.2	87,462
1744	81,542	13.5	16.2	95,665
1745	18,671	20.0	1.6	37,681
1746	55,011	16.0	12.4	79,553
1747	68,874	12.0	12.2	75,554
1748	48,957	14.0	1.7	69,769
1749	64,178	14.0	3.1	90,159
1750	44,120	16.5	1.3	74,004
1751	85,143	13.5	8.9	108,641
1752	72,561	14.0	4.6	100,348
1753	75,592	15.0	11.5	103,721
1754	51,907	17.5	13.8	80,539
1755	38,277	19.5	16.2	64,173
1756	70,429	15.0	5.6	103,066
1757	70,535	15.0	5.8	102,998
1758	75,213	14.0	7.7	100,634
1759	77,768	13.5	17.1	90,311
1760	39,518	16.0	6.9	60,732
1761	27,927	20.5	9.1	53,323

TABLE E-5 (*continued*)

Year	New Cheese Production	Price	Percentage Unsold	Product Value
1762	81,201	15.5	14.1	111,650
1763	57,381	16.0	16.0	79,532
1764	35,882	18.0	8.0	61,063
1765	86,892	14.0	20.1	100,626
1766	41,648	16.5	9.6	63,985
1767	54,929	17.5	21.2	77,902
1768	30,804	20.5	1.8	63,512
1769	62,934	20.5	18.8	107,308
1770	43,950	21.0	10.0	84,968
1771	69,603	18.0	14.5	110,107
1772	58,913	19.0	11.8	101,308
1773	45,552	21.0	10.7	87,455
1774	65,743	18.5	17.9	102,529
1775	42,988	22.0	8.3	88,691
1776	53,366	23.0	21.6	92,094
1777	50,531	23.0	11.7	98,155
1778	62,546	22.0	10.4	126,126
1779	46,750	23.0	4.2	105,186
1780	77,095	21.0	16.7	138,105
1781	70,426	20.0	10.5	129,234
1782	58,650	22.0	1.4	130,163
1783	91,423	22.0	17.4	169,848
1784	41,247	23.0	2.3	94,722
1785	69,874	23.5	8.4	153,658
1786	56,568	14.5	8.2	129,795
1787	49,065	25.6	6.0	119,873
1788	54,597	28.0	24.8	116,998
1789	35,859	30.5	20.2	88,719
1790	68,779	26.5	12.7	162,145
1791	42,599	26.8	0.5	115,708
1792	61,834	27.0	19.2	125,909
1793	59,800	24.7	6.0	141,674
1794	54,321	27.6	8.4	139,885
1795	54,539	28.0	5.9	146,245
1796	52,582	30.5	5.7	153,704
1797	66,840	29.0	2.6	192,148
1798	75,234	29.0	0	221,940
1799	36,889	40.0	1.8	146,687
1800	55,038	45.0	29.9	175,530
1801	69,314	32.0	32.5	152,162
1802	45,163	31.25	1.4	141,456
1803	43,882	39.5	12.2	154,108
1804	73,037	35.5	20.2	209,923
1805	50,066	35.25	12.7	156,267

PRODUCTION, PRICES, AND PRODUCT VALUE 297

Year	New Cheese Production	Price	Percentage Unsold	Product Value
1806	37,118	47.5	0.4	177,446
1807	55,348			
				Inventory Value
1816	41,125	37.0		154,219
1817	42,356	44.0		188,484
1818	82,832	31.0		260,921
1819	69,146	38.13		267,111
1820	61,235	32.9		204,525
1821	40,668	34.0		140,305
1822	37,677	30.5		116,799
1823	74,775	32.0		243,019
1824	78,321	25.8		205,984
1825		31.4		
1826		27.0		
1827		19.5		
1828		20.0		
1829		28.0		
1830		29.0		
1831		26.0		
1832		21.86		
1835		29.7		
1836		31.5		
1837		33.0		
1838		30.2		
1839		26.38		
1840		28.925		
1841		33.75		
1842		32.09		
1843		28.42		
1844		33.38		
1845		35.32		

Sources: Prices (1672–1729), ADLPR (cited in full in chap. 1, n. 116). The Doria prices were initially 0.5 *carlini* below the price of new cheese at Foggia (*quà*), and 1.5 *carlini* below the price at Melfi (*là*). Full record, ASFg, *Dogana,* serie I, fas. 12504–12581 (1730–1807), "Atti di voce di cascio e ricotte del corrente anno. . . ."; ASFg, *Amministrazione del Tavoliere, Scritture dell'Ufficio,* fas. 22, "Documenti e notizie relative alle voci delle lane, dei formaggi, del pane, dei cereali" (1816–1845). Prices (1730–1845) are at Foggia (*quà*).

APPENDIX F
Enlightened Reformers on the Dogana of Foggia from the 1764 Famine to the 1806 Abolition of the Dogana

1767 Nicola Fortunato. *Discoverta dell'antico Regno di Napoli col suo presente stato a pro della sovranità e de' suoi Popoli* (Naples).

1770 Salvadore Grana. *Istituzioni delle leggi della Regia Dogana di Foggia* (Naples).

1780 Filippo Briganti. *Esame economico del sistema civile* (Naples).

Ferdinando Galiani. *Trattato della moneta*, 2d ed. (Naples).

Domenico Grimaldi. *Piano di Riforma per la pubblica economia delle provincie del regno di Napoli, e per l'agricoltura delle due Sicilie* (Naples).

1781 Francesco Nicola De Dominicis. *Lo stato politico ed economico della Dogana della Mena delle pecore di Puglia*, 3 vols. (Naples).

Giuseppe Maria Galanti. *Descrizione dello stato antico ed attuale del Contado di Molise*, 2 vols. (Naples).

1783 Domenico Cimaglia. *Ragionamento . . . sull'economia che la Regia Dogana di Foggia usa co' possessori armentari e con gli agricoltori che profittano de' di lei campi, e su di ciò che disporre si potrebbe pel maggior profitto della Nazione e pel miglior comodo del Regio Erario* (Naples).

Vincenzo Patini. *Saggio sopra il sistema della Regia Dogana della Puglia, suoi difetti e mezzi di riformarlo* (Naples).

Antonio Silla. *La pastorizia difessa—Ove si fa una breve analisi sopra alcuni progetti intorno alla riforma della Regia Dogana di Foggia* (Naples).

Domenico Di Gennaro, duke of Cantalupo. *Annona o sia piano economica di pubblica sussistenza* (Nice).

1785 Diego Gatta. *Dissertazione sul privilegio della regia Dogana di Foggia per rapporto a gli ecclesiastici locati* (Naples).

Melchiorre Delfico. *Memoria sul tribunal della grascia e sulle leggi economiche nelle provincie confinanti del regno* (Naples).

1786 Luigi Targioni. *Saggi fisici politici ed economici* (Naples).

Giuseppe Maria Galanti. *Nuova descrizione storica e geografica della Siciliae* 4 vols. (1786–90) (Naples).

ENLIGHTENED REFORMERS ON THE DOGANA 299

[1787] Melchiorre Delfico. *Memoria per l'abolizione o moderazione della servitù del pascolo invernale detto de' Regi Stucchi nelle provincie marittime di Apruzzo* (n.p.).

1787 Rocco Pecori. *Riflessioni intorno ad alcuni punti legislativi giovevoli o dannosi alla popolazione* (Naples).

1788 Melchiorre Delfico. *Discorso sul Tavoliere di Puglia e sulla necessità di abolire il sistema doganale e non darsi luogo ad alcuna temporanea riforma* (Naples).

Gaetano Filangieri. *Parere presentato al Re sulla proposizione di un affitto sessennale ne così detto Tavoliere di Puglia* (Naples).

n.d. Anonymous. *Della censuazione di alcune poste domandata da molti locati della Dogana di Foggia e controdetta da pochissimi* (n.p.). (In response to the royal order of 12 January 1788).

1789 Giuseppe Palmieri. *Pensieri economici relativi al Regno di Napoli* (Naples).

Anonymous. *Idea d'un nuovo sistema pei locati ed agricoltori della Regia Dogana di Foggia* (Foggia).

Niccola Columella Onorati. *Primi esperimenti della moltiplicazione delle biade* (Naples).

1790 Francesco Longano. *Viaggi dell' Ab. Longano per lo Regno di Napoli. Viaggio per la Capitanata* (Naples).

Giuseppe Palmieri. *Della natura e sorte della coltura delle biade in Capitanta* (Naples).

Giuseppe Palmieri. *Osservazioni su vari articoli riguardanti la pubblica economia* (Naples).

1791 Niccola Columella Onorati. *Della cose rustiche*, 3 vols. (1791–95) (Naples).

1792 Francesco Saverio Camilli. *Memoria sui danni apportati allo Stato ed al fisco dalla fida delle pecore rimaste e sull'utilità di transigere in perpetuo la medesima* (Naples).

Giuseppe Palmieri. *Della richezze nazionale* (Naples).

Giuseppe Rosati. *Discorso sull' agricoltura di Puglia* (n.p.).

1794 Francesco Maria Marchesani. *Saggio dello stato attuale dell' agricoltura e del commercio frumentario delle provincie di Apruzzo Citra, Capitanata, e Contado di Molise* (Naples).

Mario Di Merino. *Memoria della divisione delle terre fiscali in Puglia* (Naples).

1796 Nicola Vivenzio. *Considerazioni sul Tavoliere di Puglia* (Naples).

1803 Niccola Columella Onorati. *Della cose rustiche*, 2d ed., 10 vols. (Naples).

Giuseppe Rosati. *Il metodo millenario per l'aumento del grano, e delle altre civaje nella semina* (Foggia).

1805 Giacinto Bellitti. *Memoria intorno alla censuazione del Tavoliere della Daunia* (San Giorgio a Cremano [NA]).

ABBREVIATIONS

ACA	Archivo de la Corona de Aragón, Barcelona
ADLPR	Archivio Doria Landi Pamphilj, Rome
AGS	Archivo General, Simancas
AHN	Archivo Histórico Nacional, Madrid
ARSJ	Archivum Romanum Societatis Jesu, Rome
ASFg	Archivio di Stato, Foggia
ASFi	Archivio di Stato, Florence
ASN	Archivio di Stato, Naples
ASP	Archivio di Stato, Pisa
ASV	Archivio di Stato, Venice
BNM	Biblioteca Nacional, Madrid
BNN	Biblioteca Nazionale, Naples
BPFg	Biblioteca Provinciale, Foggia
BRAH	Biblioteca de la Real Academia de la Historia, Madrid
BSNSP	Biblioteca della Società Napoletana di Storia Patria, Naples
BV	Biblioteca Apostolica Vaticana
HHSA	Haus-, Hof- und Staatsarchiv, Vienna

a.	anno	ins.	inserto
banc.	bancone	int.	interno
Branc.	Brancacciana	leg.	legajo
c., cc.	carta, carte	lib.	libro
ca.	circa	reg., regg.	registro, registri
c.s.	carta sciolta	MS.	manoscritto
f., ff.	foglio, fogli	n.n.	nuova numerazione
fas.	fascio	num.	numerazione
fasc.	fascicolo	scaf.	scaffale
inc.	incartamento	tav.	tavolo

NOTES

Note: A list of manuscript sources follows the notes; eighteenth-century printed sources are listed chronologically in appendix F. For all other works a complete citation is given at the first occurrence in the notes.

Introduction

1. Despite the independent origins of *La Regia Dogana della Mena delle Pecore di Puglia*, similarities between sheep transhumant institutions in Castile and southern Italy allow for this shorthand comparison. Fernand Braudel, *The Mediterranean and the Mediterranean World in the Age of Philip II*, 2 vols., trans. Siân Reynolds (New York: Harper & Row, 1972), 1: 94 quotes from a copy of a Spanish document ca. 1600 that the *dogana delle pecore* functioned "al modo de la mesta."

2. Ugo Jarussi, *Foggia. Genesi urbanistica, vicende storiche e carattere della città* (Bari: Editoriale Adda, 1975), pp. 27, 30, 34, 38, 41, 78, and tav. 1. Foggia remained a provincial backwater whose population stood at only fourteenth place in its province of Capitanata in 1532, moved to fifth by 1561, third by the end of the century, second by 1648, and not first until the hearth count of 1732.

3. For a review of the archival holdings in Foggia, see N. F. Faraglia, *Relazione al Ministero dell'Interno intorno all'Archivio della Dogana delle Pecore e del Tavoliere di Puglia in Foggia* (Naples: Tip. della R. Università, 1903); Manfredi Palumbo, *Tavoliere e sua viabilità* (Naples: Artigianelli, 1923); Dora Musto, *La regia dogana della mena delle pecore di Puglia*, Quaderni della rassegna degli "Archivi di Stato," no. 28 (Rome: Ministero dell'Interno, 1964), pp. 85–91.

4. Emmanuel Le Roy Ladurie, *The Peasants of Languedoc*, trans. John Day (Urbana: University of Illinois Press, 1974).

5. Osvaldo Baldacci, *Puglia*, vol. 14 in *Le Regioni d'Italia*, ed. Roberto Almagià (Turin: Unione Tipografico editrice Torinese, 1962), p. 297.

6. Angerio Filangieri, "La 'Dogana delle pecore' di Puglia e la struttura economico-agraria del Tavoliere," *Rivista di economia agraria* 5 (1950): 688. David Abulafia, "Southern Italy and the Florentine Economy, 1265–1370," *Economic History Review* 34, no. 3 (1981):377–88 gives the main agricultural products supplied by the Puglia-Abruzzi axis as grain, oil, and livestock. For a seven-year period reported in 1336, for example, Florentine meat and leather guildsmen purchased 50,000 sheep and goats for 30,000 florins (p. 382).

7. "Relazione del Regno di Napoli al Marchese di Mondesciar Viceré di Naples tra il 1577 e il 1579," app. III, in Camillo Porzio, *La congiura de' baroni del Regno di Napoli contra il Re Ferdinando Prima*, 2d ed. rev., ed. Ernesto Pontieri (Naples: Edizioni scientifiche italiane, 1961).

8. P. Coppola, *Geografia e Mezzogiorno* (Florence: La Nuova Italia Editrice, 1977).

9. Giuseppe Galasso, "Strutture sociali e produttive, assetti colturali e mercato dal secolo XVI all'Unità," in *Problemi di storia delle campagne meridionali nell'età moderna e contemporanea*, ed. Angelo Massafra (Bari: Dedalo libri, 1981), pp. 159–72.

10. John A. Marino, "Economic Idylls and Pastoral Realities: The 'Trickster Economy' in the Kingdom of Naples," *Comparative Studies in Society and History* 24, no. 2 (1982):211–34.

11. Benedetto Croce, "The 'Kingdom' and its internal contradictions," in his *History of the Kingdom of Naples* (orig. ed., *Storia del regno di Napoli*, 1925), trans. Frances Frenaye (Chicago: University of Chicago Press, 1970).

12. Stefano Di Stefano, *La ragion pastorale over comento su la Prammatica LXXIX de offitio Procuratoris Caesaris*, 2 vols. (Naples: Domenico Roselli, 1731).

13. Francesco Nicola De Dominicis, *Lo stato politico ed economico della Dogana della Mena delle pecore di Puglia*, 3 vols. (Naples: Vincenzo Flauto, 1781).

14. BPFg, MSS. 129 and D–A–84; and BSNSP, MS. XXI.C.6, *Notizie per il Buon Governo della Regia Dogana della mena delle pecore di Puglia* (1715), which has been edited by Pasquale di Cicco, Società Dauna di Cultura, Testi e documenti per la storia della Capitanata, no. 5 (Foggia: Editrice Apulia, 1981).

15. For a critical review of the French historiography, James L. Goldsmith, "The Agrarian History of Preindustrial France. Where do we go from here?" *Journal of European Economic History* 13, no. 1 (1984):175–199, esp. p. 193: "It is pointless to single out agriculture as the principal cause of underdevelopment and slow economic growth since the performance of agriculture was itself a product of overall underdevelopment."

16. Luigi Granata, *Economia rustica per lo Regno di Napoli*, 2 vols. (Naples: Nunzio Pasca, 1830), 2:44. The earliest printed book on the dogana, MarcAntonio Coda, *Breve discorso del principio, privilegi et istruttioni della Regia Dohana della mena delle pecore di Puglia* (Naples: Geronimo Fasulo, 1666), pp. 156–58, found it necessary to include a dictionary defining doganal terms.

17. HHSA, *Ital.-Span. Rat, Neapel, Vorträge* 1 (27 November 1709), n. 8, "Vocabulario delli Termini Dohanali": "Quantinus eorum expositio itá nescientibus fiat cognita ut tamen scientibus non sit onerosa." Gregory's text is in *Homily on Gospel*, vol. 76 in *Patrologiae Latinae*, ed. J.-P. Migne (Paris: J.-P. Migne Editorem, 1844–90), I, 13, col. 1123. My thanks to Carole Straw for locating the citation.

18. Neville Dyson-Hudson, "The Study of Nomads," *Journal of Asian and African Studies* 7, nos. 1–2 (1972):24–26 proposes a method whereby ethnographers might gather adequate knowledge of nomadic society from "the identification of relevant elements and their combination and recombination." His assumption is clear: pastoral social organization depends upon a detailed knowledge of the material culture from which it derives. The formative influence on my analysis is, above all, anthropological and may ultimately derive from a classic like E. E. Evans-Pritchard, *The Nuer* (Oxford: Clarendon Press, 1940).

19. Maurice Aymard and Jacques Revel, "Niveaux et formes de développement des économies agraires en Italie (XVe–XVIIIe siècle)" paper delivered at the Decima Settimana di Studio, Istituto "Francesco Datini," Prato, 1978; Aymard, "La transizione dal feudalesimo al capitalismo," in *Storia d'Italia, Annali: Dal feudalesimo al capitalismo*, ed. Ruggiero Romano and Corrado Vivanti (Turin: Einaudi, 1978), 1:1131–92; Aymard, "Money and Peasant Economy," *Studies in History* 2, no. 2 (1980):11–20. Also see the general model of Immanuel Wallerstein, *The Modern World-System*, 2 vols. (New York: Academic Press, 1974–80).

20. Erwin Panofsky, "*Et in Arcadia Ego*: Poussin and the Elegiac Tradition," in *Meaning in the Visual Arts* (Garden City, N.Y.: Doubleday Anchor Books, 1955), pp. 295–320 examines the dissonance between reality and imagination in pastoral settings. "It was, then, in the imagination of Virgil . . . that the concept of Arcady, as we know it, was born—that a bleak and chilly district of Greece came to be transfigured into an imaginary realm of perfect bliss. But no sooner had this new, Utopian Arcady come into being than a discrepancy was felt between the supernatural perfection of an imaginary environment and the natural limitations of human life as it is" (p. 300).

21. Gérard Delille, *Agricoltura e demografia nel Regno di Napoli nei secoli XVIII e XIX* (Naples: Guida Editore, 1977), pp. 139–42. Delille argues that population and production increases in the Kingdom after the mid eighteenth century were "false" growth because higher yields do not necessarily mean a growing economy. Real growth, on the contrary, lies in producing with a smaller outlay of labor.

1. Mediterranean Mestas and the Neapolitan Exemplar

1. Fernand Braudel, *The Mediterranean*, 1:25–102, esp. 1:85–102 (cited in full in intro., n. 1) on transhumance and nomadism; and *Comptes rendus du Congrès International de Géographie, Lisbonne 1949* (Lisbon, 1951), 3:1–105.

2. Viviana Bonazzoli, "L'economia agraria nella società della Puglia cerealicolo-pastorale nel XVIII secolo," *Annali dell'Istituto Italiano per gli Studi Storici* 4 (1973/75):105–230.

3. Catherine Delano Smith, *Western Mediterranean Europe: A Historical Geography of Italy, Spain and Southern France since the Neolithic* (New York: Academic Press, 1979), pp. 239–43. ASV, *Cinque Savi alla Mercanzia*, serie I, busta 472 bis, n. 8 (8 August 1753) exemplifies the political nature of the pastoral/agricultural, pastoral/manufacturing relationships in a constitution for the Terraferma pastoral industry of Padova.

4. Julius Klein, *The Mesta: A Study in Spanish Economic History, 1273–1836* (Cambridge, Mass.: Harvard University Press, 1920), pp. 239–43.

5. Reyna Pastor de Togneri, "La lana en Castilla y León antes de la organización de la Mesta," in *La lana come materia prima. I fenomeni della sua produzione e circolazione nei secoli XIII–XVII*, ed. Marco Spallanzani (Florence: Leo S. Olschki, 1974), p. 256.

6. Charles Julian Bishko, "The Castilian as Plainsman: The Medieval Ranching Frontier in La Mancha and Extremadura," in *The New World Looks at Its History*, ed. A. R. Lewis and T. F. McGann (Austin: University of Texas Press, 1963), p. 61. For further corrections to Klein's classic, see Bishko, "The Peninsular Background of Latin American Cattle Ranching," *Hispanic American Historical Review* 32 (1952):491–515; Jaime Vicens Vives, *Manual de Historia Economica de España*, 3d ed. (Barcelona: Editorial Vicens-Vives, 1964), pp. 222–36; Ramon Carande, *Carlos V y sus banqueros. La vida economica en Castilla (1516–1556)*, abr. ed., 2 vols. (Barcelona: Editorial Crítica, 1977), 1:26–61.

7. Jaime Vicens Vives, *Approaches to the History of Spain*, 2d ed. corrected and revised, trans. and ed. Joan Connelly Ullman (Berkeley and Los Angeles: University of California Press, 1970), pp. 64–67.

8. George D. Ramsay, "The Merchants of the Staple and the Downfall of the English Wool Traffic," in *La lana come materia prima*, Spallanzani, ed. (cited in full in n. 5), pp. 45–47; Federigo Melis, "La lana della Spagna mediterranea e della Barberia occidentale nei secoli XIV–XV," in ibid., pp. 241–51.

9. Roberto S. Lopez, "The Origin of the Merino Sheep," in *Jewish Social Studies*, Publications no. 5, The Joshua Starr Memorial Volume (New York: Conference on Jewish Relations, 1953), pp. 161–68.

10. Klein, *The Mesta*, p. 52. Enrique IV first began the policy of crown dependence.

11. Ibid., pp. 68–70. A. Floristan Samenes, "Juntas y mestas ganaderas en las Bardenas de Navarra," in *Actas del Primer Congresso Internacional del Pirineo* (Zaragoza: Heraldo de Aragón, 1951), abstract, p. 9 claims that the intertown cooperation dated from 1204.

12. Cesare De Cupis, *Le vicende dell'agricoltura e della pastorizia nell'agro Romano. L'annona di Roma* (Rome: Tipografia Nazionale di G. Berbtero & Co., 1911), p. 64; Arturo De Sanctis Mangeli, *La pastorizia e l'alimentazione di Roma nel medioevo e nell'età moderna* (Rome: P. Maglione & C. Storini, 1918), pp. 21–22. For the text, Augustin Theiner, *Codex diplomaticus dominii Temporaliis S. Saedis*, 3 vols. (Rome: Imprimerie du Vatican, 1861–62), 3:121. My conclusions were drawn before reading the most recent work on the Roman

dogana, Jean-Claude Maire Vigueur, *Les pâturages de l'église et la douane du bétail dans la province du Patrimonio (XIVᵉ–XVᵉ siècles)* (Rome: Centro di Ricerca, 1981). Vigueur, p. 105, argues incorrectly, I believe, that the Roman institution was founded by Martin V (1413–31).

13. De Cupis, *Le vicende dell'agricoltura e della pastorizia nell'agro Romano*, p. 64. The dogana of Sant'Antimo at Monte Maggiore is mentioned in some chapters of the Statutes of Rome.

14. Ibid., p. 349; Clara Gennaro, "Mercanti e bovattieri nella Roma della seconda metà del Trecento," *Istituto Storico Italiano per il Medioevo* 78 (1967):175–76; Carlo Calisse, "La costituzione del Patrimonio di S. Pietro in Tuscia nel sec. XIV," *Archivio della Società Romana di Storia Patria* 15 (1892):23.

15. BV, Cod. Vat. Lat. 8886, "Libro delli Statuti . . . a favore delle Dogana della fida, e pascoli di Roma" (7 January 1792), 1r–16v and partially transcribed in De Cupis, *Le vicende dell'agricoltura e della pastorizia nell'agro Romano*, app., doc. I, pp. 550–57.

16. Di Stefano, *La ragion pastorale*, 1:167, 2:25, 303 (cited in full in intro., n. 12); Musto, *La regia dogana*, pp. 61–62, n. 38 (cited in full in intro., n. 3); De Cupis, *Le vicende dell'agricoltura e della pastorizia nell'agro Romano*, pp. 65–71; De Sanctis Mangeli, *La pastorizia di Roma*, pp. 24–26; Antonio Anzilotti, "Cenni sulle finanze del Patrimonio di S. Pietro in Tuscia nel secolo XV," *Archivio della R. Società Romana di Storia Patria* 42 (1919):365–75. For the text of the constitutions, see BV, Cod. Vat. Lat. 8886, cc. 1–53r, which is partially transcribed in Pietro Andrea De Vecchis, *Collectio Constitutionum Chirographorum, et brevium diversorum Romanum Pontificem*, 4 vols. (Rome: Hieronymi Mainardi, 1732–34), 1:1–16.

17. For the budget estimate, Anzilotti, "Cenni sulle finanze del Patrimonio di S. Pietro," p. 373. Marie Vigueur, *Les pâturages de l'église*, pp. 127, 154, 182, 183, analyzes the extant budgets between 1347–62 and 1442–88. Mean numbers of animals for ten years in the fourteenth century are 58,248 head, and 106,530 head for seventeen years in the fifteenth century.

18. Musto, *La regia dogana*, gives a chronological overview from Roman times to 1806. For the medieval period: Gino Barbieri, "La produzione delle lane italiane dall'età dei communi al secolo XVIII," in *La lana come materia prima*, Spallanzani, ed. (cited in full in n. 5), pp. 133–48; Guiseppe De Gennaro, "La lana di Puglia nel basso medioevo," in ibid., pp. 149–67; Mario del Treppo, "Agricoltura e transumanza in Puglia nei secoli XIII/XVI: Conflitto o integrazione?" paper delivered at the Undicesima Settimana di Studio, Istituto "Francesco Datini," Prato, 1979. For the early modern period: Di Stefano, *La ragion pastorale*, 2:475–80 outlines major doganal events from 1442 to 1731; Ludovico Bianchini, *Storia del finanze del Regno delle due Sicilie* (3d ed. of orig. ed., 1859), ed. Luigi de Rosa (Naples: Edizioni Scientifiche Italiane, 1971) summarizes doganal economic history on pp. 170–72 (1414–96), pp. 242–46 (1533–1733), pp. 366–67 (1734–1806), and pp. 487–94 (1806–47); Raffaele Colapietra, "Vicende storiche ed ordinamento della Dogana di Foggia fino a Carlo di Borbone," *Rassegna di politica e di storia* 57 (1959): 13–29 tells its history from 1447 to 1734.

19. AGS, *Estado, Dos Sicilias*, leg. 5808, f. 13, letter of the Spanish ambassador in Naples to the king in Spain (15 January 1737).

20. Alfonso's charter has been published often: Coda, *Breve discorso*, pp. 4–9 (cited in full in intro., n. 16); Luca Brencola, *De jurisdictiones Regiae Dohanae menae pecudum Apuliae* (dedicated in 1724 to the viceroy Cardinal d'Althann and published from a discourse to Charles VI, n.p., 1727), pp. 12–16; Salvadore Grana, *Istituzioni delle leggi della Regia Doana di Foggia* (Naples: Stamperia Raimodi, 1770), pp. 72–79; De Dominicis, *Lo stato politico*, 1:70–74 (cited in full in intro., n. 13); Domenico De Martino, *Lavoro istorico positivo sul Tavoliere di Puglia* (Naples: Agrelli, 1859), pp. 20–25; Faraglia, *Relazione all'Archivo della*

Dogana, notes (cited in full in intro., n. 3); Nicola De Meis, *Nel Tavoliere* (Naples: Artigianelli, 1923), pp. 26–30; Palumbo, *Tavoliere e sua viabilità*, pp. 68–72 (cited in full in intro., n. 3).

21. A. Filangieri, "La 'Dogana delle pecore,' " p. 663; Pliny, *Natural History* 8.73: "Lana autem laudatissima Apulia et quae in Italia Graeci pecoris appellatur, alibi Italica."

22. Musto, *La regia dogana*, p. 14, n. 11; E. T. Salmon, *Samnium and the Samnites* (Cambridge: Cambridge University Press, 1967), pp. 67–70.

23. Albert Grenier, "La transhumance des troupeaux en Italie et son rôle dans l'histoire romaine," *Mélanges d'archéologie et d'histoire de l'Ecole Française de Rome* 25 (1905):293–328.

24. Varro, *De re rustica* (Loeb Classical Library, 1960), 2.1, is quoted by Di Stefano, *La ragion pastorale*, 1:28 and BNN, MS. I.D.21, c. 8r. Many doganal commentators invoked the dogana's ancient poetic origins to legitimize customhouse claims. Such precedents, for example, provide the proof of Philip II's need to reform the pastoral institution according to tradition. BNN, MS. I.D.21, Don Juan Enriquez, "Compendio breve dela Doana delas pecoras de Pulla dirigido por el Anno de 1578. Al serenissimo Rey Don Phelippo 2° de gloriosa" (a. 1578), 1r–37v; and its somewhat expanded Spanish exemplar, BNM, MS. 1093, "Discurso en raçonde la aduana de las pecoras de la Pulla en el Reyno de Nápoles tocante al patrimonio Real de España traducido de lengua Italiana por el licenciado Balthasar Porreño y dedicado al Rey don Philippe Tercero nuestro Señor," 1r–38v. For a review of the classical texts quoted by doganal commentators see Vincenzo Spola, "I precedenti storici della legislazione della Dogana di Foggia nel Regno di Napoli," *Archivio Storico Pugliese* 25 (1972):469–82.

25. David Abulafia, *The Two Italies: Economic Relations between the Norman Kingdom of Sicily and the Northern Communes* (Cambridge: Cambridge University Press, 1977).

26. Di Stefano, *La ragion pastorale*, 1:30; Angelo Caruso, *La Dohana Menae Pecudum— 0 Dogana di Foggia—e il suo archivio* (Naples: Centro per la Editoria Scolastica e Popolare, 1963), pp. 9–10; Spola, "I precedenti storici," pp. 476–77. The constitutions *Pervenit ad aures nostris* and *Cum per partes Apuliae* are transcribed in J.–L.–A. Huillard–Bréholles, *Historia diplomatica Friderici II*, 6 vols. (Paris: Henricus Plon 1852–61), 4:157–61.

27. Caruso, *La Dohana*, pp. 9–10; Spola, "I precedenti storici," pp. 476–77. The texts are in Huillard–Bréholles, *Friderici II*, 4:161–62.

28. BNN, MS. I.D.21, 9r-v claims that in 1244 medieval tax collectors (*ballivos*) were, like the Roman publicans, counting sheep and collecting taxes. Both, in turn, were like the latter-day doganiero.

29. A. Filangieri, "La 'Dogana delle pecore,' " p. 664.

30. For the dogana's name, Nicola Vivenzio, *Considerazioni sul Tavoliere di Puglia* (Naples: Stamperia Simoniana, 1796), p. XLVIII, n. 2 cites the "diurnali di Matteo Spinello, il più antico scrittore della lingua pugliese," now BNN, Branc. IV.B.10, "Chronica di Matteo Spinello da Giovenazzo," c. 12r, which gives the income of the dogana in July 1254 as 5,200 *onze*. Manfredi Palumbo, *I Comuni meridionali prima e dopo le leggi eversive della Feudalità*, 2 vols. (Montecorvino Rovella: Stabilmento Tipografico "L'Unione" Editore, 1910), 2:232 cites *Registro Angioino* for 1322, fol. 174, vol. 212, p. 278. For the *locazioni*, De Meis, *Nel Tavoliere*, pp. 2–3 and 24–25 transcribes ASN, *Registro Angioino*, vol. 6, fol. 255 (2 May 1270): "instrumentum locationis animalium Curiae factae quibusdam de Casalinovo," and Vivenzio, *Considerazioni sul Tavoliere*, p. L, n. 2 cites a document from 1273 which names Salpi, Orta, Ordona, Guardiola, and Bovino as having the same boundaries as under Frederick II. For the presence of transhumant sheep, Paolo Gasparinetti, "La 'Via degli Abruzzi' e l'attività commerciale di Aquila e Sulmona nel secoli XIII–XV," *Bullettino della deputazione abruzzese di storia patria* 5, nos. 54–56 (1964–66), 42, n. 23 cites a document of 1272, "Mandatum pro illis qui tempore hiemali mittunt oves de Aprutio ad Apuliam," *I*

Registri della Cancelleria Angionia, ricostruiti da Riccardo Filangieri (Naples: Presso L'Accademia Pontaniana, 1957), vol. 8, reg. 37, n. 6, p. 115. In 1271 during that same indiction, one *magistris massariis*, Thomasis de Tancredo of Foggia, held 7, 157 sheep, 1,054 goats, and 2,867 lambs along with other animals—oxen, cows, bulls, horses, etc. Ibid., reg. 35, n. 345, p. 83.

31. Pietro Gentile, "Lo stato napoletano sotto Alfonso I d'Aragona," *Archivio Storico per le Province Napoletane* 62 (1937):1-56; 63 (1938):1-56, esp. 63:21.

32. Vivenzio, *Considerazioni sul Tavoliere*, pp. LII-LVII, n. 3 transcribes the text of Giovanna's decree of 18 September 1423. Palumbo, *Tavoliere e sua viabilità*, p. 15, and pp. 67-68, n. 3 gives a partial transcription.

33. In his drive to increase doganal revenues and strengthen the Neapolitan monarchy against the barons, Alfonso hoped to lure Roman pastoralists into the Kingdom to winter their sheep. At the same time, he was also engaging in a bit of international diplomacy in an attempt to bolster his antipapal policy. Gentile, "Lo stato napoletano," 63:25.

34. ASN, *Archivio Giudice Caracciolo*, vol. 33, 271r-276v is a common text repeated in many documents as an introduction to the fiscal system of the Kingdom. On the sheepwalks and passes in Alfonso's times, Palumbo, *Tavoliere e sua viabilità*, pp. 132-36 and De Meis, *Nel Tavoliere*, pp. 33-50 cite a 1450 document no longer extant in ASN. Palumbo claims even earlier evidence of their pre-Aragonese existence and usurpation by private parties.

35. In the thirteenth century, Charles I of Anjou had already imported North African sheep into the Kingdom to improve the local breed. Spola, "I precedenti storici," p. 479; A. Filangieri, "La 'Dogana delle pecore,'" p. 664.

36. Alan Ryder, *The Kingdom of Naples under Alfonso the Magnanimous. The Making of a Modern State* (Oxford: Clarendon Press, 1976), p. 359. The baronial request, "vendere & contractare a chi li piace," is transcribed in *Privilegii et capitoli, con altre gratie concesse alla fidelis Città di Napoli, e Regno per li Serenissimo Rì di Casa de Aragona* (Venice: Per Pietro Dusinelli, ad instantia di Nicolò de Bottis, 1588), p. 4v, chap. III.

37. Ryder, *The Kingdom of Naples*, p. 360 cites Cesare Foucard, "Proposta fatta dalla Corte Estense ad Alfonso I Re di Napoli," *Archivio Storico per le Province Napoletane* 4 (1879):714 quoting Borso d'Este in 1444.

38. Klein, *The Mesta*, pp. 68-70, points out that the office of doganiero as defined by Alfonso was reminiscent of the office of *justicia* of the Casa de Ganaderos of Saragossa. Ryder, *The Kingdom of Naples*, pp. 359-61 cites ACA, *Privilegiorum Cancillería Napoles*, reg. 2902, c. 156v: in January 1443, Matheucio Vacaro, who never assumed office, was appointed doganiero for a five-year term effective from 1 September. From September 1443, Francesco Montluber held the office, with confirmation for life in Alfonso's 1447 chapter.

39. Coda, *Breve discorso*, p. 4 and others edited in n. 20. For a definition of these offices see C. Ducange, *Glossarium Mediae et infirmae Latinitates*, 10 vols. (Niort: L. Favre, 1883-87).

40. Ryder, *The Kingdom of Naples*, pp. 361, 194.

41. Ryder, *The Kingdom of Naples*, pp. 361-62; Gentile "Lo stato napoletano," 63:22. De Meis, *Nel Tavoliere*, partially transcribes the budgets, pp. 30-35.

42. Hidetoshi Hoshino, *L'Arte della lana in Firenze nel basso medioevo. Il commercio della lana e il mercato dei panni fiorentini nei secoli XIII-XV.* (Florence: Leo S. Olschki, 1980), pp. 276-82, and tab. LVIII, pp. 301-02.

43. Ibid., p. 280. Carla Rahn Phillips, "The Spanish Wool Trade, 1500-1780," *Journal of Economic History* 42, no. 4 (1982):775-95.

44. Ryder, *The Kingdom of Naples;* Ryder, "The Evolution of Imperial Government in Naples under Alfonso V of Aragon," in *Europe in the Late Middle Ages*, ed. J. R. Hale, J. R. L. Highfield, and B. Smalley (Evanston, Ill.: Northwestern University Press, 1965), pp. 332-57. Gentile, "Lo stato napolitano," 62:1-56; 63:1-56. Despite the centralizing attempts

by Alfonso, provincial administration was still dominated by the feudal barons, who remained largely autonomous. See also Mario del Treppo, "The 'Crown of Aragon' and the Mediterranean," *Journal of European Economic History* 2 (1973):161–85.

45. De Meis, *Nel Tavoliere*, pp. 11–12 reports on an eleven-item disposition of Louis XII dated 19 August 1502.

46. Gentile, "Lo stato napoletano," 63:25. Among the favorites were G. Camerario, Innico d'Avolos, 2,000 sheep; Raimondo Caldora, 10,000 sheep; and Paolo di Sangro (whose family provided later doganieri), 10,000 *animali piccoli* and 1,000 *animali grossi*. Ryder, *Kingdom of Naples*, pp. 361–62: in 1444/45 the count of Fondi was given free pasture for 1,200 sheep, and in 1450/51 Montluber admitted over 6,000 sheep without taxation.

47. De Meis, *Nel Tavoliere*, pp. 39–41, n. 38 transcribes an eleven-item instruction of 8 March 1470, ASN, *Curie della Sommaria*, vol. 7, cc. 66ff.

48. Vincenzo Spola, "Documenti del sec. XV relativi alla dogana di Foggia," *Archivio Storico Pugliese* 6, nos. 1–4 (1953):152 transcribes a royal letter of 3 January 1479 from the register of the doganiero Nicola Caracciolo, ASN, *Sommaria Partium*, vol. 545, 23r: "Dohanero. La Università de Fogia mi ha facto supplicare che considerato quella terra non have altra industria che de fare campi de grani."

49. Alberto Grohmann, *Le Fiere del Regno di Napoli in età aragonese* (Naples: Istituto Italiano per gli Studi Storici, 1969), p. 138; and Coda, *Breve discorso*, p. 23 on the creation of the office of *auditore* in the 1480s to prosecute criminal cases.

50. The two earlier documents are transcribed in De Dominicis, *Lo stato politico*, 3:349 and De Martino, *Lavoro istorico*, pp. 44–45. The 1536 request is found in Charles V's charter, item 24, cited in n. 70.

51. "Prime Grazie del Re Ferdinando I" (5 December 1470) is transcribed in Coda, *Breve discorso*, pp. 17–18; De Dominicis, *Lo stato politico*, 1:76–80; and De Martino, *Lavoro istorico*, pp. 26–31.

52. Coda, *Breve discorso*, p. 19. Bianchini, *Storia delle finanze*, p. 171 claims that only 550,000 head remained.

53. Musto, *La regia dogana*, p. 23 n. 34 cites ASN, *Sommaria Partium*, vol. 545, 1v.

54. De Dominicis, *Lo stato politico*, 1:80–83; De Martino, *Lavoro istorico*, pp. 31–34. Grazie dated 17 December 1480.

55. Coda, *Breve discorso*, p. 23; Nicol Gaetano Ageta, *Annotationes pro regio aerario ad supremi Regiae Camerae Summariae Senatus Regni Neapolis decisiones per lucelentos tractatus, et quaestiones ad rem fiscalem attinentes*, 3 vols. (Naples: Jacobi Raillard, 1692), 3:178; De Dominicis, *Lo stato politico*, 1:84; De Martino, *Lavoro istorico*, pp. 34–35. Dated 10 October 1483.

56. Ageta, *Annotationes*, 3:178–79 transcribes the commission.

57. BNM, MS. 1093, 25v points out, in a chronological review of the dogana, that the great lacuna of information from 1494 to 1533 was a result of the French Wars "por que con las guerras que siguieron [the death of Ferrante] fue esta vez la dicha Aduana muy maltratada usurpada y ocupada."

58. Bianchini, *Storia delle finanze*, p. 172 gives the economic data. De Meis, *Nel Tavoliere*, pp. 43–46, n. 43 transcribes the charter (10 August 1497).

59. Franceso Guicciardini, *Storia d'Italia*, ed. Silvana Seidel Menchi (Turin: Einaudi, 1971), bk. III, chap. 5, pp. 268–69; bk. V, chap. 7, pp. 481–83; bk. XVIII, chap. 11, pp. 1914–16. Paolo Giovio, *Storie del suo tempo*, trans. by Domenichi (Venice, 1555), bk. IV, pp. 162–67. Pietro Giannone, *Istoria Civile del Regno di Napoli* (orig. ed., 1723), ed. Antonio Marongiu, 7 vols. (Milan: Marzorati, 1972), bk 29, chap. 4, vol. 5:280–82.

60. Bianchini, *Storia delle finanze*, p. 172. For the text of the treaty, AGS, *Patronato Real*, leg. 41:21, published in José Lopez de Toro, ed. and trans., *Tratados Internacionales de los Reyes Católicos, con algunos textos complementarios* (Madrid: Imprenta Gongora, 1952), 2:173–84. A French doganal instruction of Louis XII is cited in n. 45. Louis XII also

appointed a native Neapolitan, pro-French doganiero in 1501, Federico Minadois. Scipione Mazzella, *Descrittione del Regno di Napoli* (Naples: Ad istanza di Gio. Battista Cappello, 1601; reprint, Bologna: Arnaldo Forni, 1981), p. 336.

61. De Dominicis, *Lo stato politico*, 1:86. The texts of the *grazie* are in *Privilegii et capitoli*, p. 22r, chap. XVII (27 January 1495); p. 23v, chap. X (26 October 1496); pp. 36v–37r, chap. XLVI (15 May 1503); p. 47r, chap. LXII (5 December 1505); pp. 53v–54r (5 December 1505); p. 59v, chap. XVIII (30 January 1507); and p. 63r, chap. XII (10 May 1507). On the Neapolitan parliaments, Guido D'Agostino, *Parlamento e società nel Regno di Napoli. Secoli XV–XVII* (Naples: Guida, 1979).

62. ASN, *Dipendenze della Sommaria*, serie II, vol. 57/127, 1r–4r (21 August 1506).

63. Ageta, *Annotationes*, 3:179; De Dominicis, *Lo stato politico*, 1:87. Di Stefano, *La ragion pastorale*, 2:476 reports that Antonello Di Stefano's report on the Kingdom and the dogana was delivered by his son to the king in Spain.

64. Coda, *Breve discorso*, pp. 25–27.

65. De Dominicis, *Lo stato politico*, 1:87–88. *Privilegii et capitoli*, p. 68r, Chap. XXVIII (12 December 1508).

66. Tommaso Pedío, *Napoli e Spagna nelle prima metà del Cinquecento* (Bari: Dott. Francesco Cacucci Editori, 1971), pp. 418–25, 439, 443, 453. British Library, Egestorn MS. 1905, 21v–25r chronicles LeClerc's three visits totaling forty-five days (17–24 January, 9–28 March, 8–27 April 1518), and 127v and 149v–150r give the budgetary information on income and expenses. Note especially LeClerc's historical review of doganal income for Alfonso (108v—80,000 ducats), Ferrante (109r—100,000 ducats), and Ferdinand in 1516 (109v—77,675 ducats). LeClerc points out that the doganal tax increases were introduced at the time of the Angevin Ladislas. This statement appears in a straightforward review of budgetary facts before the Habsburg propaganda machine could attribute foundations, for purposes of legitimacy, to its Aragonese predecessor Alfonso.

67. On the fire in the Foggian archives, Gaudiani, *Notizie*, p. 318, n. 161 (cited in full in intro., n. 14). AGS, *Estado, Nápoles*, leg. 1008, f. 60, "Bilancio de Introyti et exiti" (1530/31) notes that the year's income from the *dogana delle pecore* was exceptionally low because (1) soldiers from the recent wars were still raiding the sheep (undoubtedly for provisions); (2) many shepherds were seeking safer pastures in the Roman campagna and other parts of the Papal States; and (3) high sheep mortality resulted from the severe winter. Cited in Guiseppe Coniglio, *Il Regno di Napoli al tempo di Carlo V. Amministrazione e vita economico-sociale* (Naples: Edizioni Scientifiche Italiane, 1951), p. 203.

68. Karl J. Beloch, *Bevölkerungsgeschichte Italiens*, 3 vols. (Berlin: De Gruyter, 1937–61), 3:215 gives hearth (*fuochi*) information for Capitanata in 1505, 12,211; in 1532, 11,052; i.e., a decline of more than 1,000 hearths.

69. The 1533 Figueroa *reintegrazione* is preserved in ASN, *Dipendenze della Sommaria*, serie II, vol. 57/130. A photocopy and a transcription are also in ASFg, *Dogana delle pecore*, serie I, in two *fasci*, both numbered 17 bis. Simultaneously, Charles V confirmed the ancient privileges of the town of Foggia, in ACA, *Privilegiorum*, reg. 3942, 24v (26 February 1533). The graziers' petition (undated, ca. 1533–36) is transcribed only as a general introduction in De Dominicis, *Lo stato politico*, 1:94–95 and De Martino, *Lavoro istorico*, pp. 35–37.

70. Charles V's charter was signed 11 February 1536 and confirmed in camera, 29 March 1536. A transcription is in Coda, *Breve discorso*, pp. 28–34; De Dominicis, *Lo stato politico*, 1:97–103; De Martino, *Lavoro istorico*, pp. 37–44; and summarized in Ageta, *Annotationes*, 3:223–24. Baronial demands are in *Privilegii et capitoli*, p. 109r, chaps. V, VI, VII, and VIII (11–22 March 1536).

71. ASN, *Sommaria Diversi*, serie I, fas. 54, n.n. 1v–3r (26 February 1539). AGS, *Estado, Nápoles*, leg. 1025, f. 84, "La relacion que se consultara a Su Mad.d en Madrid a XX de agosto de MDXXXIX de la comission que de parte del visorey de Nápoles traxole el

regente Figueroa," transcribed by Giuseppe Coniglio, "La dogana delle pecore di Foggia nel 1539," *Archivio Storico Pugliese* 22 (1969):124–34.

72. Charles V confirmed the commission, ACA, *Privilegiorum*, reg. 3946, 53v (5 September 1539). In the parliament of 1540, even the landowners complained of abuses in pasture distribution and declining rents. *Priviligii et capitoli*, pp. 130r and 131r, chaps. XVII and XXVII (28 February 1540).

73. For the ten-year sheep average see ASN, *Sommaria Consultationum*, vol. 2, 12v–15v (13 March 1563), and BNN, MS. XI.B.39, "Della Regia Dohana delle Pecore di Puglia" (undated—mid seventeenth century), 119v. The eight-year revenue mean is taken from Coniglio, *Carlo V*, p. 202, who cites AGS, *Visítas de Italia, Nápoles*, leg. 12, which is now leg. 15:5, f. 85.

74. John A. Marino, "*Professazione voluntaria* e *pecore in aerea:* Ragione economica e meccanismi di mercato nella dogana di Foggia del secolo sedicesimo," *Rivista Storica Italiana* 94, no. 1 (1982):5–43.

75. Modern geographic evaluation of the Tavoliere is in Udo Sprengel, "La pastorizia transumante nell'Italia centro/meridionale," *Annali del Mezzogiorno* 15 (1975):276, n. 4. For a complete version of Sprengel's research, see his *Die Wanderherdenwirtschaft im mittel- und südostitalienischen Raum* (Marburg an der Lahn: Marburger Geographische Schriften, 1971). The common sense of pastoral experience confirms the wisdom of ecology in the proverb: "Pochi animali ben pasciuti rendono più che molti mal nodriti." Niccola Columella Onorati, *Dell'agricoltura pratica della pastorizia* (Naples: Angelo Trani, 1813), p. 29.

76. ASFg, *Dogana*, serie I, vol. 14 (copied in vol. 15), and ASN, *Sommaria Diversi*, serie I, vol. 103 I. Coda, *Breve discorso*, pp. 47–69, and De Dominicis, *Lo stato politico*, 1:140–70 transcribe "Il Libro della Generale Reintegrazione," in reduced form. ASN, *Sommaria Consultationum*, vol. 2, 12v–15r (13 March 1563) states that 2,060 *carra* were added to pasture for a total of 9,139.4 *carra* out of the Tavoliere's 15,641.2 *carra* used for grazing.

77. Coda, *Breve discorso*, pp. 40–46; De Dominicis, *Lo stato politico*, 1:120–36; and De Martino, *Lavoro istorico*, pp. 53–69 transcribe Toledo's instructions (19 October 1549) "per lo bon governo, beneficio, conservazione, et augmento de la detta Regia Dogana."

78. The decree of 20 October 1551 is examined in BNN, MS. Branc. V.D.14, "Discorso sopra gli erbaggi extraordinarj insoliti, e loro prezzo," 44r–46r (ca. 1613) and transcribed in Ageta, *Annotationes*, 3:214–15.

79. The original numeration *modo di vivere* is described in De Dominicis, *Lo stato politico*, 1:89–91. The state saved an annual expenditure of 4,770 ducats in salary and provisions (Ageta, *Annotationes*, 3:183) paid to the 192 *numeratori*, and helped to prevent counting frauds. Gaudiani, *Notizie*, BPFg, MS. 129, ff. 433–51 gives the general order, with "counters" and places assigned. In the new *modo di vivere* sheep numbers which were reported in tax rolls no longer corresponded to real sheep. Instead of underestimating their holdings to avoid taxes, graziers overestimated their sheep to ensure better pasture. I have found no extant document for the 1553 establishment of *professazione voluntaria*. Gaudiani, *Notizie*, p. 227 claims that the new taxation method was decreed in 1551 as part of the general reintegration. Cf. De Dominicis, *Lo stato politico*, 1:115; Marino, "*Professazione voluntaria*," p. 19.

80. *Privilegii et capitoli*, pp. 155r–v, chaps. XXI, XXII, XXIII (31 December 1554). Again in the parliament of 1556, the barons repeated their complaints against the 1548 reintegration: BNN, MS. Branc. V.B.4, "Parlamenti e Gratie della Città di Napoli," cc. 20r–v, chaps. 1–2 (25 May 1556).

81. De Dominicis, *Lo stato politico*, 1:272. In 1560 another 500 *carra* were made *terre salde* for similar reasons. Cf. *banno* of 16 January 1560 transcribed in De Dominicis, *Lo stato politico*, 1:283–85 and De Martino, *Lavoro istorico*, pp. 94–96; *consulta* dated 16 February

1560 transcribed in Palumbo, *Tavoliere e sua viabilità*, pp. 128–31; and *consulta* of 23 December 1560 in ASN, *Sommaria Consultationum*, vol. 8, 55r–60r transcribed in Dora Musto, "Sulla economia di Capitanata nel XVI secolo," *La Capitanata* 5 (1967):82–88.
82. De Dominicis, *Lo stato politico*, 1:287 dates the price rise to 20 March 1556. A copy of the edict is preserved in HHSA, *Ital.-Span. Rat, Neapel, Vorträge* 1 (27 November 1709), n. 5 (21 March 1556). Gaudiani, *Notizie*, pp. 169–70 incorrectly dates the decree 26 May 1556. He points out that it was not effectively enforced until 19 June 1574 with item 4 of Cardinal Granvelle's twenty-three instructions (n. 89 below). Granvelle's decree confirms the original date, 21 March 1556. Slightly later, in 1558, Philip II instituted new taxes on wool in Spain.
83. Marino, "*Professazione voluntaria,*" pp. 17–18, cites AGS, *Visítas de Italia, Nápoles*, leg. 43:27, "Consulta dela Camera hecha ala Visorrey," 8v–12r.
84. H. G. Koenigsberger, "The Statecraft of Philip II," *European Studies Review* 1 (1971):1–21 summarizes Philip's method of bureaucratic control. For some 20 letters see BSNSP, MS. XXVII.C.3, "Raccolta manoscritto di varii diplomi (ordini e lettere di Felippo II, 1572–86) and MS. XXVII.A.1, "Avole delle lettere di S. Mta. Lettere Reali, 1569–97"; BNN, MS. XI.A.22; and BNM, MS. 1052, "Summario de cartas de Su Mag. tocantes a este Reyno, y este Reyno, y en materia de Govierno, y otras concernientes al servicio de Su Magestad."
85. Giuseppe Coniglio, *Visitatori del Viceregno di Napoli*, Società di Storia Patria per la Puglia: Documenti e Monografie, vol. 38 (Bari: Tip. Del Sud, 1974).
86. AGS, *Visítas d' Italia, Nápoles*, leg. 15 (1559–64). For an overview of the Quiroga visit, see Roberto Mantelli, *Burocrazia e finanze pubbliche nel Regno di Napoli* (Naples: Lucio Pironti Editore, 1981).
87. De Dominicis, *Lo stato politico*, 1:302–10 and De Martino, *Lavoro istorico*, pp. 100–07 transcribe the decree dated 15 April 1563.
88. Coda, *Breve discorso*, pp. 71–75; Ageta, *Annotationes*, 3:225–26; De Dominicis, *Lo stato politico*, 1:337–45; and De Martino, *Lavoro istorico*, pp. 117–36 transcribe the document dated 7 February 1574.
89. The 19 June 1574 decree is transcribed in Coda, *Breve discorso*, pp. 76–77; Ageta, *Annotationes*, 3:224–25; De Dominicis, *Lo stato politico*, 1:319–36; and De Martino, *Lavoro istorico*, pp. 136–45. The 30 July 1574 pragmatic is transcribed in Coda, *Breve discorso*, pp. 78–84; Ageta, *Annotationes*, 3:226–28; De Dominicis, *Lo stato politico*, 1:346–62; and De Martino, *Lavoro istorico*, pp. 145–63.
90. De Dominicis, *Lo stato politico*, 1:364–71 and De Martino, *Lavoro istorico*, pp. 166–74 transcribe the commentary of 1 July 1575.
91. De Meis, *Nel Tovoliere*, pp. 14, 54–62, nn. 65–73, esp. the documents transcribed from ASN, *Processo della Regia Camera della Sommaria*, n. 8763, vol. 776, ff. 5–6 (14 January 1577), f. 4 (17 September 1577), and ff. 131–32 (31 July 1579).
92. AGS, *Secretarías Provinciales, Nápoles*, leg. 7 (15 December 1595), and leg. 11 (18 August 1609) review Fabrizio's career. He was granted the title of duke, continued to hold other offices in the bureaucracy, and enrolled his son in the order of Santiago.
93. AGS, *Visítas d'Italia, Nápoles*, leg. 23–30 (1581–84). The six doganal books include a general volume on institutional organization, one of indictments, three books of testimony, and one of miscellaneous evidence. Ageta, *Annotations*, 3:186–203 transcribes a 1581 report of the *credenziero* Gian Domenico Chirico which includes the above leg. 23:3, 263v–268v and 268v–272r, two of the eight discourses prepared on *pecores aereas*.
94. BSNSP, MS. XXVII.C.3, 211v–17v (4 November 1584) and ASN, *Dipendenze della Sommaria*, serie II, vol. 59/137, "Libro di lettere di S. M^a et consulte della R^a Cam^a et risposte, et pareri del Reg Doha delle pecore di Puyla per evietare alcuni inconvenienze, 1584."
95. BNN, MS. Branc. V.B.6, 12r–v (5 May 1587) records the 1586 *grazie*, which

focus on vassals who fraudulently claimed to be *locati*. See, Marino, *"Professazione voluntaria,"* pp. 33–34.

96. Giuseppe Coniglio, *La Dogana di Foggia nel secolo XVII* (Naples: C.E.S.P., 1964), pp. 50–62 transcribes AGS, *Secretarías Provinciales, Nápoles*, leg. 235.

97. Ageta, *Annotationes*, 3:203–08 transcribes "Discorso dello Spettabile Signor Reggente, e Luogotenente della Regia Camera Ferrante Fornaro, allora Presidente dell'istessa Reg. Cam. e Governatore della Regia Dogana delle pecore di Foggia," (ca. January or February 1588). Despite the high sheep numbers "voluntarily bid," real sheep numbered only about 1 million. Later, in 1589, Alfonso de Hermoja, a royal counselor, visited the dogana.

98. De Dominicis, *Lo stato politico*, 2:63–69 and De Martino, *Lavoro istorico*, pp. 185–91 transcribe "Istruzioni . . . al magnifico Signor Giovanni Antonio Valignano Luogotente della Regia Doganella di Apruzzo," dated 25 October 1590 in thirty-one items.

99. Musto, *La regia dogana*, p. 41, notes the 1592 instructions, but I have found no copy of the document. Philip's decree is transcribed in *Pragmaticae edicta decreta interdicta regiaeque sanctiones Regni Napolitani*, 4 vols. (Naples: Sumptibus Antonii Cervonii, 1772), 3:11, item 53.

100. BSNSP, MS. XXVII.A.1, 153v–155r.

101. Coniglio, *La Dogana nel secolo XVII*, pp. 48–50 transcribes AGS, *Estado, Nápoles*, leg. 1099, f. 70.

102. Marino, *"Professazione voluntaria."* For this reason, baronial complaints continued against fraudulent *locati* who did not engage in transhumance: BNN, MS. Branc. V.B.6, cc. 156r–57r records the 1600 *grazie* (14 November 1602).

103. Coniglio, *La Dogana nel secolo XVII*, pp. 62–92 transcribes AGS, *Secretarías Provinciales, Nápoles*, leg. 227 and 235. This is the visit for which Cervantes applied but was rejected.

104. ASN, *Sommaria Notamenti*, vol. 78, inc. (13 September 1608).

105. Ageta, *Annotationes*, 3:208–11 transcribes BNN, MS. Branc. V.D.14, 38r–43v "Sopra la materia delle pecore reali, e delle ragioni, perchè si dovesse fare il libro nuovo, stante la mortalità successa, e l'utile, che ne percepe, e può percepire per avvenire la Regia Corte," written by President de Vera in 1613.

106. Giuseppe Galasso, "Le riforme del conte di Lemos e le finanze napoletane nella prima metà del Seicento," in *Mezzogiorno medievale e moderno* (Turin: Einaudi, 1965), pp. 199–229; Giovanni Muto, *Le finanze pubbliche napoletane tra riforme e restaurazione (1520–1634)* (Naples: Edizioni Scientifiche Italiane, 1980), pp. 91–107. Documents from the deliberation of parliament are preserved in ASFg, *Dogana*, serie I, fas. 2, 181r–198v; the minutes of 4–16 May 1615 are transcribed in De Dominicis, *Lo stato politico*, 2:18–27 and De Martino, *Lavoro istorico*, pp. 198–208; the "Pubblico Istrumento" of 25 November 1615 in De Dominicis, *Lo stato politico*, 2:27–35 and De Martino, *Lavoro istorico*, pp. 208–16.

107. BNN, MS. Branc. V.D.14, 48r–53v provides accounting calculations prepared for the first *transazione*. In 1620, the total payment was 220,000 ducats; 1624, 175,000 ducats; 1633, 192,000 ducats; 1642, 192,000 ducats; 1645, 175,000 ducats. See Musto, *La regia dogana*, pp. 44–46.

108. BNN, MS. Branc. V.B.7, cc. 51r–52r records the 1617 *grazie* (19 February 1619), and 191r–193r that of 1621.

109. ASN, *Sommaria, Carte Reali*, vol. 4, 202r in a letter dated 12 June 1645 on the disposition of a perpetual *mercedes* of 2,000 ducats drawn on the dogana. On the Alarçon visit in general, Giovanni Zarrilli, "Le visite di Francesco Alarcon e Danese Casati nel Regno di Napoli," *Samnium* 38, nos. 1–2 (1965): 131–43. During Alarçon's visit, Miguel Caxa de Leruela, the *arbitrista* who later published *Restauracion de la Antigua Abundancia de España* (orig. ed., Naples, 1630), ed. Jean Paul Le Flem (Madrid: Instituto de estudios fiscales, 1976) on the Spanish Mesta, served as a fiscal officer.

110. Coniglio, *La Dogana nel secolo XVII*, pp. 92–96 cites AGS, *Secretarías Provinciales, Nápoles*, leg. 227.
111. Ibid., pp. 97–104 cites AGS, *Secretarías Provinciales, Nápoles* leg. 227.
112. ASN, *Sommaria, Carte Reali*, vol. 10, 60r–61v in two letters dated 27 July 1682 on the disposition of creditors claiming respectively 300 ducats and 3,253 ducats annually drawn on the dogana.
113. BRAH, MS. F-24, 150r–155r, "Relaçion del gran terremoto" (14 August 1627) records the effects of the 30 July 1627 earthquake: "In comparison to the ruin witnessed in our times in Puglia, with more than 20,000 dead in the most cruel and diverse manner, towns and country completely devastated, Ephesus was nothing, and Sodom and Gommorah were nothing."
114. AGS, *Secretarías Provinciales, Nápoles*, lib. 71, "Libro dove si lege come da chi e in che tempo fu eretta la Regia Dohana de Foggia con alcune istruttioni, ordini, relationi, scritture, li capituli, e la reforma dell' Al^{mo} olim Cardinale Granvela con l'in[struttione, tr]ansattione; e altro . . . por Mag^{lus} Scipion Surrentino Regente," 14v–124r.
115. De Dominicis, *Lo stato politico*, 2:51 and De Martino, *Lavoro istorico*, pp. 242–43 transcribe the decree of 27 August 1646.
116. For pastoral investment in the ninety-two-year, post-plague period (1672–1763), mean statistics reveal 9,844 sheep with a gross income of 8,315 ducats and expenses of 4,829 ducats (30 percent of which, 1,463 ducats, were paid to 87 mean total employees). In comparison, on the agricultural holdings at Forenza in 1603/04, 770 employees produced 6,300 *tomoli* of grain; but, subtracting seed and agricultural needs, 4,200 net *tomoli* were available for human consumption. With 1,380 *tomoli* destined to market at 13–15 *carlini* per *tomolo*, i.e., a maximum gross income of 2,070 ducats, the critical problem was not lower gross income, but the differential in payments to laborers. More than 60 percent of the surplus grain (2,530 *tomoli*) went to employees' wages rather than to market. Dietary needs, however, necessitated that the agricultural work force be provided with 3,850 *tomoli* (5 *tomoli* annual, media per capita × 770 employees). After market sales, therefore, even this high percentage paid to employees left a shortfall which reduced them to the brink of starvation with 34 percent less than their minimum requirements. Thus, despite the differences in the amount of land exploited by these two productive systems, the structure of labor costs vs. income and consequently the caloric squeeze enforced on labor dramatize the advantages of pastoral over agricultural production for large holders. For sheep grazing, ADLPR, banc. 21, unnumbered, "Libro mastro primo dell'Industrie dello Stato di Melfi (1671/72–1686/87)"; banc. 21/14, "Libro dell'Industrie nello Stato di Melfi (1671/72–1691/92)"; banc. 21/26, "Manuale del libro dell'Industrie (1691/92–1702/03)"; scaf. 16/54, "Manuali del libro dell'Industrie dello Stato di Melfi dal 1703/04 al 1742/43"; and scaf. 16/57, "Manuali dell'industria delle Pecore (1743/44–1763/64)." For agriculture, Silvio Zotta, "Azienda agraria e sussistenza in una terra lucana all'inizio dell'Seicento," in *Economia e classi sociali nella Puglia moderna*, ed. Pasquale Villani (Naples: Guida, 1974), p. 180.
117. *Pragmaticae edicta*, 3:192–93 transcribes the decree of 2 July 1661, and De Dominicis, *Lo stato politico*, 2:252–60 gives a fifteen-item *bando* of 22 July 1661 explaining the provisions of the new system.
118. De Dominicis, *Lo stato politico*, 2:266 and De Martino, *Lavoro istorico*, pp. 255–57 transcribe the document of 10 July 1665.
119. De Dominicis, *Lo stato politico*, 3:122–23. ASFg, *Dogana*, serie I, fas. 4, 69r (4 September 1667) ordered that in the future debts must be registered; 90r–91r (22 September 1667), and again 129r–130 (6 April 1668) ordered that *pesatori di lana* must register their account books in the doganal archive.
120. ASFg, *Dogana*, serie I, fas. 4, 498r–501r (22 December 1668) is the original printed pragmatic transcribed in *Pragmaticae edicta*, 3:239–45. Di Stefano, *La ragion pastorale*, organizes his two-volume book around the text and a commentary on each of the forty-nine chapters.

121. Coniglio, *La Dogana nel secolo XVII*, pp. 104–33 transcribes AGS, *Secretarías Provinciales, Nápoles*, leg. 227. On the Casati visit in general, see Zarrilli, "Le visite," pp. 144–166.

122. ASFg, *Dogana*, serie I, vol. 20 (1686).

123. De Dominicis, *Lo stato politico*, 3:37–39 argues that these concessions were based on "erroneous principles." Although illegal considerations which had been given by the *credenzieri* and other minor officials were prohibited by decrees of 1692 and 1694 to prevent the exploitation of the weak by the powerful (3:11–12), the dogana continued to grant official *poste fisse* through the eighteenth century.

124. Pasquale Di Cicco, "La Suddelegazione dei Cambi presso la Regia Dogana di Foggia," *La Capitanata* 10 (1970):5–18.

125. BRAH, MS. 9–21–1–3946, "Le Sette colonne," and "De Riflessioni e Ponderazioni Diverse," (Napoli, 1708). Gaudiani's unpublished manuscript, *Notizie*, bears the same dedication, ed. Di Cicco, p. 32.

126. HHSA, *Ital.-Span. Rat, Neapel, Vorträge* 1 (27 November 1709), n. 3 (10 August 1709) is the review of 17 abuses; n. 4, "Brevissimo raguaglio dell'origine della Dohana di Puglia situato in Foggia," is the chronological review; n. 8, "Vocabulario delli Termini Dohanali"; De Dominicis, *Lo stato politico*, 2:334 transcribes the price increase decree dated 15 September 1709.

127. HHSA, *Ital.-Span. Rat, Neapel, Corresp.* 194, "Giunta per la Dogana di Foggia," n. 25; esp. 25)4, 25)5, 25)6, and 25)7. De Dominicis, *Lo stato politico*, 2:329–33, with diverse documents transcribes 2:353–66; De Martino, *Lavoro istorico*, pp. 266–69 transcribes a document of 1 May 1729; Antonio Di Vittorio, *Gli Austriaci e il Regno di Napoli (1707–1744). Le finanze pubbliche* (Naples: Giannini Editore, 1969), pp. 172–75.

128. De Dominicis, *Lo stato politico*, 3:391–95 and De Martino, *Lavoro istorico*, pp. 270–75 transcribe a decree on the office of *cavallaro* in fourteen items dated 14 August 1735.

129. De Dominicis, *Lo stato politico*, 2:396–400 dated 21 May 1738.

130. *Pragmaticae edicta*, 3:250–58 and De Dominicis, *Lo stato politico*, 2:404–22 dated 10 May 1747.

131. AGS, *Estado, Dos Sicilias*, lib. 320, c. 23v (15 June 1760), and lib. 324, c. 109v (28 December 1762).

132. ASFg, *Dogana*, serie I, vol. 21, "Piante topografiche e geometriche delle ventitré locazioni del R. Tavoliere delle Puglie." Ariberto Merendi, "Il Tavoliere di Puglia nelle mappe di Agatangelo della Croce," *Archivio Storico Pugliese* 6 (1953):207–14; Raffaele Colapietra, "Ambiente e territorio della Dogana di Foggia a fine Seicento attraverso l'atlante Michele," *Studi e ricerche geografiche* 1 (1985):93–109.

133. ASFg, *Dogana*, serie I, vol. 356, n. 12628, "Atti della voce della lana del corrente anno 1779," gives 1777 wool sales: 90,411 *rubbi*, 44,192 *rubbi* exported and 46,219 remaining in the Kingdom; 1778 wool sales: 81,109 *rubbi*, 38,191 *rubbi* exported and 42,918 in the Kingdom; c. 12v claims that in normal years one-half of Puglian wool remained in the Kingdom, one-fourth was exported to the Venetian states, and one-fourth went to France.

134. Raffaele Colapietra, "Gli economisti settecenteschi dinanzi al problema del Tavoliere," *Rassegna di politica e di storia* 58 (1959):24–32; Colapietra, "Riforma e restaurazione del sistema del Tavoliere di Puglia," ibid. 60 (1960):16–22; Colapietra, "La grande polemica Ottocentesca intorno al Tavoliere di Puglia," ibid. 74 (1960):26–32 and 75(1961):21–32; Colapietra, "L'Unità d'Italia e l'affrancamento del Tavoliere di Puglia," ibid. 76 (1961):22–32 and 77(1961):17–21. Pasquale Di Cicco, *Censuazione ed affrancazione del Tavoliere di Puglia (1789–1865)*, Quaderni della rassegna degli "Archivi di Stato," no. 32 (Rome: Ministero dell'Interno, 1964); Di Cicco, "Il problema della Dogana delle Pecore nella seconda metà del XVIII secolo," *La Capitanata* 4 (1966):63–72.

135. Ferdinando Galiani, *Della moneta. Libri cinque.*, 2d ed. (Naples: Stamperia Simoniana, 1780), in his *Della moneta e scritti inediti*, ed. Alberto Merola (Milan: Feltrinelli

Editore, 1963), bk. IV, chap. 4; pp. 343–44. Eng. trans. Peter R. Toscano (Ann Arbor, Mich.: University Microfilms International, Monograph Publishing on Demand, 1977). All citations are to the Merola edition.

136. The 21 May 1806 decree is transcribed in De Martino, *Lavoro istorico*, pp. 285–89 and preserved ASFg, *Dogana,* serie 1, fas. 716.

137. Sprengel, *Die Wanderherdenwirtschaft,* p. 54 gives numbers of sheep in transhumance in modern times: 1840, 1,200,000 head; 1860, 760,000; 1877, 730,000; 1951, 400,000; and 1958, 205,000 (?). In "La pastorizia transumante," pp. 310, 322 Sprengel concludes from personal fieldwork in 1968 that 180,000–200,000 sheep were still in transhumance moving by foot, rail, and truck in about a 1:2:3 ratio. In other words, less than 10 percent of the maximum doganal capacity can still be found in transhumance, and only 36,000 sheep travel by foot.

138. In Puglia, the sheepowners held parliaments twice a year when they gathered for winter pasture in the late autumn and before leaving Foggia at the time of the spring fair. In Castile they originally held three annual meetings but limited themselves to two sessions after 1500—one in the southern plains during winter and the other in the fall before leaving summer mountain pastures. Klein, *The Mesta* pp. 49–50. In the Bardenas Real in Aragon, two *mestas* were held each year by the end of the sixteenth century, again in fall (13 November) and spring (26 April). Samenes, "Juntos y mestas ganaderos," pp. 9–10.

139. J. H. Elliott best describes the confrontation between ideal and reality in the Spanish Empire, *The Revolt of the Catalans* (Cambridge: Cambridge University Press, 1963), p. 119. Cf. his *Imperial Spain 1469–1716* (New York: New American Library, 1963).

2. The Georgics of the Tavoliere of Puglia

1. Niccola Columella Onorati, *Delle cose rustiche ovvero dell'agricoltura,* 3 vols. (1791–95) and 2d ed. rev., 10 vols. (Naples: Stamperia Flautina, 1803); Onorati, *Dell'agricoltura pratica* (cited in full in chap. 1, n. 75); Smith, *Western Mediterranean Europe,* pp. 23–26 (cited in full in chap. 1, n. 3) for a modern agricultural calendar. For the customhouse specifically, Pedro de Toledo's sixty-eight instructions (19 October 1549) (cited in full in chap. 1, n. 77); Gian Luigi di Sangro's twenty-four instructions (15 April 1563) (cited in full in chap. 1, n. 87); BNN, MS. XI.D.28, 371r–376v, "Breve notitia di quello dovrà operansi dal Dohaniero della Dohana di Foggia per invigilare al servizio di quel Real Patrimonio." For a summary of doganal space, see Pasquale Di Cicco, *La Dogana delle Pecore di Foggia. Elementi per una pianta generale del Tavoliere,* Quaderni di Foggia a cura del commune, no. 5 (Foggia: Leone, 1971).

2. Saverio La Sorsa, "La pastorizia pugliese e le sue costumanze," *Archivio "Vittorio Scioloja" per le consuetudine giuridiche agrarie e le tradizioni popolari italiane* 8–9 (1941–42), gives fullest details on division of labor, techniques like branding of sheep, costumes of shepherds, daily life, etc.

3. ADLPR cited in chap. 1, n. 116 provides statistics for ninety-two consecutive years, 1672–1763: mean number of sheep is 9,844 (with a minimum of 6,181 and maximum of 15,533); mean number of goats, 904; mean salary expenditures 1,463 ducats; mean man days of labor, 23,462; mean total employees, 87; mean full-time employees, 27; mean three-fourths-time employees, 58. This 22.7-ducat annual salary compares favorably with Onorati, *Delle cose rustiche,* 1st ed., chap. 8, p. 17, n. 14. Also see ibid., 2d ed., 3:5: one shepherd is accompanied by two dogs and paid a salary of 24 ducats per year plus the equivalent of 1 ducat in daily provisions (food, salt, oil, meat of dead sheep, milk and cheese products, pelts, etc.). Coda, *Breve discorso,* p. 94 (cited in full in intro., n. 16) gives annual shepherd salary as 20 ducats plus 13.2 ducats for bread and other provisions.

4. Smith, *Western Mediterranean Europe,* pp. 54–55; Sprengel, *Die Wanderherdenwirtschaft,* pp. 143, 147 (cited in full in chap. 1, n. 75); La Sorsa, "La pastorizia pugliese,"

pp. 8–11; Andrea A. Bissanti, "Il Tavoliere di Puglia," in Carmelo Colamonico, ed., *La casa rurale nella Puglia,* Ricerche sulle Dimore Rurali in Italia, vol. 28 (Florence: Olschki, 1970), pp. 70–91.

5. De Dominicis, *Lo stato politico* (cited in full in intro., n. 13), 1:122, item 8 of the 19 October 1549 instructions of Pedro de Toledo expand upon these restrictions.

6. Similar schedules are documented for transhumant systems in other parts of Italy: Piedmont from 1574, "Statuti di Sordevolo," cited in Grenier, "La transhumance," p. 300 (cited in full in chap. 1, n. 23) gives 8 June to 20 August as summer season, 20 August to 30 November for migration to winter pasture in graduated increments, 30 November to 1 March as winter season, and 1 March to 8 June for return to summer pasture. Padova in ASV, *Cinque Savi alla Mercanzia,* serie I, busta 472 bis, n. 8 (8 August 1758) prohibits summer descent from the mountains before 11 November and winter departure from the plains before 15 March.

7. Sprengel, "La pastorizia transumante," p. 294 (cited in full in chap. 1, n. 75). In the Spanish Mesta, sheepwalks (*cañades*) measured 830 km to Leon, and between 270 and 370 km for Segovia and La Mancha. Flocks could travel at 30 km per day in restricted sheepwalks or 10 km per day in open country. Vicens Vives, *Manual de Historia Economica,* p. 234 (cited in full in chap. 1, n. 6). Onorati, *Delle cose rustiche,* 1st ed., 3:5 states that the twenty-day journey "simulated without doubt the caravans of the Arabs."

8. ASFg, *Dogana,* serie I, vol. 3, 34r (3 February 1604); AGS, *Secretarias Provinciales, Nápoles,* lib. 71, 11 (20 June 1607); Ageta, *Annotationes,* 3:230 (25 June 1681) (cited in full in chap. 1, n. 55).

9. De Dominicis, *Lo stato politico,* 1:323, item 13 of 7 February 1574 *banno* of Fabrizio di Sangro. For a description of the physical *tratturi,* see Udo Sprengel, "Die Herdenwege auf der italienischen Halbinsel und ihre Stellung im gegenwärtigen Landschaftsbild," in C. Schott, ed., *Beiträge zur Kulturgeographie der Mittelmeerländer* (Marburg an der Lahn: Marburger Geographische Schriften, Heft 40, 1969), pp. 33–57.

10. De Dominicis, *Lo stato politico,* 1:83, item 17 of 17 December 1480 privileges conferred by Ferrante.

11. For the fine, ibid., 1:323, item 13 of 7 February 1574 *banno* of Fabrizio di Sangro; see Di Cicco, *Pianta generale,* p. 52. For the death penalty and fine, ASFg, *Dogana,* serie I, fas. 18, "Reintegrazione dei Regi Tratturi (1649–51)," 28v–30r (10 July 1575), and repeated, 30r–31r (4 March 1652).

12. The *riposi* of the Murge and the Saccione were founded during Alfonso's rule; the Montagna dell'Angelo during Ferrante's. See Musto, *La regia dogana,* p. 21 (cited in full in intro., n. 3); Caruso, *La dohana,* p. 21, n. 42 (cited in full in chap. 1, n. 26).

13. De Dominicis, *Lo stato politico* 2:82–83; Gaudiani, *Notizie,* p. 211 (cited in full in intro., n. 14); ASFg, *Dogana,* serie I, fas. 378–485.

14. De Dominicis, *Lo stato politico,* 2:81–117; Gaudiani, *Notizie,* pp. 353–65.

15. Until 1590 the doganella or *rendita delle pecore rimaste* ("income from the sheep left behind") was managed by a lieutenant nominated by the doganiero. The doganella was made up of two complex jurisdictions: the Regi Stucchi and the Poste d'Atri. Di Stefano, *La ragion pastorale,* 1:374–87 (cited in full in intro., n. 12). The Regi Stucchi were in the coldest places of the Abruzzi. About 45,000 sheep or heartier animals grazed in its forty divisions. The Poste d'Atri were divided into some twenty-five to twenty-nine posts and gave pasture to about 8,000 sheep. Sheep taxes were levied at 6.66 ducats per 100 head, i.e., one-half the regular rate in the dogana.

16. Giovanni Battista Bronzini, "Storia, strutture e funzioni delle tradizioni popolari meridionali di ambiente rurale," in *Atti del II Convegno distretti rurali e città minori* (17–19 March 1974) (Bari: Società di Storia Patria per la Puglia Convegni VIII, 1977), pp. 30–32 explains the magico-religious syncretism in the Gargano, where the cult of St. Michael the Archangel was preceded by that of the pagan, giant divinity, Gargan, who was himself a

shepherd of an enormous flock. We should also remember that the Gargano has continued its miraculous tradition into the present. The Capuchin Padre Pio (Francesco Forgione), whose stigmata was a well-publicized proof for the twentieth-century faithful worldwide, drew millions of pilgrims to San Giovanni Rotondo, where he resided from 1916 to his death in 1968.

17. On apparitions of the Virgin and pilgrim saints in Foggia—where the capital city usurps the countryside tradition, Pasquale Manerba, *Memorie sulla origine della città di Fogia e sua maggior chiesa* . . . (Naples: Presso Michele Morelli, 1798).

18. Victor and Edith Turner, *Image and Pilgrimage in Christian Culture: Anthropological Perspectives* (New York: Columbia University Press, 1978).

19. Ageta, *Annotationes*, 3:186–87.

20. Coda, *Breve discorso*, p. 37 and De Dominicis, *Lo stato politico*, 1:106 give 15,495 *carra*.

21. Coda, *Breve discorso*, pp. 37–38 and De Dominicis, *Lo stato politico*, 1:110 give 15,494 *carra*, with a 56 percent:44 percent ratio.

22. Cf. chap. 1, n. 76. ASN, *Sommaria Consultationum*, vol. 2, 12v–15v (13 March 1563). The "libri di reintegra" in Coda and De Dominicis give a 60 percent:40 percent ratio. De Dominicis, *Lo stato politico*, 1:106, 110 gives 15,495 *carra*, with a 56 percent:44 percent ratio and 558 other *carra* in litigation. Di Cicco, *Pianta generale*, pp. 25–44 gives 15,602 *carra*, with a 59 percent:41 percent ratio.

23. Cf. chap. 1, n. 81. Gaudiani, *Notizie*, p. 145 gives 41 percent pasture, 43 percent agriculture, 16 percent *terre salde*.

24. ASFg, *Dogana*, serie I, fas. 21 III, 91r.

25. Palumbo, *Tavoliere e sua viabilità*, p. 2 (cited in full in intro., n. 3).

26. Gaudiani, *Notizie*, p. 100 explains that plowed land was preferred over the virgin land (*salde*) because it provided better grass and, consequently, more cheese and healthier lambs.

27. Ibid., pp. 49–50. Grazing too high up the mountain slopes, however, made for rigorous winters.

28. Doganal thought processes operated inversely from ours. Instead of calculating how many sheep would graze on 1 *carro*, the 1548 *reintegrazione* asked ten witnesses, "How many *carra* were needed to graze 1000 sheep?" ASFg, *Dogana*, serie I, fas. 15, 6r–7r (10–18 January 1549). Why? Effective grazing did not depend on the appetite of the animals, but the quality of the pasture.

29. Calculating all other animals in terms of sheep made sheep into a kind of monetary notation. For some eighteenth-century monetary theory, Anne Robert Jacques Turgot, *Reflections on the Formation and the Distributon of Riches* (orig. ed., *Réflexions sur la formation et la distribution des richesses*, 1770), trans. William J. Ashley (New York: Augustus M. Kelley, 1971), chaps. xxxv, xxxvi, pp. 32–34: "The want of an exact correspondence between the value and the number or quantity has been made up for by a mean valuation, which becomes a sort of ideal money. In a country where there is only one race of sheep, the value of a fleece or of a sheep may easily be taken for the common measure of values, and we may easily say that a barrel of wine or a piece of stuff is worth a certain number of fleeces or of sheep." The discussion emphasizes that sheep as a measure of value is "a conventional language" and "a fictitious and abstract value" in order to clarify the inequality among commodity values and their change over time.

30. Gaudiani, *Notizie*, p. 141.

31. Giusy Laporta, "Agricoltura e pastorizia nel feudo di Monteserico nei secoli XVI e XVII," in *Problemi*, Massafra, ed. (cited in full in intro., n. 9), pp. 291–308.

32. Marino, "*Professazione voluntaria*," pp. 17–18 (cited in full in chap. 1, n. 74).

33. De Dominicis, *Lo stato politico*, 2:118–30; Bonazzoli, "L'economia agraria," pp. 148–230 (cited in full in chap. 1, n. 2) examines the role of communal land and the process of private accumulation of the commons in the *mosciali*.

34. Di Stefano, *La ragion pastorale*, 2:182–83; De Dominicis, *Lo stato politico*, 2:131–58.
35. Di Stefano, *La ragion pastorale*, 1:465–72; De Dominicis, *Lo stato politico*, 2:159–219; Gaudiani, *Notizie*, pp. 197–204.
36. Di Stefano, *La ragion pastorale*, 2:30–31; Gaudiani, *Notizie*, pp. 54–55. The importance of fennel for the shepherds' life was emphasized in the rules governing its protection and use. See, for example, item 22 in Fabrizio di Sangro's 7 February 1574 instructions (cited in full in chap. 1, n. 88).
37. De Dominicis, *Lo stato politico*, 3:31–41; Grana, *Istituzioni*, pp. 150–52 (cited in full in chap. 1, n. 20); Gaudiani, *Notizie*, pp. 165–68; Di Cicco, *Pianta generale*, pp. 22–23.
38. Granata *Economia rustica*, p. 45 (cited in full in intro., n. 16) gives 21,280 *carra* in the physical area, which would mean that the fiscal 15,645 *carra* of the 1548 cadastral survey comprised about 74 percent of the land.
39. ASFg, *Dogana*, serie I, fas. 21 III, 91r–v gives two headings: "Luoghi de' Particolari portati nelle rubriche delle Locazione," as 926 *carra* (5.0 percent), and "Altri luoghi de' Particolari oltre di sudetti," as 1,385 *carra* (7.4 percent). For the laws on private holdings, see De Meis, *Nel Tavoliere*, pp. 69–71 (cited in full in chap. 1, n. 20).
40. The consistent estimate of the *possedibile* was 1.3 million sheep. I have followed Coda, *Breve discorso*, pp. 98–102. For variant statistics, see De Dominicis, *Lo stato politico*, 1:176–77; Gaudiani, *Notizie*, pp. 51–52, 164. The normative power of the 1548 *reintegrazione* in establishing fixed limits for the *possedibile* is confirmed in BNN, MS. XI.C.46, c. 219r (15 November 1660), which gives 1,320,360 sheep from 1548 on. For the ecological limits, chap. 1, n. 75.
41. Cf. Peter J. Bowden, *The Wool Trade in Tudor and Stuart England* (London: Macmillan & Co., 1962), pp. 3–4 gives one-fourth to one-third value on the hoof for early modern English sheep as opposed to one-sixth for modern sheep, which emphasizes the greater value placed on wool then than meat now. For wool production percentages, see ASFg, *Dogana*, serie I, fas. 355, 356 "Atti della voce della lana del corrente anno [year]." For average yield, see Coda, *Breve discorso*, p. 92; Onorati, *Della cose rustiche*, 2d ed., 8:131, 155. For income see Coda, *Breve discorso*, pp. 92–93, who gives spring wool income as 32 percent of total gross income.
42. For general discussions of Puglian sheep, breeding, wool, and animal husbandry techniques for improving the breed, see Luigi Targioni, *Saggi fisici politici ed economici* (Naples: Donato Campo, 1786), pp. 43–59; Onorati, *Delle cose rustiche*, 2d ed., 8:128–73. See also De Dominicis, *Lo stato politico*, 3:109–110.
43. Gaudiani, *Notizie*, p. 262 and De Dominicis, *Lo stato politico*, 3:126 identify the three conditions by origin of summer pasture. Onorati, *Delle cose rustiche*, 2d ed., 8:146–47 claims that wool division into three categories came from Spain and corresponded to the animal's anatomy: first condition came from the back, shoulders, and neck; second condition from the sides and thighs; and third condition from the legs, underbelly, and tail. For prices, ASFg, *Dogana*, serie I, fas. 355 and 356 "Atti della voce della lana."
44. Pasquale Di Cicco, "Produzione della lana nella R. Dogana di Foggia e relativo commercio con Terra di Lavoro nella seconda metà del Seicento," *Archivio Storico Pugliese* 24 (1971):3–59 has the best summary of the mechanics of raw wool production. See also La Sorsa, "La pastorizia pugliese."
45. BNM, MS. 2659, 192r (ca. 1582/83) in a report by Ferrante Fornaro. De Dominicis, *Lo stato politico*, 3:138 cites the Roman agronomist Columella that sheep are no longer healthy and profitable after eight years. Note that normal sheep deaths averaged 15 percent per year, conforming neatly to the seven-year replacement cycle. But, male breeding sheep were replaced after two or three years to keep the stock at peak productivity.
46. I have calculated a lambing rate of 0.44 from the Doria statistics for the twenty-five years 1724–47 (chap. 1, n. 116). Antonio Silla, *La pastorizia difesa—Ove si fa una breve analisi sopra alcuni progetti intorno alla riforma della Regia Dogana di Foggia* (Naples: Stamperia

Simoniana, 1783), p. 210 gives a lambing rate of 0.45 (850 lambs per 1,900 sheep). Cf. Bowden, *The Wool Trade*, pp. 21–22 for background and English comparisons on breeding age, male/female ratio, and lambing rate, all of which varied from flock to flock and year to year. English findings are similar: on breeding age, twenty-seven months to six years; on sex ratios, three examples give 1:16, 1:20, and 1:39; on lambing rates, parameters from 0.3 to 0.95 (1.0 "rarely, if ever, achieved").

47. Silla, *La pastorizia difesa*, p. 204 gives the age/sex structure for a flock of 2,000 sheep in 1783: 1,200 sheep (60 percent) three years old or more; 350 (17.5 percent) between two and three years; 350 sheep (17.5 percent) between one and two years; 100 rams (5 percent).

48. De Dominicis, *Lo stato politico*, 3:109–110. For Doria prices, see chap. 1, n. 116.

49. The Doria account books (see chap. 1, n. 116) include a "Discarico che da al Massaro [Name] per gli animali essistenti." Again I have analyzed the data for the twenty-four-year period 1724–47. Coda, *Breve discorso*, pp. 93–95 gives a model budget for a 1,000-head flock in the seventeenth century which corroborates normal sheep demography statistics found at Melfi: 10 percent winter mortality, 5 percent summer mortality, 45 percent females fertilized. For the estimates of relative income, see chap. 9.

50. Gaudiani, *Notizie*, p. 176, n. 98; no rain fell from May to December.

51. Carlo de Cesare, *Delle condizioni economiche e morali delle classi agricole nelle tre provincie di Puglia* (Naples: Presso Tommaso Guerrero, 1859), p. 122.

52. Carlo M. Cipolla, *Before the Industrial Revolution. European Society and Economy, 1000–1700* (New York: W. W. Norton & Co., 1976) pp. 96–100.

53. ASFg, *Dogana*, serie I, fas. 42, ff. 184–87 (1755).

54. ASFg, *Dogana*, serie I, fas. 43, n. 52, 2r–v (12 January 1779).

55. ASFg, *Dogana*, serie I, fas. 36, "Notamento delle pecore, et agni morti nell' anno 14 Ind. 1560 e 1561."

56. De Dominicis, *Lo stato politico*, 2:370.

57. AGS, *Estado, Dos Sicilias*, leg. 5807, f. 61 (13 November 1736); leg. 5808, f. 11 (8 January 1737), and f. 13 (15 January 1737); leg. 5809, f. 7 (19 March 1737); leg. 5810, f. 92 (13 August 1737); leg. 5811, f. 29 (8 October 1737); leg. 5816, f. 99 (2 March 1738); and leg. 5829, f. 122 (31 March 1740) are in Spanish from the ambassador in Naples.

58. Ibid., leg. 5815, f. 58 (25 November 1738). For the grazing lands of the Tuscan *presidios*, see Braudel, *The Mediterranean*, 1:85, n. 290 (cited in full in intro., n. 1). Pastures were located on the coast and rented at 10 lire per 100 head of stock. The Tuscan *presidios* themselves were dependencies of the Spanish crown and supported by budget expenditures from Naples.

59. ASFg, *Dogana*, serie I, fas. 37 and 38 give complete accounts of individual losses, law suits, claims to regain *fida* collected, inspection of deaths to verify claims, etc.

60. Ibid., fas. 43, n. 47 (1759/60), n. 50 (1766), n. 51 (1776), n. 52 (1779), n. 53 (1782), n. 54 (1802). Giuseppe Maria Galanti, *Nuova descrizione geografica e politica delle Sicilie* (orig. ed., Naples: Soci del Gabinetto Letterario, 1786–90), ed. F. Assante and D. De Marco, 2 vols. (Naples: Edizioni Scientifiche Italiane, 1969), 2:529 claims that bad weather caused high sheep deaths four times between 1745 and 1789, but better technology and oversight would have prevented the losses.

61. Bonazzoli, "L'economia agraria," pp. 112–15, discusses Tavoliere weather; see esp. her review of the years 1788–97, taken from the records of the abbot Giuseppe Maria Giovene, *Discorso meteorologico-campestri* in *Raccolta di tutte le opere*, 3 vols. (Bari: Tipografica Fratelli Cannone, 1839–41), 2:5–278.

62. ASFg, *Dogana*, serie I, fas. 14, 3v–6r (27–28 February 1549) is copied in ibid., fas. 15; ASN, *Sommaria Diversi*, num. I, vol. 103, cc. 2–9; BNN, MS. XI.D.6, 39r–42r, and partially transcribed in Aurelio Lepre and Pasquale Villani, eds., *Il Mezzogiorno nell'età moderna e contemporanea* (Naples: Guida Editori, 1974), pp. 105–9. The 1548 *reintegrazione* text was the work of Marcello Pignone, one of the Sommaria presidents, and mentioned by

Di Stefano, *La ragion pastorale*, 1:3 as the famous "Pignone" book in the "grand archive of the Sommaria." There is a paleographic error in the transmission of the original text in the fourth respondent's testimony; fas. 14, 4v: "l'altra metà restarà in vacuo delle quale quindeci carra ne farà maiese quinde carra, et le dece resteranno vacue." This addition, five plus ten, equals fifteen. The corrupt texts, which copied fas. 15 incorrectly, transcribed *quinde carra* as *quindeci carra* and would give an addition of fifteen plus ten equals fifteen. BNN, MS. XI.D.6, 41r corrects the error by changing *quinde* to *cinque*, thus removing any doubt.

63. AGS, *Secretarias Provinciales, Nápoles*, leg. 12 (23 December 1616). In this 1616 request by a descendant, Pedro Antonio Minadois, for admission into one of the three military orders, the Minadois' history of family service is recounted in its particulars, and the family is praised as one "always most esteemed in the province of Puglia." Cf. ACA, *Privilegiorum*, reg. 3931, 57v (20 August 1518) confirmed one Antonio Minandois as doganal cashier.

64. Gaudiani, *Notizie*, p. 266 spells out the plowing and preparation of fields as a complex process requiring four separate plowings.

65. BNN, MS. XI.C.46, 219r–23r (15 November 1660) summarizes the history of land use and explains three times (220r; 221v; 222r) how a 13 March 1551 decree of the Collaterale confirmed a decree of the previous year, at the time of the cadastral survey, which changed the custom of *maiese* on the *portata* from one-third of one-half in repose to one-half of one-half. Cf. De Dominicis, *Lo stato politico*, 1:110–111, 268–69 explains the decision-making process that led to the original decree of 27 February 1550 and transcribes a revised version of 27 March 1551 (pp. 280–81). Palumbo, *Tavoliere e sua viabilità*, p. 66, n. 33 transcribes a document explaining the two-field, four-year cycle on the Tavoliere (8 November 1560). ASN, *Sommaria Partium*, fas. 544 II, 106r (16 February 1569) in which the doganiero Gian Loise di Sangro explains that land was turned over to the dogana and used as fallow every three years: "in virtù del Regio decreto generale ogni tre anni li massari de' campo si ponno permutare le terre et intrare in la parte reintegrata ad uso di duhana a fare maesi et semina in territorio." Zotta, "Momenti e problemi di una crisi agraria in uno 'stato' feudale napoletano (1585–1615)," *Mélanges de l'Ecole Français de Rome* 90, no. 2 (1978): 754 finds a proposal under discussion for this same change from what he identifies as a three-course to a two-course rotation system in a 1544 letter from the Doria estates.

66. Gaudiani, *Notizie*, pp. 267–68; Grana, *Istituzioni*, pp. 7–8; and Granata, *Economia rustica*, 2:59.

67. ASFg, *Dogana*, serie I, fas. 15, 3v, transcribed in Lepre and Villani, eds., *Il Mezzogiorno*, pp. 105–6.

68. ASFg, *Dogana*, serie I, fas. 15, 5v–6r (28 February 1549) transcribed in Lepre and Villani, eds., *Il Mezzogiorno*, pp. 108–9.

69. B. H. Slicher Van Bath, *The Agrarian History of Western Europe A.D. 500–1850*, trans. Olive Ordish (London: Edward Arnold, 1963), pp. 16–19, 21.

70. Onorati, *Delle cose rustiche*, 2d ed., 8:150. Bonazzoli, "L'economia agraria," pp. 142–43, on the contrary, cites Giuseppe Rosati, *Le industrie di Puglia* (Foggia: Presso Verrienta, 1808), p. 233 to the effect that sheep manure was more destructive than productive as fertilizer. M. L. Ryder, *Sheep and Man* (London: Duckworth, 1983), p. 735 clarifies the dung controversy: "The initial effect of fresh, concentrated dung is harmful to grass, and so the observation of its value as fertilizer must have been made on the periphery of a concentration, or on the run-off from a pen or animal house." Ryder emphasizes the high value of sheep droppings, for example, third in importance behind milk and wool, ahead of meat, in early medieval England.

71. Cipolla, *Before the Industrial Revolution*, pp. 118–22 offers a critique and amplification of Slicher Van Bath. See also Maurice Aymard, "Production et productivité agricoles: l'Italie du Sud a l'époque moderne (1450–1815)," forthcoming in *Atti* of VII International Congress of Economic History, Paris, 30 June 1977.

72. Slicher Van Bath, *Agrarian History*, p. 19.

73. Onorati, *Delle cose rustiche*, 2d ed., 3:174–75 gives grain yields in the most fertile years as 5:36, that is, 13.9 percent, almost 1:7. Silvio Zotta, "Rapporti di produzione e cicli produttivi in regime di autoconsumo e di produzione specultiva. Le vicende agrarie dello 'stato' di Melfi nel lungo periodo (1530–1730)," in *Problemi*, Massafra, ed. (cited in full in intro., n. 9), p. 227 gives 1:12, 1:8, 1:5, and 1:3 depending on land quality. Maurice Aymard, "Strutture delle aziende e studio della produzione e della produttività agricola in Italia meridionale nell'età moderna: prospettive di ricerca," in ibid., p. 23 gives 1:6 for the Jesuit *massaria* of Orta (1723–64). For Italy at large, see Aymard, "Rendements et productivité agricole dans l'Italie moderne," *Annales, E.S.C.*, 26, no. 2 (1973):475–98.

74. ASN, *Sommaria Consultationum*, vol. 2, 12v–15v (13 March 1563) is repeated in BNN, XI.B.39, c. 118r in a document, "Della Regia Dohana delle Pecore di Puglia," (ca. 1650) and again most recently by Braudel, *The Mediterranean*, 1:89. The administrative nature of this *consulta* refers to only one reason for famines; namely, soil exhaustion, and its quantitative information should be regarded with some skepticism.

75. Bonazzoli, "L'economia agraria," pp. 108–26 reconstructs the original landscape of the Tavoliere.

76. "Regime delle Precipitazione" and "Precipitazione Medie Annue," *Cartografia Ricciardi* (Rome: Consiglio Nazionale Delle Richerche, 1969) are based upon median precipitation from 1921 to 1950.

77. Ferdinando Milone, *Il Grano, Le condizioni geografiche della produzione* (Bari: Laterza, 1929), pp. 43–46. In general, cereals are greatly inferior to plants native to the Mediterranean ecological system.

78. Giovene, *Discorso*, 2:206, "Gennaio sicco, massaro ricco."

79. De Dominicis, chap. XI, "Delle semina," in his *Lo stato politico*, vol. 3, is a clear statement of agricultural procedures in the Tavoliere, esp. pp. 230–31 on kinds of grain. Granata, *Economia rustica* 1:226–27 and 2:43–50 also provides good geographical and climatic summaries of Puglia.

80. Smith, *Western Mediterranean Europe*, pp. 198–99, 206.

81. Manerba, *Memorie*, pp. 15–17. Di Stefano, *La ragion pastorale*, 1:334.

82. John Davis, *Società e imprenditori nel Regno Borbonico 1815/60* (Bari: Laterza, 1979), p. 73 cites C. Afan de Rivera, *Considerazioni sui mezzi da restituire il valore proprio a' doni che ha la natura largamente conceduto al Regno delle Due Sicilie* (Naples: Stamperia de Fibieno, 1832–42), 2:199.

83. ASFg, *Dogana*, serie I, fas. 5, 236r–v (28 January 1726) orders the two companies in Foggia on procedures and requires a detailed account book to be kept; 238r–239r (12 February 1726) gives the same order for grain deposit companies in Lucera, Manfredonia, Barletta, and Cerignola.

84. Paolo Macry, *Mercato e società nel regno di Napoli: commercio del grano e politica economica del '700* (Naples: Guida Editori, 1974), p. 496.

85. Merendi, "Il Tavoliere," pp. 210–11 (cited in full in chap. 1, n. 132) cites the earliest use of the word *tavoliere* in the documentary evidence: Ageta, *Annotationes*, 3:182–83 quotes a 27 February 1550 decree, "Verum pars territorii vocata tabulerium existens in circuitu postarum et capomandrarum non aretur"; and item 7 of Granvelle's 30 July 1574 pragmatic, "Item, quelle terre che sono state affittate vicino le poste e nelli tavolieri di quelle, cioè per due terzi di miglio distante dalla parte dinanzi e un terzo dalli lati e da dietro, e sono recadute, non si devono più affittare, ma devono insaldire." See chap. 1, n. 89.

3. Explaining Economic Expansion and Contraction

1. Grana, *Istituzioni*, p. vii (cited in full in chap. 1, n. 20).
2. John A. Marino, "I meccanismi della crisi nella dogana di Foggia nel XVII secolo," in Massafra, ed. *Problemi* (cited in full in intro., n. 9), pp. 309–20.

3. BRAH, MS. A-44, "Copia de particolari avisi havuti ultimamenti da Napoli," (1528), cc. 115r–16v is an anonymous report to the king on the disastrous state of affairs.

4. Beloch, *Bevölkerungsgeschichte*, 3:215 (cited in full in chap. 1, n. 68) gives *fuochi* information for each province. Raw data should be interpreted in light of Pasquale Villani, *Numerazioni dei fuochi e problemi demografici del Mezzogiorno in età moderna* (Naples: Istituto Grafico Italiano, 1973).

5. Alcala's *minuta* to Philip II is in AGS, *Estado, Nápoles*, leg. 1050, f. 23 (21 March 1560). BNN, MS. XI.A.22, "Cartas do la Mag.° del Rey Don Phelipe II," cc. 2v–6r (13 October 1560) is Philip's response to it and to an earlier viceregal report of 4 February 1560. BNN, MS. Branc. II.E.5, 112r–123r includes seven documents from 1561 to 1580 on the same argument of population growth and grain. See Franco Strazzullo, *Edilizia e urbanistica a Napoli dal '500 al '700* (Naples: Berisio, 1968), pp. 115–34.

6. ADLPR, scaf. 15/107, "Libro di Candela 1671 in 1692," cc. 1–2v, "Relazione di Candela," ca. 1671; banc. 21/34, "Registro per l'industrie dello Stato di Melfi (1695–1698)"; Zotta, "Momenti e problemi di una crisi agraria," pp. 717–96 (cited in full in chap. 2, n. 65).

7. Pasquale Villani, *Mezzogiorno tra riforme e rivoluzione*, 3d ed. (Bari: Laterza, 1977), pp. 1, 33.

8. Marino, "Meccanismi," p. 313.

9. Confirmation of my method can be found in Susan H. Wilson, "An Examination of California Sheep Demographic Record Sources for use in Epidemiological Studies," Master's thesis, University of California, Davis, 1977. My thanks to Calvin W. Schwabe, professor of epidemiology at Davis' School of Veterinary Medicine, for this reference and his consultation. See Marino, "Meccanismi," p. 314, n. 13 for my mathematics, and chap. 2 for a revision.

10. The classic positions are Ruggiero Romano, "Tra XVI e XVII secolo. Una crisi economica: 1619–1622," *Rivista Storica Italiana* 74 (1962):480–531 and Carlo M. Cipolla, "The Economic Decline of Italy," in *Crisis and Change in the Venetian Economy in the Sixteenth and Seventeenth Centuries*, ed. Brian Pullan (London: Methuen & Co., 1968), pp. 127–45. Note Joan Thirsk, "Agricultural Policy: Public Debate and Legislation," in *The Agrarian History of England and Wales*, vol. 2, 1640–1750: *Agrarian Change* (Cambridge: Cambridge University Press, 1985), pp. 363–64 corroborates that the effect of the declining continental supply of raw wool led to a 1614 ban on English raw wool exports that lasted for some 150 years. English manufacturers took up the slack. In 1668, the English consul in Naples claimed that the decline in the Kingdom's wool production was due to the incursion of cheap English goods. See Gigliola Pagano De Divitis, "Il Mezzogiorno d'Italia e l'espansione Inglese," *Archivio Storico per le Provincie Napoletane*, 3d. ser., 21 (1982), p. 140.

11. Ruggiero Romano, "A Florence au XVIIe siècle: Industries, textiles, et conjoncture," *Annales E.S.C.* 7 (1952), pp. 508–12. See also Cipolla, *Before the Industrial Revolution*, p. 124, 238 (cited in full in chap. 2, n. 52).

12. Domenico Sella, "The Rise and Fall of the Venetian Woollen Industry," in *Crisis and Change in the Venetian Economy*, ed. Pullan, pp. 100–26; translated from *Annales E.S.C.* 12 (1957).

13. Again cf. Thirsk, "Agricultural Policy," pp. 363–64 on England. She describes the plight of English wool sellers in the seventeenth century as follows: 1620s, low prices; 1650s, prices fell sharply; 1680s, prices fell more dramatically; 1690s, substantial recovery.

14. Felipe Ruiz Martín, "Pastos y ganaderos en Castilla: la Mesta (1450–1600)," in *La lana come materia prima*, Spallanzani, ed. (cited in full in chap. 1, n. 5), pp. 271–85, cites G. M. Jovellanos, *Informe de la Sociedad Económica de esta Corte al Real y Supremo Conseyo de Castilla en el expediente de Ley Agraria* (Madrid: en la imprenta de Sancha, 1795), pp. 41–50. Two modern historians have sorted through the complex political calculus of account books and taxation to arrive at similar conclusions. Jean Paul Le Flem, "Las cuentas de la Mesta (1510–

1709)," *Moneda y Crédito*, 121 (1972): 27–44 finds sheep and income turning points from his account books for period 1 (1511–40), period 2 (1540–63), period 3 (1563–1621), period 4 (1621–84), and period 5 (1685–1709). Carla Phillips, "The Spanish Wool Trade, 1500–1780," pp. 775–95 (cited in full in chap. 1, n. 43), finds her turning points in diverse sources of wool exports: period 1 (1500–1520s), period 2 (1520s–1582), period 3 (1582–1606), period 4 (1606–1680s), and period 5, divided into two periods of doubling (1692–1730 and 1730–80). I have also followed her analysis of Spanish market forces in periods 2 and 3. Note also that the Phillipses examine the disastrous effects upon the Spanish wool trade to the Netherlands during the Dutch Revolt. Carla Rahn Phillips, "Spanish Merchants and the Wool Trade in the Sixteenth Century," *Sixteenth Century Journal* 14, no. 3 (1983):267–68; William D. and Carla Rahn Phillips, "Spanish Wool and Dutch Rebels: The Middleburg Incident of 1574," *American Historical Review* 82 (1977):312–330.

15. Klein, *The Mesta*, pp. 139–294 (cited in full in chap. 1, n. 4) explains Mesta taxation, as does Modesto Ulloa, *La Hacienda Real de Castilla en el reinado de Felipe II*, 2d ed. (Madrid: Fundacion Universitaria Española, 1977), pp. 327–58. See also Le Flem, "Las cuentas," p. 27 and C. Phillips, "The Spanish Wool Trade," pp. 781–86.

16. Guicciardini, *Storia d'Italia*, bk. III, chap. 5, pp. 268–69 (cited in full in chap. 1, n. 59) identified this aspect of the dogana as one of the causes of renewed hostility between France and Spain during the Italian Wars.

17. Galiani, *Della moneta*, bk. 5, chap. 4, p. 304 (cited in full in chap. 1, n. 35).

18. See chap. 9, n. 85.

19. Galanti, *Nuovo descrizione*, 1:548–70 (cited in full in chap. 2, n. 60) for a balance sheet of exports and imports in 1771. Cf. Maurice Aymard, "Commerce et consommation des draps en Sicile et en Italie méridionale (XVe–XVIIIe Siècles)," in *Produzione commercio e consumo dei panni di lana (nei secoli XII–XVIII)*, ed. Marco Spallanzani (Florence: Leo S. Olschki, 1976), pp. 127–39.

20. Marino, "Meccanismi," pp. 316–17.

21. Marino, *"Professazione voluntaria,"* pp. 19–33 (cited in full in chap. 1, n. 74).

22. Ibid., pp. 20–23.

23. ASN, *Sommaria Consultationum*, vol. 2, cc. 12v–15v (13 March 1563) and 223v–24r (11 October 1567).

24. Clive Day, *A History of Commerce* (London: Longmans, Gilera & Co., 1929), p. 155 explains that the same system was used on the Royal Exchange in London in the seventeenth century. C. Phillips, "Spanish Merchants and Wool Trade," p. 280 documents *ventas de candelilla* for wool in Bruges, and in Amsterdam during the same period. In candle auctions, goods were offered with one inch of lighted candle on the desk, and prices had to be bid before the candle went out.

25. ASN, *Sommaria Consultationum*, vol. 13 I, nn. 158v–69r (8 February 1592), outlines these events with reference to earlier *consulte* of that autumn, beginning with 5 November 1591.

26. ASN, *Dipendenze della Sommaria*, vol. 25, fasc. 1, c. 17r. Out of a total 261,436.85 ducats spent on galleys, the budget of 1589/90 assigned 76,466.825 ducats of the dogana revenues for the construction of twenty-eight galleys of the Kingdom's fleet. ASN, *Sommaria Consultationum*, vol. 9, cc. 426–30r (4 July 1588) assigned 136,151.37 ducats of dogana revenues for galley expenditures in that year, 1587/88.

27. Aurelio Lepre, *Feudi e masserie, problemi della società meridionale nel 600 e nel 700* (Naples: Guida Editori, 1973), pp. 96–101.

28. HHSA, *Ital.-Span. Rat, Neapel, Vorträge* 1 (27 November 1709), n. 7 (5 August 1709). Cf. Domenico Cimaglia, *Ragionmento . . . sull'economia che la Regia Dogana di Foggia usa co' possessori armentari e congli agricoltori che profittano de' di lei campi, e su di ciò che disporre si potrebbe pel maggior profitto della Nazione e pel miglior comodo del Regio Erario* (Naples: n.p., 1783), p. 128.

29. Zotta, "Momenti e problemi di una crisi agraria," pp. 715–16 identifies eight mechanisms which "condemned Neapolitan agriculture to long-term underdevelopment: (1) structural weaknesses in the rural means of production; (2) a chronic insufficiency of capital which necessitated dependence upon mercantile capital and speculation; (3) the more privileged position of the Neapolitan capital vis-à-vis the provinces; (4) uncontrollable natural disasters (the effects of climate and disease upon both men and animals); (5) clerical and aristocratic privileges; (6) an episodic and contradictory legislative history; (7) bad harvests; and (8) the indebtedness of the agriculturists."

30. Patrick Chorley, *Oil, Silk, and Enlightenment: Economic Problems in XVIIIth Century Naples* (Naples: Istituto Italiano per gli Studi Storici, 1965), pp. 83–139; Paolo Macry, "Ceto mercantile e azienda agricola nel Regno di Napoli: il contratto alla voce nel XVIII secolo," *Quaderni storici* 21 (1972):851–909; Macry, *Mercato e società*, pp. 15–27 (cited in full in chap. 2, n. 84); and Davis, *Società e imprenditori*, pp. 66–72 (cited in full in chap. 2, n. 82).

31. ASFg, *Dogana*, serie V, regg. 1999–2551 (1623–1801), "Libri di pesatori di lana," give this formula sporadically from 1680. In 1687, 1691, 1692, 1694, and after, no entries cite actual prices.

32. Maria Nardella, "Attività creditizie e commerciali a Foggia nella prima metà del XVII secolo," in *Produzione, mercato e classi sociali nella Capitanata moderna e contemporanea*, ed. A. Massafra (Foggia: Amministrazione Provinciale di Capitanata, 1984), p. 72, n. 36.

33. See chap. 9, n. 4. Compare Castilian Mesta arrangements. Carla Phillips, "Spanish Merchants and the Wool Trade," p. 273 describes contemporary sixteenth-century criticism of advance sales contracts. Without the mechanisms of the loan, one cannot judge, but they could well be *voce* contracts. She cites Joseph Pérez, *La revolucion de las Comunidades de Castilla (1520–1521)*, trans. Juan José Faci Lacasta (Madrid: Siglo XXI de España Editores, 1977), pp. 97–100, which examines a series of 1516 observations on wool prices and contracts. The parallel monopolistic organization of buyers, one- or two-year advance contracts, and usurious complaints could not be clearer.

34. Gaudiani, *Notizie*, p. 258 (cited in full in intro., n. 14).

35. AGS, *Visítas d'Italia, Nápoles*, leg. 53:7, cc. 41–45 and 46–52.

36. AGS, *Visítas d'Italia, Nápoles*, leg. 53:8, 41 (19 June, 1582). De Dominicis, 3:193 (cited in full in intro., n. 13).

37. AGS, *Visítas d'Italia, Nápoles*, leg. 30:4, 343v–345r (1582).

38. Ibid., leg. 53:8, 41: "Talmente ch' in loro non possa nascere suspittione et trovando lo contrario ne pigliarite informatione."

39. Gaudiani, *Notizie*, chap. 18, "Della voce del pane, cascio e lana," pp. 257–63 gives a verbal description of the public price. ASFg, *Dogana*, serie I, fas. 355, "Atti della voce della lana," n. 12583 (1735) explains the mechanisms. The same personnel set the bread *voce:* fas. 2, 146r–148v (3 April 1585) and 150–151v (29 January 1586) explain that each year a committee of five (two men elected by the *generalità* of sheepowners and two by the commune of Foggia, and the doganiero) set prices for food and housing. But the commune disputed this arrangement as an infringement of its privileges. Ibid., 152r–153v (8 March 1593).

40. ASFg, *Dogana*, serie I, fas. 355, nn. 12584 and 12594, "Atti della voce . . . 1735" and "Atti della voce . . . 1745."

41. ASFg, *Amministrazione del Tavoliere. Scritture dell'Ufficio*, fas. 22, "Sulle voci del Tavoliere, 1806. Memoria per la generalità de' Locati sulle voci di lana e cacio."

42. This dual designation, *prezzo intrinseco* and *eventuale*, was common parlance. ASFg, *Dogana*, fas. 9, 171v (1 August 1787). The labor theory of value was one of the great accomplishments of Galiani's economics. See Joseph A. Schumpeter, *History of Economic Analysis*, ed. Elizabeth Boody Schumpeter (New York: Oxford University Press, 1954), pp. 188, 292–93, 300–02 for a most positive evaluation of Galiani's precocious insights. Schumpeter analyzes Galiani's "paradox of value" of 1751 as foreshadowing much later

developments like marginal utility and anticipating the value theory debate of the next century. "A little care and patience would have been sufficient to evolve from this a much more perfect body of theory than was to be presented by Adam Smith."

43. Antonio Massenzio, "Il mercato della lana in Foggia dal 1600 al 1800," Tesi di Laurea, Università degli Studi di Bari, 1963/64, p. 88.

44. Davis, *Società e imprenditori*, p. 68. Davis outlines the contradictions and criticism of the system, pp. 68–72.

45. Massenzio, "Il mercato della lana," p. 141.

46. Ibid., p. 77–78 cites a protest of the *generalità* deputies.

47. See n. 41.

48. ASFg, *Amministrazione del Tavoliere. Scritture dell'Ufficio*, fas. 22, "Progetto di Riforma sul sistema delle voci delle lane, de' formaggi, e de' cereali di Capitanata" (11 August 1827) and confirmed in three "Quadri relativo al Lavoro delle Voci delle lane de' formaggi e del pane, che si fa pel Tavoliere" (without date, ca. 1840). Note the distinction between the cereal and bread *voce*. The former applied to wheat, barley, oats, etc., and was fixed at the end of the harvest, based on high and low prices for July and August. The bread *voce*, on the other hand, was fixed for sheeppowners in Foggia in March and April and was based on bakery inventories. AGS, *Visítas d'Italia*, leg. 348:15, f. 67, "Banni dela voce del pane" (26 April 1561 and 12 April 1562).

49. Davis, *Società e imprenditori*, p. 73 cites Bianchini, *Storia delle finanze*, ed. Raffiotta, p. 256.

50. Bianchini, *Storia delle finanze*, 3d ed., p. 211 (cited in full in chap. 1, n. 18).

51. Macry, *Mercato e società*, p. 16 cities Galiani, *Della moneta* and *Pareri politici diversi*.

52. Gaudiani, *Notizie*, pp. 262–63.

53. ASFg, *Amministrazione del Tavoliere. Scritture dell'Ufficio*, fas. 22, "Quaderni relativo al Lavoro," substitutes the mean of high and low prices with the mean between the single lowest and single highest quotation.

54. ASFg, *Amministrazione del Tavoliere. Scritture dell'Ufficio*, fas. 22, "Voci della lana, del formaggio, del pane, 1852."

55. J. N. Hillgarth, *The Spanish Kingdoms 1250–1516*, 2 vols. (Oxford: Clarendon Press, 1976–78), 2:33.

56. De Dominicis, *Lo stato politico*, 1:76–80 transcribes "Prime Grazie del Re Ferdinando I," (5 December 1470), item 11.

57. Ibid., items 9 and 14 quoted in chap, 1, n. 51.

58. Ageta, *Annotationes*, 3:186–87 (cited in full in chap. 1, n. 55).

59. AGS, *Visítas d'Italia, Nápoles*, leg. 30:2, cc. 3r–8v (13 April 1583).

60. Chap. 1, n. 94 above. See Marino, *"Professazione voluntaria,"* pp. 15–19.

61. De Dominicis, *Lo stato politico*, 1:388–96; Di Stefano, 1:211 (cited in full in intro., n. 12).

62. ASFg, *Dogana*, serie I, fas. 2, 150r–151v (29 January 1586), and 152r–153v (8 March 1593).

63. Ageta, *Annotationes*, pp. 203–208.

64. De Dominicis, *Lo stato politico*, 2:8–9.

65. See chap. 2, p. 50 for a partial list of *poste fisse*.

66. HHSA, *Ital.-Span. Rat, Neapel, Collect.* 45, Zollamt in Foggia 1708–32, 2)13 (5 September 1729), 47v.

67. ASFg, *Dogana*, serie I, fas. 5, 511r–v (24 November 1735).

68. De Dominicis, *Lo stato politico*, 3:390.

69. Ibid., 3:3–4.

70. Gaudiani, *Notizie*, p. 315 quotes Tacitus, *Annals* 3.28. Translations of Tacitus are from the Loeb Classical Library, 1956, 4 vols.

4. The Graziers' Organization

1. ASFg, *Dogana*, serie I, fas. 107, n. 1738, 4r–v (10 January 1564).
2. The state administration wished to ensure that such demonstrations did not happen again. In item 18 of Viceroy Cardinal Granvelle's twenty-eight instructions of 30 July 1574 (see above, chap. 1, n. 89), the *fidati* were charged not to attend upon doganal business and justice, but to leave such matters to the *sindaci* and *procuratori* of the dogana. In 1559, 709 *locati* were registered in the *squarciafoglietti* tax rolls. AGS, *Visitas d'Italia, Nápoles*, leg. 15:5. In 1562/63, 1,374,000 sheep were reported in the dogana. De Dominicis, *Lo stato politico*, 1:293 (cited in full in intro., n. 13). With 1 shepherd employed to tend every 200 sheep, approximately 6,870 shepherds would have been in doganal service.
3. Di Stefano, *La ragion pastorale*, 1:80, 308 (cited in full in intro., n. 12).
4. The decree is transcribed in De Dominicis, *Lo stato politico*, 2:396–400 (21 May 1738) and preserved in a similar document dated one week later in ASFg, *Dogana*, serie I, fas. 109, n. 1753, 8r (29 May 1738).
5. *Pragmaticae*, 3:640–42 (cited in full in chap. 1, n. 99). For some information on the Neapolitan communes, Giovanni Muto, "Strutture e funzione finanziarie delle 'università' del Mezzogiorno tra '500 e '600," *Quaderni sardi di storia* 1 (1980):101–22.
6. Di Stefano, *La ragion pastorale*, 1:308.
7. Stefano di Stefano, "Ragioni per La Generalità de' locati ed altri sudditi della Regia Dogana della mena delle pecore di Puglia" is a legal brief on *locati* privileges printed in Naples, 11 November 1723 and preserved in the Kress Library, Harvard University.
8. Klein, *The Mesta*, p. 53 (cited in full in chap. 1, n. 4) contrasts Mesta membership with that of the Casa di Ganaderos of Saragossa whose ordinances in 1640 required citizenship in Saragossa and possession of thirty-five horses or cows, or one hundred sheep or goats.
9. Hillgarth, *The Spanish Kingdoms*, 1:279, 356; 2:191, 216, 239–40 (cited in full in chap. 3, n. 55). In 1289, a delegation of the Corts (assembly) of Catalonia collected the taxes which the assembly had voted. By 1359 the permanent delegation of the Corts became known as the *Disputació del General de Cathalunya (Generalitat)*. It eventually controlled more money than the royal treasury and had the right to defend the laws of Catalonia even against the king. The Kingdoms of Valencia and Aragon soon established institutions on the Catalan model. Similarly, the thirty-four French *généralités*, areas established in 1439 for the collection of *taille* (a tax to support the king's standing army), probably have the same late medieval origins in royal finances. Roland Mousnier, *The Institutions of France under the Absolute Monarchy 1598–1789. Society and the State*, trans. Brian Pearce (Chicago: University of Chicago Press, 1979), pp. 749–50, 755, 763.
10. Di Stefano, *La ragion pastorale*, 1:308. Domenico Aguirre, *Discursus* (Vienna: Typis Wolffgangi Schwendimann, Universitatis Typographi, 1721), pp. 8–11.
11. Di Stefano, *La ragion pastorale*, 1:308 followed Aguirre, *Discursus*, p. 10: "Quapropter Deputati Regnorum aequiparantur Viris illis Atheniensibus *Nomophylaces* nuncupatis." The *Nomophylakes* ("guardians of the laws") were Athenian magistrates who preserved the constitutionality of the laws from the late fourth century B.C. *Oxford Classical Dictionary*, 2d ed., ed. N.G.L. Hammond and H. H. Scullard (Oxford: Clarendon Press, 1970), p. 737.
12. Cf. chap. 1, nn. 20 and 32.
13. See chap. 1, n. 32 for the 1423 decree. The 23 August 1425 letter is transcribed in N. F. Faraglia, *Codice Diplomatico Sulmonese* (Lanciano: Canabba, 1888), pp. 306–7, n. 234.
14. See chap. 1, n. 51. Not only general syndics, but also particular syndics are documented from the fifteenth century. In 1479, details of the repayment of a 30,000-ducat loan mention that "twelve syndics or true men elected by the dogana" had the right to see the

accounts. ASN, *Sommaria Partium*, fas. 545, 26v (26 March 1479), and 32v (11 April 1479), which are transcribed in Spola, "Documenti," pp. 155 and 160 (cited in full in chap. 1, n. 48).

15. Gaudiani, *Notizie*, pp. 313–24 (cited in full in intro., n. 14); Grana, *Istituzioni*, pp. 229–37 (cited in full in chap, 1, n. 20). Grana gives them a different order and includes the right to sell goods to merchants—especially a wool monopoly, the right to salt, and the right of official recognition to be given to doganal *locati* only.

16. See items 9 and 14 of the 1470 *grazie*, chap. 1, p. 26.

17. For the serial record, ASFg, *Dogana*, serie V, regg. 745–1100, "Libri di squarciafogli," (1589–1788), and regg. 1101–1405, "Libri di squarciafoglietti," (1601–1805). I have chosen eleven random points for complete analysis from the serial record of *squarciafogli* in Foggia: 1591, 1604, 1619, and every twenty years thereafter: 1639, 1659, 1679, 1699, 1719, 1739, 1759, and 1779. "Libri di squarciafogli" used were reg. 747 (1591); reg. 767 (1604); reg. 795 (1619); reg. 850 (1639); reg. 876 (1659); reg. 899 (1679); reg. 933 (1699); reg. 967 (1719); reg. 1004 (1739); reg. 1044 (1759); reg. 1084 (1779). My *squarciafoglietti* statistics are taken from these *fogli* on the same principle on which the actual *foglietti* documents were drawn up.

18. Delille, *Agricoltura e demografia*, esp. pp. 103–5 (cited in full in intro., n. 2).

19. ASFg, *Dogana*, serie I, fas. 109, n. 1751, 6v (31 October 1679).

20. Silla, *La pastorizia difesa*, pp. 115–16 (cited in full in chap. 2, n. 46). My population estimate is (2,315 *locati* families + 6,000 other shepherding families) × 4.5 index number per Delille and as used on hearths / 4 million for the Kingdom in 1765 or 5 million in 1796; and 0.8 or 1.1 million for the four provinces in 1765 and 1796 respectively. See Villani, *Mezzogiorno tra riforme e rivoluzione*, p. 101 (cited in full in chap. 3, n. 7). Galasso, "Lo sviluppo demografico del Mezzogiorno prima e dopo l'unità," in *Mezzogiorno medievale e moderno* (cited in full in chap. 1, n. 106), tab. 2, p. 420 gives the shepherd population kingdomwide in 1824 as 65,045, 3.63 percent of the Kingdom's.

21. Annibale Moles, *Decisiones Supremi Tribunalis Camerae Summariae Regni Neapolis* (Naples: Egidio Longo, 1670), pp. 175–78.

22. ASFg, *Dogana*, serie V, regg. 2057–2060 (1670), 2114–2117 (1685), and 2167–2170 (1700), "Libri dei pesatori di lana."

23. De Dominicis, *Lo stato politico*, 2:276–78 describes the circumstances, while 2:299–300 and De Martino, *Lavoro istorico*, pp. 261–62 (cited in full in chap. 1, n. 20) transcribes the *banno* (24 April 1676).

24. Four different measures provide similar proportions of wealth: (1) number of locations, (2) my eleven-year *squarciafogli* survey, (3) two random years of *possedibile* sheep (1548 and 1749), and (4) averages from three random years' wool sales (1670, 1685, and 1700) as recorded by the weighers of wool.

TABLE N-1   Provincial Origins of Sheepowners

	Percentage			
	(1)	*(2)*	*(3)*	*(4)*
Abruzzo Citra	39	43	42	44
Abruzzo Ultra	30	32	25	28
Contado di Molise	13	9	18	11
Capitanata	9	10	12	8
Principato Ultra	9	6	4	5
Miscellaneous				4

Giuseppe Coniglio, "Pastori Abruzzesi in Capitanata," *Rivista Abruzzese* 20, no. 3 (1967): abstract, p. 4 arrives at the same 60–75 percent estimate based upon (1) the four doganal magistrates (*tenenze*) in Aquila, Celano, and Sulmona in the Abruzzi and Castellaneta in Basilicata; and (2) the twelve weighers of wool, three from Castel di Sangro, three from Sulmona, and six from Aquila, all in the Abruzzi. Sprengel, "La pastorizia transumante," p. 304 (cited in full in chap. 1, n. 75) calculates 75–80 percent Abruzzesi dominance.

25. ASFg, *Dogana*, serie I, fas. 109, n. 1759 (a. 1749), 23r–25r.

26. Di Stefano, *La ragion pastorale*, 1:80–81, 309. Gaudiani, *Notizie*, p. 365 made this same point: "L'industria non è forzosa, ma volontaria, e niuno spende per perdere, ma per guadagnare."

27. AGS, *Visitas d'Italia, Nápoles*, leg. 29:3, 88r–317v (Foggia, 7 May 1582); leg. 29:4, 1–318r (Foggia, 18 April 1583); leg. 30:1, 1–239r (Naples, 13 May 1583); leg. 30:1, ins. 1–115v (Foggia, 15 April 1584). Only three women, none of whom volunteered age or occupation, gave depositions. These inquiries underlined the almost exclusively male character of an institution in which sheepowners and shepherds registered in order to winter far from home without their families. Women could be *locati* since they could hold property in the dogana, but they rarely acted for themselves in person. In 1578, for example, among the 170 *locati* participating in the general parliament of 8 November, 1 woman, Julia de Nicastro, is listed, but she was represented by her son, Sempronius de Tonto of Manfredonia. AGS, *Visitas d'Italia, Nápoles*, leg. 43:28, 127r (8 November 1578).

28. ASFg, *Dogana*, serie I, fas. 7, 17r (14 January 1744) documents the founding of monasteries in the countryside with "missionaries" to teach shepherds.

29. AGS, *Visitas d'Italia, Nápoles*, leg. 43:28, 127r–137r (8 November 1578); leg. 46:1, 114r–119r (14 November 1582); 120r–124r (26 April 1583); 126r–131r (18 May 1583), but damage to the document makes it almost illegible; 132r–137v (10 November 1583).

30. Chap. 1, n. 106, "Parlamento Generale" (4–16 May 1615).

31. Di Stefano, *La ragion pastorale*, 1:309.

32. Ibid., 1:308 cited Nicolao Losaeo, *De iure universitatum tractatus* (Augustae Taurinorum: Apud Pantaleonem è Goffis, et Laurentium Vallinum socios, 1601), chap. 1 and merely translated the original, p. 5, pt. 1, chap. 2: "Universitas est plurium corporum collectio"; chap. 5: "Universitas secundum fictionem iuris repraesentat aliud diversum ab hominibus universitatis."

33. De Dominicis, *Lo stato politico*, 2:399, item 6.

34. ASN, *Sommaria Consultationum*, fas. 146, 33r–39r (29 December 1727) and fas. 168, 47v–49v (21 June 1734).

35. Di Stefano, *La ragion pastorale*, 1:309.

36. Ibid., 1:309. See John A. Marino, "The State and the Shepherds in Pre-Enlightenment Naples," *Journal of Modern History* 58, no. 1 (1986):125–42.

37. In the electoral reform of 1738, item 1; see n. 4.

38. ASFg, *Dogana*, serie I, fas. 108, n. 1740, 7r–9v (11 May 1596); n. 1742, 3r (17 May 1649); fas. 109, n. 1751, 1r (7 May 1679); fas. 108, n. 1748, 2r (26 November 1699); n. 1745, 1r (2 May 1722); n. 1743, 3r (28 May 1731); fas. 134, n. 2153, 4r (16 May 1735).

39. The representatives could be fastidious in avoiding such fines. ASFg, *Dogana*, serie I, fas. 11, 182r–183v, and 184r–v (both dated 23 December 1787) include a notarized letter from a particular syndic taken ill on the trip to Foggia and another notarized affadavit from a doctor in Chieti who recommended that his patient not risk his life "in the pernicious air of Foggia," known for the malarial swamps and infectious air along the Tavoliere coast.

40. Hillgarth, *The Spanish Kingdoms*, 2:534 points out that the nomination of one's own successors was also common practice in the Catalan *Generalitat* until a royal reform in 1493 established elections by lot in an attempt to control the deputies' unchecked power.

41. Earliest examples are found in Di Stefano, *La ragion pastorale*, 1:309–10 for the election of 1646; and ASFg, *Dogana*, serie I, fas. 3, 423r–426r for the election of 1655.
42. Di Stefano, *La ragion pastorale*, 1:310, and ASFg, *Dogana*, serie I, fas. 3, 423r (1655). Di Stefano has the same archival base at his disposal as is still conserved in Foggia, esp. serie I, fas. 107–111. If his emphasis varies from mine, the source of information is invariable.
43. ASFg, *Dogana*, serie I, fas. 3, 425r–426r (18 May 1655).
44. ASFg, *Dogana*, serie I, fas. 108, n. 1743, 6v and 13r (1731).
45. ASFg, *Dogana*, serie I, fas. 109, n. 1758, 16r–17r (17 May 1746), and fas. 110, n. 1764, 61r (3 July 1756).
46. Di Stefano, *La ragion pastorale*, 1:312–13.
47. ASFg, *Dogana*, serie I, fas. 108, n. 1748, 3r (28 November 1699).
48. HHSA, *Ital.-Span. Rat. Neapel, Corresp.*, f. 194, 25)6 (5 September 1729), pp. 89–90.
49. Ibid., p. 91.
50. HHSA, *Ital.-Span. Rat, Neapel, Collect.* 45, *Zollamt in Foggia 1708–1732*, 2)13 (5 September 1729), 39v.
51. HHSA, *Ital.-Span. Rat, Neapel, Corresp.* f. 194, 25)2 (3 August 1729).
52. Ibid., 25)3 (20 May 1729); ASN, *Sommaria Consultationum*, fas. 149, 190r–192r (21 May 1729), and 197v–200v (25 May 1729).
53. ASN, *Sommaria Consultationum*, fas. 163, 160v–163r (11 December 1732).
54. ASFg, *Dogana*, serie I, fas. 110, n. 1764, 55r–67v (3 July 1756). This same problem was repeated in the election of 5 May 1800 (fas. 134, n. 2154, 43r). Because one deputy was sick, a second died, and a third was unfamiliar with doganal affairs, a new election was held in 1801.
55. Di Stefano, *La ragion pastorale*, 1:311. On the uncertainty of the Mosca family's place of origin, Moles, *Decisiones*, p. 176 named one Manano de Moscio, which is repeated by Colapietra, "Vicende storiche," p. 23 (cited in full in chap. 1, n. 18) as the Mosca family.
56. ASFg, *Dogana*, serie I, fas. 3, 425r–426r (18 May 1655).
57. Di Stefano, *La ragion pastorale*, 1:310–311.
58. ASFg, *Dogana*, serie I, fas. 108, n. 1742 (1649), 4r.
59. Di Stefano, *La ragion pastorale*, 1:309. The 1646 banns are not extant. Similar banns, however, are preserved in ASFg, *Dogana*, serie I, fas. 108, n. 1745 (1722), 1r: "Deputati in persone de soggetti abili, idonei, ed integrita a sodisfatione delli locati"; and n. 1743 (1731), 3r: "Deputato in persone abili, idonee, e timorose di Dio per il buon governo di detta Generalità." See also an earlier document, undated, but probably ca. 1710, at the beginning of the Austrian period, HHSA, *Ital.-Span. Rat, Neapel, Collect.* 45, *Zollamt in Foggia 1708–1732*, 2)9 "Copia di Rapresentation fatta da Locati della Regia Dohana di Foggia." Abuse no. 5 concerns irregularities in syndic elections and specifies procedures and qualifications for particular syndics in order to elect general deputies who "ought to be Barons, Gentlemen, and Doctors of Law" (2r–v).
60. Di Stefano, *La ragion pastorale*, 1:311.
61. ASFg, *Dogana*, serie I, fas. 109, n. 1751 (1679), 3r–v.
62. ASFg, *Dogana*, serie I, fas. 108, n. 1745, 37v–38v (16–30 May 1722). Di Stefano, *La ragion pastorale*, 1:314 limits unauthorized syndic expenditures to 100 ducats.
63. De Dominicis, *Lo stato politico*, 2:398.
64. ASFg, *Dogana*, serie I, fas. 108, n. 1740, 7r–9v (12 May 1596).
65. Bucciarella had already been involved in doganal investment and politics for almost twenty years. As a witness during the royal visit of Lope de Guzmán in 1582, Bucciarella declared that he first had doganal experience at the age of twenty-eight in 1577. AGS, *Visítas de Italia, Nápoles*, leg. 29:3, cc. 239v–40v (22 April 1582).
66. ASFg, *Dogana.*, serie V, n. 751 (29 November 1595).

NOTES TO PAGES 103–8   331

67. Ibid., serie I, fas. 108, n. 1750, 1 bis–28v (16–21 May 1682).
68. Ibid., serie V, n. 901 (1681/82).
69. Ibid., serie I, fas. 108, n. 1745, 4r–v (1722).
70. Ibid., 8r–35r (13–14 May 1722).
71. Ibid., serie V, n. 971 (1721/22).
72. Ibid., serie I, fas. 109, n. 1753, 12r–13r (1738); 83r–v (1741); 104v–105r (1743); n. 1758, 22r–23r (1746); n. 1753, 142v–143v (1747); 150r–v (1748); n. 1760, 3r–v (1749); n. 1753, 176r–v (1751); 189r–v (1754).
73. Ibid., n. 1753, 176r–v (1751); serie V, n. 1025 (1750/51).
74. Ibid., serie I, fas. 109, n. 1753, 190r–197v (21 December 1754).
75. Di Stefano, *La ragion pastorale,* 1:314.
76. The following ordinary examples are taken from four syndic budgets, ASFg, serie I, fas. 107, n. 1739 (1569), 13r–21v (beginning 26 April 1567) and 30r–31v (18 May 1569); fas. 108, n. 1740 (1598), 22v–28v (beginning 6 June 1597) and 211r–213r (29 May 1599); fas. 109, n. 1756 (1741), 144r–156r (May 1738–May 1741); fas. 110, n. 1766 (1757), 4r–22r (June 1749–May 1756).
77. Ibid., fas. 107, n. 1738, 4r–v (10 January 1564), items 6 and 7.
78. Ibid., fas. 108, n. 1740, 212v (1596/97).
79. Ageta, *Annotationes,* 1:233 (cited in full in chap. 1, n. 55) cited in De Stefano, *La ragion pastorale,* 1:314 quotes a *relazione* prepared by Nicolas Gascon, a president of the Sommaria and regent of the Collateral Council, 25 June 1681: "Los credencieros procuraron la intercadencia del pagamento para tener los Diputados mas desarmados contro la libertad de sus operacione." AGS, *Secretarías Provinciales, Nápoles,* lib. 71, 36v (1644) gives 770 ducats.
80. ASFg, *Dogana,* serie I, fas. 109, n. 1751, 6r–v (31 October 1679).
81. Di Stefano, *La ragion pastorale,* 1:316 cites an unpreserved document of 27 May 1697 claiming 600 ducats *franchi* income in 1697 and merely asserts his 1730s figure. It is possible that 1697 was a typographical error for 1679. See also De Dominicis, *Lo stato politico,* 3:407–8 and two documents transcribed 3:418–420 (5 August 1740 and 20 April 1780). ASFg, *Dogana,* serie I, fas. 10, 264r–265r (31 August 1780) explains how the monopoly worked. The monopoly was not free of frauds, however. A 1611 order claims that the commune of Foggia was licensed to sell wine to *locati* and *fidati* in a public place outside the walls of the city, but that citizens of Foggia were buying it illegally. They were to be fined 15 *carlini* for the first offense and four times that, 6 ducats, for the second. Ibid., fas. 307, n. 10980.
82. Ibid., fas. 110, n. 1766 (1757), 4r: sheep, 2,500 ducats (46.6 percent); *franchi,* 2,400 ducats (44.7 percent) at 800 ducats per year for three years, seemingly contradicting Di Stefano; *scomissioni,* 158 ducats (2.9 percent); and salt, 311 ducats (5.8 percent). The rate of the salt tax was 12 *carlini* per *tomolo* on 260 *tomoli.*
83. De Dominicis, *Lo stato politico,* 2:318–30.
84. ASFg, *Dogana,* serie I, fas. 109, n. 1756 (1739–41), 153v.
85. Ibid., n. 1756 (1741), 109r.
86. Di Stefano, *La ragion pastorale,* 1:313–14. In 1702, 82, 165.27 *rubbi* of wool were sold in Foggia. ASFg, *Dogana,* serie V, regg. 2175–2178.
87. ASFg, *Dogana,* serie I, fas. 108, n. 1744 (1728), 4r. HHSA, *Ital.-Span. Rat, Neapel, Corresp.,* f. 194, 25)6 (5 September 1729), 87–89 records a number of *donativi* financed by the Lesina and Castiglione rent. In 1719, for example, 10,000 ducats given to the king were opposed by more than 100 *locati* and all the particular syndics. As a rule, the *locati* preferred to give 5,000 rather than 8,000 ducats.
88. ASN, *Sommaria Consultationum,* fas. 149, 203v–206r (24 May 1729) provides an example of a *generalità* initiative to intervene in the case of two *locati* who were jailed contrary to doganal law and to assert the *locati* right of exemption on bread gabelles.

89. See chap. 1, nn. 89, 90.
90. See n. 74.
91. BNM, MS 2857, "Itinerario del Reyno de Napoles di tutto lo circuito del Regno cominciando dalla prima terra di marina, et circuendo tanto il mare come la terra fatto l'anno 1559," f. 105v, "Itinerario da Napoli a Foggia/Manfredonia."
92. AGS, Visítas d'Italia,Nápoles, leg. 46:1, 120r–124r (26 April 1583).
93. Giovanni Muto, "Forme e contenuti economici dell'assistenza nel Mezzogiorno moderno: il caso di Napoli," in Timore e carità. I poveri nell'Italia moderna, ed. G. Politi, M. Rosa, F. della Peruta (Cremona, 1982), p. 251, n. 59. Among the new hospitals were Santa Maria della Vittoria (1572), which associated itself with the Spanish hospital of San Giacomo degli Spagnuoli (1540) in 1590; and the Genoese hospital, San Giorgio dei Genovesi (1587). The older hospitals of the Santissima Annunziata (before 1343), the Incurabili (1522), and San Giacomo were described among the "diverse institutions" of the Kingdom in Guzmán's 1581 visit. AGS, Visítas d'Italia, Nápoles, leg. 24:3, 11r–46r.
94. Other loans reported in the generalità budgets yielded higher rates: 6 percent on 250 ducats in 1569 yielded 15 ducats; 5 percent on 3,200 ducats in 1607 yielded 160 ducats; and 8 percent on 400 ducats in 1751 yielded 32 ducats.
95. AGS, Secretarías Provinciales, Nápoles, leg. 235, which is transcribed in Coniglio, Dogana di Foggia nel secolo XVII (cited in full in chap. 1, n. 96), p. 54.
96. ASFg, Dogana, serie I, fas. 108, n. 1740, 201r–v and 211r–213r vary slightly in their totals.
97. These charges compare favorably with the 1569 exchange rate of 1.56 percent on 3,500 ducats for a 55-ducat cost, and a 1607 rate of 1.3 percent on 3,000 ducats for 40 ducats. The remaining 1,085.9-ducat expenditures fit neatly into the normal syndic budget range, and they were spent according to the usual categories: charity, services, transport, salaries, and miscellaneous.
98. If we divide the amount of grain by the estimated 7,500 shepherds in the late sixteenth century, average cereal consumption would be 1.5 tomoli of wheat and 1.34 tomoli of barley per head. Given that shepherds were resident in the Tavoliere for only about seven months, from November through May, and that they could readily supplement cereals with animal products, the 2.85-tomoli grain allowance per head approximates the agriculturists' consumption of five tomoli per head per year ($7/12 \times 5 = 2.9$). Angelo Massafra, "Orientamenti colturali, rapporti produttivi e consumi alimentari nelle campagne molisane tra la metà del Settecento e l'Unità," in Problemi, Massafra, ed. (cited in full in intro., n. 9), pp. 423–24 documents agriculturists' diet at 5 tomoli of wheat and maize. In 1597 the weight of a loaf of wheat bread was 94 grana, while the mixed loaf of wheat and barley weighed 69 grana. ASFg, Dogana, serie I, fas. 108, n. 1740, 196r–v (13 May 1597).
99. Zotta, "Momenti e problemi di una crisi agraria," p. 784 (cited in full in chap. 2, n. 65) has a lacuna for current wheat prices at Melfi in 1596/97, but given his table of comparative prices (the voce price rose from 120 to 150 grana), prices should have been 25 percent higher than the 2.1–3.0 ducat range given for 1591–92. In other words, the generalità's grain purchase was at the low end of the inflated famine rates.
100. ASFg, Dogana, serie I, fas. 108, n. 1741, 1r–v (26 November 1606).
101. The regular squarciafoglietto of 1606/07 (ASFg, Dogana, serie V, reg. 1103), which was prepared earlier in November before this agreement, reflects the change in taxing procedure. Many new numbers are penned on top of the original figures. The grand inflation of sheep numbers bid (professazione voluntaria) in the first decade of the seventeenth century thus is convincingly explained as imaginary sheep (pecore in aerea), which were counted in the doganal tax notation to compensate for the high price of grain at this time of famine. Cf. Marino, Professazione voluntaria, pp. 23–29 (cited in full in chap. 1, n. 74).
102. AGS, Estado, Nápoles, leg, 1103, f. 135 (24 August 1606); leg. 1104, f. 8 (5 January 1607), and f. 12 (8 January 1607) attest to the city's needs. Increased population demanded 350,000 tomoli of wheat above the 960,000 tomoli procured. Puglian contracts

delivered only about 20 percent of the total need. Imports from outside the Kingdom (Germany, Flanders, France, Lombardy, England), therefore, were contracted at prices from 21 to 28 *carlini* per *tomolo* to meet the shortfall.

103. AGS, *Visítas d'Italia, Nápoles,* leg. 114:3, 72r–74r (10 September 1608).
104. Ibid., leg. 114:2 2d num., 74r–v (8 May 1609).
105. Di Stefano, *La ragion pastorale,* 1:315–16.
106. Ibid., 1:83: "una Republica, dee specialmente mirarsi all'abbondanza delle cose."
107. Ibid., 1:314.
108. For a comparative analysis of this aspect of Mediterranean pastoral societies, see Jane Schneider, "Of Vigilance and Virgins: Honor, Shame, and Access to Resources in Mediterranean Societies," *Ethnology* 10 (1971):1–24.
109. Gaudiani, *Notizie,* pp. 308–9.
110. AGS, *Estado, Nápoles,* leg. 1028, f. 7 (February 1538) is Toledo's request to the king for confirmation of office to Figueroa. In a *relazione* on the state of the dogana (ibid., leg. 1025, f. 84 [20 August 1539], chap. 1, n. 71), Figueroa recounted the episode, including further details on the terms of the 3,000-ducat loan at 12 percent which he incurred to pay back the *locati.* See also, ASN, *Sommaria Diversi* I, fas. 54, n.n. 1v–3r (26 February 1539).
111. ASFg, *Dogana,* serie I, fas. 3, n.n. 189r–191v (13 July 1627), and 298r–300r (1649) on a similar case.
112. ASN, *Sommaria, Carte Reali,* fas. 14, 880r–881r (27 October 1699) outlines judicial procedures. Ibid, fas. 15, 151r–152v (24 November 1699) names Longo to succeed Freda. ASFg, *Dogana,* serie I, n. 1747 (1699/1700), 3r gives the *locati* parliament's purchase. Ibid., Biblioteca, MS. 1030, int. 1, 2, and 3 are three printed documents of charges (18 July 1700, 5 February 1702, and 6 April 1702). ASN, *Dipendenze della Sommaria,* serie II, fas. 63/167, 9r–13r (27 November 1716) traces *credenzieri* abuses back from Freda and Giordano to the 1650s.
113. D'Agostino, *Parlamento e società,* pp. 126–27 (cited in full in chap. 1, n. 61).
114. De Martino, *Lavoro istorico,* pp. 242–43, 27 August 1646.
115. Ageta, *Annotationes,* p. 234. In the 1660s the deputies "with tears of blood" asked for the removal of one of these Sommaria presidents, Stefano Carrilo y Salzedo, because they could not negotiate with him since he had treated one of the deputies badly. BNN, MS. XI.B.26, 219r.
116. ASFg, *Dogana,* serie I, fas. 108, n. 1742, 1r (1649).
117. Di Stefano, *La ragion pastorale,* 2:457.
118. Ibid., 2:458–59 cites subsequent decrees upholding the shepherds' right to bear arms in 1547 (preserved in ASFg, *Dogana,* serie I, fas. 2, n.n. 140r–41v [5 November 1547]); in 1574 (item 15 of Fabrizio di Sangro's, 7 February 1574 constitution); by related decrees of 1604, 1607, 1608, 1610, and 1611 (two of which are preserved in ASFg, *Dogana,* serie I, fas. 3, n.n. 46r [20 December 1610], and 47r–48r [31 January 1611]); in 1617; in 1649; and by the 1668 pragmatic. Thereafter, this privilege continued to be defended. See the memorials in ASFg, *Dogana,* serie I, fas. 4, 291r–v (19 October 1686), and 308r–v (1 March 1687); De Dominicis, *Lo stato politico,* 3:417–18 (12 February 1749); and ASFg, *Dogana,* serie I, fas. 11, n.n. 162r–v (30 November 1787).
119. Di Stefano, *La ragion pastorale,* 2:457 quotes Virgil, *Georgic* 3:343–48. English translation is from Virgil, *The Georgics,* trans. Robert Wells (Manchester, England: Carcanet New Press, 1982), p. 72.

5. The Conflict between Rich and Poor

1. Mesta social stratification has been an issue of contention since the formative study of Klein, *The Mesta,* p. 60 (cited in full in chap. 1, n. 4). From one piece of fragmentary evidence of 1561, Klein maintained that the Mesta was an egalitarian institution not

dominated by large holders: 638 owners claimed 53,451 sheep, with 67 percent of the sheep in flocks of under 100 head and only 11 percent in flocks of over 1,000. Vicens Vives, *Historia Economica*, p. 236 (cited in full in chap. 2, n. 7), on the other hand, argues for extraordinary large holder influence. Nina Mickun, *La Mesta au XVIIIe siècle* (Budapest: Akadémia Kiadó, 1983), p. 171 calculates that in 1780, 2.25 million Mesta sheep in transhumance were held as follows: 90 percent of graziers held 32 percent of the sheep in flocks of under 300 head, 6.5 percent of graziers held 16 percent of the sheep in flocks of from 301 to 1,000 head, and 2.5 percent of graziers held 52 percent of the sheep in flocks of over 1,000 head.

2. Gaudiani, *Notizie*, pp. 231–32 (cited in full in intro., n. 14) outlines the manner in which *professazioni* were recorded. De Dominicis, *Lo stato politico*, 1:388–89 (cited in full in intro., n. 13) explains how a society of investors might combine their sheep under the name of one of their number, but in the global tax lists, all members of the *collettiva* would be listed with their share. ASFg, *Dogana*, serie I, fas. 3, 34r (3 February 1604) defined *padroncelli* as those possessing at least 20 sheep. Cf. chap. 2, n. 8, where 20 sheep or more are required to engage in transhumance and chap. 4, n. 18, where 80 sheep are needed to provide for a family of four. The same ratio, no mere coincidence, is used to define subsistence, *padroncelli* status, and transhumance—20 sheep per person.

3. Gaudiani, *Notizie*, pp. 232–33 explains the difference between *pecore reali fisse* and *pecore in alia tantum*. Item 8 in "Pubblico Istrumento" (25 November 1615)—see chap. 1, n. 106—requested that the *professazione* be the "true number" of sheep and assessed a fine to those *locati* not professed by 1 November.

4. AGS, *Visitas d'Italia, Nápoles*, leg. 15:15, "Locazione dela Regia doana dele pecore di puglia, 1559/60." One 1495 *squarciafoglio*, ASN, *Dipendenze della Sommaria*, serie II, fas. 62/152, "Registro della Fida delle Pecore della Dogana di Foggia," has not been included for analysis because of its early date.

5. The *credenziero* reported in 1581 that the *locazioni particolari* or *dei ricchi* pastured the sheep of "los titulados Barones, y otros particulares los mas ricos, y potentes." Ageta, *Annotationes*, 3:188 (cited in full in chap. 1, n. 55).

6. HHSA, *Ital.-Span. Rat, Neapel, Vorträge* 1 (27 November 1709), n. 3 (10 August 1709) reports on seventeen abuses and remedies compiled by the doganal governor, Andrea Guerrero. Item 1 examines the problem of double and multiple listing. It orders that only single location professions should be allowed, as was originally intended.

7. For the eleven global tax lists analyzed at fifteen- and twenty-year intervals, see chap. 4, n. 17. In addition, the following "Libri di squarciafogli" were used for the eight-location sample at five-year intervals: ASFg, *Dogana*, serie V, reg. 750 (1595); reg. 755 (1599); reg. 772 (1609); reg. 785 (1614); reg. 808 (1624); reg. 824 (1628); reg. 837 (1634); reg. 859 (1644); reg. 865 (1649); reg. 868 (1654); reg. 882 (1665); reg. 888 (1669); reg. 895 (1674); reg. 906 (1684); reg. 914 (1690); reg. 923 (1694); reg. 938 (1704); reg. 949 (1709); reg. 958 (1715); reg. 976 (1724); reg. 987 (1729); reg. 996 (1734); reg. 1015 (1744); reg. 1022 (1749); reg. 1034 (1754); reg. 1053 (1764); regg. 1063 and 1064 (1769); reg. 1074 (1774); reg. 1093 (1784). Again my abbreviated tax list statistics are taken from these *fogli* on the same principle as that on which the actual abbreviated tax list documents were drawn up. My eight sample locations, as discussed in chap. 2, were Lesina, Arignano, Orta, Ordona, Cave, Salpi, Trinità, and Canosa.

8. Marino, *"Professazione voluntaria,"* pp. 23–30, 39–40 (cited in full in chap. 1, n. 74). On the crisis of 1619–22, see above, chap, 3, n. 10.

9. A. B. Atkinson, *The Economics of Inequality* (Oxford: Clarendon Press, 1975), pp. 15–17.

10. Brian Spooner, *The Cultural Ecology of Pastoral Nomads*, An Addison-Wesley Module in Anthropology, no. 45 (Reading, Pa.: Addison-Wesley, 1973) provides a model of

pastoral society from an overview of the literature, esp. pp. 9–12, 23–25 on herd composition and social organization.

11. ASFg, *Dogana,* serie I, fas. 9, 81r–82r (10 May 1764).

12. For the 2,000-sheep definition of larger holders, see Gaudiani, *Notizie,* p. 231, who cites item 21 of the sixty-eight items in the "Istruzzioni de Don Pietro de Toledo," (19 October 1549) cited above, chap, 1, n. 77. See also item 6 in Fabrizio di Sangro's 7 February 1574 order, chap. 1, n. 88. Onorati, *Delle cose rustiche,* 2d ed., 8:10 (cited in full in chap. 2, n. 1) gives 3,000. In England large flocks had a legal limit of 2,400 head after 1533 ("'Two thousand' counted in long hundreds of 120"). Bowden, *The Wool Trade,* pp. 1–2, 111 (cited in full in chap. 2, n. 41). For the 200-sheep definition of individual small holders, see ASFg, *Dogana,* serie I, fas. 15 (1548–51) *Reintegrazione Generale,* c. 6r (10 January 1549), which gives one *brancolo* of sheep, that is, the number that one shepherd could care for, as 220 head. Similarly, a document mentioned in Di Stefano, *La ragion pastorale,* 1:3 (cited in full in intro., n. 12), the "Pecorologia" of Giovanni Battista Hogeda (1567), which is included in BNN, MS. XI.D.6, 377–405v, 401r gives flock size for a *morra* of sheep to be 320 in a large place, 200 in a constricted place. Onorati, *Delle cose rustiche,* 2d ed., 8:9 gives 300 head. A note on my statistical choices is in order. Using 3,000 sheep to define large holders would only skew the results toward middling holders, while using 220 or 300 sheep to define small holders would be an insignificant change (because of the small numbers involved) slightly increasing the ranks of the small holders. If graziers with exactly 2,000 sheep (both *padroni* alone and all *locati* in the global tax lists) counted as large rather than middling holders, the change in category of wealth is less than 5 percent in all years except 1679, when the difference is 5.1 percent for *padroni* alone and 5.7 percent for all *locati.* Since 1679 is a transitional year during the slow change from period 3 to period 4, this discrepancy fulfills our expectations that 1679 can fit into either period 3 or period 4.

13. Spooner, *Cultural Ecology of Pastoral Nomads,* p. 10 cites Warren W. Swidler, "Some Demographic Factors Regulating the Formation of Flocks and Camps among the Brahui of Beluchistan," in *Perspectives in Nomadism,* ed. W. G. Irons and N. Dyson-Hudson (Leiden: Brill, 1972), p. 74 among the Brahui in West Pakistan with 250- to 500-head flocks; and Fredrik Barth, "Capital, Investment and the Social Structure of a Pastoral Nomad Group in South Persia," in *Capital, Saving and Credit in Peasant Societies,* ed. R. Firth and B. S. Yamey (Chicago: Aldine, 1964), p. 71 among the Bassari in south Persia with 200 to 400. J. K. Campbell, *Honor, Family, and Patronage: A Study of Institutions and Moral Values in a Greek Mountain Community* (Oxford: Clarendon Press, 1964), p. 19 gives 250 animals per flock. Sprengel, "La pastorizia transumante," p. 312 (cited in full in chap. 1, n. 75) found flocks of 300–400 head, with reunions of 500–700, but rarely 100–150, for the present-day area of the dogana in the Abruzzi and Tavoliere during his research in 1967/68. Delille, *Agricoltura e demografia,* pp. 103–4 (cited in full in intro., n. 20) cites Jean Cuisenier, *Economie et parenté. Essai sur les affinités de structure entre système économique et système de parenté* (Paris: Mouton, 1975) among the Turkish populations in Anatolia with flocks of 80–100 minimum, which united to form more stable groups of between 400 or 500 and 600 head. Bruno Anatra, "Agricoltura e allevamento nella Sardegna del XVII secolo," *Quaderni sardi di storia* 3 (1981–83):92–93, 110–113 gives 289 sheep as the mean flock size in four towns between 1658 and 1662.

14. Spooner, *Cultural Ecology of Pastoral Nomads,* p. 10 cites Barth, "Capitol," p. 71 on the adverse consequences of hired labor: "A recognized consequence of this [hired labor] is somewhat less careful herding and more frequent losses, as well as a continual pilfering of the produce. The larger the total number of animals, the less effective is the owner's supervision of his shepherds, and the greater is the decrease in the rate of income." The general principle favors smaller units of production: "The rate of income decreases with increased capital." For early modern Europeans, Cervantes drew upon this same belief. Hired shepherds raided their own flock and told their employer that wolves had stolen the sheep during the night in "The

Colloquy of the Dogs," in *Three Exemplary Novels*, trans. Samuel Putnam (London: Cassell and Co., 1952), pp. 125–217. Remember Onorati's proverb, "Terra poca, terra assai: Terra assai, terra poca," and "Loda i gran campi, e il piccolo coltiva," in *Dell'agricoltura pratica*, p. 206 (cited in full in chap. 1, n. 75).

15. Delille, *Agricoltura e demografia*, pp. 105–8 demonstrates that the overall volume of production would not be an accurate measure of the amount of work expended, but that "the fundamental problem of agricultural societies . . . was . . . the efficiency of work."

16. Bowden, *The Wool Trade*, pp. 2–3 corroborates that, in sixteenth and seventeenth century England, not only were management costs lower for the large graziers; but also purchase costs, pasture acquisition, and sales contracts for wool were to their advantage.

17. Delille, *Agricoltura e demografia*, pp. 104–6, cites the 1811 statistics for Calabria Citra in U. Caldora, "La 'Statistica' murattiana del Regno di Napoli: le relazioni sulla Calabria," *Quaderni di geografia umana* (Università di Messina) 5 (1960):1–107. Some 1,374 shepherds cared for 94,600 sheep, that is, 1 man per 69 head. The 23 largest holders, however, controlled 70 percent of the sheep for a mean herd size of 2,800 each. Similarly, his own research in the Calabria holdings of Baron Barracco (1858–64) found 23 salaried employees for 4,600 sheep, about 1 man per 200 animals. My own investigations come up with similar results. On the Doria estates at Melfi (1672–1763), mean statistics reveal 9,844 sheep with 87 salaried shepherds working at least 270 days (27 full time; 58 three-fourths time), that is, 1 man per 365 sheep during seasonal inactivity, 1 per 170 sheep for 270 days per year, and 1 per 113 sheep during peak labor periods such as shearing. For Doria archival sources see chap. 1, n. 116. Onorati, *Della cose rustiche*, 2d ed., 8:10 gives 7 shepherds for 1,000 sheep, that is, 1 per 143 head. But for Tudor England, Bowden, *The Wool Trade*, pp. 1, 18 gives two examples of large holders breaking up their nontranshumant flocks into subherds. In 1521 a holding of 15,500 sheep was divided into twenty flocks; that is, a 775-head mean; and in the mid sixteenth century a holding of 10,000 sheep was divided into fourteen flocks for a 714-head mean.

18. The mean flock size in each category is roughly double that in the preceding lower one. Only the 1–50-head category among all *locati* (because of the low *professazione* of escaping vassals) exceeds the −12.8 percent maximum deviation from the doubling rule found in the other categories.

19. Marino, *Professazione voluntaria*, pp. 33–34 disproved their importance by constructing an hypothetical model that all *locati* in 1604 were escaping vassals according to the numerical criteria presented by the baronial complaint of 1586. More realistically, even if all smallest holders were these "imaginary" sheepowners, they accounted for less than 5 percent of doganal wealth and, despite their numbers, were relatively insignificant.

20. Note that little difference (−6.7 percent) between mean flock size in either measure—all *locati* or *padroni* only—ensures the validity of this comparison.

21. See n. 1; Klein gives the 1561 evidence. I have applied Mickun's questionable method of using the simple mean to calculate social stratification from her source, *Memorial ajustado del expediente de Concordia que trata el Honrado Consejo de la Mesta . . .* , 2 vols. (Madrid: B. Roman, impresor de La Real Academia de Derecho Español y Publico, 1783), 2: planos 1–7. Some 3,492 out of 8,299 graziers held flocks of under 50 head for a total of 119,212 out of 2,185,525 sheep. On her method, cf. my review in *Journal of Modern History* 58, n. 3 (1986):748–51.

22. The formula for the hypothetical category of adjusted sheep is:

adjusted sheep = *reali fisse* + (*in alia* × 32/132),

where 32/132 equals the state's tax after the rebate. An easier equation is within 1 percent of the accurate method of calculation:

adjusted sheep = *reali fisse* + (*in alia*/4).

23. Rosario Villari, *La rivolta antispagnoli a Napoli. Le origini, (1585–1647)*, 2d ed. (Bari: Laterza, 1973). Cf. Fernand Braudel, "L'Italia fuori d'Italia," esp. "Spiegare il caso di

Napoli," in *Storia d'Italia,* ed. Ruggiero Romano and Corrado Vivanti (Turin: Einaudi, 1974), vol. 2, pt. 2, 2231–33.

24. From his *Crisis of the Aristocracy 1558–1641* (London: Oxford University Press, 1965), Lawrence Stone has made the precarious nature of family inheritance a cornerstone of our understanding of early modern European elites. Between the sixteenth and nineteenth centuries, only about one family in three could transfer its inheritance from father to son through the course of a century. The seventeenth century was the most hazardous of all to navigate.

25. ASN, *Monasteri Soppressi,* 2437 (V), gives sheep numbers: 1610, 2,233; 1614, 2,805; 1643, 1,352; 1645, 1,429; 1657, 2,682; 1659, 2,272; 1660, 2,306; 1666, 2,001; 1688, 4,069; 1749, 6,271; 1756, 4,722.

26. Lepre, *Feudi e masserie,* pp. 123, 132 (cited in full in chap. 2, n. 27).

27. See chap. 1, n. 116.

28. Lepre, *Feudi e masserie,* pp. 94–96.

29. Ibid., pp. 106, 157, 168. The 1683, 1686, 1687, 1688 average is deceptive because less than 1 percent of the normal 80+ percent cereal income in 1688 was recorded. Animal income ran at an absolute level which would have been equal to about 5 percent, the mean in a normal year at that time.

30. Ibid., pp. 158, 173.

31. Item 15 in the "Pubblico Istrumento" of 25 November 1615; see chap. 1, n. 106. The narrative thread for this third period is elaborated in De Dominicis, *Lo stato politico,* 2:7–17 and Musto, *La regia dogana,* pp. 43–50 (cited in full in intro., n. 3).

32. AGS, *Secretarías Provinciales, Nápoles,* lib. 71, ff. 14v–15v (12 December 1619).

33. The 1629 agreement itemized fifty-nine specific concessions. It is preserved in BNN, Branc. V.C.10, 2d num. 1r–14r (19 May 1629).

34. AGS, *Secretarías Provinciales, Nápoles,* lib. 71, ff. 17r–21r (14 February 1634).

35. Ibid., ff. 22v–28v (21 August 1636).

36. ASFg, *Dogana,* serie V, regg. 785, 795, 808, 824, 837, "Libri di squarciafogli."

37. Cf. Charles-M. de La Roncière, "Indirect Taxes or Gabelles at Florence in the Fourteenth Century," in *Florentine Studies,* ed. N. Rubinstein (London: Faber, 1968), pp. 140–92.

38. AGS, *Secretarías Provinciales, Nápoles,* lib. 71, 99r–124r (11 February 1637) includes the extension agreement, fifty-nine itemized *locati grazie,* and a *consulta* commentary on them.

39. Ibid., 33r–34v (17 October 1637).

40. Ibid., 44v–50r (16 November 1639).

41. Ibid., 55r (19 June 1640), and 51r–v (27 October 1644).

42. De Dominicis, *Lo stato politico,* 2:16.

43. ASFg, *Dogana,* serie I, fas. 3, 283r–v (22 June 1647): "Il prezzo dell'herba che non possedeva e non possono pascolare per causa della coltura."

44. De Dominicis, *Lo stato politico,* 2:220 and two decrees, ibid., 2:242–46 (20 June 1650), and 2:247–51 (11 August 1651).

45. AGS, *Secretarías Provinciales, Nápoles,* leg. 391 (18 January 1655).

46. ASN, *Sommaria, Carte Reali,* fas. 7, 12r–14v (10 March 1661).

47. See chap. 1, n. 117.

48. AGS, *Secretarías Provinciales, Nápoles,* leg. 391 (24 September 1679).

49. See above, n. 6.

50. HHSA, *Ital.-Span. Rat, Neapel, Collect.* 45, *Zollamt in Foggia 1708–32,* 2)9 undated (ca. 1700), "Copia di Rapresentation fatta da Locati della Regia Dohana di Foggia."

51. Ibid., 2)11, undated (ca. 1721), c. 2v, "Le Regie Istruzzioni che sempre han' considerato il sollevi de Poveri sudditi, più non si osservono."

52. Di Stefano, *La ragion pastorale,* 1:310.

53. For 1764, see n. 11. For 1790, ASFg, *Dogana*, serie I, fas. 12, 23r (29 May 1790).
54. ASFg, *Dogana*, serie I, fas. 12, 391r–394v (13 July 1802).
55. Ibid., fas. 10, 415r–416v (14 November 1785).

6. Royal Patrimony, Royal Justice, Royal Office

1. Italo Calvino, comp., *Italian Folktales*, trans. George Martin (New York: Harcourt Brace Jovanovich, 1980), p. 739, n. 115, from Antonio De Nino, *Fiabe*, vol. 3 of *Usi e costumi abruzzesi* (Florence, 1883). Variants are found in shepherd localities in the Abruzzi, Puglia, Sicily, Lombardy, and Tuscany.
2. Marino, "*Professazione voluntaria*" (cited in full in chap. 1, n. 74).
3. AGS, *Visítas d'Italia, Nápoles*, leg. 27, 8v–12r, and leg. 112:8, 336r.

TABLE N-2   Fabrizio di Sangro's Term as Doganiero

Year	Professed Sheep	Income in Ducats	
		Gross	Net
1573/74	969,133	184,774.16	87,482.78
1574/75	1,622,819	225,765.98	99,785.95
1575/76	1,878,378	324,913.67	99,686.35
1576/77	1,912,120	325,117.29	241,711.98
1577/78	2,522,614	393,569.29	172,297.19
1578/79	2,978,811	454,728.83	189,851.96
1579/80	3,723,372	546,255.54	220,423.54
1580/81	4,294,822	561,104.94	199,635.18

4. AGS, *Visítas d'Italia, Nápoles*, leg. 29:3, 1–379 unnumbered ff, "Notamento delli affitti et dispensationi delle defense di Monteserico." Overall, sheep bids rose from 14,328 to 113,240 head from 1577 to 1578.
5. The differences between the total factor (7.9) and the individual mean (6.55) derive from the absence of five quotations in the previous year.
6. There is no fixed mathematical relationship between the *reali fisse* and the *alia*. For my eleven sample years, no pattern emerges for total sheep professed.

TABLE N-3   *Squarciafoglietti* Wealth

Year	Percentage	
	Reali Fisse	In Alia
1591	74	26
1604	48	52
1619	30	70
1639	22	78
1659	48	52
1679	53	47
1699	19	81
1719	51	49
1739	35	65
1759	15	85
1779	36	64

Within locations, the rate of voluntary bidding (*professazione*) of the *alia* could vary greatly, except during the time of fixed rates under the system of *transazione* (1614–60). Thereafter, rates could vary among locations in the same year. From a linear regression from my forty sample years, only the *transazione* years provide a uniform relationship between *reali fisse* and *alia* bids.

TABLE N-4   Coefficient to Determine *Alia*

Year	Coefficient	R^2	Year	Coefficient	R^2
1614	1.5	.99886	1639	3.6	.99996
1619	2.3	.99122	1644	3.7	.99999
1624	4.75	.96966	1649	1.14	.99969
1628	4.79	.98981	1654	1.02	.99677
1634	4.84	.98654	1659	1.07	.99991

The rate of calculation of the *alia* could even vary from grazier to grazier within the same location. In 1604, for example, the *locati* in Lesina who bid the largest number of *pecore in aerea* held quite different proportions of *reali fisse*/total professed than those who bid the largest *pecore reali fisse* numbers. ASFg, *Dogana*, serie V, reg. 767 (1604). Those owners with high *pecore reali fisse* bid about the same number of *pecore in aerea*, a 50:50 ratio. Those owners with high *alia* sheep declared only about 10 percent of their total in real sheep.

These bids were, remember, individual contracts worked out between sheepowners and custom house officers. Fixed contracts, therefore, meant that those graziers with old, established privileges had first priority to pasture; but high *alia* bids meant that newcomers could "buy" their way into the system.

7. Marino, "*Professazione voluntaria,*" p. 14, n. 21.
8. Guicciardini, *Storia d'Italia*, bk. III, chap. 5, pp. 268–69 (cited in full in chap. 1, n. 59).
9. Giovio. *Storia del suo tempo*, bk. IV, pp. 162–67 (cited in full in chap. 1, n. 59).
10. AGS, *Estado, Nápoles*, leg. 1004, f. 17 (1511), and f. 72 (1515).
11. Guicciardini, *Storia d'Italia*, bk. III, chap. 5, pp. 268–69.
12. AGS, *Estado, Nápoles*, leg. 1012, f. 221 (1532).
13. BNN, MS. XI.A.22, cc. 396–397r (4 March 1588).
14. Calabria, "Patrimonial Income, 1560–1600," in his "State Finances in the Kingdom of Naples in the Age of Philip II," Ph.D. diss., University of California, Berkeley, 1978, pp. 85–165, meticulously examines four compatible budgets—1560, 1574, 1583, 1600.
15. Ibid., p. 143, chart xi.
16. Gaudiani, *Notizie*, chap. IX, pp. 169–77 (cited in full in intro., n. 14).
17. De Dominicis, *Lo stato politico*, 3:125–28 (cited in full in intro., n. 13).
18. Gaudiani, *Notizie*, chap. X, pp. 179–88.
19. Ibid., chap. XI, pp. 189–92.
20. AGS, *Estado, Nápoles*, leg. 1046, f. 203 (1560) gives 10,143 ducats; and leg. 1064, f. 146 (1573), 11r gives 5,780 ducats.
21. Ibid., leg. 105 (1621), 78v. See also BNN, MS. I.D.20, 53r.
22. BNN, MS. I.D.20, 53r.
23. Gaudiani, *Notizie*, p. 184, reminds us of land values: 1608–12, 80 ducats per *carro;* down in 1613 to 60 ducats; and 1614–26, 50 ducats.
24. BNN, MS. Branc. V.D.14, 48r.
25. Di Stefano, *La ragion pastorale*, 2:501–2 (cited in full in intro., n. 12) gives 30 *terre salde* citations between 1700 and 1729 with a mean of 17,462 ducats, and 36 *terre salde* plus fallow rentals between 1670 and 1728, averaging 22,325 ducats. AGS, *Visítas d'Italia*,

Nápoles, leg. 112–8 confirms the *uso d'erba* figure in 1609/10 as 5,244 ducats. With a fixed amount of land in agricultural use, the fallow rental should have been constant.

26. Gaudiani, *Notizie*, chap. XII, pp. 193–95.
27. ASFg, *Dogana*, serie I, fas. 21 II, 115r–v, from Della Croce's survey.
28. Gaudiani, *Notizie*, chap. XIV, pp. 205–23.
29. Bianchini, *Storia delle finanze*, ed. De Rosa, p. 192 (cited in full in chap. 1, n. 18); Mazzella, *Descrittione*, p. 335 (cited in full in chap. 1, n. 60).
30. AGS, *Estado, Nápoles*, leg. 1011, f. 23 (1532).
31. ASN, *Dipendenze della Sommaria*, serie I, fas. 25, 10r–28r (1589/90).
32. AGS, *Estado, Nápoles*, leg. 1098, f. 50 (1602).
33. Ibid., leg. 1884, f. 105 (1621), 79r, and leg. 3296, f. 141 (22 May 1673), 4r.
34. ASN, *Dipendenze della Sommaria*, fas. 28, fasc. 3, 17r–21r (1701).
35. AGS, *Estado, Nápoles*, leg. 1004, f. 17 (1511), and f. 72 (1515).
36. Ibid., *Visítas d'Italia, Nápoles*, leg. 348–18.
37. Di Vittorio, *Gli Austriaci e il Regno di Napoli*, pp. 178–80 (cited in full in chap. 1, n. 127); on the duke of Modena, see Coniglio, *La Dogana nel secolo XVII*, pp. 5–21 (cited in full in chap. 1, n. 96); on the Elector Palatine, see ASFi, *Miscellanea Medicea*, vol. 125, f. 26 a, b, c, "Del Duca di Neoburg Conte Palatino e del Principe suo figlio" (ca. 1640).
38. Dora Musto," Vicende di un credito del granduca di Toscana sulle terre salde della Dogana di Foggia" (unpublished paper, 1970). He inherited them from his mother, Maria Maddalena d'Austria, and from Vittoria della Rovere, wife of the duke of Urbino.
39. But the Kingdom may not have been as economically irrational as it appears. When the Tuscan debt of 200,000 ducats was signed away in 1608, were the Sommaria accountants really unaware that *terre salde* prices would fall? Was this alienation a way of making the "investor" bear some of the risk for the annuity? By 1621 the Florentine factor in Naples laments that Tuscan income in the Kingdom was down. ASFi, *Mediceo*, fas. 4104, cc. 1–5 (1621), partially transcribed in Coniglio, *La Dogana di Foggia*, p. 12.
40. See chap. 1, n. 70, item 27 of Charles' concessions.
41. In the seventeenth century, wool gifts reflected the lower production figures, but they increased with growing production by the end of the century: 1,990.5 ducats in 1636, 1,328.95 ducats in 1648 (a small production year because of the revolt), 6,771.915 ducats in 1664, 6,570.57 ducats in 1670, 11,902 ducats in 1699, 9,500 ducats in 1710. ASN, *Dipendenze della Sommaria*, serie I, fas. 26; AGS, *Estado, Nápoles*, leg. 3296 (1670); and ASN, *Sommaria, Carte Reali*, fas. 19, 530 (1710). In the second half of the eighteenth century, these wool gifts were half white and half black wool. ASFg, *Dogana*, serie I, n. 11403 (1763). The total quantity of wool conforms neatly with this approximate 5 percent proportion. Twelve quotations between 1749 and 1780 average 4,000 *rubbi* of wool. Citations are taken from the last pages of the tax rolls [*squarciafogli*], ibid., serie V, regg. 1023 (1749), 1022 (1750), 1032 (1754), 1034 (1755), 1041 (1759), 1043 (1760), 1704–84 (1775–1780). In individual terms, Franciscan and Capuchin monasteries throughout the Kingdom received rather small gifts. In the 111 years 1611–1721, eighty-three wool gifts were given between 1637 and 1721. Median gifts per year were six; median quantity of wool, 60 *rubbi*, donated over a fixed number of years, usually six. ASN, *Sommaria, Carte Reali* (1611–1721), vols. 1 bis–29.
42. BNN, MS. I.D.20, 53r–84r, "Notizie della Dogana di Foggia."
43. H. G. Koenigsberger, *The Practice of Empire* (Ithaca, N.Y.: Cornell University Press, 1969) (emend. ed. of *The Government of Sicily under Philip II of Spain*), app. 3, "Notes on the Political Thought of Scipio di Castro," pp. 201–5 comes to the same conclusions for Spanish rule in Sicily during Philip II's reign. "The administration of justice, a warning against excessive taxation and every other virtue which he advocated, were justified solely on the grounds of expediency" (p. 204).
44. Coniglio, *La dogana nel secolo XVII*, is arguing, more or less, the much criticized

position of H. R. Trevor-Roper, "The General Crisis of the Seventeenth Century," and "Trevor-Roper's 'General Crisis': Symposium," in Trevor Aston, ed., *Crisis in Europe, 1560–1660* (Garden City, N.Y.: Anchor Books, 1967), pp. 63–123.

45. Villari, *La rivolta*, pp. 9–11 (cited in full in chap. 5, n. 23). The reverberations of the "fishmonger" Masaniello's revolt were led in Foggia by Sabato Pastore, a lawyer, not the shepherd that his name might suggest. Its concerns were not those of a simple feudal reaction but were tied to abuses in the doganal system.

46. J. H. Parry, *The Sale of Public Offices in the Spanish Indies under the Hapsburgs*, Ibero-Americana, no. 37 (Berkeley and Los Angeles: University of California Press, 1953), and Villari, *La rivolta*, app. 7, pp. 282–85 for Naples. On the problem in general and the Mediterranean in particular, Braudel, *Mediterranean*, 2:681–91 (cited in full in intro., n. 1).

47. Parry, *Sale of Public Offices*, p. 59.

48. Ibid., p. 69.

49. Villari, *La rivolta*, p. 122, n. 4 transcribes figures from ASN, *Dipendenze della Sommaria*, serie I, fas. 28, fasc. 1.

50. Villari, *La rivolta*, app. 7, pp. 283–85.

51. Ibid., p. 26.

52. Parry, *Sale of Public Offices*, p. 70.

53. AGS, *Secretarías Provinciales, Nápoles*, leg. 5 (March 1587) refers to a 27 March 1586 *consulta* which granted special exemption to the doganiero Alfonso Caracciolo to plant 30 *carra* in grain "in consideration and recompense for the will and authority he exercised, for the high cost of his office, and for the extraordinary necessity to feed Naples."

54. Federico Chabod, "Usi e abusi nell'amministrazione dello stato di Milano a mezzo il '500, in *Studi storici in onore di Gioaccino Volpe* (Florence: Sansoni, 1958), 1:180.

55. Braudel, *Mediterranean*, 2:681.

56. Parry, *Sale of Public Offices*, p. 70.

57. Ageta, *Annotationes*, 3:212–13 (cited in full in chap. 1, n. 55) transcribes a document attributed to the *avvocato fiscale* on the question of *residui*, ca. 1603–10, which concludes that the sale of the office of *percettore* was one of the causes of the loss of customhouse income.

58. ASFg, *Dogana*, serie IV contains civil cases (1540–1669); serie II contains civil cases (1700–1806).

59. Raffaelo Ajello, *Il problema della riforma giudiziaria e legislativa nel Regno di Napoli durante la prima metà del secolo XVIII. La vita giudiziaria* (Naples: Casa Editrice Dott. Eugenio Jovene, 1961), pp. 169–85.

60. Di Stefano, "Ragioni . . . con cui si mostra, che, non ostante il Capitolo XXVIII," in Kress Library, Harvard University, p. 19 is confirmed in BNN, MS. I.D.20, 53r.

61. Di Stefano, "Ragioni . . . Capitolo XXVIII," pp. 5–11.

62. Ajello, *Il problema della reforma*, p. 267.

63. ASFg, *Dogana*, serie I, fas. 24 (1603–05): for ordinary pasture, the top 11 percent of owners received 52 percent of rents while the bottom 61 percent received only 12 percent; for extraordinary usual pasture, the top 11 percent of owners received 61 percent of rents while the bottom 59 percent received only 30 percent; for extraordinary unusual pasture, the top 28 percent of owners received 80 percent of rents while the bottom 41 percent received only 6 percent.

64. Ibid., vol. 20, c. 5r. My thanks to Constance Bouchard for her insights on the inscription.

65. De Michele's maps of the locations of Camarda, Salzola, and Casalnuovo include naïve portraits of shepherds all in as realistic dress as the one inside the location of San Andrea.

66. Di Stefano, *La ragion pastorale*, 1:182: "Our legislators, seeing that these *cavallari*,

instead of playing the part of faithful sheepdogs, abuse their office and make themselves rapacious wolves."

67. Ibid., 2:491 uses this same metaphor in discussing the reestablishment of voluntary bidding in 1661: "Wherefore, in order not to end in alienating itself from the whole Kingdom, the *dogana delle pecore,* which tolerated even wolves, its implacable enemies, published" the decree condemning fraudulent bids.

68. Ibid., 2:465–80.

69. Palumbo, *Tavoliere e sua viabilità,* p. 16 (cited in full in intro., n. 3), and Gaudiani, *Notizie,* p. 325. I am not sure what kind of *"motore"* Gaudiani had in mind in 1715.

70. AGS, *Secretarías Provinciales, Nápoles,* lib. 44, "Sumario dell'offiti Regij," 35r (22 March 1594).

71. Ibid., *Visítas d'Italia, Nápoles,* leg. 15–4 VI.

72. BNN, MS. Branc. IV.D.3, 269–272v, "Del dohaniero et credenzero della dohana delle pecore de puglia de lo che hanno da osservatione sopra li affitti delli territori per uso di coltura" (26 March 1572) is an instruction in six chapters.

73. Gaudiani, *Notizie,* pp. 325–52 makes much of the pretensions and honors of the office.

74. AGS, *Estado, Nápoles,* leg. 1028, f. 7 (February 1538).

75. Ferrante di Sangro bought the office in turn from Figueroa for 12,000 or 13,000 ducats in 1542 according to the conflicting testimony of a *cavallaro* Juan Antonio Tabasco and of *credenziero* Annibale del Tinto during the Quiroga visit. AGS, *Visítas d'Italia, Nápoles,* leg. 15 I, 25r–31r, and 32r–37r (12 May 1561).

76. Alfonso Caracciolo bought the office of doganiero for 40,000 ducats in 1580. AGS, *Secretarías Provinciales, Nápoles,* leg. 4 (14 March 1580); ASN, *Sommaria Consultationum,* fas. 5, 241r–242v (17 July 1578) for an initial bid of 30,000 ducats. Lelio Caracciolo bid 28,000 ducats but was not sold the office in 1589. AGS, *Secretarías Provinciales, Nápoles,* leg. 6 (27 November 1589), with a reference in Philip II's letter, BSNSP, MS. XXVII.A.1, 130r–v (2 March 1591). Ferrante Monsorio bought it for 53,100 ducats in 1602. AGS, *Estado, Nápoles,* leg. 1100, f. 152 (24 November 1604.) Giuseppe Bernauda paid 40,000 ducats in 1624. De Dominicis, *Lo stato politico,* 2:9. Agostino Moneglia paid 37,000 ducats in 1637. AGS, *Secretarías Provinciales, Nápoles,* leg. 213 (14 November 1671).

77. Mantelli, *Burocrazia e finanze,* p. 289 (cited in full in chap. 1, n. 86) cites a letter of an ex-officer of the dogana, Pietro Corcillo to Quiroga, ca. 1560.

78. Filberto Campanile, *Historia dell'illustrissima famiglia Di Sangro* (Naples: Tarquino Longo, 1615), pp. 67–71; BNN, MS. Branc. III.E.6, 14r–16v, "Factum Pro Dnis Joane Jacobo, et Fabritio di Sangro," includes a family tree; most important, AGS, *Secretarías Provinciales, Nápoles,* leg. 11 (18 August 1609), which is a *consulta* reviewing Fabrizio's career upon his request to enroll his son Giovanni in the military order of Santiago; BNN, MS. I.D.73, cc. 103r–5v is a literary portrait in a collection of Silvio and Ascanio Corona's "La verità svelata."

79. Charles V ceded Gianfrancesco and his heirs the title of marquis because of his "great military merit." ACA, *Privilegiorum,* reg. 2083, 312r (4 June 1530).

80. AGS, *Visítas d'Italia, Nápoles,* lib. 58, transcribed in Nino Cortese, *Feudi e feudatari Napoletani della prima metà del Cinquecento* (Naples: Società Napoletani di Storia Patria, 1931), pp. 195–97, 199, 203.

81. Charles granted him a 400-ducat annuity. ACA, *Privilegiorum,* reg. 3941, 283v (17 January 1534).

82. Charles granted him a 400-ducat annuity also. Ibid., 286v, (17 January 1534).

83. AGS, *Visítas d'Italia, Nápoles,* leg. 348–18 (1549/50). ACA, *Privilegiorum,* reg. 3943, 474r (14 November 1536). Giammatista also enjoyed particular location status in 1559 with 8,700 sheep. AGS, *Visítas d'Italia,* leg. 15:15.

84. The di Sangro relationship to the Neapolitan pope, Gian Pietro Carafa, seems to

have come through marriage. Violante and Paolo's eldest son, that is, Fabrizio's first cousin and nephew, Gianfrancesco di Sangro, married into the Carafa clan. Biagio Aldimari, *Historia Genealogica della Famiglia Carafa*, 3 vols. (Naples: Giacomo Raillard, 1691), 1:137.

85. AGS, *Secretarías Provinciales, Nápoles*, leg. 4 (14 March 1580).
86. Ibid., leg. 7 (15 December 1595), leg. 155, c. 102 (26 January 1596), BNN, MS. I.D.73, cc. 103r–105v.
87. AGS, *Secretarías Provinciales, Nápoles*, leg. 162, c. 247 (9 November 1602).
88. Ibid., leg. 176, c. 150v (4 May 1613).
89. This identification is problematic. Alfonso did indeed have a sister named Laura, but she supposedly became a nun. But could this have been after her husband's death, albeit he lived so long? I have not yet found any other Laura Caracciolo. Ambrogino Caracciolo, ed., *La genealogia della famiglia Caracciolo di Francesco Fabis* (Naples: Artigianelli, 1966), tab. xxvi.
90. Neither Mantelli, *Bureaucrazia e Finanze*, p. 292 nor I have found the result of the investigation against them although the charges of fraud against doganal laws are detailed enough. Others found guilty in this investigation were twenty-eight out of thirty-three accused *cavallari* and the *mastrodatti*; one *credenziero* was found innocent. The mass of evidence is enormous and bears more sifting. AGS, *Visítas d'Italia, Nápoles*, leg. 15.
91. See chap. 1, n. 96.
92. Musto, *La regia dogana*, p. 41 (cited in full in intro., n. 3).
93. Giuseppe Coniglio, "Il contrabbando in Abruzzo intorno al 1583," *Studi economici* 10, no. 12 (1955), abstract pp. 1–5 cites ASN, *Attuari diversi*, fas. 1102, proc. 6. In 1583, 431 Abruzzesi contraband runners from sixty-three identifiable towns were fined a total of 1,155.45 ducats for illegally exporting grain, lambs, milk, cheese, wool, sheep, and a whole range of agricultural products. The ring vented its goods in the Papal States, where they were sold in the Campo dei Fiori at Rome.
94. Gaudiani, *Notizie*, pp. 328–30; Di Stefano, *La ragion pastorale*, 2:480–83.
95. BNN, MS. Branc. IV.D.3, 261v–268v, "Del Credenziere della dogana delle pecore de puglia" (8 October 1574) describes the office in nineteen chapters. Gaudiani, *Notizie*, pp. 330–40 transcribes and comments upon a thirty-two-item instruction of 25 May 1598; Di Stefano, *La ragion pastorale*, 2:503–14.
96. Di Stefano, *La ragion pastorale*, 2:483–87.
97. AGS, *Secretarías Provinciales, Nápoles*, leg. 11 (9 August 1607).
98. Ibid., leg. 112 (1631).
99. Gaudiani, *Notizie*, pp. 341–43; Di Stefano, *La ragion pastorale*, 2:524–28; De Dominicis, *Lo stato politico*, 3:379–81.
100. Gaudiani, *Notizie*, pp. 343–44; De Dominicis, *Lo stato politico*, 3:381–87.
101. Gaudiani, *Notizie*, pp. 344–45; Di Stefano, *La ragion pastorale*, 2:515–21; De Dominicis, *Lo stato politico*, 3:342–44. On salary piece rates, BPFg, MS. 4, 160r–61v (9 January 1574).
102. Gaudiani, *Notizie*, pp. 349–52, with BPFg, MS. 129, ff. 671–87, giving a fifty-chapter instruction (4 March 1617); Di Stefano, *La ragion pastorale*, 1:180–83 gives a philological analysis of the title and a historical reprise of the office; De Dominicis, *Lo stato politico*, 2:391–95 transcribes a fourteen-item instruction of 14 August.
103. ASN, *Consiglio Collaterale Consultationum*, fas. 2–7, include diverse one-page letters on sales of offices. In the twenty years between 1642 and 1662, there were eleven such sales; mean price, 297 ducats; low, 180 ducats; high, 400 ducats.
104. Coda, *Breve discorso*, pp. 95–96 (cited in full in intro., n. 16) has an undated list of officers' salaries.
105. Vincenzo Salvato, *Palazzo dogana dalle origini ai giorni nostri* (Foggia: Franco Leone Editore, 1976), tables 2–5 are reconstructed from apps. A and B, which are transcriptions of ASFg, *Dogana*, serie V, fas. 52, n. 4544, 2–6 (28 February 1732), and 8–20 (25 July 1732).

106. Salvato, *Palazzo dogana*, tables 23–26 are reconstructed in part from app. 3, which transcribes part of ASFg, *Dogana*, serie V, fas. 58, n. 4639 (17 August 1762).
107. Salvato, *Palazzo dogana*, table 33.
108. Note that even with the doubling of archival space, the king still ordered in the same year, 1788, that all criminal records before 1758 be destroyed for lack of room.
109. ASFg, *Dogana*, serie I, fas. 5, 110r–v (1 April 1723). The penalty for noncompliance was loss of office. Absenteeism was a serious problem for such bureaucratic offices, especially in April, when the spring fair increased business.
110. Braudel, *Mediterranean*, 1:456–58.
111. François Rabelais, *Gargantua and Pantagruel*, bk. 4, chaps. 5–8.
112. Domenico Franco, "La pastorizia ed il commercio della lana nella antica e nuova Cerreto," *Samnium* 39, nos. 1–2 (1966):74, n. 10.
113. AGS, *Estado, Nápoles*, leg. 1025, f. 7 (1536).

7. The Competition between Wheat and Wool

1. AGS, *Estado, Nápoles*, leg. 1038, f. 139, "Bando de la Vicaria contro los vagabundos de la cuidad de Nápoles" (29 April 1550).
2. Since the bread census did not include members of religious communities, guests of monasteries and hospitals, nobles and their servants, or children under three years old, Beloch, *Bevölkerungsgeschichte*, 1:172 (cited in full in chap. 1, n. 68) extrapolates the count to estimate 240,000 inhabitants.
3. See chap. 3, n. 5.
4. Claudia Petraccone, *Napoli dal Cinquecento all'Ottocento. Problemi di storia demografia e sociale* (Naples: Guida, 1975).
5. Alfonso La Cava, "La demografia di un comune Pugliese nell'età moderna," *Archivio Storico per le Province Napoletane* 25 (1939):25–66. Capitanata's seventy-three towns may be roughly located in three zones: (1) the Gargano peninsula (24 percent of the provincial area, with ten communes in 1595); (2) the Tavoliere and coastal plains (52 percent of total area, with ten communes in 1595); and (3) the Apennine mountain flank (24 percent of area, with fifty-three communes in 1595). Town sites in the hilly borderlands reflected earlier settlement patterns which placed a premium on defense and security, the availability of water, and the absence of malarial infection. The flat land of the Tavoliere provided none of these. The Gargano, for its part, continued to be a rather forbidding and barren wilderness except for occasional pockets of fertility.
6. Giuseppe Galasso, "Momenti e problemi di storia napolentana nell'età di Carlo V," in *Mezzogiorno medievale e moderno* (cited in full in chap. 1, n. 106), pp. 172–73.
7. Coniglio, *Il viceregno di Napoli nel secolo XVII. Notizie sulla commerciale e finanziaria secondo nuove ricerche negli archivi italiani e spagnoli* (Rome: Edizioni di Storia e Letteratura, 1955), p. 37. AGS, *Estado, Nápoles*, leg. 1104, f. 12 (8 January 1607), for example, gives 250,000 *tomoli*, 19.2 percent of the 1.3 million *tomoli* needed.
8. AGS, *Estado, Nápoles*, leg. 1030, f. 176 (27 August 1541) is cited in Coniglio, *Carlo V*, p. 123 (cited in full in chap. 1, n. 67); p. 133 gives many more examples from the 1550s, culminated in a 150,000-*tomoli* shipment in 1555.
9. ASN, *Sommaria Consultationum*, fas. 9, cc. 63r–68r (11 February 1586).
10. In 1672 a grain shortage in Sicily required extraordinary remedies to quell mounting unrest. AGS, *Estado, Nápoles*, leg. 3295, ff. 61, 62, 63, 75, 76 (14 March, 26 March, 22 and 26 April, 20 May 1672). One solution was to export 8,000 *tomoli* of Puglian wheat to Sicily itself. Ibid., f. 81 (3 June 1672) and f. 82 (6 May 1672). Cf. Braudel, *Mediterranean*, 1:602–6 (cited in full in intro., n. 1). The surplus of Puglian wheat was well known in these famine years. Requests from Spain itself for the Andalusian coast, the Bahia de Cadiz, the interior of Spain, and the city of Barcelona were forthcoming in 1677. AGS, *Estado, Nápoles*,

leg. 3300, ff. 352, 353, 403, 404 (16 September, 29 October, 29 June, 31 August 1677).

11. Galasso, "Carlo V," p. 181 quotes a Sommaria *consulta* dated 13 April 1576 in BNN, MS. I.C.41, 275v–76 on the comparative quality of grains.

12. Coniglio, *Il viceregno*, p. 37.

13. ASN, *Sommaria Consultationum*, vol. 2, cc. 228r–229r (23 November 1569). The settlement called for reimbursement at the rate of 30 ducats per *carro*, or 12 *carlini* per *tomolo*. These were not isolated incidents. The Venetian armada would engage in "evidentes actos de hostilidad" again in 1618 and 1619. AGS, *Estado, Nápoles*, leg. 1881, f. 184 (18 November 1618), and leg. 1882, f. 69 (22 June 1619).

14. Francesco Palermo, ed., "Documenti che riguardano in ispecie la storia economica e finanziera del Regno levati dal carteggio degli agenti del duca di Urbino in Napoli dall'anno 1552 sino al 1622," *Archivio Storico Italiano* 9 (1846): p. 219, n. 33 (8 November 1591). See also AGS, *Estado, Nápoles*, leg. 1092, f. 125 (13 April 1591), and f. 212 (19 December 1591). "La necessidad desta ciudad esta en quelleguen las naves que faltan o no."

15. ASN, *Sommaria Consultationum*, vol. 4, cc. 48v–50v (4 June 1575).

16. Ibid., vol. 2, cc. 237v–241r (18 December 1573), and cc. 243r–244v (30 July 1574). AGS, *Estado, Venezia*, leg. 1518, f. 56 (3 March 1576). Cf. Maurice Aymard, *Venise, Raguse, et le commerce du blé pendant la seconde moitié du XVIe siècle* (Paris, S.E.V.P.E.N., 1966), pp. 43–44.

17. ASN, *Sommaria Consultationum*, vol. 22, cc. 68r–80r includes five documents from 1608; vol. 24, cc. 169v–176r includes four renewals of the concessions dated 1613. *Consulte* begin again in 1646: vol. 48, cc. 17r–19v (1646), and 227v–228r (1647); vol. 51, cc. 142v–147v includes three renewals (1654); vol. 52, cc. 212r–251r, four renewals (1655), etc. The last of these documents appears in 1674 (vol. 72, cc. 67r–v) until the eighteenth century: vol. 94, cc. 172r–v (1703) and vol. 118, cc. 152–154r (1715).

18. AGS, *Estado, Nápoles*, leg. 1883, f. 137 (23 August 1620). A. La Cava, "Il sacco Turchesco di Manfredonia nel 1620," *Archivio Storico per le Province Napoletane* 26 (1940): 66–104. The threat of Turkish raids on the Kingdom's Adriatic coast had been a continuing fear from their 1480 seizure of Otranto. In 1560, for example, the viceroy's letter on population growth bemoaned the plundering Turkish armada, and soon thereafter, provisions for soldiers and ships were outlined. AGS, *Estado, Nápoles*, leg. 1050, f. 23 (21 March 1560); f. 43 (18 May 1560). In 1566 the Turks were again marauding on the Adriatic coast, and only a strong defense saved Serra Capriola (the important doganal town where the doganiero originally received the sheepowners' *professazioni*) on 5 August. Braudel, *Mediterranean*, 2:1033.

19. The following *consulte* describe payments to grain contractors: ASN, *Sommaria Consultationum*, vol. 10, cc. 231r–232r (23 February 1592); vol. 18, cc. 87v–90v (17 July 1604); vol. 22, cc. 81v–82r (25 October 1608).

20. Lepre, *Feudi e masserie*, pp. 85–123 (cited in full in chap. 3, n. 27) for the seventeenth century, and pp. 125–37 for the eighteenth.

21. Giuseppe Galasso, *Il Mezzogiorno nella storia d'Italia* (Florence: Felice Le Monnier, 1977); Galasso, *Economia e società nella Calabria del Cinquecento* (Milan: Feltrinelli, 1975).

22. Giuseppe Coniglio, "Annona e calmieri a Napoli durante la dominazione spagnuola. Osservazioni e rilievi," *Archivio Storico per le Provincie Napoletane* 65 (1940):105–94.

23. Giuseppe Galasso, "La Calabria nel Cinquecento," in *Atti del 3° Congresso Storico Calabrese (19–26 maggio 1963)* (Naples: Fausto Fiorentino, 1964), p. 37.

24. ASP, *Archivio Alliata*, fas. 14, "Discorso sopra la Dogana di Puglia del regnio [*sic*] di Napoli a Sua Cath. Regia Maesta," ca. 1560, partly transcribed by Coniglio, *Il Viceregno*, pp. 28–30.

25. Villari, *La rivolta*, pp. 35–58 (cited in full in chap. 5, n. 23) discusses the bread riots in Naples after prices were raised and the lynching of the people's representative, Giovanni Vincenzo Starace, in 1585. A contemporary document describing the revolt is

preserved in BRAH, MS. H-25, cc. 145r–146v, "Caso atrocissimo acaucido in la insigni ciudad de Napoles ala nube de Mayo del año 1585."

26. ASN, *Sommaria Consultationum*, vol. 13 I, nn. 145r–50v (10 October 1591) gives the *terre salde* list, and ASN, *Sommaria Consultationum*, vol. 2, cc. 223v–34r (11 October 1567) gives *mezzana* information. Musto, "Sulla economia di Capitanata," pp. 75–81 (cited in full in chap. 1, n. 81).

27. De Dominicis, *Lo stato politico*, 1:283 (cited in full in intro., n. 13) transcribes the *banno* of 16 January 1560; Palumbo, *Tavoliere e sua viabilità*, pp. 128–31 (cited in full in intro., n. 3) transcribes an almost identical *consulta* dated 16 February 1560; and Musto, "Sulla economia di Capitanata," pp. 82–88 transcribes ASN, *Sommaria Consultationum*, vol. 8, cc. 55r–60r (23 December 1560).

28. ASN, *Sommaria Consultationum*, vol. 2: 12v–15v (13 March 1563) is repeated in BNN, MS. XI.B.39, c.118r, and Braudel, *Mediterranean*, 1:89.

29. ASN, *Sommaria Consultationum*, vol. 13 I, n.n. 146r (10 October 1591).

30. AGS, *Estado, Nápoles*, leg. 1052, f. 87 (1562) transcribed in part in Francesco Caracciolo, *Il Regno di Napoli nel secoli XVI e XVII. Economia e società* (Rome: P. Tombolini, 1966), p. 158, n. 12.

31. Ruggiero Romano, "Storia dei prezzi e storia economica," *Rivista Storica Italiana* 75 (1963):243. Cf. F. Spooner and F. Braudel, "Prices in Europe, 1450–1750," in *Cambridge Economic History*, 7 vols., ed. E. E. Rich and C. H. Wilson (Cambridge: Cambridge University Press, 1967), 4:374–486.

32. Galasso, *Economia e società*, p. 217.

33. Giuseppe Coniglio, *Aspetti della società meridionale nel secolo XVI* (Naples: Fiorentino Editrice, 1978), pp. 265–75.

34. Giuseppe Galasso, "Seta e commercio del ferro nell'economia napoletana nel tardo Cinquecento," *Rivista Storica Italiana* 75 (1963):615–40.

35. Francesco Caracciolo, "Fisco e contribuiti in Calabria nel secolo XVI," *Nuovo Rivista Storica* 47 (1963):507.

36. Braudel, *Mediterranean*, 1:531.

37. Luigi De Rosa, "Una operazione d'alta finanza alla fine del '500," *Archivio Storico per la Province Napoletane* 76 (1957):267–83.

38. A. Filangieri, "La 'Dogana delle pecore,'" p. 671 (cited in full in intro., n. 6).

39. De Rosa, *I cambi esteri del Regno di Napoli dal 1591 al 1707* (Naples: Banco di Napoli, 1955), p. 34.

40. Romano, "Tra XVI e XVII Secolo," pp. 480–531 (cited in full in chap. 3, n. 10).

41. Grohmann, *Le fiere del Regno*, p. 128 (cited in full in chap. 1, n. 49) documents the June-July fair at Lucera as one of the oldest fairs in Puglia, dating from a privilege conceded in 1234 by Frederick II to fairs in Lucera, Bari, and Taranto.

42. Ibid., pp. 137–38, from notarial protocols in Aquila.

43. AGS, *Visítas d'Italia, Nápoles*, leg. 46:1, 183r (26 February 1583). The proceeds yielded some 10,080 ducats for the General Treasury of the Sommaria. Ibid., 184r (31 March 1583).

44. ASN, *Sommaria Consultationum*, fas. 9, 101r–v (18 March 1586), and 111r (8 October 1586). In the case of the November fair, the extension followed a precedent set for the 1575 Lucera fair of All Saints' Day.

45. Ibid., fas. 15, 4v (24 March 1600) is the latest entry I find. Earlier ones are numerous, e.g., fas. 10, 65r (26 February 1590) and 207r (6 October 1590).

46. "Fiera di Foggia" (14 September 1551), Document XI in Di Cicco, *Il Libro Rosso della Città di Foggia* (Foggia: Amministrazione Provinciale di Capitanata, 1965), pp. 98–103; item 1, pp. 99–100.

47. AGS, *Estado, Nápoles*, leg. 1022, f. 99 (1535). The 40,000 *rubbi* total is a calcula-

tion based upon the salary of the weighers of wool: 400 ducats paid at the rate of one *grano* per *rubbio*.

48. "*Grazie* of Charles V" (11 February 1536), item 9. See chap. 1, n. 70. It was restated by Cardinal Granvelle (30 July 1574) in item 16. See chap. 1, n. 89.

49. "Fiera di Foggia," p. 98 gives one of the reasons for issuing the 1551 instructions: "Bisogna limitare le robbe alli lochi deputati dove più comodo staranno li negocianti et sarrà benefitio della università."

50. "Concessione del Viceré Pietro di Toledo" (15 August 1541), Document VIII, in Di Cicco, *Il Libro Rosso della Città di Foggia*, p. 86.

51. De Dominicis, *Lo stato politico*, 1:146. "Fiera di Foggia," p. 99 gives the date for the first April fair as the 8th indiction (1549/50). Note that the unified fair edict corresponded to the reforms of the general reintegration of 1548/49.

52. Ibid., 3:116 cites a relation of 8 October 1561. ASN, *Sommaria Consultationum*, vol. 2, 70r–76v (8 August 1564), which copies and expands upon a 1562 *consulta* (Ibid., vol. 1, 274r–275r [25 May 1562]) gives the total salary of wool weighers as 800 ducats (75r). From that figure we can verify De Dominicis' claim of 80,000 *rubbi* of wool.

53. "Fiera di Foggia," item 3, p. 100.

54. De Dominicis, *Lo stato politico*, 3:111–12.

55. Ibid., 3:111. AGS, *Estado, Nápoles*, leg. 1011, f. 7 (22 February 1532), and leg. 1012, f. 7 (23 February 1532), "Letters of Cardinal Colonna to the King."

56. Alessio De Sariis, *Codice delle leggi del Regno di Napoli*, 9 vols. (Naples: Vincenzo Orsini, 1792–97), 4:166, n. 224 (11 September 1559).

57. De Dominicis, *Lo stato politico*, 3:118. AGS, *Visitas d'Italia, Nápoles*, leg. 46:1 (3 March 1584) reproduces a 16 May 1581 document on how increased income from wool sales was used to pay taxes.

58. See chap. 9, "Sellers' Budgets."

59. "Fiera di Foggia," item 2, p. 100. The religious procession for the feast is described in Manerba, *Memorie*, p. 71 (cited in full in chap. 2, n. 17).

60. Di Stefano, *La ragion pastorale*, 2:201 cites three Old Testament examples: 2 Samuel 13:24 (Absolom invites his father, David, and his brothers to the shearing, where he eventually murders Amnon); Genesis 38:12 (Judah ends his mourning for his wife's death by going shearing); and 1 Samuel 25:8 (David sends his servants to Nabal at shearing time).

61. ASFg, *Dogana*, serie I, fas. 9, 198r–199v (16 April 1768).

62. "Fiera di Foggia," items 4, 11, pp. 100, 102. For an example of fair-time violence and the sheep customhouse's right to keep cases in its jurisdiction rather than forward them in the normal way to the Camera of Santa Chiara, see ASFg, *Dogana*, serie I, fas. 10, 288r (29 March 1781). The case concerns a *locato* mugged by three armed men on a public street.

63. "Fiera di Foggia," items 5, 12, 13, pp. 101–3.

64. Cardinal Granvelle's instructions (30 July 1574), item 16. See Chap. 1, n. 89.

65. De Dominicis, *Lo stato politico*, 3:150.

66. Ibid., 3:143–44. Grohmann, *Le fiere del Regno*, p. 246 claims that taxes rarely exceeded 10–20 percent at the Kingdom's fairs.

67. "Fiera di Foggia," items 6–10, p. 101.

68. Foreigners, especially Bergamaschi, also sold their cloth at the Lanciano and Salerno fairs. ASV, *Sindaci Inquisitori di Terraferma*, busta 63, "Descrizione fatta da Juan da Lezze, Capitano di Bergamo della Città e Territorio del 1596," ff. 114r–v, "Modo di fabrica i Panni."

69. In the year from 1 June 1755 to 31 May 1756, 875,524 Venetian *libbre* of merchandise were shipped from Venice to nine Pugliese ports. Manfredonia, Foggia's port, accounted for 90 percent of the goods. Imports included Venetian and German cloths and hardwares, miscellaneous German goods, Bavarian wood, leather, and copper goods. Maria

Antonietta Visceglia, "Il commercio dei porti pugliesi nel Settecento. Ipotesi di ricerca," in *Economia e classi sociali*, ed. Villani (cited in full in chap. 1, n. 116), p. 220. Even native Neapolitan manufacturers got into the act. Domenico Franco, "L'industria dei panni-lana nella vecchia e nuova Cerreto," *Samnium* 3–4 (1964):187–88, n. 11 cites a notarial protocol that 367 pairs of wool shears made in Cerreto were sold at the 1723 Foggian fair.

70. De Dominicis, *Lo stato politico*, 3:150. Di Stefano, *La ragion pastorale*, 1:363–70 (cited in full in intro., n. 12) lists the oft repeated legislation ensuring these tax exemptions. Cf. ibid., 2:156–58, 323.

71. De Dominicis, *Lo stato politico*, 3:136; ASFg, *Dogana*, serie I, fas. 3, 352r–55v (22 September 1649–12 April 1652).

72. Di Stefano, *Lo stato politico*, 2:157–58; ASFg, *Dogana*, serie I, fas. 3, 464r–67r (12 June 1665).

73. ASFg, *Dogana*, serie I, fas. 2, 252r–53r (19 March 1646).

74. Di Stefano, *La ragion pastorale*, 1:329–32 gives the edict of Regent Galeota (13 April 1645).

75. ASFg, *Dogana*, serie I, fas. 3, 394r–95r (30 August 1651).

76. Ibid., serie V, nn. 3948–4022, "Fiere di Gravina ed Altamura (1693–1793)."

77. Normal wool exports from Manfredonia in the eighteenth century averaged 35,000 *rubbi*, equal to 41 percent of wool taken out of storage in Foggian depositories. I have correlated Visceglia, "Il commercio dei porti pugliesi," p. 191 with my out of storage totals.

78. ASFg, *Dogana*, serie I, fas. 355, "Atti della voce della lana . . . 1760, 1761."

79. De Dominicis, *Lo stato politico*, 3:152, 150–53; ASFg, *Dogana*, serie I, fas. 8, 166r–67v (12 June 1760), and fas. 9, 170r–73r (1 August 1787).

80. ASFg, *Dogana*, serie I, fas. 12, 49r–v (15 July 1790). Cf. Lepre, *Feudi e masserie*, pp. 114–17. The aforementioned Pietro Zannetti's renunciation of an agricultural rental contract in the 1656 plague is examined. Obviously not all merchants who bought or rented agricultural land were "fictitious." The investment of mercantile gains in land is an old tradition. Could this complaint be addressed to such new men and their new money?

81. ASFg, *Dogana*, serie 1, fas. 8, 116r–117v (13 December 1758).

82. AGS, *Visitas d'Italia, Nápoles*, leg. 53:8, 42r (31 August 1583) forbids wheat and barley purchases for speculative resale.

83. ASFg, *Dogana*, serie I, nn. 8664–8677 (1786–1806).

84. De Dominicis, *Lo stato politico*, 3:112. After the 1656 plague, special care was taken to ensure that all the houses in Foggia were cleaned out (*espurgare*) in time for the fair. BNN, MS. XI.D.21, c. 93r (3 March 1657).

85. De Dominicis, *Lo stato politico*, 3:119–20.

86. ASFg, *Dogana*, serie I, fas. 3, 88r (8 October 1619).

87. Ibid., serie V, reg. 2001 (1625). ASN, *Sommaria Consultationum*, fas. 83, 13v (31 March 1683) gives verbal confirmation that the fair's chief activity stretched from May 1 to June 15.

88. De Dominicis, *Lo stato politico*, 3:120.

89. ASFg, *Dogana*, serie V, regg. 2001 (1625), 2017 (1641), 2029 (1655), 2057–2060 (1670), 2114–2117 (1685), and 2167–2170 (1700).

90. Di Stefano, *La ragion pastorale*, 1:348–50 gives parallel examples for shearing days on holidays.

91. ASFg, *Dogana*, serie I, fas. 9, 171r (1 August 1787) tells us that wool exports continued "through the fair, that is, from the first of April through all of August."

92. De Dominicis, *Lo stato politico*, 3:151. Di Cicco, "Produzione della lana," p. 24, n. 56 (cited in full in chap. 2, n. 44) emphasizes that such later sales were made in Foggia, underlining its central importance as a permanent market.

93. ASV, *Cinque Savi alla Mercanzia*, serie I, busta 634, "Lettere dei Consoli, Barletta (1713–85)" gives monthly breakdowns.

TABLE N-5 Venetian Shipping in Capitanata

Month	Percentage	
	Manfredonia	Barletta
Apr.	7	9
May	16	21
June	15	27
July	12	15
Aug.	8	4
Sept.	19	4
Oct.	10	5
Nov.–Mar.	12	15

Goods shipped from Barletta were salt and cereals; from Manfredonia, cereals, wool, lambs, horses, salted meat and salted fish, Gargano timber, and almonds.

94. Giovanni Muto, "La economía del Mezzogiorno continental de la segunda mitad del Cinquecento a la crisis de los años cuarenta del siglo XVII," *Cuadernos de investigación histórica* 1 (1977):191–213 reviews the bibliography on Neapolitan economy and finance. Guido Quazzo, "Rifeudalizatione e ceto civile: Napoli," in *La decadenza Italiana nella storia Europea* (Turin: Einaudi, 1971), pp. 63–85 reviews the contending interpretations.

95. Giuseppe Coniglio, "L'Arte della lana a Napoli," *Samnium* 21 (1948):66. ASN, *Curia dell'arte della lana,* fas. 1–79 (1500–1867) confirms the wool conjunction in the quantity of extant documentation: 1500–1611, 33 *fasci;* 1611–1680s, only 6 *fasci;* 1680s–1806, 29 *fasci;* 1806–67, 11 *fasci.* Galasso, "Seta e ferro," outlined how the silk gabelle in Calabria had been sold to the Sanseverino family, princes of Bisignano, in 1587–88. Galasso, *Economia e società,* pp. 345–52 chronicles the silk industry's decline.

96. Luigi De Rosa, "Il Banco dei Poveri e la crisi del 1622," *Rassegna economica* 22 (1958):49–78; Giuseppe Coniglio, "La crisi monetaria napoletana del 1622 in una memoria del tempo," *Rivista "Partenope"* 2 (1961):25–46.

97. J. H. Elliott, "The Spanish Peninsula, 1598–1648," in *The Decline of Spain and the Thirty Years War 1609–48/59,* ed. J. P. Cooper (Cambridge: Cambridge University Press, 1970), vol. 4 in *The New Cambridge Modern History,* pp. 435–74; F. C. Spooner, "The European Economy 1609–1650," in ibid., pp. 67–103.

98. Coniglio, *La dogana nel XVII secolo,* p. 47 (cited in full in chap. 1, n. 96).

99. Carlo M. Cipolla, "The Economic Decline of Italy," pp. 127–45 (cited in full in chap. 3, n. 10).

8. The Fair of Foggia: Production and Prices

1. ASFg, *Dogana,* serie V, regg. 1999–2551 (1623–1801), "Libri di pesatori di lana." See Pasquale Di Cicco, "Produzione della lana," pp. 3–59 (cited in full in chap. 2, n. 44).

2. The earliest reference to the wool weighers is AGS, *Estado, Nápoles,* leg. 1022, f. 99 (1535) with three "weighing stations," two weighers from Aquila, one from Sulmona, and one from Carapella. Weighers' responsibilities are outlined in ASFg, *Dogana,* serie I, fas. 5, 31r–32r (21 September 1711); 345r–46r (7 April 1732); 416r–17v (9 April 1733); fas. 7, 162r–64r (9 April 1746); fas. 10, 237r–38v (6 April 1780), and 239r–41v (12 April 1780).

3. For weighers' salaries in 1561, ASN, *Sommaria Consultationum,* vol. 1, 274r–75r (29 May 1562); AGS, *Visitas d'Italia, Nápoles,* leg. 24:2, 300r–302r (18 March 1564); De Dominicis, *Lo stato politico,* 3:116 (cited in full in intro., n. 13). For their seventeenth-

century increase, De Dominicis, *Lo stato politico,* 3:124; Di Cicco, "Produzione della lana," n. 28.

4. ASFg, *Dogana,* serie I, fas. 446r; De Dominicis, *Lo stato politico,* 3:117. Seven salaries are extant between 1647 and 1682 in ASFg, *Dogana,* serie V, regg. 2016 (1647), 2023 (1649), 2026 (1652), 2029 (1655), 2039 (1656), 2039 (1665), and 2103 (1682). A mean total salary of 1,181 ducats confirms the 30 ducats annually for each of the forty weighers.

5. De Dominicis, *Lo stato politico,* 3:117–18 claims that weighers were elected by their community and its *locati* after a 14 November 1584 decree. AGS, *Visítas d'Italia, Nápoles,* leg. 25:1, 84v–86r (23 November 1583) traces the history of the office in royal decrees from Montluber's 1447 foundation. For the patents, ASFg, *Dogana,* serie I, fas. 334, "Spedizione delle Patenti di Pesatori di lana"; Di Cicco, "Produzione della lana," pp. 11–14 for the method of election and the formula of the licenses. By the late eighteenth century, weighers were appointed by the governor general.

6. Di Stefano, *La ragion pastorale,* 1:347–48 (cited in full in intro., n. 12) gives examples of such frauds.

7. ASN, *Sommaria Consultationum,* fas. 83, 27r–v (12 April 1583); Di Cicco, "Produzione della lana," n. 26.

8. ASFg, *Dogana,* serie I, fas. 5, 28r–v (9 October 1711).

9. Ibid., 190r–v (5 May 1725).

10. A viceregal dispatch dated 2 March 1625 ordered vigilance at the *infondacatura* and may have caused the weighers from Sulmona to send their account books to the customhouse archive. Ibid., 31r–32r (21 September 1711).

11. For archival reform documents ordering the wool weighers to register their account books, see Di Cicco, "Produzione della lana," pp. 151–57, nn. 31–38. The decrees on archival preservation of account books reinforced the establishment of *voce* pricing and grading in 1667 and, according to De Dominicis, *Lo stato politico,* 3:124, "the new policy, which was introduced into the Customhouse in the sale and storage of wool, rendered the office of *pesatori* more enviable and important."

12. Estimated from a linear regression, Hubert M. Blalock, Jr., *Social Statistics,* 2d ed. (New York: McGraw-Hill, 1972), pp. 274–83. Adjusted R^2 for Sulmona for 27 cases between 1666 and 1700 is 0.70628. Its standard error of estimate is 6,711.50. In other words, in 68 percent of the cases, Sulmona can predict total wool within ± 6,711 *rubbi;* in 95 percent of the cases, within ± 13,423 *rubbi*. The three other account books have poor confidence ratings as measured in adjusted R^2: Aquila Bianca, 0.50341; Aquila Nera, 0.25426; Castel di Sangro, 0.52374. Two other methods offer checks to the extrapolation of total wool production according to the Sulmona linear regression. First, residuals from the observed total wool sales for 1666–1700 minus predicted totals of the linear regression can be standardized and plotted. Of the twenty-six valid observations, only two points (1677 and 1700) exceed one standard deviation. On closer inspection, about 88 percent of the predictions are within ± 10 percent of the observed totals; and 54 percent, ± 5 percent. Second, wool production can be calculated from *pesatori* salaries in selected cases, noted above, n. 4 (see table N-6). Note that the three wide variations (1649, 1655, 1656) can be explained by unpredictable external factors—the disruptions following the Masaniello revolt and the uncertainty during the plague. On the whole, both comparisons increase confidence in the accuracy of the Sulmona linear regression.

13. ASFg, *Dogana,* serie V, reg. 2172 (1701) cites Ovid, *Tristia,* 4.x.3. Translation adapted from the Loeb Classical Library, 1965.

14. ASFg, *Dogana,* serie V, regg. 2001 (1625), 2017 (1641), 2029 (1655), 2057–2060 (1670), 2114–2117 (1685), and 2167–2170 (1700).

15. The Doria sources are cited in chap. 1, n. 116; the public prices in ASFg, *Dogana,* serie I, fas. 355 and 356 (1732–1805), "Atti della voce della lana del corrente anno [year]."

TABLE N-6 Comparative Wool Production

Year	Account Book	Salary Total	Difference	Percentage Difference
1647	60,023.83[a]	60,215.3	191.42	0.3
1649	51,926.67[a]	36,757.5	−15,169.17	−29.2
1652	59,923.04[a]	60,367.0	443.96	0.7
1655	51,709.66[a]	65,518.6	13,808.94	26.7
1656	48,127.97[a]	54,463.3	6,335.33	11.6
1665	53,500.43[a]	54,700.6	1,200.17	2.2
1682	52,460.69	51,539.8	920.89	1.8

[a]estimated on a linear regression.

16. De Dominicis, *Lo stato politico,* 3:132 confirms the high to be beyond 130,000 *rubbi,* more than 1.6 million sheep.

17. Again, the linear regression analysis gives an adjusted R^2 for the four account books: Aquila *bianca,* 0.73204; Aquila *nera,* 0.12179; Sulmona, 0.28178; and Castel di Sangro, 0.34902. But even Aquila *bianca* has limited value, as one other statistical measure cautions: standard error of estimate = 10,297.54.

18. De Dominicis, *Lo stato politico,* 3:123.

19. Only one source in 1564 (see chap. 7, n. 52) gives us wool production information at 80,000 *rubbi* for this earlier period of florescence. My wool estimates are based on our information on total sheep numbers.

20. ASFg, *Dogana,* serie V, unnumbered (1648) in fas. with regg. 2011–2020, and unnumbered (1657) in fas. with regg. 2021–2030. In 1650, when Foggia was still recovering from the revolt, problems were recorded at the fair because wool was sold by constraint. ASFg, *Dogana,* serie I, fas. 18, 12r–15v (28 November 1650).

21. Stefano Di Stefano, "Ragioni per la Generalità de' Locati della Mena delle Pecore di Puglia" (20 May 1705) is a printed brief preserved in ASFg, Biblioteca, MS. 1030, 31v. For 1704, Di Stefano gives 70,000 *rubbi,* and for 1705, 60,000.

22. The post season summer sales in 1670 and 1685 offer best evidence here. In 1670 the May-June mean of 93 *rubbi* per transaction was maintained in July with 95 *rubbi;* August, down to 51; but September, up to 95; and October, 104. Note, however, that prices were only discounted in the following spring, 1671, by almost 25 percent, from 21 to 16 *carlini* per *rubbio.* In 1685 the May-June mean of 140 *rubbi* was greatly superseded in July with 241 *rubbi* per transaction. ASN, *Sommaria Consultationum,* fas. 83, 15v–16r (31 March 1683): "If June 15 finds unsold wool in depositories, it should be put up for sale at whatever time possible up to the following May."

23. Ibid., 13v–16r (31 March 1683).

24. Coniglio, *Carlo V,* p. 121 (cited in full in chap. 1, n. 67); Galasso, "Momenti e problemi," pp. 169–72 (cited in full in chap. 7, n. 6); Carracciolo, *Il Regno* pp. 77–82 (cited in full in chap. 7, n. 30). Cf. H. G. Koenigsberger, "English Merchants in Naples and Sicily in the Seventeenth Century," *English Historical Review* 62 (1947):304–26.

25. Grohmann, *Le fiere del Regno,* pp. 91–92, 343–404 (cited in full in chap. 1, n. 49).

26. Armando Sapori, "Una fiera in Italia alla fine del Quattrocento," in *Studi di storia economica (Secolo XIII, XIV, XV),* 3d ed., 3 vols. (Florence: Sansoni, 1955), 1:448.

27. C. Phillips, "The Spanish Wool Trade," p. 777 (cited in full in chap. 1, n. 43) reports the same one-third export law for Castile.

28. Di Cicco, "Produzione della lana," nn. 18, 42.

29. In a direct comparison of the tabulated entries of wool in and out of deposit in the account books, 30 cases have been assembled with 20 *infondacatura* totals higher and 10

sfondacatura totals higher. In a comparison of account book totals for wool out of deposit and *voce* price production statistics, 66 cases can be compared—23 *infondacatura* and 43 *sfondacatura* totals are higher.

30. A word of caution. The *voce* lists of wool quantity put in deposit are incomplete because wool placed in storage after 15 May is not included. Their estimate is 4,000 to 5,000 *rubbi* lower. Massenzio, "Il mercato della lana" (cited in full in chap. 3, n. 43).

31. See chap. 9, n. 70.

32. ASFg, *Dogana,* serie I, fas. 355, n. 12582.

33. Ibid., fas. 356, n. 12628, esp. c.s. 50 and 51.

34. Macry, *Mercato e società,* pp. 307–18 (cited in full in chap. 2, n. 84).

35. ASFg, *Dogana,* fas. 8, 228r–29v (1762), and 256r–57v (15 May 1762).

36. Nardella, *Attività creditizie,* n. 74 (cited in full in chap. 3, n. 32), from notarial protocols in Lucera, records the exceptional case of August wool being sold at Foggia in May 1634.

37. AGS, *Visítas d'Italia, Nápoles,* leg. 15:4, 13r (1562), gives 33–34 *carlini* for April 1562; leg. 46:1, 163r (3 March 1584) copies a 16 May 1581 document with a price of 26–33 *carlini;* leg. 46:1, 174r (3 March 1584) copies an 18 May 1582 document with a price of 15–20 *carlini;* leg. 114:2, 2d num., 23v (5 April 1608) gives 30–32 *carlini* for 4 May 1606. The 1582 low, 15–20 *carlini,* proves the generalization since the document refers to this price as very low. The price of 20.3 *carlini* is confirmed in a 12 May wool merchants' contract for that year. Ibid., leg. 30:2, 219v (7 June 1582).

38. ASFg, *Dogana,* serie I, fas. 355, n. 12583, "Atti della voce . . . 1734," says prices should be higher because of increased demand that was "eating up all the wool"; n. 12594, in a document dated 29 May 1745, explains that the 1.2-ducat per *rubbio* jump in *voce* price was due to the halving of supply after that year's sheep mortality.

39. Villari, *La rivolta,* pp. 153–57 (cited in full in chap. 5, n. 23) recounts the spectacular bankruptcy of Bartolomeo D'Aquino and his circle.

40. Nardella, *Attività creditizie,* pp. 57–131.

41. Chorley, *Oil, Silk, and Enlightenment,* p. 86 (cited in full in chap. 3, n. 30).

42. AGS, *Visítas d'Italia, Nápoles,* leg. 30:2, 218r–32r (7 June 1582).

43. ASFg, *Dogana,* serie V, regg. 2057–2060 (1670).

44. ARSJ, *Fondo gesuitico,* fas. 929, fasc. 9.

45. ADLPR, scaf. 16/52, "Vendite di lana, agnelli, vaccine . . . fatte annualmente in Melfi 1705–1827," int. 7, 8, 9.

46. Ibid., int. 84, 85.

47. Here we might look ahead to the 20,000 *castrati* out of 22,000 exported to Florence, Umbria, and Ancona in 1577 (chap. 9, p. 236) and the 10,000 ducats' worth of *castrati* exported to Florence in 1624 (chap. 9, p. 236). Domestic consumption of meat was obviously unusual in 1532, when special provision had to be made to prevent its export, and then the order was countermanded (chap. 7, n. 55). By 1583, however, 8,000 *castrati* were being sent to Naples in order to feed the increasing population. AGS, *Visítas d'Italia, Nápoles,* leg. 46:1, 203r (20 March 1583). Some 1,000 *cantara* of cheese were sent to Naples in September following the 1649 revolt (see n. 44). But according to Galanti's 1771 budget, only 40 *cantara* were exported, while 135,000 *cantara* were imported from the Morea (83 percent), Sicily (10 percent), and Sardinia (7 percent). Galanti, *Nuova descrizione,* 1:551, 556 (cited in full in chap. 3, n. 19).

48. De Dominicis, *Lo stato politico,* 3:110–11 tells us that they were always in smaller number because this breeding season was considered inferior.

49. Silla, *La pastorizia difesa,* p. 210 (cited in full in chap. 2, n. 46) in his 1783 model budget for a flock of 2,000 sheep gives 850 births: 350 *primaticci* at 15 *carlini* each, 200 *vernarecci* at 10 *carlini,* and 300 *cordeschi* at 6 *carlini.* Silla's estimate would give 59 percent spring and 41 percent fall lambs.

50. Macry, *Mercato e società,* p. 64.

51. De Dominicis, *Lo stato politico*, 1:229–30. Corrado Marciani, in a series of articles and books, has studied letters of exchange, slaves, books, glass, saffron, and Jews at Lanciano.
52. Grohmann, *Le fiere del Regno*, pp. 310–25.
53. Ibid., pp. 340–42.
54. Ibid., pp. 101–2.
55. Plotting the two commodities, wheat and wool, reveals the minimal disparity in rising agricultural and pastoral prices from 1731 to 1845. The slope of the line for wheat (0.01385) rises at slightly less than twice the rate of that of wool (0.00709). For grain prices, Macry, *Mercato e società*, pp. 298–323; 487–89.
56. Ruggiero Romano, "Prezzi, salari e servizi a Napoli nel secolo XVIII," in *Napoli: dal Viceregno al Regno* (Turin: Einaudi, 1976), p. 245.
57. A similar crisis which favored cereals over wool has been documented for sixteenth- and seventeenth-century England. Wool prices failed to keep pace with wheat prices especially after 1560, and by the end of the seventeenth century, wool yielded lower returns than most other forms of agricultural investment. David Grigg, *Population Growth and Agrarian Change. An Historical Perspective* (Cambridge: Cambridge University Press, 1980), pp. 85–86 draws his graph from the price data in Joan Thirsk, ed., *The Agrarian History of England and Wales*, vol. 4, *1500–1640* (Cambridge: Cambridge University Press, 1967), pp. 815–21, 839–45. See P. J. Bowden, "Agricultural prices, farm profits, and rents," in ibid., pp. 593–695.
58. Franca Assante, *La Puglia demografica nel secolo XIX*, Biblioteca degli "Annali di Storia Economica e Sociale," no. 12 (Naples: Università degli Studi di Napoli, 1967); Assante, *Città e campagne nella Puglia del secolo XIX. L'Evolution demografica* (Geneva: Libraire Droz, 1974). See also, *Dizionario statistico de' paesi del Regno delle due Sicilie* (Naples, 1840), ed. Gabriello de Sanctis, pp. 29–30. Note however, Galasso, "Lo sviluppo demografico," (cited in full in chap. 4, n. 20) tab. 27, p. 439 gives different population figures. For 1861 he ranks provincial towns in the following order: (1) Reggio Calabria, 57,763; (2) Bari, 41,874; and (3) Foggia, 34,052. Still, according to his figures, Foggia had grown by 225 percent in 1911, when it moved up to second place (76,680) behind Bari's 116,559.

9. Sellers and Buyers at the Fair of Foggia

1. BNN, MS. XII.B.46, cc. 612–13 (13 April 1645) claims that merchants delayed purchases by waiting until the sheepowners had to leave because of the heat and, thus, hoped to "beat down prices to a very low level."
2. ASFg, *Dogana*, serie I, fas. 8, 166v–67r (12 June 1760): "senza che si cavino dal Regno l'oro, e l'argento e che la Piazza resti debitrice alle forestiere con discapito de cambi." Clearly the Neapolitan government applied Galiani's 1757 theories (chap. 3, n. 17) that exports were necessary in order to offset imports.
3. "Prime Grazie del Re Ferdinando I," (5 December 1470), item 13. See chap. 1, n. 51.
4. "*Grazie* of Charles V" (11 February 1536), item 27. See chap. 1, n. 70.
5. AGS, *Visítas d'Italia, Nápoles*, leg. 46:1 (3 March 1584) copies a document of 16 March 1581.
6. De Dominicis, *Lo stato politico*, 3:122–23 (cited in full in intro., n. 13).
7. Ibid., 3:124–25. See chap. 1, n. 120.
8. ASN, *Sommaria Consultationum*, fas. 79, 69r–v (10 June 1679).
9. De Dominicis, *Lo stato politico*, 3:126–27, 226. Governor Ulloa y Lanzina also established the state *voce* for wheat and barley in 1694.
10. Di Stefano, *La ragion pastorale*, 1:362 (cited in full in intro., n. 12). ASFg, *Dogana*, serie I, fas. 4: 424r–v (13 June 1704).

11. Gaudiani, *Notizie*, p. 257 (cited in full in intro., n. 14).
12. Di Stefano, *La ragion pastorale*, 1:355. His general principle is derived from Cicero, *De Officiis*, bk. 1, and the specific reference to Foggia is from Gian Geronimo de Filippo, *Rerum fiscalium dissertationes suis quaeque diffinitionibus illustratae* (Naples: Officina Novelli de Bonis Typographi Archiepiscopalis, 1673).
13. De Dominicis, *Lo stato politico*, 3:114. For an introduction to early monopoly theory, see Raymond de Roover, "Monopoly Theory prior to Adam Smith: A Revision," in *Business, Banking and Economic Thought in Late Medieval and Early Modern Europe*, ed. Julius Kirshner (Chicago: University of Chicago Press, 1974), pp. 273–305.
14. Giovanni Boccaccio, *Decameron*, trans. Richard Aldington (New York: Dell, 1930).
15. See chap, 2, n. 43.
16. ASV, *Cinque Savi alla Mercanzia*, serie I, busta 475, "Lana nelli magazini de Mercanti di Venezia di Puglia e Romagna" (23 October 1722).
17. Charles M. Dollar and Richard J. Jensen, *Historian's Guide to Statistics* (New York: Holt, Rinehart & Winston, 1971), pp. 50–54.
18. Le Roy Ladurie, *The Peasants of Languedoc*, pp. 4–5 (cited in full in intro., n. 4) outlines successive stages of land concentration and subdivision: consolidation in 1350, subdivision in 1500, consolidation in 1680, subdivision in 1750–70, and consolidation in 1870–73. Note the similarity to the wool conjuncture.
19. ASFg, *Dogana*, serie V, regg. 2002 (1626), 2003 (1672), 2004 (1628), 2018 (1642), 2019 (1643), 2021 (1645), and the unnumbered *libretto* in the fascio holding regg. 2011–2020 (1648). The San Severo flock size would have numbered from 10,000 to 14,000 sheep.
20. Ibid., regg. 2001 (1625) gives 406 *rubbi;* 2006 (1630), 474 *rubbi;* 2011 (1635), 645 *rubbi;* 2017 (1641), no listing; 2021 (1645), 415 *rubbi;* 2024 (1650), 426 *rubbi;* 2029 (1655), 613 *rubbi.*
21. ASN, *Monasteri soppressi*, 2437 (V).
22. Coda, *Breve discorso*, pp. 93–95 (cited in full in intro., n. 16) as corrected in Marino, "*Professazione voluntaria*," p. 31 (cited in full in chap. 1, n. 71); Cimaglia, *Ragionamento*, pp. 35–36, n. (a) (cited in full in chap. 3, n. 28); Silla, *La pastorizia difesa*, pp. 203–14 (cited in full in chap. 2, n. 46). Note that Silla also includes fixed capital outlays of close to 5,000 ducats. Initial investment for livestock and equipment made large-scale sheep farming an enterprise requiring substantial start-up capital.
23. For salaries: the Doria sheep industry records 23,462 mean work days/360 days = 65 employees; 1,463 ducats mean annual salary/65 employees = 23 ducats per year each. Coda, *Breve discorso*, pp. 93–95 gives 20 ducats per year per employee. For provisions and equipment: the Doria budgets' mean is 1,170.25/65 employees = 18 ducats. Coda gives 17.2 ducats per employee.
24. Di Cicco, "Produzione della lana," pp. 8–10 (cited in full in chap. 2, n. 44). ASFg, *Dogana*, serie V, regg. 2191 (1706), 2193 (1706), and 4547, "Affitti di fondaci." Matteo Di Padova, "Produzione e commercio della lana nella dogana delle pecore di Foggia dal 1759 al 1779," Tesi di Laurea, Università degli Studi di Bari, 1960/61, pp. 52–53 notes 134 *fondaci* and lists 22 of the largest.
25. Massenzio, "Il mercato della lana," pp. 19–21 (cited in full in chap. 3, n. 43) cites ASFg, *Dogana*, serie V, reg. 4470 (28 April 1773).
26. ASFg, *Dogana*, serie V, regg. 2028 (1654), and 2029 (1655).
27. Ibid., reg. 2029 (1655).
28. Ibid., regg. 2057–2060 (1670), 2115 (1685), 2155–2158 (1697), 2167–2170 (1700), and 2183–2186 (1704).
29. All these names appear in the weighers' account books. For these Foggian palaces, see Jarussi, *Foggia, Genesi urbanistica*, pp. 110, 117, 124–25, 133 (cited in full in intro., n. 2).

30. Di Cicco, "Produzione della lana," p. 25 identifies Pietro Zanetti, Pietro Marchetti, and Giovanni Marchetti as Foggians.

31. ASN, *Sommaria Consultationum*, fas. 124, 157r–v (24 May 1719) describes a case of contraband between Manfredonia and Venice involving another Pietro Marchetti, grandson (?) of the former. Such large public merchants could contract to send produce anywhere. In Gaudiani, *Notizie*, p. 17, n. 15, DiCicco identifies Giovanni Marchetti as one of Gaudiani's clients. He appears in a list of "well-known Venetians, public merchants and traders in the city of Foggia."

32. See chap. 9, table 31. Cerreto ranked 7, 7, and 5 among buyers' towns of origin in 1670, 1685, and 1700. Of its total wool purchases, 94 percent, 96 percent, and 99 percent respectively were of black wool. De Dominicis, *Lo stato politico*, 3:123 claims that all black wool was sent to Cerreto to be made into five hundred pieces of cloth for the royal troops. Franco, "L'industria dei panni-lana," p. 193 (cited in full in chap. 7, n. 69) cites a notarial contract of 1704 confirming particulars of prices and costs of different parts of the five hundred uniforms to be sent to the Tuscan garrisons.

33. De Dominicis, *Lo stato politico*, 3:123.

34. Nardella, *Attività creditizie*, pp. 36–37 (cited in full in chap. 3, n. 32).

35. Coniglio. "L'arte della lana a Napoli," p. 62 (cited in full in chap. 7, n. 94).

36. Ibid., p. 63; Nicola Fortunato, *Riflessioni intorno al commercio antico e moderno del Regno di Napoli* (Naples: Stamperia Simoniana, 1760), pp. 104–5 gives information on the wool guild (5 December 1463); De Dominicis, *Lo stato politico*, 3:114 explains that the 1470 *grazie* of the pastoralists were in response to monopolistic attempts on the part of these new native buyers.

37. Coniglio, "L'arte della lana a Napoli," pp. 69–79 transcribes the statutes (22 March 1536). See also, AGS, *Visítas d'Italia, Nápoles*, leg. 19:7 for a copy of the guild's constitution, privileges, and a matriculation list of members (1529–61), ASN, *Curia dell'Arte della Lana*, fas. 40, fasc. 1170, 71r–98r (1688) for revised statutes at the moment of the seventeenth-century recovery.

38. Coniglio, "L'arte della lana a Napoli," p. 67.

39. Coniglio, *Carlo V*, pp. 137–40 (cited in full in chap. 1, n. 67); Coniglio, *Il Viceregno nel secolo XVII*, pp. 83–84 (cited in full in chap. 7, n. 7); and Caracciolo, *Il Regno di Napoli*, pp. 154–66 (cited in full in chap. 7, n. 30).

40. Coniglio, *Carlo V*, p. 138, n. 140 cites three export contracts from 1545–46.

41. Aymard, "Commerce et consommation des draps," pp. 136–39 (cited in full in chap. 3, n. 19) focuses on the Salerno fair.

42. Michele Cioffi, "L'industria e il commercio della lana e dei cuoiami in S. Cipriano Picentino nei sec. XVI–XVII," *Rassegna storica salernitana* 14 (1953):208–22.

43. Michele Cioffi, "L'arte della lana nel territorio di Giffoni nel secolo XVI," *Il Picentino* 4, no. 1 (1960):5–25 and 4, nos. 3–4 (1960):8–12 gives first evidence from 1509, again with a Florentine connection.

44. F. Scandone, "L'arte della lana in Avellino dalla fine del secolo XVI all'inizio del XIX," *Samnium* 20 (1947):121–45.

45. Galanti, *Nuova descrizione*, 1:557–58 (cited in full in chap. 3, n. 19) gives the budgetary income from 1771, and 2:169–71 reviews quantity of production by towns ca. 1789.

46. If the three buyers with unverified origins mentioned above—Angelo Alfieri, Giuseppe Ricciardi, and Martino Spagnardi—turned out to be foreign buyers, then the adjusted percentage for foreign exports in 1685 would rise accordingly.

47. Nardella, *Attività creditizie*, pp. 35–36.

48. ASFg, *Dogana*, serie I, fas. 3, 256r–v (20 May 1631).

49. Domenico Sella, *Crisis and Continuity. The Economy of Spanish Lombardy in the Seventeenth Century* (Cambridge, Mass.: Harvard University Press, 1979), p. 54.

50. Ibid., p. 87.

51. Sella, "Rise and Fall of Woollen," p. 110 (cited in full in chap. 3, n. 12) emphasizes that these totals are from peak to peak along the production curve.

52. Sella, *Crisis and Continuity,* p. 113; Richard T. Rapp, *Industry and Economic Decline in Seventeenth-Century Venice* (Cambridge, Mass.: Harvard University Press, 1976), pp. 158–162.

53. Raymond De Roover, "A Florentine Firm of Cloth Manufactuers," in *Business, Banking, and Economic Thought,* ed. Kirshner, pp. 108, 118 gives two Florentine operating statutes, one from 1531 and the other from 1556–58. Raw wool accounted for 35 percent and 30 percent of cost, whereas all phases of the manufacturing process accounted for 44 percent and 46 percent, with dyeing another 18 percent and 10 percent.

54. ASV, *Sindaci Inquisitori di Terraferma,* busta 63, ff. 114r–v.

55. Rapp, *Industry and Economic Decline,* p. 162 gives a chart of the information in ASV, *Cinque Savi alla Mercanzia,* serie II, busta 121, fasc, 185, pt. 1. I have corrected a number of typographical errors from the archival document: 1685 total is 34,116 cloths; 1702 and 1703 *bassi* are 17,000 and 15,026; 1703 total is 30,042.

56. ASV, *Cinque Savi alla Mercanzia,* serie II, busta 121, 3 July 1686.

57. Ibid., fasc. 185 (22 May–15 June 1697). Foggian wools were called *panni alta Padovana, stametti, rovessi,* and *rasse.*

58. Ibid., serie I, busta 475, "Note dei fabbricatori e delle pezzi di lana e panno (1624–1770)," "Interrogazioni Risposte" (30 January 1767).

59. Ibid., busta 472 bis, fasc. "Lanificio-Bergamo fabbricche" (August and March 1782–92).

60. De Dominicis, *Lo stato politico,* 3:114, 151.

61. See chap. 8, n. 42.

62. Sella, "Rise and Fall of Woollen," p. 109. Note that the first low points in Venetian cloth production in the seventeenth century corresponded to the bad winters in Foggia: 1611, 16,079 cloths; and 1612, 16,193 cloths, down from the previous high in 1602, 28,729 cloths, 1622, 14,778 cloths; and 1623, 12,976 cloths down from the previous high in 1620, 23,000 cloths.

63. De Dominicis, *Lo stato politico,* 3:125.

64. See n. 8.

65. De Dominicis, *Lo stato politico,* 3:112.

66. ASFi, *Mediceo,* fas. 4101, "Letteri del sig. Vincenzio Vettori di Napoli (1621–1624)" (Foggia, 12 May 1624).

67. Ibid., (Foggia, 5 May 1622, and 25 April 1623).

68. Ibid., fas. 4092 (Naples, 4 July, 14 July, and 22 August 1606).

69. Here again more research on the Neapolitan wool guild and the early modern Florentine industry is needed. See Judith C. Brown and Jordan Goodman, "Women and Industry in Florence," *Journal of Economic History* 40, no. 1 (1980):77 gives a table of wool and silk cloth production, 1330–1739, by decades. The highs of the 1560s and 1570s at 31,000 pieces fell to 13,000 between 1580 and 1610, down to 10,700 in the 1610s, 9,000 in the 1620s, 6,000 between 1630 and 1649, and only one other citation, 3,500 cloths in the 1660s. We simply do not know what was going on in Florentine woolens after the seventeenth-century recovery, although Goodman's research has turned up a booming silk industry from 1600 to 1669 and even 50 percent greater output with 15,500 cloths in the 1730s. Domenico Sella, "Industrial Production in Seventeenth-Century Italy: A Reappraisal," *Explorations in Entrepreneurial History,* 2d ser., 6 (1969): 246 points out that consumer taste shifted from woolens to silks.

70. Confirming evidence of the French-Neapolitan woolen axis comes from Galanti, *Nuovo descrizione,* 2:169, who points out that Arpino engaged in the most modern native manufacturing in 1789. Its industry had been founded by a French manufacturer, Baduel, some fifty years earlier, that is, about this time in the 1730s.

71. ASFg, *Dogana*, serie I, fas. 9, 170r–173r (1 August 1767).
72. Ibid., 286r–288v (10 April 1770). Frederic C. Lane, *Venetian Ships and Shipbuilders of the Renaissance* (Baltimore: Johns Hopkins Press, 1934), pp. 36–40 explains the comparative advantages of square-rigged vessels in seaworthiness, size of cargo, reduced crew, etc., and the revolution in the rigging of Mediterranean ships which was well underway in the fourteenth and fifteenth centuries. By 1770 the Neapolitan merchant fleet was indeed behind the times.
73. Having inbound raw materials pay for the carrying charges of outbound finished products was commonplace in the political economy of Venetian shipping. See Jean-Claude Hocquet, *Le sel et la fortune de Venise*, 2 vols. (Lille: Publications de L'Université de Lille III, 1978–79) for the conscious use of salt in this regard.
74. ASFg, *Dogana*, serie I, fas. 9, 286r–88v (10 April 1770).
75. See chap. 7, n. 77 for the same figures for Venetian consumption as gleaned from the port books.
76. ASFg, *Dogana*, serie V, fas. 354, n. 12628, c.s. 50 (1r–50r).
77. Ibid., 12v.
78. Ruggiero Romano, "Il commercio franco-napoletano nel secolo XVIII," and "Il Regno di Napoli e la vita commerciale nell'Adriatico," in his *Napoli: dal Viceregno al Regno*, (cited in full in chap. 8, n. 56), pp. 83, 150–51. Note the unusually high French figures in 1776, 1779, and 1785 (a 45,000-*rubbi* mean); Galanti, *Nuova descrizione*, 1:562, gives 1,482 *balle* (44,000 *rubbi*) in 1784. The French buyers appear to have shipped in two-year supply cycles. After 1787, Romano's figures are in money value, and thus the quantity level must remain approximate.
79. Tihomir J. Markovitch, *Les industries lainières de Colbert à la Révolution* (Geneva: Droz, 1976), pp. 471–88 outlines the growth in French textiles: the period 1775/78–1785/87 witnessed an 81 percent increase from 1748/51 to 1775/78.
80. Wallerstein, *The Modern World-System*, 2:137–38 (cited in full in intro., n. 19).
81. Timothy Davies, "Changes in the Structure of the Wheat Trade in Seventeenth-century Sicily and the Building of New Villages," *Journal of European Economic History* 12, no. 2 (1983):371–405, esp. 405.
82. Aymard, "Money and Peasant Economy," p. 18 (cited in full in intro., n. 19).
83. Bowden, "Agricultural Prices," pp. 636–37 (cited in full in chap. 8, n. 57); T. H. Lloyd, "The Movement of Wool Prices in Medieval England," *Economic History Review*, suppl. no. 6 (1973), pp. 13–14.
84. Galiani, *Della moneta*, bk. V, chap. 4, pp. 303–4 (cited in full in chap. 1, n. 135).
85. The eighteenth-century estimate of the value of products exchanged at Foggia is derived from app. E: wool (375,000 ducats) + cheese (100,000 ducats) + meat (approx. 125,000 ducats). This 600,000 ducats compares to a similarly derived seventeenth-century estimate of 250,000 ducats.
86. Coniglio, *I vicerè spagnoli di Napoli* (Naples: Fausto Fiorentino, 1967), app. 10 copies a trade budget found in Mantova dated 1520. Note May wool exports during this period were only 0.4 percent.
87. Galasso, "Momenti e problemi," pp. 180–83 depends upon Porzio, *La congiura de'Baroni*, p. 346 (cited in full in intro., n. 7) and Coniglio, *Il Viceregno*, p. 87.
88. Aymard, "Commerce et consommation," pp. 133–36, 136–39.
89. Galanti, *Nuova descrizione*, 1:548–70. In ducats, major imports include silk, 965,000 (13 percent); woolens, 885,749 (12 percent); leather goods, 878,372 (11 percent); linens, 852,000 (11 percent); metals and minerals, 513,072 (7 percent); and cottons, 429,467 (6 percent) for 60 percent of 7,657,017. Major exports were olive oil, 2,600,000 (41 percent); wheat, 900,000 (14 percent); wool and woolens, 857,332 (13 percent); timber, 539,200 (8 percent); and silk, 407,670 (6 percent) for 82 percent of 6,401,277.

10. From Pastoral Models to Political Economy

1. Galiani, *Della moneta*, bk. 4, chap. 4; pp. 343-44 (cited in full in chap. 1, n. 135).
2. Some confusion surrounds the publication date. The first imprint (Naples: Raimondi, 1750) was in fact issued in 1751. Galiani, nevertheless, continued to refer to 1750 as the date of publication. See Galiani, *Della moneta*, editor's intro., p. xxxviii.
3. Franco Venturi, "The Enlightenment in Southern Italy," in *Italy and the Enlightenment. Studies in a Cosmopolitan Century*, trans. Susan Corsi (London: Longman, 1972), pp. 198-224.
4. Nicola Fortunato, *Discoverta dell'antico Regno di Napoli col suo presente stato a pro della sovranità e de' suoi Popoli* (Naples: presso Giuseppe Raimondi, 1767).
5. Nicola Fortunato, *Riflessioni*, p. 218 (cited in full in chap. 9, n. 36) mentions the sheep customhouse and Alfonso's foundation only in passing.
6. Nicola Fortunato, *Rimostranza toccante l'Annona della Città e Regno e 'l Real Tavoliere di Puglia di sua coerenza*, pp. 191-235 of *Discoverta* was published as a separate pamphlet, without date or place, in sixty-seven pages; "Digressione sul Reale Tavoliere di Puglia," pp. 214-35 of the *Discoverta*.
7. Ibid., pp. 232-33, n. B.
8. Franco Venturi, "The Position of Galiani between the Encyclopaedists and the Physiocrats," in *Italy and the Enlightenment*, pp. 180-197.
9. Filippo Briganti, *Esame economico del sistema civile* (Naples: Stamperia Simoniana, 1780), pp. 141-67.
10. Ibid., p. 167.
11. Ibid., p. 141. Note the inversion of the traditional imagery of peaceful pastoralism and warlike agriculture, where agriculture is accused of raping mother earth with the plow. Cf. Cervantes, *Don Quixote*, pt. 1, chap. 11.
12. Ronald L. Meek, *Social Science and the Ignoble Savage* (Cambridge: Cambridge University Press, 1975), examines the first stage, savagery, and the genesis of the theory in the 1750s.
13. Briganti, *Esame*, p. 156.
14. Ibid., pp. 166-67.
15. Ibid., p. 166.
16. Ibid.
17. Ibid., p. 167
18. For the Spanish case of Pedro Rodriguez Campomanes, Mickun, *La Mesta*, pp. 18-32 (cited in full in chap. 5, n. 1) explicates three Mesta documents—the memorial of 1771, the "Memorial of Concord" of 1783, and the "Memorial of the Agrarian Law" of 1784—in the context of Campomanes' Enlightened opinions on population and prosperity. Franco Venturi, "Spanish and Italian Economists and Reformers," in *Italy and the Enlightenment*, pp. 268, 274-75, 287 makes the connection between Galiani and Campomanes explicit.
19. Galanti, *Nuova descrizione*, 1:530 (cited in full in chap. 2, n. 60), "In England the sheep pasture among the plows, but the latter is the boss."
20. Aymard, "La transizione dal feudalesimo al capitalismo," pp. 1133-1192 (cited in full in intro., n. 19).
21. Le Flem, "Las cuentas de la Mesta (1510-1709)," pp. 23-24 (cited in full in chap. 3, n. 14).
22. No eighteenth-century printed text on the dogana mentions Gaudiani's work. Di Stefano was unaware of its existence, and only Grana, *Istituzioni* (cited in full in chap. 1, n. 20) seems to have made use of it anonymously. Despite its apparent oblivion, its legalistic organization presents an extremely accessible means for participants and moderns to conceptualize the sheep customhouse. See Gaudiani, *Notizie*, pp. 7-9 (cited in full in intro., n. 14).
23. Gaudiani, *Notizie*, p. 25.
24. Ibid., p. 26.

25. Ibid., p. 364.
26. Ibid., pp. 32–33, 259 cites Justus Lipsius, *Admiranda sive de magnitudine romana libri quattuor* (Paris: Apud Ambrosium Drovard, 1598), and probably found his Tacitus in Lipsius.
27. Gaudiani, *Notizie*, p. 25.
28. Ibid., p. 315. For translations of Tacitus, see chap, 3, n. 70.
29. Ibid., p. 365.
30. Ibid., p. 181.
31. Ibid., p. 185.
32. Ibid., p. 29.
33. Ibid., p. 263.
34. Ibid., p. 34. Following a review of Roman legal practice on pastoralism, Gaudiani concludes: "From which is clearly deduced the liberty, which the owners of animals hold, to rent at their own will, and liberty either in public fields or from private persons."
35. Ibid., p. 242.
36. Ibid., p. 259.
37. Ibid., p. 35.
38. For these 1668 laws, see chap. 1, n. 120.
39. Gian Vicenzo Gravina, *Della ragion poetica, libri due* (Rome: Francesco Gonzaga, 1708) in *Scritti Critici e Teorici*, ed. Amedeo Quondam (Rome: Laterza, 1973), p. 199; and for the wider Arcadian context, Marino, "The State and the Shepherds in Pre-Enlightenment Naples" (cited in full in chap. 4, n. 36).
40. Di Stefano, *La ragion pastorale*, xii–xiii (cited in full in intro., n. 12) states that these two points are "our principal objective."
41. Ibid., 1:14–24.
42. Ibid., 1:14.
43. Ibid., 1:15.
44. Ibid., 1:208.
45. De Dominicis, *Lo stato politico*, 1:ix (cited in full in intro., n. 13). This description of De Dominicis' work is given by one of the prepublication censors, P. D. Emanuele Caputo Benedettino, a Neapolitan university professor.
46. Ibid., 1:7.
47. Genovesi taught a modified "optimum population" theory. Schumpeter, *History of Economic Analysis*, p. 258 (cited in full in chap. 3, n. 42) evaluates the theory. "Genovesi saw that, from the standpoint of a population living under given conditions, numbers are capable of being either too small or too great in the sense that increase or decrease would produce greater 'happiness.'"
48. De Dominicis, *Lo stato politico*, 1:35, 39, 46.
49. Ibid., 3:149, 152, 154.
50. Ibid., 1:8.
51. Ibid., 1:1–2.
52. Venturi, "The Enlightenment in Southern Italy," p. 213 argues it would be incorrect to make hard and fast categories, but this divergent tendency between capital and provinces was evident by the early 1780s.
53. Giuseppe Palmieri, *Pensieri economici relativi al Regno di Napoli* (Naples: Vincenzo Flauto, 1789), pp. 57–119.
54. Cimaglia, *Ragionamento*, (cited in full in chap. 3, n. 28) is typical.
55. Targioni, *Saggi fisici* (cited in full in chap. 2, n. 42), and his source, Louis-Jean-Marie Daubenton, *Instruction pour les bergers et pour les propriétaires de troupeaux* (Paris: Ph-D. Pierres, 1782). This "science" even has Condorcet's imprimatur. But the information is so scientifically precise to be absurd; for example, should the shepherds be literate? Yes, but if not, someone can read this book to them. To facilitate communication, Daubenton was

translated into Italian in the year after Targioni's essays. Daubenton, *Instruzione per pastori e proprietari di gregge* (Venice: Gio. Antonio Pezzana, 1787). It must have been popular, for a fifth edition was published in 1820.

56. For a portrait of Galanti and his program, see the editors' intro., in his *Nuova descrizione* and *Riformatori Napoletani*, ed. Franco Venturi (Milan: R. Ricciardi, 1962), vol. 5 in *Illuministi Italiani*.

57. Galanti, *Nuova descrizione*, editors' intro., 1:xix quotes the royal edict of 1782.

58. Ibid., in order of citation, 1:523, 525, 526, 531, 526.

59. Ibid., 1:519.

60. Ibid., 1:520.

61. Ibid., 1:519.

62. Ibid., 1:521. Pace De Dominicis, *Lo stato politico*, 1:1–2. His pastoral vision of the "loving sisters" would not receive the ministerial favor that had greeted Di Stefano's.

63. Ibid., 1:527.

64. Ibid., 1:520.

65. Ibid., 1:530.

66. Ibid., 1:525.

67. Ibid., 2:515–40, "Relazione intorno allo stato della Capitanata," sent to the king in 1791.

68. Mario de Luca, *Gli economisti napoletane del Settecento e la politica dello sviluppo* (Naples: Morano Editore, n.d. [1969?]) examines Genovesi and Galiani in terms of modern development theory, and emphasizes the early Neapolitan school's belief in larger populations, the primacy of agriculture, the elasticity of supply, and sectoral balance.

69. Elliott, "The Decline of Spain," p. 161.

70. Grigg, *Population Growth and Agrarian Change*, p. 206 (cited in full in chap. 8, n. 57) develops the argument for the absence of a population crisis in late eighteenth- and early nineteenth-century France. He argues that rural population followed the model of earlier centuries and stopped growing so rapidly by means of declining marital fertility.

71. Robert Brenner, "Agrarian Class Structure and Economic Development in Pre-Industrial Europe," *Past and Present* 70 (1976):30–75 argues that class conflict is the mechanism for change.

72. Caroline White, *Patrons and Partisans: A Study of Politics in Two Southern Italian Comuni* (New York: Cambridge University Press, 1980), pp. 88–92.

73. Colapietra, "La grande polemica Ottocentesca intorno al Tavoliere di Puglia" (cited in full in chap. 1, n. 134) summarizes the early nineteenth-century debate. In 1853, 800,000 sheep wintered on the Tavoliere (75:31). Sprengel, *Die Wanderherdenwirtschaft*, p. 54 (cited in full in chap. 1, n. 75) gives 1,200,000 sheep in 1840; 760,000 in 1860; and still 730,000 in 1877. Colapietra, "L'Unità d'Italia e l'affrancamento del Tavoliere di Puglia," 77:17 (cited in full in chap. 1, n. 134) claims that about 50,000 people in 93 of the 127 towns in the province of Aquila were involved in pastoralism in 1863.

74. De Cesare, *Delle condizioni economiche e morali*, p. 101 (cited in full in chap. 2, n. 51). Davis, *Società e imprenditori*, p. 58 (cited in full in chap. 2, n. 82) quotes de Cesare, *Delle condizioni economiche e morali*, p. 64 to dramatize the know-nothingness of the entrepreneurs, and de Cesare continued his impassioned disdain for the new entrepreneurial landlords, *Delle condizioni economiche e morali*, p. 103.

75. Colapietra, "L'Unità d'Italia e l'affrancamento del Tavoliere di Puglia," (cited in full in chap. 1, n. 134) summarizes the debate on the change of the laws at Unification. Ryder, *Sheep and Man*, pp. 611–23 (cited in full in chap. 2, n. 70) summarizes the history of the Australian sheep industry. Sheep were introduced in Australia in the 1790s and the industry grew especially in the 1830s because of high international prices. Similarly, the 1830s marked the diffusion of artesian wells from Artois in France. Etymologically, *The Shorter Oxford English Dictionary*, 1:102 gives 1830 for its entry into English, and Robert's

Dictionaire alphabétique et analogique de la langue Française, 5:684 gives 1834 into French. For the Tavoliere, Saverio Russo, "Agricoltura e pastorizia in Capitanata nella prima metà dell'Ottocento," in *Produzione, mercato, e classi sociali,* ed. Massafra, pp. 267–320 (cited in full in chap. 3, n. 32).

76. Venturi, "The Enlightenment in Southern Italy," pp. 207–9.

77. Readers of Croce's *History of the Kingdom of Naples* (cited in full in intro., n. 11) can understand how much Croce's analysis of the *illuministi* as the dynamic segment of Neapolitan society depends upon Galanti's reading of history, methods, and plans for reform. What Croce does not admit, however, is that Naples had a common "spirit" before the Enlightened reformers. That spirit was what Galanti described as "the spirit of gain," barter and exchange. Galanti, *Della descrizione delle Sicilie,* 1:168–69. The competition and antagonisms from such exchange are the true basis of Croce's heralded Neapolitan contradictions.

78. Marshall Sahlins, *Culture and Practical Reason* (Chicago: University of Chicago Press, 1976), pp. vii–viii summarizes his thesis that utility theory does not define man's actions, but culture defines utility.

Conclusion

1. Davis, *Società e imprenditori,* p. 48 (cited in full in chap. 2, n. 82).

2. Gary S. Becker, *Economic Theory* (New York: Alfred A. Knopf, 1971), pp. 1–3 argues that economics is, in its broadest definition, the study of choice between scarce means and competing ends. George M. Foster, "Peasant Society and the Image of the Limited Good," *American Anthropologist* 67, no. 2 (1965):293–315 applies this same principle to cultural criteria in peasant settings.

3. William M. Reddy, *The Rise of Market Culture. The Textile Trade and French Society, 1750–1900* (Cambridge: Cambridge University Press, 1984) questions the idea of market culture and the failure of market language to explain the reality of market relationships even after the industrial revolution.

4. Peter Kriedte, *Peasants, Landlords and Merchant Capitalists. Europe and the World Economy, 1500–1800* (Cambridge: Cambridge University Press, 1983), p. 158 gives British manufacturing share of the physical national product in 1811 as 37 percent, French in 1803/12 as 27 percent.

5. Ferdinando Galiani, "Dell'arte del governo," (ca. 1746), in his *Della moneta,* pp. 390–92 (cited in full in chap. 1, n. 135) from a previously unpublished manuscript, BSNSP, MS. XXI.C.8, 1r–15r. The young Galiani offers an eighteenth-century definition of good government. *Il buon governo* ought to conserve and promote happiness and pleasures; that is, love, family, tradition, and property.

6. Galasso, "Strutture sociali e produttive, assetti colturali," pp. 168–70 (cited in full in intro., n. 9).

7. Jane Schneider, "Of Vigilance and Virgins," pp. 2–3 (cited in full in chap. 4, n. 108) argues that the competition between agricultural and pastoral economies for sparse resources "fragmented the social organization of each type of community and blurred the boundary between them." The result was the establishment of "their own means of social control—the codes of honor and shame—which were adapted to the intense conflict that external pressures had created within them, and between them." Clifford Geertz, *Agricultural Involution: The Process of Ecological Change in Indonesia* (Berkeley and Los Angeles: University of California Press, 1971) explores the consequences of intensification and internal complication rather than expansion.

MANUSCRIPT SOURCES

ACA   Archivo de la Corona de Aragón, Barcelona

Privilegiorum Cancillería Napoles, regg. 2902–2919 (1430–58)
Privilegiorum de Carlos V, regg. 3927–3946

ADLPR   Archivio Doria Landi Pamphilj, Rome

scaf.
  15/7, int. 1 Relationi diversi dello Stato di Melfi, 1655–1670/71
  15/40A Levamento et bilancio particolare dell'introiti del Real Patrimonio del Regno di Napoli, 1570/71
  15/76 Documenti diversi (secoli XVI–XIX)
  15/77 Documenti diversi (secoli XV–XIX)
  15/107 Libro di Candela 1671 in 1692
  16/52 Vendite di lana, agnelli, vaccine . . . fatte annualmente in Melfi, 1705–1827
  16/53, int. 3, 7, 8 Esami testimoniali nella causa di Frode nell'industrie di pecore e porci (1684–85), (1695–96), (1702)
  16/54 Manuali del Libro dell'Industrie dello Stato di Melfi, 1703/04–1742/43
  16/56 Industrie nello Stato di Melfi, 1707–84
  16/57 Manuali dell'Industrie delle pecore, 1743/44–1763/64
banc.
  21/3 Registro per l'Industrie dello Stato di Melfi, 1645–95
  21/14 Manuale del libro dell'Industrie, 1691/92–1702/03
  21/26 Libro dell'Industrie nello Stato di Melfi, 1692–1703
  21/27 Manuale del Libro dell'Industrie nello Stato di Melfi, 1692–98
  21/34 Registro per l'Industrie dello Stato di Melfi, 1695–98
  21/unnum. Libro Mastro primo dell'Industrie dello Stato di Melfi, 1671/72–1686/87

AGS   Archivo General, Simancas

Camera de Castilla
Contaduria de Mercedes
Estado
  Corona de Aragón   Nápoles
  Dos Sicilias   Roma
  Milán

Mercedes Privilegio
Quitaciones de Corte
Patronato Real
Secretarías Provinciales, Nápoles
Visítas d'Italia, Nápoles

AHN   Archivo Histórico Nacional, Madrid

Estado

ARSJ   Archivum Romanum Societatis Jesu, Rome

Fondo gesuitico
Fondo Neapolitana

ASFg   Archivio di Stato, Foggia

Biblioteca, MS. 1030 (secolo XVIII)
Dogana delle Pecore
    serie I, Carte Patrimoniali-Amministrative (1536–1816)
    serie IV, Processi civili antichi (1540–1669)
    serie V, Contabilità e Segreteria (1608–1806)
Amministrazione del Tavoliere, Scritture dell'Ufficio

ASFi   Archivio di Stato, Florence

Mediceo
Miscellanea Medicea

ASN   Archivio di Stato, Naples

Archivio Giudice Caracciolo
Consiglio Collaterale Consultationum
Curia dell'Arte della Lana
Dipendenze della Sommaria, serie I, II
Monasteri Soppressi
Piante
Sommaria
    Bannorum
    Carte Reali, 1 bis–29 (1611–1721)
    Consultationum, 1–174 (1560–1735)
    Diversi, numerazione I, II
    Notamenti
    Partium

ASP Archivio di Stato, Pisa

Archivio Alliata

MANUSCRIPT SOURCES

ASV   Archivio di Stato, Venice

Cinque Savi alla Mercanzia, serie I, II
       risposte
Sindaci Inquisitori di Terraferma

BNM   Biblioteca Nacional, Madrid

MS.
  988 Papeles Historicos-Politicos tocantes a Nápoles, tom 3 (sec. XVII)
  1502 Summario de Cartas de Su Magestad tocantes a este Reyno (sec. XVII)
  1093, 1–38v, Discurso en raconde la aduana de las pecoras. . . . (Span. trans. of BNN, MS. I.D.21)
  1935 Sumario de las cartas que su Magestad a embiado a este Reyno de officio que empieçan des de 7 de Março 1625 y por todos los 23 de Março 1639
  2490 Felipe III: Instruccion al Duque de Osuna
  2659 Varios papeles de investidura, disçursos, relaciones y cosas tocantes a las rentas y patrimonio real del Reino de Nápoles (sec. XVI–XVII)
  2857 Itinerario del Reyno de Napoles di tutto lo circuito del Regno cominciando dalla prima terra di marina, et circuendo tanto il mare come la terra fatto l'anno 1559
  5966, 1–8v, Tribunales del Reyno y Ministros dellos
  Same as Bibliothèque Nationale, Paris, MS. Esp. 127

BNN   Biblioteca Nazionale, Naples

MS.
  I.D.20 Notizie della Dogana di Foggia
  I.D.21 Compendio breve delas pecoras de Pulla dirigido por el anno de 1578 . . .
  I.D.73 Silvio e Ascanio Corona, "La verità svelata"
  I.F.12 Libro de materias tocantas á la incumbencia dela Dohana de Foja (ca. 1690)
  XI.A.22 Cartas de la Mag. del Rey Don Phelipe II
  XI.B.26 Memoriali, Viglietti, e Consulte
  XI.B.39 Miscellaneous Budgetary Information (seventeenth century)
  XI.B.40, fasc. 6, 1–80 Origine della Regia Dohana di Foggia e del governo di quella . . .
  XI.C.46 Miscellanea, 219r–223v, Degli erbaggi della regia fida sopra le pecore della Dogana di Puglia
  XI.D.6 Reintegration della Regia dohana di Puglia (sec. XVI)
  XI.D.11 Trattati diversi nella Dogana di Foggia (sec. XVII)
  XI.D.19 Lettere e Manoscritti diversi; concernono all'Abadia di San Leonardo e della Torre della Manna in Capitanata (1653–54)
  XI.D.21, 93r Espurgo delle case di Foggia per la fiera al 1657 ai timori di peste
  XI.D.26 Negotii di Camara nell'incombenza di Foggia
  XI.D.28 Incombenze di Foggia; 371r–376v, Breve notitia di quello dovrà operansi dal Dohaniero della Dohana di Foggia per invigilare al servizio di quel Real Patrimonio; Reflessioni sopra la Aduana
  XI.D.29 Incombenze di Foggia

XI.D.30 Duana di Foggia governata dal Sr. Con.ro Don Felice de Lanzina y Ulloa
XI.D.31, 246–251 Relazione delle entrate ed uscite della Dogana di Foggia
XI.D.32, 164r–179v Noticia de lo que a obrado en el govierno de la Aduana de los Ganados de Pulla el Marques de Centellas (1669) Same as ASFg, *Dogana delle pecore,* serie I, fas. 4, 145–160
XI.D.35 Dogana di Foggia (sec. XVI)
XII.B.46 Registro del Patrimonio Reale ed origini degli Arrendamenti . . . (1550–1640)
XII.D.30 [No title]
XV.B.11 Lettere Regie
MS. Brancacciano
  II.E.5 Giurisdizione Ecclesiastica
  III.E.6 Scritture giurisdizionali
  IV.B.10 Chronica di Matteo Spinello da Giovenazzo (1242–68)
  IV.D.3 Istruzioni del Real Patrimonio . . .
  IV.D.5 Istruzioni per la Dohana di Foggia
  V.B.4–9 Parlamenti e gratie della Città di Napoli . . . (1554–1642)
  V.B.10, 262r–271v Documenti relativi all Dogana delle pecore
  V.C.10, 2d num., 1r–14r Situationi 1629 pro Regia Dohana fatta in terra Foggie
  V.D.14, c. 48 Entrate della dogana delle pecore (1605/06, 1606/07)
    c. 58 Memoriale . . . a favore de' massari della Puglia (1615)
Carte Geografiche, MS. Bª 5ᴰ (15 Agatangelo della Croce (1766), "Pianta seu Mappa del Reggio Tavoliere della Puglia oltre altri corpi che non attaccano alla sudetta"

BPFg   Biblioteca Provinciale, Foggia
MS.
  4 (old 63 or 7–M.5.6) "Miscellanea di documenti della dogana delle pecore di Foggia," vol. 1
  5 (old 42 or 7–M.4.1) "Miscellanea di documenti della dogana delle pecore di Foggia," vol. 2
  129 Notizie per il buon governo della R. Dogana della mena delle pecore di Puglia . . . Andrea Gaudiani . . . 1700
  D-A-84 Notizie per il buon governo della Regia Dogana della mena delle pecore di Puglia . . . Andrea Gaudiani . . . 1715

BRAH   Biblioteca de la Real Academia de la Historia, Madrid
MS.
  A-12, 207r–v, Lettere di Annibale di Capua (10.v.1508)
  A-27, 386r–v, Merced a Hanibal de Capua (23.iv.1523)
  A-29, 123r, Merced a Lope de Soria (17.ix.1523)
  A-36, 438r–449r, Extratto deli officiali regij . . . ad vitam in le dohane, gabelle et altrj deritj regalj In lo regno (s.d., ca. 1508–23)
  F-24, 150r–155r, Relaçion del gran terremoto (14.viii.1627)
  K-72, 115r–116r, Visitador General Alarcon (16.vii.1631)
    528r–529v, Visitador General Alarcon (18.iii.1631)

K-94, 400–405, Giovanni Battista della Chiesa sopra le cose di Foggia
N-74, 236, Summaria dell'Amministratione fatta in Puglia del Duca de Vietri per commandamento di sua eccelenza nell'Anno 1612
9-21-1/3946 Diversi sul Regno fatto per Carlo III da Andrea Natale di Napoli (1708)

BSNSP Biblioteca della Società Napoletana di Storia Patria, Naples

MS.
XXI.B.14 Prammatiche Napolitane (sec. XVII)
XXI.C.6 Trattato della Dogana di Foggia, Gaudiani, 1715. Same as BPFg, MS. D-A-84
XXI.C.7 [No title]
XXI.C.9 Scritture diverse riguardano specialmente le esazioni fiscali (sec. XVI–XVII)
XXI.D.31 Rappresentenza a S.M.E. sulla Dogana di Foggia . . . dalla R. Camera della Sommaria nel 1712
XXIII.A.1 Variarum Quaestionum et rerum iurisdictionalium per reg. consiliarium
XXIII.A.3 Variarum Quaestionum et rerum iurisdictionalium per reg. consiliarium
XXIII.A.5 Variarum Quaestionum et rerum iurisdictionalium per reg. consiliarium
XXVII.A.1 Avole delle lettere di S. Mta. Lettere Reali, 1569–97
XXVII.C.3 Raccolta manoscritto di varii diplomi (Ordini e lettere di Felippo II, 1572–86)
XXXIII.A.5 [No title]

BV Biblioteca Apostolica Vaticana

MS. Cod. Vat. Lat. 8886 Libro delli statuti, Bolle, Costitutioni, sentenze . . . fatte in varij tempi . . . a favore delle Dogana della fida, e pascoli di Roma . . . (7 January 1792)

British Library, London

Egestorn MS. 1905, LeClerc Budget (1521)

HHSA Haus-, Hof- und Staatsarchiv, Vienna

Italien-Spanisher Rat, Neapel
 Collectanea
 Correspondenz
 Vorträge I

INDEX

Abruzzi fairs, 208
Accademia degli Arcadi, 8, 97, 249, 251–52. *See also* Arcadian ideology
Adjusted Sheep. *See pecore in alia tantum*
Ageta, Gaetano Nicol, 249
agrimensore. See compassatoro
Aguirre, Domenico, 86
Aguirre, Giuseppe, 99
ainina or *agnellina* (wool quality), 52–53
Ajello, Raffaelo, 163
Alarçon, Francisco Antonio de, 34, 313
Albe (fair), 208
Alcala, duke of (viceroy), 65, 176
Alfieri, Angelo, 219, 227, 229, 355
Alfiero, Fabritio de, 111
Alfonso of Aragon: centralization of government, 21–24, 308–9; charter of 1447, 19–24, 37–39, 43, 65–67, 78, 86–88, 115, 161, 255, 306–7; conquest of Naples, 19, 168; doganal appointments in 1443, 87; importation of merino sheep, 52
Alfonso II, 168
alguzzini (banditori), 173
Alliata, Giovan Battista 181–82
Altamura (fair), 187
Altamura, prince of, 187
Alvarez de Ribera, Francesco, 32
Amalfi Coast towns, 228–34
Amico, Giovanni Onufri, 87
Ancona, 178, 236, 352
Andria (location), 46–47, 49, 90, 104, 269
Andria, duca di, 219
Andria, Leone, 219
Angelis, Francesco Giuseppe de, 101
Angelis, Paolo Nicola del, 109
Angelone, Lorenzo, 99
Angelone family, 101
Anielli, Gian Caterina d', 101
Anielli, Girolamo d', 101
Anielli family, 101

Animal tax. *See fida*
Animalia in vineis, 20
Aquila, 180, 237, 350; account books (*paranze*), 195–98, 215–16, 226–27, 329, 350; sheepowner origins, 90, 94, 121; sheepwalk trailhead, 42–43; syndic origins, 20, 87, 111; wool production, 228–29, 231
Aquilani, Vincenzo, 237
Arcadian Academy of Rome. *See* Accademia degli Arcadi
Arcadian ideology, 11, 78, 116, 243, 263
archivario, 172
Arignano (location), 46–47, 91, 269, 334
Arpi, 19
arte, 113, 116
Artesian wells, 360
Atello, Angelo de, 58
Auctions *alla candela*, 72, 226, 324
auditore, 114, 139, 171–72, 174
Australian wool, 258, 360
Austrian Habsburgs, 36–37, 66–67, 143, 201
Avellino, prince of (Marino Caracciolo), 233
Avellino, sheepwalk reintegration by, 43
Aversa (fair), 180, 186
avvocato fiscale, 172, 174, 341
Aymard, Maurice, 240

Baccaro, Filippo, 99–101
Baccaro, Giacomo Antonia del, 101
Balance of payments, 17, 239–41
Bambino, Giuseppe, 239
Banco dei Poveri, 191
banditori. See alguzzini
Banu-Marin, 17
Barano, 168
Bardenas Real. *See* Saragossa, Casa de Ganaderos
Bari, 180, 226, 353
Bari, Terra di, 44, 93, 216

Barletta (location or *mosciali*), 49, 154; fair, 180; grain deposits, 322; port, 177, 187, 190, 237, 349; salt pans of, 46–47
Barone, Francesco, 207
Basaccie, duchessa di, 219
Basalis, Gaspar de, 29
Basiletti, Giovanni, 226, 228
Basilicata, 44, 49, 90, 93, 154, 177, 187, 217, 246, 329
Basilicata, *transazione* of, 50
Battinello, Anello, 228
Béjar, duke of, 117
Bellitti, Giacinto, 300
Bellovedere, Sebastiano di, 58
Benedettino, P. D. Emanuele Caputo, 359
Bergamo: wool buyers, 214, 220, 226, 228–31, 234; wool production, 67, 233, 235, 236, 260, 263
Bernauda, Giuseppe, 140–41, 342
Bernauda family, 29
Bianchini, Ludovico, 77, 157
Bisaccia, 237
Bisignano, princes of. *See* Sanseverino family
Black wool. *See negra*
Blasi, Marino, 187
Boccacio, Giovanni, 215
Bologna, 188
Bombacili, 50
Bonaparte, Joseph, 37, 66, 259
Bonare, Giovanni Giuseppe, 237
Boniface IX, 18
Boricelli, Burtolo, 228
Bourbon ascendancy in 1734, 36, 192, 246
Bovino, 219, 307
Bovino, duke of, 50, 219
Brancia family, 223
Brancio, Ferrante, 237
Braudel, Fernand, 174
Bread price. *See voce,* bread
Brescia, 230, 235
Brianza, 234
Briganti, Filippo, 247–48, 298
Brunel, Stefano, 237
Bruno, Antonio, 102–3
Bucciarella, Sinaballo, 102–3, 330
Buccio, Antonuccio di Nicola del, 87
Budgets, general syndics', 105–13; dogana of Foggia, 154–59; wool sellers', 221–26
Buffane, Gian Domenico, 228
Bugnara, 206
buon governo ("good government"), 7, 10–11, 16, 37–38, 42, 46–47, 81, 143, 159–61, 163–65, 170, 175, 214, 243, 249–51, 261–64, 361; under Alfonso of Aragon, 22–23; under the Spanish Habsburgs, 30–31

Cain and Abel, 243, 252
Calabria, Antonio, 154
Calabria family, 223
Calabritto, duke of, 104, 219
Calascio, 218–19, 269
Calendar, agrarian and pastoral, 40
Calvanese, Giulio Cesare, 101
Calvanese family, 223
Camarda (location), 46–47, 56, 90, 103, 138–39, 269
Cambini (wool company), 23
Camilli, Francesco Saverio, 37, 299
Camillo, Liberatore di, 223
Campo di Giove, 219, 269
Campomanes, Pedro Rodriguez, 248, 358
Candelaro (location), 47, 91, 96, 269
Canestriello grande, 50
Canosa (location), 46–47, 56, 103, 269, 334
Capece, Raniero, 74–75
Capece Galeota, Fabio, 43, 140, 142
Capecelatro, Ettore, 43, 142
Capitanata, 5, 6, 28, 32, 34, 40–41, 43–44, 58, 61, 65, 76, 90–91, 93, 103, 154, 168, 171, 177, 179–80, 183, 190–91, 208, 210, 215–17, 227, 241, 245, 259–60, 289, 328–29, 349
Capograsso, Restanuccio, 87
Cappella di San Giovanni of Campo di Giove, 219
Cappella di Santissimo of Pescasseroli, 219
Cappella di Santissimo Santo of Rivisondoli, 219
Capracotta, 216–17, 219, 269
Capua, Annibale de, 27
Capua, Vincenzo de (duke of Termoli), 114
Caracciolo, Alfonso, 32, 75, 80, 170, 184, 213, 341–43
Caracciolo, Baldassare, 74–75
Caracciolo, Cornelio, 58
Caracciolo, Isabella, 206
Caracciolo, Laura, 170, 343
Caracciolo, Lelio, 342
Caracciolo, Marino. *See* Avellino, prince of
Caracciolo, Nicola, 26, 309
Carafa, Antonio. *See* Corato, marchese of
Carafa, Ettore, 206, 219
Carafa, Gian Pietro. *See* Paul IV

INDEX

Carafa family, 343
Carafa War, 169
carapellesi (wool quality), 53
Carbone, Giovan Antonio. *See* Padula, marchese di
Carlo Emanuale I (duke of Savoy), 158
Carrera, Alonso Guillen de la, 34
Caroselle. See Wheat
Carroz, Francesco, 114, 167
Casa de Ganaderos. *See* Saragossa, Casa de Granaderos
Casalnuovo (location), 46–47, 90–91, 103–4, 269
Casanata, Mattia, 140
Casati, Danese, 35, 315
Casola, Giovan Giacobo, 206
Casoli, duca di, 219
Castel del Monte (Abruzzo Ultra), 91, 218, 269
Castel di Sangro: account book (*paranza*), 195–97, 216, 227, 289, 329, 350; sheep-owner origins, 91, 217; sheepwalk trailhead, 42–43
Castelli, Domenico, 99
Castellis, Aloyse de, 25
Castello, Petro, 58
Castiglione (location), 47, 81, 91, 107, 119, 179, 269, 331
Castiglione (wool buyer town, Terra di Lavoro), 229
Castiglione, Gasparo di, 25–26
Castile, 1, 2, 16–17, 20, 23, 37, 68, 130, 249. *See also* Mesta
castrati. See Meat
castratina (wool quality), 52–53, 227
Castro di Valle, 87
Castruccio, Antonio, 103
Catalan-Aragonese wool, 23
Catalans, 23
Cateau-Cambresis, Peace of, 67
Caterina, *infanta,* daughter of Philipp II, 158
Catholic kings. *See* Ferdinand the Catholic
Cava (wool buyer town, Principato Citra), 233
cavallaro, 25, 28, 32, 44, 154, 166, 168, 173, 343
Cave (location), 46–47, 269, 334
Celano, 43, 215, 329; fair, 208; sheepwalk, 42
Celentano, Saverio, 109
Centi, Gian Lorenzo, 99

Cerciello, Chapel of the Most Holy Annunciation, 138
Cereal *voce. See voce,* wheat
Cerice, Francesco Antonio (baron of Rosciano), 101
Cerice family, 101
Cerignola, 27, 237, 322
Cerreto, 213, 227, 230, 236, 355
Certosa di San Martino, Naples, 138, 179, 220
Cervantes, Miguel de, 165, 313, 335, 358
Charles II, 162
Charles III, Austrian pretender (later Holy Roman Emperor Charles VI), 35
Charles III of Anjou, 186
Charles III of Bourbon, 36–37, 86
Charles V: and doganal income, 28, 154, 158; 1536 confirmation charter, 28–29, 37, 65–66, 74, 115, 184, 187, 232, 309–10; Foggia and Foggian Fair, 185–86, 188, 310; and offices, 162; retainers and concessions of, 168–69, 175, 311; visit to Naples, 28, 164; and *voce* prices, 159, 212
Charles VI. *See* Charles III, Austrian pretender
Charles VIII, 66
Cheese, 15, 18, 22–23, 48, 52–53, 200; and income, 70–71, 185; prices, 74–77, 109, 112, 183, 213, 223, 294–97; production, 54, 207–8, 294–97. *See also voce,* cheese
Chieti, 226, 230, 245, 329
Chirico, Gian Domenico, 46, 79, 312
Christmas cribs. See *presepe*
Church's tenth. See *decima*
Ciancarella, Gian Francesco, 99
Ciancerella (lawyer) (same as Ciancarella?), 109
ciavarrina (wool quality), 53
Ciccozzi, Manlio, 219
Cimaglia, Domenico, 37, 144, 222, 298
Cimaglia, Orazio, 104, 109
Cinugui, Julio, 182
Ciotti, Donatanonio, 100
Coda, Marcantonio, 54, 101, 173, 203, 222–23, 249
Coda family, 223
ColaAngelo, Virgilio de, 94
Colabianco, Biase, 99–100
Colabianco family, 101
Colantonio, Ludovico, 228

Colapietra, Raffaele, 160
Collateral Council, 35, 46, 79, 105, 107, 115, 169–70, 173, 321
collettiva, 89, 134. See also *padroncelli*
Columella, 319
Como, 67, 234–35
compassatoro (agrimensore), 50, 173
Condorcet, marquis de, 359
Coniglio, Giuseppe, 160–61, 177, 232
Contessa, 50
contratto alla voce. See *voce*
contravenzione, 157
Corato, marchese of (Antonio Carafa), 33, 237
Corcione, Gian Luigi, 140, 172
Corcione, Sigismondo, 172
Corcione family, 172
cordeschi, 208
Cordova, Gonsalvo di, Great Captain, 27
Corleto or Cornito (location), 47, 91, 269
Cornito. See Corleto
Correa Piccola, 119
Cosimo II, 159
credenziero, 46, 115, 117, 139, 168, 171–72
Cremona, 234
Crivelli, Alfonso, 43
Croce, Agatangelo della, 36, 46–47, 50–51
Croce, Benedetto, 160, 361
Cruscole, Ignazio, 239
Cum per partes Apuliae, 19

d'Afflitto, Giovanni Battista, 109
d'Afflitto family, 29
d'Alena, Ferdinando, 98
d'Andrea, Nicola, 99–101
d'Andrea family, 101
Dante Alighieri, 252
d'Aragona, Cardinal Pasquale, 35
d'Aragona, Pietro Antonio, 35
Daubenton, Louis-Jean-Marie, 359–60
d'Austria, Maria Maddalena, 340
David, Francescantonio, 79
De Cesare, Carlo, 258
De Cesare, Cesare, 206
De Cesare, Geronimo, 206
De Cesare, Lucantonio, 206
De Cesare, Petro Paulo, 206
decima, 51, 186
De Dominicis, Francesco Nicola, 8, 36, 81, 186, 214, 243, 249, 253–54, 257, 298
d'Ecclesia, sheepwalk reintegration by, 43
de Ferrante, *avvocato fiscale*, 99

De Ferraris family, 138
De Filippo, Gian Geronimo, 214
Delfico, Melchiorre, 37, 298–99
Delille, Gérard, 90, 124
Della Chiesa, Giambattista, 141
Della Posta family, 50
De Luca family, 226, 239
Demography: of animals (*see* sheep, sheepography); of Kingdom and cities of Naples, 22–23, 65–66, 138, 176–77, 180–85, 328, 344; shepherds', 93–95
Dentice family, 168
de Vera, Diego, 313
Di Carlo, Ludovico, 119
Di Cicco, Pasquale, 47
Diet, 332
Di Gennaro, Domenico, 298
Di Matteo family, 138
Di Pila family, 223
Disease (animals), 57
disordine, 157
dispensazione, 157
Di Stefano, Antonello, 27
Di Stefano, Stefano: career as lawyer, 7–8; career as governor, 81; on the *generalità* and its syndics, 85–86, 93, 97, 100–101, 107, 112–13, 115–16, 163; on merchants, 213; on posts, 50; La ragion pastorale, 7–8, 243, 249, 251–53; on wool production, 185, 199
Di Turri family, 138
Division of labor in pastoral activities, 40–41
Dogana of Foggia, 2, 19–24, 69–70; cadastral survey of 1548, 30, 45–46, 48, 58, 61, 95, 181–82, 246, 318–19, 320–21; fixed tax agreement (*transazione*), 34, 71, 80, 96, 115, 139, 149, 156, 184, 187, 189, 339; *modo di vivere*, 71, 80, 139, 149, 311; sheep mortality of 1612, 34, 55, 57, 66, 80, 122, 125, 135, 138–39, 150, 156, 170, 183, 188, 236; *transazione (see* Fixed tax agreement)
Doganal palace, 173–74
Doganella d'Abruzzo, 33, 44–45, 143, 155, 157, 167, 170
doganiero, 22, 33, 80, 117, 139, 166–71, 325
Domestic wool market, 231–34, 239
Doria, Andrea, 65, 169, 175
Doria at Melfi: account books, 54, 138–39, 196, 203, 208, 222, 224–25; agricultural

INDEX

enterprise, 35, 65, 263; pastoral enterprise, 35, 41, 50, 54, 56, 57, 76, 90, 117, 128, 138, 206–7, 214, 222–26, 336, 354
Dutch Revolt, 68, 324

Elector Palatine, 158
Encyclopedists, 247
England, 1, 13, 23, 52, 67, 248, 319, 323, 335–36, 353
Enlightenment, 7, 36, 80, 243–49, 253–59, 261, 264
Enriquez, Don Juan, 160, 249, 307
erbaggi, 21
erbaggi or *fondi ordinari*, 44, 72, 156
erbaggi straordinari, 42, 45, 49, 144
erbaggi straordinari insoliti, 30, 32, 42, 49, 156
erbaggi straordinari soliti, 26, 42, 49, 156
Escorial, monastery of El, 117
Estates (social orders), 120, 136–37, 220–21

Fairs (other than Foggia), 208
Fallow (*maiese*), 58–59, 61, 73
Farina, Domenico, 229
Farm land. See *portate*
fellate (sheep), 53
Ferdinand II of Bourbon, 37
Ferdinand the Catholic, 17–18, 23–24, 27, 28, 37, 38, 66–67, 153, 168, 310
Ferrante, 24–27, 49, 212, 309–10; 1463 prohibition, 232; *grazie*, 25, 43, 78, 87; revolt against, 26–27
Feudo (location), 47, 103, 269
Fictitious *locati*, 163, 170
Fictitious merchants, 188, 348
fida, 21, 30, 33, 50, 72–73, 86, 124, 142, 150, 154–55, 156–57, 167, 172, 185
fida della statonica, 155
Figueroa, Juan de, 28–29, 43, 111, 114, 158, 160, 167, 169, 333
Filangieri, Gaetano, 37, 299
Filesio, Francesco, 112
Filiasi, 226, 239
Fines. See *proventi*
fiscali. See Hearth tax
Fixed tax agreement. See Dogana of Foggia
Florence, 57, 58, 67, 207, 213, 226, 232–33, 235–37, 246, 303, 340, 352, 356
Foggia, 2–3, 25, 229, 235; 1731 earthquake, 2, 56, 173, 198; population, 210, 303
Foggia fair, 70, 73, 95, 154, 184–91, 193, 291–97; buyers, 189, 193, 195, 197–98, 200–202, 205–7, 212–15, 226–41; date, 188–90, 347; prices, 74, 195–96, 203–6, 211–14, 284–89, 292–97; production, 195–202, 205, 284–90, 350–51; sellers, 189–93, 195–97, 200–202, 206–7, 212–26, 235–41; sellers' budgets, 221–26
Foiz, Odet de. See Lautrec, Monseigneur
Fontanelle, 101
Fonte, Domenico del, 87
Fonte, Nuncio de, 87
Foreign merchants, 200
Forenza, 35, 314
Forgione, Francesco. See Padre Pio
Fornaro, Ferrante, 32, 45, 75, 79, 80, 160, 170, 313
Forte, Ignazio, 239
Fortunato, Nicola, 246, 247, 253, 254, 257, 298
franchi (wine monpoly), 106, 331
Franchi, Pietro de, 178
Francis I, 28
Franiscan monasteries, 178
Francischelli, Giuseppe, 103
Frattura, Chapel of the Most Holy Sacrament, 138
Freda, Giustiniano, 115
Freda family, 172
Frederick (Neapolitan Aragonese), 27
Frederick II, 19, 20
Free bidding "tax." See *professazione voluntaria*
French Invasions of 1494, 24, 27, 66, 68, 153, 233, 263, 309
Fucino, Lago di, 52, 168, 258

Galanti, Giuseppe Maria, 37, 255–57, 298, 361
Galasso, Giuseppe, 191, 240
Galiani, Ferdinando: background, 245; career, 247; *Della Moneta*, 36–37, 70, 245, 247, 257, 298; economics, 66, 254, 325–26, 361; on pastoralism, 36–37, 247–48; value, theory of, 75–77, 325–26
Galiti, Giovanni, 226, 228–29
Gallo family, 138
Gamielli, Mutio, 228
Gargan, 317–18

Gascon, Nicolo, 91, 331
Gatta, Diego, 298
Gaudiani, Andrea: career, 8, 355; *Notizie per il buon governo*, 8, 47, 81, 249–51, 358; on landscape and practice, 48, 58, 125; on *locati*, 88, 113–14; on prices, 77, 213
Gayari, Donato Antonio, 219
Gelmi, Rocco, 229
generalità de' locati, 85–88, 90–93, 95–98, 100–105, 107–18, 144
Generalitat, 86, 327, 329
généralités, 327
General syndics. *See* Syndics, general
Genesis, 252
Genoa, 180, 200
Genovesi, Antonio, 246–47, 253–55
Georgofili Academy, 246
ghezze (wool quality), 53
Giannone, Pietro, 27
Gifoni, 229–30, 232
Gildone, 103
Giordano, Giuseppe, 115
Giordano family, 172
Giovanna II, 20–21, 24, 86–87
Giovio, Paolo, 27, 153
Giudice, Francesco (Cardinal in 1690), 219
giunta of 1729, 80, 99–100
Gombarda, 152
Good Government. *See buon governo*
Grain. *See* Wheat
Grana, Salvadore, 88, 298
Granada, Treaty of, 27, 153
Granata, Luigi, 8
grani dolci. *See* Wheat
grani forti. *See* Wheat
Granito, Angelo, 237–38
Granvelle, Cardinal (Antoine Perrenot), 31–32, 109, 312, 314, 327, 347
Gravina (fair), 187
Gravina, Gian Vincenzo, 251
grazie. *See* Ferdinand the Catholic; Ferrante
Graziers. *See locati*
Great Conspiracy of the Barons, 26
Geregory the Great, Saint, 8
Greppi, Antonio, 228–29
Greppi, Marco, 228
Grillo, Oduardo, 110
Grimaldi, Domenico, 298
Guadagno, Emilio, 226
Gualdo, Alessio, 228
Guardiola (location), 46–48, 91, 104, 154, 269, 307

Guarini, Giambattista, 252
Guerrero, Alfonso, 30
Guerrero y Torres, Andrea, 35, 143, 334
Guevara, Beltrán de, 33
Guicciardini, Francesco, 27, 153–54
Guild. *See arte*
Guzmán, Lope de, 32, 33, 79, 94, 111, 160, 169, 171, 330

Hearth (*fuochi*) tax, 154
Hermoja, Alfonso de, 313
Herrera, Juan de, 33
Hesiod, 13
Homer, 149, 252
Hospital of the Sheep Customhouse, 111
Hundred Years' War, 13, 17, 67

Iannantuono, sheepwalk reintegration by, 43
Imperiale, Prince Paolo, 104
Incarnato, Pasquale, 100
Income. *See* Budgets, general syndics'
Incoronata, 44
Infantado, duke of, 117
insoliti. *See erbaggi straordinari insoliti*
Ischitella, 168
Istanbul, 176, 177

Jesuits, 138, 179, 206, 322; budgets, 139; college in Foggia, 173; farms, 139, 179–80, 223
Jews, 188
John, duke of Anjou, 24
Joria, Sigismundo della, 143
Jovellanos, Gaspar Melchor de, 68
Juana La Loca, 158

Labor value. *See* Galiani, Ferdinando
Ladislas, 22, 310
Lanario, Francescantonio, 79
Lanciano (fair), 180, 186, 200, 208, 231
Landes, Colantonio de, 27
Lautrec, Monseigneur (Odet de Foix), 28, 66, 168
Lautrec, War of, 65
Lecce (Abruzzo Ultra), 219
Lecce (Terra d'Otranto), 180
LeClerc, Charles, 28, 310
LeFlem, Jean Paul, 69, 248
Lemos, conte de (viceroy). *See* Dogana of Foggia, fixed tax agreement
Leognano, Giovanni Jacobo, 119
Léon-Pineolo, Antonio de, 162

INDEX 375

Le Roy Ladurie, Emmanuel, 4
Lesina (location), 46–47, 56, 81, 91, 107, 269, 331, 334, 339
Lettiero, Paduano de, 94
libro maggiore, 172–74
locati, 50, 270–71, 273, 275; demography, 94–95; in the *generalità,* 85–94; literacy, 95; parliaments, 96–97; poor, 79–81. See also *generalità de' locati;* Stratification, social
Locations, 45–51, 71, 79–80, 90–92, 96–97, 269, 328
London, 177
Longano, Francesco, 37, 299
Longo, Gaetano, 115
Longo, Pasquale, 101
Lotti, G., 77
Louis XII, 27, 66, 153, 309–10
Lucera, 25, 42, 65, 210, 322; fairs, 184
Lucoli, 52, 91, 94, 100, 111, 216–17, 219, 223, 269
Lucoli (wool quality), 52, 215
lunari (sheep), 53
Luzio, Michele de, 207

Machiavelli, Niccolò, 116
Machio, Victorio, 111
madonna dell' Ospitale of Rivisondoli, 219
Madrid, 177
maiese. See Fallow
Majcitelli, Santo di Sulputio, 219
Majoriche. See Wheat
Malthus, Thomas, 143, 257
Managlia, Agostino, 141
Mancini, Giuseppe, 103
Mancini, Tomaso, 36
Manfredonia, 50, 58, 62, 322; port, 177, 178, 187–88, 190, 237, 347–49; sack of 1620, 34, 178
Manna (lawyer), 109
Manpietro, Antonio, 104
Manure, sheep, 321
Manzino, Tomasso (possibly same as Tomaso Mancini), 111
Marches, 33, 206, 226, 236
Marchesani, Francesco Maria, 37, 299
Marchesano, Francesco Antonio, 94, 103
Marchesano, Marco, 111
Marchesano family, 92, 101, 137–38
Marchetti, Giovanni, 229, 355
Marchetti, Pietro, 229, 237, 355

Marchetti, Pietro (descendant of Pietro Marchetti above), 355
Marchetti family, 227
Marco, Isidoro de, 99, 100, 107
Marco, Michele de, 187
Margarita of Austria, 158
Marinanza, Andrea, 223
Marinanza, Gianbattista and Ventura, 219
Marinanzi, Giuliano, 103
Marinanzi family, 101
Marino, Georgio de, 87
Marocco, Carolo, 206
Marseilles, 237–38
Marx, Karl, 75
Masaniello's revolt, 34, 115, 138, 341, 350
Mascitello family, 138
masseria, 41
Mastrillo, sheepwalk reintegration by, 43
mastrodatti, 155, 171–72, 343
matricina (wool quality), 23, 53, 215
Mauro, Marcello di, 32
Mayo, Giuseppe de, 99
Mazza, Giovanni Battista, 226
Mazzella, Scipione, 157
Meat, 18, 23, 48, 52–54, 56–57, 181, 200, 352; and income, 70–71, 185, 314; merchants, 108, 185, 188; prices, 74, 183, 212, 223; production, 54, 124, 207–8, 236, 292–93, 303; provisions for shepherds, 112
Melfi, prince of. *See* Doria, Andrea; Doria at Melfi
Merino, Mario Di, 37, 299
Merino sheep, 17, 21, 52
mesta, 16, 18, 38, 86, 316
Mesta, 2, 16–18, 20, 37, 85–87, 113–14, 117, 130, 248–49, 257, 317, 325, 327, 333–34; income, 68–70; wool production, 23, 68–70, 235
mezzane (draft animal pasture), 46, 51, 59–60
Michael, Saint, cult of, 40, 44, 154, 189, 317
Michele, Antonio de, 35, 164–66, 341
Mickun, Nina, 130, 334
Milan, 67, 158, 180, 198, 228–29, 234–35
Minadois, Colantonio, 27
Minadois, Federico de, 58, 60, 310
Minadois, Pedro Antonio, 321
Minerva, 152
Minervino, 56
Minervino, prince of, 220

Modena, duke of, 158
modo di vivere. See Tax assessment policy
Moles, Annibale, 32, 90, 100, 249
Moles, Maurizio, 114
Monaco, Gioacchino del, 100
Moneglia, Agostino, 342
Moneglia, Giacomo, 115
Monsorio, Ferrante, 33, 167, 170–71, 342
Monsorio family, 170
Montagna dell'Angelo, 43–45
Montalvo, Berardino Ramirez de (marchese di San Giuliano), 34, 141
Montecalvo, duke of, 50
Monteserico, 49, 51, 152, 155, 170
Montluber, Francesco, 21–22, 26, 45, 49, 87, 107, 309
montone (ram), 53
Monza, 234
Moroni, Francesco, 228
Moroni, GianBattista, 228
Mosca, Bernardo, 110
Mosca, Cristofaro, 101
Mosca, Gian Andrea, 99
Mosca, Pompaneo, 101
Mosca, Tomasso, 101
Mosca family, 100, 330
Moscio, Manano de, 330
mostra dei castrati, 185, 188–89
Murge, 43, 48

Naples, city of, 85, 98, 102–4, 107, 109–12, 115, 187, 226; grain demand, 177–80, 182, 332–33; meat demand, 188, 207, 352; population, 176–77, 188; wool demand, 188, 200, 214, 219, 228–33, 237, 239, 254, 264
Napoleonic Wars, 75, 202, 204, 209, 259
Nardis, Gian Battista di, 94
Natale, Andrea, 35
Navarra, Don Melchior de, 213
nazione (sheepowners' town of origin), 50, 52, 90–92, 121, 269
Neapolitan school of political economy, 36, 241, 245–48, 253, 256, 258. *See also* Genovesi, Antonio
negra (wool quality), 52–53, 158, 195–97, 202, 216, 218, 227, 236, 355
nera. See negra
Nicastro, Julia de, 329
Nicholas V, 18
Nido, *seggio* or *piazza*, 27, 29, 168
nocchiarica, 59, 61

Nolfi, Fabrizio de, 102, 110
Nomophylakes, 86, 327
Notorio, Corrado de, 87
numerazione (sheep census), 30, 71–72, 149, 156, 157

Occhio-in-fronte, 149
Offices, 32, 162–63, 171–75, 343
Olivares, conte de (viceroy), 170
Onorati, Niccola Columella, 61, 125, 299
Ordona (location), 46–47, 103, 137–39, 179, 207, 269, 307, 334
Orta (location), 46–47, 91, 103, 139, 179, 206, 269, 307, 322, 334
Otranto, 114
Otranto, Terra d', 44–46, 93, 154, 215–16; horse dogana, 162; per Castellaneta and per Cerreto, 50
Ottoman Empire. *See* Turks
Ovid, 196
Ovindoli, Congregazione del Sanctissima d', 100

Pace, Marino de, 94
Pace, Pace de Marino, 94
Pacentro, 269
Padova, 317
Padre Pio (Francesco Forgione), 318
padroncelli, 88–89, 118, 121–22, 125–29, 131–36, 143, 159, 334
padroni, 89, 118, 121–22, 125–29, 131–37, 272, 274, 276, 335; heads of *collettive,* 89, 118, 133–34
Padula, marchese di (Giovan Antonio Carbone), 33, 170–71
Paganese, Giovanni, 228
Paglia (location), 50
Palazios, Geronimo de, 32
Paliotti, Ignazio, 239
Palmieri, Giuseppe, 37, 258, 299
Palmiero family, 138
Papal States, 23, 99–100, 142, 256, 310, 343; *dogana dei pascoli,* 18, 20, 29, 38, 57, 305–6
paranza, 195, 349
Paris, 177
Parite, 50
Parlamento Generale of the Kingdom, 115
Parliament of the *generalità*, 95–96, 104–5, 107, 109. *See also mesta*
Parry, J. H., 162
Pascale, Giovan Maria, 206

INDEX

Pascha, Gennaro, 239
Pasquale, Madonna Santia di, 119
passate, 173
Passes, 44
Pastore, Sabato, 34, 341
Pasture. See *erbaggi*
Paterno, regent, 99
Patini, Nicola, 109
Patini, Vincenzo, 37, 298
Patrimonio di San Pietro, 18, 249. *See also* Papal States, *dogana dei pascoli*
Paul IV (Gian Pietro Carafa), 169, 342
Pauletta (lawyer), 109
Paulo, Francesco Antonio Pietro, 111
pecore in aerea, 33, 49, 67, 73, 96, 151–53, 156–57, 171, 332, 339
pecore in alia tantum, 118, 136–37, 152, 276, 336, 338–39
pecore reali fisse, 118, 136, 152, 336, 338–39
Pecori, Rocco, 299
Peligni, 269
percettore, 172–74, 341
Perini, Gerolomo, 228
pesatori di lana: account books, 8, 35, 195, 201–5, 214–17, 314, 328–39; office, 173, 195, 213, 347
Pescara, 43, 208
Pescara River, 98
Pescasseroli, 42, 43, 219, 269
Peschici, 168
Pesco Costanzo, 216–17, 269
Pesco Lanciano, 91
Petrarch, Francesco, 252
Petrea family, 223
Petricone, Fabritio, 100
Pettorano, 91, 269
pezzate, 53
Philip II: accountability of officials, 33, 162, 312; dowry gifts on the dogana, 158–59; fiscal policy, 31, 123, 152, 154, 183, 312, 340; letters on the dogana, 31, 79, 312, 342; on population of Naples, 65, 176, 181
Philip III, 162, 170
Philip IV, 162
Physiocrats, 247
Piacenza, 178
Piano della Croce (delle fosse), 2, 62
Piedimonte, 269
Piedimonte d'Alife, 154, 213, 228–32, 234, 236
Piedmont (region), 317

Pietrantonio, Giuseppe, 223
Pignatelli, Geronimo, 220
Pignatello, Cesare, 102–3
Pignone, Marcello, 320
Pisano, Petruccio, 200
Pius IV, 169
Plague, 22, 65, 138, 143, 198
Pliny, 19
Poderira, conte and contessa di, 219
Poland, king of, 158
Polish Succession, War of, 36, 198, 201
Political economy. *See* Neapolitan school of political economy
Ponce de Leon, Juan Chacon, 34
Pontalbanito (location), 47, 91, 269
portate (farm land), 51, 58, 73
possedibile (possible sheep), 48, 150, 328
Possible sheep. See *possedibile*
Poste d'Atri, 317
poste fisse (fixed posts), 35, 78
postello delle carcere, 167
Pragmatica 3 *de Procuratoribus,* 86
Pramatica LXXIX de officio Procuratoris Caesaris (1668), 35, 213, 251–52
presepe, 95, 215
prezzo alla voce (public price), 35, 74–77, 143
primaticci, 54, 292–93
Prime Grazie del Re Ferdinando I (1470). *See* Ferrante
Procine (location), 47, 269
professazione forzosa, 71, 140, 149, 251
professazione spontanea, 115
professazione voluntaria, 30–31, 34–35, 71–73, 78–80, 117, 136, 138, 140, 142, 149, 152, 164, 171, 185, 201, 205, 251, 283, 311, 332, 339
proventi (fines), 155, 157
Public price. See *prezzo alla voce*
Puglia: dogana in, 2, 87; fiscal tavoliere, 44–46, 49, 50, 52; region, 8–9, 19–21, 23, 25, 27, 30, 38, 48, 55, 58–61, 65, 68, 72, 83, 92. *See also* Tavoliere di Puglia

Quiroga y Vela, Gaspar de, 31, 118, 160, 167, 342

Rabelais, François, 174
Ragusa, 178, 180, 187
Ram, Ignazio, 99
recchiarelle, 53
Reggio di Calabria, 180

Regi Stucchi, 317
Reimbursement of land not occupied, 156–57
René of Anjou, 24
residui, 142, 151, 154, 341
restoppia, 58–59, 61
Revealed wool. See *rivelata*
Revertera, Francesco, 30, 32
Riccia, principe de, 219
Ricciardi, Giuseppe, 229, 355
Ricciardi family, 226
Ripacorsa, conte di (viceroy), 28
ripartimenti, 44
riposi, 42, 317
rivelata, 201
Rivisondoli, 91, 219, 269
Rocca del Raso, 91, 214, 216, 223, 269
Rocca Mandolfi, 269
Rocca Valle Scura, 91
Rodi, 184
Roman Republic and Empire, 19, 254
Rome, 37, 235, 249, 343. See also Papal States
Rosati, Giuseppe, 37, 299–300
Rosati family, 226, 239
Rosato, Angelo di Fulvio de, 219
Rosciano, baron of. See Cerice, Francesco Antonio
Rosito, 269
Rossi, Rosino, 219
Rovere, 223, 269
Rovere, Vittoria della, 340
Rubbeis, Domenico de, 101
Ruiz Martín, Felipe, 68
Rural credit, 205–7. See also *prezzo alla voce*
Russo family, 138

Sacchetti family, 223
Saccione, 43–45, 154
Saggese family, 223
saldo vergine, 51, 73, 79
Sale of offices. See Offices
Salerno, 227, 229–30, 232–33, 254, 264; dogana of, 108; fair, 180, 186, 200, 206, 207, 231–33
Salla, Miguel, 172
Salpi (location), 46–47, 103, 269, 307, 334
Salsola (location), 47, 103, 269
Saluzzo, Giacomo, 33, 160
Samnites, 19
San Andrea (location), 47, 91, 136, 164, 269

San Angelo Lombardo, 269
San Buono, principe di, 219
San Cipriano Picentino, 232
Sanchez, Miguel Jeronimo, 29, 114
San Demetro, 90, 269
San Giovanni Rotondo, 74–75, 318
San Giuliano (location), 46–47, 90–91, 269
San Giuliano, marchese di. See Montalvo, Berardino Ramirez de
Sangro, Adriana di, 170
Sangro, Alfonso di, 169
Sangro, Carlo di, 168
Sangro, di, family, 29, 138, 168–71
Sangro, Fabrizio di (duke of Vietri): career, 29, 32, 102, 111, 312, 342; decrees, 31, 43, 319; recall to Foggia in 1612, 34, 170; sheep and income increases, 31, 67, 152, 338
Sangro, Ferrante di, 29, 31, 169–70
Sangro, Geronimo di, 169
Sangro, Giammatista di, 169–70
Sangro, Gianfrancesco di, 168
Sangro, Gianfrancesco di (son of Paolo, marchese of Torremaggiore), 168–69, 343
Sangro, Gian Luigi (or Loise) di, 29, 31, 169–70, 316, 321
Sangro, Giovanni di, 168, 342
Sangro, Lucido di, 168
Sangro, Paolo di, 168, 309
Sangro, Paolo di (marchese of Torremaggiore), 168–69, 343
Sangro, Violante di, 169–70, 343
Sanino, Giorgio, 228
San Ippolito, baron of, 109
San Leonardo delle Matine of Siponto, abbey of, 58, 219
Sannazaro, Jacopo, 252
San Rocco (*sfossatori*), 62
San Severino, 206, 214, 229–34
Sanseverino family (princes of Bisignano), 169, 349
San Severo, 65, 153, 164, 217–18; prince of, 91, 100, 136, 168, 169, 219–20
Santa Agata, 50
Santa Maria Addolorata (Foggia), 109
Santa Maria de Tremiti. See Tremiti, abbey of
Santa Maria del Paular, 117
Santangelo, Nicola, 76–77
Santissima Annunziata (Sulmona), 50, 214, 219–20, 223
Santissima Iconavetera (Foggia), 111
Santo Pietro in Ulmo, 152

INDEX 379

Santo Stefano, 90, 101, 269
Santo Stefano (*sfossatori*), 62
Saragolle. See Wheat
Saragossa, Casa de Ganaderos, 18, 20, 249, 316, 327
Sardi, Alessandro, 110
Sassano, baron of, 100
Sassinotto (lawyer), 109
Savoy, duke of. See Carlo Emanuele I
Scanno (wool quality), 52
Scanno, 216–18, 269
Scarnera family, 223
Schifara, 50
scomissioni, 107, 157
scrivania di razione, 32, 169–70
Sella, Domenico, 234
Sellers. See Foggia fair, sellers
Senigallia, 206
Seripando and Muscettola di Leporano, duke of, 179
Serra Capriola, 345
Serrone, 50
serroni, 53
Severante, Luigi, 237
Sforza, Bona, 158
sfossatori, 62
Sheep
—breeds: *gentili*, 21, 52; *moscia*, 50, 52–53
—census (see *numerazione*)
—flock size, 124–30, 135, 334–36
—in the air (see *pecore in aerea*)
—income, 149–51
—mortality, 55–57
—numbers, 34, 68–70, 73, 149–53, 198–99, 277–83, 332, 334, 338
—sheepography, 55–57, 66, 198
—walks (see *tratturi*)
Shepherds' bread allowance. See *utilità del pane*
Sicily, 177–78, 198
Siena, War of, 169
Sierra Cimino, 170
Silk, 183, 232, 240
Silla, Antonio, 37, 90–91, 222, 298
Siniscalchi family, 226
Slicher Van Bath, B. H., 60
soliti. See *erbaggi straordinari soliti*
Sommaria, Regia Camera della, 4, 26, 30–34, 36, 46, 50, 79–80, 90, 105, 114–15, 141–43, 160, 167, 170, 172, 174, 178, 182, 184–85, 200, 236–37, 320
sorde, 53

Sotomayer, Gutierre de, 78
Spagnardi, Martion, 355
Spanish Succession, War of, 192, 198, 201, 235
Spanish wool. See Mesta
Spontaneous bidding. See *professazione spontanea*
squarciafogli, 8, 45, 89–90, 104, 117, 122, 126, 131, 133, 152, 163, 172, 270–76, 328
squarciafoglietti, 89, 117, 338
Starace, Giovanni Vincenzo, 345
sterpate, 53
Stornara, 139, 179
Stornarella, 139, 179
Stratification, social, 83, 114, 117–45, 218–21, 227–28, 270–76
Sulmona, 20, 87, 121, 190, 226, 307, 327; account book (*paranza*), 195–97, 202, 216, 218, 220, 227–28, 230, 234, 289, 329, 350; Santissima Annunziata of (see Santissima Annunziata); Santo Spirito of, 50; sheepwalk trailhead, 42–43
Summer wool, 203
Surrentino, Scipion, 314
Syndics: general, 96–98, 101–10, 112, 114–15, 144, 327; particular, 96–97, 102–4, 114, 144, 327; wealth, 102–5

Tabasco, Juan Antonio, 342
Tacitus, 8, 81, 250
Tagliacozzo (fair), 208
Tanucci, Bernardo, 36
Taranto, 180–81
Targioni, Luigi, 37, 298
Tartary, 248, 255
Tasso, Torquato, 252
Tauro, Felippo, 228
Tavoliere di Puglia, 4, 5, 13, 15, 24, 30, 37, 40–44, 46, 50–52, 54–58, 61–63, 65, 73, 79, 86–87, 179, 322; jurisdiction after 1806, 66. See also Puglia
Tax assessment policy, 34, 71–72, 78, 139, 149
Tax collection, 71–72
Taxes, 68–69, 149–51, 154–57, 186, 237
Termoli, duke of. See Capua, Vincenzo de
terre demaniali salde, 20
terre salde, 46, 51, 72–73, 85, 88, 113, 151, 155–56, 158–59, 173, 182
terre salde a coltura, 30, 182
Textile industry, national, 231–34, 239

Textiles, 240
Thirty Years' War, 34, 263
Tinacio, Agostino di Paolo, 87
Tinto, Annibale del, 342
Toledo, Pedro de, 30, 114, 176; sixty-eight instructions, 311, 316–17; viceroy, 28, 37, 65, 175, 184–85
Tonto, Sempronius de, 329
Torre, Bartolomeo della, 87
transazione. *See* Dogana of Foggia
tratturi, 42–43, 123, 317
Tremiti, abbey of, 50, 178
Tressanti (location), 47, 103, 138, 179, 220, 269
Trigno, 44–45
Trigno River, 43–44, 98
Trinità (location), 46–47, 269, 334
Troia, 25, 179, 216–18
Troia, principe di, 229
Turks, 34, 178, 184, 345
Tuscan garrisons, 57, 320, 355

Umbria, 18, 206, 236, 352
Unification of Italy, 37, 210, 258, 261
università de' padroni di animali, 85
uso d'erba, 155
Ut delicti, 20
utilità del pane, 112, 155–56

Valignano, Giovanni Antonio, 313
Vallano, Michelangelo, 228
Vallecannella (location), 47, 91, 269
Value, theory of. *See* Galiani, Ferdinando
Varro, 19, 252
Vasto, marchese di, 219
vecchie, 53
Venice, 177, 180, 186–88, 206, 213–14, 228–30, 234, 236, 239, 246, 250; cloth, 227, 233, 347, 356; consul, 190; market, 178, 206–7; piracy, 178, 345; shipping, 226, 235, 237, 349, 357; Terraferma, 206, 214, 236; wool imports, 231, 238; wool manufacturing, 67, 234–36, 263
Ventura, Francesco, 99
vernarecci, 54, 208, 292–93
Vespa, donato, 219
Vespa, Giuseppe Antonio, 104
Vespoli, Girolamo, 99
Vettori, Vincenzo, 236–37
Vidman, Vincenzo, 143
Vietri, duke of. *See* Sangro, Fabrizio di
Vignano, Andrea, 229

Villari, Rosario, 137–38, 160–62
Virgil, 116, 252, 304
Vitale, Giovanni, 229
Vitorando, Giovanni Domenico, 101
Vivenzio, Nicola, 37, 299
voce: bread, 77, 80, 325–26; cheese, 76–77, 196, 209–10; contracts, 205, 325; credit, 122; pricing system, 74–77, 109, 112, 138–39, 196, 201, 204, 207, 213, 350; wheat, 196, 209–10, 326; wool, 76, 159, 196, 209–10, 236, 238

Wallerstein, Immanuel, 238
Wars of the Roses, 23
Wheat, 15, 23, 30, 35, 40, 81, 122, 124, 200, 205, 240–41, 259, 261, 263–64 (see also *voce*, wheat); field rotation system, 58–63; government policy, 180–83, 189–90; prices, 72–75, 209–11; provisioning for Naples, 177–78; provisioning for shepherds, 111–12
William I, 19
William II, 19
Wool, 81, 91, 109, 124, 130, 186–88, 261, 263
—buyers, 108, 187–88, 200–202, 205–7, 212–15, 226–41
—demand, 200–202, 234–38 (see also *voce*, wool)
—price, 112, 122, 203–4, 284–89
—production, 181, 183, 195, 259, 263, 284–89
—product value, 204–5, 284–89
—quality, 197, 202–3, 235–36; *agnellina* or *ainina*, 52–53; *canina*, 53; *carfagna*, 52–53; *castratina*, 53; *cordeschi*, 54, 208; first condition, 52–53, 215; *maggiorina*, 52, 202; second condition, 52–53, 215; third condition, 53
—quantity, 190–91, 195, 216–17, 227–33; in depositories, 185, 189, 195, 202, 213, 223, 284–89; out of depositories, 284–89
—sellers, 187–88, 200–202, 205–7, 212–26, 235–41
—sold at Foggia, 185, 188–91, 199, 205, 290
—supply, 200–202
—weighers (see *pesatori di lana*)

Yields, 61, 322

Zanetti, Federico, 226
Zanetti, Pietro, 187, 226, 228–29, 348
Zenucchi, Giovanni, 226, 229
Zenucchi, Giuseppe, 229
Zimma, Francesco Antonio, 226, 228

Designed by Martha Farlow.
Composed by the Composing Room of Michigan, Inc., in Garamond #3.
Printed by Bookcrafters, Inc., on 50-lb. S. D. Warren's Sebago Eggshell Cream and bound in GSB cloth.

LIBRARY OF DAV